The High School Edition of Lotus® 123®
RELEASE 2.3

Applications for Students

The Writing Team for The High School Edition of Lotus 1-2-3, Release 2.3

Curriculum Guide
Theda Siebert, Burlingame High School, California

Applications for Students
Terrence O'Donnell, Business Media Resources
Harry Phillips, Santa Rosa Junior College
Gloria Wheeler
Douglas Wolf

Applications Exercises
Barbara Mathis, Cooper City High School, Florida
Jeff Mock, Diablo Valley College, California
John Steffee, Robert E. Lee High School, Texas
Ric Williams, Riverside Community College and
    University of California, Riverside

The High School Edition of Lotus 1-2-3

RELEASE 2.3

Applications for Students

Editorial Review Board

Elaine Besalki, Buccholz High School, Florida
Carol Doschadis, Champlin Park High School, Minnesota
Mary Jett, Edison High School, California
Barbara Mathis, Cooper City High School, Florida
Dr. Virginia Mosier, Richardson High School, Texas
Theda Siebert, Burlingame High School, California
John Steffee, Robert E. Lee High School, Texas
Louis Webb, San Francisco County Regional Occupation
    Program, California

Addison-Wesley Publishing Company, Inc.

Benjamin/Cummings Publishing Company, Inc.

Reading, Massachusetts ▪ Redwood City, California ▪ New York
Don Mills, Ontario ▪ Wokingham, England ▪ Amsterdam ▪ Bonn
Sydney ▪ Singapore ▪ Tokyo ▪ Madrid ▪ San Juan ▪ Milan ▪ Paris

The High School Edition of Lotus 1-2-3, Release 2.3, Applications for Students, is published by Addison-Wesley Publishing Company, Inc. and The Benjamin/Cummings Publishing Company, Inc.

Contributors

Alan Jacobs, Sponsoring Editor
Cindy Johnson, Project Manager
Business Media Resources, Concept & Development
Terrence O'Donnell, Development Editor
Mary Coffey, Software Production Manager
Folkert Van Karssen, Production Project Manager
Jean Hammond, Text and Cover Designer
Brian Miller, Validator
Steve Toebes, Validator
David Toebes, Validator
Barbara Borzecki, Validator
Trish Gordon, Media Manufacturing Supervisor
Janet Drumm, Sales and Marketing Manager
Allison Associates, Compositor

The High School Edition of Lotus 1-2-3, Release 2.3, Applications for Students
Copyright © 1992, Addison-Wesley Publishing Company, Inc.

All rights reserved. No part of this publication may be reproduced, stored in a retrieval system, or transmitted in any form or by any means, electronic, mechanical, photocopying, recording, or otherwise, without the prior written permission of the publisher.

Printed in the United States of America.

ISBN 0-201-60508-2
3 4 5 6 7 8 9 10 - BAM - 98 97 96 95 94 93

Preface

The High School Edition of Lotus® 1-2-3®, Release 2.3 is a complete introduction to the use of spreadsheets, specially designed for high school students. It includes the complete Lotus 1-2-3, Release 2.3 software, this student textbook, and a teacher's guide—everything you and your teacher need to learn and use the world's most popular spreadsheet.

The goal of this program is to encourage you to explore the use of spreadsheets, in general, and Lotus 1-2-3, in particular, to solve problems you will encounter in school, on the job, or at home. Never before has the computer been such a necessary part of a good education. And the use of the spreadsheet is now as important to working with numbers as the word processor is necessary for term papers and reports. As you work through the applications and activities in this book, The High School Edition of Lotus 1-2-3, Release 2.3 will help you see how you can use the spreadsheet as a problem-solving tool in almost *all* of your courses, as well as in college and on the job.

Take a closer look at the book and software you will be using.

The Software

The High School Edition of Lotus 1-2-3, Release 2.3 includes the latest release in the Lotus 1-2-3, Release 2 family. This new release is updated with many new features to make "the industry standard" even more powerful and easy to use. Through special arrangement with Lotus Development Corporation, this High School Edition is virtually the same product being offered commercially. It includes many new features, such as

- ▶ Dialog boxes that can be edited directly, providing users with time-saving alternatives to using the command menus
- ▶ A what-you-see-is-what-you-get (Wysiwyg) graphic display for instant on-screen formatting, producing publishing-quality output, and quick print preview
- ▶ Over 200 graph styles for improved graphing flexibility
- ▶ Built-in mouse support (optional)

The High School Edition of Lotus 1-2-3, Release 2.3 also includes data files (shipped with the Lotus 1-2-3 software) for student and teacher use. These data files are used in selected exercises to allow you to focus on relevant objectives without excessive data entry. Your teacher will provide you with work disks that contain the files you need.

The Student Textbook

Applications for Students, the student book designed for The High School Edition of Lotus 1-2-3, Release 2.3, is really two books in one: a hands-on manual for learning how to use 1-2-3 commands and operations, and an applications book with over 120 exercises for applying 1-2-3 to situations in business and other high school courses.

Hands-on Exercises

Each of the 12 lessons in the book has a series of explicit, step-by-step exercises designed to help you learn by doing. You will step through 1-2-3 commands and operations to apply spreadsheet concepts to a real-world business. The exercises are built around Mollie's Music Shoppe, a fictitious small business where student employees assist the store's owner with administrative tasks, forecasts, and budgeting problems by using 1-2-3.

Applications

Each lesson concludes with a set of ten applications selected from typical high school experiences. The applications continue from lesson to lesson, allowing you to develop sophisticated spreadsheet applications as you work through the book. Whether you complete one or all of the continuing applications, these realistic situations provide a tangible means of integrating your spreadsheet skills with the rest of your high school courses. You may even be able to use the applications as projects in other courses! You can choose from among the following applications:

Three business applications for

- analyzing sales performance for the branch offices in a nationwide sales force
- planning production for a small business that manufactures windsurfing boards
- completing a general accounting worksheet, income statement, and balance sheet for a bicycle manufacturer

Three social studies applications for

- analyzing the results of a questionnaire that rates student attitudes toward school functions and facilities
- analyzing present and estimated world populations by continent for a geography project
- analyzing popular versus electoral college votes in three past presidential elections for an American government project

Two science and mathematics applications for

- studying the solar system and relationships of planetary orbits and attributes for an astronomy project
- solving various mathematical problems, including calculating amounts of money raised from a student recycling drive and a charity bowling tournament, a uniform motion problem, creating an instant multiplication table, and payroll allocation for a group of employees

Two heath and fitness applications for

- monitoring nutrient intake in a typical daily diet
- tracking the batting statistics for a high school softball team

Study and
Review Resource

You can also use this text for reference and review. Spreadsheet concepts at the end of each lesson summarize concepts that apply to *all* spreadsheet software. You can use the 1-2-3 command summaries as a quick reference while you complete the applications exercises and for review. If you need to review DOS commands for formatting disks or managing files, refer to Appendix A. If the system you are using has a mouse, you can read Appendix B to learn how to use the mouse with Lotus 1-2-3.

Acknowledgments

The High School Edition of Lotus 1-2-3, Release 2.3 is the result of years of cooperation between the Lotus Development Corporation and Addison-Wesley Publishing Company. This partnership has made it possible for more than half a million students to learn and work with Lotus 1-2-3. Addison-Wesley brings 50 years of experience in producing quality educational materials to the collaboration, which pioneered the concept of pairing best-selling professional software with manuals written especially for students.

The publishers would like to thank the many individuals who participated in making The High School Edition of Lotus 1-2-3 a reality. A large number of high school teachers helped us by responding to our survey, attending our focus groups, reviewing the manuscript, class-testing, and contributing applications exercises. Their suggestions and shared insights were invaluable in making the concept and design meet the needs of the high school student.

Addison-Wesley Publishing Company
Benjamin/Cummings Publishing Company
February, 1992

How To Use This Book

Textbook Conventions

The step-by-step instructions in the exercises are designed to be read comfortably and easily while sitting at a computer terminal. As you work through the step-by-step exercises, please be aware of the following conventions.

All text, numbers, or symbols to be typed by you appear in boldface with the numbered instruction. For example:

4 ▶ Type **Mollie's Music Shoppe**

The Slash key (/) is always treated as a separate command for accessing the 1-2-3 Main Menu of commands. For example:

1 ▶ Press the Slash key (/) to access the Main Menu.

All significant keyboard keys, other than the alphabet keys (A-Z) and numbers (0–9), are represented in a special "keycap" font. For example:

5 ▶ Press [HOME] to move the cell pointer to cell A1.

20 ▶ Press [CAPS LOCK] to switch to uppercase mode.

Two keyboard keys that are to be pressed and released, one right after the other, are represented separately. For example:

23 ▶ Press [END], and then press [→].

Sometimes two keys must be pressed at the same time, that is, one key is pressed and held, the other is pressed, and then both are released. Keys to be pressed in this manner appear as "keycaps" joined by a hyphen, as follows:

25 ▶ Press [CTRL]-[BREAK] to return to ready mode.

Lotus 1-2-3 commands can be selected by typing the first letter of the command (usually). The "Type" instruction is always used for this method of command selection, and the command's letter is always uppercase and boldface. For example:

29 ▶ Type **WG** to select the Worksheet and Global commands.

How to Study From This Book

Your teacher will provide specific assignments for you to complete as you learn Lotus 1-2-3, but there are a number of elements in *Applications for Students* that can help you get the most from the course. Here's how to use them.

▶ Work through the exercises in each lesson as directed by your teacher, comparing your results to the screens shown in the book and making corrections as needed. Save your work as directed onto the student work disk (or directory) provided by your instructor.

▶ Complete as many of the applications exercises at the end of each lesson as you need to to feel comfortable with the 1-2-3 skills you have learned. If your teacher gives you a choice of exercises, select those you think you will find most interesting. If you complete all the applications and would like to try some more, ask your teacher for additional exercises.

▶ After each lesson, read the Concept Summaries to review what you have learned about spreadsheets. Use the term definitions in the margins and the command summaries to review and study.

▶ If you need to review a command or a term from a previous lesson, use the index in the back of the book to find the lesson where it was covered.

▶ If you need to review how to use the disk operating system, DOS, to format data disks or manage your files, refer to Appendix A.

▶ If you are using a mouse with your computer, Appendix B provides information about using the mouse with Lotus 1-2-3.

▶ As you become proficient, look for applications of 1-2-3 at home, at work, and in other courses. Use this book as a reference in taking on problems of your own and devising spreadsheet solutions.

Contents

Introduction
What is a Spreadsheet?   1

Lessons

1 ▶ Getting Acquainted with 1-2-3   3

1.1 Starting 1-2-3 from DOS   4
1.2 Getting to Know the 1-2-3 Display   6
1.3 Accessing 1-2-3 Command Menus   13
1.4 Entering Data   17
1.5 Naming and Saving Worksheet Files   22
1.6 Quitting 1-2-3   24
Concept and Command Summary   25
Business Applications   26
Social Studies Applications   31
Science Applications   32
Mathematics Applications   32
Health Applications   33

2 ▶ Editing and Printing a Worksheet   36

2.1 Retrieving a Worksheet File   37
2.2 Displaying the Current Filename   39
2.3 Creating Formulas   42
2.4 Editing Worksheet Data   45
2.5 Copying Data and Selecting Cell Ranges   49
2.6 Printing a Worksheet Range   52
2.7 Erasing a Worksheet   55
Concept and Command Summary   56
Business Applications   57
Social Studies Applications   59
Science Applications   63
Mathematics Applications   64
Health Applications   65

3 ▶ Formatting a Worksheet and Getting Help   68

3.1 Formatting Values   69
3.2 Adjusting Column Widths   74
3.3 Formatting Labels   77
3.4 Inserting and Deleting Columns and Rows   80
3.5 Adjusting a Selected Range   84
3.6 Getting Help   87
Concept and Command Summary   90
Business Applications   91
Social Studies Applications   94
Science Applications   97
Mathematics Applications   98
Health Applications   99

4 ▶ Using 1-2-3 @Functions and Checking Their Accuracy   102

4.1 Creating and Copying 1-2-3 @Functions   103
4.2 Reformatting the Worksheet   108
4.3 Erasing a Range   110
4.4 Using the @AVG Function   115
4.5 Locking Worksheet Titles   117
4.6 Moving a Range   120
Concept and Command Summary   125
Business Applications   126
Social Studies Applications   130
Science Applications   132
Mathematics Applications   133
Health Applications   134

5 ▶ Building a Model to Solve What-If problems   137

5.1 Setting Up a Worksheet Model   138
5.2 Combining Date from Other Files   142
5.3 Using Relative & Absolute Sale References   146
5.4 Splitting the Worksheet Area into Windows   153
5.5 Solving What-If Problems   155
Concept and Command Summary   159
Business Applications   160
Social Studies Applications   163
Science Applications   165
Mathematics Applications   166
Health Applications   167

xii   Contents

6 ▶ Creating Budgets and Using a Worksheet Template 171

6.1 Linking Worksheet Files 172
6.2 Using Mixed Cell References 177
6.3 Using the @IF Function 182
6.4 Creating a Worksheet Template 187
6.5 Protecting a Worksheet 189
6.6 Protecting Worksheets with Passwords 192
Concept and Command Summary 195
Business Applications 196
Social Studies Applications 200
Science Applications 202
Mathematics Applications 202
Health Applications 203

7 ▶ Advanced Printing Features 205

7.1 Adjusting Margins 206
7.2 Setting Print Borders 210
7.3 Printing Headers and Footers 213
7.4 Hiding Columns 217
7.5 Printing Data with Condensed Print 222
7.6 Printing Cell Formulas 225
Concept and Command Summary 226
Business Applications 228
Social Studies Applications 229
Science Applications 230
Mathematics Applications 231
Health Applications 231

8 ▶ Graphing Worksheet Data 233

8.1 Creating and Displaying a Line Graph 234
8.2 Naming and Saving a Graph 239
8.3 Creating Bar and Pie Graphs 240
8.4 Selecting and Enhancing Named Graphs 244
8.5 Creating a Graph with Multiple Data Ranges 249
8.6 Using the Lotus PrintGraph Utility to Print Graphs 253
Concept and Command Summary 258
Business Applications 260
Social Studies Applications 263
Science Applications 266
Mathematics Applications 267
Health Applications 268

9 ▶ Using Wysiwyg to Create Presentation-Quality Documents 270

9.1 Attaching and Using the Wysiwyg Add-In 271
9.2 Changing Fonts and Font Attributes 277
9.3 Enhancing Ranges with Lines and Shading 282
9.4 Using Wysiwyg to Add a Graph to a Document 287
9.5 Using a Wysiwyg to Format Text 292
9.6 Using Wysiwyg to Print a Document 295
Concept and Command Summary 297
Business Applications 299
Social Studies Applications 302
Science Applications 304
Mathematics Applications 304
Health Applications 305

10 ▶ Creating Worksheet Databases 307

10.1 Introduction to Databases 308
10.2 Creating a Database 310
10.3 Inserting and Deleting Records to Maintain a Database 315
10.4 Sorting Records 317
Concept and Command Summary 323
Business Applications 324
Social Studies Applications 326
Science Applications 327
Mathematics Applications 328
Health Applications 329

11 ▶ Database Queries and @Functions 330

11.1 Creating, Naming and Defining Input, Criteria, and Output Ranges 331
11.2 Locating and Extracting Records 335
11.3 Specifying Multiple Criteria 340
11.4 Using 1-2-3 Database @Functions 343
Concept and Command Summary 348
Business Applications 349
Social Studies Applications 351
Science Applications 354
Mathematics Applications 354
Health Applications 355

12 ▶ Automating Your Work with Macros   357

12.1 Writing, Naming, and Running Macros   358
12.2 Writing a Command Macro   361
12.3 Testing a Macro IN STEP Mode   363
12.4 Recording Macro Keystrokes in a Learn Range   366
12.5 Writing an Interactive Macro   370
12.6 Creating and Using a Macro Library   373
Concept and Command Summary   376
Business Applications   377
Social Studies Applications   381
Science Applications   383
Mathematics Applications   383
Health Applications   385

Appendix A
Using DOS and DOS Commands   387

Starting Your Computer   387
Using the DOS Prompt   389
Moving Between Disk Drives   389
Entering DOS Commands   389
Data Disks   389
Managing Data in Files   390
Managing Files in Directories   391
Using The DIR Command   393
Using Wildcard Characters   393
Using the FORMAT Command to Prepare Floppy Disks   394
Using the COPY Command   396
Using the DELETE and ERASE Commands   398

Appendix B
Using a Mouse with 1-2-3   401

What is a Mouse?   401
Identifying the Mouse Pointer and Icons   402
Basic Mouse Techniques   402
Switching Mouse Buttons   403
Moving the Cell Pointer   403
Accessing Help   404
Selecting 1-2-3 Commands   404
Selecting Wysiwyg Commands   405
Selecting Ranges   405
Changing Column Widths While Wysiwyg is Attached   406
Splitting the Worksheet Area into Windows   406

Index   408

Introduction

What Is a Spreadsheet?

Lotus 1-2-3, Release 2.3 is a powerful, easy-to-use spreadsheet and graphics software package designed for personal computers. The 1-2-3 spreadsheet is probably the most popular electronic spreadsheet used in business today. You can also use it in school, your personal life, social or club activities, or anything else that requires organizing and analyzing data.

A spreadsheet is a tool that is used to store, organize, and do mathematical calculations on numeric data. But it is also much more than that. It can be used to analyze data, make important decisions, or solve complex problems in any enterprise.

A spreadsheet looks like an accountant's ledger, or columnar pad—sheets of paper for recording sums of money received and paid, or any other numeric data. Such pages typically contain horizontal and vertical lines that form columns and rows. Each column–row intersection forms a box into which data (a number, letter, or character) can be written, as shown in Figure 1.1.

Figure 1.1

In the past, spreadsheet data was entered by hand on a columnar pad.

Like ledgers, electronic spreadsheets display columns and rows on a computer screen. The column–row intersections are called cells, and each cell stores and displays data.

What Is a Spreadsheet?

WORKSHEET
Another name for an electronic spreadsheet.

In the past, a spreadsheet (or *worksheet*, as it is often called) was used to build a model of a financial or budget problem. You might get a solution to the problem after working hours—or even days—on math calculations. And if a mistake was later found, redoing the worksheet could become a huge job!

Today, computers and spreadsheet software—such as Lotus 1-2-3—can be used to make models of problems and get solutions much faster and more accurately. Errors can be corrected quickly, and new results can be recalculated in seconds! So an electronic worksheet has great benefits: efficient data entry and management, fast recalculation, and time savings.

Spreadsheet software such as Lotus 1-2-3 also includes many formatting and printing features to enhance the printed pages that present worksheet data. And spreadsheet software often includes graphic capabilities. Graphs can make your presentations visually powerful by emphasizing trends or solutions.

This book gives full instruction on spreadsheet concepts and operations using Lotus 1-2-3, Release 2.3. You will find the 1-2-3 spreadsheet to be an invaluable problem-solving tool you can use in many ways.

1 ▶ Getting Acquainted with 1-2-3

Objectives

- Turn on the computer.
- Locate the 1-2-3 program files on your hard disk.
- Load 1-2-3 into the computer's memory.
- Identify the control panel.
- Identify the worksheet area.
- Identify the status line.
- Move the cell pointer.
- Discover the outer reaches of a 1-2-3 worksheet.
- Use the Go To command (F5) to go directly to a specific cell.
- Use the Slash key (/) to access the Main Menu.
- Access 1-2-3 command menus.
- Select command options.
- Enter labels into a worksheet.
- Enter values into a worksheet.
- Change the current directory.
- Save a 1-2-3 worksheet file.
- Quit the 1-2-3 program.

In this lesson you will start 1-2-3 from *DOS*, and become familiar with the 1-2-3 worksheet and display. You will also enter data into a worksheet, save and name a worksheet file, and quit (leave) the 1-2-3 program.

Exercise 1.1

Starting 1-2-3 from DOS

Objectives

After completing this exercise, you will be able to
- Turn on the computer.
- Locate the 1-2-3 program files on your hard disk.
- Load 1-2-3 into the computer's memory.

DOS
Short for *disk operating system*—a computer program that readies the computer and manages its operation while other software, such as 1-2-3, is loaded and in use.

You will begin the lesson by turning on the computer and *loading* the 1-2-3 program. This book assumes you are using a computer that has a hard disk drive with DOS installed. If you do not have a hard disk drive, refer to the first three sections in *Appendix A, Using DOS and DOS Commands*. If you need help, ask your instructor.

Note: If you are using a dual floppy disk drive computer, insert your DOS disk in drive A.

1 ▶ Turn on the computer and the monitor (if the monitor has its own power switch).

Depending on your system, a message on screen may ask you to enter today's date.

DOS PROMPT
An operating system indicator that displays the current disk drive in use (for example, C:\> or A>). On some systems, the prompt also displays a path or current directory.

Note: Some computer systems may display a *DOS prompt* (for example, C:\>) without asking you to enter the current date and time. If you see a DOS prompt at this point, skip to step 6.

2 ▶ If this occurs, type today's date, using numbers in this format: MM/DD/YY.

For example, if today's date is October 7, 1996, type "10/7/96."

3 ▶ Press ⏎.

Today's date is entered. A prompt displayed on screen may ask you to enter the current time.

4

1 ▶ Getting Acquainted with 1-2-3

4 ▶ If this occurs, type the current time in the format HH:MM:SS:00.

For example, if the current time is 9:30 A.M., type "09:30." If the current time is 2:15 P.M., type "14:15."

Note: You do not have to enter seconds or fractions of seconds.

5 ▶ Press ⏎.

A DOS prompt appears (for example, C:\> or A>). You are now in the main or root *directory* on the current disk drive.

DIRECTORY
A named disk subdivision where a group of related files are stored. A directory on a disk can be thought of as a folder in a file cabinet drawer. A directory acts as a folder by holding a group of files.

Note: If you are using a dual floppy disk drive computer, remove your DOS disk from drive A, and insert your Lotus 1-2-3 program disk in drive A. Then go to step 8.

From the root directory, you will go to the directory that holds the 1-2-3 program files. You will do this by using the DOS command CD, which is short for Change Directory. If you need more information about this DOS command, see the "Making a Directory Current" section in *Appendix A, Using DOS and DOS commands*.

Note: On your system, the directory that contains the 1-2-3 program files may have a name different from the name used in step 6 (next). For example, the directory may be named 123, LOTUS, L123, LR23, or something similar. If it is something other than 123R23, type that other name in step 6.

6 ▶ Type **CD\123R23**

7 ▶ Press ⏎.

The current directory on your system should contain the 1-2-3 program files.

8 ▶ Type **123**

9 ▶ Press ⏎.

LOADING
The action by which a computer reads a disk to locate program files, and then copies the program files to the computer's temporary (RAM) memory.

Lotus 1-2-3 is loaded, and the 1-2-3 *opening screen* appears, as shown in Figure 1.2. Welcome to 1-2-3!

Starting 1-2-3 from DOS 5

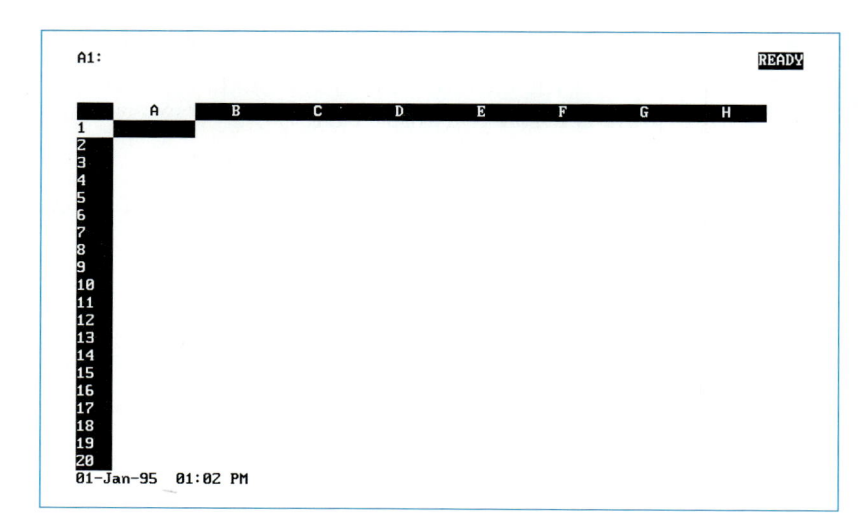

```
A1:                                                    READY
    A     B     C     D     E     F     G     H
 1
 2
 3
 4
 5
 6
 7
 8
 9
10
11
12
13
14
15
16
17
18
19
20
01-Jan-95  01:02 PM
```

Figure 1.2

After you load the 1-2-3 application into your computer's memory, the 1-2-3 opening screen appears.

Exercise 1.2

Getting to Know the 1-2-3 Display

Objectives

After completing this exercise, you will be able to
- Identify the control panel.
- Identify the worksheet area.
- Identify the status line.
- Move the cell pointer.
- Identify the outer reaches of a 1-2-3 worksheet.
- Use the Go To command (F5) to go directly to a specific cell.

WORKSHEET AREA
The window through which only a small portion of an entire spreadsheet or worksheet is visible. On the opening 1-2-3 display, the worksheet area shows the first 20 rows and the first eight columns (A through H).

Look at the 1-2-3 opening screen shown in Figure 1.3. It has three parts: the control panel, the worksheet area, and the status line. The *worksheet area* takes up most of the screen. It can be thought of as a window through which you see a very small part of a whole worksheet. Across the top and down the left side of the screen are the *borders*. The top border displays column letters *A* through *H*. The left border displays rows 1 through 20 on the opening 1-2-3 screen.

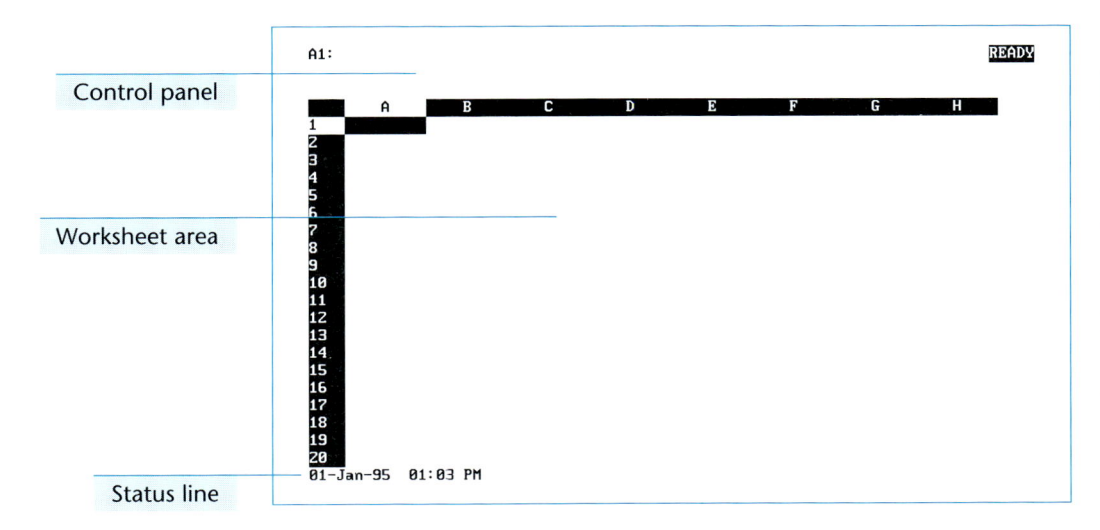

Figure 1.3

The 1-2-3 screen display is made up of the control panel at the top, the status line at the bottom, and the worksheet area. The worksheet area shows the upper-left corner of the entire worksheet.

Labels on figure: Control panel, Worksheet area, Status line

CELL
The basic unit of a worksheet in which data is stored or a calculation is performed. A cell is formed by the intersection of a column and a row.

The entire worksheet has 256 columns and 8192 rows. The *columns* are vertical, and the *rows* are horizontal. Each column and row intersection forms a *cell*, which is the basic unit of a worksheet. Each cell has a unique *cell address* made up of the column letter and row number (for example, A1). The cell address identifies the cell. The worksheet area also contains the *cell pointer*. This is the rectangular highlight that you move from cell to cell by pressing specific keys. As shown in Figure 1.4, on the 1-2-3 opening screen the cell pointer is on cell A1.

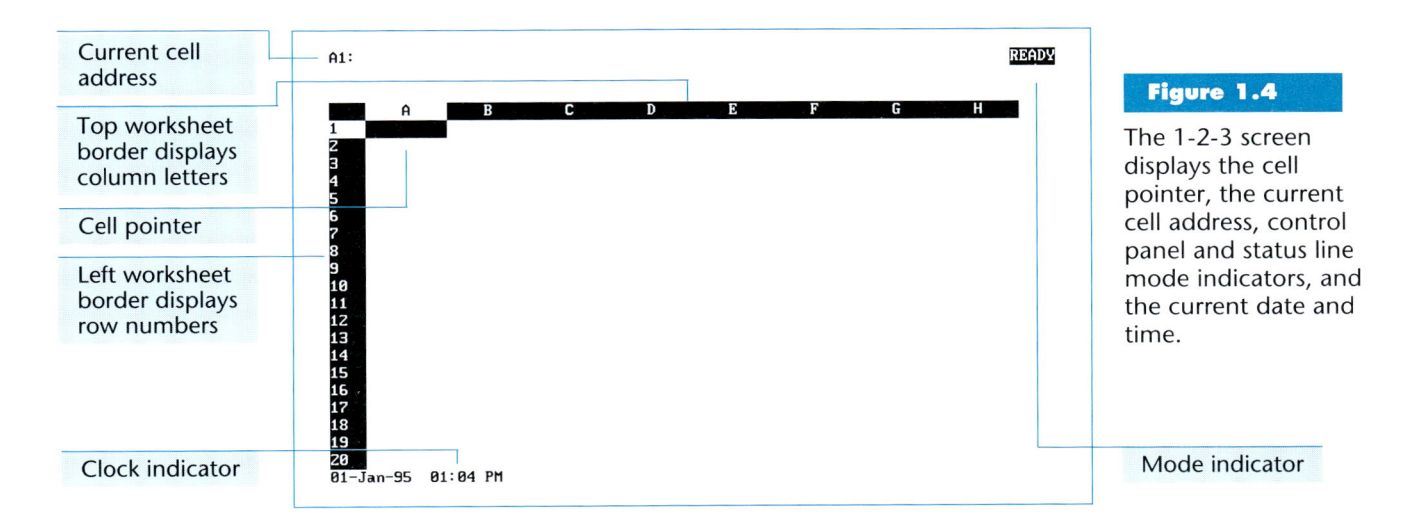

Figure 1.4

The 1-2-3 screen displays the cell pointer, the current cell address, control panel and status line mode indicators, and the current date and time.

Labels on figure: Current cell address, Top worksheet border displays column letters, Cell pointer, Left worksheet border displays row numbers, Clock indicator, Mode indicator

CONTROL PANEL
The first three lines at the top of the 1-2-3 display. The control panel displays the contents of the current cell, 1-2-3 mode indicators, command menus, and command prompts.

The *control panel* is the area at the top. It is above the top border and includes the first three lines on the screen (see Figure 1.3). You use the control panel to enter data into a cell, edit data in a cell, or select 1-2-3 commands. The left side of the control panel's first line displays the current cell address. This is the current location of the cell pointer. Notice in Figure 1.4 that you can quickly spot the cell pointer's location by looking at the worksheet borders. The column letter and row number that indicate the cell pointer location are highlighted. On your monitor, they may appear blacked out.

Getting to Know the 1-2-3 Display

MODE INDICATOR
A control panel indicator in the upper-right corner of the screen. The mode indicator shows the current operating state in which you can perform particular 1-2-3 operations.

The right side of the control panel's top line displays the current 1-2-3 *mode indicator*, READY. This means that you can enter data in the current cell or access the 1-2-3 command menus.

As discussed later, the second and third lines on the control panel can display several items, depending on the mode you are using. For example, the second line displays data you are typing into a cell, command menu options, or special *command prompts*. The third line displays command *submenus* or messages that describe a command's use. You will learn more about commands later in this lesson.

STATUS LINE
The single line at the bottom of the 1-2-3 screen that displays the current date and time or the current worksheet filename. The status line also displays error messages or command descriptions and 1-2-3 status indicators.

At the bottom of the screen is the *status line*. The left side of the status line displays the current date and time (if your system's internal clock is set correctly). The status line also displays error messages and status indicators. The *status indicators* are like the mode indicator on the control panel. They tell you if certain command or keyboard modes are active (turned on). For example, NUM is displayed if the *numeric keypad* numbers are active. And CAPS is displayed if the CAPS LOCK key has been pressed to lock alphabetic characters in uppercase.

If you are using a standard keyboard and the NUM status indicator is displayed on the status line, press NUM LOCK. This turns off the numbers on the numeric keypad so that you can use the Arrow keys to move the cell pointer. Your keyboard may be an enhanced keyboard. Enhanced keyboards have a separate set of Arrow keys between the alphabet keys and the numeric keypad. If you are using an enhanced keyboard, use this separate set to move the cell pointer.

NUMERIC KEYPAD
A separate set of keys on a computer keyboard that are used to either input numbers or move a cursor, depending on whether the NUM LOCK toggle is on or off.

> Note: If your system has a mouse, your 1-2-3 opening screen may show a rectangular mouse pointer and five mouse icons. The mouse icons are on the right edge of the screen, directly below the control panel's mode indicator. The four directional icons (they look like arrowheads) are used to move the cell pointer with the mouse. The question mark (?) icon is used to access the 1-2-3 Help facility. This book does not discuss using the mouse. If you want more information on using the mouse, refer to *Appendix B, Using a Mouse with Lotus 1-2-3, Release 2.3*.

CELL POINTER
The rectangular highlight that identifies the current cell.

Now you will use the keyboard to move the cell pointer around the worksheet.

1 ▶ Press →.

   The cell pointer is on cell B1, and the control panel displays B1:. The column letter B and row number 1 are highlighted on the borders.

2 ▶ Press ↓ twice.

   The cell pointer is on cell B3.

3 ▶ Press ← once.

   The cell pointer is on cell A3.

STATUS INDICATOR
Similar to the mode indicator, a status indicator is a highlighted word or abbreviation on the status line. It is displayed when certain command or keyboard conditions are active.

4 ▶ Press ⬆ once.

   The cell pointer is on cell A2.

5 ▶ Press CAPS LOCK.

   The CAPS status indicator displays on the status line.

6 ▶ Press NUM LOCK.

   The NUM status indicator displays on the status line.

   Note: If the NUM indicator was displayed before you did step 6, press NUM LOCK again to turn it back on.

TOGGLE
A keystroke or command that switches something on or off.

The CAPS LOCK and NUM LOCK keys are called *toggle* keys because they switch these keyboard modes on and off. You press a toggle key once to turn an option on, and you press it again to turn it off.

7 ▶ Press CAPS LOCK once, and press NUM LOCK once.

   The status indicators are no longer displayed on the status line.

   Note: If you are using an enhanced keyboard, press NUM LOCK again to turn on the numeric keypad's numbers.

8 ▶ Press HOME.

   The cell pointer is on cell A1. No matter where you are on the worksheet, you can always return to cell A1 by pressing HOME.

9 ▶ Press ⬇ 15 times.

   The cell pointer moves down one row at a time to cell A16.

10 ▶ Press ⬇ 5 times.

SCROLLING
The movement of the worksheet as the cell pointer is moved in the worksheet area.

   The cell pointer is on cell A21. Notice that the worksheet area displays rows 2 through 21. As you move the cell pointer downward, the worksheet seems to move upward, displaying rows beyond row 20. This movement is called *scrolling*. You scroll the worksheet to see different parts in the worksheet area. Figure 1.5 shows the relationship between the worksheet area and the entire worksheet.

Getting to Know the 1-2-3 Display

Figure 1.5

The worksheet area is a window through which you view a very small part of the entire 1-2-3 worksheet.

Worksheet area

BORDER
The highlighted areas on the 1-2-3 screen display that border the worksheet area on the top and left sides. The top border displays column letters, and the left border displays row numbers.

11 ▶ Press ⬅.

Your computer beeps, telling you that you cannot move left of the worksheet border.

12 ▶ Press HOME.

The cell pointer returns to cell A1.

13 ▶ Press TAB.

The cell pointer is on cell I1. The worksheet scrolls to display one screenful to the right, as shown in Figure 1.6.

Note: You can also make the same movement by pressing CTRL-➡.

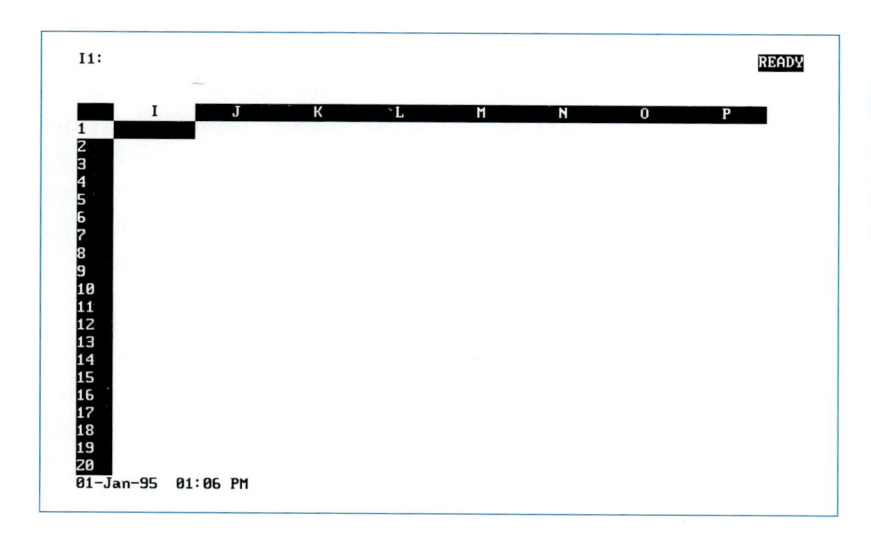

Figure 1.6

Press TAB (or CTRL-➡) to scroll the worksheet one screenful to the right.

10   1 ▶ Getting Acquainted with 1-2-3

14 ▶ Press PGDN.

   The cell pointer is on cell I21. The worksheet scrolls to display the next screenful down (columns I–P and rows 21–40).

15 ▶ Press SHIFT-TAB.

   The cell pointer is on cell A21. The worksheet scrolls to display one screenful to the left.

   Note: You can also make the same movement by pressing CTRL-←.

Now you will discover the outer reaches of the worksheet. The quickest way to do this is to use the END key to turn on the END status line indicator. When the END indicator is displayed, pressing an Arrow key moves the cell pointer in the selected direction to the next cell that contains data. If no cell with data is encountered, the cell pointer moves to the last cell in the row or column.

16 ▶ Press END.

   The END status indicator appears on the status line.

17 ▶ Press ↓.

   The cell pointer moves down to cell A8192. Row 8192 is the very last row in the worksheet.

18 ▶ Press END and then press →.

   The cell pointer is on cell IV8192. This is the very last cell in the entire worksheet. After column Z, 1-2-3 assigns two letters to each column, beginning with AA, AB, AC, and so on all the way to column IV.

Now you will use a *function key* to tell 1-2-3 to move the cell pointer to a particular cell.

19 ▶ Press F5 (the Go To command).

   The second line on the control panel displays a prompt. It asks you to enter the cell address where you want to move the cell pointer, as shown in Figure 1.7.

ROW
A horizontal division of a worksheet that is identified by a number. There are 8192 rows in a 1-2-3 worksheet.

COLUMN
A vertical division of the worksheet that is identified by an alphabetic letter. There are 256 columns in a 1-2-3 worksheet.

FUNCTION KEYS
A set of keys on the computer keyboard that execute specific commands, depending on the software application. The function keys are labeled F1 through F10 (or F1 through F12 on enhanced keyboards). Generally, function keys are command short-cuts, reducing the number of keystrokes required to execute the command.

Getting to Know the 1-2-3 Display

Figure 1.7

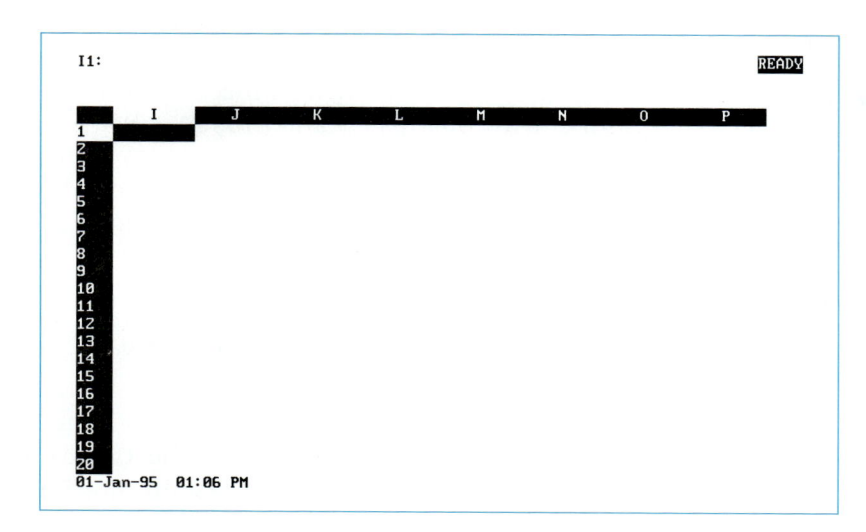

When you press [F5] (Go To command), 1-2-3 prompts you to enter the cell address where you want to move the cell pointer.

20 ▶ Type **dx4046**

The cell address appears on the control panel to the right of the prompt.

21 ▶ Press ⏎.

The cell pointer is on cell DX4046, as shown in Figure 1.8. Notice that the worksheet has scrolled so that cell DX4046 is in the upper-left corner of the worksheet area. The current cell address is displayed on the control panel.

CELL ADDRESS
The column letter and row number location that identify a particular cell (for example, cell D12). Every cell in a worksheet has a unique address.

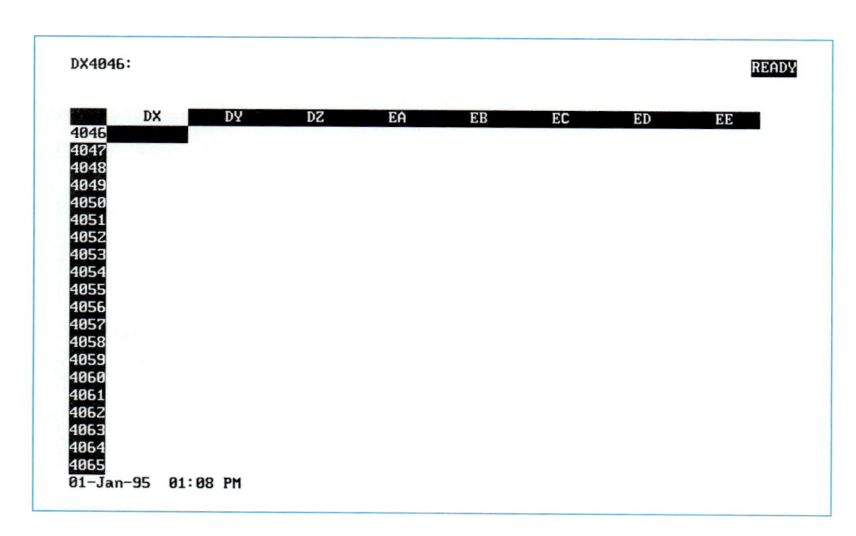

Figure 1.8

When you press [F5] (Go To command) and enter a cell address, 1-2-3 moves the cell pointer to that cell. The worksheet also scrolls so that the current cell is in the upper-left corner of the worksheet area.

22 ▶ Press [HOME].

The cell pointer returns to cell A1.

12   **1 ▶ Getting Acquainted with 1-2-3**

Exercise 1.3
Accessing 1-2-3 Command Menus

Objectives

After completing this exercise, you will be able to
- Use the Slash key (/) to access the Main Menu.
- Access 1-2-3 command menus.
- Select command options.

SLASH KEY (/)
The key that is pressed to switch 1-2-3 to MENU mode and display the 1-2-3 Main Menu.

Lotus 1-2-3 provides a branched command menu system for accessing command options. You access the command menus by pressing the *Slash key* (/), which is usually next to the right SHIFT key. When you press the Slash key, 1-2-3 switches to MENU mode and the *Main Menu* appears on the control panel. The *menu pointer* appears on the left side of the Main Menu line, highlighting the first command—the Worksheet command. The control panel's third line displays the next level of options, or submenu, for the Worksheet command. To select a command menu option, press → or ← to highlight an option and press ⏎.

> Note: In MENU mode, you can press HOME to move the menu pointer to the current menu's first option (extreme left) and END to move the menu pointer to its last option (extreme right).

Now you will familiarize yourself with the 1-2-3 command menu system.

1 ▶ Press the Slash key (/).

MAIN MENU
The set of commands displayed on the second line of the control panel when the Slash key (/) is pressed to access MENU mode.

The 1-2-3 Main Menu appears on the control panel, and the MENU mode indicator appears, as shown in Figure 1.9. Because the Worksheet command is highlighted by the menu pointer, the Worksheet command's submenu is shown on the control panel's third line.

Active 1-2-3 Main Menu

Worksheet command submenu

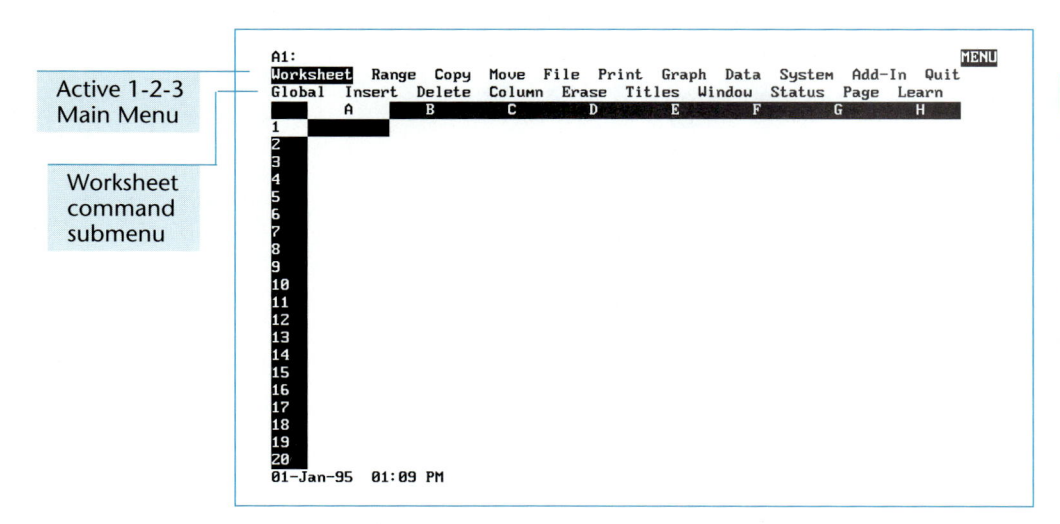

Figure 1.9

When you press the Slash key (/), 1-2-3 switches to MENU mode, and the Main Menu displays on the second line of the control panel. The Worksheet command submenu displays on the third line.

MENU POINTER
The rectangular highlight that is used to move between command options on the second line of the control panel.

SUBMENU
The next level of options that become active when you select the highlighted command on the control panel's second line. Submenus are initially displayed on the third line of the control panel.

2 ▶ Press → 4 times.

The menu pointer moves to the File command on the Main Menu. The File command's submenu appears on the control panel's third line.

3 ▶ Press END.

The menu pointer highlights the Quit command. A message explaining what it does appears on the control panel's third line.

4 ▶ Press → once.

The menu pointer highlights the Worksheet command. Lotus 1-2-3 command menus are "circular." That is, when you move the menu pointer to the right of the last option, it moves to the first option on the current menu.

5 ▶ Press ⏎.

The Worksheet command is selected. The Worksheet command's submenu moves to the control panel's second line. Its options are now available, as shown in Figure 1.10.

14   **1 ▶ Getting Acquainted with 1-2-3**

Active worksheet command submenu

Global command submenu

Figure 1.10

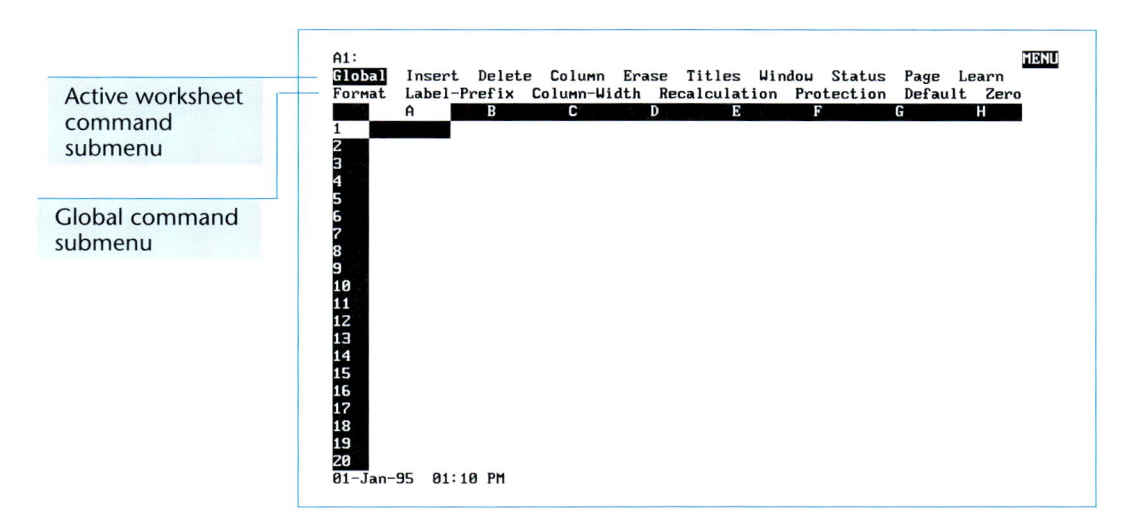

Selecting any command option on the second line of the control panel takes you one level deeper into the 1-2-3 menu structure.

There is a faster way to select commands. You can choose command options by simply pressing the first uppercase letter in the command's name, which in most cases is the first letter of the command name.

Note: This book uses the word "Type" for command selection, as shown in step 6 (next).

DIALOG BOX

A box or frame that surrounds various setting options and appears over the current worksheet when a specific command is selected. A submenu usually appears on the control panel when a dialog box first appears. The dialog box can be activated so you can select and change settings.

SETTINGS

Conditional options that control the 1-2-3 operating environment and that can be readily changed by the user.

6 ▶ Type **G** to select the Global command.

The Global command's submenu appears on the control panel's second line. The Format command's submenu appears on the control panel's third line. The Global Settings dialog box also appears, as shown in Figure 1.11. A *dialog box* gives you another way to change *settings* in addition to the command menu. You will learn more about dialog boxes in Lesson 2.

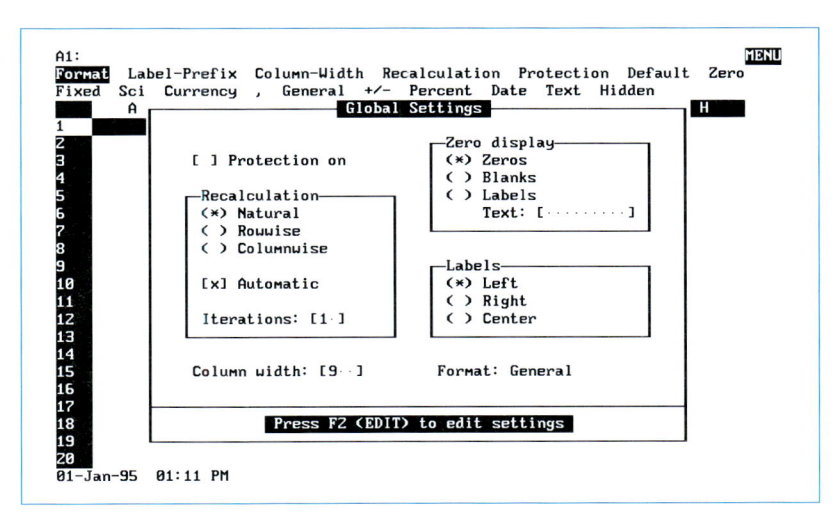

Figure 1.11

The Global Settings dialog box appears when you select the /Worksheet Global command (/WG). Dialog boxes display settings that can be changed either directly in the dialog box or by using the command menus.

Accessing 1-2-3 Command Menus

15

Do not worry if you select a command that takes you to a menu level you do not want. You can get back to the previous level by pressing the ESC key. Press ESC as many times as necessary to get back to the menu level you want. If you want to leave the command menu system from any menu level, press and hold down CTRL and press BREAK. Then release both keys at the same time. In this book, keys to be pressed this way are linked with a hyphen (for example, CTRL-BREAK).

7 ▶ Press ESC.

The Worksheet command's submenu returns to the control panel's second line, and the Global command is highlighted. The Global Settings dialog box is no longer displayed.

8 ▶ Press ESC.

The Main Menu is now available, and the Worksheet command is highlighted.

9 ▶ Press ESC.

Lotus 1-2-3 returns to READY mode. You have left the command menu system.

10 ▶ Press the Slash key (/).

The Main Menu appears.

11 ▶ Type **WS** to select the Worksheet and Status commands.

The Worksheet Status information screen appears.

This screen shows memory size and other system information. Notice that the STAT mode indicator appears on the control panel, telling you that 1-2-3 is in "status" mode. There is no menu of options displayed. Unlike a dialog box, an *information screen* cannot be edited.

12 ▶ Press CTRL-BREAK.

Lotus 1-2-3 returns to READY mode.

INFORMATION SCREEN
A box or frame that displays over the worksheet and shows current settings and other status information. The displayed settings can be adjusted only by using the command menu system. Unlike dialog boxes, information screens cannot be activated for editing.

Exercise 1.4

Entering Data

Objectives

After completing this exercise, you will be able to
- Enter labels into a worksheet.
- Enter values into a worksheet.

DATA
Any information entered into a cell.

In this exercise, you will begin building a worksheet by entering *data* into specific cells. Entering data into a worksheet is very simple. You move the cell pointer to a cell, type the label or value, and press ⏎.

In the rest of the exercises in this book, you will use 1-2-3 to do administrative work for a fictional music store business: Mollie's Music Shoppe. This store sells CDs, new and used albums, cassette tapes, videotapes, and other recording products. Recently, the owner bought Lotus 1-2-3, Release 2.3 to help with business administration. The owner wants you to get acquainted with the software. She asks you to make a worksheet that shows sales figures for the recording items the store sold during the summer.

First, you will make sure you have a blank worksheet on screen and the cell pointer is on cell A1. You will begin by entering the name of the store and a title for the worksheet. This information will be stored as labels in the first two rows. *Labels* are text data that give meaning to the values in a worksheet. As soon as you type the first text character in a label, 1-2-3 switches to LABEL mode and inserts the *apostrophe formatting prefix*, which left-aligns the label in the current cell.

LABEL
Any string of text (alphanumeric characters) stored in a cell. Labels are used to make numeric data understandable. Labels can be up to 240 characters long.

1 ▶ Type **Mollie's Music Shoppe**

The label's text appears on the control panel. Notice that the control panel's mode indicator changes to LABEL. As soon as you typed the "M", 1-2-3 interpreted the entry as a label.

APOSTROPHE FORMATTING PREFIX
A symbol that 1-2-3 places in front of any label automatically as soon as a text (non-numeric) character is typed. The apostrophe formatting prefix distinguishes a label from a value and left aligns a label in a cell.

What can you do if you make a mistake while typing data (before pressing ⏎)? Simply press BACKSPACE as many times as necessary to delete the character or characters you do not want. Then retype.

2 ▶ Press ⏎.

The label is entered and displayed in cell A1.

Because cell A1 is the current cell, its content, the label 'Mollie's Music Shoppe,' is displayed to the right of the cell address on the control panel. Notice that 1-2-3 inserted the apostrophe formatting prefix in front of the label and has returned to READY mode.

Entering Data **17**

3 ▶ Press ⬇.

    The cell pointer is on cell A2.

As you enter the next label, you will type a mistake on purpose. This will give you practice making a correction before pressing ⏎. Later you will learn how to edit data in a cell *after* pressing ⏎.

4 ▶ Type **Summer Recording Sqles**

    A "q" is placed where you meant to type an "a." The cursor on the control panel follows the letter "s."

5 ▶ Press BACKSPACE 4 times.

    The characters "qles" are erased.

6 ▶ Type **ales** and press ⏎.

    The label is entered into cell A2 and is displayed on the control panel.

Often you must enter a lot of data into a worksheet. Pressing ⏎ each time you type data into a cell can slow you down. Instead, you can press an Arrow key after typing the data. This enters the data in one cell and moves the cell pointer to the next cell where you can enter more data—all in one motion.

7 ▶ Press ⬇ 3 times.

    The cell pointer is on cell A5.

8 ▶ Type **CDs**

9 ▶ Press ⬇.

    The label is entered in cell A5, and the cell pointer is on cell A6.

10 ▶ Type **Albums**

11 ▶ Press ⬇.

    The label is entered in cell A6, and the cell pointer is on cell A7.

12 ▶ Type **Cassettes**

13 ▶ Press ⬇.

    The label is entered, and the cell pointer is on cell A8.

14 ▶ Type **Videotape**

15 ▶ Press ⏎.

    The column A labels are entered. Your worksheet should look like Figure 1.12.

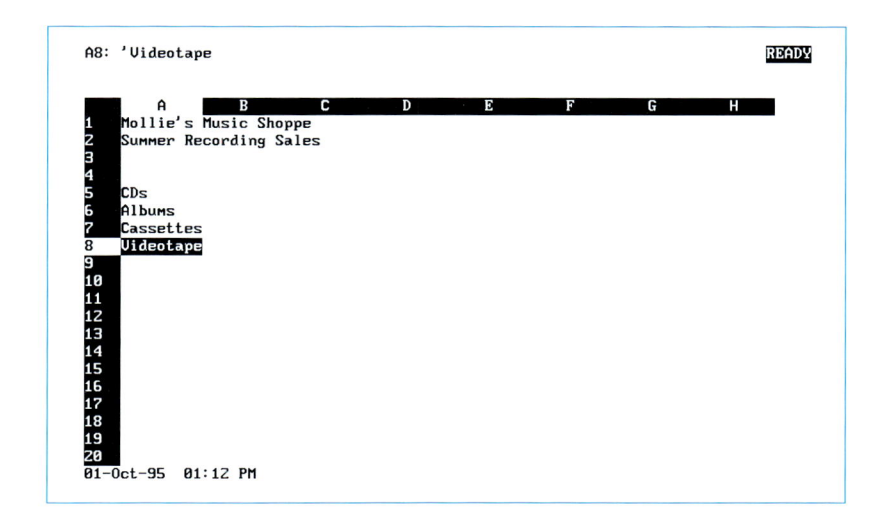

Figure 1.12

After entering the column A labels, your worksheet should look like this.

16 ▶ Press ⬆ 4 times.

The cell pointer is on cell A4.

17 ▶ Press ➡ once.

The cell pointer is on cell B4.

18 ▶ Press [CAPS LOCK].

The CAPS indicator appears on the status line. The alphabetic characters are in uppercase mode.

19 ▶ Type **JUNE**

20 ▶ Press ➡.

The label is entered, and the cell pointer is on cell C4.

21 ▶ Type **JULY**

22 ▶ Press ➡.

23 ▶ Type **AUGUST**

24 ▶ Press ➡.

25 ▶ Type **SEPT**

26 ▶ Press ⏎.

27 ▶ Press [CAPS LOCK] to turn it off.

The cell pointer is on cell E4. Your worksheet should look like the one shown in Figure 1.13.

Entering Data

Figure 1.13

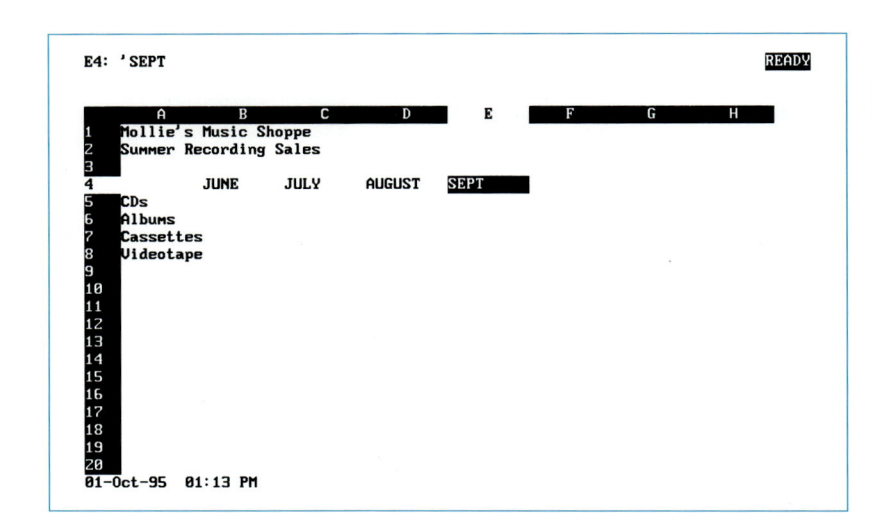

After entering the column heading labels in row 4, your worksheet should look like this.

Now you will enter some values into the worksheet. *Values* are numbers that represent dollars, percentages, units, or any other numeric data. When you enter values, 1-2-3 switches to VALUE mode. Data is interpreted as a value as soon as you type a number (0–9) or any of the following special characters: + − * $ % @ (# or . (period). You will continue with the exercise by first moving the cell pointer to cell B5.

28 ▶ Move the cell pointer to cell B5.

29 ▶ Type **$4,579.88**

Notice that the VALUE mode indicator appears on the control panel. As soon as you typed "$", 1-2-3 interpreted the data as a value entry.

30 ▶ Press ↓.

Your computer "beeps," 1-2-3 switches to EDIT mode, and the cursor jumps to the beginning of the entry. Lotus 1-2-3 does not accept the comma as a thousandths' place separator. The program automatically switches to EDIT mode so you can correct the problem.

31 ▶ Press → twice.

The cursor moves beneath the comma.

32 ▶ Press DEL.

The comma is erased, and the numbers to the right are moved left to fill up the space left by the comma.

33 ▶ Press ↓.

The value 4579.88 is entered in cell B5, and the cell pointer is on cell B6. Notice that 1-2-3 stripped off the dollar sign you typed. In Lesson 3 you will learn how to format values to display dollar signs.

34 ▶ Type **2150.42**

35 ▶ Press ↓.

The value is entered, and the cell pointer is on cell B7.

36 ▶ Type **1617.35**

37 ▶ Press ↓.

38 ▶ Type **3744.55**

39 ▶ Press ↵.

> The column B values are entered. Your screen should look like Figure 1.14.

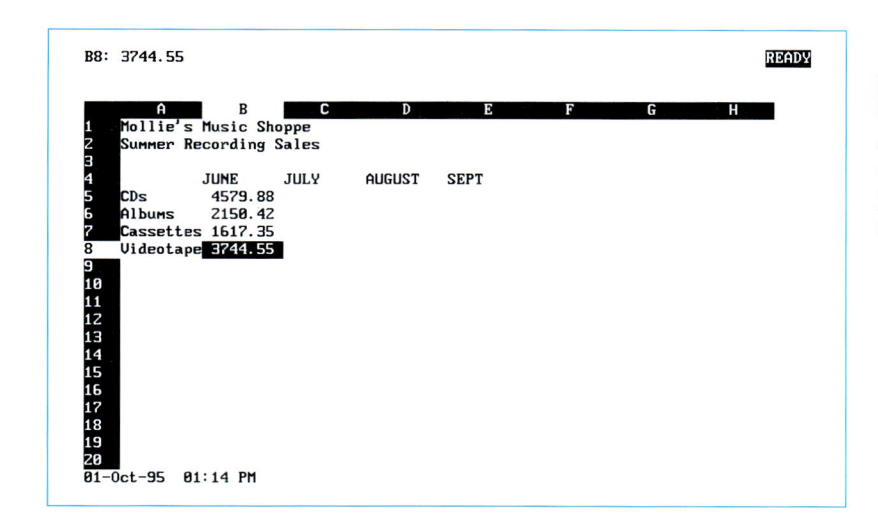

Figure 1.14

After entering the column B sales values, your worksheet should look like this.

40 ▶ Move the cell pointer to cell C5.

41 ▶ Enter the remaining values in columns C, D, and E, and then press HOME so that your worksheet looks like the worksheet shown in Figure 1.15.

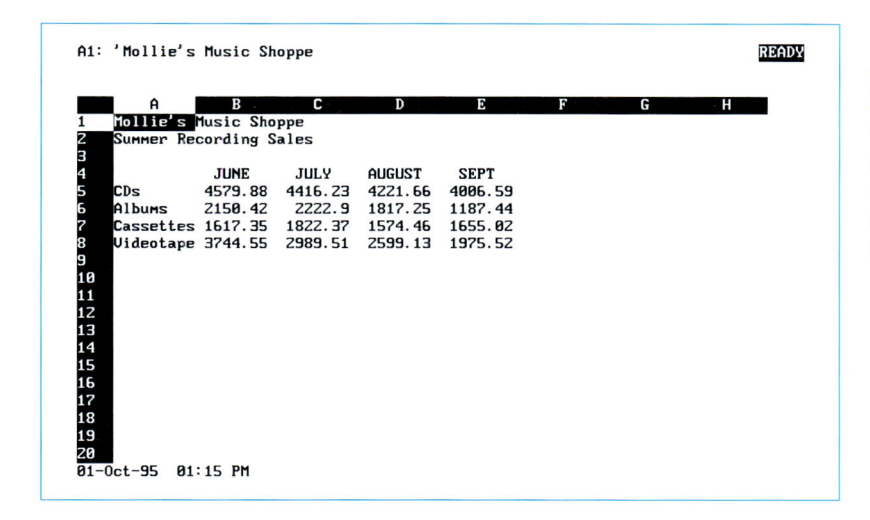

Figure 1.15

Enter the additional sales values shown in columns C, D, and E so that your worksheet looks like this.

Entering Data

Exercise 1.5

Naming and Saving Worksheet Files

Objectives

After completing this exercise, you will be able to
- Change the current directory.
- Save a 1-2-3 worksheet file.

SAVE
The action used to store a named collection of data on disk permanently.

FILE
A named collection of data electronically stored on a disk. Lotus 1-2-3 worksheet files are saved with the .WK1 filename extension.

FILENAME
In DOS applications, a one- to eight-character name for a file that can include an optional one- to three-character extension. Within the same directory, each filename must be unique.

In this exercise, you will *save* the worksheet you just created in a file. The file can be stored on your student data disk or on any other disk. If you will be saving files on a new floppy disk, the disk must be formatted first. See the "Using the FORMAT Command to Prepare Floppy Disks" section in *Appendix A, Using DOS and DOS Commands*, for more information on formatting disks.

When working with 1-2-3, the worksheet you see on screen is only held temporarily in your computer's RAM (random access memory). If you shut off your computer or if a power failure occurred before you saved your work, you would lose everything. So you should save your work often—perhaps every 10 to 15 minutes. By saving your work to disk in a *file*, you can always go back to it later to update your figures.

To save a worksheet, begin by pressing [HOME] so that the cell pointer is on cell A1. This is a good habit to get into. The cell pointer location is saved with the file, so it will always be on cell A1 when you later retrieve the file. (In Lesson 2, you will learn how to retrieve a file.) Next, select the /File Save command (/FS) and type a *filename* that follows standard DOS filename rules.

> Note: See the "Managing Data in Files" section in *Appendix A, Using DOS and DOS Commands*, for standard DOS rules for naming files.

Before you save a file, however, you must tell 1-2-3 the disk location where you want the file stored. Lotus 1-2-3 stores files in the current directory. The *current directory* is the disk location where 1-2-3 manages files. You use the /File Directory command (/FD) to change the current directory. It is a good idea to set your current directory immediately after you load 1-2-3.

You will begin this exercise by inserting your student data disk into drive A (or drive B if you do not have a hard drive).

Note: Your system may be set up differently or the student data files may have been stored on a hard disk. Ask your instructor for the right disk and drive location to enter in step 5 in the following sequence.

1 ▶ Insert your student data disk into drive A (or drive B, if you do not have a hard drive and your program disk is in drive A).

2 ▶ Press [HOME].

The cell pointer is on cell A1.

3 ▶ Press the Slash key (/) to access the Main Menu.

4 ▶ Type **FD** to select the File and Directory commands.

The following prompt appears on the control panel:

Enter current directory: C:\123R23\

CURRENT DIRECTORY
The disk location or work area setting that tells 1-2-3 where to store worksheet files that you save or where to retrieve the files you want to use.

Note: The drive and path to the right of the prompt may be different on your system.

5 ▶ Type **A:** (or type **B:** if you do not have a hard drive).

6 ▶ Press [↵].

The current directory is changed, and 1-2-3 returns to READY mode.

7 ▶ Press the Slash key (/) to access the Main Menu.

8 ▶ Type **FS** to select the File and Save commands.

The following prompt appears on the control panel:

Enter name of file to save: A:*.wk1

Note: The drive and path to the right of the prompt may be different on your system.

EXTENSION
An optional one- to three-character element in a filename that follows a period (for example, FILE-NAME.EXT). Typically, filename extensions are used to indicate the type of file saved to disk. For instance, 1-2-3 adds the .WK1 extension to worksheet files saved during a 1-2-3 session.

Notice that the first five filenames in the current directory appear across the control panel's third line.

9 ▶ Type **SUMSALES**

The filename you just typed appears to the right of the prompt.

10 ▶ Press [↵].

The file SUMSALES.WK1 is saved. Lotus 1-2-3 automatically adds the .WK1 *extension* to the filename.

Naming and Saving Worksheet Files   23

Exercise 1.6

Quitting 1-2-3

Objective

After completing this exercise, you will be able to
- Quit the 1-2-3 program.

QUITTING
Exiting (leaving) the 1-2-3 program by removing it from memory (RAM) and returning to the DOS prompt.

You complete a 1-2-3 work session by *quitting* the program. You select the /Quit command (/Q) to quit the program. Quitting 1-2-3 removes all data and program files from your computer's RAM and returns you to the operating system prompt. Be sure to save your work before quitting 1-2-3.

> Note: Do not just turn the computer off when you finish using 1-2-3. If you do, you risk losing valuable data.

You will complete Lesson 1 by quitting the 1-2-3 program.

1 ▶ Press the Slash key (/) to access the Main Menu.

2 ▶ Type **Q** to select the Quit command.

The control panel's second line displays the options No and Yes. Because the menu pointer highlights the No option, a message describing its result appears on the control panel's third line. This option allows you to abandon the Quit operation.

3 ▶ Type **Y** to select the Yes option.

You exit from 1-2-3 and return to the DOS prompt.

> Note: If you had not saved your work before selecting the Yes option, your system would have beeped. Also, the control panel would have displayed the following prompt:
>
> WORKSHEET CHANGES NOT SAVED! End 1-2-3 anyway?

This prompt is also accompanied by No and Yes options. If it ever appears and you want to return to 1-2-3 so that you can save your latest changes before quitting, select the No option. Then save your work, and quit 1-2-3. Otherwise, select Yes to abandon your changes.

1 ▶ Getting Acquainted with 1-2-3

Congratulations! You have successfully completed Lesson 1. You can either go on to Lesson 2 or do the applications that follow the Concept Summary.

Concept Summary

- A spreadsheet is a tool that is used to store, organize, and do mathematical calculations on numeric data. It looks much like an accountant's ledger or columnar pad, which has columns and rows that organize data.

- Spreadsheets can be used for much more than business. You can use spreadsheets to analyze data, make important decisions, or solve problems in any situation that requires you to use numeric data.

- Electronic spreadsheets—such as Lotus 1-2-3—can handle data very fast and with great accuracy. Spreadsheets are often called worksheets. Such software lets you format, edit, print, and even graph worksheet data to make professional-quality presentations.

- A cell is the basic worksheet unit. It is the intersection of a row and a column. A cell stores text and numeric data and does simple to complex math, displaying the results in various formats. Every cell in a worksheet has its own cell address.

- Electronic worksheet files allow you to store related data on a disk. The data can be brought back later for printing, updating, or reviewing. Worksheet files created with 1-2-3 are automatically given the .WK1 extension by the program.

Command Summary

F5 (Go To command)
moves cell pointer to a specific cell

/ (Slash key)
displays the 1-2-3 Main Menu

/Worksheet Global (/WG)
displays Global command submenu and Global Settings dialog box

/Worksheet Status (/WS)
displays information screen of worksheet settings

/File Directory (/FD)
changes the current directory setting

/File Save (/FS)
saves worksheet data to disk in a file

/Quit (/Q)
exits (leaves) the 1-2-3 program

Moving a Range

Applications

For each of the following applications, start 1-2-3 (if necessary) and do the application. Save the file and then quit the 1-2-3 program. Begin by placing your student data disk in drive A (or drive B if you do not have a hard disk).

Business

Sales Analysis

1. For your business class, you are going to help the owner of a fictitious business make a simple spreadsheet. You will compare last year's sales figures with this year's for each sales branch office. Start 1-2-3, and make a worksheet that lists the following office branches and sales figures.

BRANCH	LAST YEAR	THIS YEAR
Los Angeles	20000	21460
Houston	15000	13980
New Orleans	12080	13450
Chicago	17700	16680
St. Louis	14350	12450
Boston	18200	19080
New York	30600	27470
Miami	24500	23270

   To create the worksheet, do the following:

   a. Enter column headings in row 3, list the cities in column A, and list the sales figures in columns C and D.

   > Note: If you type the wrong character(s), press BACKSPACE to delete the character(s).

   b. Enter the following title in cell A1: "SALES COMPARISON FOR BRANCH OFFICES".

   c. Use the /File Directory command (/FD) to make drive A (or drive B), which contains the student data disk, current.

   d. Press [HOME], and use the /File Save command (/FS) to save the worksheet in a file named SALES1.WK1.

   e. Use the /Quit command (/Q) to quit the 1-2-3 program.

Business

Small Business

2. For your business class, you are assigned to play the role of owner and president of a company that manufactures windsurfing boards. Your instructor gives you the following information about the company:

   Marketing says that the most competitive price for your product is $1,500.

   Production calculates that it costs $1,250 to manufacture, market, and distribute each board.

   Accounting tells you that fixed costs for the company, such as salaries, insurance, and loan payments, are $150,000.

   You need to perform a break-even analysis. This tells you how many windsurfing boards the company needs to sell at $1,500 before it breaks even and begins making a profit. To perform a break-even analysis, you create the worksheet shown in Figure 1.16 by following these steps:

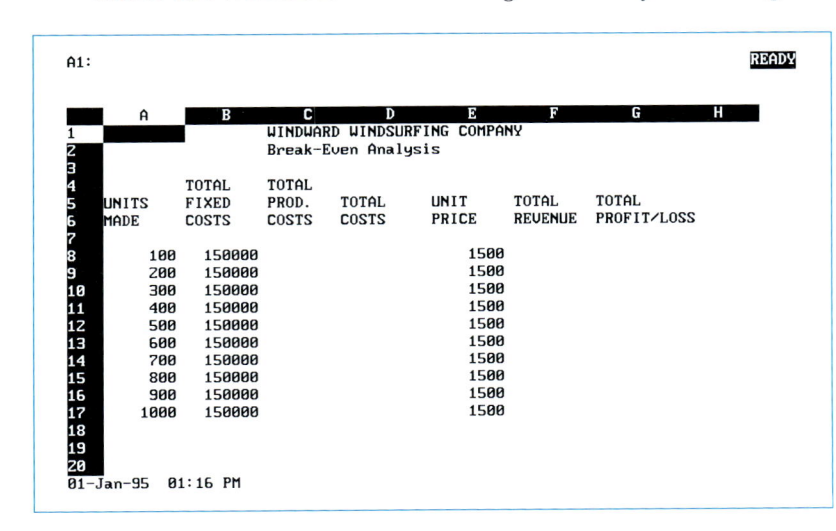

Figure 1.16

Follow the instructions in application 2 (Small Business) to create this worksheet.

   a. Enter the title label "WINDWARD WINDSURFING COMPANY" in cell C1. Be sure to use CAPS LOCK.
   b. Enter the subtitle label "Break-Even Analysis" in cell C2.
   c. Enter the column headings as shown in Figure 1.16.
   d. In column A, enter the values that show the number of units made, as shown in the figure.
   e. In column B, enter the values that show total fixed costs, as shown in the figure.
   f. In column E, enter the values that show unit price, as shown in the figure.
   g. Use the /File Directory command (/FD) to make drive A (or drive B), which contains the student data disk, current.
   h. Press HOME, and use the /File Save command (/FS) to save the worksheet in a file named PROFIT1.WK1.
   i. Use the /Quit command (/Q) to quit the 1-2-3 program.

Applications

Business

Accounting

3. Your accounting instructor has given you a semester project in which you take the role of a junior staff accountant. The company is a bicycle manufacturer called Big Peak Mountain Bicycles. You are given a ledger of accounts for the month of April. To start, you will use 1-2-3 to begin setting up a trial balance. A trial balance is used periodically to test the equality of the ledger. In a trial balance, you list debits to any account in one column and credits to any account in another column. The trial balance test is successful when the sums of both columns are equal. Use the following instructions to make the partial trial balance shown in Figure 1.17.

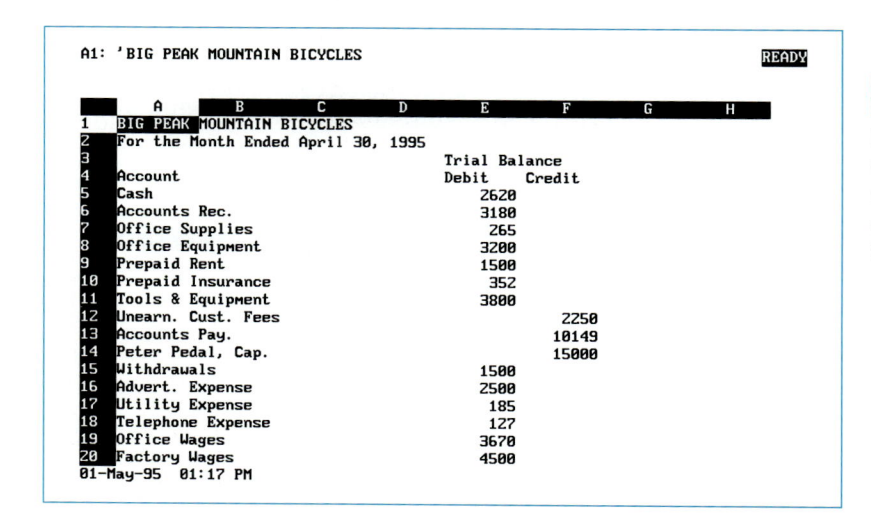

```
A1: 'BIG PEAK MOUNTAIN BICYCLES                                          READY

        A          B          C          D          E          F          G          H
 1  BIG PEAK MOUNTAIN BICYCLES
 2  For the Month Ended April 30, 1995
 3                                            Trial Balance
 4  Account                                   Debit      Credit
 5  Cash                                       2620
 6  Accounts Rec.                              3180
 7  Office Supplies                             265
 8  Office Equipment                           3200
 9  Prepaid Rent                               1500
10  Prepaid Insurance                           352
11  Tools & Equipment                          3800
12  Unearn. Cust. Fees                                    2250
13  Accounts Pay.                                        10149
14  Peter Pedal, Cap.                                    15000
15  Withdrawals                                1500
16  Advert. Expense                            2500
17  Utility Expense                             185
18  Telephone Expense                           127
19  Office Wages                               3670
20  Factory Wages                              4500
01-May-95   01:17 PM
```

Figure 1.17

Follow the instructions in application 3 (Accounting) to begin creating this trial balance.

a. Enter the title "BIG PEAK MOUNTAIN BICYCLES" in cell A1.
b. Enter the subtitle "For the Month Ended April 30, 1995" in cell A2.
c. Enter the label "Trial Balance" in cell E3.
d. Enter the column headings "Debit" and "Credit" in cells E4 and F4, as shown in Figure 1.17.
e. Enter the column A labels for the ledger accounts, as shown in the figure.
f. Enter the values for the debits and credits posted in April, as shown in the figure.
g. Use the /File Directory command (/FD) to make drive A (or drive B), which contains the student data disk, current.
h. Press (HOME), and use the /File Save command (/FS) to save the worksheet in a file named BALANCE1.WK1.
i. Use the /Quit command (/Q) to quit the 1-2-3 program.

Social Studies

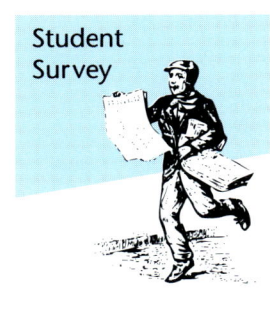

Student Survey

4. For your sociology class, you are examining student attitudes toward the school's sports program, facilities, and social events. To perform the study, you prepare a questionnaire that you distribute to over 700 students. To analyze the results of the questionnaire, you enter the results into a 1-2-3 worksheet, as shown in Figure 1.18. To create this worksheet, follow these steps:

```
A1:                                                              READY

        A       B       C       D       E       F       G       H
 1                      School Activities Questionnaire
 2
 3                      Excellent Good   Fair    Poor    No Opinion
 4      SPORTS
 5      Football        132     314     118     57      89
 6      Baseball        205     363     94      23      67
 7      Basketball      67      248     221     35      189
 8      Water Polo      42      262     109     11      252
 9
10      FACILITIES
11      Cafeteria       56      114     334     214     12
12      Library         179     183     193     34      145
13      Gym             201     245     97      52      103
14
15      EVENTS
16      Prom            156     279     178     23      89
17      Sadie Hawkins Danc 78   168     201     78      125
18      Homecoming      132     285     102     76      89
19      Can Drive       92      159     132     91      96
20
01-Mar-95  01:18 PM
```

Figure 1.18

Follow the instructions in application 4 (Student Survey) to create this worksheet.

a. Enter the title "School Activities Questionnaire" in cell C1.
b. Enter the column heading labels in row 3, as shown in Figure 1.18.
c. Enter the column A labels, as shown in the figure.

  Note: Be sure to press CAPS LOCK to enter the labels that are in all uppercase letters.

d. Enter the values for columns C, D, E, F, and G.
e. Use the /File Directory command (/FD) to make drive A (or drive B), which contains the student data disk, current.
f. Press HOME, and use the /File Save command (/FS) to save the worksheet in a file named SURVEY1.WK1.
g. Use the /Quit command (/Q) to quit the 1-2-3 program.

Applications

Social Studies

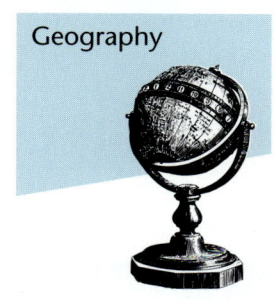

Geography

5. For your geography class, you are studying world population growth. To do so, you create the worksheet shown in Figure 1.19 by following these steps:

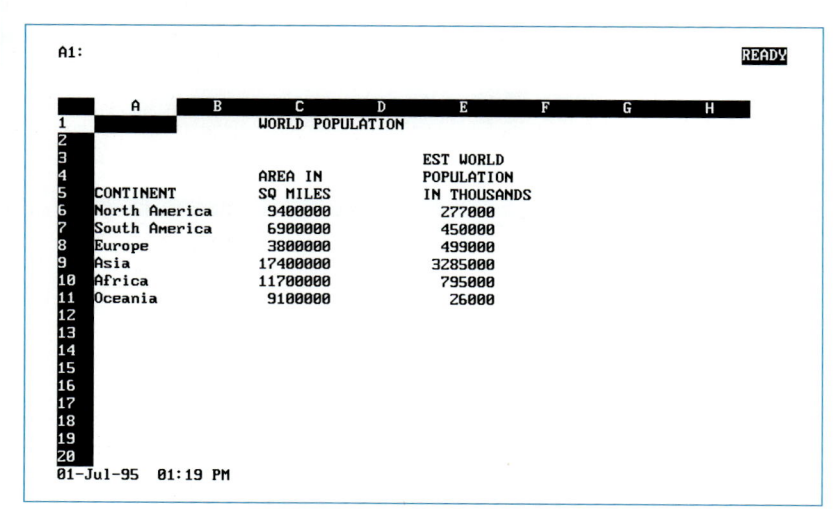

```
A1:                                                      READY
        A         B         C         D         E         F         G         H
1                          WORLD POPULATION
2
3                                              EST WORLD
4                          AREA IN             POPULATION
5    CONTINENT             SQ MILES            IN THOUSANDS
6    North America         9400000             277000
7    South America         6900000             450000
8    Europe                3800000             499000
9    Asia                  17400000            3285000
10   Africa                11700000            795000
11   Oceania               9100000             26000
12
13
14
15
16
17
18
19
20
01-Jul-95  01:19 PM
```

Figure 1.19

Follow the instructions in application 5 (Geography) to create this worksheet.

a. Enter "WORLD POPULATION" in cell C1. Be sure to press CAPS LOCK.

b. Enter the labels "CONTINENT" in cell A5, "AREA IN" in cell C4, and "SQ MILES" in cell C5. Enter the labels "EST WORLD" in cell E3, "POPULATION" in cell E4, and "IN THOUSANDS" in cell E5, as shown in Figure 1.19.

c. Starting in cell A6, enter the continent names, as shown in the figure.

d. Starting with cell C6, enter the area in square mile values, as shown in the figure.

e. Starting with cell E6, enter the population amounts, as shown in the figure.

f. Use the /File Directory command (/FD) to make drive A (or drive B), which contains the student data disk, current.

g. Press HOME, and use the /File Save command (/FS) to save the worksheet in a file named WRLDPOP1.WK1.

h. Use the /Quit command (/Q) to quit the 1-2-3 program.

Social Studies

American Government

6. For your American government class, you are studying the electoral college system in presidential elections. You want to see if the system has ever failed to do what its designers intended it to do. As you may recall, in presidential elections the winner is the candidate with the most electoral votes. Electoral votes are not popular votes. They are votes cast by each state according to which candidate had the majority vote in that state. *The winner takes all electoral votes*. As a result, it is possible for a candidate to earn the majority of national votes and still lose an election!

   To see if a winning candidate ever lost an election, you will compare popular votes with electoral votes. Your comparison will look at three presidential elections. To do so, start 1-2-3 and create the worksheet shown in Figure 1.20 by following these steps:

   Figure 1.20
   Follow the instructions in application 6 (American Government) to create this worksheet.

   ```
   A1: 'COMPARING POPULAR AND ELECTORAL VOTES IN THREE PRESIDENTIAL ELECTIONS    READY

            A         B         C         D         E         F         G         H
    1  COMPARING POPULAR AND ELECTORAL VOTES IN THREE PRESIDENTIAL ELECTIONS
    2
    3       1960               Poplr Vot%          Elec Vote%
    4  Kennedy                 34221334                  303
    5  Nixon                   34106671                  219
    6  Others                    500945                   15
    7
    8       1976
    9  Carter                  40825839                  297
   10  Ford                    39147770                  240
   11  Others                   1629737                    1
   12
   13       1988
   14  Bush                    48881278                  426
   15  Dukakis                 41805374                  111
   16  Others                    898168                    1
   17
   18
   19
   20
   01-Nov-95  01:22 PM
   ```

   a. Enter the following title in cell A1: "COMPARING POPULAR AND ELECTORAL VOTES IN THREE PRESIDENTIAL ELECTIONS". Be sure to press [CAPS LOCK].

   b. Enter the year value "1960" in cell A3.

   c. Enter the labels "Poplr Vot" in cell C3 and "Elec Vote" in cell E3. Enter the label "%" in cells D3 and F3.

   d. Enter the labels "Kennedy" in cell A4, "Nixon" in cell A5, and "Others" in cell A6.

   e. Enter the other column A year values and labels, as shown in Figure 1.20.

   f. Enter the values in columns C and E, as shown in the figure.

   g. Use the /File Directory command (/FD) to make drive A (or drive B), which contains the student data disk, current.

   h. Press [HOME], and use the /File Save command (/FS) to save the worksheet in a file named ELECTN1.WK1.

   i. Use the /Quit command (/Q) to quit the 1-2-3 program.

Applications

Science/Mathematics

Astronomy

7. For your astronomy class, you are given an ongoing assignment to study relationships among the planets in the solar system. Begin by creating a worksheet that lists the nearest and farthest orbital distances from the sun for each planet. Follow the instructions outlined in the following steps:

PLANET	NEAR	FAR
Mercury	28600	43200
Venus	66800	67000
Earth	91400	94500
Mars	125800	154900
Jupiter	468080	507000
Saturn	830000	932000
Uranus	1700000	1860000
Neptune	2754000	2821000
Pluto	2748000	4571200

   a. Enter the title "Orbital Distances from the Sun" in cell A1.
   b. Enter the label "distances are in thousands of miles" in cell A2.
   c. Enter the column heads in row 5.
   d. List the planets in column A, the nearest distances in column B, and the farthest distances in column C.
   e. Use the /File Directory command (/FD) to make drive A (or drive B), which contains the student data disk, current.
   f. Press (HOME), and use the /File Save command (/FS) to save the worksheet in a file named PLANETS1.WK1.
   g. Use the /Quit command (/Q) to quit the 1-2-3 program.

Science/Mathematics

Mathematics

8. Your school recently held a recycling drive to raise money for the school's computer lab. The money will be used to purchase new software. The local recycling center pays 35 cents for every pound of tin or aluminum cans collected, and 3 cents for every inch of stacked newspaper. It pays 4 cents for every glass bottle. As an incentive, the class that raises the most money will receive a field trip to an aquarium. For an extra-credit assignment, you are asked to count how much recyclable material each class collected. You will also figure out how much money each class raised, based on these rates. Begin by using the following instructions to set up the worksheet shown in Figure 1.21.

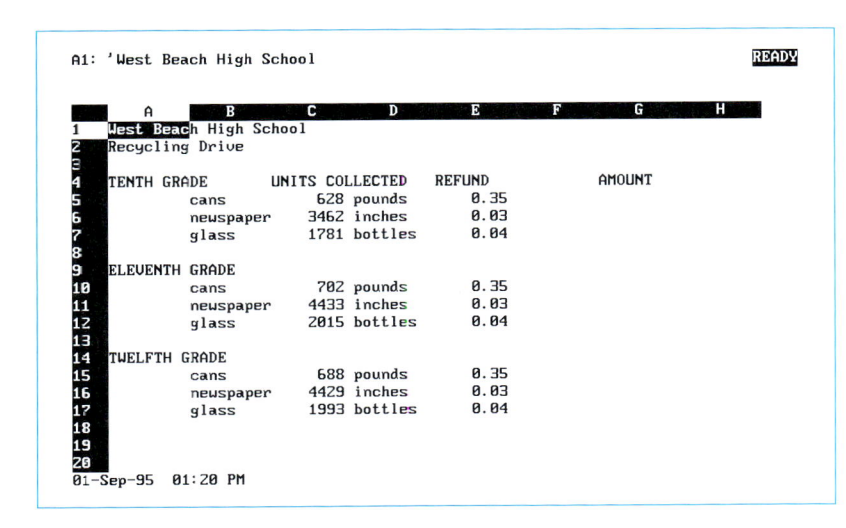

```
A1: 'West Beach High School                                    READY

        A       B       C       D       E       F       G       H
    1  West Beach High School
    2  Recycling Drive
    3
    4  TENTH GRADE      UNITS COLLECTED   REFUND          AMOUNT
    5          cans          628 pounds    0.35
    6          newspaper    3462 inches    0.03
    7          glass        1781 bottles   0.04
    8
    9  ELEVENTH GRADE
   10          cans          702 pounds    0.35
   11          newspaper    4433 inches    0.03
   12          glass        2015 bottles   0.04
   13
   14  TWELFTH GRADE
   15          cans          688 pounds    0.35
   16          newspaper    4429 inches    0.03
   17          glass        1993 bottles   0.04
   18
   19
   20
   01-Sep-95  01:20 PM
```

Figure 1.21

Follow the instructions in application 8 (Mathematics) to set up this worksheet.

- a. Enter the titles "West Beach High School" and "Recycling Drive" in cells A1 and A2, as shown in Figure 1.21.
- b. Enter the row 4 and column A and B labels as shown in the figure. Be sure to press CAPS LOCK to enter the labels shown in all uppercase characters.
- c. Enter values for the units collected in column C, as shown in the figure.
- d. Enter the unit labels in column D, as shown in the figure.
- e. Enter the refund rate values in column E, as shown in the figure.
- f. Use the /File Directory command (/FD) to make drive A (or drive B), which contains the student data disk, current.
- g. Press HOME, and use the /File Save command (/FS) to save the worksheet in a file named RECYCLE1.WK1.
- h. Use the /Quit command (/Q) to quit the 1-2-3 program.

Health

Nutrition

9. For your health class, you are given an assignment to determine whether you are keeping your fat intake within a healthy range. The Food and Drug Administration suggests that you limit your daily fat intake to 30 percent or less of your daily total calorie intake. Begin by creating the worksheet shown in Figure 1.22. The worksheet lists your typical daily diet and its caloric or energy content, as outlined in the following steps:

```
A1: 'Daily Nutritional Information                                    READY
          A         B        C         D         E         F       G       H
    1  Daily Nutritional Information
    2
    3  BREAKFAST                   Prot.     Carb.     Lipids
    4  Toast                          4        25          2
    5  Orange Juice                   2        20
    6  Melon                          2        30
    7  Scrambled Eggs                13                   11
    8
    9  LUNCH
   10  Noodles                       15        74          4
   11  Mozzarella                    18         3         16
   12  Olives                                   1          8
   13  Mushrooms                      2        15          2
   14  Apple                                   24
   15
   16  DINNER
   17  Broccoli                       5         7
   18  Butter                                             26
   19  Chicken                       32        12         25
   20  Ice Cream                      5        45         23
   01-Feb-95  01:21 PM
```

Figure 1.22

Follow the instructions in application 9 (Nutrition) to create this worksheet.

a. Enter the title "Daily Nutritional Information" in cell A1.

b. Enter the column A labels. Be sure to press [CAPS LOCK] for the category labels in cells A3, A9, and A16.

c. Enter the column heading labels in row 3, as shown in Figure 1.22.

d. Enter the protein, carbohydrates, and lipids values, as shown in the figure.

e. Use the /File Directory command (/FD) to make drive A (or drive B), which contains the student data disk, current.

f. Press [HOME], and use the /File Save command (/FS) to save the worksheet in a file named NUTRINF1.WK1.

g. Use the /Quit command (/Q) to quit the 1-2-3 program.

Health

Physical Education

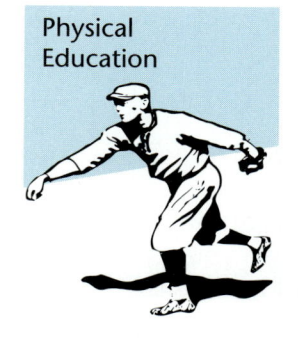

10. You are the official scorer for your school's softball team. Each time a batter goes to bat, you record what happened. At the end of the game, you calculate batting averages for each player by creating the worksheet shown in Figure 1.23. To do so, follow these steps:

```
A1:                                                                  READY
          A         B        C         D         E         F       G       H
    1                    WASHINGTON HIGH SCHOOL SOFTBALL TEAM
    2
    3                       COMPOSITE BATTING
    4
    5  NAME      POSITION AT BAT    RUNS      HITS     DOUBLES  TRIPLES  HOME RUNS
    6
    7  Bernhart  OF           8         1         6         1         0         1
    8  Taylor    SS           7         3         5         1         0         0
    9  Hepburn   3B           6         2         4         0         1         1
   10  Monroe    OF           6         3         3         3         0         0
   11  d'Arc     2B           5         7         2         1         0         1
   12  Victoria  OF           7         6         7         3         1         2
   13  Wood      1B           5         1         3         1         0         0
   14  Smith     C            4         0         1         1         0         0
   15  Turner    P            4         0         2         0         0         0
   16
   17
   18
   19
   20
   03-Sep-91  01:23 PM
```

Figure 1.23

Follow the instructions in application 10 (Physical Education) to create this worksheet.

a. Enter "WASHINGTON HIGH SCHOOL SOFTBALL TEAM" in cell C1. Be sure to press CAPS LOCK.
b. Enter "COMPOSITE BATTING" in cell C3.
c. Enter the column heading labels in row 5, as shown in Figure 1.23. Be sure to press CAPS LOCK.
d. Enter the label "RBI" (for "runs batted in") in cell I5 (not shown in the figure).
e. Enter the players' names in column A, starting in cell A7, as shown in Figure 1.23.
f. Enter the column B position labels, as shown in the figure. Be sure to include an apostrophe formatting prefix for the labels that begin with numbers.
g. Enter the values for at bats in column C, runs in column D, hits in column E, doubles in column F, triples in column G, and home runs in column H.
h. Enter the following column I RBI values starting in cell I7:
    5
    3
    4
    6
    2
    1
    2
    0
    0
i. Use the /File Directory command (/FD) to make drive A (or drive B), which contains the student data disk, current.
j. Press HOME, and use the /File Save command (/FS) to save the worksheet in a file named SBGAME1.WK1.
k. Use the /Quit command (/Q) to quit the 1-2-3 program.

2 Editing and Printing a Worksheet

Objectives

- Retrieve a worksheet file.
- Activate a dialog box.
- Edit settings in a dialog box.
- Display the current filename on the status line.
- Enter formulas into a worksheet.
- Point to cells in POINT mode to create a formula.
- Use EDIT mode to change data in a cell.
- Replace the contents of a cell.
- Observe automatic recalculation when data is changed.
- Anchor the current cell.
- Select a range in POINT mode.
- Copy a cell range.
- Select a print range.
- Print a range of data.
- Erase worksheet data from the display.

Often you must edit data you have entered into a worksheet and enter formulas that operate on values. In this lesson you will reload 1-2-3, and retrieve the worksheet file you created in Lesson 1. Then you will edit a dialog box setting to display the worksheet's filename on the status line. Finally, you will learn a variety of 1-2-3 operations to edit data, create formulas, specify cell ranges, and print data in the worksheet.

Exercise 2.1 — Retrieving a Worksheet File

Objective

After completing this exercise, you will be able to
- Retrieve a worksheet file.

RETRIEVE
The action of opening or loading a 1-2-3 worksheet file into memory and displaying its data on screen.

You will begin this lesson by retrieving the SUMSALES.WK1 file you created in Lesson 1. You *retrieve* a worksheet file by selecting the /File Retrieve command (/FR). As with the /File Save command (/FS), 1-2-3 switches to FILES mode when you select the /File Retrieve (/FR) command. In FILES mode, 1-2-3 displays the first five filenames in the current directory. But what do you do if the file you want is not among the first five listed?

You can press the → key until the filename you want appears on the control panel. The control panel displays the next five filenames when you move the menu pointer past the last filename on the right. However, it is easier to select a file from a list of all the files in the current directory by pressing F3, the Name command. The Name command displays a full-screen menu of all the files in the current directory when 1-2-3 is in FILES or NAMES mode. When the files are displayed, use any of the Arrow keys to move the menu pointer to the filename you want to retrieve and press ←. Now you will retrieve the file SUMSALES.WK1.

1 ▶ If necessary, start 1-2-3. Use the /File Directory command (/FD) to change the current directory setting to the drive that contains your student data disk.

2 ▶ Press the Slash key (/) to access the Main Menu.

3 ▶ Type **F** to select the File command.

The File command's submenu is active on the control panel's second line.

4 ▶ Type **R** to select the Retrieve option.

The FILES mode indicator is displayed, and the following prompt appears on the control panel:

Name of file to retrieve: A:*.wk1

> **Note:** The drive and/or path to the right of the prompt may be different on your screen.

The first five files on the student data disk are listed across the control panel's third line.

5 ▶ Press F3 (the Name command).

A full-screen list of the files on your student data disk appears, as shown in Figure 2.1. (If you are using high density disks, your data disk may contain more files than shown here.)

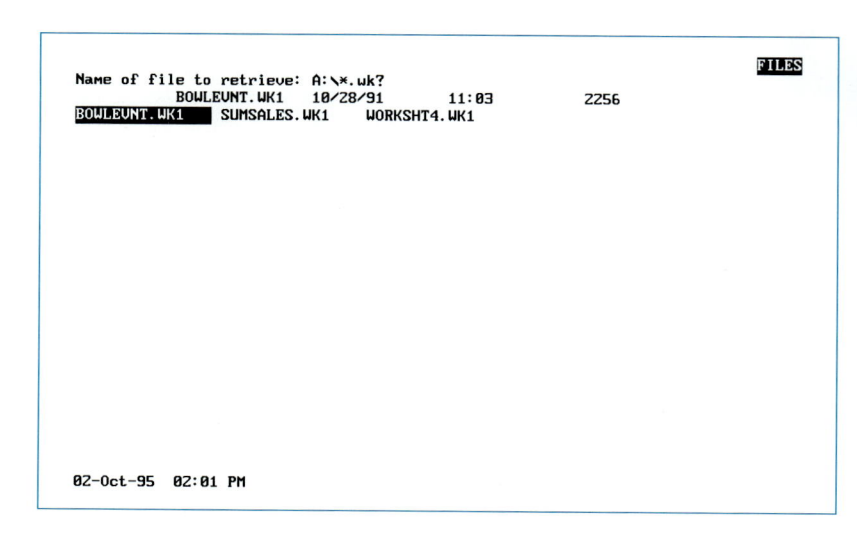

```
Name of file to retrieve: A:\*.wk?                                    FILES
            BOWLEVNT.WK1   10/28/91       11:03         2256
BOWLEVNT.WK1    SUMSALES.WK1    WORKSHT4.WK1




02-Oct-95  02:01 PM
```

Figure 2.1

Press F3 (the Name command) to display a full-screen list of files in the current directory when 1-2-3 is in FILES mode.

6 ▶ Move the menu pointer to the filename SUMSALES.WK1.

7 ▶ Press ⏎.

The SUMSALES.WK1 worksheet appears, and 1-2-3 switches to READY mode.

2 ▶ Editing and Printing a Worksheet

Exercise 2.2

Displaying the Current Filename

Objectives

After completing this exercise, you will be able to
- Activate a dialog box.
- Edit settings in a dialog box.
- Display the current filename on the status line.

When working with 1-2-3, it is often useful to see the name of the file with which you are working. Right now your screen probably shows the current date and time (if your computer's internal clock has been properly set). You can change the clock setting so that it displays the name of the file that is currently loaded. There are two ways to do this: (1) Select the /Worksheet Global Default Other Clock Filename (/WGDOCF) command; or (2) select the /Worksheet Global Default (/WGD) command and change the clock setting in the Default Settings dialog box, shown in Figure 2.2. *Dialog boxes* are a new feature with this 1-2-3 release. You will use the Default Settings dialog box to change the clock setting.

DIALOG BOX
A special 1-2-3 screen that displays current worksheet or computer system settings. Dialog boxes can be activated for editing to change settings. Settings can also be changed by using 1-2-3 command menu options.

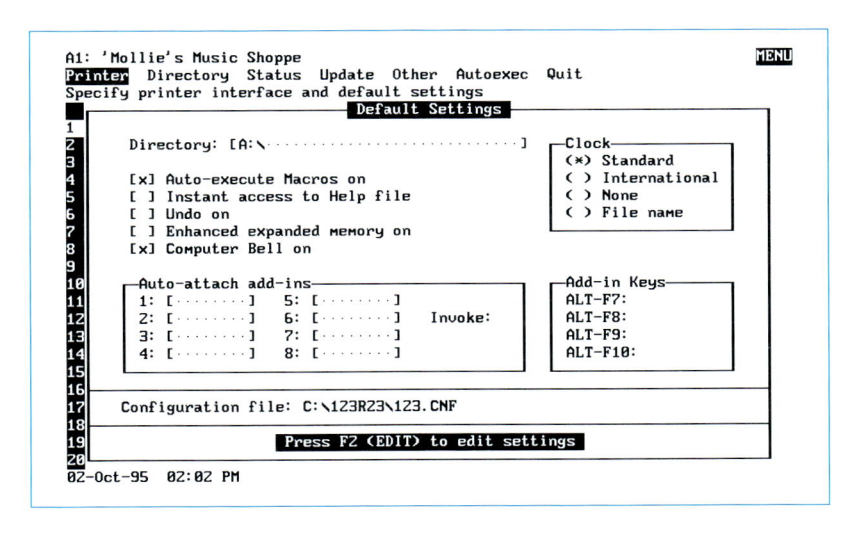

Figure 2.2

When you select the /Worksheet Global Default (/WGD) command, the Default Settings dialog box displays. It shows default settings for the current worksheet. The Default command submenu is still active in MENU mode.

Note: If you use the /Worksheet Global Default Other Clock Filename (/WGDOCF) command, select the Quit option on the Default command submenu to return to READY mode after doing so.

You activate a dialog box by pressing F2 (the Edit command). This key also lets you edit the contents in a cell, and you will learn more about this later.

Displaying the Current Filename 39

When you press F2, 1-2-3 switches from MENU mode to SETTINGS mode. In SETTINGS mode, you can move the pointer in the dialog box to edit (change) settings. You can use the Arrow keys to move the pointer. However, a quicker method is to type the underlined letter in the name of the setting you want to change.

Some settings have a group of options, such as the Clock setting. The pointer moves to the first option in the group when you type the C. To change any setting, press the ↓ or ↑ key to move the pointer to an option and press ↵. Or, type the underlined letter in the option's name. After changing any settings, press ↵. Then press any combination of Arrow keys to move the pointer to the OK command button at the bottom of the dialog box. Press ↵ again to return to MENU mode.

Now you will change the clock setting in the Default Settings dialog box.

1 ▶ Press the Slash key (/) to access the Main Menu.

2 ▶ Type **WGD** to select the Worksheet, Global, and Default commands.

The Default Settings dialog box appears. The Default command's submenu is active on the control panel, as shown in Figure 2.2.

3 ▶ Press F2 to activate the dialog box.

The Default Settings dialog box is activated, and 1-2-3 switches to SETTINGS mode. Notice that no menu is displayed on the control panel, as shown in Figure 2.3.

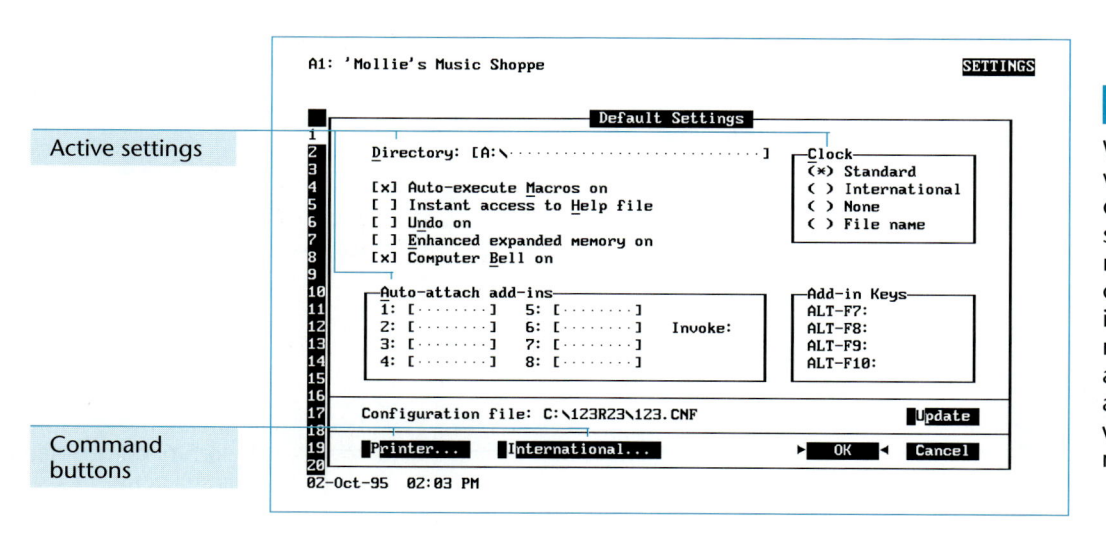

Figure 2.3

When you press F2 with a dialog box displayed, 1-2-3 switches to SETTINGS mode and the command menu is inactive. You can move the pointer to any dialog box setting and make changes while in SETTINGS mode.

Before you change the Clock setting in the dialog box, practice moving the pointer around to get a feel for how it moves from setting option to setting option in a dialog box.

4 ▶ Press ↓ twice.

The pointer moves to the Directory setting. Notice that your current directory setting is A:\, so you do not need to make any adjustment.

5 ▶ Press ⬇ once.

   The pointer moves to the Clock setting. However, before you change this setting, move the pointer around to other dialog box options.

6 ▶ Press ⬆ 5 times.

   The pointer should be on the Printer... command button. (If it is not, press an Arrow key until it is.)

7 ▶ Press ⏎.

   The Default Printer Settings dialog box appears over the Default Settings dialog box, as shown in Figure 2.4.

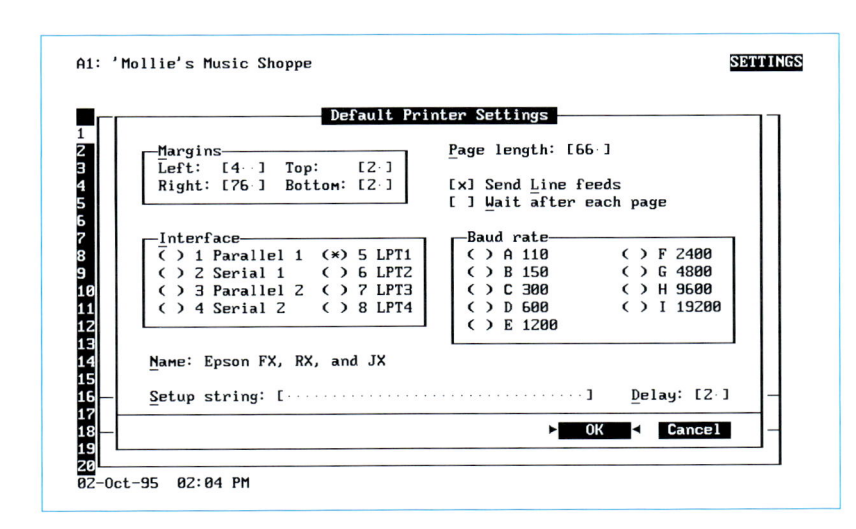

Figure 2.4

When you select a command button with ellipses in a dialog box, another dialog box with additional options appears over the existing dialog box. In this case, the Printer... command button displays the Default Printer Settings dialog box.

Certain command buttons in dialog boxes have ellipses (...). This means that another dialog box of setting options is displayed when you select the command button. Notice that when you select a command button, the new dialog box is already activated.

8 ▶ Press ESC.

   The Default Settings dialog box appears.

   Note: You could also select the OK button to return to the previous dialog box.

Now you will change the Clock setting to display the current worksheet filename on the status line.

9 ▶ Type **C** to move the pointer to the Clock setting options.

10 ▶ Press ⬆ once.

   The pointer moves to the File name option.

Displaying the Current Filename

11 ▶ Press ⏎.

> The File name option for the Clock setting is selected. The asterisk now is displayed in the parentheses next to the File name option. The pointer returns to the OK option.

12 ▶ Press ⏎.

> The Default option menu reappears on the control panel, and 1-2-3 returns to MENU mode.

Notice that this menu has a Quit option. You can use this option to leave MENU mode and return to the worksheet in READY mode.

13 ▶ Type **Q** to select the Quit option.

> You return to the worksheet in READY mode. The filename SUMSALES.WK1 appears on the status line, as shown in Figure 2.5.

Current filename

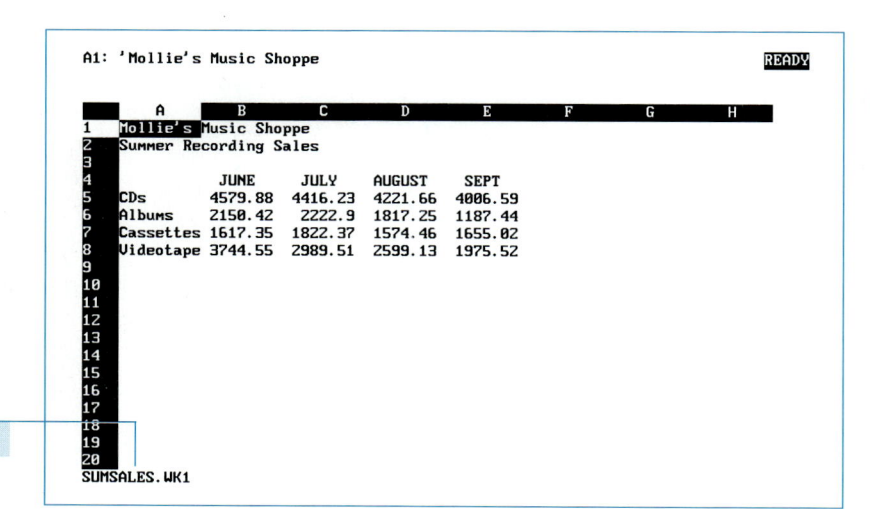

Figure 2.5

After you change the clock setting to the File name option, the current worksheet's filename appears on the status line.

Exercise 2.3 Creating Formulas

Objectives

After completing this exercise, you will be able to
- Enter formulas into a worksheet.
- Point to cells in POINT mode to create a formula.

So far, you could have just as easily set up the SUMSALES.WK1 worksheet with pencil and paper. In this exercise, you will begin to experience the

42 2 ▶ Editing and Printing a Worksheet

power of spreadsheet software by building formulas that calculate a result automatically.

Formulas are mathematical calculations that contain one or more operands and operators. *Operands* are numbers that are used in the calculation. *Operators* are symbols that represent an arithmetic operation, such as addition or subtraction.

In 1-2-3, *formulas* are mathematical expressions that you enter into cells to do calculations with data stored in other cells. You can use 1-2-3 as a calculator by entering numbers in a formula (for example, 300+150). However, you will use 1-2-3's power better if you enter cell addresses into a formula (for example, +B5+B6). This may not seem like such a big deal. But if you later change one or more values in cells that are referenced in a formula, the formula adjusts automatically. In contrast, a formula built with numbers would need editing whenever data changed.

When you build formulas that contain cell addresses, you begin by entering an operator. Usually you enter the plus sign (+), which switches 1-2-3 to VALUE mode. Then you enter the cell addresses and operators you need for the calculation. The first operator is necessary. If you were to begin a formula with a column letter in a cell address, 1-2-3 would interpret that entry as a label.

When creating formulas, you must be aware of the order in which 1-2-3 does the arithmetic based on the operators in the formula. Lotus 1-2-3 uses a special order called the operator order of precedence. *Order of precedence* is the order or number in which each arithmetic operation is calculated when there are two or more operators in the formula. Table 2.1 shows the order of precedence that 1-2-3 uses for each arithmetic operator. If two or more operators are the same, 1-2-3 does their calculations in sequence from left to right.

OPERAND
A number or a cell reference in a formula on which a mathematical operation is performed.

OPERATOR
A symbol in a formula that represents an arithmetic operation or a relationship between two values. Lotus 1-2-3 recognizes the following symbols as operators: plus sign (+) for addition, minus sign (-) for subtraction, asterisk (*) for multiplication, and slash (/) for division.

FORMULA
A mathematical expression that calculates a result.

Operation	Operator	Precedence
exponentiation	^	first
negative/positive	-/+	second
multiplication or division	* or /	third
addition or subtraction	+ or -	fourth

Table 2.1

Operator Order of Precedence

You can override 1-2-3's operator order of precedence by enclosing operations in parentheses in the formula. Operations inside parentheses are performed first. The same operator order of precedence applies within parentheses. The following example demonstrates how parentheses in a formula can affect its result.

 -5+3/2*4+7=8

 -5+3/2*(4+7)=11.5

Now you will create a formula with cell addresses to get an expense total for June in the current worksheet.

Creating Formulas

1 ▶ Move the cell pointer to cell B9.

2 ▶ Type **+**

The plus operator appears on the control panel, and 1-2-3 switches to VALUE mode.

3 ▶ Type **b5+b6+b7+b8**

The formula appears on the control panel as you type.

4 ▶ Press ⏎.

The formula is entered. Notice that the result 12092.2 appears in the cell, but the formula is displayed on the control panel as the cell's content.

You typed all the formula's cell addresses and operators into cell B9. However, there is a problem in building formulas this way. You can very easily make mistakes (typos), especially if you are entering a long or complex formula, or many formulas.

POINTING
When you are building a formula, the method in which the Arrow keys are used to point to specific cells to insert cell addresses into the formula.

Lotus 1-2-3 gives you another way to build formulas that is more accurate. This method is called *pointing*. When you build a formula, you can use the Arrow keys to move the cell pointer and point to the cells you want to include in the formula. Go ahead and try this method by getting an expense total for July in column C.

5 ▶ Move the cell pointer to cell C9.

6 ▶ Type **+**

The operator and the VALUE mode indicator appear on the control panel.

7 ▶ Press ↑ 4 times.

The cell pointer is on cell C5, and +C5 appears on the control panel.

8 ▶ Type **+**

The cell pointer returns to cell C9, and +C5+ appears on the control panel.

9 ▶ Press ↑ 3 times.

The cell pointer is on cell C6, and +C5+C6 appears on the control panel.

10 ▶ Type **+**

The cell pointer returns to cell C9, and +C5+C6+ appears on the control panel.

2 ▶ Editing and Printing a Worksheet

11 ▶ Press ↑ twice.

The cell pointer is on cell C7.

12 ▶ Type **+**

13 ▶ Press ↑ once.

The cell pointer is on cell C8 and +C5+C6+C7+C8 appears on the control panel.

14 ▶ Press ↵.

The formula is entered. The result 11451.01 appears in cell C9, and the formula is displayed on the control panel.

Exercise 2.4 — Editing Worksheet Data

Objectives

After completing this exercise, you will be able to
- Use EDIT mode to change data in a cell.
- Replace the contents of a cell.
- Recognize automatic recalculation when data is changed.

In Lesson 1 you learned how to correct typos before pressing ↵ to store data in a cell. However, very often you need to go back and edit data that has already been entered. Basically, there are two ways to edit existing data: (1) replace the cell's contents with new data or (2) edit the data in EDIT mode.

EDIT MODE KEYS
The set of keys that allow you to position the cursor, overtype, insert, or delete characters in EDIT mode.

INSERT
The default keyboard mode in which characters are inserted at the cursor position. The existing characters to the right of the cursor move right to accommodate the inserted characters.

The first step in editing data is to move the cell pointer to the cell you want to edit. If the data is to be replaced entirely, enter the new data into the cell that contains the existing data. The new data simply replaces the old data. However, if you want to change only some of the data, press F2 (the Edit command) to switch 1-2-3 to EDIT mode. In EDIT mode, the content of the current cell appears on the control panel along with a cursor. Use the appropriate *EDIT mode keys,* shown in Table 2.2, to move the cursor anywhere within the entry. Other EDIT mode keys let you *insert, delete,* or *overtype* characters, as necessary, to make changes.

Table 2.2

EDIT Mode Keys

EDIT Mode Keys	Description
F2	Toggles between VALUE or LABEL mode and EDIT mode.
→ or ←	Moves the cursor one character to the right or left.
↑ or ↓	Enters the edited data in the current cell, moves the cell pointer to the next cell up or down, and returns 1-2-3 to READY mode. Also switches 1-2-3 to POINT mode if the cursor is on a cell or range address.
CTRL-→ or CTRL-←	Moves the cursor five characters to the right or left.
HOME or END	Moves the cursor to the beginning or end of the entry on the control panel.
BACKSPACE	Erases one character to the left of the cursor.
DEL	Erases the character at the cursor position.
ESC	Erases all the entry's characters on the control panel.
INS	Toggles between insert and overtype keyboard modes.
←	Enters the edited data in the current cell, which remains current as 1-2-3 returns to READY mode.
ALT-F1 \ (Compose)	Creates characters that are not available on the keyboard.
F9 (Calc)	Converts a formula to its current value.

DELETE
To erase one or more characters by pressing BACKSPACE or DEL.

OVERTYPE
A keyboard mode in which existing characters are replaced by new characters as they are typed. The INS key is used to toggle between insert and overtype status modes.

Characters can automatically be inserted at the cursor position. To overtype characters, press INS to display the OVR indicator on the status line. The INS key toggles between insert (INS) and overtype (OVR) status modes. When you have finished making changes, press ← or the ↑ or the ↓ key to store the changes.

You will now edit some data in your worksheet. You will begin by editing two product labels in column A. Then you will replace the June sales figure for compact discs (CDs), because you were given an incorrect amount.

1 ▶ Move the cell pointer to cell A5, which contains the label "CDs."

The label in cell A5 appears to the right of the cell address on the control panel.

2 ▶ Press F2.

The data in cell A5 appears on the control panel with a cursor, and 1-2-3 switches to EDIT mode.

46   **2 ▶ Editing and Printing a Worksheet**

3 ▶ Press ← twice.

The cursor on the control panel moves to the "D."

4 ▶ Type **ompact**

5 ▶ Press **SPACEBAR** once.

A space is inserted after the word "Compact."

6 ▶ Press → once.

The cursor moves to the "s."

7 ▶ Type **isc**

Your control panel should look like the one shown in Figure 2.6. If it does not, edit it until it does.

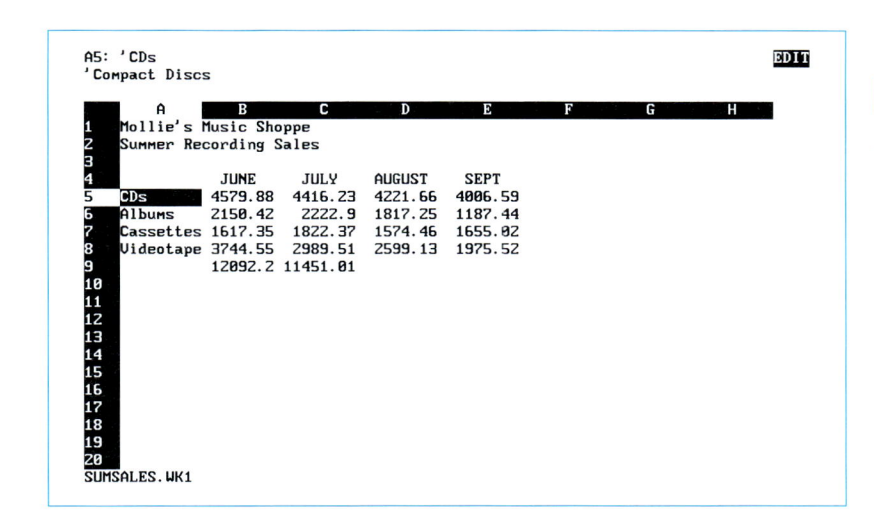

Figure 2.6

After you edit the label in cell A5 in EDIT mode, your control panel should look like this.

8 ▶ Press ←.

The product label in cell A5 is edited and stored.

TRUNCATION
The shortening of a label display when (1) it contains more characters than will fit in the cell width and (2) the next cell to the right contains data.

DEFAULT SETTING
The settings that 1-2-3 or any computer program uses automatically until you change them.

Notice that part of the edited label in cell A5 has been cut off. This is called truncation. *Truncation* means that only part of a label appears in a cell. Lotus 1-2-3 truncates the label's display because the label is longer than will fit in the width of the column. Also, there is data in cell B5. By default, 1-2-3 worksheet columns are 9 characters wide. A *default setting* is one that is used by 1-2-3 automatically. If no data is in the cell to the right of a long label, then the label spills over into as many cells as it needs. For example, look at the label for the worksheet's title in cell A1. The label is 21 characters (counting the spaces), but the whole label appears because there is no data in cell B1. In cell A5, your new label is 13 characters, but 1-2-3 truncates its display because there is a value in cell B5. Truncation only affects a label's display. All the label's characters are stored in the cell, as you can see on the first line of the control panel.

Editing Worksheet Data

In Lesson 3, you will learn how to adjust the width of columns to display long labels. For now, you will continue with this exercise by editing another label in EDIT mode.

9 ▶ Move the cell pointer to cell A7.

The cell pointer is on the cell that contains the label "Cassettes."

10 ▶ Press F2.

The data in cell A7 appears on the control panel with a cursor, and 1-2-3 switches to EDIT mode.

11 ▶ Press HOME.

The cursor moves to the apostrophe formatting prefix on the control panel.

12 ▶ Press →.

The cursor moves to the "C."

13 ▶ Type **Audio**

14 ▶ Press SPACEBAR.

15 ▶ Press ←.

Cell A7's label is edited, and the change is stored.

Now you will correct the June sales figure for compact discs.

16 ▶ Press ↑ twice and → once.

The cell pointer is on cell B5, which contains the June sales for compact discs.

17 ▶ Type **5565.15**

The new value appears on the control panel's second line, while the original value remains displayed on the first line, as shown in Figure 2.7.

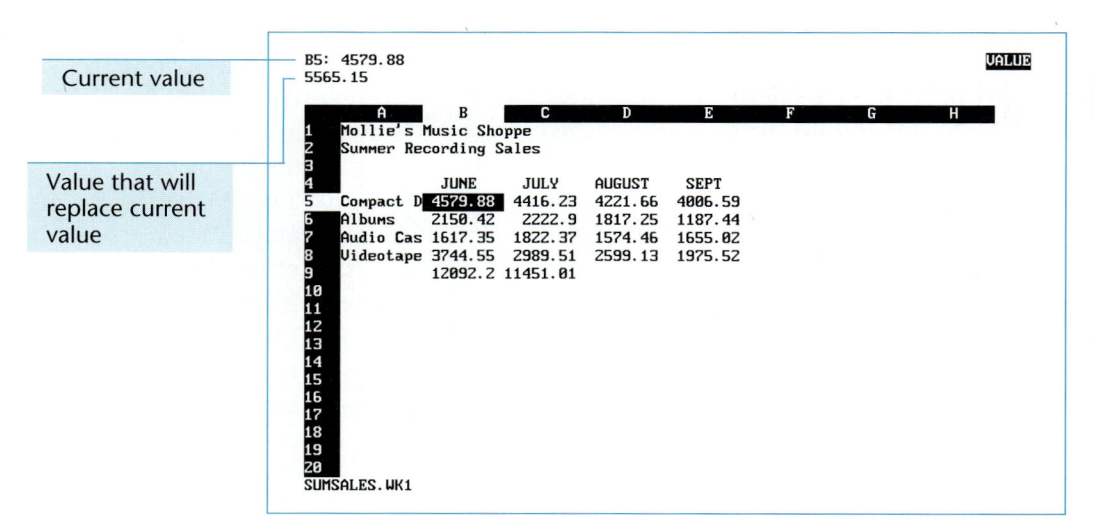

Current value

Value that will replace current value

Figure 2.7

Before you press ←, the control panel displays the current contents of cell B5 on the control panel's first line. The new value you have just typed appears on the second line.

2 ▶ Editing and Printing a Worksheet

AUTOMATIC RECALCULATION
An electronic spreadsheet feature in which formulas containing cell addresses recalculate automatically after a change is entered into a cell referenced in the formula.

18 ▶ Press ⏎, and observe the change in cell B9.

   The new value replaces the old value, and the formula's result in cell B9 changes to 13077.47.

The formula in cell B9 contains the cell address B5. The formula's result reflects the change you made to the data in cell B5. This powerful electronic spreadsheet feature is called *automatic recalculation*. Change another value to observe automatic recalculation again.

19 ▶ Move the cell pointer to cell C8, which contains the July sales for videotape.

20 ▶ Type **3001.49**

21 ▶ Press ⏎.

   The new value replaces the old value, and the formula's result in cell C9 changes to 11462.99.

22 ▶ Press HOME to move the cell pointer to cell A1.

Exercise 2.5 — Copying Data and Selecting Cell Ranges

After completing this exercise, you will be able to
- Anchor the current cell.
- Select a range in POINT mode.
- Copy a cell range.

RANGE
A rectangular group of adjacent cells, including a single cell, a column, a row, or several adjacent rows and columns.

RANGE ADDRESS
The location of a range, designated by the cell addresses of two diagonally opposite cells, separated by two periods (for example, A1..IV8192).

Many 1-2-3 operations require you to specify or select cell ranges. A *range* is any rectangular group or block of cells. A single cell is also considered a range. Like cells, you refer to a range by its range address. A *range address* includes any two cells within the range that are in diagonally opposite corners.

Often you select a range in response to 1-2-3 command prompts. You can respond accurately to such prompts by using the Arrow keys to highlight the range in POINT mode. To highlight a range in POINT mode, you must first establish the anchor cell. The *anchor cell* is the first cell address that you lock in place. You lock the anchor cell so that the highlight can be expanded from that cell to specify the range.

For instance, you will soon learn to use the /Copy command (/C) to perform a copy operation. The *copy* operation is very useful when you need to enter duplicate information into other worksheet ranges. The /Copy command (/C) can be used to copy labels, values, and formulas. To copy data, you must

ANCHOR CELL
The cell that is fixed in POINT mode so that a range can be expanded (highlighted) from that cell.

COPY
The action used to duplicate data in a cell or range and to place the duplicate data into another cell or range.

specify the range to be copied and the range where the copied information is to be placed. For example, if you select this command with the cell pointer in cell B9, the following prompt appears on the control panel:

Copy what? B9..B9

Because a full range address is displayed when you select the /Copy command (/C), 1-2-3 is telling you that cell B9 is already anchored. This means you can press the Arrow keys to expand (highlight) any size range from that location. After you highlight the range you want to copy, press ⏎ and the following prompt appears on the control panel:

To where? B9

Because a single cell address (the current cell) is displayed at this prompt, 1-2-3 is telling you that cell B9 is not anchored. If you press an Arrow key, the cell pointer moves to another cell but does not expand the highlight from the current cell. To anchor a cell, move the cell pointer to a desired location and type a period (**.**). The current cell becomes the anchor cell, and you can highlight the range and then complete the operation. You will use the /Copy command (C) to practice selecting ranges and copy a formula to another range.

1 ▶ Move the cell pointer to cell B9.

2 ▶ Press the Slash key (/) to access the Main Menu.

3 ▶ Type **C** to select the Copy command.

The prompt "Copy what? B9..B9" appears on the control panel. The full range address tells you that cell B9 is anchored.

4 ▶ Press ⏎ to select cell B9 as the "Copy what?" range.

The range is entered, and the prompt "To where? B9" appears on the control panel. Cell B9 is not anchored because a cell address (B9), not a range address, follows the prompt.

5 ▶ Press → twice.

The cell pointer is on cell D9.

6 ▶ Type **.** (a period).

The control panel prompt now reads "To where? D9..D9." This tells you that cell D9 is anchored.

7 ▶ Press →.

The range "D9..E9" appears on the control panel, and the range is highlighted in the worksheet area, as shown in Figure 2.8.

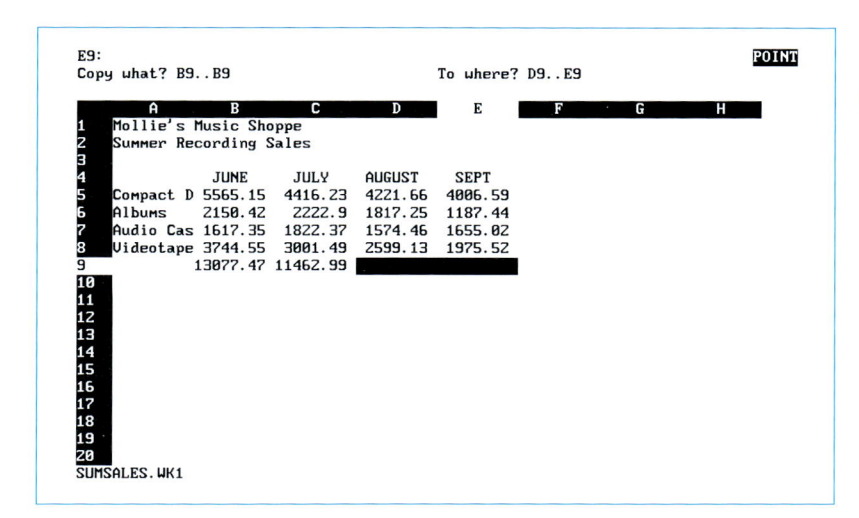

Figure 2.8

After you type the period to anchor the current cell, you can extend the highlight to specify the Copy command's "To where" range.

8 ▶ Press ⏎.

The formula in cell B9 is copied to the range "D9..E9." Notice that the results in cells D9 and E9 have been accurately calculated, as shown in Figure 2.9.

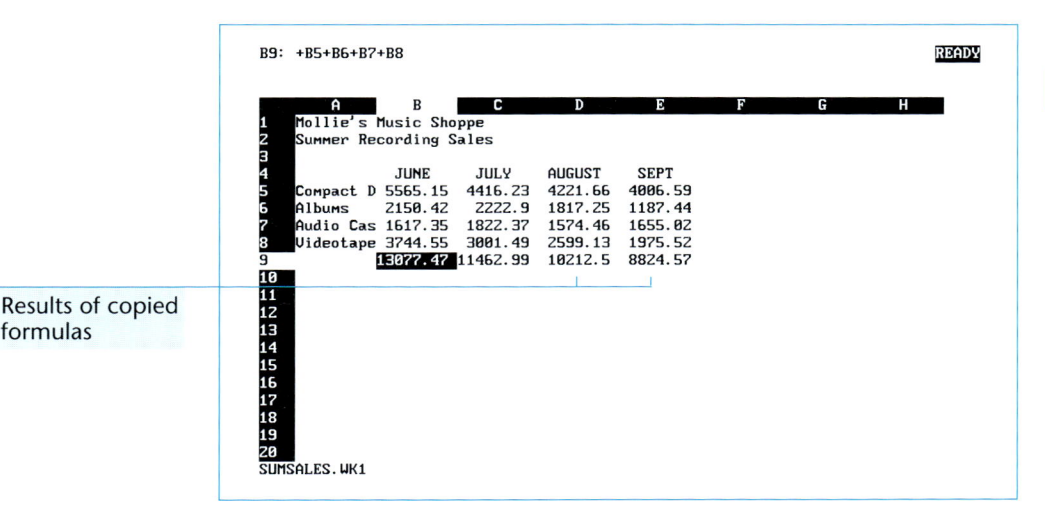

Figure 2.9

After you copy the formula in cell B9, the formulas in the range D9..E9 adjust to calculate the values in their respective columns.

Results of copied formulas

9 ▶ Move the cell pointer to cell D9, which contains the formula that sums the August sales for all products.

10 ▶ Look at the formula in the current cell on the control panel.

Lotus 1-2-3 adjusted the cell addresses in the formula to total the column D values. In Lesson 5 you will learn more about how 1-2-3 is able to make this adjustment to copied formulas.

Copying Data and Selecting Cell Ranges

Exercise 2.6

Printing a Worksheet Range

Objectives

After completing this exercise, you will be able to
- Select a print range.
- Print a range of data.

HARD COPY
A paper copy of printed text or data that was generated using a software program.

Often you will need to print a hard copy of all or a portion of the data you have worked with in a worksheet. A *hard copy* of worksheet data is a paper copy that is useful for editing or providing others with information. In 1-2-3, you select the /Print Printer command (/PP) to begin the printing operation. In order to print worksheet data, you must tell 1-2-3 the range of data you want to print. You do this in the same way that you selected ranges when you learned to use the /Copy command (C).

Before printing a range of data, it is good practice to first save the latest changes to your worksheet file. That way you will not lose any changes to your file in case your system hangs up during printing because of a technical problem. When you select the /File Save command (/FS) to save a file that you have saved before, 1-2-3 displays the existing filename. Press ⏎ to save the file under the same name. After you press ⏎, the following three options appear on the control panel:

> Cancel Replace Backup

Select the Replace option to update the existing file with your latest changes. The Cancel option allows you to abandon the save operation. If you select the Backup option, 1-2-3 saves the current version with the .WK1 extension and retains a copy of the previous version with the .BAK extension. Now you will save the current version of your SUMSALES.WK1 worksheet and then print a range of data.

1 ▶ Press HOME.

   The cell pointer is on cell A1.

2 ▶ Press the Slash key (/) to access the Main Menu.

3 ▶ Type **FS** to select the File and Save commands.

   Lotus 1-2-3 prompts you to enter the filename. The filename SUMSALES.WK1 appears to the right of the prompt.

4 ▶ Press ⏎.

2 ▶ Editing and Printing a Worksheet

The existing filename is entered, and the three save options appear on the control panel.

5 ▶ Type **R** to select the Replace option.

The latest changes to SUMSALES.WK1 are saved.

Now you will print the range of data that you see on your screen.

6 ▶ Press the Slash key (/) to access the Main Menu.

7 ▶ Type **PP** to select the Print and Printer commands.

The Printer command's submenu is active on the control panel. The Print Settings dialog box appears, as shown in Figure 2.10.

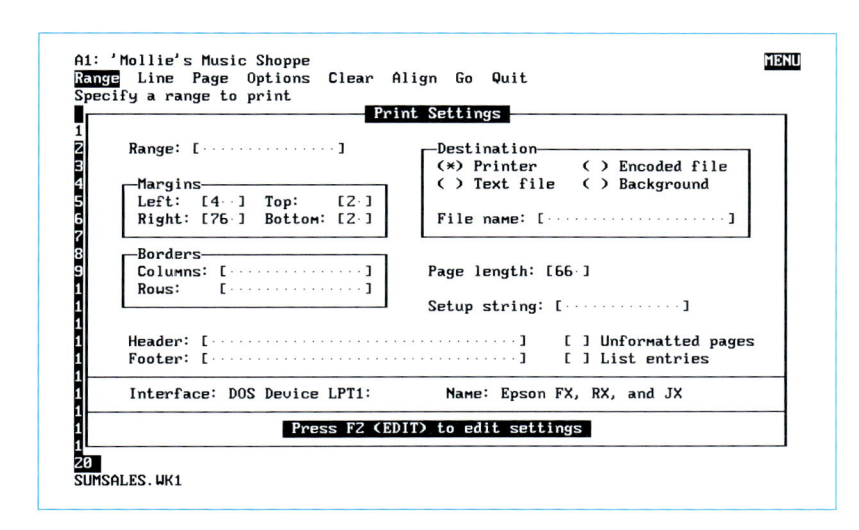

Figure 2.10

The /Print Printer command (/PP) displays the worksheet's current print settings in the Print Settings dialog box. The current settings shown on your screen may differ from those shown here.

8 ▶ Type **R** to select the Range command.

The Print Settings dialog box disappears. Lotus 1-2-3 switches to POINT mode and prompts you to enter the print range. Notice that A1, the current cell address, is displayed to the right of the prompt. Cell A1 is not anchored.

9 ▶ Type **.** (a period).

Now the range address "A1..A1" appears to the right of the prompt. Cell A1 is anchored.

10 ▶ Press ⬇ 8 times.

The cell pointer is on cell A9, and the range address on the control panel is "A1..A9." The range is highlighted in the worksheet area.

11 ▶ Press ➡ 4 times.

The cell pointer is on cell E9, and the range address on the control panel is "A1..E9." The range is highlighted in the worksheet area, as shown in Figure 2.11.

Printing a Worksheet Range

53

```
E9: +E5+E6+E7+E8                                              POINT
Enter print range: A1..E9
         A         B        C        D        E        F    .    G        H
1    Mollie's Music Shoppe
2    Summer Recording Sales
3
4              JUNE      JULY    AUGUST     SEPT
5    Compact D 5565.15   4416.23  4221.66  4006.59
6    Albums    2150.42   2222.9   1817.25  1187.44
7    Audio Cas 1617.35   1822.37  1574.46  1655.02
8    Videotape 3744.55   3001.49  2599.13  1975.52
9             13077.47  11462.99 10212.5   8824.57
10
11
12
13
14
15
16
17
18
19
20
SUMSALES.WK1
```

Highlighted print range

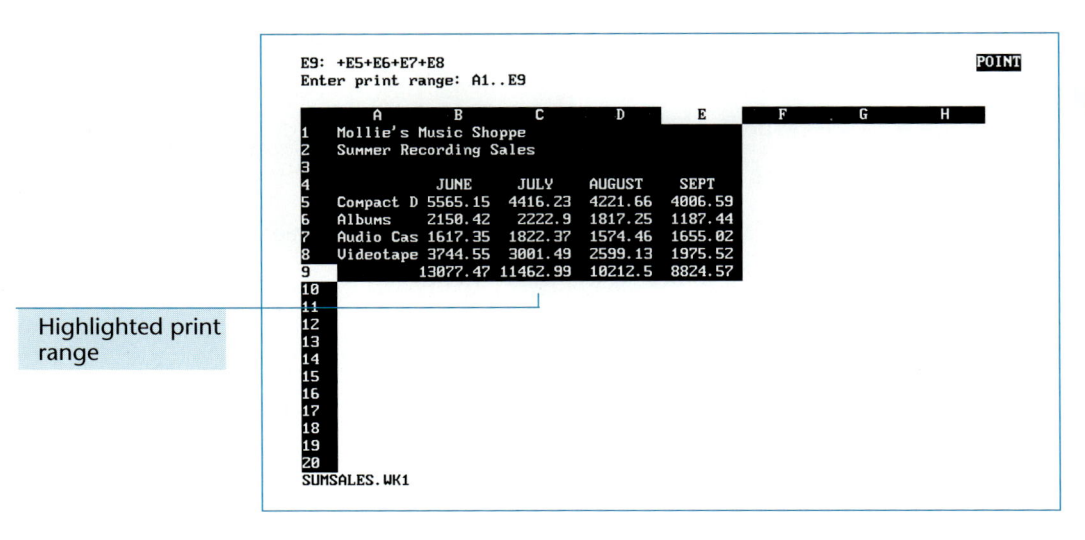

Figure 2.11

After you point to the desired print range, the range is highlighted in the worksheet area.

12 ▶ Press ⏎.

The Print Settings dialog box reappears. Notice that the range "A1..E9" is now the current print range setting.

Before you actually send the data range to the printer, always check and make sure that your printer has paper. Also check that the paper is properly aligned in the printer and that the printer is on line. Then select the Align command to tell 1-2-3 that your printer is ready. Nothing will seem to happen when you select the Align command. Next, select the Go command to start the printing operation. After the range is printed, select the Page command to advance the paper in the printer.

13 ▶ Check that your printer is turned on, is on line, and has paper. Make sure the paper is properly aligned.

14 ▶ Type **A** to select the Align command.

Nothing will seem to happen, but you have told 1-2-3 that your printer is ready.

15 ▶ Type **G** to select the Go command.

The range prints.

Note: The range prints if you are using a dot-matrix printer. If you are using a laser printer, you may see a flashing light on the printer. This tells you that the printer is processing the data.

16 ▶ Type **P** to select the Page command.

Note: If you are using a dot-matrix printer, the Page command advances the continuous-feed paper to the top of the next page. If you are using a laser printer, the Page command ejects the page with the printed data range.

2 ▶ Editing and Printing a Worksheet

17 ▶ Type **Q** to select the Quit option.

The worksheet reappears, and 1-2-3 returns to READY mode.

Because print settings are saved with a worksheet file, it is good practice to save the worksheet again. This saves the current print range with the file. You will do this the same way you updated the file before the printing operation.

18 ▶ Press HOME to move the cell pointer to cell A1, if it is not already there.

19 ▶ Press the Slash key (/) to access the Main Menu.

20 ▶ Type **FS** to select the File and Save commands.

21 ▶ Press ⏎ to save the file under the same filename.

22 ▶ Type **R** to select the Replace option.

The file is saved with the current print range setting.

Exercise 2.7 Erasing a Worksheet

Objective

After completing this exercise, you will be able to
- Erase worksheet data from the display.

ERASE
A process that removes all the currently loaded data from memory (RAM) and clears the worksheet area.

You can *erase* worksheet data and return to a blank, or clear, worksheet area using the /Worksheet Erase Yes command (/WEY). This allows you to begin creating a new worksheet without having to quit and reload 1-2-3. Always be sure to save your work before executing this command. Otherwise, you will lose any changes you have made since the last time you saved. You will complete this lesson by erasing the SUMSALES.WK1 worksheet data. Because you saved your work at the end of Exercise 2.6, you can go ahead and erase the worksheet now.

1 ▶ Press the Slash key (/) to access the Main Menu.

2 ▶ Type **WE** to select the Worksheet and Erase commands.

As with the Quit command you learned in Lesson 1, 1-2-3 displays the No and Yes options.

3 ▶ Type **Y** to select the Yes option.

The worksheet data is erased, and the worksheet area is clear.

Erasing a Worksheet   55

You can now begin the Lesson 2 applications that follow the Concept Summary, or you can go on to Lesson 3. Otherwise, quit 1-2-3 if you are through with this session.

Concept Summary

- Spreadsheet software provides commands to retrieve worksheet files for updating, printing, or extensive editing.

- Formulas are mathematical calculations that can be created and stored in a worksheet cell. Formulas contain operands (numbers and cell addresses) and operators (symbols that perform operations on operands or show relationships between operands).

- In many spreadsheet software packages, a formula usually begins with an operator so that the software does not misinterpret column letters in cell addresses as text.

- Editing lets you replace or change data in worksheets.

- When working with formulas and commands, the pointing method lets you point to specific cells and highlight ranges. This method lets you enter the formula into the worksheet accurately, so it can operate on the correct data.

- A big advantage in using spreadsheet software is that formulas with cell addresses automatically recalculate when data in a referenced cell is changed.

- Ranges are any rectangular group of cells, including a single cell, adjacent cells in a row, adjacent cells in a column, or several rows and columns of adjacent cells.

- A range is identified by a range address, which is composed of the addresses of the top left and bottom right cells.

- Electronic spreadsheets let you copy data in any size range to other ranges of any size. The copy feature makes data entry even easier when duplicate information must be entered into the worksheet.

- The printing capacity in spreadsheet software lets you make a hard copy of worksheet data for editing and presentation.

Command Summary

/File Retrieve (/FR)
loads a worksheet file into memory (RAM)

/Worksheet Global Default Other Clock Filename (/WGDOCF)
displays the current filename on the status line

/Worksheet Global Default (/WGD)
displays the Default Settings dialog box

F2 (Edit command)
switches 1-2-3 to EDIT mode

/Copy (/C)
copies a range of data to another range

/Print Printer (/PP)
displays the Printer command submenu and Print Settings dialog box

/Print Printer Range (/PPR)
sets the range of data to be printed

/Print Printer Align Go (/PPAG)
tells 1-2-3 that the printer is ready and prints the current print range

/Print Printer Page (/PPP)
advances the printer's paper after printing a range

/File Save Replace (/FS ⏎ R)
saves changes to an existing file

/Worksheet Erase Yes (/WEY)
erases all worksheet data to clear the worksheet area

Applications

Begin doing the applications by loading 1-2-3, if necessary. Place your student data disk in drive A (or drive B if you do not have a hard disk). Change the current directory to the drive that contains the student data disk. Also, change the clock setting in the Default Settings dialog box to display the current filename on the status line.

Business

Sales Analysis

1. Retrieve the SALES1.WK1 file you created in Lesson 1. If necessary, edit any mistakes you may have entered in the worksheet in Lesson 1. After you complete the following tasks, your worksheet should look like the one shown in Figure 2.12.

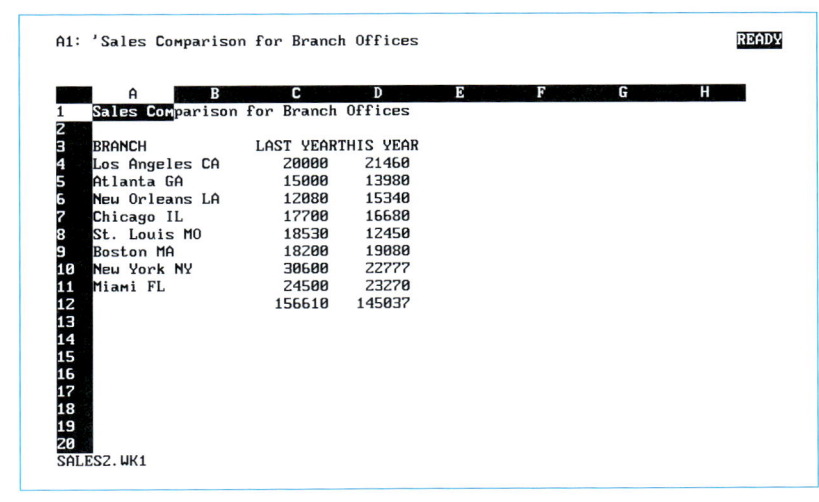

    Figure 2.12

    Follow the instructions in application 1 (Sales Analysis) to create this worksheet.

    a. Change the label "Houston" to "Atlanta".
    b. In EDIT mode, edit each label in column A so that the city name is followed by a space and a state abbreviation (for example, "Los Angeles CA").
    c. Use the pointing method to create a formula in cell C12 that sums the values in the column.
    d. Use the /Copy command (/C) to copy the formula in cell C12 to cell D12.
    e. Press HOME, and save the file as SALES2.WK1.
    f. Change the value in cell C8 to 18530, the value in cell D6 to 15340, and the value in cell D10 to 22777. What are the new totals in cells C12 and D12?
    g. Check the printer to make sure it is turned on and has paper. Make sure the paper is properly aligned. Print the range A1..D12.

Business

Small Business

2. The accounting office calls to say their first estimate—that fixed costs totaled $150,000—was wrong. Fixed costs are actually $145,000. To correct the worksheet, retrieve the file PROFIT1.WK1 from your student data disk and edit cells where needed by doing the following:

   h. Use the /File Save Replace command (/FS ⏎ R) to save the latest changes to SALES2.WK1.

   i. Use the /Worksheet Erase Yes command (/WEY) to erase the worksheet.

   a. Replace the fixed costs value in cell B8 with the value 145000.

   b. Use the /Copy command (/C) to copy the value in cell B8 to the range B9..B17.

   c. In EDIT mode, change the label "PROFIT/LOSS" in cell G6 to "PROFIT(LOSS)".

   d. Press HOME, and use the /File Save command (/FS) to save the worksheet as PROFIT2.WK1.

   e. Check the printer to make sure it is turned on and has paper. Make sure the paper is properly aligned. Print the range A1..H17.

   f. Use the /File Save Replace command (/FS ⏎ R) to save the latest changes to PROFIT2.WK1.

   g. Use the /Worksheet Erase Yes command (/WEY) to erase the worksheet.

Business

Accounting

3. To continue creating the trial balance that you began in Lesson 1, you decide to edit the account names so they match those in the ledger. Also you realize that some of the debit and credit values were incorrect so you want to correct those as well. To do so, retrieve the file BALANCE1.WK1. Do the following tasks to edit the worksheet so that the first 20 rows appear like those shown in Figure 2.13.

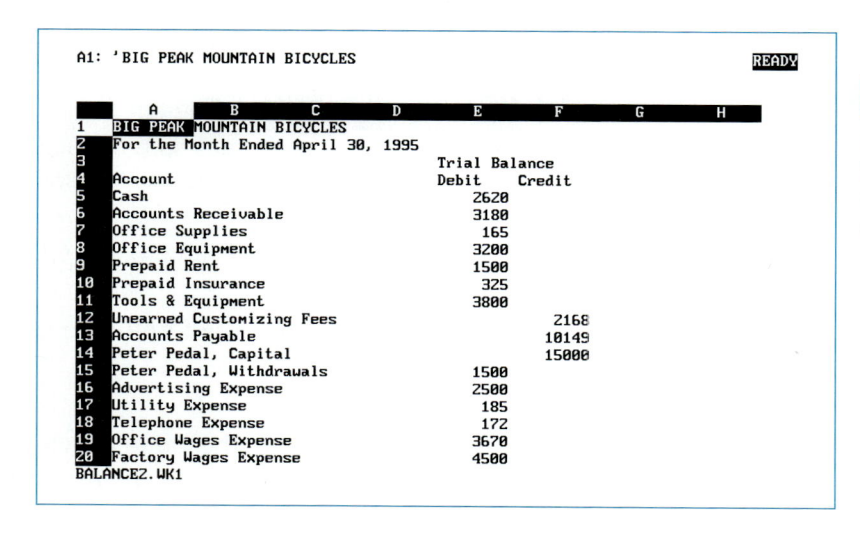

```
A1: 'BIG PEAK MOUNTAIN BICYCLES                                    READY

         A           B           C           D        E        F        G        H
 1  BIG PEAK MOUNTAIN BICYCLES
 2  For the Month Ended April 30, 1995
 3                                            Trial Balance
 4  Account                                   Debit    Credit
 5  Cash                                      2620
 6  Accounts Receivable                       3180
 7  Office Supplies                            165
 8  Office Equipment                          3200
 9  Prepaid Rent                              1500
10  Prepaid Insurance                          325
11  Tools & Equipment                         3800
12  Unearned Customizing Fees                          2168
13  Accounts Payable                                  10149
14  Peter Pedal, Capital                              15000
15  Peter Pedal, Withdrawals                  1500
16  Advertising Expense                       2500
17  Utility Expense                            185
18  Telephone Expense                          172
19  Office Wages Expense                      3670
20  Factory Wages Expense                     4500
BALANCE2.WK1
```

Figure 2.13

Follow the instructions in application 3 (Accounting) to create this worksheet.

a. In EDIT mode, edit each of the abbreviated account names in cells A6, A12, A13, A14, A16, A19, and A20 so that they appear as shown in Figure 2.13.

b. Change the label "Withdrawals" in cell A15 to "Peter Pedal, Withdrawals".

c. Change the debit value for office supplies to 165, the prepaid insurance debit value to 325, and the telephone expense debit value to 172.

d. Use the pointing method to enter a formula in cell E21 that totals the debit column values.

e. Use the /Copy command (/C) to copy the formula in cell E21 to cell F21.

f. You notice that the debit column does not equal the credit column. After checking the ledger, you realize that the credit value for the Unearned Customizing Fees account was not accurately posted. Change the credit value for this account to 2168, and observe the change in cell F21. Both columns should balance at 27317.

g. Press (HOME), and use the /File Save command (/FS) to save the worksheet as BALANCE2.WK1.

h. Check the printer to make sure it is turned on and has paper. Make sure the paper is properly aligned. Print the range A1..F21.

i. Use the /File Save Replace command (/FS ⏎ R) to save the latest changes to BALANCE2.WK1.

j. Use the /Worksheet Erase Yes command (/WEY) to erase the worksheet.

Social Studies

Student Survey

4. To start analyzing the questionnaire's results, you decide to total the results of each column and row. To do so, retrieve the file SURVEY1.WK1, build a formula, and copy the formula where necessary. Also, to clarify entries, you decide to edit certain labels and values, as outlined next. When completed, your worksheet should look like the one shown in Figure 2.14.

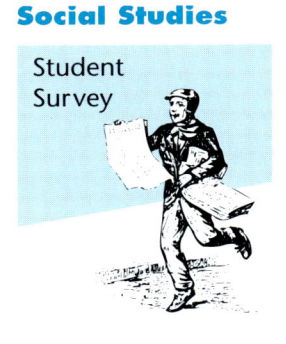

```
A1:                                                              READY

        A         B         C        D       E       F        G        H
 1                    School Activities Questionnaire
 2
 3                      Excellent Good    Fair    Poor   No Opinio TOTAL
 4  SPORTS
 5  Varsity Football     132      314     118      57       89      710
 6  Varsity Baseball     205      363      94      23       67      752
 7  Varsity Basketball    67      248     221      35      189      760
 8  Sophomore Water Po    42      262     109      11      252      676
 9                                                                    0
10  FACILITIES                                                        0
11  Cafeteria             56      114     334     214       12      730
12  Library              179      183     193      34      145      734
13  Gym                  201      245      97      52      103      698
14                                                                    0
15  EVENTS                                                            0
16  Prom Dance           156      279     178      23       89      725
17  Sadie Haukins Danc    78      168     201      78      125      650
18  Homecoming           132      285     102      76       89      684
19  Can Drive             92      159     132      91       96      570
20  Car Wash             127      201      55      19      203      605
SURVEY2.WK1
```

Figure 2.14

Follow the instructions in application 4 (Student Survey) to create this worksheet.

a. In EDIT mode, change the label "Football" to "Varsity Football", the label "Baseball" to "Varsity Baseball", the label "Basketball" to "Varsity Basketball", and the label "Water Polo" to "Sophomore Water Polo".

> Note: The value in cell C8 causes the label in cell A8 to truncate.

b. In EDIT mode, change the label "Prom" in cell A16 to "Prom Dance".
c. In row 20, enter the following labels and values in the appropriate columns:

   Car Wash   127   201   55   19   203
d. Enter the formula +C5+D5+E5+F5+G5 in cell H5.
e. Use the /Copy command (/C) to copy the formula in cell H5 to the range H6..H20.
f. Enter a formula in cell C21 that totals the values in column C.
g. Use the /Copy command (/C) to copy the formula in cell C21 to the range D21..H21.
h. Enter the label "TOTAL" in cells A21 and H3.
i. Press (HOME), and use the /File Save command (/FS) to save the worksheet as SURVEY2.WK1.
j. Check the printer to make sure it is turned on and has paper. Make sure the paper is properly aligned. Print the range A1..H21.
k. Use the /File Save Replace command (/FS ⬅ R) to save the latest changes to SURVEY2.WK1.
l. Use the /Worksheet Erase Yes command (/WEY) to erase the worksheet.

Social Studies

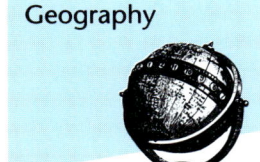

Geography

5. To start analyzing world population, you decide to total the results of each column in the file that you created in Lesson 1. Also, to clarify entries, you decide to edit certain labels and values. When completed, your worksheet should appear as shown in Figure 2.15. Retrieve the file WRLDPOP1.WK1 and follow these steps:

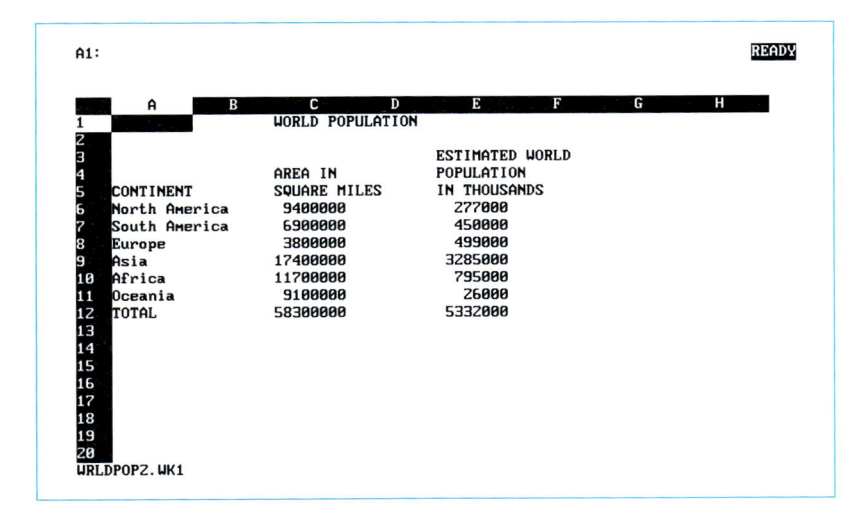

Figure 2.15

Follow the instructions in application 5 (Geography) to create this worksheet.

```
A1:                                                              READY

        A           B         C         D         E         F         G         H
 1                          WORLD POPULATION
 2
 3                                              ESTIMATED WORLD
 4                        AREA IN               POPULATION
 5   CONTINENT           SQUARE MILES           IN THOUSANDS
 6   North America         9400000                 277000
 7   South America         6900000                 450000
 8   Europe                3800000                 499000
 9   Asia                 17400000                3285000
10   Africa               11700000                 795000
11   Oceania               9100000                  26000
12   TOTAL                58300000                5332000
13
14
15
16
17
18
19
20
WRLDPOP2.WK1
```

a. In EDIT mode, change the label "EST WORLD" to "ESTIMATED WORLD".

b. In EDIT mode, change the label "SQ MILES" to "SQUARE MILES".

c. Enter the label "TOTAL" in cell A12.

d. Use the pointing method to enter a formula in cell C12 that sums the values in the column.

e. Use the /Copy command (C) to copy the formula in cell C12 to cell E12.

f. Press [HOME], and use the /File Save command (/FS) to save the worksheet as WRLDPOP2.WK1.

g. Check the printer to make sure it is turned on and has paper. Make sure the paper is properly aligned. Print the entire range of data.

h. Use the /File Save Replace command (/FS ← R) to save the current print settings to the same file.

i. Use the /Worksheet Erase Yes command (/WEY) to erase the worksheet data from memory.

Applications

Social Studies

American Government

6. To start analyzing electoral results, you decide to total the results of each column and row in the file that you created in Lesson 1. Also, to clarify entries, you decide to edit certain labels and values. When completed, your worksheet should appear as shown in Figure 2.16. Retrieve the file ELECTN1.WK1, and follow these steps:

```
A1: 'COMPARING POPULAR AND ELECTORAL VOTES IN THREE PRESIDENTIAL ELECTIONS   READY

        A         B       C        D        E       F        G       H
1   COMPARING POPULAR AND ELECTORAL VOTES IN THREE PRESIDENTIAL ELECTIONS
2
3       1960            Popular V%        Electoral%
4   Kennedy             34221334              303
5   Nixon               34106671              219
6   Others                500945               15
7   TOTAL               68828950              537
8       1976
9   Carter              40825839              297
10  Ford                39147770              240
11  Others               1629737                1
12  TOTAL               81603346              538
13      1988
14  Bush                48881278              426
15  Dukakis             41805374              111
16  Others                898168                1
17  TOTAL               91584820              538
18
19
20
ELECTN2.WK1
```

Figure 2.16

Follow the instructions in application 6 (American Government) to create this worksheet.

    a. In EDIT mode, change the label "Poplr Vot" in cell C3 to "Popular Vote". (Notice that the label in cell C3 truncates to "Popular V.")

    b. In EDIT mode, change "Elec Vote" in cell E3 to "Electoral Vote".

    c. Enter the label "TOTAL" in cells A7, A12, and A17.

    d. Enter the formula **+C4+C5+C6** in cell C7, and then use the /Copy command (/C) to copy the formula to cell E7.

    e. Enter the formula **+C9+C10+C11** in cell C12, and copy the formula to cell E12.

    f. Enter the formula **+C14+C15+C16** in cell C17, and copy the formula to cell E17.

    g. Press (HOME), and use the /File Save command (/FS) to save the worksheet as ELECTN2.WK1.

    h. Check the printer to make sure it is turned on and has paper. Make sure the paper is properly aligned. Print the entire range of data.

    i. Use the /File Save Replace command (/FS ⇐ R) to save the current print settings to the same file.

    j. Use the /Worksheet Erase Yes command (/WEY) to erase the worksheet.

2 ▶ Editing and Printing a Worksheet

Science/ Mathematics

Astronomy

7. Retrieve the PLANETS1.WK1 file that you created in Lesson 1, and use the following steps to create the worksheet shown in Figure 2.17:

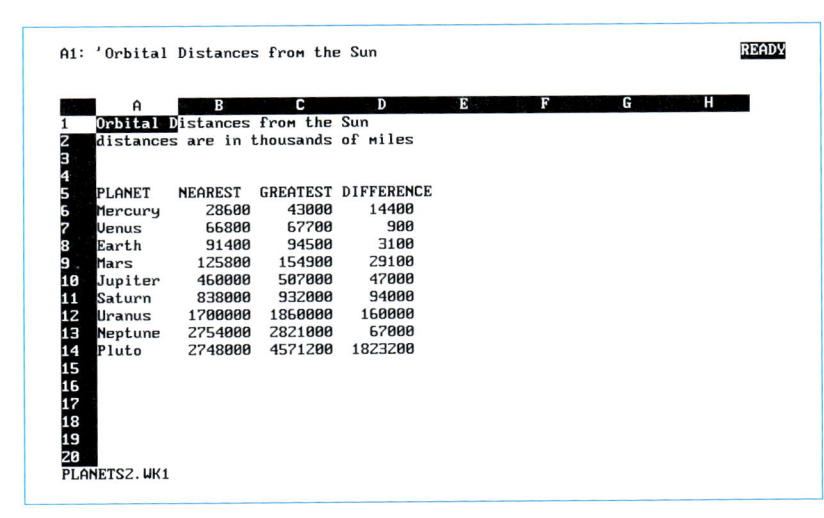

Figure 2.17

Follow the instructions in application 7 (Astronomy) to create this worksheet.

```
A1: 'Orbital Distances from the Sun                              READY
         A         B         C         D       E       F       G       H
   1  Orbital Distances from the Sun
   2  distances are in thousands of miles
   3
   4
   5  PLANET    NEAREST   GREATEST  DIFFERENCE
   6  Mercury     28600     43000      14400
   7  Venus       66800     67700        900
   8  Earth       91400     94500       3100
   9  Mars       125800    154900      29100
  10  Jupiter    460000    507000      47000
  11  Saturn     838000    932000      94000
  12  Uranus    1700000   1860000     160000
  13  Neptune   2754000   2821000      67000
  14  Pluto     2748000   4571200    1823200
  15
  16
  17
  18
  19
  20
  PLANETS2.WK1
```

a. In EDIT mode, change the label in cell B5 so that it reads "NEAREST".

b. Replace the label in cell C5 with the label "GREATEST".

c. Enter a formula in cell D6 that subtracts the value in cell B6 from the value in cell C6. This formula finds the difference between Mercury's farthest and nearest orbital distances from the sun.

d. Use the /Copy command (/C) to copy the formula in cell D4 down the column. This will calculate the difference between greatest and nearest orbital distances for each planet.

e. Replace the distance value in cell C6 with 43000, the value in cell C7 with 67700, the value in cell B10 with 460000, and the value in cell B11 with 838000. Notice the effect each change has on the results in column D.

f. Enter the label "DIFFERENCE" in cell D5.

g. Press HOME, and use the /File Save command (/FS) to save the file as PLANETS2.WK1.

h. Check the printer to make sure it is turned on and has paper. Make sure the paper is properly aligned. Print the range A1..C14.

Note: Do not include the data in column D in the print range.

i. Use the /File Save Replace command (/FS ⏎ R) to save the print settings to the current file.

j. Use the /Worksheet Erase Yes command (/WEY) to erase the worksheet.

Applications 63

Science/ Mathematics

Mathematics

8. Retrieve the file RECYCLE1.WK1, and continue working with the worksheet you created in Lesson 1 by editing some labels and values. Also, enter and copy formulas that calculate both of the following:

   ▶ The refunds for cans, newspapers, and bottles that each class collected

   ▶ The total amount of money raised by each class

   After completing the following steps, your worksheet should look like the one shown in Figure 2.18.

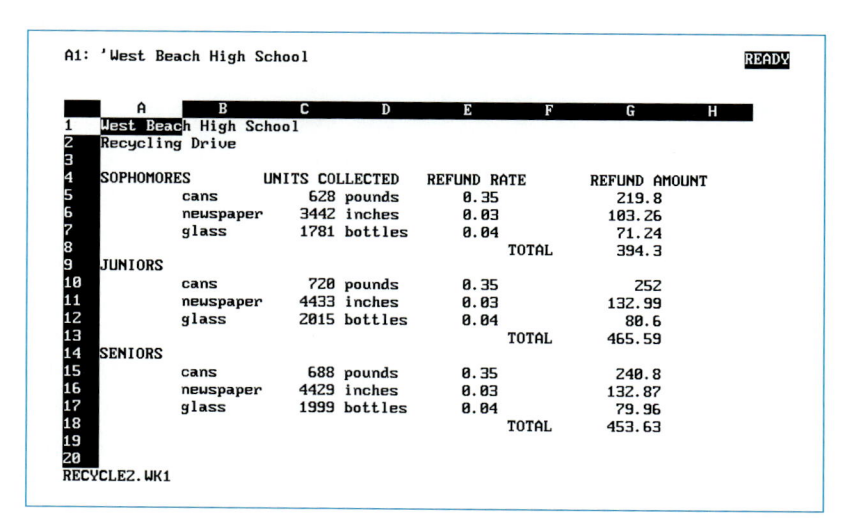

   ```
   A1: 'West Beach High School                                      READY
          A          B          C        D      E        F        G       H
    1  West Beach High School
    2  Recycling Drive
    3
    4  SOPHOMORES          UNITS COLLECTED    REFUND RATE      REFUND AMOUNT
    5              cans        628  pounds     0.35                 219.8
    6              newspaper  3442  inches     0.03                 103.26
    7              glass      1781  bottles    0.04                  71.24
    8                                                    TOTAL      394.3
    9  JUNIORS
   10              cans        720  pounds     0.35                 252
   11              newspaper  4433  inches     0.03                 132.99
   12              glass      2015  bottles    0.04                  80.6
   13                                                    TOTAL      465.59
   14  SENIORS
   15              cans        688  pounds     0.35                 240.8
   16              newspaper  4429  inches     0.03                 132.87
   17              glass      1999  bottles    0.04                  79.96
   18                                                    TOTAL      453.63
   19
   20
   RECYCLE2.WK1
   ```

   Figure 2.18
   Follow the instructions in application 8 (Mathematics) to obtain the results shown in this worksheet.

   a. In EDIT mode, change the label in cell E4 to "REFUND RATE" and the label in cell G4 to "REFUND AMOUNT".

   b. Replace the class labels in column A, as shown in Figure 2.18.

   c. Enter a formula in cell G5 that multiplies the refund rate for cans in column E and the amount that the tenth-graders collected in column C.

   d. Use the /Copy command (/C) to copy the formula to the appropriate ranges in column G.

   e. Enter the label "TOTAL" in cell F8, and then copy the label to cells F13 and F18.

   f. Enter a formula in cell G8 that sums the tenth-grade results in column G. Copy this formula to cells G13 and G18 to sum the results for the other two classes. Which class won the field trip?

   g. Change the value representing inches of stacked newspaper that the sophomores collected to 3442.

   h. Change the value for pounds of cans that the juniors collected to 720. Change the value representing the number of bottles that the seniors collected to 1999.

2 ▶ Editing and Printing a Worksheet

i. Press [HOME], and use the /File Save command (/FS) to save the file as RECYCLE2.WK1.

j. Check the printer to make sure it is turned on and has paper. Make sure the paper is properly aligned. Print the range A1..H18.

k. Use the /File Save Replace command (/FS ⏎ R) to save the print settings to the current file.

l. Use the /Worksheet Erase Yes command (/WEY) to erase the worksheet.

Health

Nutrition

9. Retrieve the worksheet file NUTRINF1.WK1 that you created in Lesson 1, and do the following tasks to edit the worksheet:

   a. In EDIT mode, change the label in cell D3 to "Protein" and the label in cell E3 to "Carbohydrate".

   b. Replace the label "Lipids" in cell F3 with the label "Fat".

   c. Use the pointing method to enter a formula in cell D8 that totals the grams of proteins consumed at breakfast.

   d. Use the /Copy command (/C) to copy the formula in cell D8 to the range E8..F8 to calculate total carbohydrates and fats consumed at breakfast.

   e. Enter a similar formula in cell D15 and use the /Copy command (/C) to copy the formula to the range E15..F15 to total nutrients consumed at lunch.

   f. Repeat step e for cell D21 and the range E21...F21 to total nutrients consumed at dinner.

   g. Enter the label "TOTAL" in cell C8. Be sure to use the [CAPS LOCK] key. Copy the label to cells C15 and C21.

   h. Press [HOME], and use the /File Save command (/FS) to save the worksheet as NUTRINF2.WK1.

   i. Check the printer to make sure it is turned on and has paper. Make sure the paper is properly aligned. Print the entire range of data.

   j. Use the /File Save Replace command (/FS ⏎ R) to save the current print settings to the same file.

   k. Use the /Worksheet Erase Yes command (/WEY) to erase the worksheet.

Applications

Health

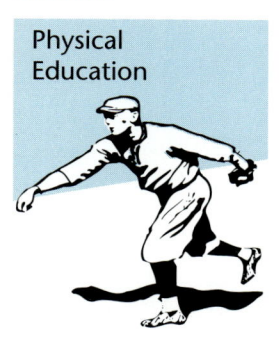

Physical Education

10. The Washington High School softball team completed its second game of the season, winning 22–14. You want to update the team's batting statistics by retrieving the file SBGAME1.WK1 that you created in Lesson 1. To clarify the worksheet, you will edit certain labels. You will also create formulas to reflect the two games played thus far, as outlined in the following steps. When completed, columns C through J should appear as shown in Figure 2.19.

Figure 2.19

After following the instructions in application 10 (Physical Education), columns C through J in your worksheet should look like this.

a. Replace the label "NAME" in cell A5 with the label "PLAYER".

b. Change the values in columns C through H to formulas by adding the following totals from the second game's scorecard to the first game's totals:

HINT

Edit each cell in EDIT mode to add the new value from the scorecard to the existing value.

Player	At Bats	Runs	Hits	Doubles	Triples	HRs	RBIs
Bernhart	7	4	4	1	0	2	2
Taylor	7	2	6	0	0	0	2
Hepburn	7	5	4	0	0	1	4
Monroe	6	1	1	0	0	1	2
d'Arc	5	1	2	1	0	1	3
Victoria	7	5	6	2	0	0	4
Wood	5	2	2	1	0	1	3
Smith	5	2	2	0	1	0	1
Turner	0	0	0	0	0	0	0

2 ▶ Editing and Printing a Worksheet

c. You notice that the worksheet does not include the names of the remaining players on the team. Add the following names and numbers, starting in row 16:

Welch	P	3	0	1	0	0	1	1
Loren	OF	2	0	1	0	0	0	0
Mabely	IF	2	0	1	1	0	0	0
Braga	C	3	1	2	1	0	0	1

d. Enter the label "TOTAL" in cell A20.

e. Use the pointing method to enter a formula in cell C20 that totals the team's at bats in column C.

f. Use the /Copy command (/C) to copy the formula in cell C20 to the range D20..I20.

g. Now figure the players' batting averages after two games. First, enter the label "AVERAGE" in cell J5.

h. Enter a formula in cell J7 that divides hits (in column E) by at bats (in column C) for Bernhart.

i. Use the /Copy command (/C) to copy the formula down the column. This will calculate averages for all players plus the team average in row 20.

j. Press HOME and use the /File Save command (/FS) to save the worksheet as SBGAME2.WK1.

k. Check the printer to make sure it is turned on and has paper. Make sure the paper is properly aligned. Print the range A1..H20.

l. Use the /File Save Replace command (/FS ⏎ R) to save the current print settings to the same file.

m. Use the /Worksheet Erase Yes command (/WEY) to erase the worksheet.

3 Formatting a Worksheet and Getting Help

Objectives

- Format a range of values.
- Use the Range command (F4) to preselect a range before selecting a command.
- Change the width of a single column.
- Change the widths of columns.
- Select a column range before changing column widths.
- Enter formulas into a worksheet.
- Insert and delete columns and rows.
- Use the backslash formatting prefix (\) to enter a repeating-character label.
- Change the anchor cell in a selected range.
- Expand or contract a range from the anchor cell.
- Access the 1-2-3 on-line Help facility.
- Use context-sensitive Help.

Formatting a worksheet is as important as editing to make sure that its data is presented clearly and accurately. In this lesson, you will continue working with the worksheet for Mollie's Music Shoppe. You will format the display of values, adjust column widths, format labels, and insert and delete columns and rows. Finally, you will be introduced to 1-2-3's Help facility, which gives you help information for almost any 1-2-3 operation.

Exercise 3.1

Formatting Values

Objectives

After completing this exercise, you will be able to
- Format a range of values.
- Use the Range command (F4) to preselect a range before selecting a command.

Worksheets can be enhanced by formatting the display of labels and values. You will learn how to format labels later in this lesson. When you enter a value into a worksheet, 1-2-3 displays the stored value in general format. This is the *default setting*, or automatic value format setting. Lotus 1-2-3's value *format* options are summarized in Table 3.1.

DEFAULT SETTING
The setting that 1-2-3 or any computer program uses automatically until you change it.

FORMAT
The manner in which values are displayed. Value format options control the number of decimal places and insert symbols that indicate what the values represent (for example, currency, percentages, decimals, and scientific notation).

Table 3.1

Value Formats

Format		Description
Fixed	123.00	Values are displayed with a fixed number of decimal places up to 15. Trailing zeros are displayed up to the specified number of decimal places. Negative values are displayed with a minus sign. A leading zero is displayed for values less than 1.
Sci	1.2E+8	Values are displayed in scientific (exponential) notation with up to 15 decimal places. The exponent ranges from −99 to +99.
Currency	$1,230.00	Values are displayed with dollar signs, commas that separate thousandths' places, and up to 15 decimal places. Negative numbers are displayed in parentheses or with a minus sign, depending on the current global worksheet setting.
, (comma)	1,230.00	Values are displayed with the same characteristics as the Currency option, but without the dollar signs.

Format		Description
General	123	Values are displayed with no comma separators for thousandths and no trailing zeros to the right of the decimal point. Displays as many numbers to the right of the decimal point as will fit in the width of the cell. Displays values in scientific notation when numbers to the left of the decimal point exceed the cell width minus 1. Negative numbers are displayed with a minus sign.
+/-		Values are displayed as a bar of plus signs (+++) or minus signs (- - -), depending on the whole-number value of their digits (positive or negative). A period is displayed for values between -1 and 1.
Percent	1.23%	Values are displayed as percentages (multiplied by 100) with percent signs and up to 15 decimal places.
Text		Formulas (instead of results) are displayed as entered in cells. Numbers are displayed in General format.
Hidden		Values are not displayed but still exist.
Reset		Values reset to General format.

Table 3.1

Value Formats (continued)

As you have seen, 1-2-3 strips any value format characters that you type, such as dollar signs or percent signs, and just displays the value. For example, you can type "$250.00," but 1-2-3 only stores and displays "250." A percent sign (%) is also not displayed when you enter it with a value. However, 1-2-3 does interpret the value as a percentage. For example, you can type "25%," and 1-2-3 displays "0.25" in the cell.

To display values in currency or any other format, you must use the /Range Format command (/RF). From its submenu you select a value format option for a specific range of values. You can also change a global worksheet setting so that a value entered in any cell in the worksheet is formatted automatically. You do this by selecting the /Worksheet Global Format command (/WGF). Or you can use the /Worksheet Global command (/WG) to change the setting in the Global Settings dialog box.

COLUMN WIDTH
The number of characters that are displayed in a cell. The default column width is nine characters.

When you format certain values, the extra characters in the formatted value may cause them to not fit within the default *column width* (9 characters). If so, 1-2-3 displays a string of asterisks (*********) in the cell. Although the asterisks are displayed in the worksheet area, the value is still stored in the cell. Later in this lesson you will learn how to adjust column widths to display formatted values. For now, you will begin by starting 1-2-3, if necessary, and retrieving the SUMSALES.WK1 worksheet that you worked with in Lessons 1 and 2.

1 ▶ If necessary, start 1-2-3, and use the /File Directory command (/FD) to change the current directory to the drive that contains the student data disk.

70   **3 ▶ Formatting a Worksheet and Getting Help**

2 ▶ If necessary, use the /File Retrieve command (/FR) to retrieve the SUMSALES.WK1 worksheet file.

3 ▶ If necessary, change the Clock setting in the Default Settings dialog box so that the current filename is displayed.

4 ▶ Press the Slash key (/) to access the Main Menu.

5 ▶ Type **WG** to select the Worksheet and Global commands.

The Global Settings dialog box appears, as shown in Figure 3.1.

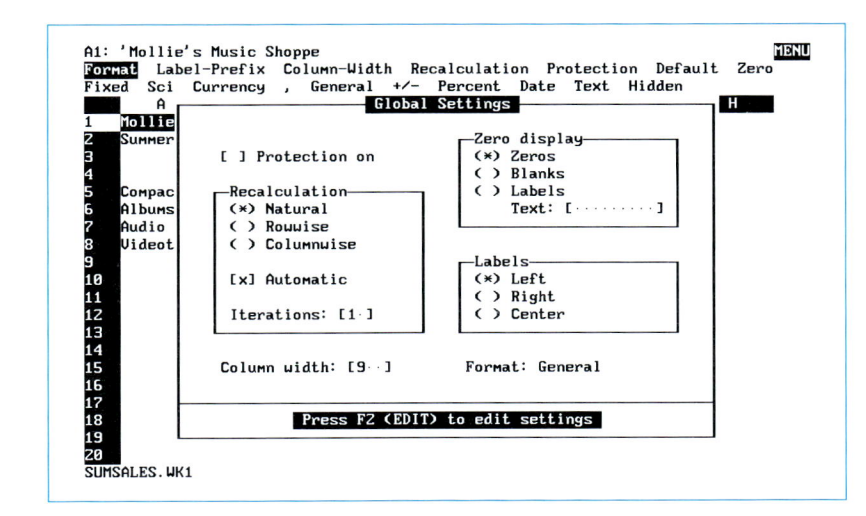

Figure 3.1

The /Worksheet Global (/WG) command displays the Global Settings dialog box in MENU mode.

6 ▶ Press F2 to activate the dialog box.

7 ▶ Type **F** to select the Format option.

A pop-up dialog box that lists the format options appears, as shown in Figure 3.2. The pointer highlights the General option, which is the current (default) format in effect for the worksheet.

Pop-up dialog box

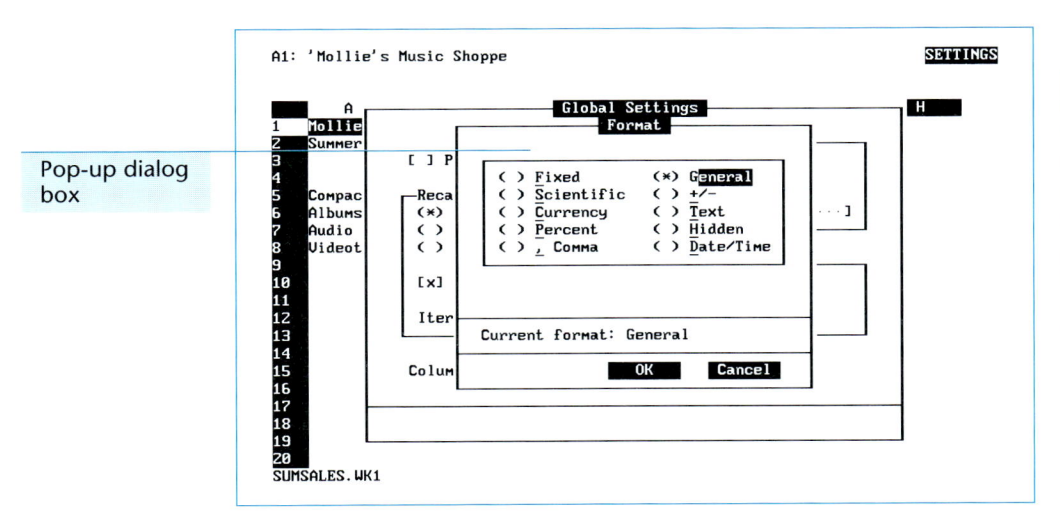

Figure 3.2

When you select the Format option in the Global Settings dialog box, 1-2-3 displays a pop-up dialog box that lists format options. By default, the General option is currently selected.

8 ▶ Press ← once to move the pointer to the comma option.

Formatting Values   **71**

9 ▶ Press ⏎.

The Decimal Places text box appears and prompts you to enter the number of decimal places. The numeral "2" appears to the right of the prompt.

10 ▶ Press ⏎ to accept "2" as the number of decimal places.

11 ▶ Press ⏎ again.

The Global command submenu is active on the control panel.

12 ▶ Press CTRL-BREAK to return to READY mode.

The global value format setting is changed. Your screen should look like Figure 3.3. Notice that asterisks appear in the range B9..D9 because those values are too wide to fit in those columns.

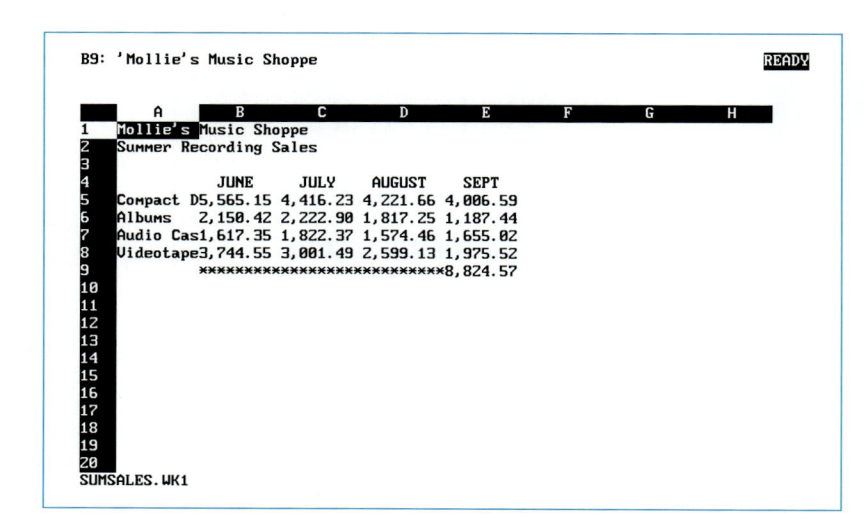

Figure 3.3

After you change the worksheet's global value format setting, some of the formatted values appear as a series of asterisks. This happens because the column widths are too narrow to display the entire values.

Note: Later in this lesson you will adjust the widths of the columns to display the values.

Now you will format two value ranges with the Currency format option.

13 ▶ Move the cell pointer to cell B5.

14 ▶ Press the Slash key (/) to access the Main Menu.

15 ▶ Type **RF** to select the Range and Format commands.

The Format command submenu is active on the second line of the control panel.

16 ▶ Type **C** to select the Currency command.

The following command prompt appears on the control panel:

Enter number of decimal places (0..15): 2

17 ▶ Press ⏎ to accept "2" as the number of decimal places.

3 ▶ Formatting a Worksheet and Getting Help

Lotus 1-2-3 prompts you to enter the range to format. Cell B5 is anchored.

18 ▶ Press (END), and then press (→).

The range B5..E5 is highlighted.

19 ▶ Press (←).

The selected range is formatted. Asterisks appear in each cell because the columns are not wide enough to display the formatted values.

20 ▶ Press (END) and (↓) to move the cell pointer to cell B9.

Before you format this range, try preselecting the range you want to format. Lotus 1-2-3 Release 2.3 lets you select a range before you do something that requires a range address. This feature is very useful when you have to perform more than one operation on the same range. The range remains highlighted until you press an Arrow key to move the cell pointer. To preselect a range, you can press the (F4) key when 1-2-3 is in READY mode to display the following prompt:

> Range: A1..A1

This prompt automatically anchors the current cell, so all you need to do is (1) press any combination of Arrow keys to highlight a range and (2) press (←). The range will be highlighted in the worksheet area, ready for you to select a command. When you select a command to operate on the preselected range (for example, /Range Format), 1-2-3 skips the prompt that asks you to enter a range address and carries out the operation.

Now you will do the steps to preselect the range of total sales for each month before you select the /Range Format command (/RF).

21 ▶ Make sure 1-2-3 is in READY mode.

22 ▶ Press (F4).

Lotus 1-2-3 prompts you to enter a range.

23 ▶ Press (END), and then press (→).

The range B9..E9 is highlighted, and its address is displayed to the right of the prompt.

24 ▶ Press (←).

The range B9..E9 is highlighted in the worksheet area.

25 ▶ Press the Slash key (/) to access the Main Menu.

26 ▶ Type **RFC** to select the Range, Format, and Currency commands.

Lotus 1-2-3 prompts you to enter the number of decimal places.

27 ▶ Press (←) to accept "2" as the number of decimal places.

Lotus 1-2-3 skips the prompt for the range to format and formats the preselected range. Notice that asterisks appear in each cell because the

Formatting Values

columns are not wide enough to display the formatted values, as shown in Figure 3.4.

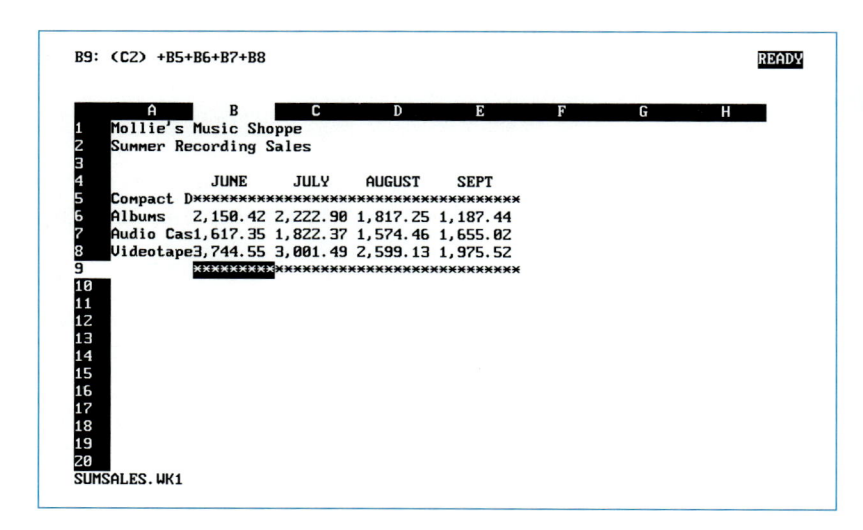

Figure 3.4

The range of monthly totals is formatted as currency with two decimal places, and is displayed as a series of asterisks. This happens because the columns are too narrow to display entire values.

28 ▶ Press HOME to move the cell pointer to cell A1.

Exercise 3.2

Adjusting Column Widths

Objectives

After completing this exercise, you will be able to
- Change the width of a single column.
- Change the widths of columns.
- Select a column range before changing column widths.

In the last exercise, you formatted two value ranges with the Currency format. Because the formatted values were too long to fit within the current column width, 1-2-3 displayed a string of asterisks instead. You can replace the asterisks with the formatted values by adjusting the widths of the columns. A column's width is expressed as numbers of characters. Widths can be adjusted for single columns, a range of columns, or all worksheet columns.

Use the /Worksheet Column Set-Width command (/WCS) to increase (or decrease) the width of the column that contains the cell pointer. Increasing a column's width replaces asterisks with formatted values or displays long labels that were truncated. This command prompts you to enter the number of characters for the column width. You can enter any width between 1 and

3 ▶ Formatting a Worksheet and Getting Help

240 characters by typing a number. Or you can use → or ← to increase or decrease the column's width while viewing the adjustment in the worksheet area.

Now you will use the /Worksheet Column Set-Width command (/WCS) to adjust column A's width in your worksheet.

1 ▶ Make sure the cell pointer is on cell A1.

2 ▶ Press the Slash key (/) to access the Main Menu.

3 ▶ Type **WCS** to select the Worksheet, Column, and Set-Width commands.

  The following prompt appears:

  Enter column width (1..240): 9

4 ▶ Press → 7 times.

  The column's width increases in the worksheet area. The width is adjusted to 16 characters on the control panel, as shown in Figure 3.5.

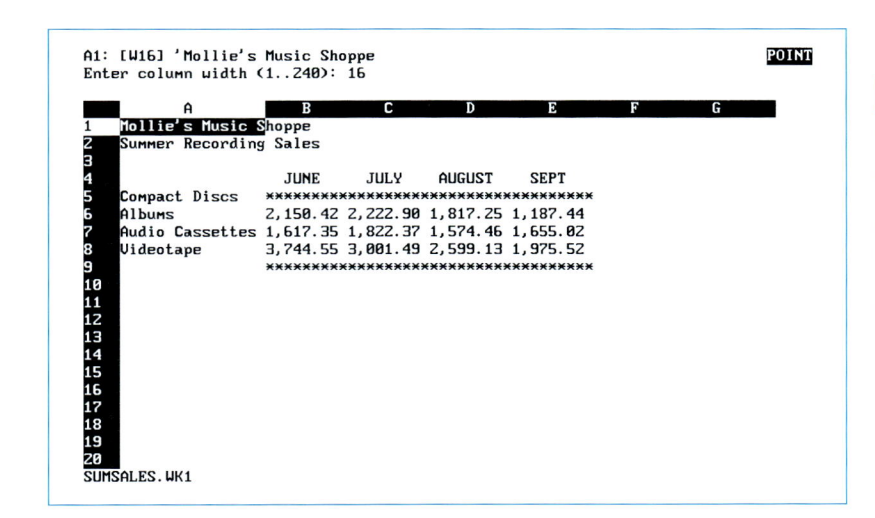

Figure 3.5

When you select the /Worksheet Column Set-Width command (/WCS), you can press → or ← to increase or decrease the width of the column that contains the cell pointer.

5 ▶ Press ←.

  The width of column A is now 16 characters. The "Compact Discs" label previously truncated in cell A7 now appears in full.

You can also adjust a range of columns so that they are all the same width. To do this, use the /Worksheet Column Column-Range Set-Width command (/WCCS). This command prompts you to select any number of columns (a column range) to be adjusted. However, you can preselect the column range before you select the command, as you learned to do earlier in this lesson.

Now you will adjust the widths for a column range to display the Currency-formatted values.

6 ▶ Press → to move the cell pointer to column B.

7 ▶ Press F4.

Lotus 1-2-3 prompts you to enter a range.

8 ▶ Press → 3 times.

The range B1..E1 appears to the right of the prompt.

9 ▶ Press ←.

Row 1 cells in columns B, C, D, and E are highlighted.

10 ▶ Press the Slash key (/) to access the Main Menu.

11 ▶ Type **WCCS** to select the Worksheet, Column, Column-Range, and Set-Width commands.

Lotus 1-2-3 prompts you to enter the width for each column.

12 ▶ Press → 3 times.

The asterisks are replaced by the currency values in the worksheet area. The widths for the columns are changed to 12 characters on the control panel.

13 ▶ Press ←.

The widths for columns B, C, D, and E are changed to 12 characters. Notice that now only columns A through E are visible. Your worksheet should look like Figure 3.6.

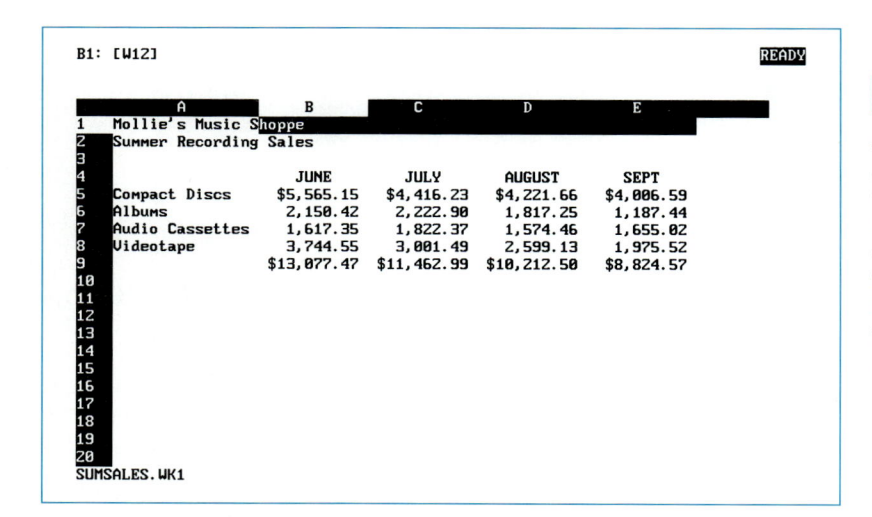

Figure 3.6

After you use the /Worksheet Column Column-Range Set-Width command (/WCCS) to increase the widths of columns B, C, D, and E, your worksheet should look like this.

14 ▶ Press HOME to move the cell pointer to cell A1.

Exercise 3.3

Formatting Labels

After completing this exercise, you will be able to
- Use label-formatting prefixes.
- Use the /Range Label command (/RL) to align labels.

Objectives

ALIGNMENT
The manner in which a label is displayed within a cell. Labels can be left-aligned (default), right-aligned, or centered.

LABEL-FORMATTING PREFIX
A 1-2-3 symbol that designates data as a label and controls its alignment.

Labels are formatted by adjusting their *alignments* within cells. In Lesson 1 you learned that 1-2-3 inserts the apostrophe formatting prefix (') automatically when you type a text character. Besides designating the entry as a label, the apostrophe formatting prefix left-aligns a label in a cell. You can control a label's alignment as you enter it by typing another label-formatting prefix in front of the label text. Table 3.2 summarizes the four 1-2-3 *label-formatting prefixes*. You will learn more about the backslash formatting prefix later in this lesson.

Formatting Prefix	Label Alignment	Example
' apostrophe	left	Label
" quotation mark	right	Label
^ caret	center	Label
\ backslash	repeats characters	LabelLabe

Table 3.2

Label-Formatting Prefixes

Label-formatting prefixes also allow you to enter labels that begin with numbers. For example, suppose you enter as labels the year "1999" or the address "789 Spring St." Lotus 1-2-3 interprets either entry as a value and switches to VALUE mode as soon as you type the first character. To enter a label that begins with a number, type a label-formatting prefix first (for example, type **'1999**). If you want to format a label with another alignment, type the appropriate label-formatting prefix. For example, type **^789 Spring St.** if you want to center this address label.

Lotus 1-2-3 also provides you with the option to realign a range of labels. You do this with the /Range Label command (/RL). This command allows you to left-align, center, or right-align a range of labels. As with other commands that operate on ranges, you can press [F4] to select the range before you realign the labels. In this exercise, you will change the worksheet's title and align other labels in your worksheet.

1 ▶ Make sure the cell pointer is on cell A1.

Formatting Labels 77

2 ▶ Press ⬇ to move the cell pointer to cell A2.

3 ▶ Type **'1995 Summer Sales**

4 ▶ Press ⬇.

The worksheet's subtitle label, which begins with a number, is entered in cell A2. The cell pointer moves to cell A3.

5 ▶ Type **Recordings**

6 ▶ Press ⏎.

An additional label is displayed in row 3.

7 ▶ Move the cell pointer to cell A9.

8 ▶ Type " (a quotation mark).

The quotation mark formatting prefix that will right-align a label appears on the control panel.

9 ▶ Type **Totals:**

> Note: Be sure to include the colon (:).

10 ▶ Press ⏎.

The right-aligned label is displayed in the cell.

11 ▶ Move the cell pointer to cell B4.

Now you will use the /Range Label command (/RL) to center the month column heading labels in row 4. You will begin by selecting the range of labels.

12 ▶ Press F4.

Lotus 1-2-3 prompts you to enter a range.

13 ▶ Press END, and then press →.

The range B4..E4 is displayed to the right of the prompt.

14 ▶ Press ⏎.

The range of column heading labels is highlighted in the worksheet area.

15 ▶ Press the Slash key (/) to access the Main Menu.

16 ▶ Type **RL** to select the Range and Label commands.

The Label command submenu is displayed on the control panel.

17 ▶ Type **C** to select the Center option.

The column labels in the range B4..E4 are centered. Your worksheet should look like Figure 3.7.

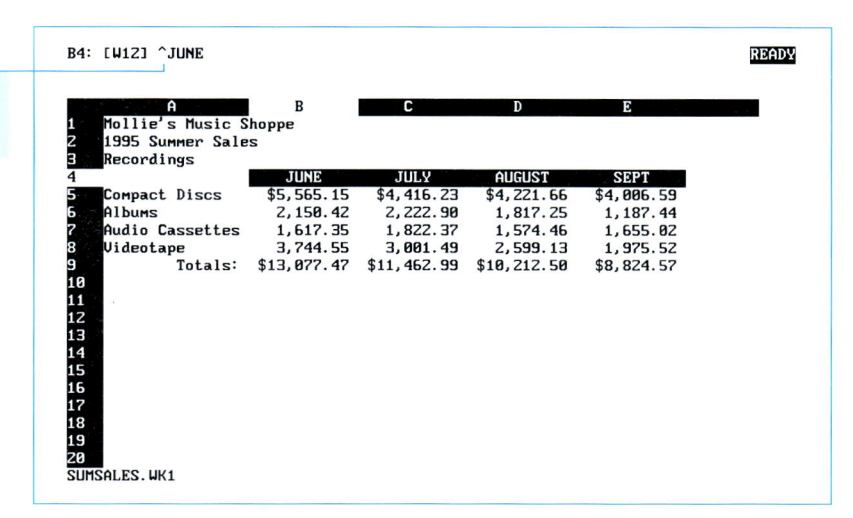

Figure 3.7

After you use the /Range Label command (/RL) to center the column heading labels, your worksheet should look like this.

Caret formatting prefix centers label

```
B4: [W12] ^JUNE                                            READY

        A            B          C          D          E
1  Mollie's Music Shoppe
2  1995 Summer Sales
3  Recordings
4                  JUNE       JULY      AUGUST      SEPT
5  Compact Discs $5,565.15  $4,416.23  $4,221.66  $4,006.59
6  Albums         2,150.42   2,222.90   1,817.25   1,187.44
7  Audio Cassettes 1,617.35  1,822.37   1,574.46   1,655.02
8  Videotape      3,744.55   3,001.49   2,599.13   1,975.52
9        Totals: $13,077.47 $11,462.99 $10,212.50  $8,824.57
10
...
20
SUMSALES.WK1
```

Now you will save the worksheet and then print the same range of data.

18 ▶ Press HOME to move the cell pointer to cell A1.

19 ▶ Press the Slash key (/) to access the Main Menu.

20 ▶ Type **FS** to select the File and Save commands.

21 ▶ Press ⏎ to save your changes to the same file.

Lotus 1-2-3 prompts you to select a save option.

22 ▶ Type **R** to select the Replace command.

23 ▶ Press the Slash key (/) to access the Main Menu.

24 ▶ Type **PPR** to select the Print, Printer, and Range commands.

The original print range that was saved with the file is highlighted in the worksheet area. Its address is displayed to the right of the prompt on the control panel.

25 ▶ Press ⏎ to accept the current print range.

The Print Settings dialog box appears, and the Printer command submenu is active on the control panel's second line.

26 ▶ Make sure that your printer is turned on and has paper. Make sure the paper is properly aligned.

27 ▶ Type **AG** to select the Align and Go commands.

If you have a dot-matrix printer, the print range is printed. If you have a laser printer, it processes the data.

28 ▶ Type **P** to select the Page command.

If you have a dot-matrix printer, the printed page is advanced. If you have a laser printer, the printed page is ejected.

29 ▶ Type **Q** to leave MENU mode and return to the worksheet.

Formatting Labels

Exercise 3.4

Inserting and Deleting Columns and Rows

Objectives

After completing this exercise, you will be able to
- Insert and delete columns and rows.
- Use the backslash formatting prefix (\) to enter a repeating-character label.

You can make worksheet data easier to read by inserting columns or rows to add space between ranges. Columns or rows can also be inserted when you want to insert data within a range. Use the /Worksheet Insert Column command (/WIC) to insert one or more columns. Use the /Worksheet Insert Row command (/WIR) to insert one or more rows. These commands prompt you to enter a column or row range, as does the /Worksheet Column Column-Range Set-Width command you learned earlier. You can type the number of columns or rows. Or you can use the Arrow keys to highlight the number of columns or rows you want to insert. You can also preselect the range with the F4 key.

When you insert columns, data in all the columns to the right move to the right to make room for the new columns. Similarly, when you insert rows, data in all the rows below the inserted rows move down.

The /Worksheet Delete Column (/WDC) and /Worksheet Delete Row (/WDR) commands delete columns or rows. Use extreme caution when deleting columns and rows. If you accidentally delete a row or column that contains data you want, you may not be able to get the data back.

In this exercise, you will complete your 1995 summer sales worksheet by inserting rows and a column. You will also add separation lines. You will begin by inserting a column and decreasing its width to create space in the worksheet.

1 ▶ Make sure the cell pointer is on cell A1.

2 ▶ Press the Slash key (/) to access the Main Menu.

3 ▶ Type **WIC** to select the Worksheet, Insert, and Column commands.

Lotus 1-2-3 prompts you to enter the column insert range.

4 ▶ Press ⏎.

A new column A is inserted, and the data moves one column to the right.

5 ▶ Press the Slash key (/) to access the Main Menu.

6 ▶ Type **WCS** to select the Worksheet, Column, and Set-Width commands.

Lotus 1-2-3 prompts you to enter the column's width.

7 ▶ Press ← 6 times.

8 ▶ Press ←.

The column's width is reduced to three characters.

Now you will insert several rows to add some spacing between the worksheet's subtitle labels and the range of data.

9 ▶ Press ↓ 3 times.

The cell pointer is on cell A4, the blank cell below the label "Recordings."

10 ▶ Press the Slash key (/) to access the Main Menu.

11 ▶ Type **WIR** to select the Worksheet, Insert, and Row commands.

Lotus 1-2-3 prompts you to enter the row insert range.

12 ▶ Press ↓ twice to highlight cells in rows 4, 5, and 6.

The control panel displays the range A4..A6.

13 ▶ Press ←.

Three blank rows are inserted into the worksheet.

The worksheet probably would look better if you inserted two more rows: one below the column headings in row 7 and one between the sales figures and the totals in row 12.

14 ▶ Move the cell pointer to cell A8.

15 ▶ Press the Slash key (/) to access the Main Menu.

16 ▶ Type **WIR** to select the Worksheet, Insert, and Row commands.

Lotus 1-2-3 prompts you to enter the row insert range.

17 ▶ Press ← to select one row.

A single blank row is inserted. All data below row 7 move down one row.

18 ▶ Move the cell pointer to cell A13, and repeat steps 15, 16, and 17 to insert a row between rows 12 and 13.

Your screen should look like Figure 3.8.

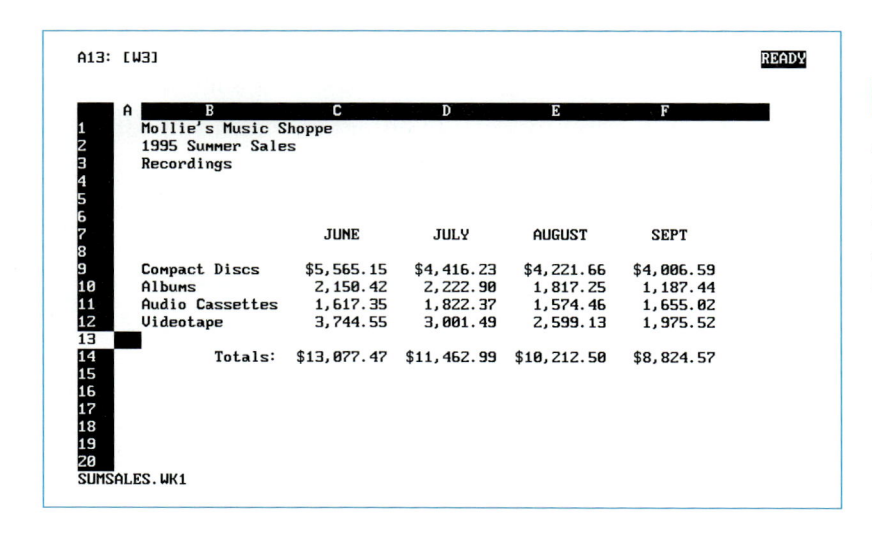

Figure 3.8

After you use the /Worksheet Insert Row command (/WIR) to insert rows, your worksheet should look like this.

SEPARATOR LINES
Dashed lines that separate totals from a column of values or double-dashed lines that underscore totals.

Your worksheet's appearance can be improved by entering a dashed line that separates the row of sales totals from the sales figures. This *separator line* helps the totals stand out, making the worksheet's data easier to read. Totals also stand out better when you underscore them with a double-dashed line. Dashed lines and double-dashed lines are created by using the backslash formatting prefix (\) to create a repeating-character label. You can then copy the repeating-character label across a range of cells in a row to create a line. The backslash formatting prefix (\) repeats any character(s) that follow it across the width of the cell.

Now, you will use the backslash formatting prefix (\) and the /Copy command (/C) to enter separator lines into the worksheet.

19 ▶ Move the cell pointer to cell C13.

20 ▶ Type \ (the backslash character).

The backslash formatting prefix appears on the control panel.

21 ▶ Type - (the hyphen character).

22 ▶ Press ⏎.

A dashed line fills the current cell.

23 ▶ Press the Slash key (/) to access the Main Menu.

24 ▶ Type **C** to select the Copy command.

25 ▶ Press ⏎ to accept cell C13 as the "Copy what?" range.

Lotus 1-2-3 prompts you to enter the "To where?" range. Cell C13 is not anchored.

26 ▶ Type **.** (a period).

Cell C13 is anchored.

27 ▶ Press → 3 times.

The range C13..F13 is highlighted.

28 ▶ Press ⏎.

> The repeating-character label copies to the specified range. A dashed line fills the range C13..F13.

Now you will place a double-dashed line in row 15 beneath the totals.

29 ▶ Move the cell pointer to cell C15.

30 ▶ Type \=

31 ▶ Press ⏎.

> A double-dashed line fills the cell.

32 ▶ Press the Slash key (/) to access the Main Menu.

33 ▶ Type **C** to select the Copy command.

34 ▶ Press ⏎ to accept cell C15 as the "Copy what?" range.

35 ▶ Type **.** (a period) to anchor cell C15.

36 ▶ Press → 3 times.

> The range C15..F15 is highlighted.

37 ▶ Press ⏎.

> The repeating-character label copies to the range C15..F15, creating a double-dashed line.

A little too much space seems to separate the subtitle labels from the data. You will delete one of the blank rows above the range of data.

38 ▶ Move the cell pointer to cell C4.

39 ▶ Press the Slash key (/) to access the Main Menu.

40 ▶ Type **WDR** to select the Worksheet, Delete, and Row commands.

> Lotus 1-2-3 prompts you to enter the range of rows to be deleted.

41 ▶ Press ⏎.

> The row containing the cell pointer is deleted, and the data below move up one row. Your screen should look like Figure 3.9.

Inserting and Deleting Columns and Rows

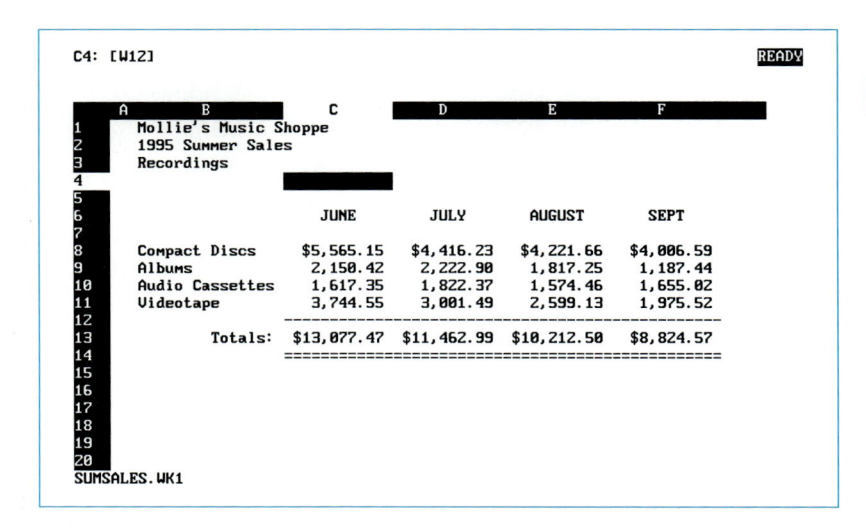

```
C4: [W12]                                                                READY

     A         B           C          D          E          F
1          Mollie's Music Shoppe
2          1995 Summer Sales
3          Recordings
4
5
6                        JUNE       JULY       AUGUST     SEPT
7
8          Compact Discs  $5,565.15  $4,416.23  $4,221.66  $4,006.59
9          Albums          2,150.42   2,222.90   1,817.25   1,187.44
10         Audio Cassettes 1,617.35   1,822.37   1,574.46   1,655.02
11         Videotape       3,744.55   3,001.49   2,599.13   1,975.52
12                        ─────────  ─────────  ─────────  ─────────
13             Totals:    $13,077.47 $11,462.99 $10,212.50  $8,824.57
14                        ═════════════════════════════════════════
15
16
17
18
19
20
SUMSALES.WK1
```

Figure 3.9

After you use the /Worksheet Delete Row command (/WDR) to delete a row, your worksheet should look like this.

Now you will save the changes to the worksheet.

42 ▶ Press HOME to move the cell pointer to cell A1.

43 ▶ Press the Slash key (/) to access the Main Menu.

44 ▶ Type **FS** to select the File and Save commands.

45 ▶ Press ⏎ to save the changes to the same file.

46 ▶ Type **R** to select the Replace command.

The changes to the worksheet are saved.

Exercise 3.5 — Adjusting a Selected Range

Objectives

After completing this exercise, you will be able to
- Change the anchor cell in a selected range.
- Expand or contract a range from the anchor cell.

At the end of this exercise, you will print the current worksheet. When you select the commands to print the worksheet, you will notice that 1-2-3 has adjusted the print range. Because you have inserted rows, the program expands the print range to keep its original data within the range. You will learn how to expand a highlighted range to include data you may have added outside the current print range.

3 ▶ Formatting a Worksheet and Getting Help

When a range is highlighted in the worksheet area, you can readily identify the anchor cell because it contains a cursor. Also, its column letter and row number are not highlighted on the worksheet borders. This cell is also the corner from which you can expand or contract the highlighting to change the selected range. If necessary, 1-2-3 lets you change the anchor cell by pressing the period key (.). Each time you press the period key (.), the anchor cell rotates clockwise to another corner of the highlighted range.

You will expand your current print range to include the double-dashed line in row 14 and the spacer column (column A).

1 ▶ Press the Slash key (/) to access the Main Menu.

2 ▶ Type **PPR** to select the Print, Printer, and Range commands.

The original print range (A1..E9) saved with the worksheet has adjusted. It is now B1..F13. Notice, however, that it does not include the spacer column (column A) or the double-dashed line in row 14, as shown in Figure 3.10. The anchor cell is cell F13.

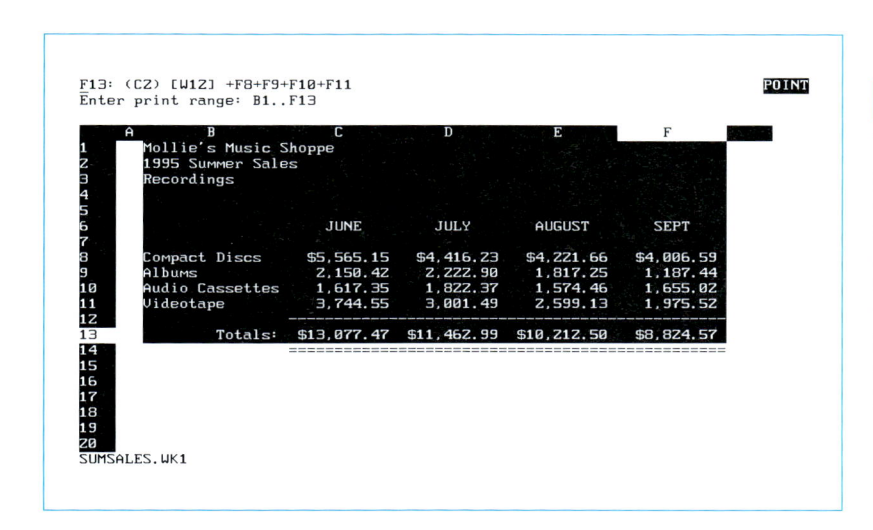

Figure 3.10

The current print range adjusted to keep the original data after you made changes to the worksheet. However, the print range does not include additional entries outside the range.

Take a look at your screen (or Figure 3.10). Notice that cell F13, which contains the total recording sales for September, has a cursor. This is the current anchor cell from which you can expand the highlighted range, if necessary. You need to change the anchor cell so you can expand the range to include column A and the double-dashed line in row 14.

3 ▶ Type **.** (a period).

The anchor cell moves clockwise to cell B13. The highlighting can be expanded off this corner of the range.

4 ▶ Press ⬅, and then press ⬇.

The highlighted range expands. Notice that its address on the control panel is F1..A14, as shown in Figure 3.11.

Adjusting a Selected Range   85

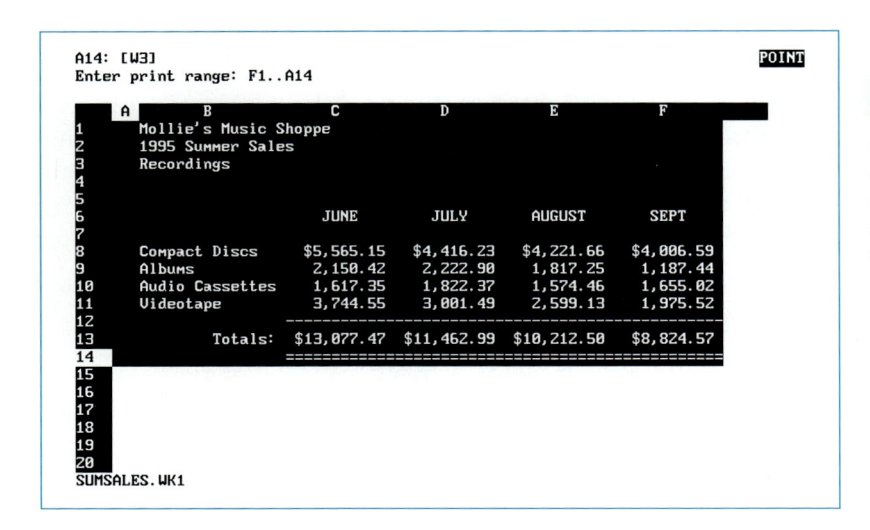

Figure 3.11

After you press the period key (.), the anchor cell rotates clockwise and you can expand the print range.

5 ▶ Press ⏎ to accept the print range.

The Printer Settings dialog box appears. Notice that the Print range setting is A1..F14.

6 ▶ Check that your printer is turned on and has paper. Make sure the paper is properly aligned.

7 ▶ Type **AG** to select the Align and Go commands.

If you have a dot-matrix printer, the print range is printed. If you have a laser printer, it processes the data.

8 ▶ Type **P** to select the Page command.

If you have a dot-matrix printer, the printed page is advanced. If you have a laser printer, the printed page is ejected.

9 ▶ Type **Q** to leave MENU mode and return to the worksheet.

10 ▶ Press HOME and use the /File Save Replace command (/FS ⏎ R) to update SUMSALES.WK1 with the new print settings.

3 ▶ Formatting a Worksheet and Getting Help

Exercise 3.6

Getting Help

After completing this exercise, you will be able to
- Access the 1-2-3 on-line Help facility.
- Use context-sensitive Help.

HELP FACILITY
A 1-2-3 feature that provides on-screen information about 1-2-3 commands and operations while you use the program.

Lotus 1-2-3 provides an on-line *Help facility* that gives you information about 1-2-3 commands and operations. You access the Help facility by pressing [F1]. If you are in READY mode when you press [F1], 1-2-3 displays the 1-2-3 Main Help Index screen, as shown in Figure 3.12. To see information about a specific topic, press [↓] or [↑] to move the pointer to a topic and press [←].

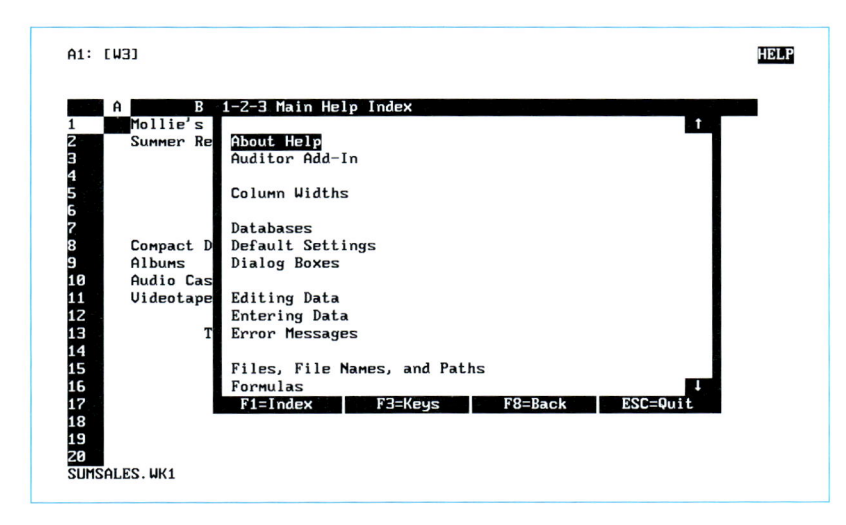

Figure 3.12
The 1-2-3 Main Help Index screen appears when you press [F1].

CONTEXT-SENSITIVE
A characteristic of the 1-2-3 on-line Help facility that enables it to display information about a specific command or operation that is currently in use.

The Help facility is context sensitive. This means that you can get information about the command or operation with which you are currently working. In this exercise, you will get acquainted with the 1-2-3 Help facility. And whenever you need to get help, use the 1-2-3 Help facility to find the information you need. (If your system does not have a hard disk, you may not be able to use 1-2-3's Help facility.)

1 ▶ Press [F1] to access the 1-2-3 Help facility.

The 1-2-3 Main Help Index appears.

Note: If you are using 1-2-3 on a floppy disk, replace the program disk with the Help disk before pressing [F1].

First, you will look up information on the keys that allow you to move around the Help facility.

2 ▶ Press [F3].

A screen of information on the keys used to move around the Help facility appears.

3 ▶ Briefly scan the information shown.

4 ▶ Press [PGDN].

The next screen of information appears.

5 ▶ Press [PGDN] again.

The rest of the information on the Help facility keys appears.

6 ▶ Press [F8] to return to the 1-2-3 Main Help Index.

7 ▶ Press [↓] twice.

The topic "Column Widths" is highlighted.

8 ▶ Press [←].

A screen of information on the /Worksheet Column Set-Width command appears.

9 ▶ Press [↓] 4 times.

The screen scrolls line by line until the first topic under "OTHER TOPICS" is highlighted at the bottom of the Help screen.

10 ▶ Press [←].

A screen of information on the /Worksheet Column Column-Range Set-Width command appears.

11 ▶ Press [F8].

A screen of information on the previous topic, the /Worksheet Column Set-Width command, appears.

12 ▶ Press [F1] to return to the 1-2-3 Main Help Index.

13 ▶ Press [PGDN] twice.

14 ▶ Press [↓] 4 times.

The 1-2-3 Command Index option is highlighted.

15 ▶ Press [←].

The 1-2-3 Command Index appears.

16 ▶ Press [END].

The last command in the index, "/Worksheet Window," is highlighted.

3 ▶ Formatting a Worksheet and Getting Help

17 ▶ Press `HOME`.

The first command in the index, "/Add-In," is highlighted.

18 ▶ Press `PGDN` 3 times.

19 ▶ Press `↓` 13 times.

The "/Move" command option is highlighted.

20 ▶ Press `↵`.

Information about the /Move command (/M) appears. You will learn how to use this command in the next lesson. For now, briefly scan the information shown.

21 ▶ Press `ESC`.

You exit from the 1-2-3 Help facility and return to the worksheet in READY mode.

22 ▶ Press `CTRL`-`F1`.

The screen of information on the /Move command appears.

BOOKMARK
A 1-2-3 Help facility feature that lets you return to the last screen of information that appeared the last time you used the Help facility in the current 1-2-3 session.

Note: The 1-2-3 Help facility's *bookmark* feature, `CTRL`-`F1`, displays the last Help screen you viewed the last time you used the Help facility.

23 ▶ Press `ESC`.

You exit from the 1-2-3 Help facility and return to the worksheet in READY mode.

Now you will try accessing the Help facility while using a command menu, to get context-sensitive information.

24 ▶ Press the Slash key (/) to access the Main Menu.

25 ▶ Type **P** to select the Print command.

26 ▶ Press `F1` to access the Help facility.

A screen of information on the /Print Printer command appears. The 1-2-3 Help facility is *context sensitive*—it displays information about the command that is currently highlighted.

27 ▶ Press `ESC`.

The 1-2-3 Help facility screen no longer is displayed. Notice that the Print command submenu is still active on the control panel's second line.

28 ▶ Press `CTRL`-`BREAK` to cancel the current command and return to READY mode.

You will complete this lesson by erasing the current worksheet.

29 ▶ Press the Slash key (/) to access the Main Menu.

Getting Help 89

30 ▶ Type **WEY** to select the Worksheet, Erase, and Yes commands.

The worksheet area is clear.

You can now begin the Lesson 3 applications that follow the Concept Summary, or you can go on to Lesson 4. Otherwise, quit 1-2-3 if you are through with this session.

Concept Summary

■ Range format options allow you to display values in a variety of formats. Format options include currency (for example, $1,230.00); percentages (for example, 1.23%); scientific notation (for example, 1.23E+08); or fixed numbers of decimal places (for example, 1230.00). Format options only affect the display of values, not the actual values.

■ Most spreadsheet software uses a string of symbols (for example, asterisks) to represent large formatted values that cannot be displayed. Formatted values cannot be displayed when the current column width is too narrow. Therefore, spreadsheet software includes commands that let you increase (or decrease) column widths so you can display formatted data on screen.

■ Labels can be aligned within cells so that they are left-aligned, centered, or right-aligned. Many spreadsheet software packages include special symbols that control the alignment of labels.

■ Spreadsheet software provides many worksheet enhancement features. Such features include the ability to insert and delete columns and rows or add separation lines to make totals or other ranges stand out. Most spreadsheet software allows you to expand or contract highlighted ranges.

■ Spreadsheet software generally includes an on-line Help feature that provides you with on-screen information about specific commands and operations. Some software packages provide context-sensitive help, which means that information about a command operation in current use can be obtained immediately.

3 ▶ Formatting a Worksheet and Getting Help

Command Summary

/Range Format (/RF)
formats the display of a range of values (for example, Currency format)

/Worksheet Column Set–Width (/WCS)
adjusts the width of a single column

/Worksheet Column Column–Range Set–Width (/WCCS)
adjusts the width of several columns

/Range Label (/RL)
changes the alignment of labels within a range

/Worksheet Insert Column (/WIC)
inserts one or more columns into the worksheet

/Worksheet Insert Row (/WIR)
inserts one or more rows into the worksheet

/Worksheet Delete Column (/WDC)
deletes one or more columns from a worksheet

/Worksheet Delete Row (/WDR)
deletes one or more rows from a worksheet

Applications

Begin doing the applications by loading 1-2-3, if necessary. Place your student data disk in drive A (or drive B if you do not have a hard disk). Change the current directory to the drive that contains the student data disk. Also, change the Clock setting in the Default Settings dialog box so that the current filename displays.

Business

Sales Analysis

1. On review of your sales comparison worksheet, the owner notices that there is no data for the San Francisco branch. Also, she would like you to add a column of data that shows the difference in sales between years. While you are at it, you decide to improve the worksheet's appearance. Begin by retrieving the file SALES2.WK1 and doing the following tasks:

    a. Format all the values as currency with no decimal places.

    b. Move the cell pointer to cell B9, and insert one row.

    c. Delete column B.

    d. Enter the following data in the new row 9:

    San Francisco CA   16524   17983

    e. Widen column A to 18 characters, and then widen columns B and C to 11 characters.

    f. Replace the labels in cells B3 and C3 with the right-aligned labels "1994 Sales" and "1995 Sales", respectively.

    g. Enter a formula in cell D4 that calculates the difference between the

1995 and 1994 sales figures for the Los Angeles branch. Copy the formula down the column to calculate differences for each city.

    h. Enter the right-aligned label "Change" in cell D3.

    i. Press HOME, and save the file as SALES3.WK1.

    j. Check the printer to make sure it is turned on and has paper. Make sure the paper is properly aligned. Print the range A1..D12.

    k. Save the current print settings to the same file.

    l. Erase the worksheet.

Business

Small Business

2. You are now ready to begin analyzing the break-even point for producing windsurfing boards. You decide to calculate total production costs, total costs, total revenue, and the total profit or loss. To do so, retrieve the file PROFIT2.WK1, build and copy formulas, and format data as outlined in the following steps. When completed, your worksheet should appear as shown in Figure 3.13.

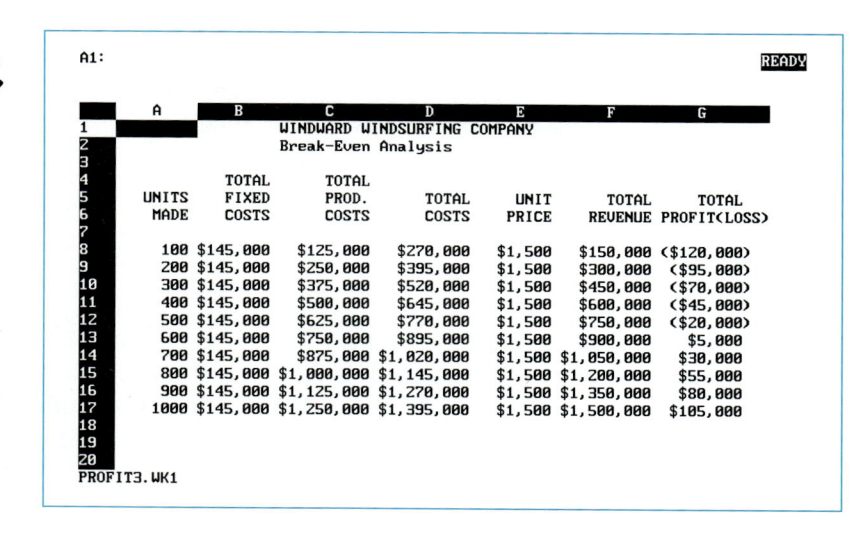

Figure 3.13

Follow the instructions in application 2 (Small Business) to create this worksheet.

    a. Right-align all labels in the range A4..G6.

    b. Enter the formula **1250*A8** in cell C8, and copy the formula down the column to calculate total production costs.

    c. Enter the formula **+C8+B8** in cell D8, and copy the formula down the column to calculate total costs.

    d. Enter the formula **+E8*A8** in cell F8, and copy the formula down the column to calculate total revenue.

    e. Enter the formula **+F8-D8** in cell G8, and copy the formula down the column to calculate profit or loss.

    f. Format the values in the range B8..G17 as currency with no decimals.

g. Increase the widths of columns C, D, F, and G so that all values are displayed.

h. Look at the data and notice that the break-even point, the point when the company starts to make a profit, is after 600 units are sold.

i. Press (HOME), and save the worksheet as PROFIT3.WK1.

j. Check the printer to see that it is turned on and has paper. Make sure the paper is properly aligned. Print the range A1..D17.

k. Save the latest changes to PROFIT3.WK1.

l. Erase the worksheet.

Business
Accounting

3. Complete the trial balance portion of your worksheet for Big Peak Mountain Bicycles' accounts during the month of April. Retrieve the file BALANCE2.WK1. Use various formatting techniques to improve the worksheet's appearance by doing the following tasks:

a. Insert a new row 3, a new row 5, a new row 7, and a new row 24. Insert a blank column between columns E and F.

b. Delete columns C and D.

c. Increase the width of column A to 26 characters.

d. Decrease the width of columns B, D, and F to one character.

e. Use a formatting prefix and the vertical bar character (|) to enter a vertical line down column B that extends from row 5 to row 26.

f. Copy the range of labels that make the vertical line in column B to columns D and F.

g. Use the backslash formatting prefix to enter dashed lines in rows 5, 7, and 24 that extend from columns A to F.

h. Format all values in the worksheet with the comma format option and no decimal places.

i. In EDIT mode, place three spaces in front of the label "Trial Balance" to center it over the "Debit" and "Credit" headings.

j. Use the /Range Label command (/RL) to center the headings "Debit" and "Credit" in their cells.

k. Use the backslash formatting prefix to enter double-dashed lines in cells C26 and E26, below the "Debit" and "Credit" column totals.

l. Press (HOME), and save the worksheet as BALANCE3.WK1.

m. Check the printer to see that it is turned on and has paper. Make sure the paper is properly aligned. Print the range A1..F26.

n. Save the current changes to the same file.

o. Erase the worksheet.

Applications

Social Studies

Student Survey

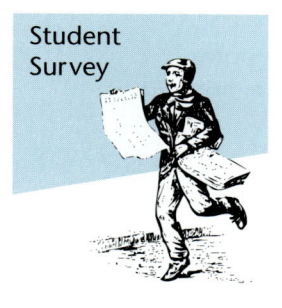

4. Continue analyzing the results of the questionnaire on student attitudes. You decide to calculate percentages for each total and clarify the worksheet by formatting data. To do so, retrieve the file SURVEY2.WK1. Change some column widths, create formulas to calculate percentages, and format data, as outlined in the following steps. When the steps are completed, rows 3 through 22 in your worksheet should appear as shown in Figure 3.14.

```
A3: [W11]                                                          READY

      A              B         C         D         E         F         G
 3                        Excellent   Good      Fair      Poor  No Opinion
 4   SPORTS
 5   Varsity Football       132       314       118        57        89
 6   Varsity Baseball       205       363        94        23        67
 7   Varsity Basketball      67       248       221        35       189
 8   Sophomore Water Polo    42       262       109        11       252
 9
10   FACILITIES
11   Cafeteria               56       114       334       214        12
12   Library                179       183       193        34       145
13   Gym                    201       245        97        52       103
14
15   EVENTS
16   Prom Dance             156       279       178        23        89
17   Sadie Hawkins Dance     78       168       201        78       125
18   Homecoming             132       285       102        76        89
19   Can Drive               92       159       132        91        96
20   Car Wash               127       201        55        19       203
21   TOTAL                 1467      2821      1834       713      1459
22   PERCENTAGE TOTAL     17.69%    34.01%    22.11%     8.60%    17.59%
SURVEY3.WK1
```

Figure 3.14

After you follow the instructions in application 4 (Student Survey), rows 3 through 22 in your worksheet should look like this.

a. Right-align the column headings in the range C3..G3.

b. Widen column A to 11 characters and column G to 10 characters.

c. Enter the label "PERCENTAGE TOTAL" in cell A22.

d. Enter the formula +C21/H21 in cell C22, which divides the total of "Excellent" responses by the total of all responses.

e. Enter similar formulas in cells D22, E22, F22, and G22 that divide each column's response total by the total of all responses.

f. Format the range C22..G22 as percentages with two decimal places.

g. Press (HOME), and save the worksheet as SURVEY3.WK1.

h. Check the printer to see that it is turned on and has paper. Make sure the paper is properly aligned. Print the range A1..G22.

i. Save the current print settings to the same file.

j. Erase the worksheet.

Social Studies

Geography

5. To continue analyzing world population for your Geography class, retrieve the file WRLDPOP2.WK1. You decide to create formulas that calculate percentages for each total. You also want to improve the worksheet by formatting data, changing column widths, and inserting rows, as outlined in the following steps. When completed, your worksheet should look like Figure 3.15.

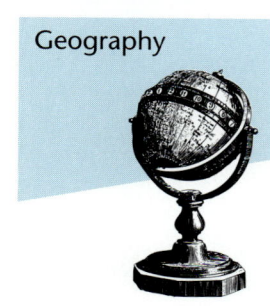

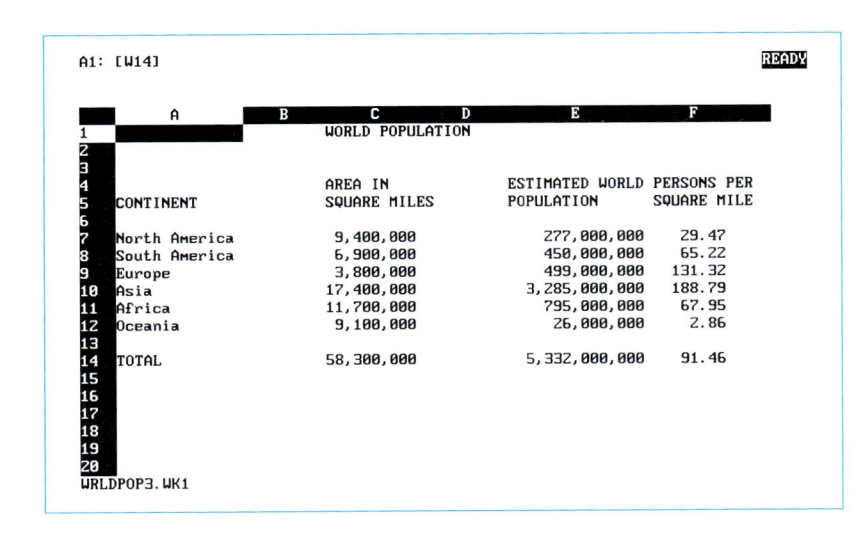

```
A1: [W14]                                                              READY

        A              B       C         D         E           F
  1                         WORLD POPULATION
  2
  3
  4                          AREA IN          ESTIMATED WORLD PERSONS PER
  5   CONTINENT              SQUARE MILES     POPULATION      SQUARE MILE
  6
  7   North America          9,400,000        277,000,000       29.47
  8   South America          6,900,000        450,000,000       65.22
  9   Europe                 3,800,000        499,000,000      131.32
 10   Asia                  17,400,000      3,285,000,000      188.79
 11   Africa                11,700,000        795,000,000       67.95
 12   Oceania                9,100,000         26,000,000        2.86
 13
 14   TOTAL                 58,300,000      5,332,000,000       91.46
 15
 16
 17
 18
 19
 20
WRLDPOP3.WK1
```

Figure 3.15

Follow the instructions in application 5 (Geography) to create this worksheet.

a. Increase the width of column A to 14 characters and the width of column C to 11 characters.

b. Use the /Range Format Comma command (/RFC) to format the values in column C with commas and no decimal places.

c. In EDIT mode, add three zeros (000) to the end of each value in column E. (Note that each value appears in exponential format.)

d. Insert a new row 6 and a new row 13.

e. Increase the width of column E to 16 characters.

f. Format the values in column E with commas and no decimal places.

g. Enter the label "PERSONS PER" in cell F4 and the label "SQUARE MILE" in cell F5.

h. Copy the labels in the range E3..E4 to E4..E5. Delete the label in E3.

i. Enter a formula in cell F7 that divides North America's total population in cell E7 by the continent's total area value in cell C7.

j. Copy the formula in cell F7 to the range F8..F14 to calculate person-per-square-mile ratios for the other continents. Delete the formula in cell F13.

k. Format the values in column F as fixed values with two decimal places.

l. Press HOME, and save the worksheet as WRLDPOP3.WK1.

m. Check the printer to see that it is turned on and has paper. Make sure the paper is properly aligned. Print the entire range of data.

n. Save the worksheet again to save the current print settings to the same file.

o. Erase the worksheet.

Social Studies

American Government

6. Continue with your assignment to analyze the electoral college system from a historical perspective. Begin by retrieving the file ELECTN2.WK1 and calculating percentages for each total. Also, use several formatting techniques to help clarify the worksheet, as outlined in the following steps. When completed, your worksheet should look like Figure 3.16.

```
A1: 'COMPARING POPULAR AND ELECTORAL VOTES IN THREE PRESIDENTIAL ELECTIONS  READY

         A         B         C         D         E         F         G
1    COMPARING POPULAR AND ELECTORAL VOTES IN THREE PRESIDENTIAL ELECTIONS
2
3        1960              Popular Vote    %      Electoral    %
4    Kennedy              34,221,334     49.72%      303     56.42%
5    Nixon                34,106,671     49.55%      219     40.78%
6    Others                  500,945      0.73%       15      2.79%
7    TOTAL                68,828,950                 537
8
9        1976
10   Carter               40,825,839     50.03%      297     55.20%
11   Ford                 39,147,770     47.97%      240     44.61%
12   Others                1,629,737      2.00%        1      0.19%
13   TOTAL                81,603,346                 538
14
15       1988
16   Bush                 48,881,278     53.37%      426     79.18%
17   Dukakis              41,805,374     45.65%      111     20.63%
18   Others                  898,168      0.98%        1      0.19%
19   TOTAL                91,584,820                 538
20
ELECTN3.WK1
```

Figure 3.16

Follow the instructions in application 6 (American Government) to create this worksheet.

a. Edit the year values in cells A3, A9, and A15 to make them right-aligned labels.

b. Center the labels "%" in row 3.

c. Widen column C to 13 characters, and widen column E to 10 characters.

d. Insert a new row 8 and a new row 14.

e. Enter a formula in cell D4 that divides the 1960 popular votes for Kennedy by the total popular votes.

f. Enter similar formulas in cells D5 and D6 that divide the 1960 popular votes for Nixon and the other candidates, respectively, by the total 1960 popular votes.

g. Enter similar formulas in cells F4, F5, and F6 that divide the 1960 electoral votes for each candidate by the total 1960 electoral votes.

h. Enter similar formulas in the appropriate column D and F locations to calculate percentages for each candidate in the other election years.

i. Format the values in columns D and F as percentages with two decimals.

j. Format the values in column C with commas and no decimals.

k. Press (HOME), and save the worksheet as ELECTN3.WK1.

l. Check the printer to see that it is turned on and has paper. Make sure the paper is properly aligned. Print the entire range of data.

m. Save the current print settings to the same file.

n. Erase the worksheet.

Science/Mathematics

Astronomy

7. Continue working with the solar system analysis worksheet by retrieving the file PLANETS2.WK1. Enter some additional data that compares each planet's diameter and gravitational pull to Earth's. Then use various techniques to improve the worksheet's formatting, as outlined in the following steps. When completed, your worksheet should look like Figure 3.17.

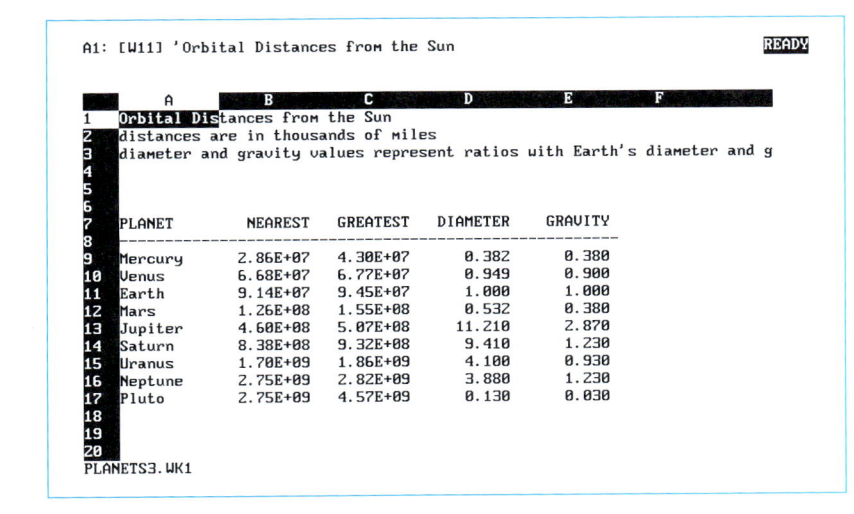

Figure 3.17

Follow the instructions in application 7 (Astronomy) to create this worksheet.

```
A1: [W11] 'Orbital Distances from the Sun                    READY

        A          B         C         D         E        F
 1  Orbital Distances from the Sun
 2  distances are in thousands of miles
 3  diameter and gravity values represent ratios with Earth's diameter and g
 4
 5
 6
 7  PLANET      NEAREST   GREATEST  DIAMETER  GRAVITY
 8  ------------------------------------------------
 9  Mercury     2.86E+07  4.30E+07   0.382    0.380
10  Venus       6.68E+07  6.77E+07   0.949    0.900
11  Earth       9.14E+07  9.45E+07   1.000    1.000
12  Mars        1.26E+08  1.55E+08   0.532    0.380
13  Jupiter     4.60E+08  5.07E+08  11.210    2.870
14  Saturn      8.38E+08  9.32E+08   9.410    1.230
15  Uranus      1.70E+09  1.86E+09   4.100    0.930
16  Neptune     2.75E+09  2.82E+09   3.880    1.230
17  Pluto       2.75E+09  4.57E+09   0.130    0.030
18
19
20
PLANETS3.WK1
```

a. Enter the following label in cell A3: "diameter and gravity values represent ratios with Earth's diameter and gravitational pull".

b. Insert two new rows between the blank row 4 and row 5, which contains the column headings.

c. Delete column D.

d. Enter the label "DIAMETER" in cell D7 and the label "GRAVITY" in cell E7.

e. Enter the column D and E ratios (values) that compare the diameter and gravity measures for each planet to Earth's, as shown in Figure 3.17.

f. In EDIT mode, add three zeros to each distance value in columns B and C. After you have edited the values, notice that 1-2-3 displays all values over 8 digits in scientific notation with two decimal places.

g. Format the distances in columns B and C so they all are displayed in scientific notation with two decimal places.

h. Format the ratios in columns D and E so they are displayed in fixed decimal format with three decimal places.

i. Right-align the column heading labels in the range B7..E7.

j. Insert a new row 8. Enter a repeating-character label and use the /Copy command to enter a dashed line in the range A8..E8.

k. Increase the widths of columns A through E to 11 characters.

l. Save the file as PLANETS3.WK1.

m. Check the printer to see that it is turned on and has paper. Make sure the paper is properly aligned. Print the range A7..E17.

n. Save the current print settings to the same file.

o. Erase the worksheet.

Science/Mathematics

Mathematics

8. Complete the Recycling Drive worksheet by doing some additional calculations and formatting the worksheet's appearance. Begin by retrieving the file RECYCLE2.WK1, and then do the following steps. When the steps are completed, rows 4 through 23 in your worksheet should look like Figure 3.18.

```
G23: (C2) [W12] +G8+G14+G20                                    READY

       A          B         C         D          E        F         G
  4  SOPHOMORES           UNITS COLLECTED    REFUND RATE       REFUND AMOUNT
  5              cans        628 pounds       $0.35                219.80
  6              newspaper 3,442 inches       $0.03                103.26
  7              glass     1,781 bottles      $0.04                 71.24
  8                                                    TOTAL:    $394.30
  9                                                   % COLLECTED  30.02%
 10  JUNIORS
 11              cans        720 pounds       $0.35                252.00
 12              newspaper 4,433 inches       $0.03                132.99
 13              glass     2,015 bottles      $0.04                 80.60
 14                                                    TOTAL:    $465.59
 15                                                   % COLLECTED  35.45%
 16  SENIORS
 17              cans        688 pounds       $0.35                240.80
 18              newspaper 4,429 inches       $0.03                132.87
 19              glass     1,999 bottles      $0.04                 79.96
 20                                                    TOTAL:    $453.63
 21                                                   % COLLECTED  34.54%
 22
 23                                              GRAND TOTAL:  $1,313.52
RECYCLE3.WK1
```

Figure 3.18

After you follow the instructions in application 8 (Mathematics), rows 4 through 23 in your worksheet should look like this.

a. Insert a new row 9 and a new row 15.

b. Format the refund rate values in column E as currency with two decimal places.

c. Format the refund amounts for each recycled item in each class with the comma format and two decimal places.

d. Format the refund amount totals in cells G8, G14, and G20 as currency with two decimal places.

e. Enter the label "% COLLECTED" in cells F9, F15, and F21. Be sure to use a label-formatting prefix.

f. Enter the label "GRAND TOTAL:" in cell F23.

g. Right-align all the labels in column F.

h. Enter a formula in cell G23 that sums the total refund amounts for the three classes and format the cell as currency with two decimal places.

i. Enter formulas in cells G9, G15, and G21 to calculate percentages of the grand total that each class's refund amount represents.

j. Format the results of the formulas you entered in step i as percentages with two decimal places.

k. Widen columns F and G to 12 characters.

l. Save the worksheet as RECYCLE3.WK1.

m. Check the printer to see that it is turned on and has paper. Make sure the paper is properly aligned. Print the entire range of data.

n. Save the current print settings to the same file.

o. Erase the worksheet.

Health

Nutrition

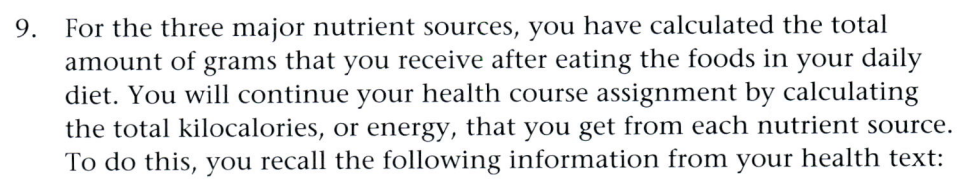

9. For the three major nutrient sources, you have calculated the total amount of grams that you receive after eating the foods in your daily diet. You will continue your health course assignment by calculating the total kilocalories, or energy, that you get from each nutrient source. To do this, you recall the following information from your health text:

   Fat contains 9 kilocalories per gram.

   Protein and carbohydrates each contain 4 kilocalories per gram Retrieve the file NUTRINF2.WK1, and do the following steps to make the calculations and reformat the worksheet.

   a. Replace the row 3 column heading labels so that they are in all uppercase letters. Right-align these labels.

   b. Delete column B.

   c. Widen columns B through E to 12 characters.

   d. Insert a new row 19 and enter the following data in the new row:

	PROTEIN	CARBOHYDRATES
Rice	4	25

   e. In order, insert the following new rows: row 4, row 9, rows 11 and 12, row 19, rows 21 and 22, and row 29.

   f. In rows 9, 19, and 29, enter a repeating-character label and use the /Copy command (/C) to enter a dashed line in columns C through E.

   g. Enter dashed lines in rows 12 and 22 that span columns A through E.

   h. Delete the label "TOTAL" in column B and enter the labels "Total Grams" in column A.

   i. Below the label "Total Grams", enter the label "Energy in kilocalories".

   j. Enter a formula in cell C11 that calculates the total breakfast protein kilocalories. The formula must multiply the total grams of breakfast protein by the number of kilocalories per gram that protein contains.

   k. Because carbohydrate contains the same amount of kilocalories per gram as protein, copy the formula in cell C11 to cell D11.

   l. Enter a similar formula in cell E11 that calculates the total fat kilocalories for breakfast.

   m. Copy the formulas you have entered in row 11 to rows 21 and 31.

   n. Format all the values in the worksheet with the fixed decimal option and one decimal place.

   o. Save the worksheet as NUTRINF3.WK1.

Applications

p. Check the printer to see that it is turned on and has paper. Make sure the paper is properly aligned. Print the entire range of data.

q. Save the current print settings to the same file.

r. Erase the worksheet.

Health

Physical Education

10. The Washington High School softball team lost their third game 31–21. The following stats were taken from the game's scorecard:

Player	At Bats	Runs	Hits	Doubles	Triples	HRs	RBIs
Bernhart	7	3	3	0	0	1	2
Taylor	7	3	4	1	1	0	2
Hepburn	7	3	3	1	0	0	3
Monroe	6	2	2	0	0	0	2
d'Arc	6	2	3	0	0	0	3
Victoria	6	3	3	1	0	1	4
Wood	5	2	1	0	0	1	3
Smith	5	1	2	0	0	0	1
Turner	2	0	0	0	0	0	0
Welch	0	0	0	0	0	0	0
Loren	2	1	1	0	0	0	0
Mabely	1	0	0	0	0	0	0
Braga	2	1	1	0	0	1	1

Retrieve the file SBGAME2.WK1, and update the formulas by editing each cell so that the new value is added to the current formula. Then do the following steps to format the worksheet. When the steps are completed, column J in your worksheet should show the batting averages shown in Figure 3.19.

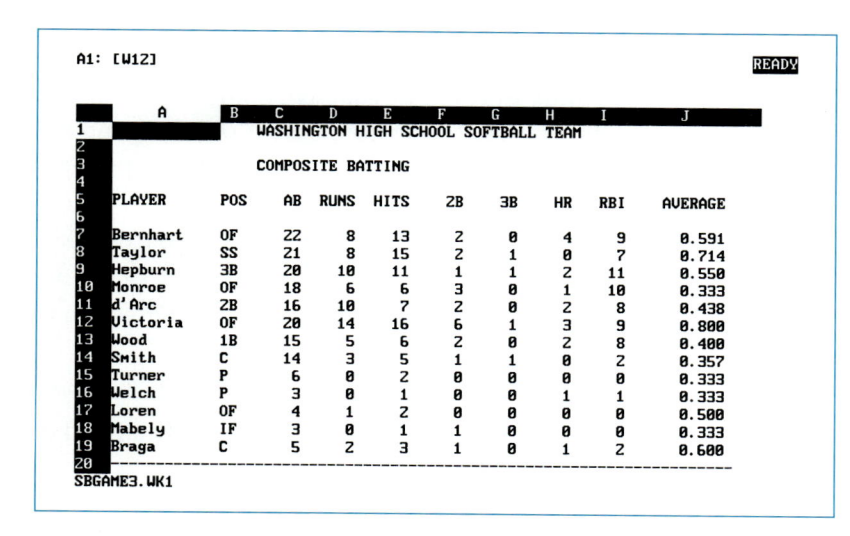

Figure 3.19

After you edit the worksheet with game 3's statistics, column J in your worksheet should display these batting averages.

3 ▶ Formatting a Worksheet and Getting Help

a. Widen column A to 12 characters, and widen column J to 11 characters.
b. Narrow column B to 4 characters, and narrow columns C through I to 6 characters.
c. Replace the column headings in the range B5..H5 as follows:

   POS   AB   RUNS   HITS   2B   3B   HR

   > Note: Be sure to enter a label-formatting prefix for the labels that begin with a number.

d. Format the labels in the range C5..J5 so that they are right aligned.
e. Format the batting average values in column J as fixed with three decimal places. What is the team batting average after three games?
f. Insert a new row 20, enter a repeating-character label in cell A20, and use the /Copy command to enter a dashed line in the range A20..J20.
g. Press (HOME), and save the worksheet as SBGAME3.WK1.
h. Check the printer to see that it is turned on and has paper. Make sure the paper is properly aligned. Print the entire range of data.
i. Save the current print settings to the same file.
j. Erase the worksheet.

4 Using 1-2-3 @Functions and Checking Their Accuracy

Objectives

- Describe how to use 1-2-3 @functions.
- Enter an @SUM function to add a range of values.
- Reformat the worksheet to keep its appearance consistent.
- Insert an additional row of data.
- Use the SCROLL LOCK key to scroll the worksheet.
- Erase a range of data.
- Replace simple formulas with @SUM functions.
- Enter an @AVG function to calculate an average.
- Freeze, or lock, worksheet titles.
- Clear worksheet titles.
- Move a range.

In this lesson you will learn two powerful 1-2-3 @functions, which are special formulas that do specific calculations quickly. You will also learn how to erase and move ranges and reformat the worksheet so it will have a consistent appearance.

Exercise 4.1: Creating and Copying 1-2-3 @Functions

Objectives

After completing this exercise, you will be able to
- Describe how to use 1-2-3 @functions.
- Enter an @SUM function to add a range of values.

1-2-3 @FUNCTIONS
Special types of formulas built into 1-2-3 for performing routine or complex computations.

@SUM
A function that calculates a total for a range of values.

ARGUMENT
A condition or information, enclosed in parentheses, that is required by a 1-2-3 @function to perform an operation. An argument can be a cell, a range, a value, or a text string.

Lotus 1-2-3 has special formulas called *@functions* that automatically do specific computations or calculations for you. These @functions extend 1-2-3 capabilities by doing complex calculations *without* your having to build the formulas.

The most commonly used 1-2-3 @function is the *@SUM* function (pronounced "at SUM"). As its name suggests, it calculates a total or sum by adding up a range of numbers. When you use the @SUM function, you must include an argument that tells 1-2-3 the range of values you want to add. An *argument* is a range or series of cell addresses that an @function needs in order to perform its calculation. The argument for a function is always put inside parentheses. You enter the argument for the @SUM function by typing "@SUM" and then the range address enclosed in parentheses. For example, if you want to use the @SUM function to add up monthly sales figures for one year stored in the range B5..M5, you type the following @SUM function:

@SUM(B5..M5)

You could enter the formula +B5+C5+D5+E5+F5+G5+H5+I5+J5+K5+L5+M5 to calculate the same total; but as you can see, the @SUM function requires fewer keystrokes. It can be entered more quickly than the formula, and there is less chance of typing an error.

An @function's argument can also contain a series of cell addresses and/or ranges. For example, you may want to do a calculation on values that are not next to each other in a range. In this case, you must separate each cell address or range with a comma (,) in the @function's argument. For example, the @function @SUM(B5,C12,D90..D99) will add the values stored in those ranges.

You can also use the pointing method that you learned in Lesson 3 to enter a range argument in an @function. The pointing method ensures even greater accuracy.

You will use the @SUM function to calculate the total sales of compact discs, albums, audio cassettes, and videotapes for June through September in your worksheet for Mollie's Music Shoppe. Begin by adjusting certain column widths to improve spacing.

1 ▶ If necessary, start 1-2-3, and use the /File Directory command (/FD) to change the current directory to the drive that contains the student data disk.

2 ▶ If necessary, use the /File Retrieve command (/FR) to retrieve the SUMSALES.WK1 file.

3 ▶ If necessary, use the /Worksheet Global Default command (/WGD) to change the Clock display to the File name option in the Default Settings dialog box.

4 ▶ Move the cell pointer to cell C6.

The cell pointer is on the first column in the range that you want to adjust.

5 ▶ Press [F4].

Lotus 1-2-3 prompts you to enter a range.

6 ▶ Press [END], and then press [→].

The range C6..F6 is highlighted.

7 ▶ Press [↵].

The range of columns is selected.

8 ▶ Press the Slash key (/) to access the Main Menu.

9 ▶ Type **WCCS** to select the Worksheet, Column, Column-Range, and Set-Width commands.

Lotus 1-2-3 prompts you to select a width for the column range.

10 ▶ Press [↵] once.

11 ▶ Press [↵].

The column widths are adjusted to 11 characters. Notice that column G is now visible.

12 ▶ Move the cell pointer to cell G6.

You will enter another title as a column heading in this cell.

13 ▶ Press [CAPS LOCK].

14 ▶ Type **^TOTAL**, and press [↓] twice.

The centered label is entered in cell G6, and the cell pointer is on cell G8. In this cell you will enter an @SUM function to total sales for compact discs.

15 ▶ Type **@SUM(**

> The VALUE mode indicator appears. The first part of the @SUM function appears on the control panel, as shown in Figure 4.1.

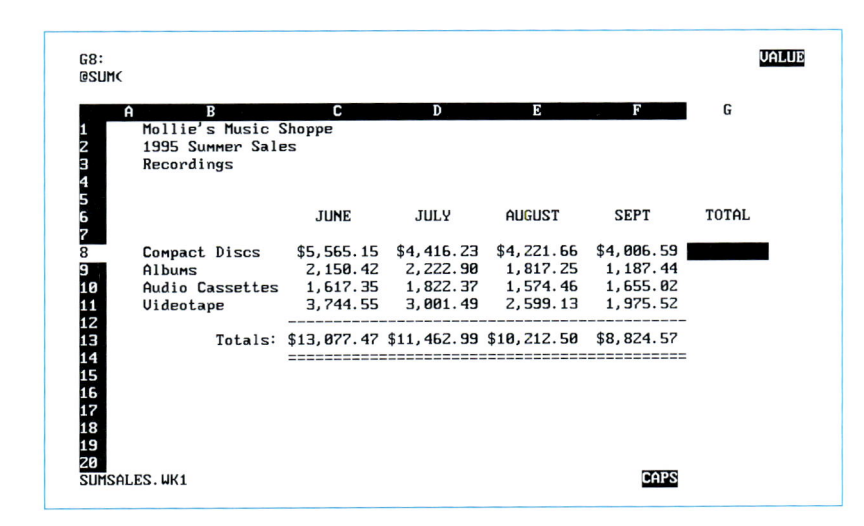

Figure 4.1

As soon as you type the at sign (@), 1-2-3 switches to VALUE mode. After typing the @function name and opening parenthesis, you are ready to point to the range of values you want to sum.

Now you will use the pointing method to enter the range for the @SUM function's argument, instead of manually typing the range address.

16 ▶ Press ← 4 times.

> The cell pointer is on cell C8, which contains the compact disc sales for June. The cell address is to the right of the opening parenthesis, "(", on the control panel, as shown in Figure 4.2.

Current cell is added to @function

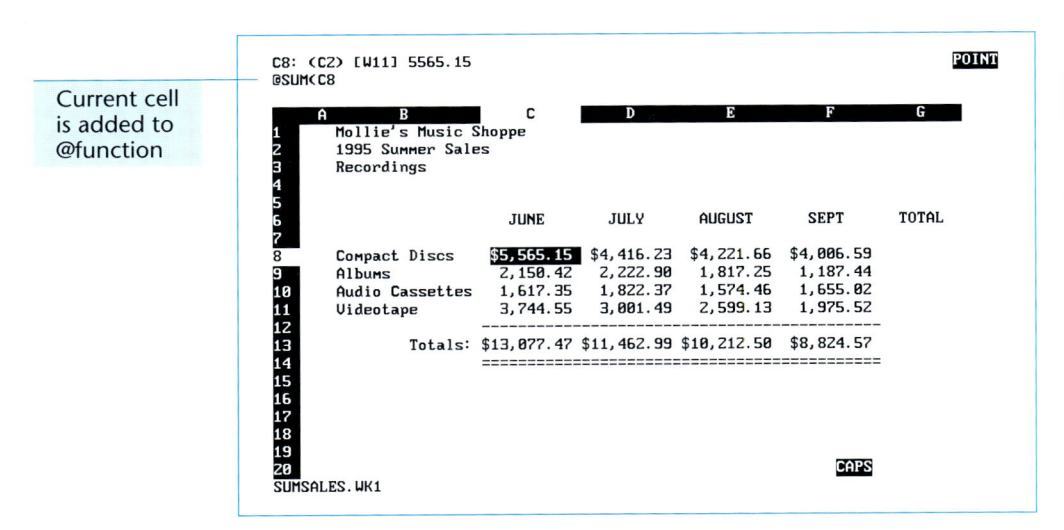

Figure 4.2

As soon as you press an Arrow key, 1-2-3 switches to POINT mode. The current cell is displayed to the right of the opening parenthesis on the control panel.

17 ▶ Type **.** (a period) to anchor the current cell.

18 ▶ Press → 3 times.

> The range expands to include cells C8, D8, E8, and F8. This range

Creating and Copying 1-2-3 @Functions 105

contains the sales for compact discs for June, July, August, and September, as shown in Figure 4.3.

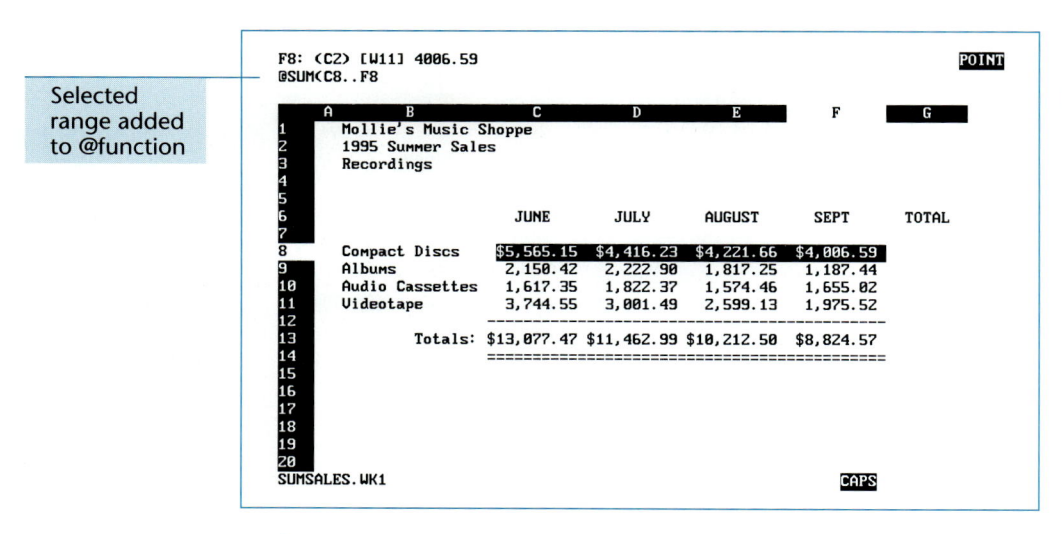

Figure 4.3

After you select the value range in POINT mode for the @SUM function, the range address appears to the right of the opening parenthesis on the control panel.

Selected range added to @function

19 ▶ Type **)** (a closing parenthesis).

The cell pointer returns to cell G8, as shown in Figure 4.4, where the function will be stored.

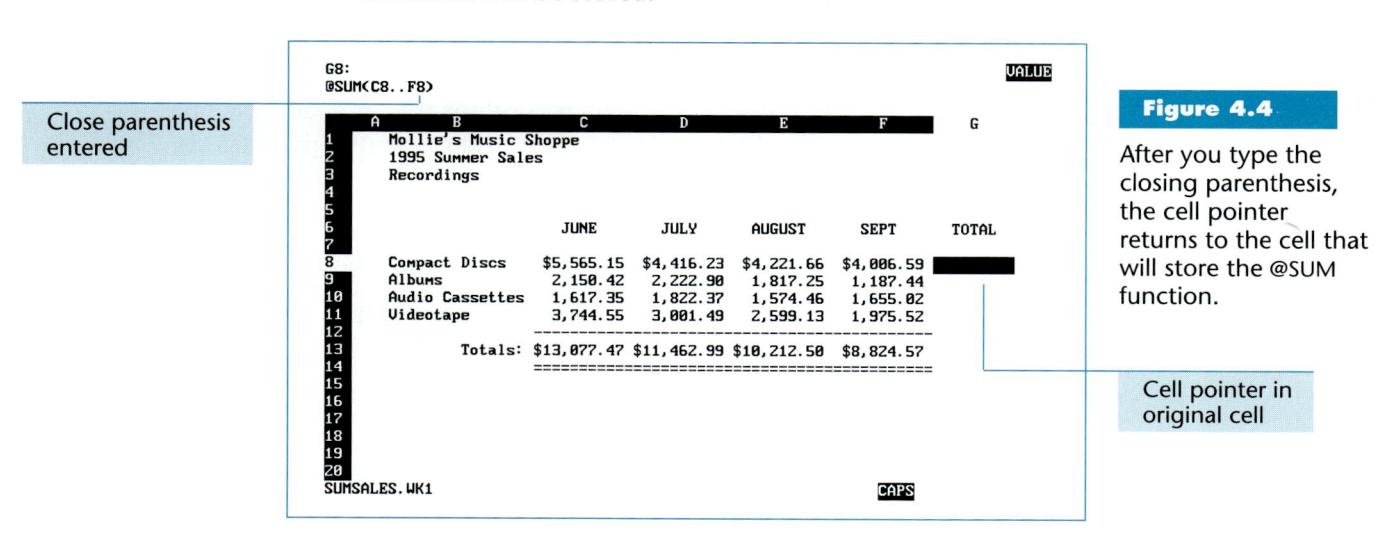

Figure 4.4

After you type the closing parenthesis, the cell pointer returns to the cell that will store the @SUM function.

Close parenthesis entered

Cell pointer in original cell

20 ▶ Press ⏎.

The @SUM function is entered, displaying a series of asterisks. The width of the column needs to be adjusted to accommodate the formatted value.

21 ▶ Press the Slash key (/) to access the Main Menu.

22 ▶ Type **WCS** to select the Worksheet, Column, and Set-Width commands.

Lotus 1-2-3 prompts you to enter the column width.

23 ▶ Press → twice.

24 ▶ Press ⏎.

The column's width is adjusted to 11 characters, and the formatted total is displayed. Notice that the worksheet area has adjusted and displays columns B through G, but not column A.

25 ▶ Press CAPS LOCK to turn off uppercase status.

The @SUM function you entered in cell G8 totals the values in the range C8..F8. You also have to calculate totals for the other ranges in this worksheet. So the next logical step is to copy this @function down the column.

Like formulas, you can copy @functions not only to save time and effort but also to maintain accuracy. And 1-2-3 automatically adjusts cell addresses in the copied @function's argument so that the @function uses the correct range of values. In Lesson 5, you will learn more about how 1-2-3 does this.

Now you will use the next set of steps to copy the @SUM function you just entered so that you can total summer sales figures for the other products.

26 ▶ Make sure the cell pointer is on cell G8.

This cell contains the @SUM function that totals summer compact disc sales.

27 ▶ Press the Slash key (/) to access the Main Menu.

28 ▶ Type **C** to select the Copy command.

Lotus 1-2-3 prompts you to enter the "Copy what?" range.

29 ▶ Press ↵.

Lotus 1-2-3 prompts you to enter the "To where?" range.

30 ▶ Type **.** (a period) to anchor the current cell.

31 ▶ Press ↓ 3 times.

The range expands to include the cells G8, G9, G10, and G11.

32 ▶ Press ↵.

The @function copies to each cell in the range, displaying the calculated values for each product, as shown in Figure 4.5.

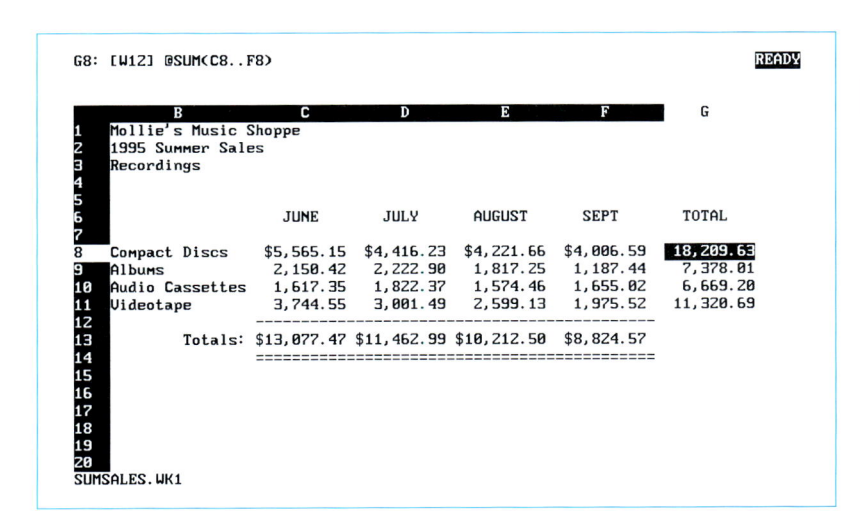

Figure 4.5

The @SUM function in cell G8 is copied to the range G9..G11, and the summer totals for each product are displayed.

Creating and Copying 1-2-3 @Functions

107

33 ▶ Press ⬇ once.

    The cell pointer is on cell G9, which contains the first @SUM function entered by the copy operation.

Check the control panel. Notice that the range address in this @SUM function was adjusted during the copy operation. It now refers to the values on this row. Check the other cells that contain @SUM functions, and note the changes 1-2-3 made to the range addresses in their arguments. Now you will continue this exercise by copying an @SUM function to cell G13. This will produce a grand total for sales of all items for the summer period.

34 ▶ Move the cell pointer to cell G11.

    The cell pointer is on the cell that contains the @SUM function that totals videotape sales.

35 ▶ Press the Slash key (/) to access the Main Menu.

36 ▶ Type **C** to select the Copy command.

    Lotus 1-2-3 prompts you to enter the "Copy what?" range.

37 ▶ Press ⏎ to select the current cell.

    Lotus 1-2-3 prompts you to enter the "To where?" range.

38 ▶ Press ⬇ twice.

    The cell pointer is on cell G13.

39 ▶ Press ⏎.

    The @SUM function copies to cell G13 and calculates a grand total for sales of all recording products during the summer.

Exercise 4.2 — Reformatting the Worksheet

Objective

After completing this exercise, you will be able to
- Reformat the worksheet to maintain a consistent appearance.

As you use a worksheet, you will find that you need to keep repeating many formatting techniques. You must do this to make sure the worksheet data is formatted consistently.

Look at the worksheet that you have been using in this lesson. Notice that the worksheet can be improved in two ways. First, the compact disc sales total in cell G8 is not displayed in the same format as the rest of the data on row 8. Neither is the grand total in cell G13. So you need to apply the Currency format to these cells. Second, use the /Copy command (/C) to extend the dashed and double-dashed lines to column G.

1 ▶ Move the cell pointer to cell G8.

   This cell contains the total sales for compact discs.

2 ▶ Press the Slash key (/) to access the Main Menu.

3 ▶ Type **RFC** to select the Range, Format, and Currency commands.

   Lotus 1-2-3 prompts you to enter the number of decimal places.

4 ▶ Press ⏎ to accept the default option of two decimal places.

   Lotus 1-2-3 prompts you to enter the range that you want to format.

5 ▶ Press ⏎ to select the current cell.

   The value in cell G8 is displayed in Currency format.

6 ▶ Move the cell pointer down this column to cell G13.

   This cell contains the grand total.

7 ▶ Repeat steps 2–5 to display this value in Currency format.

Next, you will copy the repeating-character labels in rows 12 and 14 to extend the dashed and double-dashed lines to column G.

8 ▶ Move the cell pointer to cell F12.

   The cell pointer is on the cell that contains the repeating-character label that forms a dashed line.

9 ▶ Press the Slash key (/) to access the Main Menu.

10 ▶ Type **C** to select the Copy command.

11 ▶ Press ⏎ to select the current cell as the "Copy what?" range.

12 ▶ Press → once.

13 ▶ Press ⏎.

   The repeating-character label copies to the next cell, extending the dashed line to column G.

14 ▶ Press ↓ twice.

   The cell pointer is on cell F14, which contains the repeating-character label that makes the double-dashed line.

15 ▶ Repeat steps 9–13 to copy the label in cell F14 to cell G14.

Now that you have modified the worksheet, you will save your work.

16 ▶ Press HOME, and use the /File Save Replace command (/FS ⏎ R) to save the current changes to the same file.

Reformatting the Worksheet

Exercise 4.3

Erasing a Range

Objectives

After completing this exercise, you will be able to
- Insert an additional row of data.
- Use the Scroll Lock key to scroll the worksheet.
- Erase a range of data.
- Replace simple formulas with @SUM functions.

In the middle of working, you suddenly realize that you have not included data on the sales of reel-to-reel tapes. You will insert an additional row of data for reel-to-reel tapes. You will begin by moving the cell pointer to the place where you will insert the new row.

1 ▶ Move the cell pointer to cell B11.

The cell pointer is on the cell that contains the label "Videotape."

2 ▶ Press the Slash key (/) to access the Main Menu.

3 ▶ Type **WIR** to select the Worksheet, Insert, and Row commands.

Lotus 1-2-3 prompts you to enter the number of rows to insert.

4 ▶ Press ⏎.

A blank row is inserted before the row with the sales data for videotapes.

SCROLL LOCK KEY

A toggle key that, when turned on, locks the cell pointer on the current cell, so that the worksheet, and not the cell pointer, is moved with the arrow keys. When this key is turned off, the cell pointer unlocks so that it can be moved from cell to cell.

As you enter sales figures for reel-to-reel tapes, it might be more convenient to see the last column with the totals. You can use the SCROLL LOCK key to scroll the worksheet with the cell pointer locked in place. This lets you adjust your view of the worksheet without having to press the Arrow keys over and over. When you press SCROLL LOCK a second time, the cell pointer unlocks and you can move it from cell to cell.

5 ▶ Press SCROLL LOCK.

The SCROLL indicator appears on the status line in the lower right corner of the screen, and the cell pointer locks on the current cell.

6 ▶ Press → once.

The worksheet scrolls, and the worksheet area displays columns B through G.

7 ▶ Press SCROLL LOCK.

The SCROLL indicator disappears, and the cell pointer can be moved with the Arrow keys.

8 ▶ Type **Reel to Reel**

9 ▶ Press →.

> The label is entered in cell B11. The cell pointer is on cell C11, where you can enter the June sales figure for this item.

Before you enter this value, note the total sales for the month of June in cell C14.

10 ▶ Type **2816.98**

11 ▶ Press ←.

> The value is entered, but the total sales for June in cell C14 do not change. Check the formula stored in that cell.

12 ▶ Move the cell pointer to cell C14, and look at the formula on the control panel, as shown in Figure 4.6.

Cell C11 is not in formula

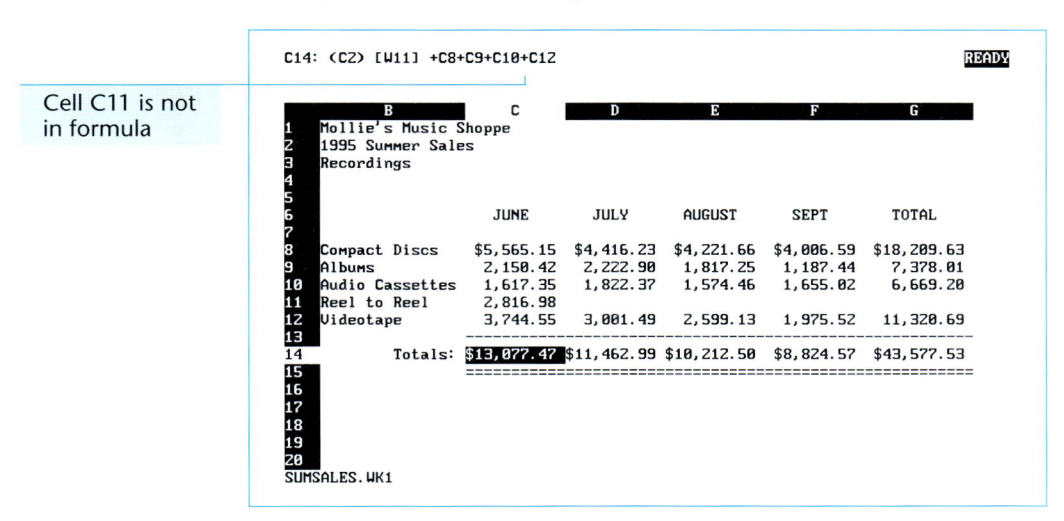

```
C14: (C2) [W11] +C8+C9+C10+C12                                    READY

        B              C          D         E         F         G
1   Mollie's Music Shoppe
2   1995 Summer Sales
3   Recordings
4
5
6                    JUNE       JULY     AUGUST      SEPT      TOTAL
7
8   Compact Discs  $5,565.15  $4,416.23 $4,221.66 $4,006.59 $18,209.63
9   Albums          2,150.42   2,222.90  1,817.25  1,187.44   7,378.01
10  Audio Cassettes 1,617.35   1,822.37  1,574.46  1,655.02   6,669.20
11  Reel to Reel    2,816.98
12  Videotape       3,744.55   3,001.49  2,599.13  1,975.52  11,320.69
13                  ----------------------------------------------------
14       Totals:  $13,077.47 $11,462.99 $10,212.50 $8,824.57 $43,577.53
15                  ====================================================
16
17
18
19
20
SUMSALES.WK1
```

Figure 4.6

Notice that the formula in cell C14 does not contain the cell address C11. When you inserted a new row 11, 1-2-3 adjusted the cell address for the June videotape sales figure. However, the value in cell C11 is not added to the computation.

The formula contains cell addresses that reference the values for compact discs, albums, audio cassettes, and videotapes. It does not include a cell address that references the value for reel-to-reel tapes. The formula in this cell cannot add a cell address for the row you inserted into the worksheet. So you need to somehow change the formula so that the June sales figure for reel-to-reel tapes is included. You have two options: you can edit the existing formula, or you can replace the formula with an @SUM function.

In this case, an @SUM function is the better choice because the range in its argument will expand if rows or columns are inserted. You could enter the @SUM functions over the formulas to replace them. However, now is a good time to learn another useful 1-2-3 command that lets you erase a range of data.

The /Range Erase command (/RE) erases the data in a range, but it does not erase the formatting associated with cells in the range. Use the /Range Erase command (/RE) to erase data in more than one cell. However, if you want to quickly erase data in the current cell, you can simply press the DEL key. Now,

Erasing a Range

you will erase the range C14..F14 in your worksheet, and then enter @SUM functions in that range.

13 ▶ Make sure the cell pointer is on cell C14.

14 ▶ Press the Slash key (/) to access the Main Menu.

15 ▶ Type **RE** to select the Range and Erase commands.

Lotus 1-2-3 prompts you to enter the range to erase. Cell C14 is anchored.

16 ▶ Press → 3 times.

The range C14..F14 is highlighted.

> Caution: Do not highlight cell G14 in the column with the totals.

17 ▶ Press ←.

The range of values is erased, as shown in Figure 4.7. Notice that the current cell contains the currency format with two decimal places. This is indicated by the code (C2) on the control panel.

Currency format code

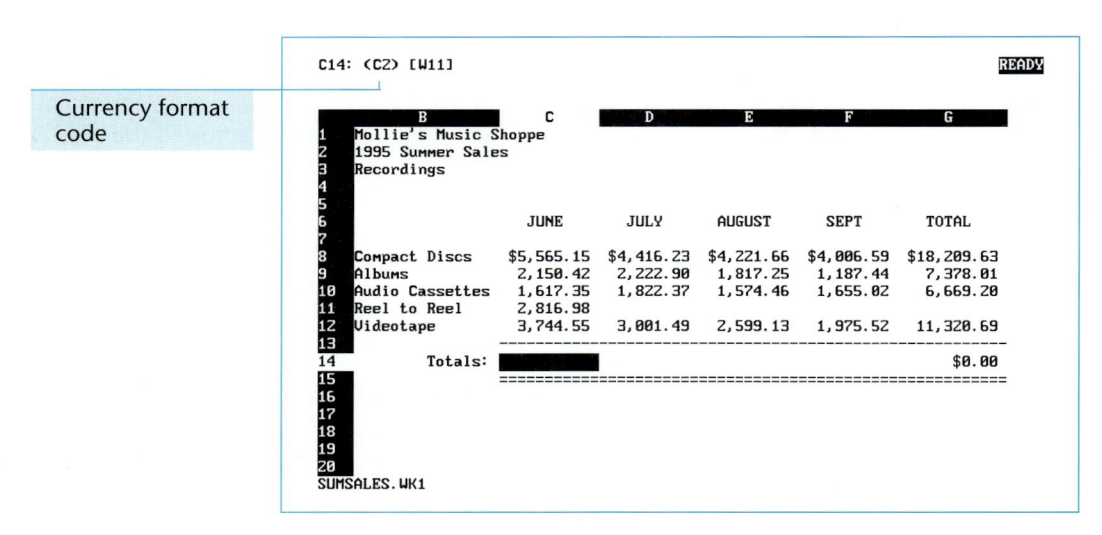

```
C14: (C2) [W11]                                                    READY

         B              C          D          E          F          G
 1   Mollie's Music Shoppe
 2   1995 Summer Sales
 3   Recordings
 4
 5
 6                    JUNE       JULY     AUGUST       SEPT      TOTAL
 7
 8   Compact Discs  $5,565.15  $4,416.23  $4,221.66  $4,006.59  $18,209.63
 9   Albums          2,150.42   2,222.90   1,817.25   1,187.44    7,378.01
10   Audio Cassettes 1,617.35   1,822.37   1,574.46   1,655.02    6,669.20
11   Reel to Reel    2,816.98
12   Videotape       3,744.55   3,001.49   2,599.13   1,975.52   11,320.69
13   ------------------------------------------------------------------
14          Totals:                                                 $0.00
15   ==================================================================
16
17
18
19
20
SUMSALES.WK1
```

Figure 4.7

The /Range Erase command (/RE) erases the data in the specified range, but any cell formatting in the range remains intact. Notice that the format code (C2) is displayed on the control panel for the current cell.

Notice that 1-2-3 recalculated a new total in cell G14. This occurred because cell G14 stores an @SUM function that references the range you erased. Each empty cell in the range represents a value that equals zero, so 1-2-3 calculates a zero total. When you enter new @SUM functions to calculate the monthly totals, 1-2-3 will recalculate the grand total in cell G14.

18 ▶ Make sure the cell pointer is on cell C14.

The cell pointer is on the cell that will store the total sales for June.

19 ▶ Type **@sum(**

20 ▶ Press ⬆ 6 times.

The cell pointer is on cell C8, which stores the June sales figure for compact discs.

21 ▶ Type **.** (a period) to anchor the current cell.

22 ▶ Press ⬇ 4 times.

The range C8..C12 is highlighted.

23 ▶ Type **)** (a closing parenthesis).

The cell pointer returns to cell C14.

24 ▶ Press ⬅.

The @SUM function is entered and calculates a new total for this range. The range includes the June sales for reel-to-reel tapes in cell C11. Notice that the @SUM function in cell G14 recalculates the grand total.

Now, you will copy this @function across the row and produce @functions that total sales figures for the next three months.

25 ▶ Press the Slash key (/) to access the Main Menu.

26 ▶ Type **C** to select the Copy command.

27 ▶ Press ⬅.

Lotus 1-2-3 prompts you to enter the "To where?" range.

28 ▶ Type **.** (a period) to anchor the current cell.

29 ▶ Press ➡ 3 times.

The range C14..F14 is highlighted.

30 ▶ Press ⬅.

The @SUM function copies to the range C14..F14 and calculates totals for each month. Notice also that the @SUM function in cell G14 displays the grand total. It summed the range of @SUM functions, as shown in Figure 4.8.

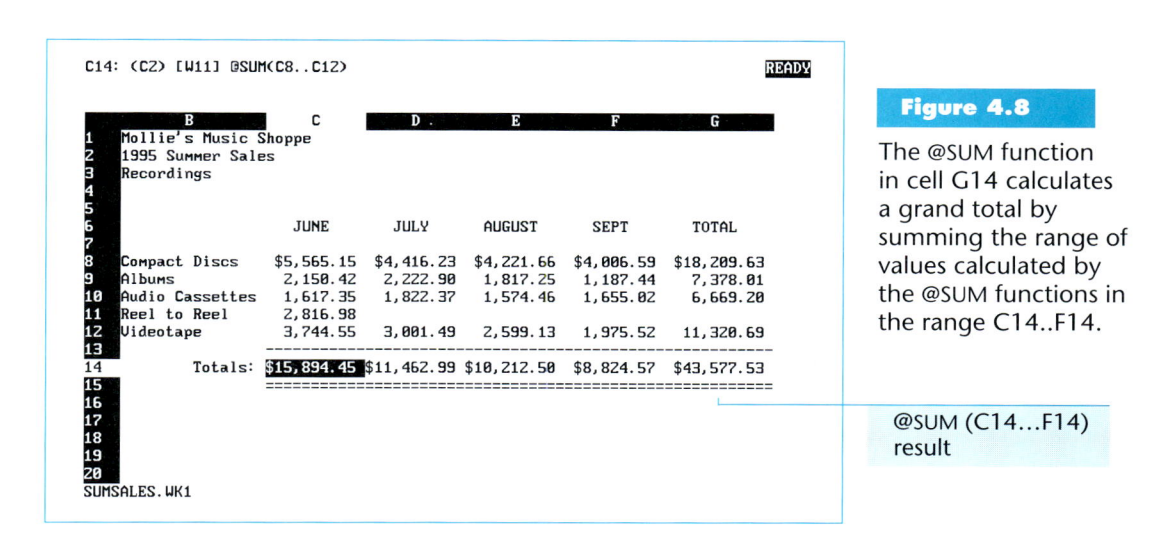

Figure 4.8

The @SUM function in cell G14 calculates a grand total by summing the range of values calculated by the @SUM functions in the range C14..F14.

@SUM (C14...F14) result

Erasing a Range 113

After making these adjustments, you are ready to enter the rest of the sales data for reel-to-reel tapes.

31 ▶ Move the cell pointer to cell D11.

The cell pointer is on the cell that will store the July sales figure for reel-to-reel tapes.

32 ▶ Type **3251.22**

33 ▶ Press ⟶.

A new total for the July sales is recalculated in cell D14.

Cell D11 is within the range of values referenced in the @SUM function. So the @SUM function in cell D14 recalculates a total. At the same time, the grand total in cell G14 also is recalculated because its @SUM function references the July total in cell D14.

34 ▶ Type **3191.23**

35 ▶ Press ⟶.

The @SUM functions in cells E14 and G14 are recalculated.

36 ▶ Type **2970.79**

37 ▶ Press ⟶.

The totals in cells F14 and G14 are recalculated.

To complete this row, you will enter an @SUM function to calculate the total sales for reel-to-reel tapes. Rather than type the formula, you will copy the @SUM function that calculates the total sales for audio cassettes in cell G10.

38 ▶ Move the cell pointer to cell G10.

The cell pointer is on the cell that contains the @SUM function that totals sales for audio cassettes.

39 ▶ Use the /Copy command (/C) to copy the @SUM function in the current cell to cell G11.

40 ▶ After completing the copy operation, move the cell pointer to cell G11.

Check the @SUM function displayed on the control panel. Again, 1-2-3 adjusted the range reference in the copied @SUM function so that it references values on the row where it is stored. In Lesson 5, you will learn more about how 1-2-3 is able to do this.

41 ▶ Press (HOME), and use the /File Save Replace command (/FS ⟵ R) to save the latest changes to SUMSALES.WK1.

This exercise emphasizes the importance of checking the accuracy of your formulas and @functions. It is good practice to spot-check calculations and make sure that the resulting values are close to what you expect. This is very important when you are changing the structure of the worksheet.

Exercise 4.4

Using the @AVG Function

Objective

After completing this exercise, you will be able to
- Enter an @AVG function to calculate an average.

@AVG
A function that calculates an average for a range of values.

In addition to total sales for each item, the owner of Mollie's Music Shoppe wants to see average summer sales for each item. Lotus 1-2-3 has an @function that calculates an average, or mean value, for a range of values. This is the *@AVG* function. Like the @SUM function, its argument is the range, or series of separate cell addresses, that contains the values you want to average.

You may recall from a math course how an average, or mean, is found. You add a series of values and then divide the sum by the number of values in the series. This is the computation that the @AVG function performs on a range of values.

In this exercise, you will set up an additional column that contains @AVG functions. These functions will average the range of sales figures that the @SUM functions in column G total.

1 ▶ Move the cell pointer to cell H6.

> The cell pointer is one cell to the right of the cell that stores the label "TOTAL."

Notice that you cannot see the column headings in Column B because 1-2-3 can only fit columns C through H on the screen.

2 ▶ Press [CAPS LOCK].

3 ▶ Type **^AVERAGE**

4 ▶ Press [↓] twice.

> The centered label is entered. The cell pointer is on cell H8, where you will enter the first @AVG function. The @AVG function will calculate the sales average for compact discs over the summer.

5 ▶ Type **@AVG(**

6 ▶ Press [←] 5 times.

> The cell pointer is on cell C8, which contains the June sales figure for compact discs.

Using the @AVG Function

115

7 ▶ Type **.** (a period) to anchor the current cell.

8 ▶ Press → 3 times.

The range C8..F8 is highlighted.

> Caution: Do *not* select cell G8 in the total column.

9 ▶ Type **)** (a closing parenthesis).

The cell pointer returns to cell H8.

10 ▶ Press ⏎.

The @AVG function is entered. Its result—average sales for compact discs—is displayed, as shown in Figure 4.9.

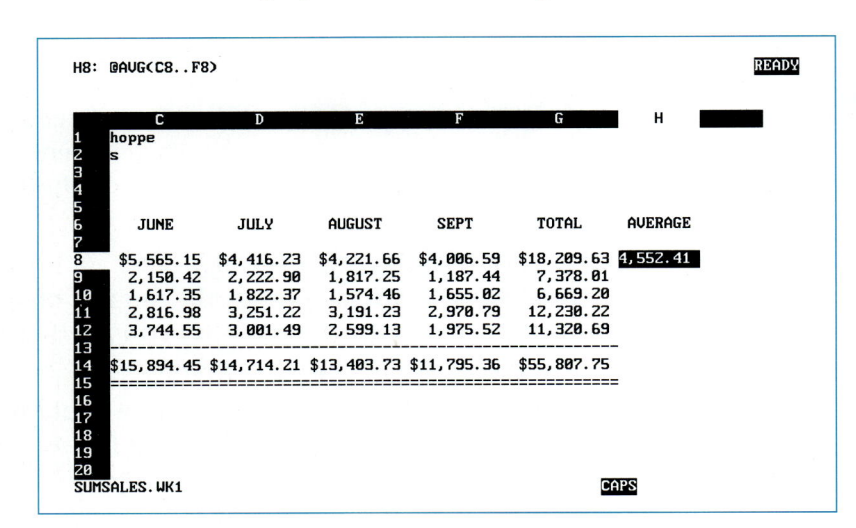

Figure 4.9

The @AVG function calculates the average sales of CDs for the four months in row 8.

```
H8: @AVG(C8..F8)                                              READY

         C         D         E         F         G        H
1   hoppe
2   s
3
4
5
6       JUNE      JULY    AUGUST      SEPT     TOTAL    AVERAGE
7
8   $5,565.15 $4,416.23 $4,221.66 $4,006.59 $18,209.63  4,552.41
9    2,150.42  2,222.90  1,817.25  1,187.44   7,378.01
10   1,617.35  1,822.37  1,574.46  1,655.02   6,669.20
11   2,816.98  3,251.22  3,191.23  2,970.79  12,230.22
12   3,744.55  3,001.49  2,599.13  1,975.52  11,320.69
13  --------------------------------------------------
14  $15,894.45 $14,714.21 $13,403.73 $11,795.36 $55,807.75
15  ==================================================
16
17
18
19
20
SUMSALES.WK1                                           CAPS
```

11 ▶ Press CAPS LOCK to turn off uppercase status.

Before you copy this function down the column, you decide you want to see the row headings while you work in this column.

116 **4 ▶ Using 1-2-3 @Functions and Checking Their Accuracy**

Exercise 4.5

Locking Worksheet Titles

Objective

After completing this exercise, you will be able to
- Freeze, or lock, worksheet titles.

WORKSHEET TITLES
Labels for column and row headings that remain fixed in place on the screen as you move the cell pointer around a worksheet.

As you move the cell pointer around a large worksheet, the worksheet scrolls. As it scrolls, different parts of the worksheet can be seen in the worksheet area. This makes column and/or row headings move off the screen. But when these *worksheet titles* are not in view, you have no way to understand the data being displayed. This increases the chance that you will put errors into the worksheet. For example, you may not be sure which value you are changing or on which range you are working.

The /Worksheet Titles command (/WT) lets you freeze, or lock in place, either the column headings or row headings, or both. Then they stay on screen as you move the cell pointer to scroll the worksheet. Before using this command, you must place the cell pointer to the right of any columns and/or below any rows that you want to lock. The locked "titles" will stay fixed in place until you use the /Worksheet Titles Clear command (/WTC) to unlock them.

In the SUMSALES.WK1 worksheet, you will lock the column B row headings (titles) in place. They will stay on screen as you scroll to the right to work in column H. You will begin by positioning the cell pointer before you select the /Worksheet Titles command (/WT).

1 ▶ Make sure the cell pointer is on cell H8.

2 ▶ Press END, and then press ←.

  The cell pointer moves to cell B8, which contains the label "Compact Discs."

3 ▶ Press → to move the cell pointer to cell C8.

4 ▶ Press the Slash key (/) to access the Main Menu.

5 ▶ Type **WT** to select the Worksheet and Titles commands.

  The following submenu appears on the control panel:

  Both   Horizontal   Vertical   Clear

The Both option freezes, or locks, all rows above and all columns to the left of the cell pointer. The Horizontal option locks all rows above the cell pointer. The Vertical option locks all columns to the left of the cell pointer. The Clear option unlocks any titles that you have previously locked.

6 ▶ Type **V** to select the Vertical command.

The labels in column B are locked as vertical titles, and 1-2-3 returns to READY mode.

7 ▶ Press ←.

Your system beeps, and the cell pointer remains on cell C8. You cannot move the cell pointer into cells within columns and/or rows that are locked while working in READY mode.

> Note: There is one exception to this. You can use the Go To command (F5) to move the cell pointer to a cell that contains a locked title. This is useful if you want to edit a label without first clearing the worksheet titles.

8 ▶ Press → 5 times.

The cell pointer moves to cell H8, which contains the average sales for compact discs.

Notice that as you moved the cell pointer to the right past the last column on screen, the columns to the left moved left off the screen. However, column B, which is locked in place, stays on screen, as shown in Figure 4.10.

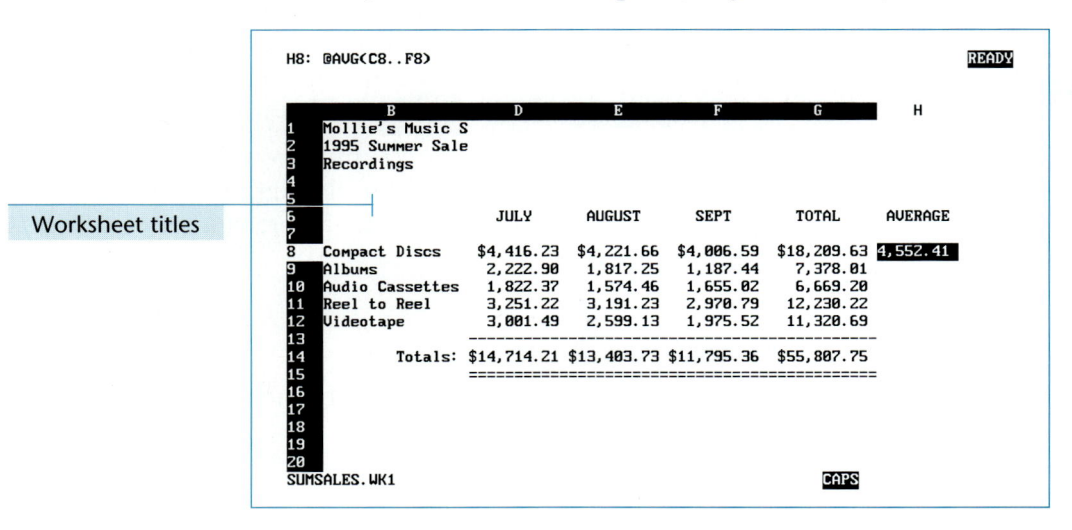

Figure 4.10

The /Worksheet Titles command (/WT) freezes, or locks, the column B labels so that they remain displayed as the other columns move left off screen. Notice here that column D is next to column B, and column C has moved left off screen.

118 4 ▶ Using 1-2-3 @Functions and Checking Their Accuracy

Now you know what the value in cell H8 represents because you can see the row headings (titles). The /Worksheet Titles command (/WT) is useful for worksheets that have more columns and/or rows than will display in the worksheet area. You will now use the /Copy command (/C) to copy the @AVG function in cell H8 down the rest of the column.

9 ▶ Make sure the cell pointer is on cell H8.

10 ▶ Use the /Copy command (/C) to copy the @AVG function in the current cell to the range H9..H12.

11 ▶ Move the cell pointer down one cell at a time, and look at the range addresses in the functions' arguments.

Note that each range address references values on the row where that @AVG function is stored.

12 ▶ Move the cell pointer to cell H12.

The cell pointer is on the cell that contains the last @AVG function in the column.

13 ▶ Use the /Copy command (/C) to copy the @AVG function in the current cell to cell H14.

The copied @AVG function will calculate an average for the monthly sales totals.

Notice that a series of asterisks (***) appears in cell H14. This means you will have to increase the width of the column.

14 ▶ Press the Slash key (/) to access the Main Menu.

15 ▶ Type **WCS** to select the Worksheet, Column, and Set-Width commands.

16 ▶ Press ⇒ twice.

17 ▶ Press ⏎.

The column's width is adjusted to 11 characters.

18 ▶ Move the cell pointer down to cell H14, and look at the @AVG function and its range address.

The range in the @AVG function's argument adjusted to calculate an average for the values stored on the same row, as shown in Figure 4.11.

Locking Worksheet Titles

119

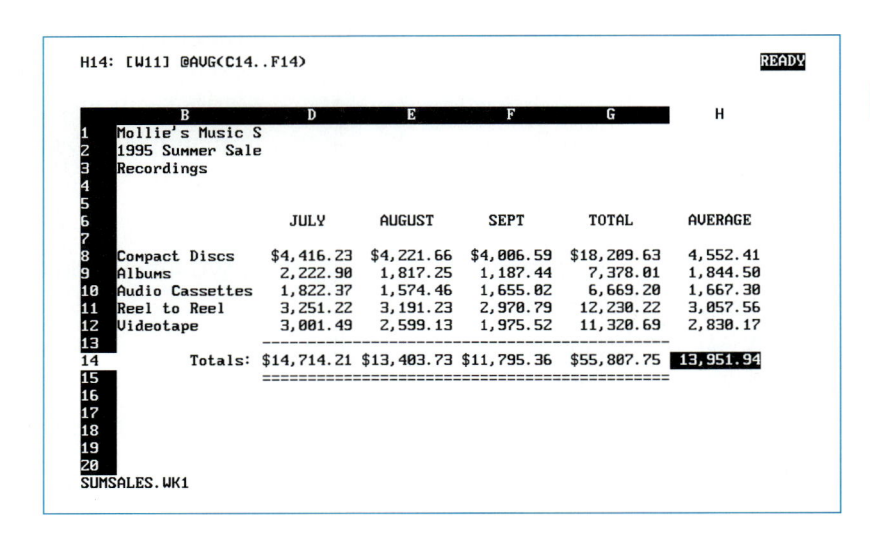

Figure 4.11

The copied @AVG function calculates an average for the respective values in its row. You will learn more about how 1-2-3 does this in Lesson 5.

Now you will save the latest changes to the worksheet.

19 ▶ Press HOME.

Notice that the cell pointer moved to cell C1.

The cell pointer cannot go to cell A1 because you have locked columns A and B with the /Worksheet Titles command (/WT). If you want to move the cell pointer to cell A1, you can use the Go To command (F5). Or you can unlock the titles in columns A and B. For now, however, you will save the worksheet and go on to the next exercise.

20 ▶ Use the /File Save Replace command (/FS ⬅ R) to save the latest changes to SUMSALES.WK1.

Exercise 4.6 — Moving a Range

Objectives

After completing this exercise, you will be able to
- Clear worksheet titles.
- Move a range.

To complete this worksheet, you will add some formatting touches. For instance, you want to extend the dashed and double-dashed lines in rows 13 and 15 to column H. You also want to format some values in column H to be consistent with the rest of the values. You would also like to move the worksheet's title and subtitles (range B1..B3) so that they appear centered over the worksheet's data. You can do this with the /Move command (/M).

The /Move command (/M) is very similar to the /Copy command. However, instead of copying data from one range to another, it physically moves a range from one location to another. The /Move command (/M) also moves any formatting associated with the data being moved. To move the titles in the SUMSALES.WK1 worksheet, you need to move the cell pointer to column B. However, in order to move the cell pointer to that column, you will first unlock the column B titles.

1 ▶ Press the Slash key (/) to access the Main Menu.

2 ▶ Type **WT** to select the Worksheet and Titles commands.

   The Titles command submenu appears on the control panel.

3 ▶ Type **C** to clear any worksheet titles.

   The worksheet titles are unlocked, and 1-2-3 returns to READY mode.

4 ▶ Press [HOME].

   The cell pointer moves to cell A1 because columns A and B are no longer locked.

5 ▶ Move the cell pointer to cell B1.

   The cell pointer is on the cell that contains the label "Mollie's Music Shoppe."

6 ▶ Press the Slash key (/) to access the Main Menu.

7 ▶ Type **M** to select the Move command.

   Lotus 1-2-3 displays the following prompt:

   Move what? B1..B1

   Cell B1 is anchored.

8 ▶ Press [↓] twice.

   The range to be moved is highlighted.

9 ▶ Press [←].

   Lotus 1-2-3 displays the following prompt:

   To where? B1

   Cell B1 is not anchored.

10 ▶ Press [→] twice.

   The cell pointer is on cell D1, where you want to move the title labels.

11 ▶ Press [←].

   The titles in the range B1..B3 move to the range D1..D3, as shown in Figure 4.12.

Moving a Range 121

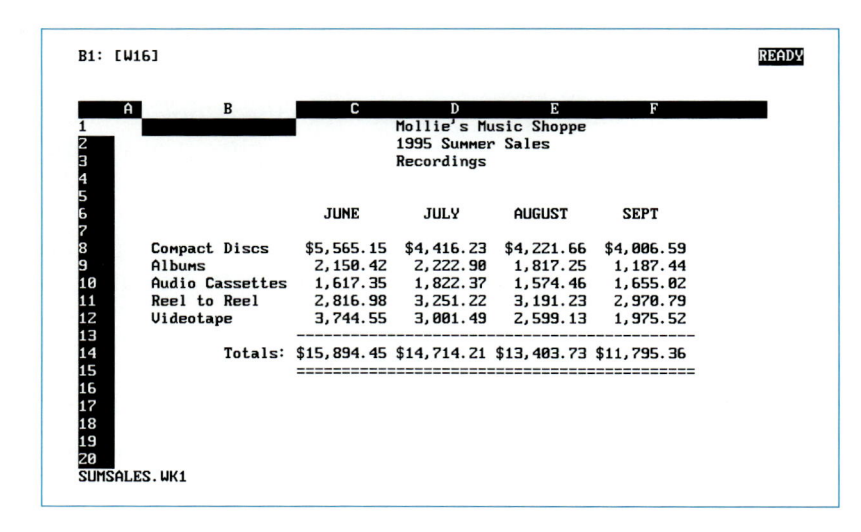

```
B1: [W16]                                                      READY

     A         B           C         D          E          F
 1                                Mollie's Music Shoppe
 2                                1995 Summer Sales
 3                                Recordings
 4
 5
 6                              JUNE      JULY      AUGUST     SEPT
 7
 8        Compact Discs      $5,565.15  $4,416.23  $4,221.66  $4,006.59
 9        Albums              2,150.42   2,222.90   1,817.25   1,187.44
10        Audio Cassettes     1,617.35   1,822.37   1,574.46   1,655.02
11        Reel to Reel        2,816.98   3,251.22   3,191.23   2,970.79
12        Videotape           3,744.55   3,001.49   2,599.13   1,975.52
13                          ----------------------------------------------
14              Totals:    $15,894.45 $14,714.21 $13,403.73 $11,795.36
15                          ==============================================
16
17
18
19
20
SUMSALES.WK1
```

Figure 4.12

The /Move command (/M) allows you to move any range of data from one location to another.

The /Move command (/M) can be used to move any range from one location to another. However, make sure that the range that you are moving to is empty. Otherwise, 1-2-3 will replace any data that is already there.

Now you will edit the labels in the range D2..D3 so that the two subtitles appear centered over the worksheet data.

12 ▶ Move the cell pointer to cell D2.

   The cell pointer is on the cell that contains the label "1995 Summer Sales."

13 ▶ Press [F2].

   Lotus 1-2-3 switches to EDIT mode.

14 ▶ Press [HOME], and then press [→] once.

   The cursor moves to the "1."

15 ▶ Press SPACEBAR twice.

16 ▶ Press [↓].

   The label is edited to appear centered, and the cell pointer moves to cell D3, which contains the label "Recordings."

17 ▶ Press [F2].

18 ▶ Press [HOME], and then press [→].

   The cursor is on the "R."

19 ▶ Press SPACEBAR 5 times.

20 ▶ Press [↵].

   The subtitles appear centered over the worksheet data.

4 ▶ Using 1-2-3 @Functions and Checking Their Accuracy

Now you will complete this exercise by formatting the values that are not consistent with the rest of the worksheet.

21 ▶ Move the cell pointer to cell H8.

The cell pointer is on the cell that contains the average sales for compact discs.

22 ▶ Press the Slash key (/) to access the Main Menu.

23 ▶ Type **RFC** to select the Range, Format, and Currency commands.

Lotus 1-2-3 prompts you to enter the number of decimal places.

24 ▶ Press ⏎ to accept the default option of two decimal places.

Lotus 1-2-3 prompts you to enter the range to format.

25 ▶ Press ⏎ to select the current cell.

The first value in column H is in Currency format.

26 ▶ Move the cell pointer to cell H14, and repeat steps 22–25 to display this value in Currency format.

Finally, you will use the /Copy command (/C) to extend the dashed and double-dashed lines to column H.

27 ▶ Move the cell pointer to cell G13.

The current cell contains the repeating-character label that makes a dashed line.

28 ▶ Use the /Copy command (/C) to copy the label in the current cell to cell H13.

29 ▶ Press ↓ twice.

The cell pointer is on cell G15, which contains the repeating-character label that makes a double-dashed line.

30 ▶ Use the /Copy command (/C) to copy the label in the current cell to cell H15.

Now you will save the latest changes to the same file.

31 ▶ Press HOME, and use the /File Save Replace command (/FS ⏎ R) to save the latest changes to SUMSALES.WK1.

The owner tells you that she wants a hard copy of your worksheet, but she does not need the column of average sales. Unfortunately, there is not enough room on an 8 ½ × 11-inch page to fit columns A through G on a single page. If you added column G to the current print range, 1-2-3 would print columns A through F on one page and column G on a second page. Therefore, to get the data on one page, you decide to delete the blank column A (the spacer column). When you do this, you will have to specify your print range again. Lotus 1-2-3 clears the current print range when you delete the first or last cell in the print range address.

Moving a Range

32 ▶ Make sure the cell pointer is in column A.

33 ▶ Press the Slash key (/) to access the Main Menu.

34 ▶ Type **WDC** to select the Worksheet, Delete, and Column commands.

Lotus 1-2-3 prompts you to enter the range of columns to be deleted.

35 ▶ Press ⏎.

The blank spacer column is deleted, and all the data shifts one column to the left.

36 ▶ Press the Slash key (/) to access the Main Menu.

37 ▶ Type **PP** to select the Print and Printer commands.

The Print Settings dialog box displays. Notice that the Range setting is blank.

38 ▶ Type **R** to select the Range command.

Lotus 1-2-3 switches to POINT mode and prompts you to enter a print range.

39 ▶ Type **.** (a period) to anchor the current cell.

40 ▶ Press END, and then press HOME.

The range A1..H15 is highlighted.

41 ▶ Press ⏎ twice.

The range A1..F15 is highlighted.

42 ▶ Press ⏎.

The Print Settings dialog box redisplays, and the Printer command submenu is active on the control panel.

43 ▶ Make sure your printer is turned on, has paper, and that the paper is properly aligned.

44 ▶ Type **AG** to select the Align and Go commands.

If you are using a dot-matrix printer, the data prints. If you are using a laser printer, the printer processes the data.

45 ▶ Type **P** to select the Page command.

If you are using a dot-matrix printer, the paper advances one page. If you are using a laser printer, the printed page ejects.

46 ▶ Type **Q** to select the Quit option.

The worksheet redisplays in READY mode.

47 ▶ Use the /File Save Replace (/FS ⏎ R) to save the print settings to SUMSALES.WK1.

48 ▶ Use the /Worksheet Erase Yes command (/WEY) to erase the worksheet.

You can now begin the Lesson 4 applications that follow the Concept Summary, or you can go on to Lesson 5. Otherwise, quit 1-2-3 if you are through with this 1-2-3 session.

Concept Summary

▶ ▶ ▶ ▶ ▶

- Spreadsheet software often includes specialized formulas or functions that perform specific calculations on ranges of worksheet data.

- Lotus 1-2-3 gives you over 100 @functions (pronounced "at-functions"). Together, the set of @functions is a powerful and versatile tool for doing computations and analyzing worksheet data.

- Although each @function does a different operation, all the @functions are set up in much the same way. Each 1-2-3 @function starts with the "at" symbol (@). This tells 1-2-3 that the @function is a value entry. Next is the name of the @function, which indicates the type of operation performed. Most @functions need an argument, or additional information, that is enclosed in parentheses. The argument is needed for 1-2-3 to carry out the calculation.

- Function arguments are often put in parentheses, and they generally reference a range or series of separate cells.

- The @SUM and @AVG functions provide convenient methods for calculating totals and averages. In many cases, summing and averaging functions need fewer keystrokes than if formulas were built to do the same thing.

- Many spreadsheet software packages let you freeze, or lock, one or more columns and/or rows that contain labels. This keeps the labels on screen as a large worksheet is scrolled. Thus, values in other areas of the worksheet can be easily referenced, reducing the risk that the wrong data will be used.

- Most spreadsheet software packages have a command that lets you move data from one range to another. Usually this type of command carries any associated formatting to the new range, leaving the original range clear of any formatting.

Command Summary

▶ ▶ ▶ ▶ ▶

/Range Erase (/RE)
erases (clears) a range of data

/Worksheet Titles Vertical (/WTV)
locks one or more columns of labels on screen

/Worksheet Titles Horizontal (/WTH)
locks one or more rows of labels on screen

/Worksheet Titles Both (/WTB)
locks one or more columns and rows of labels on screen

/Worksheet Titles Clear (/WTC)
unlocks any rows and/or columns of labels

/Move (/M)
moves a range of data (and its formatting) to another range

Applications

Begin doing the applications by loading 1-2-3, if necessary. Place your student data disk in drive A (or drive B if you do not have a hard disk). Change the current directory to the drive that contains the student data disk. Also, change the Clock setting in the Global Settings dialog box so that the current filename appears on the status line.

Business

Sales Analysis

1. Understandably, the president is deeply concerned by the drop in sales since last year. Because she must meet with the board to discuss possible solutions, she wants you to make the worksheet more presentable. To do so, retrieve the file SALES3.WK1 and do the following tasks:

   a. Erase the totals in the range B13..D13.

   b. Enter @SUM functions in row 14 that total sales for 1994 and 1995 and the overall difference (change) between years.

   c. Enter the right-aligned labels "Total:" in cell A14 and "Average:" in cell A16.

   d. Enter an @AVG function in cell B16 that calculates the average sales for 1994, and then copy the @AVG function in column B to columns C and D. This will produce averages for 1995 sales and the change between years.

   e. Format the calculated values in row 16 as currency, with 0 decimal places.

   f. Insert a row below the row with column headings.

   g. Enter a repeating-character label, and copy it to create a dashed line under the column headings in the range B4..D4. Then copy the dashed line to the range B14..D14.

   h. Enter a repeating-character label, and copy it to create a double-dashed line between the totals in row 15 and the averages in row 17.

   i. Lock the column A labels as worksheet titles. Scroll the worksheet so that only the change column (column D) is visible to the right of the worksheet titles. Which branch had the biggest drop in sales? Which had the biggest increase?

   j. Clear the worksheet titles, press (HOME), and save the worksheet as SALES4.WK1.

   k. Print the range A1..D17, and save the file again.

   l. Erase the worksheet.

Business

Small Business

2. Continue enhancing the worksheet that helps you to analyze the break-even point for the windsurfing board manufacturer. Retrieve the file PROFIT3.WK1. You decide to improve the worksheet's appearance. You will insert blank rows between each row of data, insert a spacer column, and create lines between each row, as outlined in the following steps. When completed, the first 20 rows of your worksheet should look like Figure 4.13.

Figure 4.13

After you follow the instructions in application 2 (Small Business) the first 20 rows of your worksheet should look like this.

a. Insert a blank row between each row of data.
b. Insert two blank columns between the "UNITS MADE" and "TOTAL FIXED COSTS" columns.
c. Decrease the widths of column A to 6 characters and column B to 1 character. Then increase the widths of columns C and D to 12 characters.
d. Enter the label "'|" into cell B4 to begin creating a vertical separator line. Copy the label in cell B4 to the range B5..B26 to create a vertical line.
e. Enter and copy a repeating-character label in each blank row to create dashed lines.
f. Move all the data in column I to the blank column C.
g. Press (HOME), and save the worksheet as PROFIT4.WK1.
h. Print the range A1..F26, and save the file again.
i. Erase the worksheet.

Business Accounting

3. Now that you have set up the trial balance part of the accounting worksheet, it's time to make some adjustments. To begin, retrieve the file WORKSHT4.WK1. This file has been set up with the first seven columns of an accounting worksheet. It includes the trial balance you worked with in the first three lessons. Post the debit and credit entries to the appropriate accounts in the "Adjustments" section of the worksheet. Then enter @SUM functions to check the balances for each section.

   a. One month's rent ($895) has expired. Debit the Rent Expense account, and credit the Prepaid Rent account.

   b. One month's insurance premium ($112) has expired. Debit the Insurance Expense account, and credit the Prepaid Insurance account.

   c. The company received $1,400 for payment on a shipped bicycle. Debit the Cash account, and credit Accounts Receivable.

   d. The company paid a $2,100 outstanding bill for tires. Debit Accounts Payable, and credit the Cash account.

   e. A total of $79 worth of office supplies were used. Debit the Office Supplies Expense account, and credit the Office Supplies account.

   f. Delete the formulas that total the debit and credit columns for the trial balance in cells C27 and E27. Then enter @SUM functions in the same cells to total the columns.

   g. Enter @SUM functions in cells G35 and I35 to total the debit and credit columns in the "Adjustments" section. Enter double-dashed lines below the results.

   h. Lock the account names in column A as worksheet titles.

   i. Post the adjustment results to the "Adjusted Trial Balance" section. Enter formulas in the appropriate columns that add debits and subtract credits for debit accounts or add credits and subtract debits for credit accounts. For example, you would enter the formula +C9–E9+G9–I9 in cell K9 to post the adjustment to the Cash account, which normally holds a debit balance. Do this for every account.

   j. Enter @SUM functions in cells K35 and M35 to check the accuracy of your postings. Enter double-dashed lines below the results. The Adjusted Trial Balance columns should balance at 29,123.

   k. Clear the worksheet titles and save the worksheet as BALANCE4.WK1.

   l. Print the range F3..N37, to check your work on hard copy, and then save the file again.

   m. Erase the worksheet.

Social Studies

Student Survey

4. Continue using the worksheet that helps you analyze the student attitudes questionnaire results. Retrieve the file SURVEY3.WK1, replace summing formulas with @SUM functions, and use a variety of techniques to improve the worksheet's appearance. You will also insert columns where necessary and enter formulas that calculate percentages for each rating category, as outlined in the following steps. When completed, your worksheet should appear as shown in Figure 4.14.

```
A1: [W20]                                                    READY

         A              B        C        D        E        F
  1                       School Activities Questionnaire
  2
  3                   Excellent Percent   Good   Percent    Fair
  4    SPORTS
  5    Varsity Football    132   18.59%   314    44.23%     118
  6    Varsity Baseball    205   27.26%   363    48.27%      94
  7    Varsity Basketball   67    8.82%   248    32.63%     221
  8    Sophomore Water Polo 42    6.21%   262    38.76%     109
  9
 10    FACILITIES
 11    Cafeteria            56    7.67%   114    15.62%     334
 12    Library             179   24.39%   183    24.93%     193
 13    Gym                 201   28.80%   245    35.10%      97
 14
 15    EVENTS
 16    Prom Dance          156   21.52%   279    38.48%     178
 17    Sadie Hawkins Dance  78   12.00%   168    25.85%     201
 18    Homecoming          132   19.30%   285    41.67%     102
 19    Can Drive            92   16.14%   159    27.89%     132
 20    Car Wash            127   20.99%   201    33.22%      55
 SURVEY4.WK1
```

Figure 4.14

Follow the instructions in application 4 (Student Survey) to modify the worksheet as shown.

a. Enter an @SUM function in cell C21 that adds all values in column C. (Note that the formulas in row 22 will display ERR messages until all totals are calculated.)

b. Copy the @function to the range D21..H21.

c. Move the range C3..H22 one column left, beginning at cell B3.

d. Increase the width of column A to 20 characters.

e. Insert one column between columns B and C.

f. Enter the right-aligned label "Percent" in cell C3.

g. Repeat steps e and f to create "Percent" columns between all the response columns.

h. Enter a formula in cell C5 that divides the "Excellent" response in column B by the total of all responses for varsity football. Then copy the formula to all appropriate cells in column C.

i. Enter a formula in cell E5 that divides "Good" responses in column D by the total responses for Varsity Football in column L. Copy the formula to all appropriate cells in column E.

j. Enter and copy similar formulas for columns G, I, and K.

k. Format the values in columns C, E, G, I, and K as percentages with two decimal places.

l. Increase the width of column J to 10.

m. Insert a blank row at row 21, and enter a dashed line in the range B21..L21.

n. Save the worksheet as SURVEY4.WK1.

o. Print the entire range of data, and then save the file again.

p. Erase the worksheet.

Social Studies
Geography

5. Continue working with the worksheet that helps you to analyze world population. Retrieve the file WRLDPOP3.WK1. Follow the instructions below to enter @SUM functions in place of the existing formulas and move a range of data. Also, use a variety of formatting techniques to improve the worksheet's appearance.

   a. Delete column B, and then delete column C.

   b. Increase the width of column B to 16 characters, and increase the width of column D to 14 characters.

   c. Move the worksheet's title to column C.

   d. Enter an @SUM function in cell B14 to find the total area in square miles of all the continents. Copy the @SUM function to column C to calculate total estimated world population.

   e. Copy one of the formulas in column D to cell D14.

   f. Right align all labels in the range A4..D5, and then right align the label "TOTAL" in cell A14.

   g. Enter a dashed line between the range of totals and the values above. Copy the dashed line to the range B15..D15.

   h. Enter the right-aligned label "AVERAGES" in cell A16.

   i. Enter an @AVG function in cell B16 that calculates the average area in square miles for the continents. Copy the @function to column C to calculate the average estimated population for the continents.

   j. Save the worksheet as WRLDPOP4.WK1.

   k. Print the entire range of data, and then save the file again.

   l. Erase the worksheet.

Social Studies
American Government

6. Before you show your vote comparison worksheet to your instructor, you decide to really jazz it up by reformatting it. Begin by retrieving the file ELECTN3.WK1, and then do the following steps to make your worksheet look like Figures 4.15 and 4.16.

   a. Erase the title label in cell A1.

   b. Insert a new column A.

   c. Enter new worksheet title labels in cells A1 and A2, as shown in Figure 4.15.

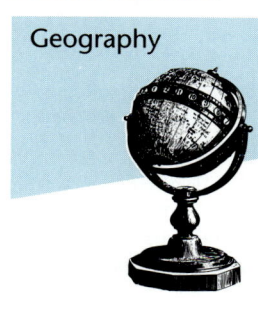

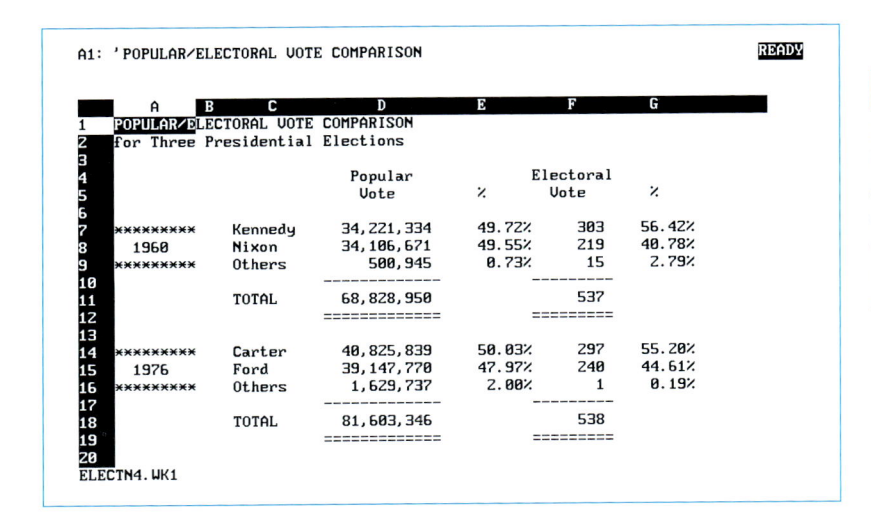

Figure 4.15

```
A1: 'POPULAR/ELECTORAL VOTE COMPARISON                              READY

        A      B    C          D          E         F         G
 1  POPULAR/ELECTORAL VOTE COMPARISON
 2  for Three Presidential Elections
 3
 4                          Popular           Electoral
 5                           Vote       %       Vote      %
 6
 7  *********  Kennedy    34,221,334  49.72%    303    56.42%
 8     1960    Nixon      34,106,671  49.55%    219    40.78%
 9  *********  Others        500,945   0.73%     15     2.79%
10                        ----------            ---
11             TOTAL      68,828,950            537
12                        ==========            ===
13
14  *********  Carter     40,825,839  50.03%    297    55.20%
15     1976    Ford       39,147,770  47.97%    240    44.61%
16  *********  Others      1,629,737   2.00%      1     0.19%
17                        ----------            ---
18             TOTAL      81,603,346            538
19                        ==========            ===
20
ELECTN4.WK1
```

Follow the instructions in application 6 (American Government) to reformat rows 1–20 so they look like this.

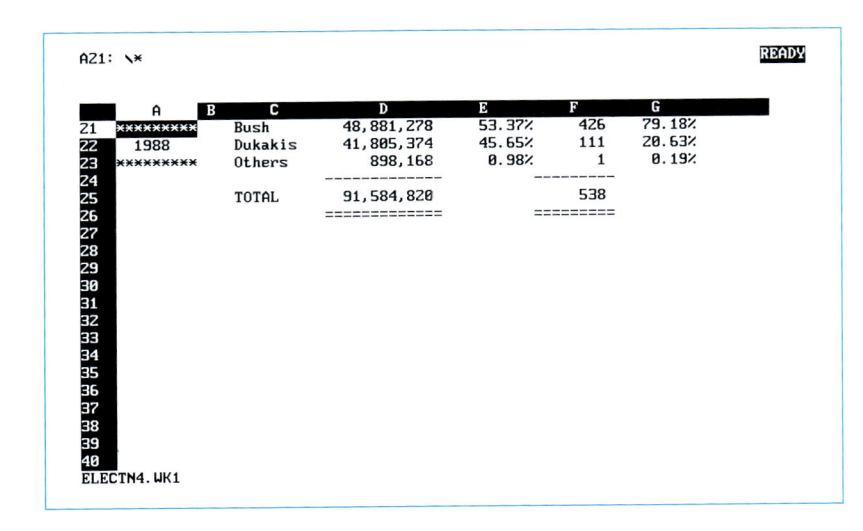

Figure 4.16

```
A21: \*                                                           READY

        A      B    C          D          E         F         G
21  *********  Bush       48,881,278  53.37%    426    79.18%
22     1988    Dukakis    41,805,374  45.65%    111    20.63%
23  *********  Others        898,168   0.98%      1     0.19%
24                        ----------            ---
25             TOTAL      91,584,820            538
26                        ==========            ===
27
28
29
30
31
32
33
34
35
36
37
38
39
40
ELECTN4.WK1
```

Rows 21–40 should look like this.

    d. Use EDIT mode and the /Move command (/M) to modify and rearrange the column heading labels, as shown in Figure 4.15.

    e. Move the year labels in column B to cells A8, A15, and A22, as shown in both figures.

    f. Use the /Copy, /Move, /Worksheet Insert (Column Row), /Worksheet Delete (Column Row) commands, and repeating-character labels, as necessary, to finish reformatting the worksheet. When you complete these formatting steps, your worksheet should appear as shown in Figures 4.15 and 4.16.

    g. Save the worksheet as ELECTN4.WK1.

    h. Print the entire range of data, and save the file again.

    i. Erase the worksheet.

Applications

Science/ Mathematics

Astronomy

7. To extend your comparative analysis of planets in the solar system, retrieve the file PLANETS3.WK1. Do the following steps to add additional data and improve the worksheet's appearance. When you have finished, your worksheet should look like Figure 4.17.

```
A1:                                                              READY
        A        B         C         D         E       F        G
 1                    Orbital Distances from the Sun
 2
 3
 4
 5                                        DIAMETER           GRAVITY
 6            NEAREST   GREATEST  AVERAGE  COMPARISON         COMPARISON
 7  PLANET    DISTANCE  DISTANCE  DISTANCE TO EARTH  DENSITY  TO EARTH
 8  ---------------------------------------------------------------
 9  Mercury   2.86E+07  4.30E+07  3.58E+07  38.2%    5.440    38.0%
10  Venus     6.68E+07  6.77E+07  6.73E+07  94.9%    5.270    90.0%
11  Earth     9.14E+07  9.45E+07  9.30E+07 100.0%    5.520   100.0%
12  Mars      1.26E+08  1.55E+08  1.40E+08  53.2%    3.950    38.0%
13  Jupiter   4.60E+08  5.07E+08  4.84E+08 1121.0%   1.310   287.0%
14  Saturn    8.38E+08  9.32E+08  8.85E+08  941.0%   0.704   123.0%
15  Uranus    1.70E+09  1.86E+09  1.78E+09  410.0%   1.210    93.0%
16  Neptune   2.75E+09  2.82E+09  2.79E+09  388.0%   1.660   123.0%
17  Pluto     2.75E+09  4.57E+09  3.66E+09   13.0%   1.000     3.0%
18
19
20
PLANETS4.WK1
```

Figure 4.17

Follow the instructions in application 7 (Astronomy) to create this worksheet.

a. Erase the labels in the range A2..A3.

b. Move the worksheet's title to column C, and then move the labels "NEAREST" and "GREATEST" to the range B6..C6.

c. Insert a column between the "GREATEST" and "DIAMETER" columns.

d. Enter the label "AVERAGE" in cell D6, enter the label "DISTANCE" in cell D7, and then copy the label in cell D7 to the range B7..C7.

e. Enter an @AVG function in cell D9 to calculate an average orbital distance for the planet Mercury. Copy the @function down the column to calculate average distances for the other planets.

f. Format the average distances as scientific notation with two decimal places.

g. Move the labels "DIAMETER" and "GRAVITY" to the range E5..F5.

h. Enter the label "COMPARISON" in cell E6 and the label "TO EARTH" in cell E7. Copy the labels to the range F6..F7.

i. Format the values in columns E and F as percentages with one decimal place.

j. Insert a column between the "DIAMETER" and "GRAVITY" columns.

k. Enter the label "DENSITY" in cell F7, a dashed line in cell F8, and the values shown in Figure 4.17.

l. Right-align the column heading labels in the range B5..G7.

m. Format the values in column F as fixed with 3 decimal places.

n. Save the worksheet as PLANETS4.WK1.

o. Print the entire range of data, and then save the file again.

p. Erase the worksheet.

4 ▶ Using 1-2-3 @Functions and Checking Their Accuracy

Science/Mathematics

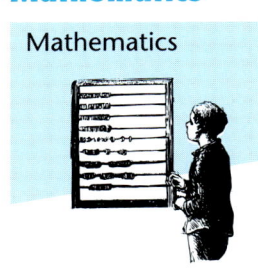

Mathematics

8. Three of your fellow students represented your school in a charity bowling event. They competed against two other schools to raise money for a local charity. Various sponsors agreed to collectively pay $2.75 for every pin knocked down. Each player bowled three games. At the event you noted scores, and now you will enter them into a worksheet model. The model will total scores, calculate players' averages, and determine the amount of money raised for charity. The teams eagerly await your results because the team with the highest score wins a free pizza party. Also, the player with the highest average wins free concert tickets. Retrieve the file BOWLEVNT.WK1, and complete the worksheet model as outlined in the following steps:

   a. Enter the following scores in the appropriate cells:

		Games	
PLAYER	**1**	**2**	**3**
Ross	192	217	201
Nyro	199	198	188
Slick	203	206	202
Daltry	195	218	220
Burdon	208	207	224
Plant	211	210	217
Santana	216	209	221
Berry	223	187	211
Townshend	212	209	203

   b. Enter an @SUM function in column E to total Ross's scores for the three games. Copy the @SUM function to the appropriate ranges to total the scores for all players.

   c. Enter an @SUM function in cell E10 that calculates the total team score for Singer High School. Copy the @SUM function to the appropriate cells to calculate total scores for the other schools.

   d. Enter an @AVG function in column F to calculate Ross' bowling average. Copy the @AVG function to the appropriate ranges in column F to calculate averages for all the players.

   e. Take a look at the average results in column F. The decimal parts of bowling averages are always averaged down. However, if you formatted the averages to get rid of the decimals, the averages for Slick and Plant would round up. Correct their results by subtracting 0.6666 from their averages in EDIT mode.

   f. Format the averages in column F as fixed, with no decimal places.

   g. Enter formulas in cells G10, G17, and G24 that multiply the total pins for each team by the $2.75 pledge. Which team won the pizza dinner by raising the most money? Which player won the concert tickets for highest average?

Applications

h. Enter an @SUM function in row 26 to calculate the total number of pins knocked down in the event, and then enter a formula that calculates the total amount of money raised.

i. Use the /File Save command (/FS) to save the worksheet as MATH4.WK1, and print the entire range of data.

> Note: Columns F and G may print on a second page.

j. Use the /File Save Replace command (/FS ⏎ R) to save the print settings to the same file.

k. Use the /Worksheet Erase Yes command (/WEY) to erase the worksheet.

Health

Nutrition

9. Continue tracking your daily nutrient intake by retrieving and working with the file NUTRINF3.WK1. Enter @SUM functions in place of addition formulas, and reformat the worksheet's appearance, as outlined in the following steps. After you enter an @AVG function to determine the number of kilocalories of energy provided per meal, rows 18 through 37 in your worksheet should look like Figure 4.18.

```
D37: [W12] @AVG(F12,F23,F34)                                      READY

         A     B              C           D          E          F
    18         Mushrooms                 2.0        15.0        2.0
    19         Apple                                24.0
    20         -------------------------------------------------------
    21         Total Grams              35.0       117.0       30.0
    22         Energy in kilocalories  140.0       468.0      270.0
    23         Total Energy (kilocalories):                   878.0
    24
    25         -------------------------------------------------------
    26         Broccoli                  5.0         7.0
    27         Butter                                          26.0
    28  DINNER Rice                      4.0        25.0
    29         Chicken                  32.0        12.0       25.0
    30         Ice Cream                 5.0        45.0       23.0
    31         -------------------------------------------------------
    32         Total Grams              46.0        89.0       74.0
    33         Energy in kilocalories  184.0       356.0      666.0
    34         Total Energy (kilocalories):                  1206.0
    35
    36
    37  Average kilocalories/meal:                 861.7
    NUTRINF4.WK1
```

Figure 4.18

After entering an @AVG function to determine the number of kilocalories per meal in your diet, rows 18 through 37 in your worksheet should look like this.

a. Insert a new column A, and increase its width to 10 characters.

b. Insert one new row between the rows that contain the "Energy in kilocalories" labels and the dashed lines.

> Note: This will give you new blank rows 12, 23, and 34.

c. Move the label "BREAKFAST" to cell A7, the label "LUNCH" to cell A17, and the label "DINNER" to cell A28.

d. Enter the label "Total Energy (kilocalories):" in cell B12, above the dashed line.

134   **4 ▶ Using 1-2-3 @Functions and Checking Their Accuracy**

e. Enter an @SUM function in cell F12 that totals the breakfast energy results in the range D11..F11.

f. Copy the data in row 12 to rows 23 and 34.

g. Erase the ranges of addition formulas in the ranges D10..F10, D21..F21, and D32..F32.

h. Enter an @SUM function in cell D10 that totals the breakfast protein. Copy the @function to columns E and F. Enter and copy @SUM functions in the ranges D21..F21 and D32..F32.

i. Enter the label "Average kilocalories/meal:" in cell A37.

j. Enter an @AVG function in cell D37 that calculates the average number of kilocalories intake per meal.

k. Save the worksheet as NUTRINF4.WK1.

l. Print the entire range of data, and then save the file again.

m. Erase the worksheet.

HINT
Use commas to separate the individual cells in the @AVG function's argument.

Health

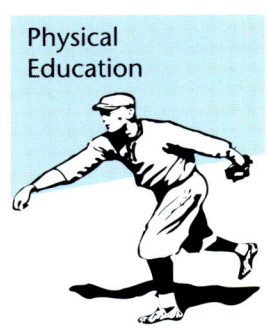

Physical Education

10. Alas, the softball team lost again; this time getting shelled 32–10. Retrieve the worksheet SBGAME3.WK1, and add the scores from the following scorecard to continue tracking the team's batting statistics. In addition, enter @AVG functions and formulas to compile some more statistics, as outlined in the following steps.

Player	At Bats	Runs	Hits	Doubles	Triples	HRs	RBIs
Bernhart	5	0	1	0	0	0	0
Taylor	6	1	2	1	0	0	0
Hepburn	6	1	1	1	0	1	1
Monroe	5	2	2	1	0	0	2
d'Arc	5	0	3	0	0	0	0
Victoria	5	0	2	0	0	1	1
Wood	4	2	2	2	0	0	2
Smith	4	1	1	0	0	0	0
Turner	3	0	1	0	1	0	0
Welch	1	0	0	0	0	0	0
Loren	2	0	0	0	0	0	0
Mabely	2	0	0	0	0	0	0
Braga	3	3	3	1	0	2	4

Applications

a. Erase the label in cell C3.
b. Enter three spaces and the label "TEAM BATTING" in cell A2.
c. Move the label in cell C1 to cell A1.
d. Erase the summing formulas in the range C21..I21. Do not erase the team batting average formula in cell J21.
e. Enter an @SUM function in cell C21 to total the number of at bats, and then copy the @SUM function to the range D21..I21.
f. Enter the label "TEAM AVERAGES:" in cell A23.
g. Enter an @AVG function in cell C23 to calculate the players' average number of times at bat. Copy the @function to the range D23..I23 to calculate average numbers of runs scored, hits, doubles, triples, home runs, and runs batted in.
h. Enter the labels "PER GAME" in cell A25 and "AVERAGES:" in cell A26.
i. Enter a formula in cell C26 that divides the total number of at bats by the number of games played (4). Copy the formula to the range D26..I26.
j. Format all values in rows 23 and 26 as fixed with one decimal place.
k. Enter a double-dashed line in the cell beneath the team batting average.
l. Lock the column heading labels as worksheet titles, and use the [SCROLL LOCK] key to scroll the worksheet so that your worksheet area looks like Figure 4.19.

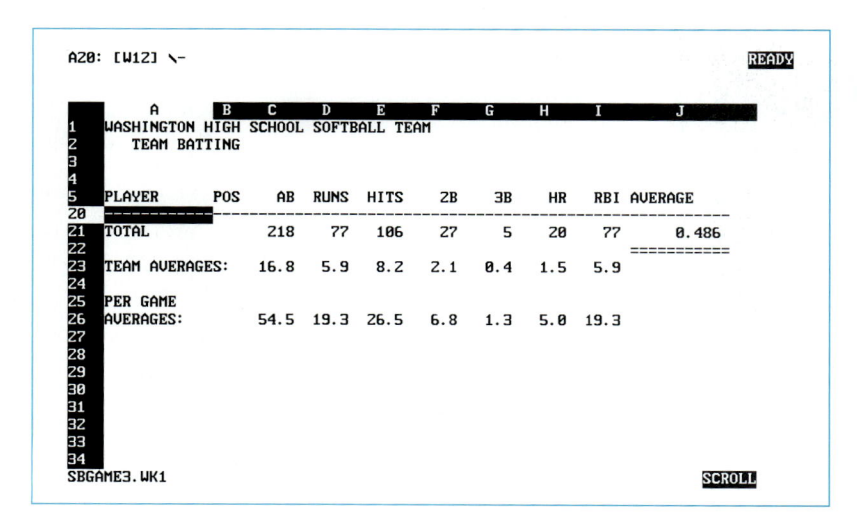

Figure 4.19

After you lock worksheet titles, press [SCROLL LOCK], and scroll the worksheet, your worksheet should look like this.

m. Clear the worksheet titles, and save the worksheet as SBGAME4.WK1.
n. Print the entire range of data, and then save the file again. Erase the worksheet.

5 Building a Model to Solve What-If Problems

Objectives

- Set up a worksheet model.
- Copy labels from a stored file to the current worksheet.
- Combine values from a stored file to the current worksheet.
- Enter formulas with operators for addition and multiplication.
- Use relative cell addresses.
- Use absolute cell addresses.
- Use the Absolute command (F4).
- Split the worksheet area into two windows to view different parts of the same worksheet.
- Use the Window command.
- Enter assumptions to solve what-if problems.

In this lesson, you will use the skills you have already learned, along with some additional 1-2-3 features, to build a worksheet model. You will use the worksheet model to make some sales estimates based on certain assumptions. You will also learn how 1-2-3 can adjust cell addresses when you copy formulas and how you can enter a cell address in a formula so that it does not adjust when you copy the formula.

Exercise 5.1

Setting Up a Worksheet Model

After completing this exercise, you will be able to
- Set up a worksheet model.

Objective

The owner of Mollie's Music Shoppe has asked you to project sales for the rest of the year. The projections will be based on the average sales during the past four months. To do this, you will build a worksheet model that (1) shows different rates of growth in sales over the next three months and (2) determines which rate of growth will result in total sales of $75,000 by the year's end.

MODEL
A worksheet that is planned and set up for a specific situation and makes it easy to change assumptions to see different results.

A worksheet *model* sets up a specific problem or situation. The model is set up to make it easy to change assumptions so that the worksheet can calculate the results quickly. For example, you might set up a model that calculates the monthly payments on a car loan. Then you can change the interest rate or loan amount to see the effect on the monthly payments.

When building a model, it is best to plan the worksheet on paper before setting up the model in 1-2-3. Figure 5.1 shows one way in which you might plan the sales projection model. You will begin setting up the worksheet by changing the global column width and format settings.

	Adjustable Sales Growth Percentage (GP)				
	Avg. Sales		Projected Sales		
	June–Sept.	Oct.	Nov.	Dec.	Total
CDs		Avg. Sales increased by G.P.	Oct. Sales increased by G.P.	Nov. Sales increased by G.P.	Projected sum (Oct., Nov., Dec.) for each product
Albums					
R-R Tapes					
Videotapes					
Totals	Total Avg. Sales	Total Oct.	Total Nov.	Total Dec.	Projected Grand Total for quarter

Figure 5.1

Here is an example of how you might first plan your sales projection model. You should always plan your worksheet models before you set them up.

1 ▶ If necessary, start 1-2-3, and change the current directory to the drive that contains the student data disk. Change the default clock setting to display the current filename on the status line.

2 ▶ If necessary, use the /Worksheet Erase Yes (/WEY) command to clear the worksheet area.

3 ▶ Press the Slash key (/) to access the Main Menu.

4 ▶ Type **WG** to select the Worksheet and Global commands.

The Global Settings dialog box displays.

5 ▶ Press F2.

The dialog box is activated in SETTINGS mode.

6 ▶ Press ↑ 3 times.

The pointer moves to the Column Width setting option.

7 ▶ Press ↵.

8 ▶ Type **11** and press ↵.

The pointer returns to the OK option.

9 ▶ Press ↑ twice.

The pointer moves to the Format setting option.

10 ▶ Press ↵.

The Format pop-up dialog box appears.

11 ▶ Type **,** (a comma).

A text box appears that prompts you to enter the number of decimal places for the global format.

Setting Up a Worksheet Model

12 ▶ Press ⏎ twice.

The default number of decimal places (two) and comma format are selected, and 1-2-3 returns to MENU mode. The Global command submenu is active on the control panel.

13 ▶ Press CTRL-BREAK.

Lotus 1-2-3 returns to READY mode.

Now you will change the width of column A to 16 characters to accommodate long row headings.

14 ▶ Make sure the cell pointer is on any cell in column A.

15 ▶ Press the Slash key (/) to access the Main Menu.

16 ▶ Type **WCS** to select the Worksheet, Column, and Set-Width commands.

Lotus 1-2-3 prompts you to enter the column width.

17 ▶ Type **16** and press ⏎.

Now you will enter some titles for the model.

18 ▶ Move the cell pointer to cell C1.

19 ▶ Type **Mollie's Music Shoppe** and press ↓.

20 ▶ Press SPACEBAR 3 times.

21 ▶ Type **Projected Sales** and press ⏎.

22 ▶ Move the cell pointer to cell A5.

23 ▶ Type **Growth in Sales:**

24 ▶ Press →.

25 ▶ Type **10%** and press ⏎.

Note: Make sure you type the percent sign (%) so 1-2-3 enters the value as the decimal 0.10 rather than as a whole number.

26 ▶ Press the Slash key (/) to access the Main Menu.

27 ▶ Type **RFP** to select the Range, Format, and Percent commands.

Lotus 1-2-3 prompts you to enter the number of decimal places.

28 ▶ Type **1** and press ⏎ twice.

Now you will enter column headings and center them within their cells.

29 ▶ Move the cell pointer to cell B7.

30 ▶ Press CAPS LOCK.

31 ▶ Type **AVERAGE** and press ↓.

5 ▶ Building a Model to Solve What-If Problems

32 ▶ Type **'(JUN-SEP)** and press →.

> Note: Be sure to type the apostrophe, or 1-2-3 will assume you are entering a formula.

33 ▶ Type **OCTOBER** and press →.
34 ▶ Type **NOVEMBER** and press →.
35 ▶ Type **DECEMBER** and press →.
36 ▶ Type **TOTAL** and press ←.
37 ▶ Press CAPS LOCK to turn off uppercase status.
38 ▶ Press F4.

Lotus 1-2-3 prompts you to enter a range.

39 ▶ Press END, and then press ←.
40 ▶ Press ↑.
41 ▶ Press ←.

The range of column heading labels is highlighted.

42 ▶ Press the Slash key (/) to access the Main Menu.
43 ▶ Type **RLC** to select the Range, Label, and Center commands.

The range of heading labels is centered.

44 ▶ Press HOME to move the cell pointer to cell A1.

Now you need to enter the inventory items as row headings. Although you could type them, you know they already exist in the file SUMSALES.WK1. There is also other data in that file that you will want to enter in the current worksheet. So you would like to combine selected data from SUMSALES.WK1 into your model. Fortunately, 1-2-3 lets you do just that.

Setting Up a Worksheet Model

141

Exercise 5.2

Combining Data from Other Files

Objectives

After completing this exercise, you will be able to
- Copy labels from a stored file to the current worksheet.
- Combine values from a stored file to the current worksheet.

You might find that you need to create worksheets that will store data that already exist in another worksheet file. Rather than enter the data again and again, you can use the /File Combine command (/FC) to combine data from another file to the current worksheet. This command is especially useful when you want to enter values that are the results of calculations in another file.

When you use the /File Combine command (/FC), 1-2-3 lets you combine either an entire file or a selected range of data from a file stored on disk in the current directory. The Combine command submenu has three command options: Copy, Add, and Subtract.

You will continue setting up the model you began in the last exercise. You will combine (copy) the product labels in the range A8..A12 in SUMSALES.WK1 into the current model. You will also combine into the current model the average sales figures for June through September from the range G8..G12 in SUMSALES.WK1. You will begin by saving the file first. It is good practice to save the current worksheet before you select the /File Combine command (/FC). The copied or imported data will overwrite any data that existed in the range before you combined data. By saving the file first, you can always retrieve it if the combined data overwrites data you want to keep.

> Note: You may not always remember the exact address for the range that stores the data you want to combine. If this happens, retrieve the worksheet file and jot down the correct address.

1 ▶ Use the /File Save command (/FS) to save the current worksheet as PRJSALES.WK1.

2 ▶ Move the cell pointer to cell A10.

This is the first cell in the range where you want to copy the product labels from the file SUMSALES.WK1.

3 ▶ Press the Slash key (/) to access the Main Menu.

4 ▶ Type **FC** to select the File and Combine commands.

The Combine command submenu appears on the control panel.

5 ▶ Type **C** to select the Copy option.

Another submenu appears that gives you the option of copying all the data in the file or a selected range.

6 ▶ Type **N** to select the Named/Specified Range option.

Lotus 1-2-3 prompts you to enter the range of data you want to copy from the file.

7 ▶ Type **A8.A12**

8 ▶ Press ⏎.

Lotus 1-2-3 prompts you to enter the filename from which you want to combine data.

9 ▶ Press F3.

A full-screen list of the worksheet files in the current directory appears.

10 ▶ Move the pointer to the filename SUMSALES.WK1.

11 ▶ Press ⏎.

The product labels in the range A8..A12 in SUMSALES.WK1 copy to the range A10..A14 in the current worksheet.

12 ▶ Move the cell pointer to cell A16.

13 ▶ Type "**Totals:** and press ⏎.

The right–aligned label appears in the cell.

You have set up the model, as shown in Figure 5.2. Now you need to enter the information that will be used as the basis for your sales estimates for the next three months.

> **TIP**
> 7 ▶ When entering a range address in response to a command prompt, you can type just one period (.) between the beginning and ending cell.

Combining Data from Other Files

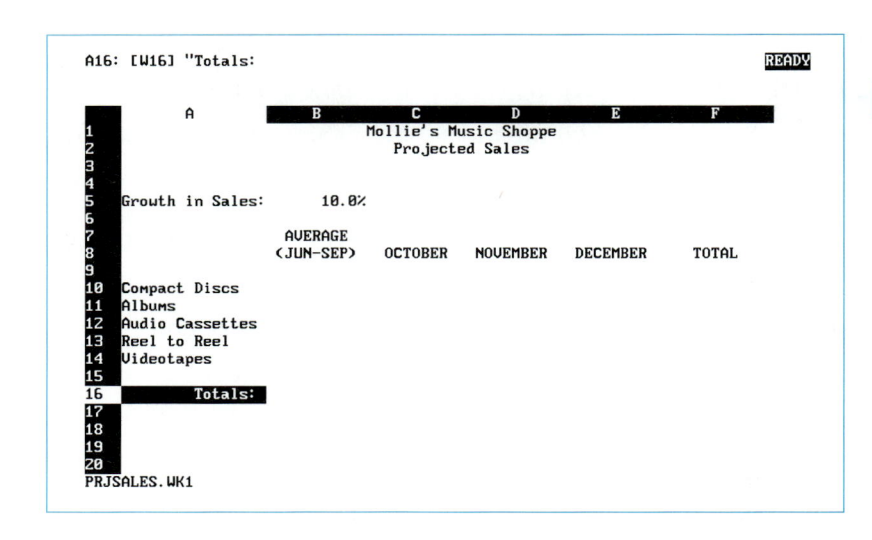

Figure 5.2

Your worksheet model should look like this.

Recall that you entered @AVG functions in the range G8..G12 in SUMSALES.WK1. The @AVG functions calculated average sales figures for each product from June through September. You will combine the results of those @AVG functions into the current model. If you want to combine a range of results from formulas or @functions, use the Add option, not the Copy option. The Copy option will copy formulas or @functions to the current worksheet but not their results. This is because the ranges in the original formulas or @functions will probably not reference the correct values in the current worksheet.

14 ▶ Move the cell pointer to cell B10.

The cell pointer is on the cell that will contain the average compact disc sales for the previous four-month period.

15 ▶ Press the Slash key (/) to access the Main Menu.

16 ▶ Type **FC** to select the File and Combine commands.

The Combine command submenu is activated on the control panel.

17 ▶ Type **A** to select the Add option.

Another submenu appears that gives you the option of copying all the data in the file, or just a selected range.

18 ▶ Type **N**

Lotus 1-2-3 prompts you to enter the range address for the data you want to combine.

19 ▶ Type **G8.G12**

20 ▶ Press ⏎.

Lotus 1-2-3 prompts you to select the filename from which you want to combine data.

21 ▶ Press F3.

A full-screen list of filenames in the current directory appears.

5 ▶ Building a Model to Solve What-If Problems

22 ▶ Move the menu pointer to the filename SUMSALES.WK1.

23 ▶ Press ⏎.

> The @AVG function results in the range G8..G12 in SUMSALES.WK1 are displayed as values in the range B10..B14 in the current worksheet.

Notice the value format for the combined data. Even though you have formatted the current worksheet cells with the comma format, the combined values carried over their formatting from SUMSALES.WK1. The average of the compact disc sales for June through September is displayed in Currency format. Now you will reformat this value.

24 ▶ Make sure the cell pointer is on cell B10.

25 ▶ Press the Slash key (/) to access the Main Menu.

26 ▶ Type **RF** to select the Range, Format, and , (comma) commands.

> Lotus 1-2-3 prompts you to enter the number of decimal places.

27 ▶ Press ⏎ to accept 2 decimal places.

28 ▶ Press ⏎.

> The range is formatted.

Quickly look over the worksheet model. Check the accuracy of your entries by comparing your worksheet to the one shown in Figure 5.3. Make any necessary corrections before you save your work.

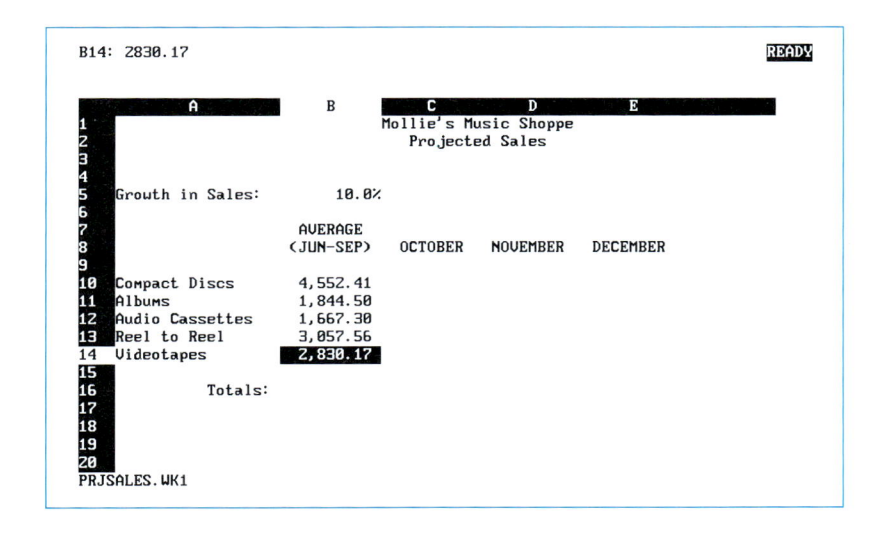

Figure 5.3

After you set up the projected sales worksheet model, your worksheet should look like this. If it does not, edit it until it does.

29 ▶ Press HOME, and use the /File Save Replace command (/FS ⏎ R) to save the current changes to the worksheet.

You are now ready to enter the formulas that will calculate projected sales for the next three months.

Combining Data from Other Files 145

Exercise 5.3

Using Relative and Absolute Cell References

Objectives

After completing this exercise, you will be able to
- Enter formulas with operators for addition and multiplication.
- Use relative cell addresses.
- Use absolute cell addresses.
- Use the F4 key (ABS command).

Your worksheet model will make two assumptions. First, you will assume that October sales will be 10 percent higher than average sales for June through September. And, second, you will assume that sales will increase 10 percent per month for each item from October through December.

The first formula you will enter will calculate the projected compact disc sales for October. Then you will copy that formula to the rest of the range to calculate the other products' projected sales for each month. To calculate projected compact disc sales for October, you will create a formula that increases the average compact disc sales for June through September by 10 percent. To do this, you must multiply the average sales figure by 10 percent. Then add the product to the same average sales figure. The formula should look like this: +B10+B10*B5. Use the pointing method to create the formula.

1 ▶ Move the cell pointer to cell C10.

The cell pointer is on the cell that will contain the projected compact disc sales for October.

2 ▶ Type +

Lotus 1-2-3 switches to VALUE mode.

3 ▶ Press ←.

The cell pointer moves to the cell that contains the average sales for compact discs.

4 ▶ Type +

The cell pointer returns to cell C10.

5 ▶ Press ←.

The pointer is again on the cell that contains the average sales figure for compact discs.

5 ▶ Building a Model to Solve What-If Problems

6 ▶ Type *

   The multiplication operator is entered, and the cell pointer returns to cell C10.

7 ▶ Move the pointer to cell B5.

   The cell pointer is on the cell that contains 10 percent.

8 ▶ Press ⏎.

   The result, 5,007.65, is displayed. This is the projected sales for October, as shown in Figure 5.4.

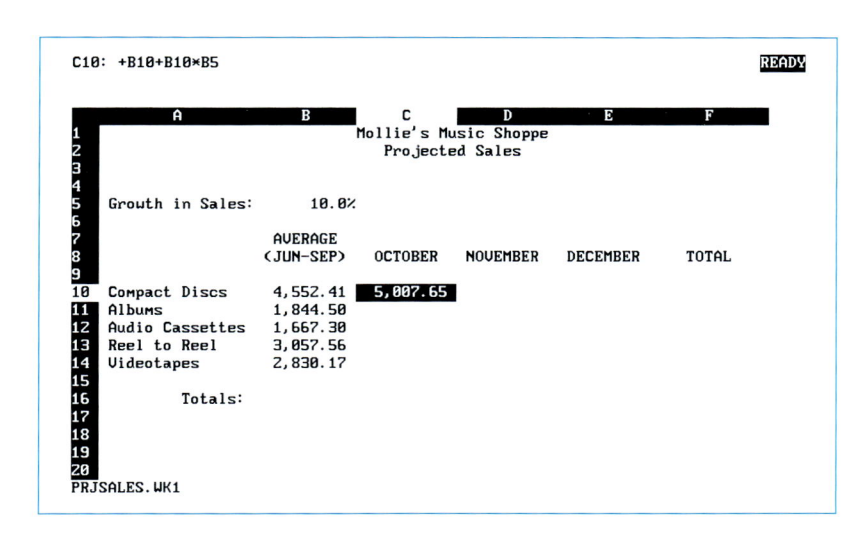

Figure 5.4

The result of the formula is displayed in cell C10.

```
C10: +B10+B10*B5                                                    READY

              A              B            C           D          E         F
 1                                  Mollie's Music Shoppe
 2                                     Projected Sales
 3
 4
 5      Growth in Sales:          10.0%
 6
 7                              AVERAGE
 8                              (JUN-SEP)   OCTOBER   NOVEMBER  DECEMBER   TOTAL
 9
10      Compact Discs          4,552.41    5,007.65
11      Albums                 1,844.50
12      Audio Cassettes        1,667.30
13      Reel to Reel           3,057.56
14      Videotapes             2,830.17
15
16            Totals:
17
18
19
20
PRJSALES.WK1
```

Now you will copy the formula to the rest of the range.

9 ▶ Make sure the cell pointer is on cell C10, which contains the formula that calculates projected sales for October.

10 ▶ Press the Slash key (/) to access the Main Menu.

11 ▶ Type **C** to select the Copy command.

12 ▶ Press ⏎.

   The current cell is selected as the "Copy what?" range.

13 ▶ Type **.** (a period) to anchor the current cell.

14 ▶ Press → twice.

15 ▶ Press ↓ 4 times.

   The range C10..E14 is highlighted.

16 ▶ Press ⏎.

   The formula copies to the range and displays calculated values, as shown in Figure 5.5.

Using Relative and Absolute Cell References

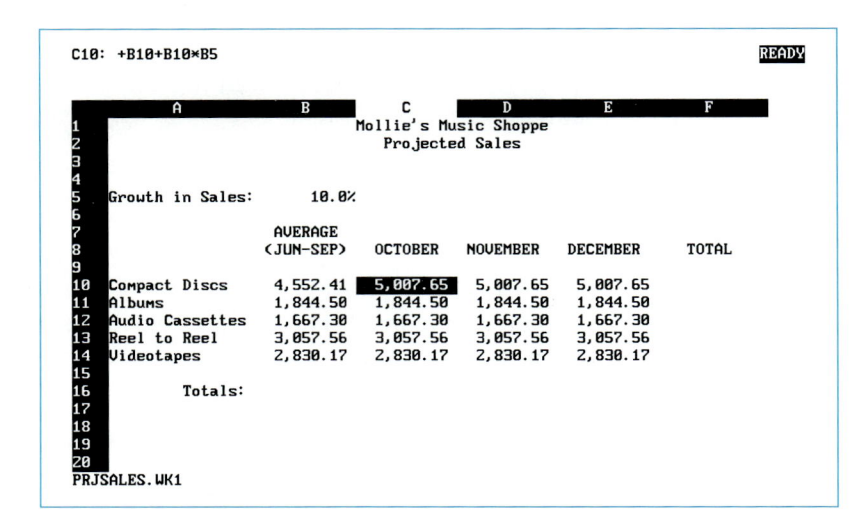

Figure 5.5

The projected sales formula copies to the range C10..E14.

Notice that there are two problems. First, the projected compact disc sales for November and December are the same as for October—they did not increase by 10 percent per month. Second, the projected sales for the other products did not increase either. The obvious, and correct, assumption is that the copy operation did not create accurate formulas.

Unlike other formulas you have copied so far, this formula contains a value that you want to remain constant, or fixed. That is, you want each and every formula in the range C10..E14 to multiply by the same factor, 10 percent growth in sales.

Take a look at the original formula for the projected October compact disc sales: +B10+B10*B5. If you move the cell pointer to the cell that contains the projected November compact disc sales, you will notice that the formula in that cell is +C10+C10*C5. All the cell addresses in the original formula are relative cell references. As you have already seen, *relative cell references* adjust when a formula is copied. This adjustment maintains a relationship between the formula's cell references and the cell that contains the formula. To understand this relationship, consider the original formula in cell C10. Relative cell reference B5 is one column to the left and five rows up from cell C10. When the formula in cell C10 is copied to cell D10, the relative cell reference B5 becomes C5. Cell C5 is one column to the left and five rows up from cell D10. When a formula is copied, relative cell references adjust to maintain this cell location relationship.

In your model, you want the first two relative cell references to cell B10 to adjust when the formula is copied. That is, you want the projected sales for November to be based on the October sales in cell C10. However, the relative cell reference C5 in the copied formula is empty, which tells 1-2-3 to multiply the value in cell C10 by 0, not 10 percent. The same problem occurs with the projected compact disc sales for December: the relative cell reference B5 adjusts to D5, which also refers to an empty cell.

Check the formulas that calculate the projected sales for each of the other items for October. The formulas contain adjusted relative cell references that refer to other empty cells or cells that contain labels. When these formulas

RELATIVE CELL REFERENCE

A cell address in a formula or 1-2-3 @function that represents a specific location relationship with the current cell. (For example, cell C5 is one cell right and two cells down from cell B3.) When a formula or @function with a relative cell reference is copied to another location, the relative cell reference adjusts to maintain a similar or "relative" relationship with the cell into which the copied formula or function is placed.

were copied down column C, 1-2-3 adjusted the row numbers in the relative cell references.

You want the cell address B5 in the formula to stay the same when the formula is copied to another location. To do this, you must use an absolute cell reference. An *absolute cell reference* is a cell address that does not change, no matter where you copy the formula. To create an absolute cell reference, you include a dollar sign ($) in front of the column letter and the row number in the cell reference (for example, B5). In the original formula in cell C10 of your worksheet, you will change the relative cell reference B5 to the absolute cell reference B5. Although you could fix the formula in EDIT mode, you will instead erase the inaccurate formulas in the range C10..E14 first. Then you will enter a new formula.

ABSOLUTE CELL REFERENCE
A cell address in a formula or 1-2-3 @function that represents a fixed cell location, which usually contains a constant value. When a formula or @function with an absolute cell reference is copied, the cell address always remains the same (absolute) no matter where the copied formula or @function is placed.

17 ▶ Move the cell pointer to cell C10.

The cell pointer is on the cell that contains the projected compact disc sales for October.

18 ▶ Press the Slash key (/) to access the Main Menu.

19 ▶ Type **RE** to select the Range and Erase commands.

Lotus 1-2-3 prompts you to enter the range to erase.

20 ▶ Press (END), and then press (→).

21 ▶ Press (END), and then press (↓).

The range of formulas is highlighted.

22 ▶ Press (←┘).

The formulas in the range C10..E14 are erased.

You could enter the formula manually by typing the operators and cell references, but you will use the pointing method to make sure the formula is entered accurately.

23 ▶ Type **+**

Lotus 1-2-3 switches to VALUE mode.

24 ▶ Press (←).

The cell pointer is on cell B10, which contains the average compact disc sales for summer.

25 ▶ Type **+**

The cell pointer returns to cell C10.

26 ▶ Press (←).

The cell pointer returns to the average compact disc sales figure in cell B10.

27 ▶ Type *****

The multiplication operator is entered, and the cell pointer returns to cell C10.

Using Relative and Absolute Cell References

149

ABS COMMAND [F4]
A function key command that changes a relative cell reference to an absolute cell reference.

28 ▶ Move the cell pointer to cell B5.

The cell pointer is on the cell that contains the value 10 percent.

Using the pointing method, you have put the relative cell reference B5 in the formula. You will change this relative reference to an absolute reference by pressing the [F4] key (*ABS command*) once.

29 ▶ Press [F4].

The relative cell reference B5 changes to B5 on the control panel, as shown in Figure 5.6.

Absolute cell reference

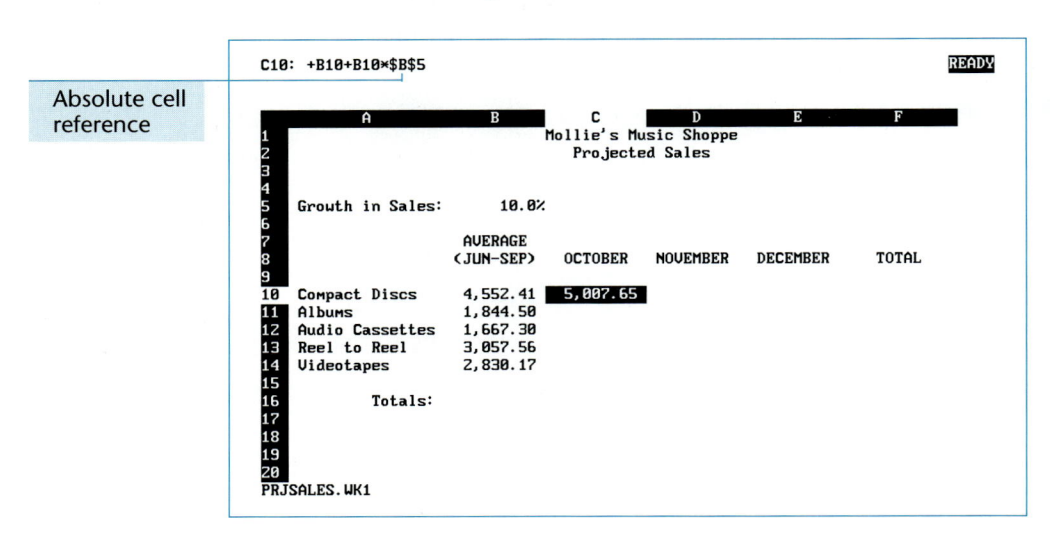

```
C10: +B10+B10*$B$5                                          READY

         A              B           C         D         E         F
 1                          Mollie's Music Shoppe
 2                             Projected Sales
 3
 4
 5  Growth in Sales:       10.0%
 6
 7                         AVERAGE
 8                         (JUN-SEP)   OCTOBER   NOVEMBER   DECEMBER   TOTAL
 9
10  Compact Discs         4,552.41   5,007.65
11  Albums                1,844.50
12  Audio Cassettes       1,667.30
13  Reel to Reel          3,057.56
14  Videotapes            2,830.17
15
16        Totals:
17
18
19
20
PRJSALES.WK1
```

Figure 5.6

When you press [F4] (the ABS command) while building a formula, the cell reference at the cursor position on the control panel changes to an absolute reference.

Note: If you accidentally press [F4] more than once, keep pressing it until you see B5 again.

30 ▶ Press ⏎.

The formula is entered, and the result, 5,007.65, is displayed in cell C10.

31 ▶ Make sure the cell pointer is on cell C10.

32 ▶ Use the /Copy command (/C) to copy the formula in cell C10 to the range C10..E14.

When you complete the copy operation, the results should display as shown in Figure 5.7.

150 5 ▶ Building a Model to Solve What-If Problems

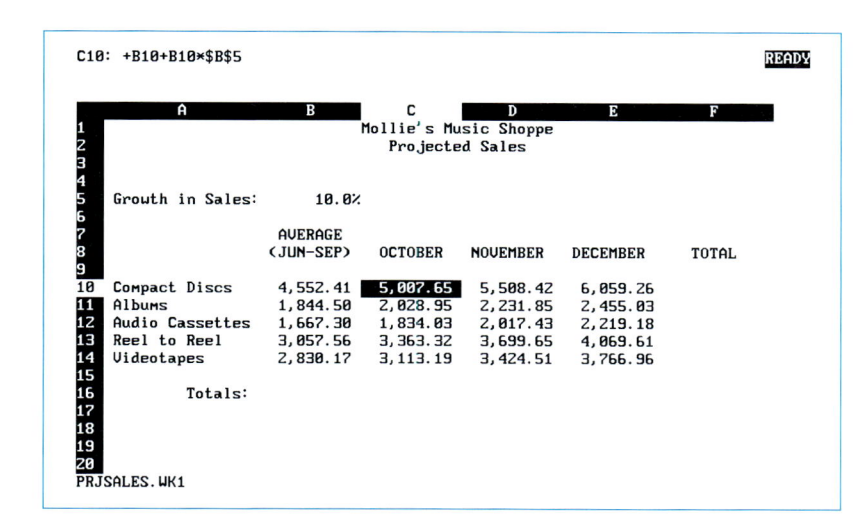

```
C10: +B10+B10*$B$5                                                    READY

            A           B           C           D           E           F
                              Mollie's Music Shoppe
 1                              Projected Sales
 2
 3
 4
 5  Growth in Sales:      10.0%
 6
 7                      AVERAGE
 8                      (JUN-SEP)   OCTOBER    NOVEMBER    DECEMBER    TOTAL
 9
10  Compact Discs       4,552.41   5,007.65    5,508.42    6,059.26
11  Albums              1,844.50   2,028.95    2,231.85    2,455.03
12  Audio Cassettes     1,667.30   1,834.03    2,017.43    2,219.18
13  Reel to Reel        3,057.56   3,363.32    3,699.65    4,069.61
14  Videotapes          2,830.17   3,113.19    3,424.51    3,766.96
15
16         Totals:
17
18
19
20
PRJSALES.WK1
```

Figure 5.7

The results of the copied formulas reflect the 10 percent increases because the original formula contains the absolute cell reference B5.

33 ▶ Move the cell pointer from cell to cell in this range and check the formulas.

Notice that all the formulas contain the absolute cell reference B5.

The absolute cell reference did not adjust when you copied the formula from column to column and row to row. Therefore, each formula accurately references the value that is to stay fixed.

34 ▶ Press [HOME], and use the /File Save Replace command (/FS ⏎ R) to save the current changes to PRJSALES.WK1.

You will complete this exercise by entering @SUM functions that calculate totals for each row and for each column.

35 ▶ Move the cell pointer to cell F10.

The pointer is on the cell that will contain the total projected compact disc sales for October through December.

36 ▶ Type **@SUM(**

37 ▶ Press ⬅ 3 times.

The cell pointer is on cell C10, which contains the projected compact disc sales for October.

38 ▶ Type **.** (a period) to anchor the current cell.

39 ▶ Press ➡ twice.

The range C10..E10, which contains the projected CD sales for October through December, is highlighted.

40 ▶ Type **)** (a closing parenthesis), and press ⏎.

Lotus 1-2-3 stores the @function and the result, 16,575.32, appears.

Note: If you obtain another result, check the @SUM function and make sure that its argument contains the range C10..E10 and not B10..E10.

Using Relative and Absolute Cell References 151

You will copy this @SUM function down the column to produce the rest of the formulas you need.

41 ▶ Use the /Copy command (/C) to copy the @SUM function in cell F10 to the range F11..F14.

After you copy the @SUM function to the specified range, the projected sales result for each item should be displayed, as shown in Figure 5.8.

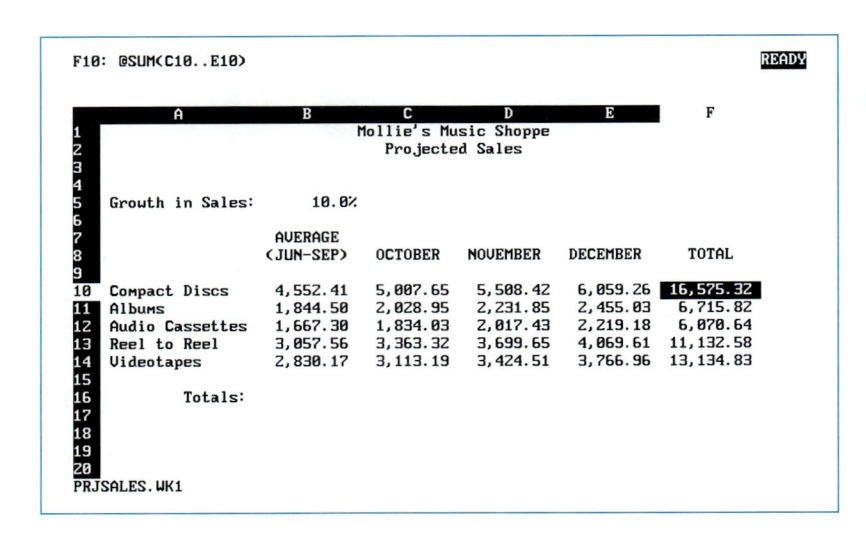

```
F10: @SUM(C10..E10)                                          READY

            A           B         C         D         E         F
                            Mollie's Music Shoppe
                               Projected Sales

    Growth in Sales:      10.0%

                        AVERAGE
                       (JUN-SEP)  OCTOBER   NOVEMBER  DECEMBER   TOTAL
  10  Compact Discs    4,552.41   5,007.65  5,508.42  6,059.26  16,575.32
  11  Albums           1,844.50   2,028.95  2,231.85  2,455.03   6,715.82
  12  Audio Cassettes  1,667.30   1,834.03  2,017.43  2,219.18   6,070.64
  13  Reel to Reel     3,057.56   3,363.32  3,699.65  4,069.61  11,132.58
  14  Videotapes       2,830.17   3,113.19  3,424.51  3,766.96  13,134.83
  15
  16       Totals:

  PRJSALES.WK1
```

Figure 5.8

After you copy the @SUM function to the range F10..F14, your worksheet should look like this.

Now you will enter the row 16 @SUM functions to calculate total average sales for June through September, total projected sales for each month, and the total projected sales for this three-month period.

42 ▶ Move the cell pointer to cell B16.

The cell pointer is on the cell that will contain the total average sales for June through September.

43 ▶ Type **@SUM(**

44 ▶ Press ↑ 6 times.

The cell pointer is on the cell that contains the average compact disc sales for June through September.

45 ▶ Type **.** (a period) to anchor the current cell.

46 ▶ Press ↓ 4 times.

The range B10..B14, which contains average sales for each item during June through September, is highlighted.

47 ▶ Type **)** (a closing parenthesis).

48 ▶ Press ↵.

The @SUM function is entered and the total average sales for June through September, 13,951.94, displays.

49 ▶ Use the /Copy command (/C) to copy the @SUM function in cell B16 to the other columns in row 16.

After you copy the @SUM function, the average sales totals for each month and a grand total should appear as shown in Figure 5.9.

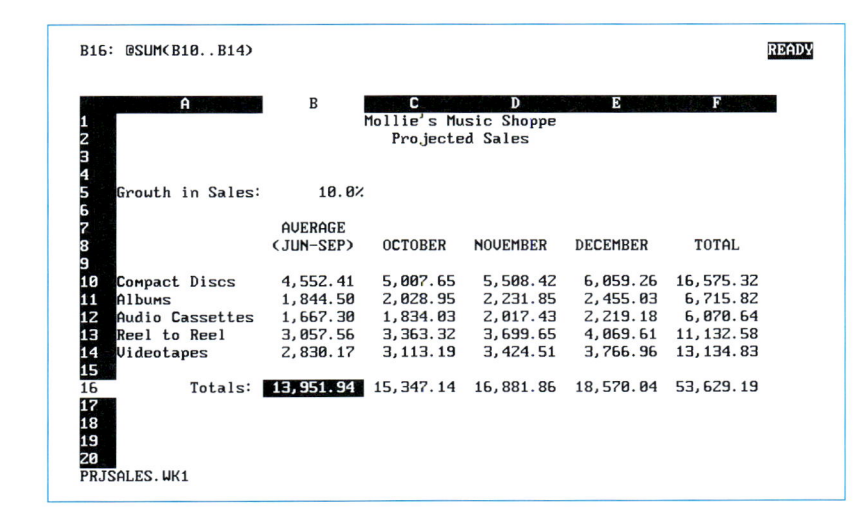

Figure 5.9

After you copy the @SUM function that calculates average sales totals for each month, your worksheet should look like this.

```
B16: @SUM(B10..B14)                                              READY

        A           B         C         D         E         F
 1                        Mollie's Music Shoppe
 2                          Projected Sales
 3
 4
 5  Growth in Sales:     10.0%
 6
 7                     AVERAGE
 8                    (JUN-SEP)  OCTOBER   NOVEMBER  DECEMBER  TOTAL
 9
10  Compact Discs      4,552.41  5,007.65  5,508.42  6,059.26  16,575.32
11  Albums             1,844.50  2,028.95  2,231.85  2,455.03   6,715.82
12  Audio Cassettes    1,667.30  1,834.03  2,017.43  2,219.18   6,070.64
13  Reel to Reel       3,057.56  3,363.32  3,699.65  4,069.61  11,132.58
14  Videotapes         2,830.17  3,113.19  3,424.51  3,766.96  13,134.83
15
16         Totals:    13,951.94 15,347.14 16,881.86 18,570.04  53,629.19
17
18
19
20
PRJSALES.WK1
```

50 ▶ Press HOME, and use the /File Save Replace command (/FS ⏎ R) to save the current changes to PRJSALES.WK1.

You have now completed your worksheet model. You are about ready to test different assumptions to solve what-if problems. However, let's first look at a feature that allows you to split the worksheet area into windows so that you can view different areas of the worksheet at the same time.

Exercise 5.4 — Splitting the Worksheet Area into Windows

Objective

After completing this exercise, you will be able to
- Split the worksheet area into two windows to view different parts of the same worksheet.

WINDOW
A division or split in the worksheet area that lets you view different portions of the same worksheet.

At any time, you can split the worksheet area into two horizontal or vertical *windows*. This feature lets you see different parts of the same worksheet by scrolling the worksheet in any direction in either window. Use the /Worksheet Window command (/WW) to split the worksheet area vertically or horizontally. This feature is very useful when you want to solve what-if problems or if you want to see the effects of changes on a large worksheet.

Splitting the Worksheet Area into Windows

153

WINDOW COMMAND F6

A function key that moves (toggles) the cell pointer from one window to the next when the worksheet area has been split into windows.

When you split the worksheet area into windows, the cell pointer is in the left window in a vertical split or in the top window in a horizontal split. To move the cell pointer between windows, press the F6 key (the *Window command*). This key acts as a toggle by moving the cell pointer from one window to the other each time it is pressed. When you are through working with windows, select the /Worksheet Window Clear command (/WWC). The worksheet area will become a single window again.

1 ▶ Move the cell pointer to cell C5.

The cell pointer is one cell to the right of the 10 percent growth in sales figure.

2 ▶ Press the Slash key (/) to access the Main Menu.

3 ▶ Type **WW** to select the Worksheet and Window commands.

The control panel displays the following Window command submenu:

   Horizontal   Vertical   Sync   Unsync   Clear

4 ▶ Type **V** to select the Vertical option.

The worksheet area splits into two vertical windows, as shown in Figure 5.10. Notice that another vertical border with row numbers appears between columns B and C. The cell pointer is on cell B5 in the left window.

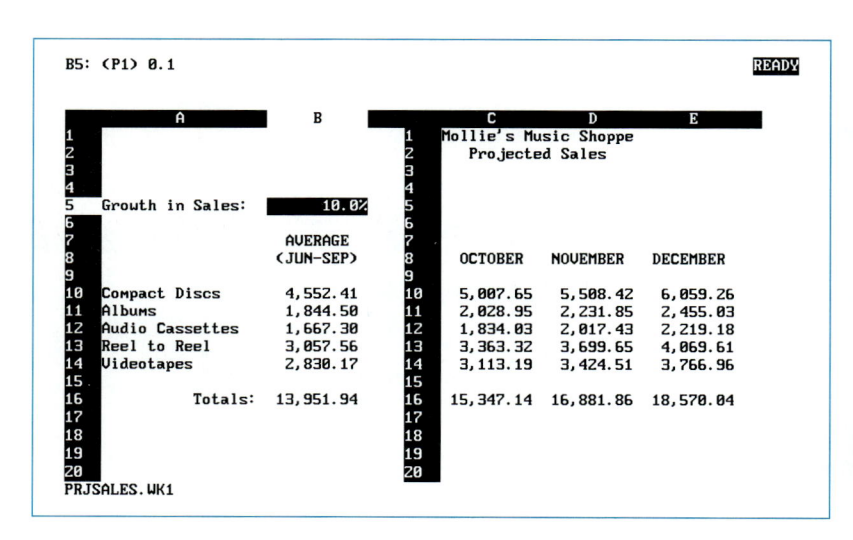

```
B5: (P1) 0.1                                              READY

            A              B              C         D         E
                                    1  Mollie's Music Shoppe
                                    2     Projected Sales
                                    3
                                    4
 5  Growth in Sales:       10.0%    5
 6                                  6
 7                     AVERAGE      7
 8                     (JUN-SEP)    8  OCTOBER   NOVEMBER  DECEMBER
 9                                  9
10  Compact Discs      4,552.41    10   5,007.65  5,508.42  6,059.26
11  Albums             1,844.50    11   2,028.95  2,231.85  2,455.03
12  Audio Cassettes    1,667.30    12   1,834.03  2,017.43  2,219.18
13  Reel to Reel       3,057.56    13   3,363.32  3,699.65  4,069.61
14  Videotapes         2,830.17    14   3,113.19  3,424.51  3,766.96
15                                 15
16        Totals:     13,951.94    16  15,347.14 16,881.86 18,570.04
17                                 17
18                                 18
19                                 19
20                                 20
PRJSALES.WK1
```

Figure 5.10

The /Worksheet Window Vertical command (WWV) splits the worksheet area into vertical windows. The windows are divided by another vertical border with row numbers, and the cell pointer is in the left window.

5 ▶ Press F6.

The cell pointer moves to cell C5 in the right window.

6 ▶ Press SCROLL LOCK.

The SCROLL indicator appears on the status line in the lower-right corner of the screen. The cell pointer is locked.

5 ▶ Building a Model to Solve What-If Problems

7 ▶ Press →.

The worksheet scrolls one column, and the column of totals appears.

8 ▶ Press SCROLL LOCK.

The cell pointer can be moved.

9 ▶ Press F6.

The cell pointer returns to cell B5 in the left window.

Before solving what-if problems in a worksheet model, it is good practice to save the worksheet. That way, if you need to see the original values, you can retrieve the file again. You can save a file when you have the worksheet area split into windows. In fact, 1-2-3 saves the window split with the file. This can be handy if you have set up the worksheet area for a particular task but need to leave your work for a while. To see how 1-2-3 does this, you will save the latest version of your model, erase the worksheet, and then retrieve it.

10 ▶ Use the /File Save Replace command (/FS ⏎ R) to save changes to PRJSALES.WK1.

11 ▶ Use the /Worksheet Erase Yes command (/WEY) to erase the worksheet.

12 ▶ Use the /File Retrieve command (/FR) to retrieve the file PRJSALES.WK1.

The worksheet appears with the worksheet area split into vertical windows. The cell pointer is on cell B5. This is exactly how your worksheet area was set up when you last saved the file.

Exercise 5.5 — Solving What-If Problems

Objective

After completing this exercise, you will be able to
- Enter assumptions to solve what-if problems.

The owner of the music store tells you her desired sales projection, or estimate, for October through December. She believes sales should match or exceed the sales for June through September. She wants to know how much sales should increase per month on average to come close to the total sales for June through September: $55,795.77.

WHAT-IF PROBLEM SOLVING
A process of looking at different situations by changing assumptions in a worksheet model. The changing assumptions help you to find answers to questions or to solve problems.

To answer this question, you will use the model you have made in this lesson to solve a what-if problem. A *what-if problem* is a question that you ask based on an assumption or estimate. For example, you might ask, "How much will sales of audio cassettes be in November *if* sales increase by 8 percent over October's sales?" To solve this what-if problem, you can enter 8% (the assumption) in the cell that contains the growth-in-sales percentage. You immediately get your answer when the formulas and @functions are recalculated.

In your model, you have one assumption: the percentage (10 percent) by which you expect sales to increase on a monthly basis. When you built your model, you assumed that sales would increase 10 percent per month. So the first thing you do is check the total for projected sales of all items, which is $50,799.00. This amount is below the total for average sales during June through September. So you will test different growth percentages to solve the following what-if problem: by what percentage must sales increase each month in the next three months to match sales income from June through September?

1 ▶ Make sure the cell pointer is on cell B5.

This cell contains your starting assumption, 10.0 percent.

2 ▶ Type **15%** and press ⏎.

The model's formulas and @functions are recalculated based on the revised value in cell B5, as shown in Figure 5.11. Notice that the change you made in the left window caused the total result in the right window to be recalculated.

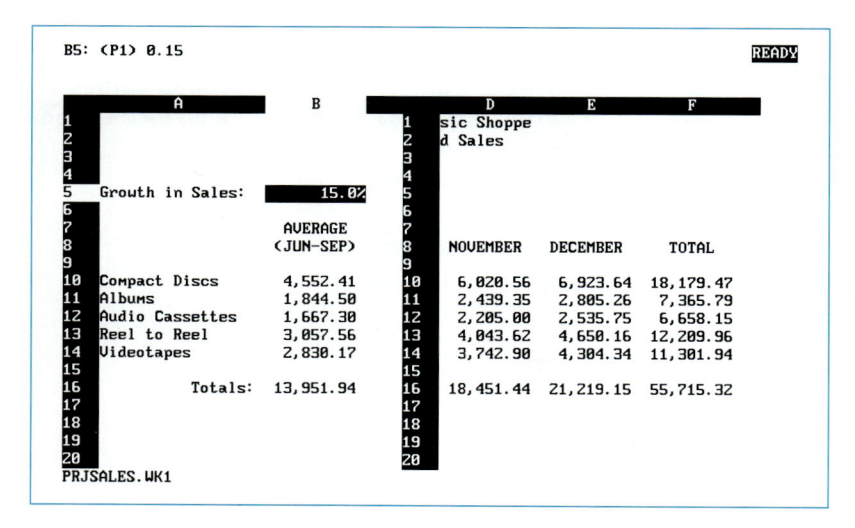

Figure 5.11

When you change the sales growth percentage in cell B5, all the formulas and @SUM functions recalculate to help you solve your what-if problem.

The total projected sales of all items for October through December is $55,715.32. This amount is close to the total sales for June through September. Now you will see how much closer an extra half percentage point gets you.

156   5 ▶ Building a Model to Solve What-If Problems

3 ▶ Type **15.5%**

4 ▶ Press ⏎.

> The formulas and @functions are recalculated. The total projected sales for October through December are now $56,223.85.

You tell the owner that the store must increase its sales by an average of 15 percent per month to make as much money during October through December as it did in June through September. She asks you to find out what total projected sales would be if monthly sales increased 20 percent and 25 percent.

5 ▶ Make sure the cell pointer is on cell B5.

6 ▶ Type **20%**

7 ▶ Press ⏎.

> The projected sales total for October through December is 60,942.06.

8 ▶ Type **25%**

9 ▶ Press ⏎.

> The projected sales total is now 66,489.70.

You tell the owner that the projected sales total for October through December is almost $61,000 if sales increase 20 percent per month. Projected sales are almost $66,500 if sales increase 25 percent per month. She tells you that the current economic situation indicates that the next quarter will be a good business period—particularly the month of December. She feels that the store can gross $75,000 if she spends more money on advertising. She asks you to find out how much monthly sales should increase, on average, to make $75,000 by the end of December.

10 ▶ Make sure the cell pointer is on cell B5.

> The cell pointer is on the cell that contains the 25 percent assumption.

11 ▶ Type **30%**

12 ▶ Press ⏎.

> The total projected sales is now 72,368.70.

13 ▶ Type **35%**

14 ▶ Press ⏎.

> The projected sales total is 78,589.52.

You know that the increase you are looking for is between 30 and 35 percent.

15 ▶ Type **31%**

Solving What-If Problems

157

16 ▶ Press ⏎.

> The projected sales total is 73,585.18.

17 ▶ Type **32%**

18 ▶ Press ⏎.

> The projected sales total is 74,815.42—quite close to the $75,000 goal.

Your latest what-if problem assumptions tell you that the store can make the $75,000 sales goal if average monthly sales increase between 32 and 33 percent. Now you will clear the window split and save the model.

19 ▶ Press HOME.

20 ▶ Press the Slash key (/) to access the Main Menu.

21 ▶ Type **WWC** to select the Worksheet, Window, and Clear commands.

22 ▶ Use the /File Save Replace command (/FS ⏎ R) to save the changes to PRJSALES.WK1.

23 ▶ Print the entire range of data.

> Note: The data in column F may print on a second sheet of paper. In Lesson 7, you will learn how to break pages where you want when you print.

24 ▶ Save the print settings to the same file, and erase the worksheet.

You can now begin the Lesson 5 applications that follow the Concept Summary, or you can go on to Lesson 6. Otherwise, quit 1-2-3 if you are through with this 1-2-3 session.

Concept Summary

- When you create formulas that reference values in the current worksheet, most spreadsheet software gives you the choice of using either relative cell references or absolute cell references.

- When a formula or function is copied, relative cell references adjust automatically. The adjustment maintains the same relative location relationship with the cell that contains the formula.

- Absolute cell references do not adjust when a formula or function is copied. Commonly, a dollar sign or some other symbol precedes the column letter and row number to make a cell reference absolute. An absolute cell reference always refers to a cell that contains a value that you want to remain fixed or constant.

- A worksheet model sets up a specific problem or situation in which you can change assumptions to see different results.

- Spreadsheet software often contains a feature that lets you copy or combine data between files. This is generally done by importing either all or selected data from a file stored on disk to the current worksheet.

- Most spreadsheet software contains a feature that splits the worksheet area or view into vertical or horizontal windows. Windows let you see different parts of the same worksheet at the same time. You can use windows to make changes in one area of a large worksheet and see the effects in another area.

- Solving what-if problems is a technique with which you can test assumptions and analyze results to answer questions and solve problems. You solve what-if problems by entering different values, representing assumptions or estimates, into a cell that is referenced in other formulas. Automatic recalculation gives you an immediate answer. Before you change assumptions, you can evaluate the effects that occur.

Command Summary

/File Combine Copy (/FCC)
copies data from a file stored on disk to the current worksheet

/File Combine Add (/FCA)
combines data, including formula results, from a file stored on disk to the current worksheet

F4 (ABS command)
changes a relative cell reference to an absolute cell reference

/Worksheet Window Horizontal (/WWH)
splits the worksheet area into top and bottom windows

/Worksheet Window Vertical (/WWV)
splits the worksheet area into left and right windows

/Worksheet Window Clear (/WWC)
clears a window split so the worksheet area is a single window

Applications

To begin doing the applications, load 1-2-3, if necessary. Place your student data disk in drive A (or drive B if you do not have a hard disk). Change the current directory to the drive that contains the student data disk. Also, change the clock setting in the Global Settings dialog box so that the current filename displays on the status line.

Business

Sales Analysis

1. The president of the company wants to figure out how some of the slumping sales branches can recover. She wants you to project 1996 sales, given an 8 percent increase across the board. To do this, you will insert some comparison data and then solve some what-if problems. Retrieve the file SALES4.WK1 and begin by inserting new columns, as shown in Figure 5.12.

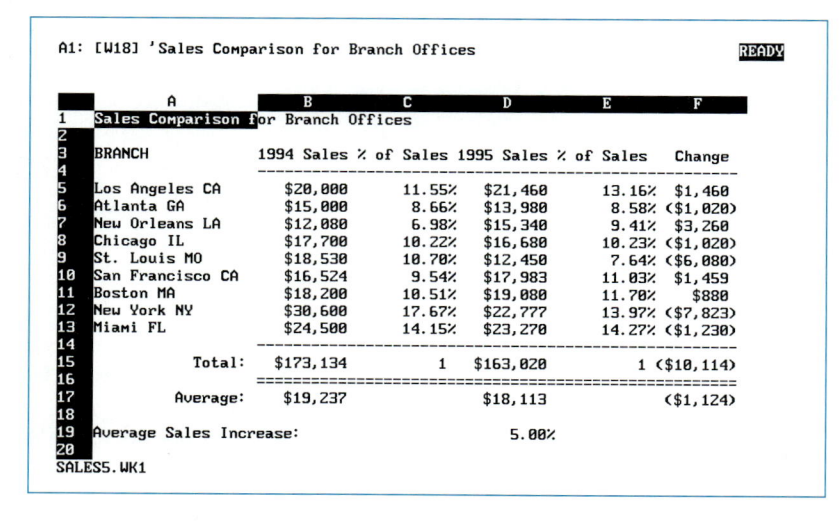

```
A1: [W18] 'Sales Comparison for Branch Offices                    READY

             A              B         C         D         E         F
 1  Sales Comparison for Branch Offices
 2
 3  BRANCH               1994 Sales % of Sales 1995 Sales % of Sales  Change
 4  ------------------------------------------------------------------------
 5  Los Angeles CA         $20,000     11.55%   $21,460    13.16%    $1,460
 6  Atlanta GA             $15,000      8.66%   $13,980     8.58%   ($1,020)
 7  New Orleans LA         $12,080      6.98%   $15,340     9.41%    $3,260
 8  Chicago IL             $17,700     10.22%   $16,680    10.23%   ($1,020)
 9  St. Louis MO           $18,530     10.70%   $12,450     7.64%   ($6,080)
10  San Francisco CA       $16,524      9.54%   $17,983    11.03%    $1,459
11  Boston MA              $18,200     10.51%   $19,080    11.70%      $880
12  New York NY            $30,600     17.67%   $22,777    13.97%   ($7,823)
13  Miami FL               $24,500     14.15%   $23,270    14.27%   ($1,230)
14  ------------------------------------------------------------------------
15           Total:       $173,134        1    $163,020        1  ($10,114)
16           ========================================================
17         Average:        $19,237              $18,113             ($1,124)
18
19  Average Sales Increase:                       5.00%
20
SALES5.WK1
```

Figure 5.12

Follow the instructions in application 1 (Sales Analysis) to modify the worksheet as shown.

a. Insert a new column between the columns for 1994 and 1995 sales, and insert a new column between the columns for 1995 sales and change.

b. Enter the label "% of Sales" as the column heading for each of the two new columns, and change their widths to 11 characters.

c. Enter a formula in column C that divides 1994 sales for the Los Angeles branch by the total sales for 1994. Use an absolute cell reference to make the total sales for 1994 a constant.

d. Copy the formula down the column, and format the results in this column, using the Percent option with two decimal places.

e. Enter a similar formula in column E that divides 1995 sales for the Los Angeles branch by the total sales for 1995. Use an absolute cell reference to make the total sales for 1995 a constant.

160   5 ▶ Building a Model to Solve What-If Problems

f. Copy the formula down the column, and format the results, using the Percent option with two decimal places.

g. Fill the gaps in the dashed and double-dashed lines.

h. Enter the label "Average Sales Increase:" in cell A19, and then enter and format an 8 percent value in cell D19.

i. In column G, enter the column heading "1996 Projected."

j. Enter a formula in column G that increases the 1995 sales figure for the Los Angeles branch by the average sales growth amount you entered in cell D19. Be sure to use an absolute cell reference. Copy the formula down the column.

k. For all the branch offices with sales slippages between 1994 and 1995, solve a series of what-if problems to find the percentages by which 1996 sales must increase over 1995 sales so these offices will meet their 1994 sales levels.

l. Save the file as SALES5.WK1, and then erase the worksheet.

Business

Small Business

2. Marketing now tells you it was wrong about $1,500 being the best price at which to sell the windsurfing boards. After surveying several focus groups, it now recommends $1,650. Rather than redo the worksheet each time a variable changes, you decide to modify an earlier version of the break-even analysis worksheet. The modification will make it easy to adjust whenever there is a change. This will also let you solve some what-if problems more efficiently. Begin by retrieving the file PRF_LOSS.WK1 from the student data disk, and doing the following tasks to modify the worksheet:

a. Insert three new rows at row 3.

b. Enter the label "FIXED COSTS =" in cell A3, the label "UNIT PRICE =" in cell A4, and the label "PROD. COSTS =" in cell A5.

c. Starting in cell B3, enter the values 145000 for fixed costs, 1500 for unit price, and 1250 for production costs.

d. Replace the value in row 11 for total fixed costs per 100 units with the absolute cell reference +B3.

Note: Be sure to enter the plus sign.

Copy the absolute cell reference down the column.

e. In EDIT mode, edit the formula in cell D11 by replacing the value with an absolute cell reference for the "PROD COSTS" value in column B. Copy the edited formula down the column.

f. Replace the value in cell F11 with an absolute cell reference to the "UNIT PRICE" value in column B.

Note: Be sure to enter the plus sign.

Applications

Copy the absolute cell reference down the column.

g. Change the unit price in cell B4 to 1650 to solve the following what-if problem: how many units do you need to sell now to break even?

h. Suppose production costs increase to $1,480 per board. How many units do you need to sell to break even?

i. Suppose fixed costs increased to $146,500 and production costs were $1,375 per board, while the unit price of the boards remained at $1,650. How many units do you need to sell to break even? What will the total costs be at that point?

j. Save the worksheet as PROFIT5.WK1, and erase the worksheet.

Business

Accounting

3. As part of your accounting project, you must prepare an income statement that calculates cost of goods sold (COGS) for April. COGS is the value of the bicycle inventory sold during the month. The income statement also calculates net income for the month. Net income is equal to net sales less the sum of COGS and operating expenses. Begin by retrieving the file INCOME.WK1 from the student data disk. This file contains a partially completed income statement for the month. You will enter formulas with absolute values and @SUM functions, and then combine data from the file BALANCE4.WK1 to complete the worksheet, as outlined in the following steps:

a. Enter a formula in cell B9 that calculates the discount from gross sales. Be sure to use an absolute cell reference.

HINT
a. Use multiplication to calculate the discount.

b. Copy the formula in cell B9 to cell B18 to calculate the purchase discount.

c. Enter a formula in cell E11 that calculates net sales by subtracting the discount from gross sales.

d. Enter a formula in cell C20 that subtracts the purchase discount from the total purchases to calculate the net cost of purchases.

e. Enter an @SUM function in cell D22 that totals beginning inventory and net cost of purchases to give you the cost of goods available for sale.

f. Use the /Worksheet Titles command (/WT) to freeze the column of account names as worksheet titles.

g. Enter a formula in cell E27 that calculates COGS by subtracting the ending inventory from the cost of goods available for sale.

h. Move the cell pointer to cell C31, and use the /File Combine Add command (/FCA) to combine the expense account debits from the range K21..K32 in BALANCE4.WK1.

i. Use the /Move command (/M) to move the values you just combined from the range C39..C41 up to the range C36..C39.

j. Enter an @SUM function in cell E40 that calculates Total Operating Expenses (sums expenses).

k. Enter a formula in cell F43 that calculates net income by subtracting COGS from net sales. Then subtract the total operating expenses from net income.

l. Solve these what-if problems. First, what effect is there on net income if the discounts increase to 7.2 percent? Second, what happens to net income if the beginning inventory is corrected to 7,750?

m. Save the worksheet as INCOME5.WK1, and then print the entire range of data.

n. Save the current print settings to the same file, and then erase the worksheet.

Social Studies

Student Survey

4. Use the worksheet you have created and modified in Lessons 1–4 to solve some what-if problems. Before you do, enter a row of formulas that calculate percentages of responses for each response category in relation to the totals. Begin by retrieving the file SURVEY4.WK1 and performing the tasks outlined in the following steps:

   a. Enter the label "PERCENTAGE TOTALS" in cell A24.

   b. Enter a formula in cell B24 that divides the total number of "Excellent" responses by the total number of all responses. Use an absolute cell reference to represent the total number of responses.

   c. Copy this formula to cells D24, F24, H24, and J24.

   d. Format the formula results in row 24 as percentages with two decimal places.

   e. Given the formulas' results, which response category collected the highest percentage of responses in relation to the total? Which collected the lowest?

   f. Split the worksheet area into two horizontal windows, and then scroll the worksheet in both windows to set up the worksheet area's view so that it looks like Figure 5.13.

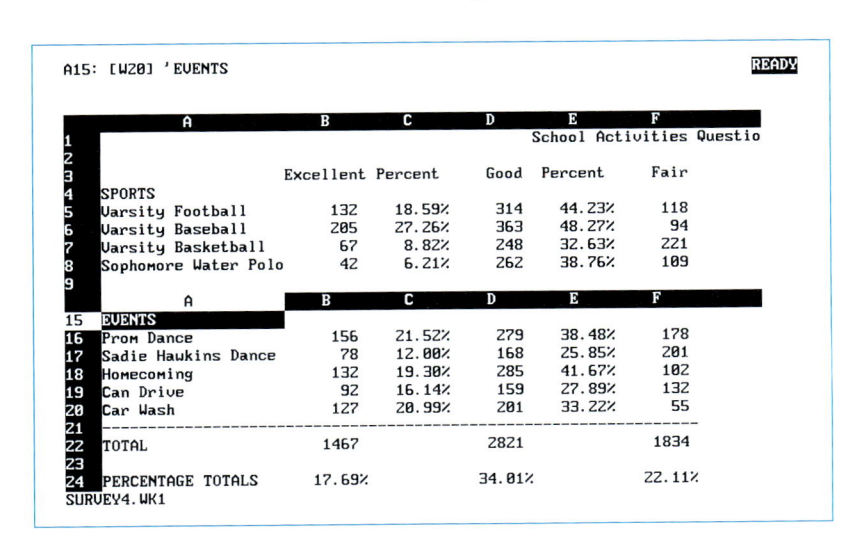

Figure 5.13

After you split the worksheet area into two horizontal windows and then scroll the worksheet in each, your screen should look like this. This view will make it convenient for you to see results when solving what-if problems.

Applications 163

g. Solve the following what-if problem: what is the total percentage of "Excellent" responses if you correct the number of "Excellent" responses for varsity football to 232?

h. Solve the following what-if problem: what is the total percentage of "Excellent" responses if you correct the number of "Excellent" responses for the "Can Drive" event to 192?

i. Save the worksheet as SURVEY5.WK1.

j. Lock the activities' labels in column A as worksheet titles in each window. Scroll the worksheet in each window so that columns H through L is displayed.

k. Solve the following what-if problems: What is the percentage of "No Opinion" responses (in column K) for the homecoming event in relation to total responses for this event if you correct the number of responses to 155? What is the effect on the total percentage of "No Opinion" responses?

l. Erase the worksheet *without* saving the file.

Social Studies

Geography

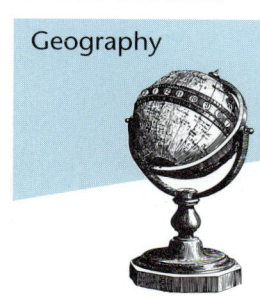

5. You will now analyze population growth by entering formulas with absolute values and solving some what-if problems. Begin by retrieving the file WRLDPOP4.WK1 and performing the tasks outlined in the following steps:

  a. Enter the label "GROWTH %:" in cell A3.

  b. Enter the value 10 percent in cell B3, and format the value as a percentage with two decimal places.

  c. Insert a row between rows 3 and 4.

  d. Insert a column between columns C and D.

  e. Increase the width of column D to 15 characters.

  f. Enter the label "GROWTH" in cell D4, and enter the label "PROJECTIONS" in cell D5.

  g. Enter a formula in cell D8 that increases the estimated world population for North America by the 10 percent growth factor you entered in cell B3. Copy the formula down the column.

  h. Use the /Copy command (/C) to enter an @SUM function in cell D15 that totals growth projections and an @AVG function in cell D17 that calculates a mean growth projection.

  i. Format the projection values in column D with the comma option and no decimal places. Copy the dashed lines into cells D14 and D16.

  j. Solve the following what-if problem: What is the estimated growth projection for South America if you change the world growth factor to 20 percent? What is the change for Africa? What is the change in total projection?

  k. Solve the following what-if problem: What is the estimated total growth projection for the world if you change the growth factor to 30 percent? What effect does this change have on the projections' mean?

5 ▶ Building a Model to Solve What-If Problems

l. Save the worksheet as WRLDPOP5.WK1, and erase the worksheet.

Social Studies

American Government

6. Retrieve the file ELECTN4.WK1, and erase the ranges of vote percentages in columns E and G. Re-enter formulas in cells E7, E14, E21, G7, G14, and G21 with the appropriate absolute cell references. Then copy each formula to the appropriate ranges. Save the file as ELECTN5.WK1, and then solve the following what-if problems:

   a. In the 1960 election, how would the percentages of popular and electoral votes for Kennedy have compared if he had received 35.5 million votes?

   b. How many more popular votes would Carter have needed in the 1976 election to match the same percentage of popular votes that Bush received in the 1988 election?

   c. Erase the worksheet without saving it.

Science/Mathematics

Astronomy

7. In your astronomy class, you learned the following formula, which lets you calculate the rotation of each planet around the sun in Earth years:

$$\sqrt{(2.985 \times 10^{-25}) \times (D \times 1.6093)^3}$$

Your instructor gives the class a homework assignment to calculate the rotations for all the planets using the formula. The instructor explains that the *D* represents the average orbital distance. The constant 1.6093 converts the average distance in miles to kilometers. You know you can enter the formula into your solar system analysis worksheet. However, you are not sure how to make the square root calculation in 1-2-3. After scanning the 1-2-3 help facility, you discover that 1-2-3 provides the @SQRT function. The @SQRT function calculates the square root for any value, formula, or @function in the @SQRT function's argument.

> Note: Enter the @SQRT function into your worksheet the same way as an @SUM or @AVG function.

Begin by retrieving the file PLANETS4.WK1 and entering additional data to set up the assigned calculation.

   a. Enter the label "miles to kilometers" in cell A3, and the label "conversion factor:" in cell A4.

   b. Enter the conversion constant value (1.6093) in cell C4.

   c. Enter the right-aligned labels "ROTATION" in cell H5, "IN EARTH" in cell H6, and "YEARS" in cell H7, as well as a repeating-character label in cell H8 to extend the dashed line.

   d. Enter the following @function in cell H9:

   @SQRT((2.985*10^-25)*(D9*C4)^3)

   e. Copy the @SQRT function in cell H9 down the column.

   f. Format the results in column H as fixed values with four decimal places.

Applications

g. Split the worksheet area into vertical windows between columns D and E, and then scroll the worksheet in the right window so that your screen looks like Figure 5.14.

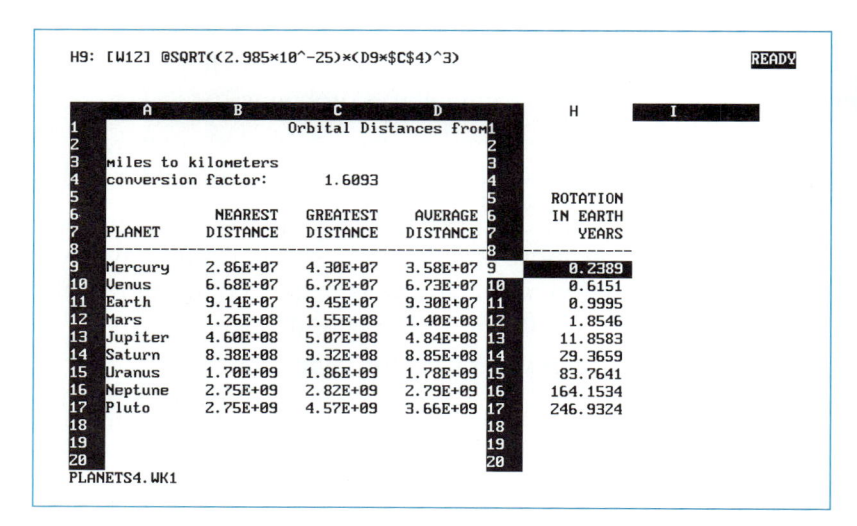

Figure 5.14

After you split the worksheet area into vertical windows and scroll the worksheet in the right window, you can view the calculations in column H next to the columns of orbital distances.

h. Save the worksheet as PLANETS5.WK1, and erase the worksheet.

Science/Mathematics

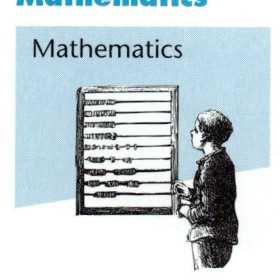

Mathematics

8. For your mathematics course, you are given an assignment to find the solution to the following uniform motion problem:

    A bicyclist leaves home riding at 18 miles per hour (mph). Three hours later, a car leaves the same location and travels in the same direction at the rate of 40 mph. How long will it take the car to overtake the bicyclist?

    To help solve the uniform motion problem, you will create the worksheet model shown in Figure 5.15, as outlined in the following steps:

Figure 5.15

Follow the instructions in application 8 (Mathematics) to create this worksheet.

a. Enter the title "Uniform Motion Problem" in cell A1.

166   **5 ▶ Building a Model to Solve What-If Problems**

b. Decrease the width of column C to one (1) character. Increase the width of columns D and E to 12 characters.

c. Enter the labels, dashed lines, and the rate values as shown in Figure 5.15.

d. Enter the values representing the amounts of time on the bicycle down column B, in quarter-hour increments, as shown in the figure. The quarter-hour values begin with 3 in cell B9 and end with 7 in cell B25. Format these values as fixed with 2 decimal places.

e. Enter a formula in cell D9 that multiplies the amount of time the bicycle has traveled by the bicycle's rate of speed. Copy the formula down the column.

f. Enter a formula in cell E9 that subtracts 3 hours from the amount of time the bicycle has traveled and multiplies the difference by the car's rate of speed. Copy this formula down the column.

HINTS

e. Use an absolute cell reference that refers to the bicycle's rate of speed.

f. Use parentheses in the formula to set off the difference in the formula.

g. Format the results in columns D and E as fixed with one decimal place.

h. Given the rates of speed you entered, in how many hours will the car catch up with the bicycle?

i. Solve the following what-if problem: in how many hours will the car catch up with the bicycle if the bicycle averages 25 mph and the car averages 55 mph?

j. Solve the following what-if problem: in how many hours will the car catch up with the bicycle if the bicycle averages 15 mph and the car averages 35 mph?

k   Save the worksheet as MATH5.WK1, and then print the entire range of data.

l. Save the current print settings to the same file, and erase the worksheet.

Health

Nutrition

9. Continue your health class assignment in which you are analyzing your daily nutrient intake. You will enter some additional data and formulas that will calculate daily totals, meal percentages of nutrient grams, and the energy in kilocalories they produce. Begin by retrieving the file NUTRINF4.WK1 and performing the tasks outlined in the following steps:

   a. Enter the centered labels "MEAL" in cell G2, "DAILY" in cell H2, "TOTALS" in cell G3, and "PERCENTAGE" in cell H3.

   b. Enter an @SUM function in cell G10 to calculate total grams of nutrients from breakfast. Copy the @SUM function to the ranges G11, G21..G22, and G32..G33 to calculate total grams and kilocalories for each meal.

   c. Because the information in rows 12, 23, and 34 duplicates the @SUM function results in cells G11, G22, and G33, delete row 12, then delete row 22, and then delete row 32.

d. Enter 8 spaces followed by the label "DAILY GRAMS:" in cell E36, and then enter 9 spaces followed by the label "DAILY Kcal:" in cell E37.

e. Enter an @SUM function in cell G36 that sums the total grams per meal in column G. Copy the @SUM function to cell G37, which will calculate daily energy in kilocalories.

> **HINT**
>
> e. Separate the appropriate cells with commas in the @SUM function's argument.

f. Split the worksheet area into horizontal windows, freeze the column headings as worksheet titles, and scroll the worksheet in each window so that your screen looks like Figure 5.16.

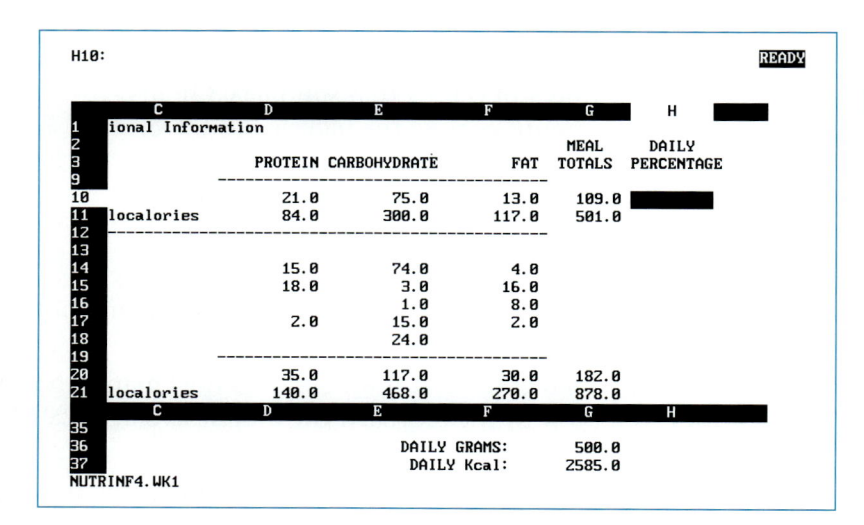

Figure 5.16

Split your worksheet area into two horizontal windows and scroll the worksheet in each window so that your screen looks like this. This will make it easier to build formulas.

g. Enter a formula in cell H10 that divides the total breakfast nutrient grams by the daily gram total. Be sure to use an absolute cell reference to refer to the daily gram total. Copy the formula to cells H20 and H30 to calculate percentages for lunch and dinner.

h. Enter a similar formula in cell H11 that divides total breakfast kilocalories by the daily total. Be sure to use an appropriate absolute cell reference.

i. Format the column G results as fixed decimals with one decimal place, and then format the column H results as percentages with one decimal place.

j. Solve the following what-if problem: what are the changes in totals and percentages if you correct the number of carbohydrate grams for rice to 41?

k. Save the worksheet as NUTRINF5.WK1, and erase the worksheet.

Health

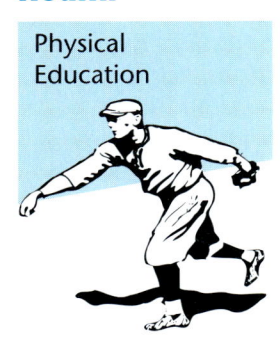

Physical Education

10. The Washington High softball team survived their closest game of the season 10–9 (an exhausting pitchers' duel). Here is the scorecard that summarizes the team's batting. Retrieve the file SBGAME4.WK1. Update the batting statistics worksheet by adding the game 5 scores to the summing formulas for each statistic.

Player	At Bats	Runs	Hits	Doubles	Triples	HRs	RBIs
Bernhart	6	1	1	0	0	0	0
Taylor	6	0	2	1	0	0	1
Hepburn	6	1	2	0	0	0	1
Monroe	6	2	2	1	0	0	1
d'Arc	6	0	1	0	0	0	0
Victoria	6	2	2	0	0	0	1
Wood	4	1	2	0	0	1	3
Smith	5	1	2	0	1	0	2
Turner	2	1	0	0	0	0	0
Welch	1	0	0	0	0	0	0
Loren	1	0	0	0	0	0	0
Mabely	2	0	0	0	0	0	0
Braga	5	1	2	1	0	0	1

Also, the players asked if you would calculate their slugging averages. Slugging averages are computed by dividing players' number of bases (one for a single, two for a double, and so on) for all their hits by their number of at bats. Because your worksheet does not track singles as a separate category, your formula must account for differences between number of at bats and total extra-base hits. Modify the worksheet as outlined in the following steps:

a. Enter the labels "SLUGGING" in cell K4 and "AVERAGE" in cell K5.

b. Create a quick table of constants to help you figure each player's slugging average. Enter the right-aligned labels "BASES:" in cell A28, "2B =" in cell B28, "3B =" in cell B29, and "HR =" in cell B30. Then enter the values 2, 3, and 4 in each cell in the range C28..C30.

c. Enter a formula in cell K7 that calculates Bernhart's slugging average. The formula must divide the player's total bases, based on the number of singles and extra-base hits, by the player's total at bats. You can construct this formula in various ways; here are a few guidelines.

- You can use an @SUM function to calculate the total number of bases. The @SUM function's argument would contain four separate formulas.
- The first formula in the argument subtracts the sum of extra-base hits from the total hits to calculate the number of singles.
- The next three formulas in the argument multiply the numbers of extra-base hits (for each type) by the appropriate constant in the table. Be sure to use absolute cell references to refer to the constants.

Applications

Note: If you need some help constructing the formula, refer to the control panel in Figure 5.17.

d. Copy the formula in cell K7 down the column and format column K as fixed with 3 decimals. Also copy the formula to cell K21 to calculate the team's slugging average. Which player has the highest slugging average? Which player has the lowest?

e. Use the /Copy command (/C) to extend the dashed line in row 20.

f. Save the worksheet as SBGAME5.WK1.

g. Split the worksheet area into vertical windows, and scroll the worksheet in the right window so that your screen looks like Figure 5.17.

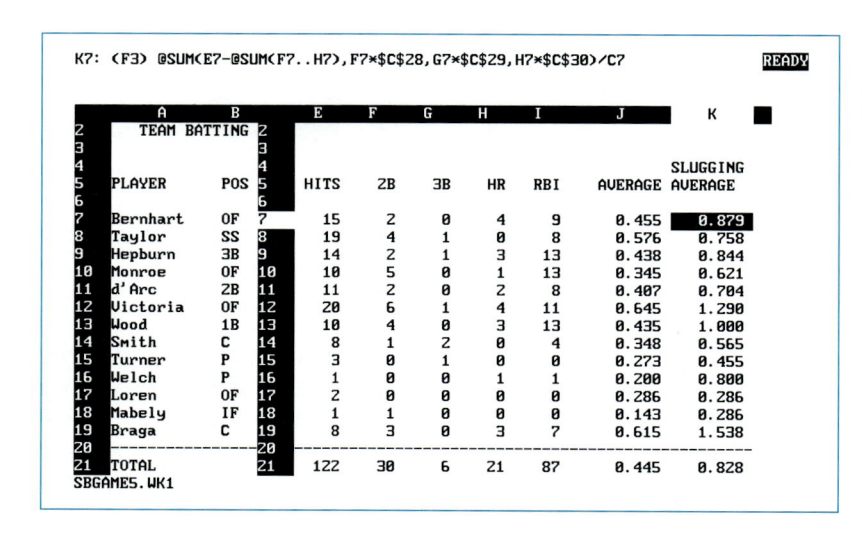

```
K7: (F3) @SUM(E7-@SUM(F7..H7),F7*$C$28,G7*$C$29,H7*$C$30)/C7           READY

        A         B         E      F     G    H     I       J         K
     TEAM BATTING
                                                           SLUGGING
     PLAYER      POS       HITS    2B    3B   HR    RBI   AVERAGE AVERAGE

     Bernhart    OF         15     2     0    4     9     0.455    0.879
     Taylor      SS         19     4     1    0     8     0.576    0.758
     Hepburn     3B         14     2     1    3     13    0.438    0.844
     Monroe      OF         10     5     0    1     13    0.345    0.621
     d'Arc       2B         11     2     0    2     8     0.407    0.704
     Victoria    OF         20     6     1    4     11    0.645    1.290
     Wood        1B         10     4     0    3     13    0.435    1.000
     Smith       C           8     1     2    0     4     0.348    0.565
     Turner      P           3     0     1    0     0     0.273    0.455
     Welch       P           1     0     0    1     1     0.200    0.800
     Loren       OF          2     0     0    0     0     0.286    0.286
     Mabely      IF          1     1     0    0     0     0.143    0.286
     Braga       C           8     3     0    3     7     0.615    1.538
     --------------------------------------------------------------------
     TOTAL                  122   30     6    21    87    0.445    0.828
SBGAME5.WK1
```

Figure 5.17

Split your worksheet area into vertical windows at column C, and scroll the worksheet in the right window so that your screen looks like this.

h. Solve the following what-if problems: Suppose Braga hits 5 singles in 5 at bats. What happens to Braga's batting average? What happens to Braga's slugging average?

i. Solve the following what-if problems: Suppose Victoria gets 0 hits in 7 at bats. What happens to Victoria's batting and slugging averages?

j. Erase the worksheet without saving the changes.

6 ▶ Creating Budgets and Using a Worksheet Template

Objectives

- Link worksheet files.
- Enter linking formulas.
- Describe the relationship between source and target files.
- Update linked files.
- Enter formulas that contain mixed cell references.
- Use the ABS command (F4) to enter a mixed cell reference.
- Use the logical @IF function.
- Create a worksheet template.
- Protect worksheets.
- Password-protect worksheets.

Business people commonly use 1-2-3 to create budgets so that they can plan income and expenses for a coming period. A budget is an example of a complex worksheet structure that is used over and over again. In this lesson, you will learn some powerful 1-2-3 techniques to build a budget worksheet. You will also create a template worksheet from your budget worksheet. Templates are worksheet structures that can be used again and again to create similar worksheets.

Exercise 6.1 Linking Worksheet Files

After completing this exercise, you will be able to

Objectives
- Link worksheet files.
- Enter linking formulas.
- Describe the relationship between source and target files.
- Update linked files.

BUDGET
A report that shows a company's projected income, expenses, and the resulting profit after total expenses are subtracted from total income.

The owner of Mollie's Music Shoppe wants you to create a budget worksheet. A *budget* is a financial report that shows estimated income and expenses. Income is the money a company makes by selling its merchandise or services. An expense is the money a company spends to run its business (for example, an electricity bill).

Budgets also show estimated profit. In simple terms, a budget subtracts expenses from income to determine profit. This is the money the company makes after expenses are paid. Budgets, or similar financial reports, sometimes show actual income and expenses for a period that has already happened. "Actual" values are income that has already been made and expenses that have already been paid.

Budgets are commonly divided into time periods called quarters. A *quarter* is one-fourth (1/4) of a year, or three months. Businesses often operate on what is called a fiscal year. A *fiscal year* is a 12-month accounting period. It can begin on January 1, like a calendar year. However, it is more common for fiscal years to begin on June 1 or July 1.

The fiscal year for Mollie's Music Shoppe begins on July 1. So your budget will show the store's "actual" income, expenses, and profit for the first quarter, which has already ended. It will also show the estimated budget amounts for the rest of the fiscal year.

The actual first-quarter income figures are stored in another file. The owner is checking the figures, so you may have to make some changes later. Instead of typing the figures again to enter them in the budget, why not somehow

LINKING

An electronic spreadsheet feature in which a *linking formula* in the current worksheet (the target file) imports data that is stored in a specific cell in another worksheet (the source file), which is stored on disk. The two worksheet files are linked because the target file updates the linked data if any change has been made to the data in the source file.

import them from the other file? You could use the /File Combine command (/FC) to import the data, but changes made to the other file will not update the budget. Linking the data stored on disk to the current worksheet solves this problem. *Linking* is an operation that brings data stored in a file into the current worksheet. The linking operation brings in data that is in a single cell. The two files are "linked" because the data will be updated in the current worksheet if it is changed in the other file.

To link two files, you must enter a linking formula in a cell in the current worksheet. A *linking formula* contains a filename enclosed in double angle brackets (<< >>) and a cell address, as follows:

+<<FILENAME.WK1>>A1

The filename belongs to a file stored on disk, and the cell address is where the data is stored in the file. This file is called the source file. As shown in Figure 6.1, the *source file* contains data that you want to link with the current worksheet. The current worksheet is called the *target file* because it receives the data from the source file.

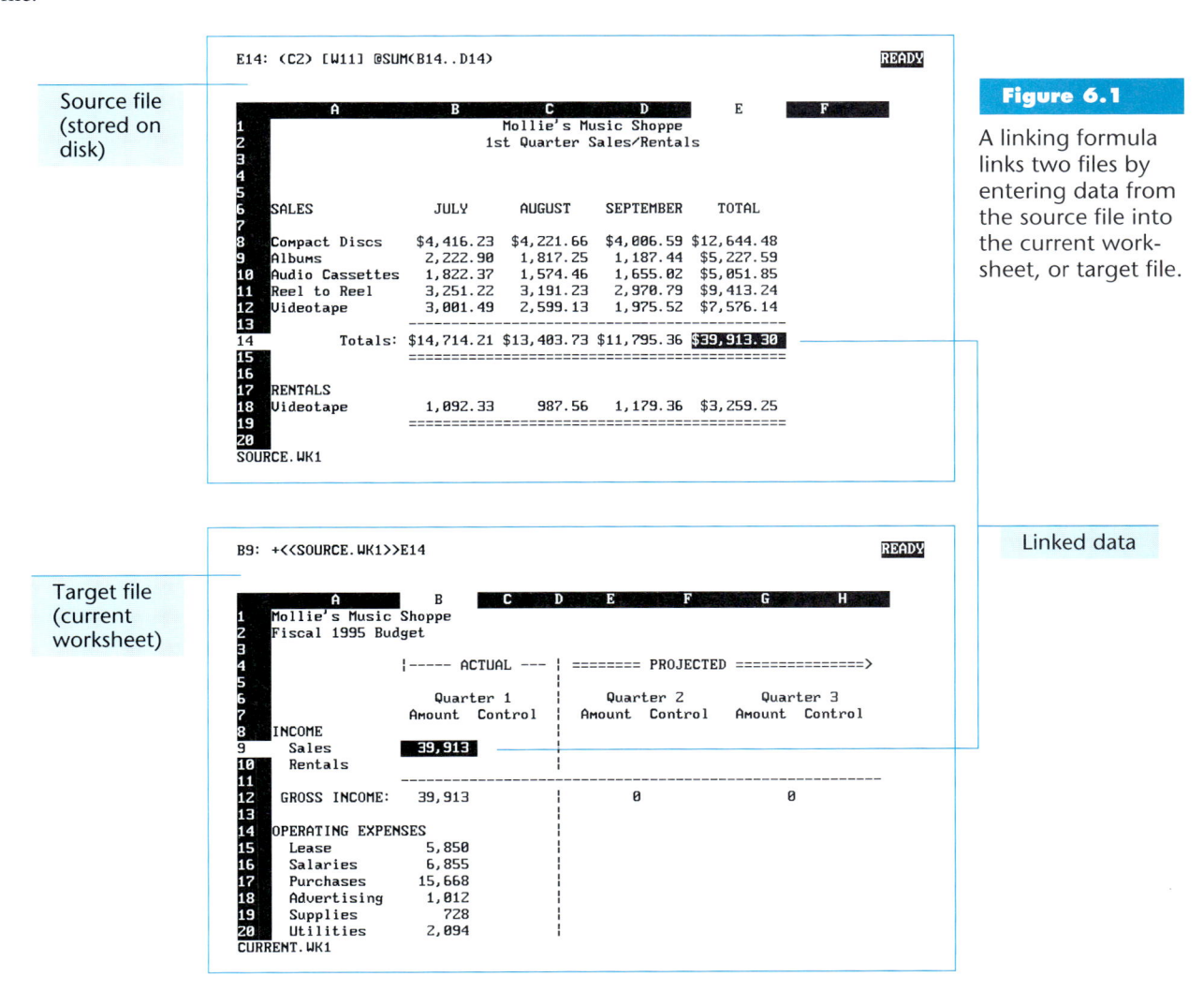

Figure 6.1

A linking formula links two files by entering data from the source file into the current worksheet, or target file.

Source file (stored on disk)

Target file (current worksheet)

Linked data

Linking Worksheet Files

173

When you enter a linking formula in a cell, you must first type a plus sign (+). Otherwise, 1-2-3 will display the Main Menu when you type the first angle bracket (<).

You will now begin building the budget by linking the first-quarter income data. First you will retrieve the file that contains the income data. This will let you see the source file data that you will link to your budget.

SOURCE FILE
In a linking formula, the name of a file stored on disk that contains data to be imported into the current worksheet (target file).

1 ▶ If necessary, start 1-2-3. Change the current directory to the drive that contains your data disk. Change the Clock setting so that the current filename is displayed on the status line.

> Note: If 1-2-3 is already loaded, make sure you clear the worksheet area.

2 ▶ Retrieve the file INCMLINK.WK1.

A file with actual first-quarter income is displayed, as shown in Figure 6.2.

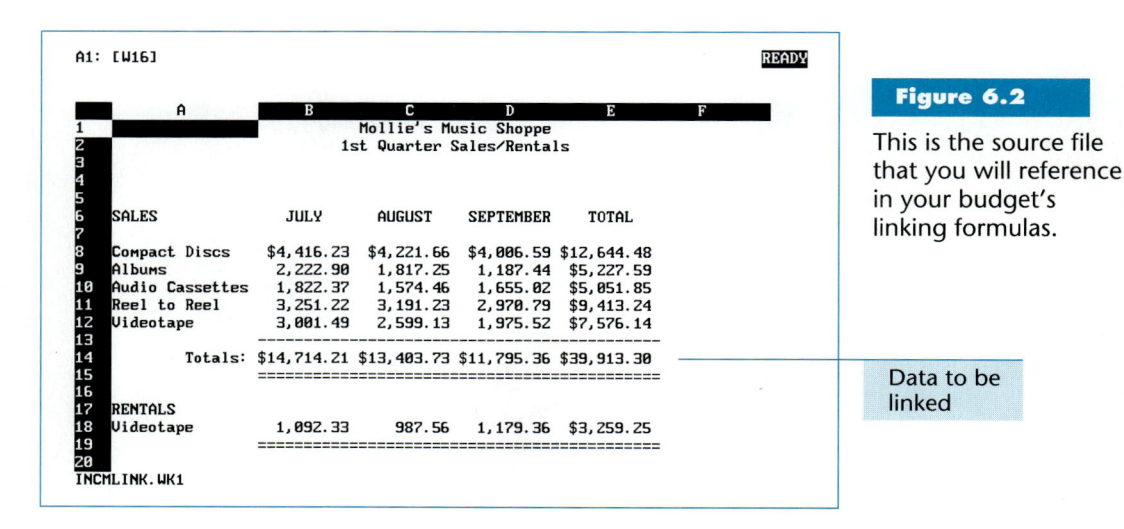

Figure 6.2

This is the source file that you will reference in your budget's linking formulas.

Data to be linked

3 ▶ Take a look at the worksheet.

Notice that the worksheet contains income information on sales of merchandise and rentals for the first quarter. (The store also rents out videotapes as a secondary source of income.) Also, note that totals for the quarter are listed in column E.

4 ▶ Retrieve the file FISCAL95.WK1.

> Note: Because you did not change any data in INCMLINK.WK1, you can retrieve another file without erasing the worksheet. The retrieved file simply replaces the previous one.

6 ▶ Creating Budgets and Using a Worksheet Template

TARGET FILE
The current worksheet that contains a linking formula, which imports data from a source file stored on disk.

A budget worksheet is displayed, as shown in Figure 6.3. To save time, this worksheet has been partially set up for you. Notice that the actual expenses for the first quarter and several @SUM functions have been entered. This worksheet is the target file.

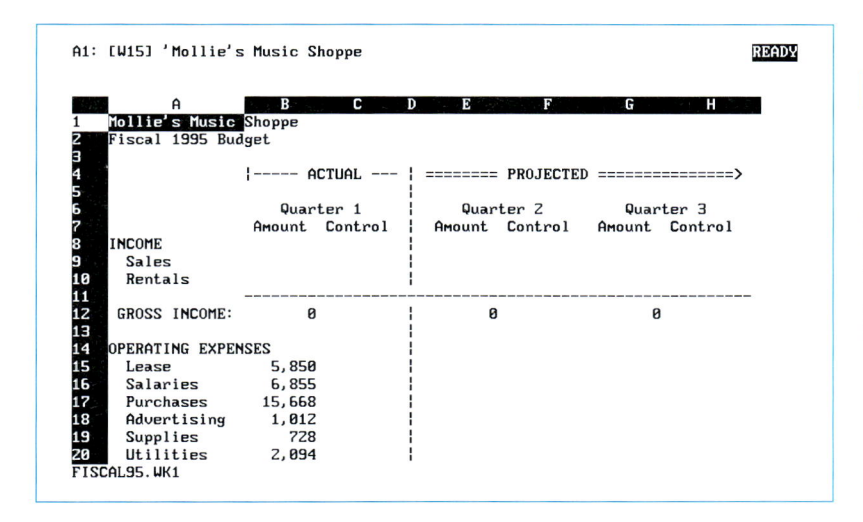

Figure 6.3

This is the target file into which you will enter the linking formula. The linking formula will bring in the first-quarter sales data from the source file.

LINKING FORMULA
A special 1-2-3 formula that enters data stored in another file into the current worksheet. A linking formula is composed of the source filename, enclosed in double angle brackets (<< >>), and a cell reference. The filename must include a directory path if the file is not in the current directory.

Linking formula

5 ▶ Move the cell pointer to cell B9.

This is the cell where you will enter a linking formula to bring in the total sales stored in cell E14 in INCMLINK.WK1.

6 ▶ Type +<<**incmlink**>>**e14**

The linking formula is entered on the control panel, as shown in Figure 6.4. If your linking formula looks different, edit it so that it appears exactly as shown in the figure.

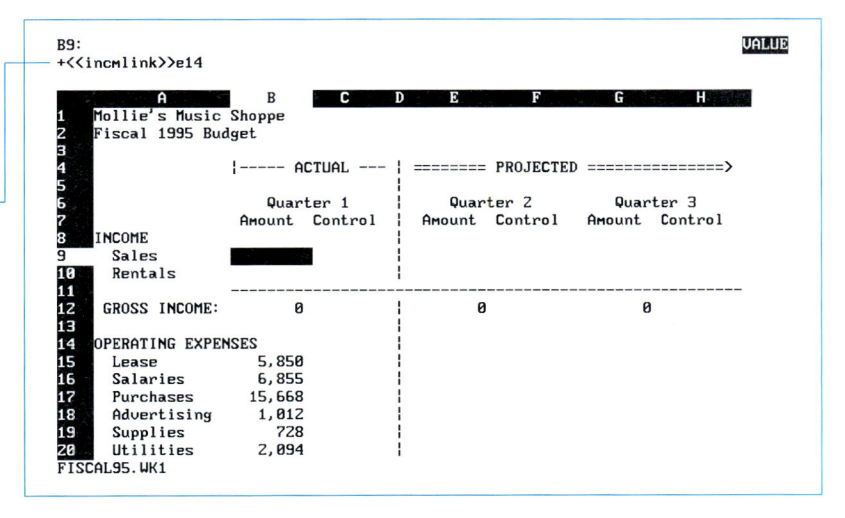

Figure 6.4

The linking formula contains the source filename, enclosed in double angle brackets, and a cell address. The cell address is the location of the source file data you want to link with the target file.

Linking Worksheet Files   **175**

> Caution: If the source file is not in the current directory, be sure to enter the correct path with the filename. The path tells 1-2-3 where the file is. Here is an example of a complete path in a linking formula:
>
> **+<<C:\123R23\DATA\FILENAME.WK1>>E14**
>
> *(handwritten: +<<A:\incmlink.>>E.14)*

7 ▶ Press ⏎.

The linking formula is entered in cell B9, and the value stored in cell E14 in INCMLINK.WK1 is displayed. Also, the @SUM function in cell B12 calculates the current gross income.

> **HINT**
> You need not type the .WK1 extension when entering a filename in a linking formula.

Now you will enter another linking formula to bring in the income from rentals. Instead of typing the formula this time, copy the linking formula you just entered.

8 ▶ Make sure the cell pointer is on cell B9.

9 ▶ Use the /Copy command (/C) to copy the linking formula in cell B9 to cell B10.

After you copy the linking formula to cell B10, an equals sign (=) appears. The linking formula in cell B9 contains the relative cell reference E14. The copy in cell B10 adjusted the relative cell reference and brought in the source file data in cell E15. Cell E15 in INCMLINK.WK1 contains a repeating-character label (\=). However, the linking formula did not bring in the backslash formatting prefix. Linking formulas only bring in the raw data; they do not bring in cell formats.

Now you will edit the linking formula in cell B10 so it brings in the correct data.

10 ▶ Move the cell pointer to cell B10.

11 ▶ Press F2.

Lotus 1-2-3 switches to EDIT mode.

12 ▶ Press BACKSPACE.

The 5 in the cell address erases.

13 ▶ Type **8**

14 ▶ Press ⏎.

The rental income for the first quarter (3,259) is displayed in cell B10, and the gross income in cell B12 is recalculated.

15 ▶ Press HOME, and save the worksheet as BUDGET95.WK1.

The owner has checked the first-quarter figures. She tells you that the September sales figures for compact discs and videotapes were wrong. You will now retrieve the source file, INCMLINK.WK1, and change

176   6 ▶ Creating Budgets and Using a Worksheet Template

those figures. Before you do, note the current gross income in cell B12: 43,173.

16 ▶ Retrieve the file INCMLINK.WK1.

17 ▶ Move the cell pointer to cell D8.

The cell pointer is on the cell that contains the September sales figure for compact discs.

18 ▶ Type **4326.40**

19 ▶ Press ⬇ 4 times.

The cell pointer is on cell D12, which contains the September sales for videotapes.

20 ▶ Type **1823.15**

21 ▶ Press ⏎.

22 ▶ Press HOME, and save the changes to the same file.

23 ▶ Retrieve the file BUDGET95.WK1.

The budget worksheet is displayed. Notice that the linked first-quarter sales figure in cell B9 has been updated automatically. Also, the @SUM function in cell B12 recalculated the gross income.

24 ▶ Save the changes to the same file.

Now you will learn how to use mixed cell references as you continue building the budget.

Exercise 6.2 Using Mixed Cell References

Objectives

After completing this exercise, you will be able to
- Enter formulas that contain mixed cell references.
- Use the ABS command (F4) to enter a mixed cell reference.

Look at the BUDGET95.WK1 worksheet. Notice that there are columns labeled "Control" to the right of the "Amount" columns. In these columns, you will enter cost-control formulas. A cost-control formula calculates the percentage (portion) of quarterly income that the company spends for each expense. These percentages help you control expenses based on income level. For example, if income increases considerably, a business owner might budget more money for salaries to hire additional people.

The cost-control formulas you will enter in column C will divide each expense amount by the first quarter's gross income. The results will be percentages of first-quarter gross income that the expenses represent. Notice that you will be entering similar formulas in columns F, H, J, and L. For this reason, you need to enter the column C formulas so they can be copied accurately to those columns.

In Lesson 5, you learned how to change a relative cell reference to an absolute cell reference. However, an absolute cell reference to the first-quarter gross income (B12) will not work when you copy the formulas. Why not? Because the formulas in column H, for example, would divide each second-quarter expense by the first-quarter gross income. However, you want the column H formulas to divide second-quarter expenses by the second-quarter gross income in column G.

To make the formulas copy accurately, the cell references to the gross income values must adjust their column letters. However, the row numbers in the cell references must remain fixed on row 12. You can do this by making the cell reference to gross income in the original formula a mixed cell reference. A *mixed cell reference* is half relative and half absolute. The relative half (column letter or row number) adjusts when the formula is copied. The absolute half remains fixed.

MIXED CELL REFERENCE
A cell reference in which either the column letter or row number is absolute. If the column letter is absolute, the row number is relative (for example $B12). If the row number is absolute, the column letter is relative (for example B$12).

A mixed cell reference contains a dollar sign ($) before either the column letter or the row number (for example, $B12 or B$12). You can use the ABS command ([F4]) to change a cell address on the control panel to a mixed cell reference. Recall that you press [F4] once to create an absolute cell reference. To create a mixed cell reference, press [F4] twice to make only the row number absolute. Press it three times if you want to make only the column letter absolute. Table 6.1 shows the types of cell references that are created, depending on the number of times [F4] is pressed.

Cell reference displayed on control panel	Press [F4] to change cell reference to
A1	A1
A1	A$1
A$1	$A1
$A1	A1

Table 6.1

The [F4] key is used to create absolute and mixed cell references.

You will begin this exercise by entering estimated income and expenses for the next three quarters. Then you will enter the first-quarter cost-control formulas and copy them to the columns for the other quarters.

1 ▶ Move the cell pointer to cell E9.

The cell pointer is on the cell that will contain the estimated quarter 2 sales.

2 ▶ Type **65000** and press ⬇.

The estimated sales goal for quarter 2 is entered. The cell pointer is on the cell that will contain estimated income on rentals.

3 ▶ Type **4750** and press ⬅.

The estimated income for quarter 2 is entered, and the estimated gross income in cell E12 is calculated.

4 ▶ Move the cell pointer to cell G9.

The cell pointer is on the cell that will contain estimated sales for quarter 3.

5 ▶ Type **48000** and press ⬇.

6 ▶ Type **3500** and press ⬅.

The estimated income for quarter 3 is entered.

7 ▶ Copy the estimated income in the range G9..G10 to the range I9..I10 to enter the same estimated income for quarter 4.

8 ▶ Move the cell pointer to cell B15.

9 ▶ Copy the amount in cell B15 to cells E15, G15, and I15 to carry the lease expense across all quarters. The lease expense is the same in each quarter.

10 ▶ Move the cell pointer to cell E16.

The cell pointer is on the cell that will contain the salary expense for quarter 2.

11 ▶ Type **11000** and press ⬇.

12 ▶ Type **26500** and press ⬇ twice.

The quarter 2 purchases expense is entered. Purchases represent the cost of stocking (buying) CDs, albums, tapes, etc. The cell pointer is on cell E19, which will contain the supplies expense.

> Note: The advertising expense will require a special calculation later in this lesson.

13 ▶ Type **1100** and press ⬇.

14 ▶ Type **2500** and press ⬅.

15 ▶ Move the cell pointer to cell G16.

The cell pointer is on the cell that will contain estimated salaries for quarter 3.

16 ▶ Type **8000** and press ⬇.

17 ▶ Type **18500** and press ⬇ twice.

Using Mixed Cell References

18 ▶ Type **850** and press ↓.

19 ▶ Type **2200** and press ↵.

The estimated expenses for quarter 3, except for advertising, are entered.

Now you will copy the estimated expenses you just entered for salaries, purchases, supplies, and utilities to column I. This will carry the same estimates over to quarter 4.

20 ▶ Use the /Copy command (/C) to copy the range G16..G20 to the range I16..I20.

Except for advertising, which will require a special calculation, the estimated expenses are entered, as shown in Figure 6.5.

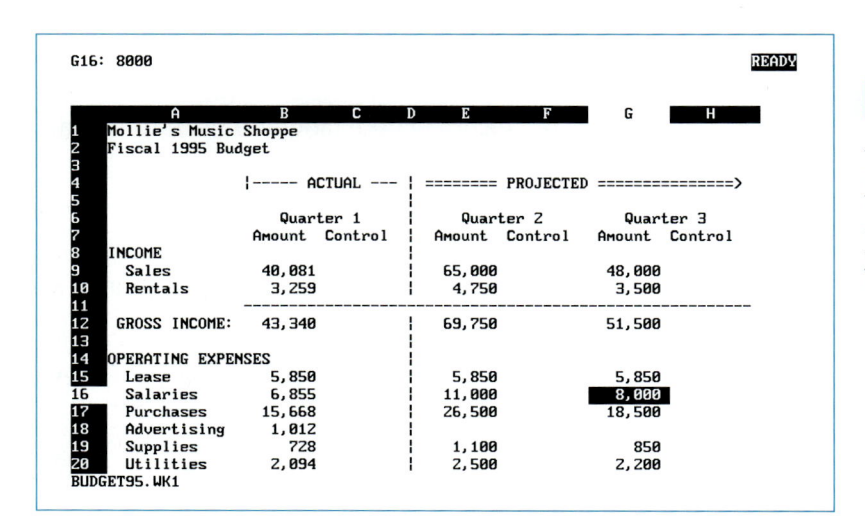

```
G16: 8000                                                              READY

         A          B       C       D       E       F       G       H
 1  Mollie's Music Shoppe
 2  Fiscal 1995 Budget
 3
 4                  |----- ACTUAL ---|======== PROJECTED ==============>
 5                  |                |
 6                  Quarter 1        Quarter 2        Quarter 3
 7                  Amount  Control  Amount  Control  Amount  Control
 8  INCOME
 9     Sales        40,081           65,000           48,000
10     Rentals       3,259            4,750            3,500
11                  --------------------------------------------------
12  GROSS INCOME:   43,340           69,750           51,500
13
14  OPERATING EXPENSES
15     Lease         5,850            5,850            5,850
16     Salaries      6,855           11,000            8,000
17     Purchases    15,668           26,500           18,500
18     Advertising   1,012
19     Supplies        728            1,100              850
20     Utilities     2,094            2,500            2,200
BUDGET95.WK1
```

Figure 6.5

After you enter projected expenses for the second, third, and fourth quarters, your screen should look like this.

Now you are ready to enter the formulas that will calculate the cost-control formulas in columns C, F, H, and J.

21 ▶ Move the cell pointer to cell C15.

The cell pointer is on the cell that will store the cost-control formula for the first-quarter lease expense.

22 ▶ Type **+** (a plus sign).

23 ▶ Press ↵.

The cell address B15 appears to the right of the addition operator on the control panel.

24 ▶ Type **/** (a slash).

The division operator is entered into the formula.

25 ▶ Move the cell pointer to cell B12.

The cell address B12 appears to the right of the division operator on the control panel.

26 ▶ Press F4.

   The relative cell reference B12 changes to the absolute cell reference B12.

27 ▶ Press F4.

   The absolute cell reference B12 changes to the mixed cell reference B$12. This is the mixed cell reference you want in the formula.

28 ▶ Press ↵.

   The formula is entered, and the result is displayed in cell C15.

The formula's result means that the $5,850 lease expense represents 13.5 percent of the first-quarter gross income. Now you will copy the formula down column C to calculate percentages for the other first-quarter expenses. Then you will copy the column C formulas to the other cost-control columns to calculate estimated cost-control percentages.

29 ▶ Use the /Copy command to copy the formula in cell C15 to the range C16..C20.

30 ▶ Move the cell pointer down the column to each copied formula in column C.

   Notice that each formula contains the mixed cell reference B$12.

Note: For the step 29 copy operation, an absolute cell reference for gross income would have worked. However, as you will see, an absolute cell reference will not work when you copy the formulas to the other columns.

31 ▶ Use the /Copy command (/C) to copy the formula in cell C15 to the ranges F15..F20, H15..H20, and J15..J20.

   After you perform the three copy operations, your worksheet should look like Figure 6.6.

Mixed cell reference

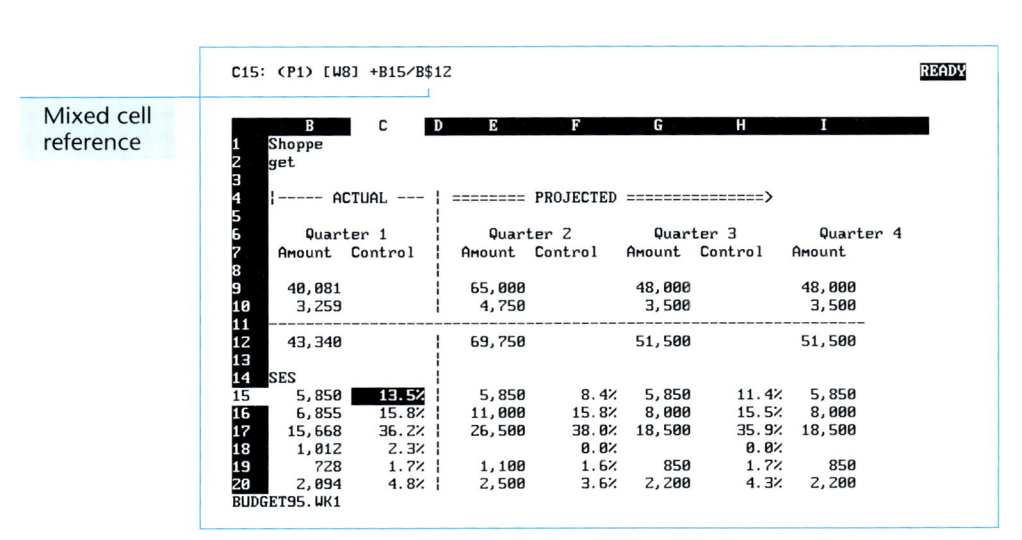

Figure 6.6

After you copy the cost-control formulas to columns F, H, and J, columns B through I in your worksheet should look like this.

Using Mixed Cell References

181

32 ▶ Move the cell pointer to cell F17.

The cell pointer is on the cell that contains the cost-control percentage for second-quarter purchases. Notice that the mixed cell reference is E$12.

33 ▶ Press (HOME), and save the changes to the same file.

When you copied the formulas to column F, 1-2-3 adjusted the relative column letter and did not adjust the absolute row number. A mixed cell reference was necessary to copy the formulas accurately to the other cost-control columns.

Exercise 6.3 Using the @IF Function

Objective

After completing this exercise, you will be able to
- Use the logical @IF function.

The owner asked you not to include estimated advertising expenses for the rest of the fiscal year. These amounts require some special considerations. For instance, she knows that the store must increase the advertising expense in the second quarter. The extra advertising should boost sales for the busiest time of the year. During the second quarter, the store will try to meet the $65,000 sales goal. The owner expects to spend less on advertising during the third quarter, which is the slowest period. Therefore, the budgeted advertising expense for each quarter must be based on a condition. The condition is the level of sales for the previous quarter.

LOGICAL @FUNCTION
A group of @functions that test a condition to see if the condition is true or false.

To solve this problem, you can use the logical @IF function. The @IF function lets you return or display one of two values or labels, based on an existing *condition* within the worksheet. The @IF function is a *logical @function*. That is, it tests whether a condition is true or false. Then it displays one of two results based, on the outcome of the test.

The @IF function has three elements separated by commas in its argument. The first element is the condition you want to test. The second element is a value, formula, or text string that is to be displayed if the condition is true. The third element is a value, formula, or text string that is to be displayed if the condition is false.

A text string is text, or a label, that you want to display. For example, you might enter an @IF function that tests whether an exam score is a passing or failing grade. The @IF function displays either "PASS" or "FAIL," based on the result of its test. The @IF function is written in the following format:

@IF(condition,option1,option2)

Often the condition is a statement that contains a logical operator. *Logical operators* are symbols that make specific types of comparisons to test the relationship between two values. Table 6.2 summarizes the logical operators recognized by 1-2-3.

LOGICAL OPERATORS
Symbols that represent specific types of comparisons between two values. Often the condition in a logical @function contains a logical operator that compares two values as a test.

Operator	Name	Operation
=	equal to	tests to see if value on the left is equal to value on the right
<>	not equal to	tests to see if value on the left is not equal to value on the right
<	less than	tests if value on the left is smaller than value on the right
>	greater than	tests to see if value on the left is larger than value on the right
<=	less than or equal to	tests to see if value on the left is smaller than or equal to value on right
>=	greater than or equal to	tests to see if value on the left is larger than or equal to value on the right

Table 6.2

Logical Operators

In your budget, you want to enter an estimated advertising expense for each quarter, based on that quarter's sales. The percentage of sales used for advertising will depend on the previous quarter's sales.

The owner tells you to calculate each quarter's advertising expense as follows. If the previous quarter's sales are less than $45,000, enter a value that is 4.5 percent of the estimated sales. If the previous quarter's sales are more than $45,000, enter a value that is 2.8 percent of the quarter's estimated sales. The resulting @IF function for the second quarter will be entered as follows:

@IF(B9<45000,E9*.045,E9*.028)

In English, this @function means "If the value in cell B9 is less than $45,000, multiply the value in cell E9 times 4.5 percent and display the result. Otherwise, multiply the value in cell E9 times 2.8 percent and display the result."

Using the @IF Function   **183**

Now you will use the pointing method to enter this @IF function into the budget worksheet. You will then copy it to enter the advertising expense for each quarter.

1 ▶ Move the cell pointer to cell E18.

The cell pointer is on the cell that will contain the second quarter's advertising expense.

2 ▶ Type **@if(**

The @function name and opening parenthesis are displayed on the control panel.

3 ▶ Move the cell pointer to cell B9.

The cell pointer is on the cell that contains the actual first-quarter sales. Its cell address is displayed on the control panel.

4 ▶ Type **<45000,**

CONDITION
A value, formula, or text string tested by the logical @function. The condition is the first element in a logical @function's argument.

The @IF function's condition is displayed on the control panel.

Note: Be sure you type the comma (,).

5 ▶ Move the cell pointer to cell E9.

The cell pointer is on the cell that contains the estimated second-quarter sales.

6 ▶ Type ***.045,**

The control panel displays the formula that calculates the advertising expense if the condition is true.

Note: Be sure you type the comma (,).

7 ▶ Move the cell pointer back to cell E9.

8 ▶ Type ***.028**

The formula that calculates the advertising expense if the condition is false is displayed on the control panel.

9 ▶ Type **)** (a closing parenthesis).

The entire @IF function is displayed on the control panel. After you type the closing parenthesis, ")", the cell pointer returns to cell E18.

10 ▶ Press ⏎.

184 **6 ▶ Creating Budgets and Using a Worksheet Template**

The @IF function is entered in cell E18. The condition tested true. The result equals 4.5 percent of the estimated second-quarter sales in cell E9, as shown in Figure 6.7.

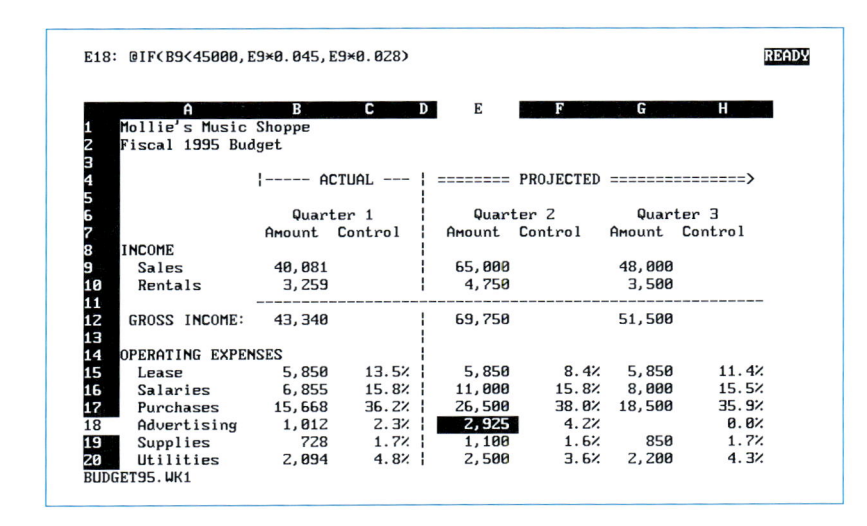

```
E18: @IF(B9<45000,E9*0.045,E9*0.028)                              READY

         A         B        C     D     E        F        G        H
 1  Mollie's Music Shoppe
 2  Fiscal 1995 Budget
 3
 4                  |----- ACTUAL ---  | ======== PROJECTED ===============>
 5
 6                  Quarter 1          | Quarter 2        Quarter 3
 7                  Amount   Control   | Amount  Control  Amount  Control
 8  INCOME                             |
 9    Sales         40,081             | 65,000           48,000
10    Rentals        3,259             |  4,750            3,500
11                  ---------------------------------------------------------
12  GROSS INCOME:   43,340             | 69,750           51,500
13
14  OPERATING EXPENSES                 |
15    Lease          5,850     13.5%   |  5,850    8.4%    5,850   11.4%
16    Salaries       6,855     15.8%   | 11,000   15.8%    8,000   15.5%
17    Purchases     15,668     36.2%   | 26,500   38.0%   18,500   35.9%
18    Advertising    1,012      2.3%   |  2,925    4.2%              0.0%
19    Supplies         728      1.7%   |  1,100    1.6%      850    1.7%
20    Utilities      2,094      4.8%   |  2,500    3.6%    2,200    4.3%
BUDGET95.WK1
```

Figure 6.7

The first-quarter sales figure in cell B9 is less than $45,000. This means the condition in the @IF function is true. Therefore, the projected sales figure for the second quarter is multiplied by 4.5 percent, which equals 2,925. If you have a different result, make sure your @IF function matches the one shown here.

Now you will copy the @IF function to columns G and I. This will calculate the estimated advertising expenses for the third and fourth quarters.

11 ▶ Make sure the cell pointer is on cell E18.

The cell pointer is on the cell that contains the @IF function for the advertising expense.

12 ▶ Use the /Copy command (/C) to copy the @IF function in cell E18 to cells G18 and I18.

You need to edit the two @IF function copies in columns G and I. The relative cell references in their conditions did not adjust accurately because there is an extra column (column D). The extra column stores the vertical line between the quarter 1 and quarter 2 columns. You will edit the @IF functions in columns G and I so that their conditions operate on the correct values.

13 ▶ Move the cell pointer to cell G18.

14 ▶ Press F2.

Lotus 1-2-3 switches to EDIT mode.

15 ▶ Move the cursor to the "D" in the first cell reference (D9).

16 ▶ Press DEL.

17 ▶ Type **E** and press ↵.

The @IF function for the estimated third-quarter advertising expense is edited to test the estimated sales value for the second quarter.

Using the @IF Function 185

18 ▶ Move the cell pointer to the @IF function in column I.

19 ▶ Edit the @IF function in EDIT mode to change the first cell reference to G9.

20 ▶ Press HOME, and save the changes to the same file.

You have learned to use mixed cell references and the @IF function to prepare a budget. To complete the budget, you will enter formulas in row 24 to calculate the actual net profit for the first quarter. Then you will copy the formula to calculate profit for quarters 2, 3, and 4.

21 ▶ Move the cell pointer to cell B24.

> The cell pointer is on the cell that will contain the net profit for the first quarter.

22 ▶ Type + (a plus sign).

> Lotus 1-2-3 switches to VALUE mode.

23 ▶ Move the cell pointer to cell B12.

> The cell pointer is on the cell that contains the gross income for the first quarter.

24 ▶ Type – (a minus sign).

25 ▶ Move the cell pointer to cell B22.

> The cell pointer is on the cell that contains the total expenses for the first quarter.

26 ▶ Press ⏎.

> The formula is entered. Total expenses are subtracted from gross income to calculate first-quarter profit.

27 ▶ Use the /Copy command (/C) to copy the net profit formula to cells E24, G24, and I24.

> After you copy the formulas, net profit for all four quarters is calculated.

28 ▶ Scroll the worksheet so that the total budget figures for the fiscal year in column K are visible.

> Based on the formulas and @functions you have entered to create the budget, the @SUM functions in column K calculate the total fiscal year budget figures.

29 ▶ Press HOME, and save the current changes to the same file.

30 ▶ Use the /Print Printer command (/PP) to print the range A1..F25.

> This print range contains actual quarter 1 figures and estimated quarter 2 figures.

31 ▶ Save the current print settings to the same file.

6 ▶ **Creating Budgets and Using a Worksheet Template**

Exercise 6.4

Creating a Worksheet Template

Objective

After completing this exercise, you will be able to
- Create a worksheet template.

In Lessons 1 through 5 you created and used worksheets to analyze monthly sales. You also learned to create worksheets that let you change assumptions to solve problems. In some cases, you may want to use these worksheets again to analyze new sets of data or solve similar problems. In fact, it is a good idea to design worksheets so they can be used again. That way, you do not have to spend valuable time recreating complex formulas for new worksheets. For example, the budget you created in this lesson can be used year after year. The easiest way to design "reusable" worksheets is to create worksheet templates.

TEMPLATE
A worksheet with a specific structure that is set up so that many similar worksheets can be created from it. Template worksheets contain labels and formulas, but no values. To create other worksheets, the template is retrieved, modified, and saved under a different filename.

A *template* is a worksheet that contains the basic structure for a particular type of worksheet (for example, budgets). It includes labels and formulas, but no values. The values are provided by you or any other user who uses the template to create a worksheet. As data is entered into the template, the pre-existing formulas and/or @functions in the template calculate the results. After entering data, you can save the template file under a new name. This creates a worksheet file that was built from the template, while the template file remains unchanged.

One advantage of worksheet templates is that you can use them again and again. Another reason for creating templates is to give other users a structure that is already set up. Other users can create a consistent-looking document without having to build formulas and create the worksheet from scratch.

The owner of Mollie's Music Shoppe is impressed with the budget you have put together for the current fiscal year. With a few modifications, she wants you to save the budget's structure as a template. The template can then be used by other employees to create budgets for other fiscal years. To begin, you will make sure that you have saved the current file, BUDGET95.WK1. Then you will modify it, erase the 1995 values, and save the worksheet as a budget template.

1 ▶ Press HOME, and save the current version of BUDGET95.WK1.

2 ▶ Move the cell pointer to cell A2.

3 ▶ In EDIT mode, change the label to read "Fiscal Budget."

4 ▶ Delete rows 4 and 5.

5 ▶ Move the cell pointer to cell B7.

   The cell pointer is on the cell that contains the actual total sales for the first quarter.

6 ▶ Press [F4].

   Lotus 1-2-3 prompts you to enter a range.

7 ▶ Press [↓].

8 ▶ Press [→] 7 times.

   The range B7..I8 is highlighted.

9 ▶ Press [↵].

   The range is highlighted in the worksheet area.

10 ▶ Press the Slash key (/) to access the Main Menu.

11 ▶ Type **RE** to select the Range and Erase commands.

   The range of income values are erased. Notice that the cost-control formulas display "ERR."

12 ▶ Move the cell pointer to any cell in column D.

13 ▶ Press the Slash key (/) to access the Main Menu.

14 ▶ Type **WDC** to select the Worksheet, Delete, and Column commands.

15 ▶ Press [↵].

   The old column D containing the vertical line is deleted.

16 ▶ Move the cell pointer to cell B13.

   The cell pointer is on the cell that contains the lease expense for the first quarter.

17 ▶ Press [F4].

   Lotus 1-2-3 prompts you to enter a range.

18 ▶ Press [↓] 5 times.

19 ▶ Press [↵].

   The range B13..B18 is highlighted in the worksheet area.

20 ▶ Press the Slash key (/) to access the Main Menu.

21 ▶ Type **RE** to select the Range and Erase commands.

   The first-quarter expense values are erased.

22 ▶ Move the cell pointer to cell D13, and repeat steps 17–21 to erase the range of expense values for the second quarter.

23 ▶ Perform similar procedures to erase the range of expense values for quarters 3 and 4.

24 ▶ Press HOME, and save the worksheet as BDGTMPLT.WK1.

You have completed the budget template, as shown in Figure 6.8.

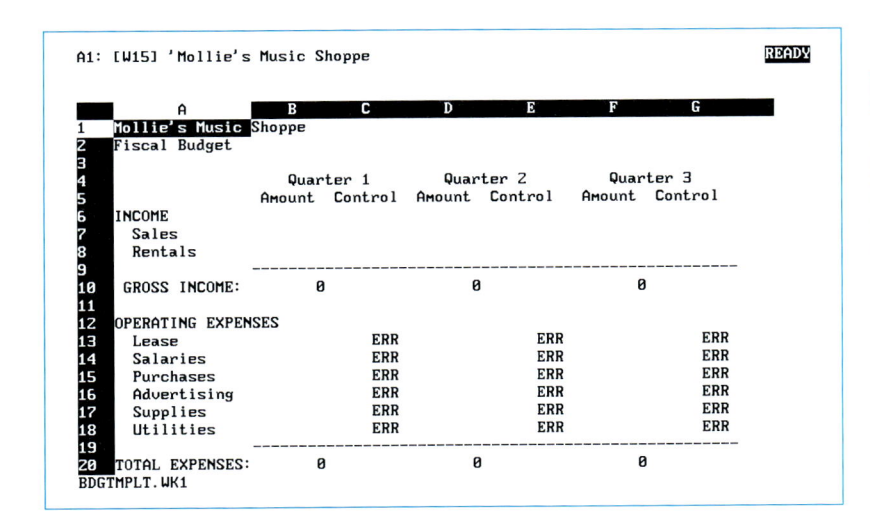

```
A1: [W15] 'Mollie's Music Shoppe                                    READY
         A          B        C        D        E        F        G
 1  Mollie's Music Shoppe
 2  Fiscal Budget
 3
 4                    Quarter 1         Quarter 2         Quarter 3
 5                  Amount  Control   Amount  Control   Amount  Control
 6  INCOME
 7    Sales
 8    Rentals
 9                  -------           -------           -------
10  GROSS INCOME:       0                 0                 0
11
12  OPERATING EXPENSES
13    Lease                  ERR               ERR               ERR
14    Salaries               ERR               ERR               ERR
15    Purchases              ERR               ERR               ERR
16    Advertising            ERR               ERR               ERR
17    Supplies               ERR               ERR               ERR
18    Utilities              ERR               ERR               ERR
19                  -------           -------           -------
20  TOTAL EXPENSES:     0                 0                 0
BDGTMPLT.WK1
```

Figure 6.8

After you modify the budget worksheet into a template structure, your screen should look like this.

Exercise 6.5

Protecting a Worksheet

After completing this exercise, you will be able to
- Protect worksheets.

Objective

You have spent a lot of time building the budget worksheet and template. Now you want to be sure the formulas and @functions will not be changed by another user. Fortunately, 1-2-3 lets you protect cells in a worksheet. This will keep important formulas, @functions, or data from being deleted by mistake.

The best way to protect a worksheet is to use the /Worksheet Global Protection command (/WGP) to protect the entire worksheet. Then use the /Range Unprotect command (/RU) to remove the protection from those ranges into which another user will enter data. This guarantees that another

Protecting a Worksheet

user can only enter or edit data in specific cells. Any important formulas, @functions, or data will not be changed.

Now you will globally protect the BDGTMPLT.WK1 worksheet. Then you will remove the protection from those cells that you want another user to access for data entry.

1 ▶ Make sure the file BDGTMPLT.WK1 is currently loaded.

2 ▶ Press the Slash key (/) to access the Main Menu.

3 ▶ Type **WG** to select the Worksheet and Global commands.

4 ▶ Type **P** to select the Protection command.

Lotus 1-2-3 prompts you to enable or disable the global worksheet protection feature.

5 ▶ Type **E** to select the Enable command.

Protection for the entire worksheet has been enabled. Notice the PR code on the control panel. This indicates that the current cell is protected. Right now, every cell in the worksheet is protected. To test the protection feature, try entering data into a cell.

6 ▶ Type **label**

7 ▶ Press ⏎.

Your system beeps and displays an ERROR message text box. The message tells you that the cell is protected. You cannot enter data into a protected cell.

8 ▶ Press ESC.

Lotus 1-2-3 returns to READY mode.

Now you will remove the protection status from the ranges that will contain income and expense data.

9 ▶ Move the cell pointer to cell B7.

This cell is where a user would enter an income projection value for the first quarter.

10 ▶ Press F4.

Lotus 1-2-3 prompts you to enter a range.

11 ▶ Press ↓ once.

12 ▶ Press → 7 times.

13 ▶ Press ⏎.

The range B7..I8 is highlighted in the worksheet area.

14 ▶ Press the Slash key (/) to access the Main Menu.

190   **6 ▶ Creating Budgets and Using a Worksheet Template**

15 ▶ Type **RU** to select the Range and Unprotect commands.

   The range where income information can be entered is unprotected.

Now you will try entering a value in the current cell.

16 ▶ Type **2500**

17 ▶ Press ⏎.

   The value is entered because the cell is no longer protected. Notice that the @SUM function in cell B10 calculates a total.

18 ▶ Press DEL to erase the value in cell B7.

Now you will unprotect the range where estimated first-quarter expense amounts can be entered.

19 ▶ Move the cell pointer to cell B13.

20 ▶ Press F4.

21 ▶ Press ↓ 5 times.

22 ▶ Press ⏎.

   The selected range is highlighted in the worksheet area.

23 ▶ Press the Slash key (/) to access the Main Menu.

24 ▶ Type **RU** to select the Range and Unprotect commands.

   The range for estimated first-quarter expenses is no longer protected.

25 ▶ Move the cell pointer to cell D13, and repeat steps 20–25 to unprotect the range for estimated second-quarter expenses.

26 ▶ On your own, unprotect the ranges F13..F18 and H13..H18.

27 ▶ Press HOME, and save the current changes to BDGTMPLT.WK1.

You have protected all of the cells in the worksheet and then disabled that protection for selected ranges. Now other users can create budget worksheets without disturbing any of the formulas and @SUM functions. To complete this lesson, you will retrieve the budget you created for fiscal year 1995 and password-protect that worksheet so that only you and the owner can access the file.

Protecting a Worksheet   **191**

Exercise 6.6

Protecting Worksheets with Passwords

Objective

After completing this exercise, you will be able to
- Password-protect worksheets.

PASSWORD
A reference or name of up to 15 characters that you assign to a file. A 1-2-3 password is case sensitive, and it protects the file from being retrieved by anyone who does not know the password.

As a security measure, the owner asks you to assign the *password* "*FY95BUDGET*" to the budget worksheet you created. Only you and she will be able to access this file.

You can assign a password to a worksheet file when you use the /File Save command (/FS) to save the file. When 1-2-3 prompts you to enter the filename, type the name (if necessary). Then type a space and the letter "P." When you press ⏎, 1-2-3 prompts you to enter the password. A password can be any text up to 15 characters. As you type the password, 1-2-3 displays only little highlighted boxes (■) on the control panel. These boxes represent each character you type. This is so that nobody can look over your shoulder and see the password as you type it.

1 ▶ Make sure you have saved the budget template file BDGTMPLT.WK1.

2 ▶ Retrieve the file BUDGET95.WK1.

3 ▶ Press the Slash key (/) to access the Main Menu.

4 ▶ Type **FS** to select the File and Save commands.

   Lotus 1-2-3 prompts you to enter the filename. The current filename BUDGET95.WK1 is displayed to the right of the prompt.

5 ▶ Press **SPACEBAR**.

6 ▶ Type **p**

7 ▶ Press ⏎.

   Lotus 1-2-3 prompts you to enter a password.

8 ▶ Press CAPS LOCK.

   Uppercase status mode is turned on.

9 ▶ Type ***FY95BUDGET***

   As you type the password, highlighted boxes appear, as shown in Figure 6.9.

192   6 ▶ Creating Budgets and Using a Worksheet Template

Figure 6.9

As you type a password, 1-2-3 displays highlighted boxes, representing the characters you type, on the control panel.

Boxes represent typed password characters

```
A1: [W15] 'Mollie's Music Shoppe                                    EDIT
Enter password: ▪▪▪▪▪▪▪▪▪▪▪▪▪
          A        B         C      D       E         F       G          H
  1  Mollie's Music Shoppe
  2  Fiscal 1995 Budget
  3
  4                   |----- ACTUAL ---  | ======= PROJECTED ==============>
  5
  6                       Quarter 1         Quarter 2          Quarter 3
  7                     Amount  Control   Amount  Control    Amount  Control
  8  INCOME
  9    Sales           40,081             65,000             48,000
 10    Rentals          3,259              4,750              3,500
 11                   ----------------------------------------------------
 12  GROSS INCOME:     43,340             69,750             51,500
 13
 14  OPERATING EXPENSES
 15    Lease            5,850   13.5%  |   5,850    8.4%      5,850   11.4%
 16    Salaries         6,855   15.8%  |  11,000   15.8%      8,000   15.5%
 17    Purchases       15,668   36.2%  |  26,500   38.0%     18,500   35.9%
 18    Advertising      1,012    2.3%  |   2,925    4.2%      1,344    2.6%
 19    Supplies           728    1.7%  |   1,100    1.6%        850    1.7%
 20    Utilities        2,094    4.8%  |   2,500    3.6%      2,200    4.3%
BUDGET95.WK1
```

Note: The asterisks are included in the password to reduce the chances of someone guessing the password. They are not necessary.

10 ▶ Press ⏎.

Lotus 1-2-3 prompts you to enter the password again to verify that it is the password you meant to enter.

11 ▶ Type ***FY95BUDGET***

12 ▶ Press ⏎.

The Save command submenu of options is displayed on the control panel.

Note: If an ERROR message text box appears because the passwords do not match, go back to step 3. Do the save operation again to re-enter the password.

13 ▶ Type **R** to select the Replace command.

The existing file is updated with the current changes and is now password protected.

The next time you retrieve this file, 1-2-3 will ask you for the password. You must not forget the password; if you do, you will be unable to retrieve the worksheet. You might want to write down your passwords, and keep them in a safe place. Now, you will erase the screen and retrieve the password-protected budget worksheet to test the password.

14 ▶ Erase the current worksheet.

Protecting Worksheets with Passwords

15 ▶ Press the Slash key (/) to access the Main Menu.

16 ▶ Type **FR** to select the File and Retrieve commands.

17 ▶ Press F3.

A list of the filenames in the current directory are displayed.

18 ▶ Move the pointer to the filename BUDGET95.WK1.

19 ▶ Press ⏎.

Lotus 1-2-3 prompts you to enter the password, as shown in Figure 6.10.

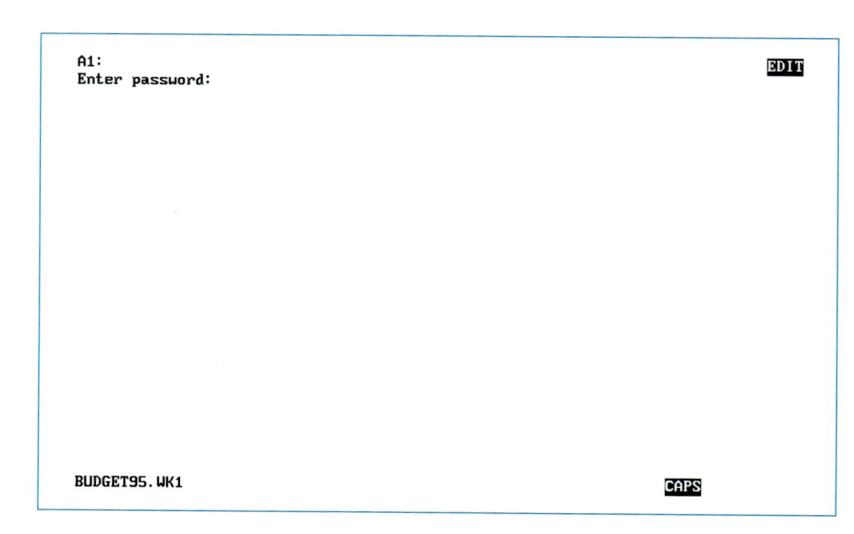

```
A1:
Enter password:                                         EDIT




















BUDGET95.WK1                                            CAPS
```

Figure 6.10

When you try to retrieve a password-protected file, 1-2-3 prompts you to enter the password. You must remember the passwords to your password-protected files, or else you will not be able to retrieve them.

20 ▶ Type ***FY95BUDGET***

Highlighted boxes representing the characters you have typed are displayed on the control panel.

21 ▶ Press ⏎.

The password-protected file BUDGET95.WK1 is displayed.

22 ▶ Press CAPS LOCK.

Uppercase status mode is turned off.

23 ▶ Erase the worksheet.

Note: Lotus 1-2-3 passwords are case sensitive. You would not have been able to retrieve the worksheet if you had typed "*fy95budget*" or "*Fy95Budget*."

You can now begin the Lesson 6 applications that follow the Concept Summary, or you can go on to Lesson 7. Otherwise, quit 1-2-3 if you are through with this session.

6 ▶ Creating Budgets and Using a Worksheet Template

Concept Summary

- Newer versions of spreadsheet software let you dynamically link two worksheet files. Generally, this is done by entering a special formula into the current worksheet. The formula brings in a value or formula result from a worksheet file stored on disk.

- When files are linked, the file stored on disk is called a source file. The file that contains the linking formula is called the target file. The target file receives the data from the source file. If a change is made to the linked data in the source file, the data is updated in the target file automatically. The update to the target file occurs the next time it is retrieved.

- In addition to relative and absolute cell references, you can use mixed cell references in formulas or functions. In a mixed cell reference, either the column letter or row number is absolute, while the other remains relative.

- Most spreadsheet software contains logical functions that test whether a condition in a worksheet is true or false. A widely used logical function in 1-2-3 is the @IF function.

- The @IF function displays either of two options, depending on whether a condition is true or false. If the condition is true, the function returns a value, formula result, or text string as one option; if the condition is false, the function returns a value, formula result, or text string as the second option.

- A worksheet template is a structure or framework from which other similar worksheets can be created. A template contains labels and formulas, so that another user only needs to enter values to build a new worksheet.

- Ranges or entire worksheets can be protected so that their contents cannot be altered. This feature keeps complex formulas from being deleted by mistake.

- Worksheet files can be password protected so that only certain users can have access to the files.

Command Summary

ABS command (F4)
changes an absolute cell reference to a mixed cell reference or a relative cell reference

/Worksheet Global Protection (/WGP)
protects all cells in a worksheet so data cannot be changed

/Range Unprotect (/RU)
disables protection status in a range so that data can be changed

Applications

Begin doing the applications by loading 1-2-3, if necessary. Place your student data disk in drive A (or drive B if you do not have a hard disk). Change the current directory to the drive that contains the student data disk. Also, change the Clock setting in the Global Settings dialog box so that the current filename is displayed on the status line.

Business

Sales Analysis

1. Before the company sends the sales comparison worksheet to branch managers, the president wants the branches with slumping sales to submit financial reports to the headquarter office. Also, the worksheet is to be password protected, so that only those who know the password will have access to the file. Begin by retrieving the file SALSCMP6.WK1. This worksheet is much like the one you used in Lessons 1–5. Do the following steps to prepare the worksheet for the branch managers. When completed, your worksheet should look like Figure 6.11.

Figure 6.11

Follow the instructions in application 1 (Sales Analysis) to modify this worksheet.

a. Insert a new column A, and decrease its width to 3 characters.
b. Enter a right-aligned label composed of three asterisks (***) in cell C4.
c. Enter the label that begins in cell D4, as shown in Figure 6.11.
d. Enter the following @IF function in cell A9:

   @IF($G9<0,$C$4," ")

This @IF function tests whether the change in sales value in cell G9 is less than 0. If the condition is true, the label in cell C4 will be entered in cell A9; if the condition is false, cell A9 will appear blank.

196 **6 ▶ Creating Budgets and Using a Worksheet Template**

Note: To make a cell appear blank, the second option in the @IF function's argument is a space character entered as a text string. Text strings are enclosed in quotation marks ("). To enter this text string correctly, type a quotation mark, press SPACEBAR, and type another quotation mark.

    e. Copy the @IF function in cell A9 down the column. Asterisks will appear next to the branches whose sales dropped between 1994 and 1995.

    f. Copy the @IF function in cell A9 to the range I9..I17. Because of the mixed and absolute cell references in the @IF function, the same results occur.

    g. Save the file as SALES6.WK1 with a password. Use any password you want that is 15 characters or fewer. Do not forget the password.

    h. (optional) Modify the worksheet by editing years out of labels, erasing values, and changing any formatting you desire. Save the file under a new name to create a template file for the branch sales comparison.

    i. Erase the worksheet, retrieve the file to test the password, and then erase the worksheet again.

Business

Small Business

2. In continuing with your class assignment, you have been given three separate worksheet files that calculate gross sales for each office. These are gross sales for the first six months of the year. You want to consolidate the gross sales reports into one worksheet that will calculate how much the company grossed in sales. In addition, you want to see by how much money the company's sales were under the $1 million mark. To create this worksheet, perform the tasks outlined in the following steps:

    a. Retrieve and briefly look over the following three worksheet files: WWCSD.WK1, WWCLA.WK1, and WWCSF.WK1. Take note of which cells contain the total units sold and the gross sales totals. Because the worksheets were created from a template, the total amounts appear in the same cells in each worksheet.

    b. Retrieve the file WWCSMMRY.WK1. You will use this template to create your consolidated summary worksheet. Notice that the worksheet is protected except for certain cell ranges.

    c. Enter a linking formula in cell B7 that enters the total units sold from the file WWCSD.WK1.

    d. Copy the linking formula down the column for the Los Angeles and San Francisco offices. Edit the filenames in each formula so they link with the appropriate files.

    e. Copy the linking formulas in column B to column D, and then edit each formula so that they link to the cells in the other files that contain total gross sales (cell E15).

HINT

c. Make the cell reference absolute so you can type the formula once and then copy it to other cells.

f. Calculate the percentage of sales for the San Diego office by dividing the office's six-month gross sales by the total gross sales. Because you will copy this formula to column G, change the cell reference for the company's total gross sales to a mixed reference that keeps the row absolute.

g. Copy the formula down the column, and then copy it to column G. The copied formulas in column G will display "ERR" until you enter values in column F.

h. To figure out how much money each office is short of their contribution to the total of $1 million in gross sales, enter the following @IF function in cell F7:

@IF(D11>1000000,0,E7*(1000000-D11))

This @function enters a zero in the current cell if the total gross sales value is over $1 million. Otherwise, it multiplies each office's percentage of sales times $1 million less total gross sales.

i. Copy the @IF function to cells F8 and F9. After you copy the @functions, your worksheet should look like Figure 6.12.

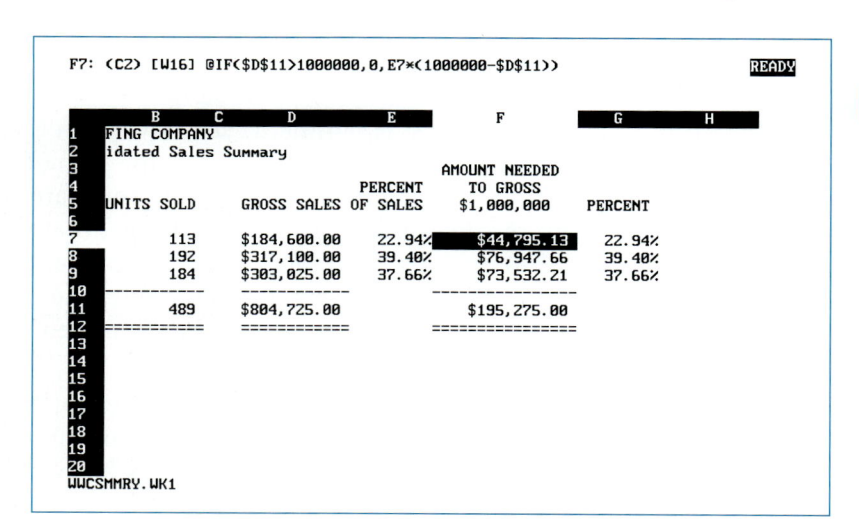

Figure 6.12

After you perform the steps in application 2 (Small Business), your worksheet should look similar to this.

j. Save the file as PROFIT6.WK1, and assign a password to the file as you do. The password can be any text you choose.

k. Retrieve the file WWCLA.WK1, change the number of units sold in June to 46, and save the changes to the file. Then, retrieve the file WWCSF.WK1, change the number of units sold in March to 25, and save the changes to the file.

l. Retrieve the file PROFIT6.WK1. Be sure to use your password. Notice that the linked data is updated in the file. What effect did the changes have on total gross sales?

m. Save the changes to PROFIT6.WK1, and then erase the worksheet.

Business

Accounting

3. Now that you have completed the company's income statement, you will return to your general worksheet. In the general worksheet, you will link various results from an income statement file similar to the one you prepared in Lesson 5. The results will be linked to the appropriate debit and credit columns in the worksheet's income statement columns. After you complete your entries across all worksheet columns, the debit and credit columns for your trial balance, adjusted trial balance, income statement, and balance sheet portions should all balance. Begin by retrieving the file INCSTMNT.WK1, and note the following results:

   net sales in cell E11

   beginning inventory in cell C15 and ending inventory in cell D24

   net cost of purchases in cell C20

   net income in cell F43

   After reviewing the INCSTMNT.WK1 worksheet, retrieve the file WORKSHT6.WK1. Do the following steps:

   a. Enter a linking formula in cell C12 that links the beginning inventory from INCSTMNT.WK1. Make the cell reference absolute so you can copy the formula to the debit columns in the adjusted trial balance and income statement parts of the worksheet.

   b. Enter a linking formula in cell Q12 that links the ending inventory from INCSTMNT.WK1. Make the cell reference absolute. Because this amount must be posted as a debit in the balance sheet, copy the linking formula to cell S12.

   c. Enter a linking formula in cell E23 that links net sales from INCSTMNT.WK1. Copy it to columns M and Q to post net sales as credits to the adjusted trial balance and income statement.

   d. Enter a linking formula in cell C24 that links net cost of purchases from INCSTMNT.WK1. Copy it to columns K and O to post the net cost of purchases as debits to the adjusted trial balance and income statement.

   e. Enter @SUM functions in row 39 to total the debit and credit columns for the income statement and balance sheet. Do the debit and credit columns balance in the income statement and balance sheet portions of the worksheet?

   f. To balance the income statement and balance sheet for this worksheet, you need to make two more entries. You need to debit the net income calculated in the file INCSTMNT.WK1 to the income statement. You also need to credit the net income to the balance sheet. Do this by entering linking formulas in cells O40 and U40. Now do the debits and credits balance?

   g. Press HOME, and save the file as BALANCE6.WK1 with a password of your choice.

   h. Print the entire range of data, and then save the print settings to the same file.

   i. Erase the worksheet.

Social Studies

Student Survey

4. As chair of the Student Activities Committee, you decide to identify those activities or facilities that received fewer than 25 percent "Excellent" ratings. You want to focus on them to improve school spirit. Retrieve the file SURVEY5.WK1, and do the following steps. After you modify the worksheet, the upper-left corner of your worksheet should look like Figure 6.13.

```
A1: [W20]                                                    READY

              A              B        C       D       E        F
 1                       Excellent Rating Standard   15.0%
 2
 3                         Rating  Variance Excellent Percent  Good
 4   SPORTS
 5   Varsity Football      GOOD     13.6%    232     28.64%    314
 6   Varsity Baseball      GOOD     12.3%    205     27.26%    363
 7   Varsity Basketball    IMPROVE  -6.2%     67      8.82%    248
 8   Sophomore Water Polo  IMPROVE  -8.8%     42      6.21%    262
 9
10   FACILITIES
11   Cafeteria             IMPROVE  -7.3%     56      7.67%    114
12   Library               GOOD      9.4%    179     24.39%    183
13   Gym                   GOOD     13.8%    201     28.80%    245
14
15   EVENTS
16   Prom Dance            GOOD      6.5%    156     21.52%    279
17   Sadie Hawkins Dance   IMPROVE  -3.0%     78     12.00%    168
18   Homecoming            GOOD      2.6%    132     17.60%    285
19   Can Drive             GOOD     13.7%    192     28.66%    159
20   Car Wash              GOOD      6.0%    127     20.99%    201
SURVEY6.WK1
```

Figure 6.13

Follow the instructions in application 4 (Student Survey) to modify the worksheet as shown.

a. Insert two columns between columns A and B.

b. Enter the labels "Rating" and "Variance," as shown in Figure 6.13.

c. Enter your initial assumption by first entering the label "Excellent Rating Standard" in cell B1 and the value 25% in cell E1. Format the value as a percentage with one decimal place.

d. Enter a formula in cell C5 that subtracts the rating standard percentage in cell E1 from the percentage of excellent responses for varsity football. Be sure to use an absolute cell reference for the rating standard percentage. Then this constant will be referenced in all the copied formulas.

e. Copy the formula down column C to produce variance results for each of the other activities. This will show how close each activity comes to a 25 percent approval. Format the results as percents with one decimal place.

f. Enter the following @IF function in cell B5:

@IF(E5>E1,"GOOD","IMPROVE")

This @IF function will test whether the percentages of excellent responses for each activity are greater than the rating standard percentage. If they are greater, the label "GOOD" will appear in the rating column. Otherwise, the label "IMPROVE" will appear.

> Note: The result options for this @IF function are text strings. Be sure to enter the quotation marks as shown so that the @IF function will display a label rather than a value.

200 6 ▶ Creating Budgets and Using a Worksheet Template

g. Copy the @IF function down column B to produce new formulas for each activity or facility. The results of this function show you that eight activities or facilities need improvement.

h. You decide to lower your standards and see how many activities or facilities have less than a 20 percent "Excellent" response rating. Change the rating standard to 20 percent. After recalculation, the worksheet shows that five areas need improvement. Then try 15 percent. After recalculation, the worksheet shows that four areas need improvement.

i. Press HOME, and save the worksheet as SURVEY6.WK1 with a password of your choice. Try to retrieve the password-protected file, and then erase the worksheet.

Social Studies

Geography

5. Continue working with your worksheet that helps you analyze world population for your geography class. Retrieve the file WRLDPOP5.WK1. Insert columns as shown in Figure 6.14. These columns let you enter formulas that calculate percentages of total land area and estimated population for each continent.

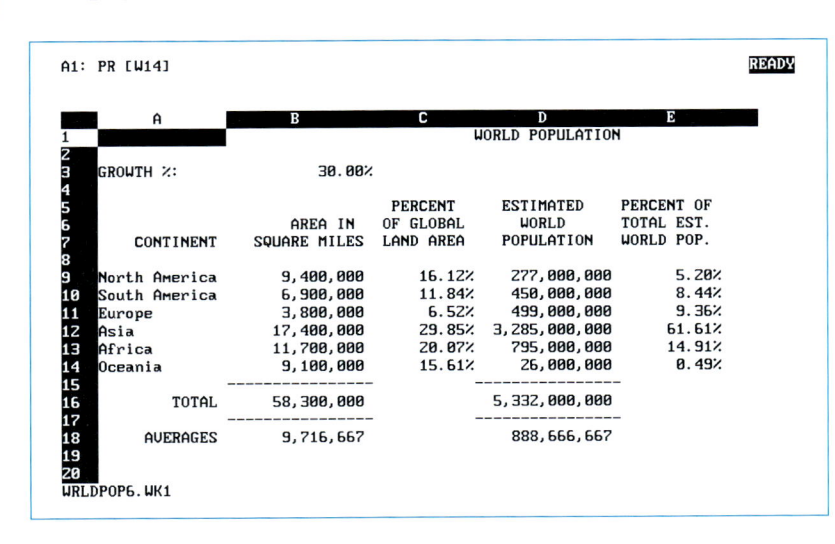

Figure 6.14

After you complete the instructions in application 5 (Geography), your worksheet should look like this.

```
A1: PR [W14]                                                          READY

           A              B             C             D             E
  1                                           WORLD POPULATION
  2
  3  GROWTH %:                     30.00%
  4
  5                              PERCENT     ESTIMATED     PERCENT OF
  6                    AREA IN   OF GLOBAL     WORLD       TOTAL EST.
  7     CONTINENT   SQUARE MILES LAND AREA   POPULATION    WORLD POP.
  8
  9  North America    9,400,000    16.12%    277,000,000      5.20%
 10  South America    6,900,000    11.84%    450,000,000      8.44%
 11  Europe           3,800,000     6.52%    499,000,000      9.36%
 12  Asia            17,400,000    29.85%  3,285,000,000     61.61%
 13  Africa          11,700,000    20.07%    795,000,000     14.91%
 14  Oceania          9,100,000    15.61%     26,000,000      0.49%
 15                  ----------                  ----------
 16       TOTAL      58,300,000              5,332,000,000
 17                  ----------                  ----------
 18      AVERAGES     9,716,667                888,666,667
 19
 20
WRLDPOP6.WK1
```

Enter labels and modify the other labels as shown in the figure. The formula that calculates a percentage of total land area for each continent will contain a mixed cell reference. The mixed cell reference refers to the total, so you can copy the formula to the appropriate ranges. After completing the formulas, protect the entire worksheet and then unprotect cell B3 and the range D9..D14. Save the worksheet as WRLDPOP6.WK1 with a password of your choice. Erase the worksheet.

Applications

Social Studies

American Government

6. You want to create a template out of the election analysis worksheet that can be used for the results of the upcoming presidential election. Retrieve the file ELECTN5.WK1, and add a section for the new election. The new section will include the appropriate year and the candidates' names, if you know who they are. Otherwise, leave the candidates' cells blank. Be sure to copy the formulas that calculate vote percentages. Protect the entire entire worksheet, and then unprotect the ranges that will store numbers of votes. Save the file as ELECTN6.WK1, and give it a password. Retrieve the file to check your password, and then erase the worksheet. If you want more practice, try creating a summary worksheet that just shows the vote percentages for each candidate in each election year. Link the worksheets by entering linking formulas to enter the percentages from ELECTN6.WK1 into the summary worksheet. Save the file with any filename you want.

HINT
Use the /Copy command.

Science/Mathematics

Astronomy

7. Retrieve the file PLANETS5.WK1, and enter and copy two @IF functions. The first @IF function will be entered and copied down column I for each planet. It will test whether each rotation result in column H is less than 1. If the value is less than 1, the @IF function will enter the product of the value in column H multiplied by 365 to express the rotation in number of days. Otherwise, it will enter the value in column H to express the value in years. The @IF function you enter in column J will perform the same test on the column H value. If the value is less than 1, the @IF function will enter the label "DAYS"; otherwise, it will enter the label "YEARS". Format the column I results as fixed values with two decimal places. Save the worksheet as PLANETS6.WK1, and erase the worksheet.

Science/Mathematics

Mathematics

8. Now that you have learned how to use mixed cell references, put your knowledge to work by creating a multiplication table for a quick reference to the product of any two numbers between 0 and 50.

   a. Start with a blank worksheet. Enter consecutive integers (0, 1, 2, 3, and so on) up to 50 (or more if you like) down column A in each cell, starting in row 4. Then do the same in row 3, consecutively entering an integer in each column, starting with column B.

   b. Change the worksheet's global column width to 5 characters.

   c. Enter the product formula in cell B4 by multiplying the first integer in row 3 (0) by the first integer in column A (0).

   d. Use mixed cell references for each cell so that column A is absolute in the first reference and row 3 is absolute in the second.

   e. Copy the formula to every cell in the table.

   f. Protect the entire worksheet, save it as MATH6.WK1, and erase the worksheet.

Health

Nutrition

9. The FDA suggests that your total daily fat intake should not exceed 30 percent of your total daily intake of all nutrients. Retrieve the file NUTRINF5.WK1. Now you are ready to check to see if this particular daily diet exceeds this percentage. After you do, you will edit the worksheet and protect certain ranges to save it as a template, as outlined in the following steps:

   a. Enter an @IF function in cell C43 that tests whether the total grams of fat divided by the total daily nutrient grams in cell G36 are less than or equal to 30 percent. If the fat intake is less than or equal to 30 percent, the @IF function enters the label "MEETS FDA RECOMMENDATION". If the fat intake is over 30 percent, it enters the label "EXCEEDS FDA RECOMMENDATION".

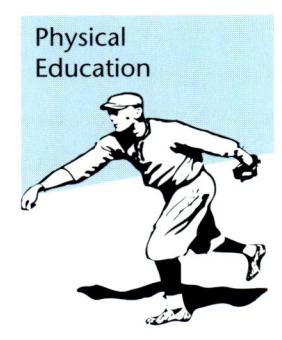

   HINT
   Make the condition in the @IF function a formula that sums the grams of fat for breakfast, lunch, and dinner, and then divides the result by the total nutrient grams.

   b. For presentation purposes, enter a formula in cell B3 that calculates the percentage of daily fat intake in grams to total grams of nutrient intake. Format the cell as a percentage with two decimal places. Enter the right-aligned label "Fat:" in cell A43.

   c. If you want to test the accuracy of the @IF function, increase the grams of fat for any one food item by a large amount. Did the label in cell C43 change?

   d. Press (HOME), and save the worksheet as NUTRINF6.WK1.

   e. Protect the entire worksheet, and then unprotect and erase only the ranges that contain the nutrient gram values for each food item. Do not unprotect and erase any ranges with formulas. Then unprotect and erase the range of food items in column B.

   f. Press (HOME), and save the template as NUTRTMPL.WK1. Erase the worksheet.

Health

Physical Education

10. The softball team won their next game 15–10. The team's game batting scores follow. Retrieve the file SBGAME5.WK1, and add the new scores to the addition formulas in each cell, which combine all the game's scores. Then do the following steps:

Player	At Bats	Runs	Hits	Doubles	Triples	HRs	RBIs
Bernhart	7	2	4	1	0	0	4
Taylor	7	1	2	0	0	0	0
Hepburn	7	0	2	0	0	0	1
Monroe	6	1	2	0	0	0	1
d'Arc	6	2	3	0	0	2	2
Victoria	6	1	2	0	0	0	1
Wood	5	1	3	0	0	1	1
Smith	5	1	2	0	0	0	1

continued

Player	At Bats	Runs	Hits	Doubles	Triples	HRs	RBIs
Turner	0	0	0	0	0	0	0
Welch	1	0	0	0	0	0	0
Loren	4	3	3	1	1	0	4
Mabely	4	2	2	1	0	0	0
Braga	4	1	0	0	0	0	0

a. After entering the scores from the recent game, what is the team's current batting average? Its slugging percentage? Who has the best batting average after six games? Who has the worst?

b. The coach tells you he wants to give some extra batting practice to those players who have batting averages under .333. Enter an @IF function in cell L7 that tests whether Bernhart's batting average is less than .333. If it is, the @IF function will enter the label "EXTRA BP". Otherwise, it will enter a space (leave the cell empty). Copy the @IF function down the column. Which players will have to do extra batting practice?

c. Press (HOME), and save the worksheet as SBGAME6.WK1.

d. Make the worksheet a batting score template by protecting the entire worksheet and then unprotecting and erasing the range of scores in columns C through I for each player.

e. Press (HOME), and save the worksheet as BATTMPLT.WK1. Erase the worksheet.

7 Advanced Printing Features

Objectives

- Adjust margin settings.
- Set print borders.
- Print a header at the top of each page.
- Print a footer at the bottom of each page.
- Hide columns of data before printing.
- Enter a setup string that contains a printer control code.
- Print a range of data in condensed print.
- Print cell formulas.

Up to this point you have produced hard copies of worksheet data by selecting print ranges and then printing them. However, you have had limited control over the appearance of the printed document. In this lesson, you will learn to use 1-2-3 print settings to control the way printed data ranges look.

Exercise 7.1 — Adjusting Margins

Objective

After completing this exercise, you will be able to
- Adjust margin settings.

When you print a range of worksheet data using the /Print Printer command (/PP), 1-2-3 uses specific settings, called *default print settings*. These are already set when you install the software. However, as you work with data ranges of different sizes, you often need to adjust these print settings. You adjust these settings to make the printed data both presentable and understandable.

MARGIN
The area of blank space along the edges of a page that borders the printed data.

You may have already noticed that 1-2-3 fits as many columns of data between the margins as it can. *Margins* are the borders of empty space between printed data and the page edges. Any extra columns are printed on the next page or pages. The number of columns that fit on a page varies, depending on the width of the columns and current margin settings. The default margin settings are as follows:

left margin	=	4 characters from left paper edge
right margin	=	76 characters from left paper edge
top margin	=	2 lines from the top paper edge
bottom margin	=	2 lines from the bottom paper edge

To determine the number of columns that 1-2-3 can print across a page, you must calculate the number of characters that fit between the left and right margins. Most popular dot-matrix printers print 80 characters (12-point Courier) across the width of a page. Figure 7.1 shows you how the default margin settings affect the number of columns that print across an 80-character–wide page. The number of characters that can fit between the left and right margins is equal to the full page width (80) minus the sum of the left and right margins (8, by default). The calculation for the default margin settings is as follows:

$$80-(4+(80-76))=72$$

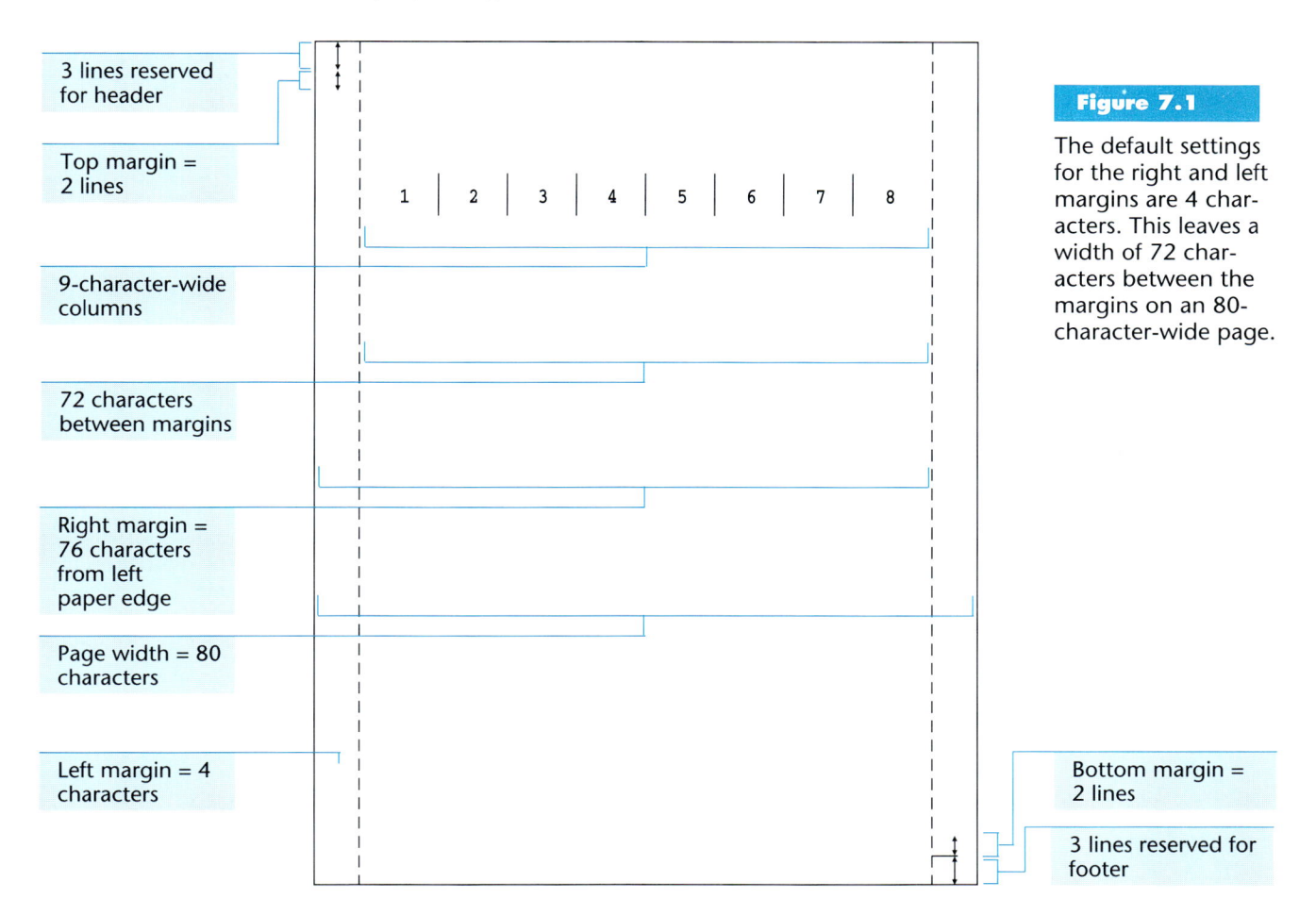

Figure 7.1

The default settings for the right and left margins are 4 characters. This leaves a width of 72 characters between the margins on an 80-character-wide page.

- 3 lines reserved for header
- Top margin = 2 lines
- 9-character-wide columns
- 72 characters between margins
- Right margin = 76 characters from left paper edge
- Page width = 80 characters
- Left margin = 4 characters
- Bottom margin = 2 lines
- 3 lines reserved for footer

Recall that columns are 9 characters wide by default. If you divide the number of characters that fit between margins (72) by the default column width (9), you get 8 columns. This means that 1-2-3 prints 8 columns between the left and right margins if the margin settings and column widths are all set at their default settings. Obviously, if you increase column widths or increase the width of margins, 1-2-3 will print fewer columns across the page. If you decrease the settings, 1-2-3 will print more columns across the page.

In this exercise, you will retrieve a budget worksheet that is very similar to the one you created in Lesson 6. This worksheet is too wide to fit all the columns of data on one page. Therefore, you will begin adjusting print settings by changing the left and right margins.

1. ▶ If necessary, start 1-2-3. Change the current directory to the drive that contains the student data disk. Change the Clock setting so that the current filename will be displayed on the status line.

Adjusting Margins 207

2 ▶ Retrieve the file PRNTBDGT.WK1.

A budget worksheet appears. This budget is very similar to the worksheet you created in Lesson 6.

3 ▶ Take a moment to scroll through the worksheet to see how it is set up.

The budget shows projected revenue and expenses for each quarter in fiscal year 1995.

4 ▶ Press HOME after scrolling around the worksheet.

5 ▶ Press the Slash key (/) to access the Main Menu.

6 ▶ Type **PP** to select the Print and Printer commands.

The Print Settings dialog box appears, as shown in Figure 7.2. Notice that the default margin settings are displayed in the dialog box and that a print range has not yet been specified.

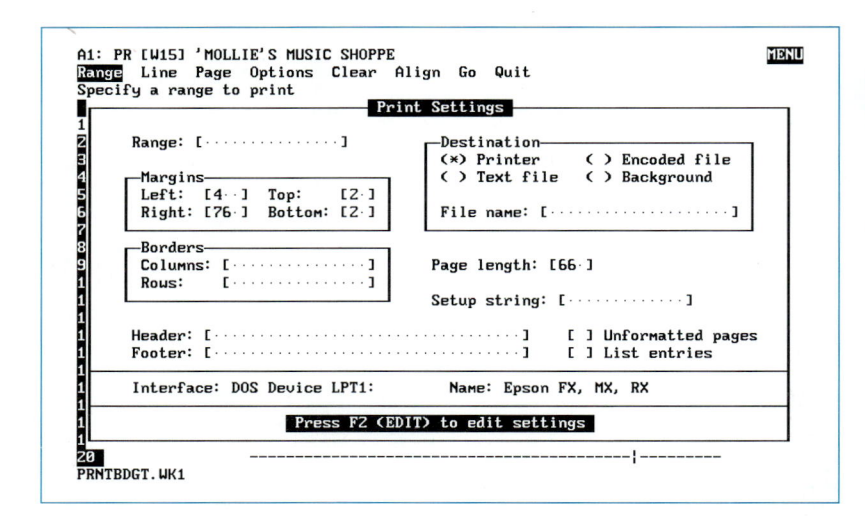

Figure 7.2

The Print Settings dialog box displays the default print settings for the current worksheet.

Note: It is possible that your version of 1-2-3 has other margin-setting values.

7 ▶ Type **R** to select the Range command.

The current worksheet is displayed.

8 ▶ Make sure the cell pointer is on cell A1.

9 ▶ Type **.** (a period) to anchor the current cell.

10 ▶ Press END, and then press HOME.

The range A1..Z24 is highlighted.

11 ▶ Press ↵.

The print range is selected, and the Print Settings dialog box again is displayed. Notice that the range you selected is displayed to the right of the Range setting.

208   7 ▶ Advanced Printing Features

12 ▶ Press F2.

   The Print Settings dialog box is active.

13 ▶ Type **ML** to move the pointer to the Left margin setting in the dialog box.

14 ▶ Type **2** and press ⏎.

   The left margin is set at 2, and the pointer moves to the Right margin setting.

15 ▶ Type **R** to move the cursor to the Right margin setting in the dialog box.

16 ▶ Type **80** and press ⏎.

   The right margin is set at 80, and the pointer moves to the Top margin setting.

17 ▶ Press ESC.

18 ▶ Press ↑ 4 times.

   The pointer moves to the OK command button.

19 ▶ Press ⏎.

   The Printer command submenu is again active on the control panel.

Now you will print the worksheet.

20 ▶ Check your printer to make sure it is turned on and has paper. Make sure that the paper is properly aligned.

21 ▶ Type **AG** to select the Align and Go commands.

   If you have a dot-matrix printer, the print range is printed; if you have a laser printer, the data is processed.

22 ▶ Type **P** to select the Page command.

   If you have a dot-matrix printer, the last printed page is advanced. If you have a laser printer, the last printed page ejects, if it has not ejected already.

Take a look at your printed hard copy. The number of columns printed across the page may vary, depending on the printer connected to your system. For example, if you are using a dot-matrix printer, the data range probably printed across three pages. Notice that the row labels in column A printed on page 1 only. You cannot tell which revenues and expenses correspond to the values listed on pages 2 and 3. You will learn how you can print the column A labels as a print border in the next exercise. For now, you will save the current print settings to the same file.

23 ▶ Type **Q** to select the Printer command submenu's Quit option.

24 ▶ Press HOME, if necessary, and save the current print settings to the same file.

Adjusting Margins

Exercise 7.2

Setting Print Borders

Objective

After completing this exercise, you will be able to
- Set print borders.

BORDER
A range of labels arranged in columns or rows that are printed on each page of a multi-page document.

In this exercise, you will use the Borders command on the Printer command submenu to set a print border. A print *border* is a range of labels arranged in a column or row. The border prints on each page of a multipage document.

For example, you can print a border of row heading labels on the left side of each page. Set a column of row labels as a print border when there are more columns than will fit on a page. That way, any column of data can be referenced easily by the reader. To set a border of row labels, you select the Columns option on the Borders command submenu. Similarly, you can select the Rows option to set a row of column headings as a print border. Use the Rows option when the worksheet has many rows of data. The border of column headings will print at the top of each page. You can also select both options to set print borders that include one or more columns and rows of labels.

> Note: Be sure you do not include the print border column(s) and/or row(s) in the print range. If you do, 1-2-3 will print the print border range twice on the first page. It will print once as the border and again as part of the print range.

As you can see, the current worksheet is very wide. You will set a print border in Column A that consists of the row heading labels.

1 ▶ Make sure the cell pointer is on cell A1.

2 ▶ Press the Slash key (/) to access the Main Menu.

3 ▶ Type **PP** to select the Print and Printer commands.

The Print Settings dialog box is displayed.

4 ▶ Type **O** to select the Options command.

The Options command submenu is activated on the control panel.

5 ▶ Type **B** to select the Borders command.

The Borders command submenu is displayed on the control panel, and the Columns option is highlighted.

6 ▶ Press ⏎.

The Columns option is selected, and 1-2-3 prompts you to enter the range of columns for the print border.

7 ▶ Press ⏎.

Column A is selected as the border range. Notice that the Print Settings dialog box displays the Border Columns setting range A1..A1, as shown in Figure 7.3.

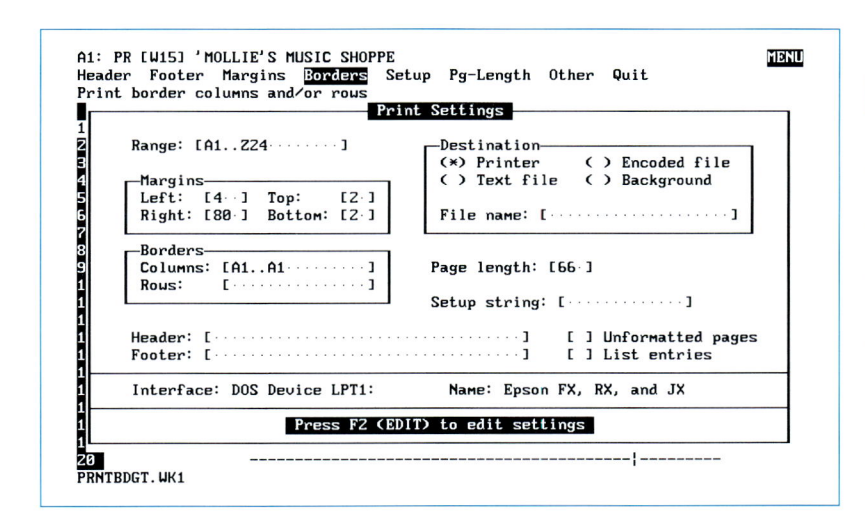

Figure 7.3

The Print Settings dialog box shows print settings for the current worksheet. Notice that the Borders Columns option is set to the range A1..A1.

Now you will adjust your print range so that the print border labels do not print twice on the first page.

8 ▶ Press F2.

The Print Settings dialog box is activated.

9 ▶ Type **R**

The pointer moves to the Range setting.

10 ▶ Press ⏎ 6 times.

The cursor is on the "1" in the cell address A1.

Setting Print Borders   211

11 ▶ Press BACKSPACE.

The column letter "A" is erased.

12 ▶ Type **b**

13 ▶ Press ⏎.

The print range is adjusted, and the pointer moves to the OK command button.

14 ▶ Press ⏎.

The Options command submenu is activated on the control panel.

15 ▶ Type **Q** to select the Options command submenu's Quit command.

The Printer command submenu is active on the control panel.

Now you will print the same data range again.

16 ▶ Check your printer to make sure it is turned on and has paper. Make sure that the paper is properly aligned.

17 ▶ Type **AG** to select the Align and Go commands.

If you have a dot-matrix printer, the print range is printed; if you have a laser printer, the data is processed.

18 ▶ Type **P** to select the Page command.

If you have a dot-matrix printer, the last printed page is advanced. If you have a laser printer, the last printed page ejects, if it has not ejected already.

19 ▶ Type **Q** to select the Printer command submenu's Quit option.

Lotus 1-2-3 returns to READY mode.

20 ▶ Press (HOME), if necessary, and save the current print settings to the same file.

Look at your hard copy. As you can see, 1-2-3 printed the worksheet's titles and the column of row labels on each page. Everything in column A printed as a print border. Now you will learn about another print feature that you can use to enhance your worksheet hard copies.

212 7 ▶ Advanced Printing Features

Exercise 7.3

Printing Headers and Footers

Objectives

After completing this exercise, you will be able to
- Print a header at the top of each page.
- Print a footer at the bottom of each page.

HEADER
A line of information that is printed at the top of each page in a document.

FOOTER
A line of information that is printed at the bottom of each page in a document.

In 1-2-3, headers and footers are single lines of information that print on each page of a multipage document. *Headers* print at the top of a page, and *footers* print at the bottom. Headers and footers can be used to identify a document, print the current date, or print page numbers. Or you can print any other information you want to be repeated on each page of the document.

Lotus 1-2-3 reserves three lines at the top and at the bottom of each page for a header and a footer. This additional space affects the size of the top and bottom margins when you print. If you do not include a header, then your top margin will include three additional blank lines. Likewise, your bottom margin will include three additional blank lines if you do not include a footer. For example, if the top margin is four lines and there is no header text, 1-2-3 leaves seven blank lines at the tops of pages. The lines (three blank lines plus four margin lines) will be between the top of the page and the first line of data. So take into account whether you will be printing a header or footer when you change the size of margins.

VERTICAL BAR (OR PIPE)
A keyboard symbol that in 1-2-3 is used to align text in a header or footer. The first vertical bar tells 1-2-3 to center the text that follows it. The second vertical bar tells 1-2-3 to right-align the text that follows it.

When you create a header or footer, you can align text with the use of the vertical bar (|). On many keyboards, the *vertical bar* is broken or appears to be two stacked, vertical hyphens (¦). Sometimes this symbol is called a *pipe*. Text that follows the first vertical bar in header or footer text will be centered on the printed page. For example, enter the following as your header (or footer) text if you want to center the text:

|Mollie's Music Shoppe

If you use two vertical bars, the text that follows will print aligned on the right. For example, to right-align this header or footer, type:

||Mollie's Music Shoppe

You can also use different alignments for text within the header or footer. In the following example, the company's name prints left-aligned and the document's description ("Annual Budget") prints right-aligned:

Mollie's Music Shoppe||Annual Budget

If you want to include the current date in a header or footer, enter the at sign (@). The at sign (@) tells 1-2-3 to print the current date, if your system's internal clock has been set properly. The printed date will be in the following default format:

27-Jul-95

If you want to include the current page number in a header or footer, you type the pound sign (#). Enter the pound sign where you want the page number to appear within the header or footer text. Lotus 1-2-3 keeps track of each page number as it prints the print range. The program inserts the correct page number on each page (if you have selected the Align command before printing). For example, enter the following to print centered page numbers in a header or footer:

|#

Or you can enhance the page number by entering the header or footer text as follows:

|-#-   or   **|Page #**

Now you will continue adjusting print settings for the budget worksheet. You will create a header that identifies the document and the name of the business. You will also create a footer that prints the date and page numbers. Finally, you will adjust your margins to improve the document's appearance.

1 ▶ Make sure the cell pointer is on cell A1 and 1-2-3 is in READY mode.

2 ▶ Press the Slash key (/) to access the Main Menu.

3 ▶ Type **PPOH** to select the Print, Printer, Options and Header commands.

Lotus 1-2-3 prompts you to enter the header information.

4 ▶ Type **Fiscal 1995 Budget||Mollie's Music Shoppe**

> Note: Be sure to type two vertical bars between the words "Budget" and "Mollie's."

5 ▶ Press ⏎.

The header information is entered.

6 ▶ Type **F** to select the Footer option.

7 ▶ Type **@|Page #**

8 ▶ Press ⏎.

The footer text is entered. The footer will print a left-aligned date and a centered page number at the bottom of each page. Your Print Settings dialog box should look like Figure 7.4.

7 ▶ Advanced Printing Features

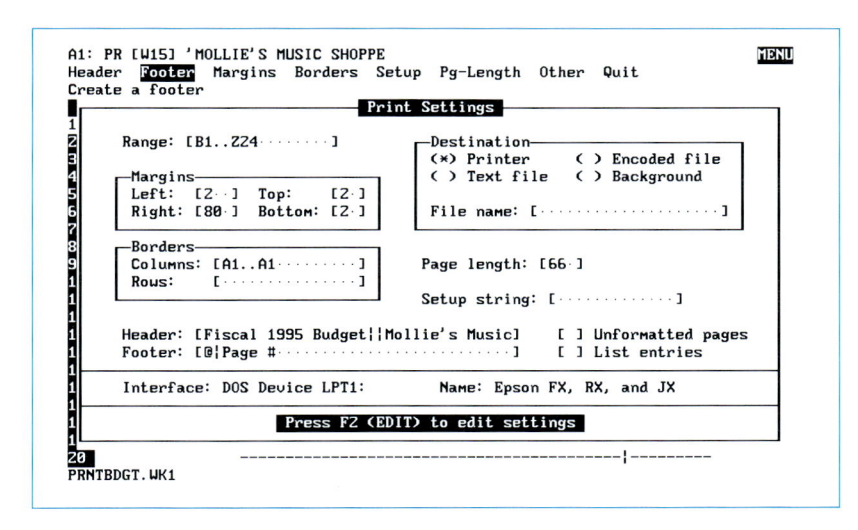

```
A1: PR [W15] 'MOLLIE'S MUSIC SHOPPE                              MENU
Header Footer Margins Borders Setup Pg-Length Other Quit
Create a footer
                        ┌──────── Print Settings ────────┐
   Range: [B1..Z24·······]
                                    ┌─Destination─────────────────┐
   ┌─Margins─────────────────┐      │ (*) Printer  ( ) Encoded file│
   │ Left:  [2·] Top:    [2·]│      │ ( ) Text file ( ) Background │
   │ Right: [80] Bottom: [2·]│      │ File name: [··············] │
   └─────────────────────────┘
   ┌─Borders─────────────────┐
   │ Columns: [A1..A1·······]│        Page length: [66·]
   │ Rows:    [·············]│
   └─────────────────────────┘        Setup string: [············]

   Header: [Fiscal 1995 Budget|¦Mollie's Music]   [ ] Unformatted pages
   Footer: [@¦Page #·························]   [ ] List entries

   Interface: DOS Device LPT1:      Name: Epson FX, RX, and JX

             ┌────── Press F2 (EDIT) to edit settings ──────┐
```

Figure 7.4

After you enter header and footer text, your Print Settings dialog box should look like this.

9 ▶ Type **Q** to select the Option command submenu's Quit option.

The Printer command submenu is activated on the control panel.

Now you will edit the Print Settings dialog box to change some margin settings. You want to try and adjust the settings so that the information for each quarter prints on a separate page.

10 ▶ Press F2.

The Print Settings dialog box is activated.

11 ▶ Type **ML** to move the pointer to the Left margin setting.

12 ▶ Type **8** and press ⏎.

The pointer moves to the Right margin setting.

13 ▶ Press ⏎.

14 ▶ Type **72**

15 ▶ Press ⏎.

The Right margin setting is changed, and the pointer moves to the Top margin setting.

16 ▶ Press ⏎.

17 ▶ Type **4**

18 ▶ Press ⏎.

The Top margin setting is changed to four lines, and the pointer moves to the Bottom margin setting.

19 ▶ Press ⏎.

20 ▶ Press ↑ 4 times.

The pointer moves to the OK command button.

Printing Headers and Footers

215

21 ▶ Press ⏎.

The Printer command submenu is again active on the control panel.

Now you will print the current print range. The first page of your document should appear similar to Figure 7.5.

```
Fiscal 1995 Budget                              Mollie's Music Shoppe

MOLLIE'S MUSIC SHOPPE
FISCAL BUDGET
                                  FIRST QUARTER
                          JUL     AUG     SEPT    TOTAL      %
        REVENUE
          Sales         14,750  14,750  14,750   44,250
          Rentals        1,010   1,010   1,010    3,030

        GROSS INCOME:   15,760  15,760  15,760   47,280

        OPERATING EXPENSES
          Lease          1,950   1,950   1,950    5,850    12.4%
          Salaries       2,285   2,285   2,285    6,855    14.5%
          Purchases      5,223   5,223   5,223   15,668    33.1%
          Advertising      337     337     337    1,012     2.1%
          Supplies         243     243     243      728     1.5%
          Utilities        225     225     225      675     1.4%

        TOTAL EXPENSES: 10,263  10,263  10,263    2,415

        NET PROFIT                               44,865




        1-Jul-96                 Page 1
```

Figure 7.5

After you print the budget worksheet, the first page should look like this.

22 ▶ Make sure that your printer is turned on and has paper. Make sure that the paper is properly aligned in the printer.

23 ▶ Type **AG** to select the Align and Go commands.

If you have a dot-matrix printer, the range prints; if you have a laser printer, the data is processed.

24 ▶ Type **P** to select the Page command.

If you have a dot-matrix printer, the last printed page advances. If you have a laser printer, the last printed page ejects, if it has not ejected already.

Take a look at your latest hard copy. Notice that the header printed at the top of each page and the footer printed at the bottom. Because you adjusted the right and left margins, the data for each quarter printed on a separate page. This gives the entire document a neat, organized appearance.

25 ▶ Type **Q** to select the Printer command submenu's Quit option.

Lotus 1-2-3 returns to READY mode.

26 ▶ Press [HOME], if necessary, and save the current print settings to the same file.

> Note: If the footer text printed on the top of your pages, change the Page Length setting to a value less than 66.

Notice that 1-2-3 left two blank rows between the header and the first row of the print range. Notice also that on pages 2–5 the word "Shoppe" is cut from the label in cell A1. This is because the label extends into column B and only column A is specified as a print border. To fix this problem, you will delete the labels in column A. The column A labels repeat information already in the header anyway.

27 ▶ Make sure the cell pointer is on cell A1.

28 ▶ Use the /Range Erase command (/RE) to delete the labels in the range A1..A2.

Before you print the worksheet again, take a look at another advanced 1-2-3 printing feature.

Exercise 7.4 — Hiding Columns

Objective

After completing this exercise, you will be able to
- Hide columns of data before printing.

The owner of Mollie's Music Shoppe wants you to print a document that shows only the projected totals for each quarter. The document will also show the projected 1995 fiscal year totals. In other words, she does not want to see the figures for each particular month, just the totals.

The current worksheet is structured so that each quarter's total column follows the three columns for each month in the quarter. You will print only the columns with each quarter's totals and cost-control percentages. The document will also contain the projected total figures in the last column. You can use the /Worksheet Column Hide command (/WCH) to hide those columns that you do not want to print. This command is very useful if you ever need to print columns that are not next to each other.

1 ▶ Move the cell pointer to cell B1.

   The cell pointer is in the first column in the range that you want to hide.

2 ▶ Press the Slash key (/) to access the Main Menu.

3 ▶ Type **WC** to select the Worksheet and Column commands.

   The Column command submenu is activated on the control panel.

4 ▶ Type **H** to select the Hide command.

5 ▶ Type **.** (a period) to anchor the current cell.

6 ▶ Press → twice.

   Columns B, C, and D are selected to be hidden.

7 ▶ Press ⏎.

   Lotus 1-2-3 hides columns B, C, and D, as shown in Figure 7.6.

Figure 7.6

After you use the /Worksheet Column Hide command (/WCH), columns B, C, and D in the current worksheet are hidden.

```
E1: PR                                                                  READY

         A              E        F    G    H         I         J        K
1
2
3
4                                              SECOND QUARTER
5                              ---------  ------------------------------------
6                               TOTAL  %  !   OCT       NOV       DEC     TOTAL
7     REVENUE                             !
8        Sales                 44,250     !  21,667    21,667    21,667   65,000
9        Rentals                3,030     !   1,583     1,583     1,583    4,750
10                             ---------  !------------------------------------
11    GROSS INCOME:            47,280     !  23,250    23,250    23,250   69,750
12                                        !
13    OPERATING EXPENSES                  !
14       Lease                  5,850 12.4%!  1,950     1,950     1,950    5,850
15       Salaries               6,855 14.5%!  3,667     3,667     3,667   11,000
16       Purchases             15,668 33.1%!  8,833     8,833     8,833   26,500
17       Advertising            1,012  2.1%!    975       975       975    2,925
18       Supplies                 728  1.5%!    367       367       367    1,100
19       Utilities                675  1.4%!    833       833       833    2,500
20                             ---------  !------------------------------------
PRNTBDGT.WK1
```

Now you will hide three more columns. This time, however, try preselecting the range of columns to be hidden.

8 ▶ Move the cell pointer to cell H1.

   The cell pointer is on the first column in the next column range you want to hide.

9 ▶ Press F4.

10 ▶ Press → twice.

11 ▶ Press ↵.

The first cells in columns H, I, and J are highlighted.

12 ▶ Press the Slash key (/) to access the Main Menu.

13 ▶ Type **WCH** to select the Worksheet, Column, and Hide commands.

Columns H, I, and J are hidden.

14 ▶ Move the cell pointer to cell N1.

15 ▶ Repeat the procedure in steps 9–13 to hide columns N, O, and P.

16 ▶ Repeat the procedure in steps 9–13 to hide columns T, U, and V.

17 ▶ Press HOME to move the cell pointer to cell A1.

After you hide the 12 columns, your worksheet should look like the one shown in Figure 7.7.

```
A1: PR [W15]                                                         READY

           A            E      F   G     K       L   M     Q       R   S    W
1
2
3
4
5                  --------------- --------------- --------------- ---------
6                    TOTAL     %  |  TOTAL     %  |  TOTAL     %  |  TOTAL
7   REVENUE                       |               |               |
8     Sales          44,250       |  65,000       |  48,000       |  48,000
9     Rentals         3,030       |   4,750       |   3,500       |   3,500
10                 ---------------|---------------|---------------|---------
11   GROSS INCOME:   47,280       |  69,750       |  51,500       |  51,500
12                                |               |               |
13  OPERATING EXPENSES            |               |               |
14    Lease           5,850  12.4%|   5,850   8.4%|   5,850  11.4%|   5,850
15    Salaries        6,855  14.5%|  11,000  15.8%|   8,000  15.5%|   8,000
16    Purchases      15,668  33.1%|  26,500  38.0%|  18,500  35.9%|  18,500
17    Advertising     1,012   2.1%|   2,925   4.2%|   1,344   2.6%|   1,344
18    Supplies          728   1.5%|   1,100   1.6%|     850   1.7%|     850
19    Utilities         675   1.4%|   2,500   3.6%|   2,200   4.3%|   2,200
20                 ---------------|---------------|---------------|---------
PRNTBDGT.WK1
```

Figure 7.7

After you hide columns B, C, D, H, I, J, N, O, P, T, U, and V, columns A through W in your worksheet should look like this.

As you can see, in the worksheet area, the columns you want to print are all next to each other. However, you cannot tell which quarter corresponds to which column of totals. So you will need to enter some temporary labels before you print the worksheet.

18 ▶ Enter the numbers 1, 2, 3, and 4 as centered labels in cells E4, K4, Q4, and W4, respectively.

Enter a new label in cell A1.

19 ▶ Press HOME to move the cell pointer to cell A1.

20 ▶ Type **QUARTERLY TOTALS** and press ↵.

Now you will change the left and right margin settings. In total, the columns you want to print (A–W) contain 78 characters. Therefore, you will adjust the margins to accommodate 78 characters.

21 ▶ Press the Slash key (/) to access the Main Menu.

22 ▶ Type **PP** to select the Print and Printer commands.

The Print Settings dialog box is displayed.

23 ▶ Press [F2].

The Print Settings dialog box is activated.

24 ▶ Type **ML** to move the cell pointer to the Left margin setting.

25 ▶ Type **2**

26 ▶ Press [←] twice.

27 ▶ Type **80**

28 ▶ Press [←].

29 ▶ Press [ESC].

30 ▶ Press [↑] 4 times.

The pointer moves to the OK command button.

31 ▶ Press [←].

The Printer command submenu is activated on the control panel.

Now you will print the budget's quarterly totals and grand total columns. The current settings should print the quarterly totals on page 1 and the grand total column on page 2.

32 ▶ Make sure that your printer is turned on and has paper. Make sure that the paper is properly aligned.

33 ▶ Type **AG** to select the Align and Go commands.

If you have a dot-matrix printer, the range prints; if you have a laser printer, the data is processed.

34 ▶ Type **P** to select the Page command.

If you have a dot-matrix printer, the last printed page advances. If you have a laser printer, the last printed page ejects, if it has not ejected already.

35 ▶ Type **Q** to select the Printer command submenu's Quit option.

Lotus 1-2-3 returns to READY mode.

After hiding columns, you can always go back and redisplay the columns by selecting the /Worksheet Column Display command (/WCD). Now you will redisplay the columns that are currently hidden, and then you will erase the temporary labels.

36 ▶ Press the Slash key (/) to access the Main Menu.

37 ▶ Type **WCD** to select the Worksheet, Column, and Display commands.

Lotus 1-2-3 prompts you to specify the hidden columns to redisplay. Notice that the currently hidden columns are redisplayed (temporarily). Asterisks appear to the right of the column letters in the worksheet border, as shown in Figure 7.8. The asterisks indicate that the columns are currently hidden.

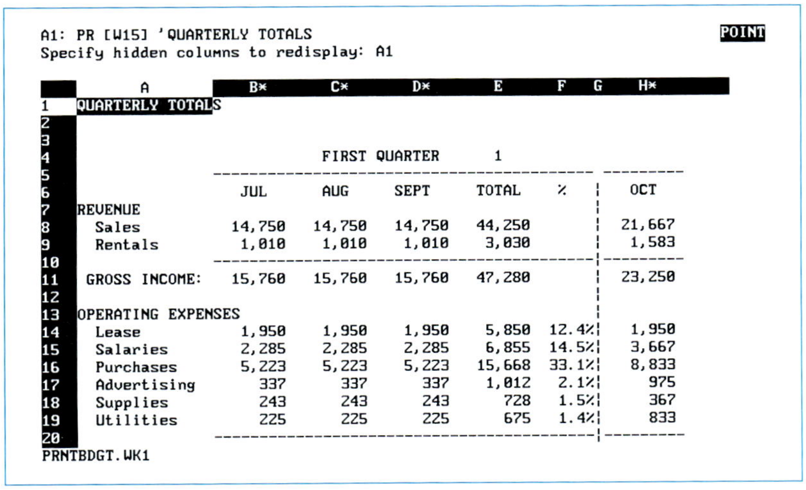

A1: PR [W15] 'QUARTERLY TOTALS   POINT
Specify hidden columns to redisplay: A1

	A	B*	C*	D*	E	F	G	H*
1	QUARTERLY TOTALS							
2								
3								
4			FIRST QUARTER		1			
5								
6		JUL	AUG	SEPT	TOTAL	%	¦	OCT
7	REVENUE						¦	
8	Sales	14,750	14,750	14,750	44,250		¦	21,667
9	Rentals	1,010	1,010	1,010	3,030		¦	1,583
10								
11	GROSS INCOME:	15,760	15,760	15,760	47,280		¦	23,250
12								
13	OPERATING EXPENSES						¦	
14	Lease	1,950	1,950	1,950	5,850	12.4%	¦	1,950
15	Salaries	2,285	2,285	2,285	6,855	14.5%	¦	3,667
16	Purchases	5,223	5,223	5,223	15,668	33.1%	¦	8,833
17	Advertising	337	337	337	1,012	2.1%	¦	975
18	Supplies	243	243	243	728	1.5%	¦	367
19	Utilities	225	225	225	675	1.4%	¦	833
20								

PRNTBDGT.WK1

Figure 7.8

When you select a command that affects a range, hidden columns are displayed with an asterisk next to each column's letter.

38 ▶ Type **.** (a period) to anchor the current cell.

39 ▶ Press (→) 21 times.

40 ▶ Press (↵).

All of the previously hidden columns are redisplayed.

41 ▶ Delete the temporary labels in cells E4, K4, Q4, and W4.

42 ▶ Press (HOME), and save the changes to the same file.

Now you will learn another 1-2-3 feature that allows you to reduce the size of print.

Exercise 7.5

Printing Data with Condensed Print

Objectives

After completing this exercise, you will be able to
- Enter a setup string that contains a printer control code.
- Print a range of data in condensed print.

CONDENSED PRINT
A printer mode in which the size of printed characters is reduced to 16 characters per inch. This lets the printer fit more data on a single line.

SETUP STRING
A special instruction preceded by a backslash character (\) that contains one or more printer control codes.

PRINTER CONTROL CODE
A sequence of non-printing characters that set certain settings in a printer or change print modes. Printer control codes are different for each printer model.

Sometimes you will have documents that have many columns and rows of data. Even after adjusting print settings, the data in such multipage documents can be difficult to read. For example, in a later lesson you will learn to work with special worksheet files, called *databases*. Documents printed from these files contain large amounts of listed information, such as names and addresses or inventories. Information in columns that do not fit across a page are printed on another page. However, you can give your printer a special instruction to change the printer's printing mode to condensed print. *Condensed print* reduces the size of the printed characters to 16 characters per inch. Having more characters per inch means you can fit more printed data on a single line.

The special instruction you send to your printer is called a *setup string*. You enter a setup string after selecting the /Print Printer Options Setup command (/PPOS). A setup string contains characters that make up a *printer control code*. The code tells your printer to switch to condensed-print mode. The characters that make up the printer control code vary depending on the particular printer model. Table 7.1 lists setup strings for condensed print for a few of the more popular printer models. If the table does not list your printer model, ask your instructor for the correct setup string or refer to your printer's reference manual.

Printer	Setup String
Epson FX, MX, or RX	\015
Epson LQ1500	\027x0\015
Apple ImageWriter II	\027q
Hewlett-Packard LaserJet	\027&k2S

Table 7.1

Condensed Print Setup Strings for Various Printer Models

Now you will print another version of the 1995 fiscal year budget for Mollie's Music Shoppe. In this exercise, you will enter a setup string that switches your printer to condensed print mode. See Table 7.1, your printer's reference manual, or your instructor for the correct printer control code.

1 ▶ Make sure 1-2-3 is in READY mode.

2 ▶ Press the Slash key (/) to access the Main Menu.

3 ▶ Type **PPOS** to select the Print, Printer, Options, and Setup commands.

Lotus 1-2-3 prompts you to enter a setup string.

4 ▶ Type **\015**

> Note: The setup string shown here switches most dot-matrix printers to condensed print mode. The 0 is a zero. Check the reference manual for your printer, or ask your instructor or technical support person, for your printer's setup string.

5 ▶ Press ⏎.

The setup string is entered. Notice that it is displayed to the right of the Setup option in the Print Settings dialog box.

6 ▶ Type **Q** to select the Options command submenu's Quit option.

The Printer command submenu is active on the control panel.

Now you must adjust the left and right margin settings to accommodate the condensed print. Condensed-print mode will print more characters across the page, so you will increase both margin settings.

7 ▶ Press F2.

The Print Settings dialog box is activated.

8 ▶ Type **ML**

The pointer moves to the Left margin setting.

9 ▶ Type **15**

10 ▶ Press ⏎ twice.

The pointer moves to the Right margin setting.

11 ▶ Type **120**

12 ▶ Press ⏎.

13 ▶ Press ESC.

14 ▶ Press ↑ twice.

The pointer moves to the Range setting.

15 ▶ Press ⏎.

16 ▶ Press ESC.

The current print range address clears.

17 ▶ Type **b1.y24**

18 ▶ Press ⏎.

The pointer moves to the OK command button.

Printing Data with Condensed Print

19 ▶ Press ⏎.

20 ▶ Check your printer to make sure it is turned on and has paper. Make sure that the paper is properly aligned.

21 ▶ Type **AG** to select the Align and Go commands.

If you have a dot-matrix printer, the range prints; if you have a laser printer, the data is processed.

22 ▶ Type **P** to select the Page command.

If you have a dot-matrix printer, the last printed page advances. If you have a laser printer, the printed pages eject.

> Note: The setting adjustments you have made in this exercise should print the first- and second-quarter information on the first page, as shown in Figure 7.9. The third- and fourth-quarter information should print on the second page. If you get different results, you may have to experiment with different settings.

```
Fiscal 1995 Budget                                              Mollie's Music Shoppe

QUARTERLY TOTALS
                        FIRST QUARTER                          SECOND QUARTER
                JUL    AUG    SEPT   TOTAL    %         OCT    NOV    DEC    TOTAL    %
REVENUE
  Sales       14,750 14,750 14,750  44,250          21,667 21,667 21,667  65,000
  Rentals      1,010  1,010  1,010   3,030           1,583  1,583  1,583   4,750

GROSS INCOME: 15,760 15,760 15,760  47,280          23,250 23,250 23,250  69,750

OPERATING EXPENSES
  Lease        1,950  1,950  1,950   5,850 12.4%     1,950  1,950  1,950   5,850  8.4%
  Salaries     2,285  2,285  2,285   6,855 14.5%     3,667  3,667  3,667  11,000 15.8%
  Purchases    5,223  5,223  5,223  15,668 33.1%     8,833  8,833  8,833  26,500 38.0%
  Advertising    337    337    337   1,012  2.1%       975    975    975   2,925  4.2%
  Supplies       243    243    243     728  1.5%       367    367    367   1,100  1.6%
  Utilities      225    225    225     675  1.4%       833    833    833   2,500  3.6%

TOTAL EXPENSES: 10,263 10,263 10,263  2,415         16,625 16,625 16,625   6,525

NET PROFIT                           44,865                               63,225


1-Jul-96                          Page 1
```

Figure 7.9

After you print the budget in condensed print mode, the first page should look like this.

23 ▶ Type **Q** to select the Printer command submenu's Quit option.

Lotus 1-2-3 returns to READY mode.

24 ▶ Press HOME, and save the current print settings to the same file.

You will complete this lesson by learning how to print a special list of the cell contents in your worksheet.

Exercise 7.6 Printing Cell Formulas

Objective

After completing this exercise, you will be able to
- Print cell formulas.

By default, 1-2-3 prints a range of worksheet data as it is displayed on the screen. However, 1-2-3 can print a list of cells' contents, rather than what you see displayed in the worksheet area. This is useful if you want to list formulas in a worksheet, rather than their results.

The owner of Mollie's wants you to give her a list of the formulas that calculate all budget totals.

1 ▶ Press the Slash key (/) to access the Main Menu.

2 ▶ Type **PPO** to select the Print, Printer, and Options commands.

The Options command submenu is active on the control panel.

3 ▶ Type **O** to select the Other command.

The Other command submenu is active on the control panel.

4 ▶ Type **C** to select the Cell-Formulas command.

The Options command submenu is again activated on the control panel.

5 ▶ Type **Q** to select the Quit option and return to the Printer command submenu.

6 ▶ Make sure that your printer is turned on and has paper. Make sure that the paper is properly aligned.

7 ▶ Type **AG** to select the Align and Go commands.

If you have a dot-matrix printer, the range prints; if you have a laser printer, the data is processed.

8 ▶ Type **P** to select the Page command.

If you have a dot-matrix printer, the last printed page advances. If you have a laser printer, the printed pages eject.

Take a look at the hard copy. It is a line item list of all the formula entries in the budget worksheet. Also, the repeating-character labels that form the horizontal and vertical separation lines are listed. Notice that each line lists the cell's address and its protection status code. The list also shows each cell's width code (if the width was changed). Finally, the cell's content (label, value, formula, or @function) is listed.

You will change the cell formula setting so you can print in the worksheet format again, if necessary.

9 ▶ Type **OO** to select the Options and Other commands.

10 ▶ Type **A** to select the As-Displayed command.

The Options command submenu is active on the control panel.

11 ▶ Type **QQ** to return to READY mode.

12 ▶ Save the changes to the current worksheet, and then erase the worksheet.

You can now begin the Lesson 7 applications that follow the Concept Summary, or you can go on to Lesson 8. Otherwise, quit 1-2-3 if you are through with this 1-2-3 session.

Concept Summary ▶▶▶▶▶

- One of the more important operations that you perform with any spreadsheet software package is printing ranges of worksheet data. The hard copy can be used for editing, included in a report, or presented to associates or supervisors.

- All spreadsheet software contains special print settings that can be adjusted to enhance the appearance of a printed document. Commonly, margin settings can be adjusted to control the borders of clear space that surround the printed data on a page.

- When you print multipage documents, you can set special print borders that contain column and/or row heading labels that appear on each page. In this way, columns and/or rows of data printed on any additional pages are readily identified.

- You can set up headers or footers that print one line of information on each page of a document. Headers and footers commonly contain such information as titles, dates, page numbers, and other descriptive text.

- Spreadsheet software commonly includes a feature that lets you hide specific columns of data that you do not want printed in a document.

- If necessary, you can print a special list of the formulas that are in specific cells in a worksheet, instead of the displayed results. This feature lets you generate a permanent record of how you constructed a particular worksheet.

- Most software, including spreadsheet software, lets you enter a special instruction for a printer, called a setup string. Setup strings contain printer control codes that control certain settings or modes for a printer, such as bold, italic, or condensed-print modes.

Command Summary

/Print Printer Options Margins (Left Right Top Bottom)
changes margin settings to adjust the border of clear space around the edges of a document page

/Print Printer Options Borders Columns (/PPOBC)
sets one or more columns of labels as a border that prints on every page of a multipage document

/Print Printer Options Borders Rows (/PPOBR)
sets one or more rows of labels as a border that prints on every page of a multipage document.

/Print Printer Options Header (/PPOH)
sets a header that prints text at the top of every page in a multi-page document

/Print Printer Options Footer (/PPOF)
sets a footer that prints text at the bottom of every page in a multipage document

/Print Printer Options Setup (/PPOS)
sets a setup string, which sends a special printer-control code to a printer to change print modes

/Print Printer Options Other Cell-Formulas (/PPOOC)
prints the current print range in a list format that shows the content and format status of each cell

/Print Printer Options Other As-Displayed (/PPOOA)
prints the current print range in a worksheet format

/Print Printer Clear (/PPC)
clears all or selected print settings

/Worksheet Column Hide (/WCH)
hides the display of one or more columns

/Worksheet Column Display (/WCD)
redisplays hidden columns

Applications

Begin doing the applications by loading 1-2-3, if necessary. Place your student data disk in drive A (or drive B if you do not have a hard disk). Change the current directory to the drive that contains the student data disk. Also, change the clock setting in the Global Settings dialog box to display the current filename on the status line.

Business

Sales Analysis

1. You want to print the sales comparison worksheet and send copies to the branch managers. Retrieve the file SALSRPT7.WK1. You also want to adjust the print settings so that the final output is a two-page document that shows the data in the range C5..I20. The first page will show the data in columns A through G, and the second page will show the data in columns H and I. Set columns A and B and rows 1 through 4 as print borders. Enter a header that prints the left-aligned company name "KISMET INDUSTRIES" and the right-aligned date. Enter a footer that prints a centered page number. Save the current print settings in a file called SALES7.WK1, print the document, and then erase the worksheet.

Business

Small Business

2. Your instructor wants you to hand in the break-even analysis for the windsurfing board manufacturer. Retrieve the file BRKEVEN7.WK1. Scroll through the worksheet. You will notice that it is similar to the worksheet model you created earlier. However, the analysis was expanded to show figures up to 2,500 units produced. Adjust print settings as follows to print a hard copy of the analysis:

   a. Set the print range address to A12..G59.
   b. Set the right margin to 80 characters and the top margin to 4 lines.
   c. Set a print border that includes rows 1–11.
   d. Enter a header that prints the left-aligned text "Business Class Project", the centered text "Assignment 1", and the right-aligned date.
   e. Enter a footer that prints a centered page number and your name (right-aligned).
   f. Save the current print settings in the file PROFIT7.WK1, and then print the document.
   g. Erase the worksheet.

Business

Accounting

3. You are ready to print your general worksheet and income statement so you can turn in part of your assigned project. Retrieve the file WORKSHT7.WK1. Adjust the print settings as follows:

   a. Set the print range as A3..V43.
   b. Set the margins as follows: left = 4, right = 135, top = 4, and bottom = 2.
   c. Enter a setup string that switches your printer to condensed-print mode.

   > Note: If you are using a dot-matrix printer, the setup string for condensed-print mode is commonly \015. (The 0 is a zero.) If your printer requires a different printer control code, consult the printer's reference manual or your instructor.

   d. Enter a header that prints the centered text "Accounting Term Project" and your name (right-aligned).

228 7 ▶ Advanced Printing Features

- e. Enter a footer that prints the date (left-aligned) and the right-aligned text "GENERAL WORKSHEET".
- f. Save the current print settings to the file BALANCE7.WK1, and print the document.
- g. Retrieve the file INCSTMNT.WK1. Set the print range as A1..F44. Enter the same header described in step d, and then enter a footer that prints the date (left-aligned) and the right-aligned text "INCOME STATEMENT".
- h. Save the print settings to the file INCOME7.WK1, and print the document. Erase the worksheet after printing the document.

Social Studies

Student Survey

4. You want to print a worksheet document that shows the results of the student attitudes questionnaire. Retrieve the file SRVRSLTS.WK1, and adjust the print settings as follows:
   - a. Set the print range address to B1..N24.
   - b. Set column A as a print border.
   - c. Enter a header with the left-aligned text "Student Activities Questionnaire" and a right-aligned date.
   - d. Enter a footer that prints the left-aligned word "Page" and a page number.
   - e. Set the left and right margin settings so that page 1 prints the border column and columns B–G, page 2 prints the border column and columns H–M, and page 3 prints column N.

   > Note: For most dot-matrix printers, set the left margin to 4 characters and the right margin to 80 characters.

   - f. Save the current print settings to the file SURVEY7.WK1, and print the document.
   - g. Hide the Rating and Variance columns. Adjust the right margin to accommodate condensed print, enter a setup string to switch the printer to condensed-print mode, and then print the document again.
   - h. Redisplay the hidden columns, save the current changes to the same file, and erase the worksheet.

Applications

Social Studies

Geography

5. You need to print a polished document with your world population analysis worksheet data to hand in the assignment to your instructor. Retrieve the file POPULATN.WK1, and adjust the print settings as follows to print the document:

    a. Set the print range address to B4..G18.

    b. Enter a header that prints the left-aligned text "WORLD POPULATION ANALYSIS" and your name (right-aligned). Enter a footer that prints a centered page number.

    c. Set column A as a print border.

    d. Save the current print settings to the file WRLDPOP7.WK1, and print the document.

    e. Print a list of cell contents for the worksheet. After printing the list, change the cell-formula list setting back to "As-Displayed."

    f. Erase the worksheet.

Social Studies

American Government

6. You need to print the results of your election analysis worksheet to hand in your work the next time you are in your American government class. Retrieve the file VOTECOMP.WK1 and adjust the print settings as follows to print the document:

    a. Set the print range address to A1..G26.

    b. Enter a header that prints the left-aligned text "American Government", a centered date, and your name (right-aligned). Enter a footer that prints your school's name (centered).

    c. Change the left margin to 6 characters and the right margin to 78 characters.

    d. Save the current print settings to the file ELECTN7.WK1, and print the document.

    e. Hide columns D and F, and print the document again.

    f. Redisplay the hidden columns, save the changes to the same file, and erase the worksheet.

Science/ Mathematics

Astronomy

7. You will print a document that lists your solar system analysis data. Retrieve the file SOLRSYST.WK1, and adjust selected print settings as follows to print the document:

    a. Set the print range address to A1..J17.

    b. Set the left margin to 20 and the right margin to 130 to accommodate condensed print.

    c. Enter a setup string that switches your printer to condensed-print mode.

    d. Enter a header that prints the left-aligned text "Astronomy" and the right-aligned text "Solar System Analysis".

    e. Enter a footer that prints the date left-aligned and your name right-aligned.

    f. Save the current print settings to the file PLANETS7.WK1, and print the document.

g. Change the appropriate setting to print a list of cell contents for the worksheet data. Print the list.

h. Erase the worksheet without saving the file.

Science/Mathematics

Mathematics

8. Recall that in Lesson 6 you used 1-2-3 to create a multiplication table. Retrieve the file TMSTABLE.WK1, which contains a multiplication table similar to the one you created. Adjust selected print settings as follows to print the table:

   a. Set the print range address to C2..#AF35.

   b. Set columns A and B as a print border.

   c. Set the left margin setting to 2 characters and the right margin setting to 135 characters to accommodate condensed print.

   d. Enter a setup string that switches your printer to condensed-print mode.

   e. Enter a header that prints the left-aligned text "MATHEMATICS", the centered text "***MULTIPLICATION TABLE***", and your name (right-aligned).

   f. Enter a footer that prints a centered page number enclosed by hyphens (-).

   g. Save the current print settings to the file MATH7.WK1, and print the table.

   Note: Printing will require several minutes, as the table is large.

   Erase the worksheet when printing has completed.

Health

Nutrition

9. Because you want to hand in your health class assignment, you will print the daily nutritional information worksheet, which shows that your typical dietary intake of fat does not exceed 30 percent. Retrieve the file DLYDIET7.WK1, and adjust the print settings as follows to print the document:

   a. Set the print range address to A1..G43.

   b. Set the left margin to 4 characters and the right margin to 80 characters.

   c. Enter a header that prints the left-aligned text "HEALTH", the centered text "Daily Nutritional Analysis," and the date (right-aligned).

   d. Enter a footer that prints your name (right-aligned).

   e. Save the current print settings to the file NUTRINF7.WK1, and print the document.

   f. Print a list of the cell contents, and then erase the worksheet without updating the file.

Applications

Health

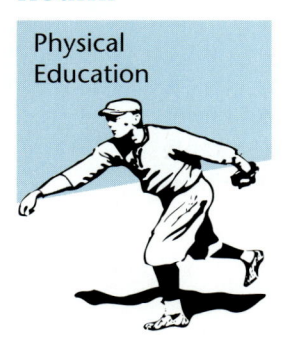

Physical Education

10. The softball team coach would like to receive a list of the team's current batting statistics. In addition, the coach would also like a list that just shows at bats, runs, hits, and batting and slugging averages. Both lists will show which players are slated for extra batting practice. Retrieve the file SOFTBALL.WK1, and adjust the print settings as follows to print the document:

   a. Set the print range address to A1..L26.

   b. Set the Left margin setting to 20 characters and the Right margin setting to 125 characters to accommodate condensed print.

   c. Enter a setup string that switches the printer to condensed-print mode.

   d. Enter a header that prints the left-aligned text "Physical Education", a centered date, and the right-aligned text "Softball Team Statistics".

   e. Enter a footer that prints the left-aligned text "* BP=Batting Practice".

   f. Save the current print settings to the file SBGAME7.WK1, and print the document.

   g. Hide the display of columns F through I. Reset the margin settings to their default values, and remove the setup string for condensed-print mode.

   h. Print the document, and then erase the worksheet without updating the file.

8 ▶ Graphing Worksheet Data

Objectives

- Create a line graph.
- Display a graph.
- Name a graph.
- Save a graph in a graph file.
- Create, name, and save a bar graph.
- Create, name, and save a pie graph.
- Select a graph to make it current.
- Enhance a bar graph.
- Enhance a pie graph.
- Separate a slice from a pie graph.
- Create a graph that plots multiple data ranges.
- Label graph components with worksheet labels.
- Enter legends to identify graphed data ranges.
- Enhance a graph with horizontal grid lines.
- Access the Lotus PrintGraph utility.
- Print 1-2-3 graph files.

Graphing is a very important 1-2-3 feature. You can create graphs to represent, or illustrate, worksheet data. A graphic representation of data can have more impact on an audience than a document full of numbers and text. In this lesson, you will learn how to create and enhance a variety of graphs. Graphs can be displayed on your monitor or printed as hard copy.

Exercise 8.1: Creating and Displaying a Line Graph

Objectives

After completing this exercise, you will be able to
- Create a line graph.
- Display a graph.

Lotus 1-2-3's graphics capability lets you graphically represent information stored in a worksheet. Viewing a graph gives you, or your audience, an additional tool for interpreting and understanding worksheet data. You can spot changes, trends, and patterns in a graph more easily than you can in a worksheet. You can use the 1-2-3 graphing feature to create line graphs, bar graphs, pie charts, and other types of graphs.

To get a better perspective on sales during the summer period, you will create a line graph. The line graph will show the trend in sales for June through September.

LINE GRAPH
A type of graph that plots values as points and connects those points with lines. Line graphs represent patterns or trends over a period of time.

In a *line graph,* values are plotted on the graph as points and the points are connected by lines. A line graph is useful for seeing how values change over time and plotting a large number of values.

To create a graph, you select the /Graph command (/G). This displays the Graph command menu. From this menu, you choose the type of graph that you want to create. Then you identify one or more ranges in the worksheet that contain the data that you want to represent. You can also specify the x-axis range, which is usually a range of labels that identifies which values are plotted on the graph. You also often include titles and other labels to clarify the represented data for the reader.

1 ▶ If necessary, start 1-2-3. Use the /File Directory command to change the current directory to the drive that contains the student data disk.

2 ▶ Retrieve the file SUMSALES.WK1.

The file you last saved in Lesson 4 appears.

8 ▶ Graphing Worksheet Data

3 ▶ Press the Slash key (/) to access the Main Menu.

4 ▶ Type **G** to select the Graph command.

The Graph Settings dialog box is displayed and the Graph command submenu is active on the control panel, as shown in Figure 8.1.

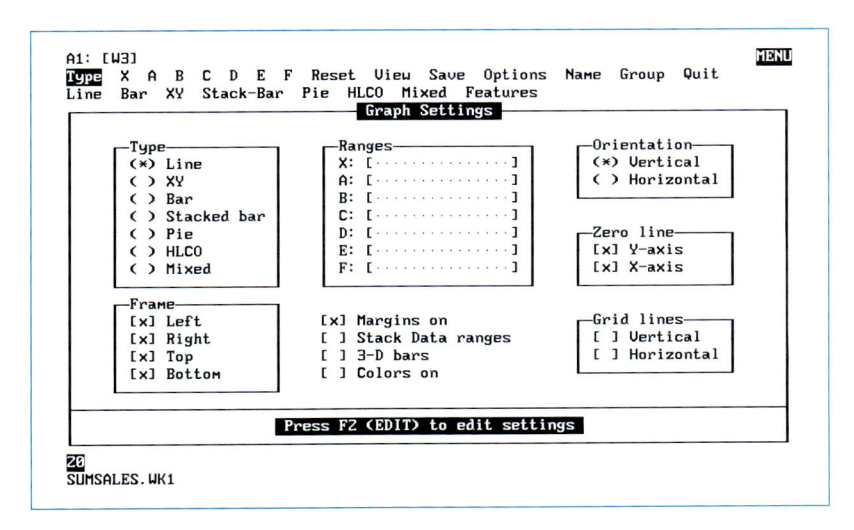

Figure 8.1

The Graph Settings dialog box allows you to specify the range of worksheet data you want to graph. You also use this dialog box to change current graph settings.

The Graph Settings Dialog Box shows you the current, or default, settings that are installed automatically with 1-2-3. Notice in the upper-left corner of the dialog box that the default graph type is a line graph. As you select settings for your graph, 1-2-3 will update the settings displayed on the screen. Settings can be adjusted either through the command menu or by editing the Graph Settings dialog box.

When you create a graph, usually the first step is to select the type of graph. However, in this instance, the line graph option is already selected, so you can save one step. Your next step is to specify the range of values to plot on the graph.

5 ▶ Type **A** to specify the first data range.

The worksheet reappears, and 1-2-3 prompts you to enter the first range of data that will be plotted on the graph.

6 ▶ Move the cell pointer to cell B14.

The cell pointer is on the cell that contains the total sales for June.

7 ▶ Type **.** (a period) to anchor the current cell.

8 ▶ Press → 3 times.

9 ▶ Press ↵.

The first data range is selected, and the Graph Settings dialog box is displayed again. Notice that the range address is shown in the Ranges settings group.

Creating and Displaying a Line Graph

235

10 ▶ Type **X** to specify a range of labels for the graph's x-axis.

The worksheet reappears, and 1-2-3 prompts you to enter the X-axis range.

11 ▶ Move the cell pointer to cell B6.

The cell pointer is on the cell that contains the label "JUNE."

12 ▶ Type **.** (a period) to anchor the pointer.

13 ▶ Press → 3 times.

14 ▶ Press ←.

The X data range is selected, and its address is displayed in the Graph Settings dialog box.

15 ▶ Type **O** to select the Options command.

The Options command submenu is active on the control panel.

16 ▶ Type **T** to select the Titles command.

The Graph Legends & Titles dialog box is displayed, as shown in Figure 8.2, and 1-2-3 displays the following submenu of options:

    First   Second   X-Axis   Y-Axis

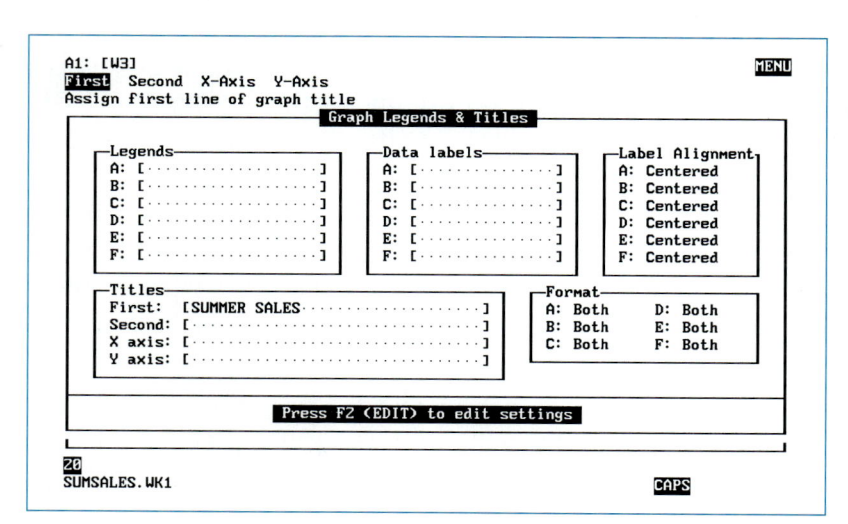

Figure 8.2

When you select the /Graph Options Titles command (/GOT), the Graph & Titles dialog box is displayed. The Titles command submenu is active on the control panel.

17 ▶ Type **F** to select the First command.

Lotus 1-2-3 prompts you to enter the first, or primary, title for the graph.

18 ▶ Type **SUMMER SALES** and press ←.

The Options command submenu is activated on the control panel.

8 ▶ Graphing Worksheet Data

19 ▶ Type **T** to select the Titles command.

    The Graph Legends & Titles dialog box is displayed, and the Titles command submenu is activated on the control panel.

This time you will edit the displayed dialog box to enter the graph's second title or subtitle.

20 ▶ Press F2.

    The Graph Legends & Titles dialog box is active.

21 ▶ Type **TS**

    The pointer moves to the Titles Second setting.

22 ▶ Type **June - September 1995**

23 ▶ Press TAB.

    The second title's text is entered, and the pointer moves to the X-axis title setting.

24 ▶ Type **Months**

25 ▶ Press TAB.

    The x-axis label is entered, and the pointer moves to the Y-axis title setting.

26 ▶ Type **Dollars**

27 ▶ Press ↵.

    The y-axis label is entered, and the pointer moves to the OK command button.

28 ▶ Press ↵.

    The Titles command submenu is activated on the control panel.

29 ▶ Press ESC.

    The Options command submenu is activated on the control panel.

30 ▶ Type **Q** to select the Options command submenu's Quit option.

    The Graph command menu is activated on the control panel.

31 ▶ Type **V** to select the View command.

    The current line graph is displayed, as shown in Figure 8.3.

Creating and Displaying a Line Graph

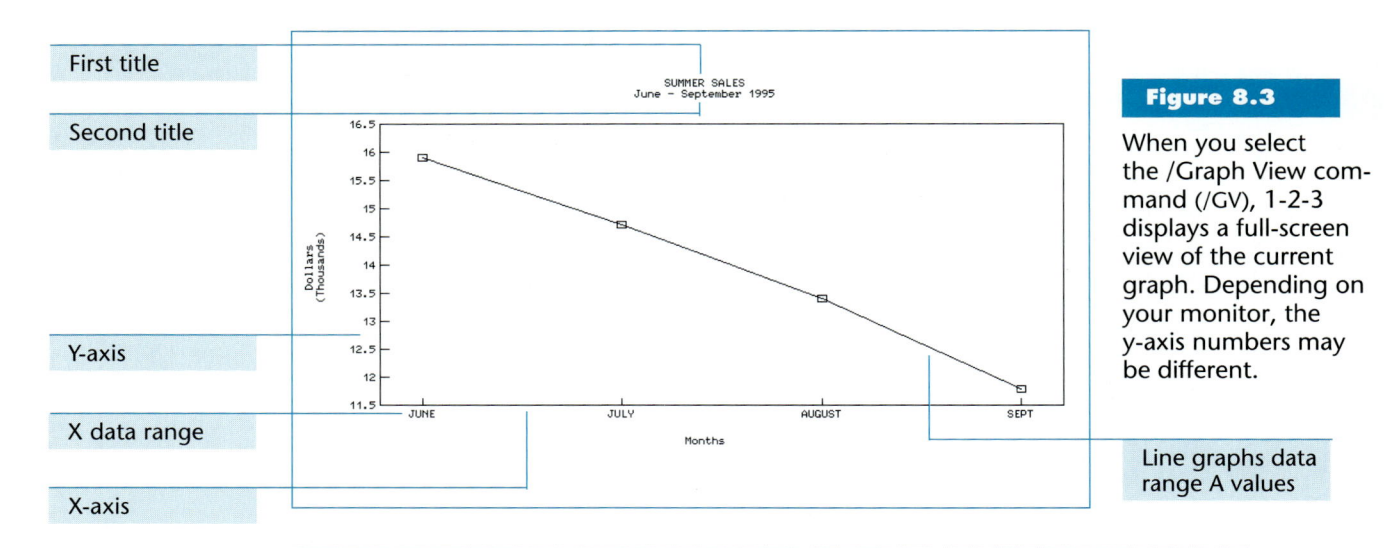

[Figure 8.3 diagram with labels: First title, Second title, Y-axis, X data range, X-axis, Line graphs data range A values. The graph shows SUMMER SALES June – September 1995, with Dollars (Thousands) on the y-axis ranging from 11.5 to 16.5, and Months on the x-axis showing JUNE, JULY, AUGUST, SEPT.]

Figure 8.3

When you select the /Graph View command (/GV), 1-2-3 displays a full-screen view of the current graph. Depending on your monitor, the y-axis numbers may be different.

Note: If you do not see the graph displayed, your system may not have a graphics card for your monitor that supports the display of 1-2-3 graphs.

Y-AXIS
The vertical line that serves as the left border of the graph area. The y-axis displays a range of values or a time period for which data is plotted.

X-AXIS
The horizontal line that borders the graph area on the bottom. The x-axis displays a range of values from which data is plotted.

Lotus 1-2-3 scales the y-axis automatically for the range of values you selected as data range A. The *y-axis* is the vertical axis on the left side of the graph. The indicator "(Thousands)" tells you that the numbers on this axis represent thousands. The label "Dollars" that you specified with the /Graph Options Titles Y-Axis command (/GOTY) tells you that the y-axis values represent thousands of dollars.

Note: The y-axis numbers displayed on your screen may be different depending on the graphics card in your system.

Along the x-axis, 1-2-3 equally spaces the labels you selected as the X range. The *x-axis* is the horizontal axis at the bottom of the graph. The main title and subtitle are centered above the graph.

The four values representing sales for the summer months are plotted as points on the graph. They are spaced according to the time period. The points are connected by lines. The graph shows that sales dropped steadily throughout the summer. You might conclude that this graph represents a typical sales pattern for this particular time period.

32 ▶ Press ⏎, or any other key.

Lotus 1-2-3 returns to the Graph command menu.

33 ▶ Type **Q** to return to READY mode.

34 ▶ Save the changes to the file SALSDATA.WK1.

Now you will go on to the next exercise and learn how to name graph settings and save a graph to a special graph file.

Exercise 8.2

Naming and Saving a Graph

Objectives

After completing this exercise, you will be able to
- Name a graph.
- Save a graph in a graph file.

GRAPH NAME
A name from 1 to 15 characters that identifies a particular set of graph settings. A graph name is saved along with the worksheet file. The graph name can be used to make the settings current and display a particular graph.

After you create a graph, you can assign a name to the current graph settings that you have used to create the graph. *Graph names* are stored with the worksheet file. If you create more than one graph for a worksheet, be sure to name each specific group of settings. Then you can view or modify any of the graphs later. Now you will create a name for the current line graph's settings.

1 ▶ Make sure 1-2-3 is in READY mode.

2 ▶ Press the Slash key (/) to access the Main Menu.

3 ▶ Type **G** to select the Graph command.

The Graph command menu and Graph Settings dialog box are displayed.

4 ▶ Type **N** to select the Name command.

5 ▶ Type **C** to select the Create command.

Lotus 1-2-3 prompts you to enter a name for the current graph settings. The name can be 15 characters or fewer.

6 ▶ Type **LINE-95SUMSALES** and press ⏎.

Lotus 1-2-3 assigns the name to the current set of line graph settings.

GRAPH FILE
A special type of file that you create to store 1-2-3 graph information. Graph files can be printed later with the Lotus PrintGraph utility. Graph filenames can be up to eight characters and must conform to DOS filename rules. Lotus 1-2-3 assigns the .PIC extension to graph filenames automatically.

To print a graph, you must use the PrintGraph utility program that is included with 1-2-3. The PrintGraph utility can only be used to print 1-2-3 graph files. Graph files are created with the /Graph Save command (/GS). A *graph file* is a file that contains the particular settings for printing a graph. When you save a graph file, 1-2-3 adds the file extension .PIC to the name you provide. This extension allows the PrintGraph program to recognize which files contain graph images.

7 ▶ Make sure that the Graph command menu is currently displayed.

8 ▶ Type **S** to select the Save command.

Lotus 1-2-3 prompts you to enter a graph filename. The filename must be 8 characters or fewer.

9 ▶ Type **95SALELN**

10 ▶ Press ⏎.

The current graph settings are saved to the file 95SALELN.PIC. The Graph command menu is active on the control panel, and the Graph Settings dialog box is displayed.

11 ▶ Type **Q** to return to READY mode.

12 ▶ Save the current changes to the file.

Later you will learn how to print the line graph you have created in this lesson. For now, go on to the next exercise to learn how to create other types of graphs.

Exercise 8.3 — Creating Bar and Pie Graphs

Objectives

After completing this exercise, you will be able to
- Create, name, and save a bar graph.
- Create, name, and save a pie graph.

BAR GRAPH
A type of graph that represents data ranges with vertical bars. The height of a vertical bar represents the significance of values in the range.

A *bar graph* is a graph in which values are represented by the height of vertical bars. A bar graph is useful when you want to compare values in a data range or plot more than one data range.

You decide that you want to create a bar graph that shows the change in sales from June to September. You have already created a line graph that shows a similar comparison. You can change the graph type but keep the other settings intact to create a new graph. You will change the current graph type to display the current settings as a bar graph rather than a line graph.

1 ▶ If 1-2-3 is in READY mode, press the Slash key (/) to access the Main Menu.

2 ▶ Type **G** to select the Graph command.

The Graph command menu and Graph Settings dialog box are displayed.

3 ▶ Press F2.

The Graph Settings dialog box is activated.

4 ▶ Type **T**

The pointer moves to the Type setting.

5 ▶ Type **B**

The Bar graph type option is selected, and the pointer moves to the OK command button.

6 ▶ Press ⏎.

The Graph command menu is active on the control panel.

7 ▶ Type **V** to select the View command.

A bar graph appears. It plots sales for June through September. Each value is now represented by a vertical bar, as shown in Figure 8.4.

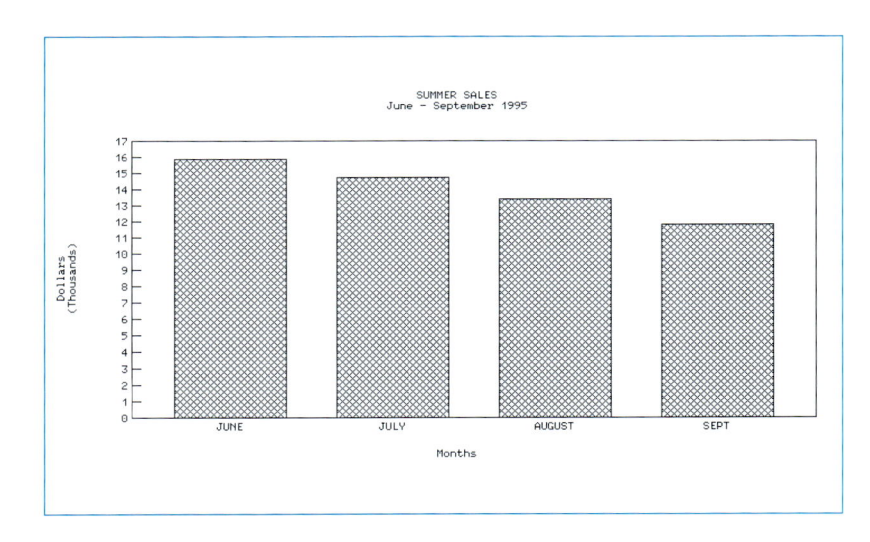

Figure 8.4

After you change the current graph type to Bar, the original line graph settings are represented in this bar graph.

Like the line graph, the bar graph shows the same decrease in sales over this period of time. However, the comparison is in a different graphic format. The decrease seems more gradual because 1-2-3 scaled the y-axis differently.

You decide to name this set of graph settings and then save the graph in a graph file so it can be printed later.

8 ▶ Press ⏎, or any other key, to return to the Graph command menu.

Creating Bar and Pie Graphs

9 ▶ Type **NC** to select the Name and Create commands.

Lotus 1-2-3 prompts you to enter the name for the current graph settings. Notice that the name you assigned to the line graph settings is displayed on the third line of the control panel.

10 ▶ Type **BAR-95SUMSALES**

11 ▶ Press ⏎.

The current graph settings are named, and 1-2-3 returns to the Graph command menu.

12 ▶ Type **S** to select the Save command.

Lotus 1-2-3 prompts you to enter a filename for the current graph. Notice that the graph filename 95SALELN.PIC is displayed on the third line of the control panel.

13 ▶ Type **95SALEBR**

14 ▶ Press ⏎.

The bar graph is saved to a graph file, and 1-2-3 returns to the Graph command menu.

Now you will create one more graph that displays sales for this four-month period—a pie graph.

PIE GRAPH
A type of graph in which data ranges are represented as pie slices or wedges. Each pie slice or wedge represents a value as a part in relation to a whole.

A *pie graph* is one of the simplest types of graphs. Pie graphs represent a single data range. The total of all the values in the range is represented by the pie. In a pie graph, the pie (a circle) is divided into "slices." Each slice represents one value in the range plotted on the graph. A pie graph is useful when you want to compare the values in a small range to each other. Pie graphs also show clearly the relationship between each slice (value) and the total or whole.

You will plot sales for June through September on a pie graph. Again, you can use the same settings that you used for the line and bar graphs.

15 ▶ Make sure that the Graph command menu is active and the Graph Settings dialog box is displayed.

16 ▶ Press F2.

The Graph Settings dialog box is active.

17 ▶ Type **TP**

The Pie graph setting option is selected, and the pointer returns to the OK command button.

18 ▶ Press ⏎.

The Graph command menu is active on the control panel.

19 ▶ Type **V** to select the View command.

A pie graph appears that plots total sales for June through September. Each value is now represented by a pie slice, as shown in Figure 8.5.

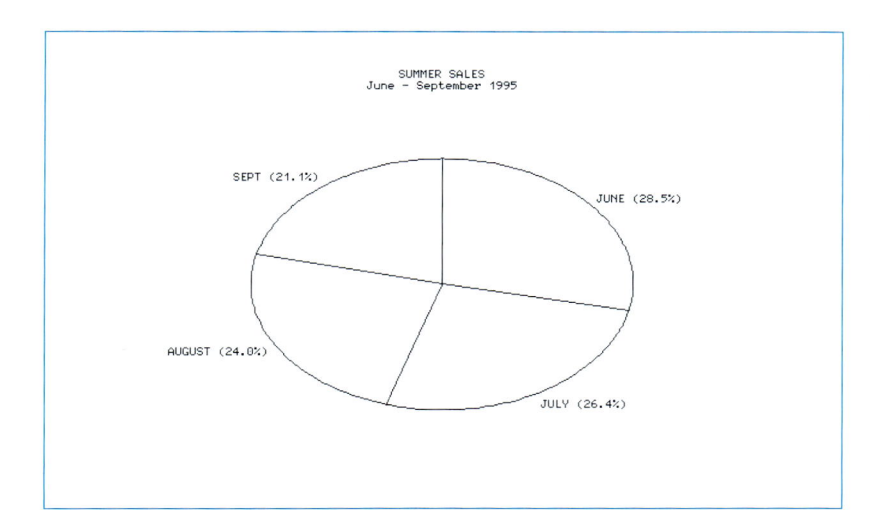

Figure 8.5

After you change the current graph's type to Pie, the original line and bar graph settings are represented in a pie graph.

Notice that there is some additional information on the pie graph. It displays percentages next to each label. The percentages indicate the parts of the whole that each value represents. For example, the current graph shows that August sales are 24.0 percent of the total sales for this four-month period.

Now you will name the current graph settings. Then you will save the graph to a graph file that can be printed later.

20 ▶ Press ⏎, or any other key, to return to the Graph command menu.

21 ▶ Type **NC** to select the Name and Create commands.

Lotus 1-2-3 prompts you to enter a name for the current graph settings. Notice that the names you assigned to the line and bar graph settings are displayed on the third line of the control panel.

22 ▶ Type **PIE-95SUMSALES**

23 ▶ Press ⏎.

The current graph settings are named, and 1-2-3 returns to the Graph command menu.

24 ▶ Type **S** to select the Save command.

Lotus 1-2-3 prompts you to enter a graph filename. Notice that the graph filenames for the line and bar graphs are displayed on the third line of the control panel.

25 ▶ Type **95SALEPI**

26 ▶ Press ⏎.

The current graph is saved to the file 95SALEPI.PIC, and 1-2-3 returns to the Graph command menu.

27 ▶ Type **Q** to return to READY mode.

Creating Bar and Pie Graphs

28 ▶ Save the current settings to the same file.

Later you will learn how to print a graph file with the PrintGraph utility. For now, go on to the next exercise to learn how to make a named graph current so that you can modify it.

Exercise 8.4 — Selecting and Enhancing Named Graphs

Objectives

After completing this exercise, you will be able to
- Select a graph to make it current.
- Enhance a bar graph.
- Enhance a pie graph.
- Separate a slice from a pie graph.

Once you have assigned a name to a group of graph settings, you can use the name to make the named graph current. You do this by selecting the /Graph Name Use command (/GNU). Only one set of graph settings can be current at one time.

Right now the current graph is a pie graph. You will make the bar graph that you created earlier in this lesson the current graph.

1 ▶ Make sure 1-2-3 is in READY mode. Press the Slash key (/) to access the Main Menu.

2 ▶ Type **G** to select the Graph command.

The Graph command menu is activated on the control panel, and the Graph Settings dialog box is displayed.

3 ▶ Type **N** to select the Name command.

4 ▶ Type **U** to select the Use command.

Lotus 1-2-3 prompts you to select the named graph you want to make current. An alphabetical list of the graph names associated with the current worksheet is displayed on the third line of the control panel.

5 ▶ If necessary, move the menu pointer to the graph name BAR-95SUMSALES and press ⏎.

The settings for the bar graph are current, and 1-2-3 displays the bar graph on screen.

8 ▶ Graphing Worksheet Data

6 ▶ Press ⏎, or any other key, to return to the Graph command menu.

Lotus 1-2-3 provides many features that let you enhance graphs for presentation. Now you will edit the Graph Settings and Graph Legends & Titles dialog boxes to enhance the appearance of the graph.

7 ▶ Press F2.

The Graph Settings dialog box is active.

8 ▶ Type **3** to select the 3-D bars setting.

An "x" appears next to this option in the check box, indicating that it is selected.

9 ▶ Press ⏎ twice.

The selection is stored, and the Graph command menu is displayed.

10 ▶ Type **V** to select the View command.

A three-dimensional bar graph appears, as shown in Figure 8.6.

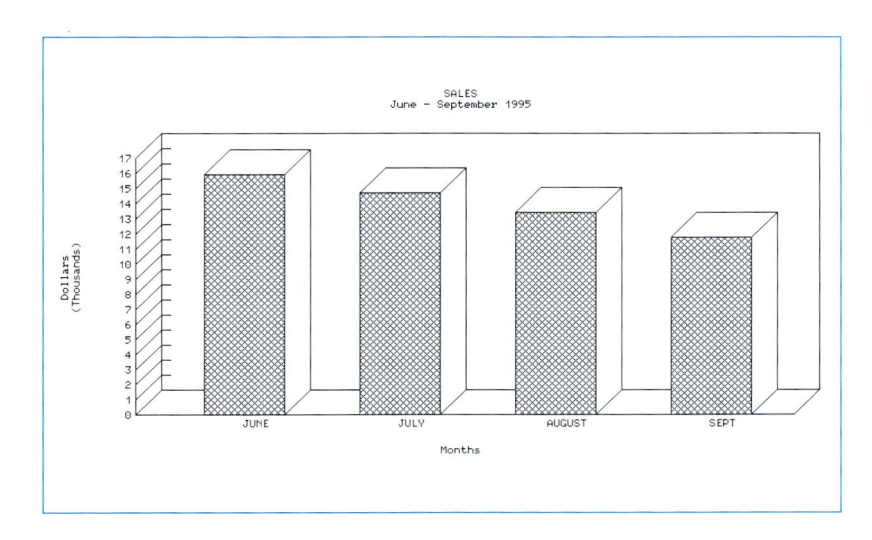

Figure 8.6

The 3-D bars option enhances the current graph by making the vertical bars three-dimensional.

Because you have made a change to this graph, you will replace the previous version with the current version.

11 ▶ Press ⏎, or any other key, to return to the Graph command menu.

12 ▶ Type **NC** to select the Name and Create commands.

Lotus 1-2-3 prompts you to enter a name for the current graph settings.

13 ▶ If necessary, move the menu pointer to the graph name BAR-95SUMSALES and press ⏎.

The current graph settings replace the previous version, and 1-2-3 returns to the Graph command menu. When you use the same name

Selecting and Enhancing Named Graphs

assigned to the previous graph, you update the named graph with the current settings.

So that you can print this version of the bar graph, you will update the graph file 95SALEBR.PIC with the current changes.

14 ▶ Type **S** to select the Save command.

Lotus 1-2-3 prompts you to enter the filename for the current graph.

15 ▶ Move the menu pointer to the filename 95SALEBR.PIC, and press ⏎.

Lotus 1-2-3 prompts you to replace the existing file with the current changes or cancel the operation.

16 ▶ Type **R** to replace the previous version of the file.

The current graph, including the 3-D bars enhancement, is saved to a graph file.

As you make changes to a graph or to the represented worksheet values, you will likely want to save the changes. Use the /Graph Name Create command (/GNC) to update the graph settings associated with a particular graph. Use the /Graph Save command (/GS) to save the changes to a graph file that you want to print.

Also, remember to use the /File Save command (/FS) to save all the named graph settings with the worksheet. Even if you do not change any worksheet data, 1-2-3 considers any adjustments to graph settings to be worksheet changes. Therefore, you must save any named graph settings with the worksheet. Otherwise, you will not be able to use those settings the next time you load the worksheet. Now you will save the current worksheet and enhance your pie graph.

17 ▶ Type **Q** to select the Graph command menu's Quit option.

Lotus 1-2-3 returns to READY mode.

18 ▶ Save the current changes to the same file.

You can enhance the display of a pie graph by adding hatch patterns or shading to distinguish the pie slices. Also, you can emphasize a particular value or part of the whole by separating a slice from the pie. A *hatch pattern*, or shading, is applied to a pie slice when you specify a B data range. The B data range must be the same size as the A data range. In each cell of the B data range, you enter a number between 1 and 8. Each number represents a specific hatch pattern. Furthermore, you can separate, or explode, one or more slices from the pie by adding 100 to a hatch pattern number. For example, suppose you enter the number 102 in a B data range cell. The corresponding pie slice will have the number 2 hatch pattern, and it will be separated from the pie.

HATCH PATTERN
A pattern made up of parallel and/or crisscrossing diagonal lines. Hatch patterns shade a graph element, such as a bar or a pie slice. Seven hatch patterns are available for graph elements in 1-2-3.

Now you will make current the pie graph settings you created earlier, and then you will enhance the pie graph with hatch patterns.

19 ▶ Press the Slash key (/) to access the Main Menu.

20 ▶ Type **GNU** to select the Graph, Name, and Use commands.

> A list of the current worksheet's named graphs is displayed on the third line of the control panel.

21 ▶ Move the menu pointer to the graph name PIE-95SUMSALES.

22 ▶ Press ⏎.

> The pie graph is current and is displayed.

23 ▶ Press ⏎, or any other key.

24 ▶ Type **Q** to select the Graph command menu's Quit option.

> The current worksheet is displayed, and 1-2-3 is in READY mode.

25 ▶ Move the cell pointer to cell B4.

> The cell pointer is two cells above the label "JUNE." This will be the first cell in the pie graph's B data range.

26 ▶ Type **101**

27 ▶ Press →.

> The hatch pattern number for the "JUNE" pie slice is entered. The value assigns hatch pattern 1 to the slice and separates the slice from the rest of the pie.

28 ▶ Type **2**

29 ▶ Press →.

30 ▶ Type **3**

31 ▶ Press →.

32 ▶ Type **4**

33 ▶ Press ⏎ 3 times.

> The B data range values are entered, and the cell pointer is on cell B4.

34 ▶ Press the Slash key (/) to access the Main Menu.

35 ▶ Type **GB** to select the Graph command and B data range option.

36 ▶ Type **.** (a period) to anchor the current cell.

37 ▶ Press END, and then press →.

> The range B4..E4 is highlighted.

38 ▶ Press ⏎.

> The B data range is selected, and the Graph Settings dialog box reappears.

Selecting and Enhancing Named Graphs

39 ▶ Type **V** to select the View command.

The pie graph is displayed, as shown in Figure 8.7. Notice that each slice has a hatch pattern, and the "JUNE" sales slice is separated from the pie.

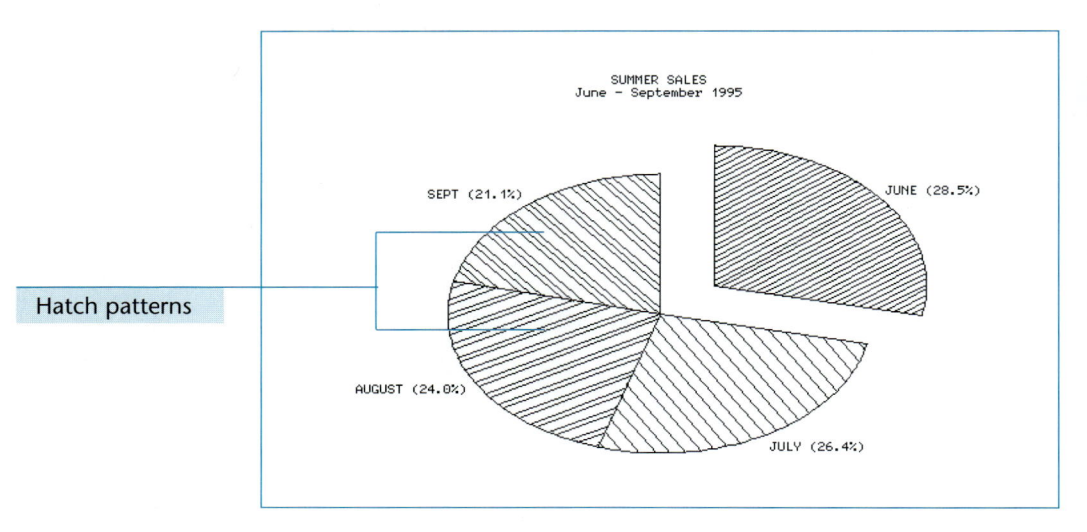

Figure 8.7

After you enter the B data range, which contains hatch pattern numbers, the slices in the pie graph each have a unique hatch pattern. The "JUNE" sales slice is separated from the pie to emphasize the summer month that produced the most sales.

Hatch patterns

Now you will update the named graph settings for the current graph and then update its graph file.

40 ▶ Press ⏎, or any other key.

The Graph Settings dialog box reappears.

41 ▶ Type **NC** to select the Name and Create commands.

42 ▶ Move the menu pointer to the graph name PIE-95SUMSALES.

43 ▶ Press ⏎.

The current graph settings are stored with the selected graph name.

44 ▶ Type **S**

Lotus 1-2-3 prompts you to enter a name for the graph file. Graph filenames in the current directory display on the control panel.

45 ▶ Move the menu pointer to the filename 95SALEPI.PIC.

46 ▶ Press ⏎.

47 ▶ Type **R** to replace the previous version of the file.

48 ▶ Type **Q** to select the Graph command menu's Quit option.

Lotus 1-2-3 returns to READY mode.

49 ▶ Press (HOME), and save the current changes to the same file.

248   **8 ▶ Graphing Worksheet Data**

Exercise 8.5

Creating a Graph with Multiple Data Ranges

Objectives

After completing this exercise, you will be able to
- Create a graph that plots multiple data ranges.
- Label graph components with worksheet labels.
- Enter legends to identify graphed data ranges.
- Enhance a graph with horizontal grid lines.

You can plot up to six ranges of data in all types of graphs except the pie graph. This lets you create more complex representations or illustrations of worksheet data. When using 1-2-3's graphing capability, you will often want to create different graphs for the same worksheet. In some cases, you may want to start over and create a completely different graph from the current graph. You can use the /Graph Reset Graph command (/GRG) to clear all the current graph settings.

At the owner's request, you will create a bar graph that plots summer sales for all the recording merchandise.

1 ▶ Make sure 1-2-3 is in READY mode.

2 ▶ Press the Slash key (/) to access the Main Menu.

3 ▶ Type **G** to select the Graph command.

4 ▶ Type **RG** to clear all current graph settings.

5 ▶ Type **TB** to select the Type and Bar commands.

6 ▶ Type **A** to select the first data range option.

7 ▶ Move the cell pointer to cell B8.

   The cell pointer is on the cell that contains the compact disc sales for June.

8 ▶ Type **.** (a period) to anchor the current cell.

9 ▶ Press ↓ 4 times.

   June sales figures for all merchandise are highlighted.

10 ▶ Press ↵.

   The A data range is selected, and the Graph command menu appears.

11 ▶ Type **B** to select the second data range option.

12 ▶ Move the cell pointer to cell C8.

The cell pointer is on the cell that contains the compact disc sales for July.

13 ▶ Type **.** (a period) to anchor the current cell.

14 ▶ Press ⬇ 4 times.

July sales figures for all merchandise are highlighted.

15 ▶ Press ⏎.

The B data range is selected.

16 ▶ Type **C** to select the third data range option.

17 ▶ Move the cell pointer to cell D8.

The cell pointer is on the cell that contains compact disc sales for August.

18 ▶ Type **.** (a period) to anchor the current cell.

19 ▶ Press ⬇ 4 times.

August sales figures for all merchandise are highlighted.

20 ▶ Press ⏎.

The C data range is selected.

21 ▶ Type **D** to select the fourth data range.

22 ▶ Move the cell pointer to cell E8.

The cell pointer is on the cell that contains the compact disc sales for September.

23 ▶ Type **.** (a period) to anchor the current cell.

24 ▶ Press ⬇ 4 times.

September sales figures for all merchandise are highlighted.

25 ▶ Press ⏎.

The D data range is selected.

26 ▶ Type **X** to select the X data range option.

27 ▶ Move the cell pointer to cell A8.

The cell pointer is on the cell that contains the label "Compact Discs."

28 ▶ Type **.** (a period) to anchor the current cell.

29 ▶ Press ⬇ 4 times.

The labels in the range A8..A12 are highlighted.

30 ▶ Press ⏎.

250 **8 ▶ Graphing Worksheet Data**

Now you will enter some titles, labels, and other enhancements to the current graph. When entering titles for a graph, you may find it easier to use labels that already exist in the worksheet. You can do this by entering a backslash character (\) and the cell address that contains the label. The cell address can be entered at a command prompt or directly into the appropriate dialog box setting.

31 ▶ Type **OT** to select the Options and Titles commands.

32 ▶ Press F2.

The Graph Legends & Titles dialog box is active.

33 ▶ Type **TF**

The pointer moves to the Titles First setting.

34 ▶ Type **\c1**

35 ▶ Press TAB.

The cell reference to a worksheet label is entered, and the pointer moves to the Titles Second setting.

36 ▶ Type **\c2**

37 ▶ Press TAB twice.

The cell reference to a worksheet label is entered, and the pointer moves to the Titles Y axis setting.

38 ▶ Type **Dollars**

39 ▶ Press ⏎.

The y-axis label is entered, and the pointer moves to the OK command button.

LEGEND
A 1-2-3 graph element that identifies the information represented by bars, points, or pie slices in a graph.

When you create a graph with more than one data range, it is helpful to include legends. *Legends* identify each of the data ranges plotted on the graph. In bar graphs, a legend consists of a box with a hatch pattern next to a label. The label identifies the data represented by the bar. Now you will enter legends into the current worksheet. As with other titles and labels in your graph, you can use cell addresses to label legends with worksheet labels.

40 ▶ Type **LA** to select the Legend and A data range setting options.

The pointer moves to the A data range setting in the Legend group.

41 ▶ Type **\b6**

42 ▶ Press TAB.

43 ▶ Type **\c6**

44 ▶ Press TAB.

45 ▶ Type **\d6**

46 ▶ Press TAB.

47 ▶ Type **\e6**

Creating a Graph with Multiple Data Ranges

48 ▶ Press ⏎ twice.

The Titles command submenu is active on the control panel.

49 ▶ Press ESC.

The Graph command menu and Graph Settings dialog box appear.

Finally, you will add two more enhancements to the current bar graph. Look at the Graph Settings dialog box. Notice that there is a group of grid line settings. You can use grid line settings to add vertical, horizontal, or both vertical and horizontal grid lines to the graph. Grid lines serve as a valuable aid for reading graphs. To complete the current bar graph, you will add grid lines and turn on the 3-D bars enhancement.

50 ▶ Press F2.

The Graph Settings dialog box is activated.

51 ▶ Type **GH** to select the Grid lines and Horizontal settings.

52 ▶ Press ⏎.

53 ▶ Type **3**

The 3-D bars setting is turned on.

54 ▶ Press ⏎ twice.

The Options command submenu is activated on the control panel.

55 ▶ Type **Q** to select the Options command submenu's Quit option.

The Graph command menu appears.

56 ▶ Type **V** to select the View command.

The current bar graph is displayed, as shown in Figure 8.8.

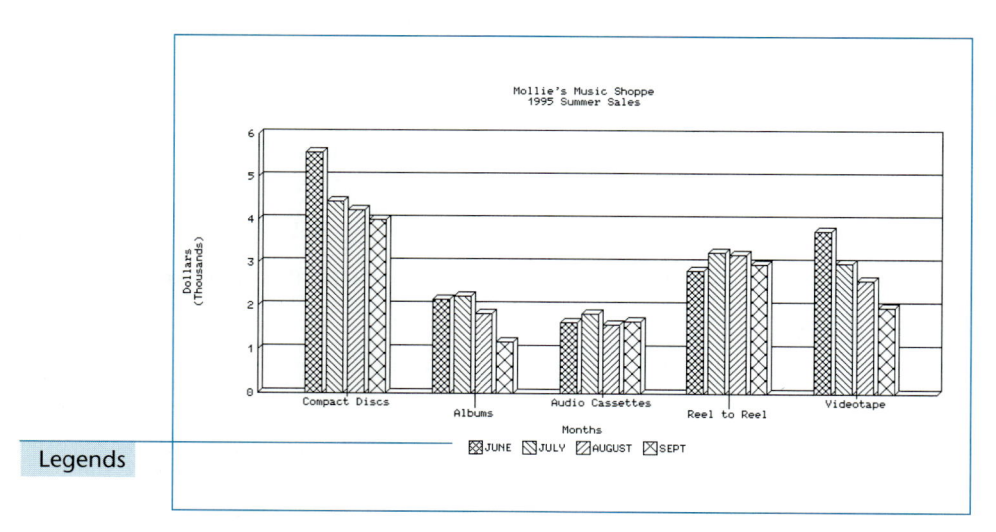

Figure 8.8

After you select the bar graph's data ranges and add other enhancements, your current graph should look like this.

For each product along the x-axis, 1-2-3 displays four vertical bars that represent the products' sales for each month. The first bar in each group represents June sales, the second represents July sales, and the third

252   8 ▶ Graphing Worksheet Data

represents August sales. The fourth represents September sales. As you can see, the legends are important because they identify each data range plotted on the graph. Now you will name and save the current bar graph.

57 ▶ Press ⏎, or any other key, to return to the graph menu.

58 ▶ Type **NC** to select the Name and Create commands.

59 ▶ Type **Summer Sales 95** and press ⏎.

The name is assigned to the current graph settings, and 1-2-3 returns to the Graph command menu.

60 ▶ Type **S** to select the Save command.

61 ▶ Type **3DBSALES** and press ⏎.

The current graph is stored in a 1-2-3 print file.

62 ▶ Type **Q**

Lotus 1-2-3 returns to READY mode.

63 ▶ Save the current changes to the same worksheet file.

Now you will go on to the next exercise to learn how to print 1-2-3 graph files with the PrintGraph utility.

Exercise 8.6 Using the Lotus PrintGraph Utility to Print Graphs

Objectives

After completing this exercise, you will be able to
- Access the Lotus PrintGraph utility.
- Print 1-2-3 graph files.

PRINTGRAPH UTILITY
A utility program that comes with the Lotus 1-2-3, Release 2.3 package. This program allows you to print special graph files you create in 1-2-3 with the /Graph Save command (/GS).

You use 1-2-3 to create graphs, name graph settings and save graph print files. However, to print graphs that you have saved to graph files, you must use the Lotus PrintGraph utility. The Lotus *PrintGraph utility* is a special program that allows you to print graph files that have the .PIC filename extension. To use the PrintGraph utility, you must first exit from the 1-2-3 application and then access the Lotus Access System. *The Lotus Access System* is a menu screen from which you can access 1-2-3 or one of several utility programs. The other utility programs are PrintGraph, Translate, and Install. Translate is used for transporting data between 1-2-3 and other software applications. The Install program allows you to make changes to certain hardware or other default 1-2-3 settings whenever necessary.

LOTUS ACCESS SYSTEM
A menu environment that lets you access the 1-2-3 Translate, PrintGraph, or Install programs. Using the access system makes it easier for you to switch between 1-2-3 and the other utility programs; however, it does use roughly 2KB of memory.

Like the 1-2-3 application, the PrintGraph utility can be accessed in either of two ways. First, you can type LOTUS at the DOS prompt and press ⏎ to access the Lotus Access Menu screen. Then select the PrintGraph option, which starts the PrintGraph utility. Or (second) you can simply type the command PGRAPH at the DOS prompt to enter the PrintGraph utility directly. (If you are working with 1-2-3 on a floppy diskette, you will have to replace the 1-2-3 program disk with the disk that contains the PrintGraph program before you type PGRAPH.)

In this exercise, you will print the graph files you created in this lesson for the owner of Mollie's Music Shoppe. You will do so by quitting 1-2-3 and then accessing PrintGraph from the Lotus Access Menu.

1 ▶ Make sure you have saved the current worksheet.

2 ▶ Press the Slash key (/) to access the Main Menu.

3 ▶ Type **Q** to select the Quit command.

4 ▶ Type **Y** to select the Yes option.

Depending on how your system has been set up, you will see either the Lotus Access System screen or a DOS prompt on your monitor. If you see the Lotus Access System screen, as shown in Figure 8.9, skip steps 5 and 6.

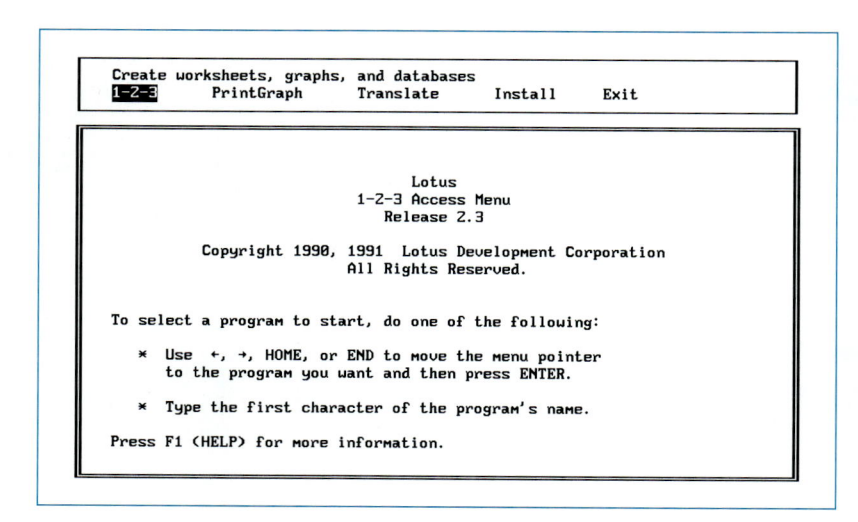

Figure 8.9

The Lotus Access System screen displays a menu of utility program options. You can access the 1-2-3 application, the PrintGraph utility, the Translate utility, the Install program, or exit from the Lotus Access System.

5 ▶ Type **lotus** (or type **pgraph** if you are using a dual floppy system.)

6 ▶ Press ⏎.

The Lotus Access System screen appears, as shown in Figure 8.9. (If you are using a dual floppy system, and the PrintGraph utility's opening screen appears, as shown in Figure 8.10, skip step 7.)

Now you will start the Lotus PrintGraph utility.

254   8 ▶ Graphing Worksheet Data

7 ▶ Type **P** to select the PrintGraph option.

The PrintGraph utility's opening screen appears, as shown in Figure 8.10.

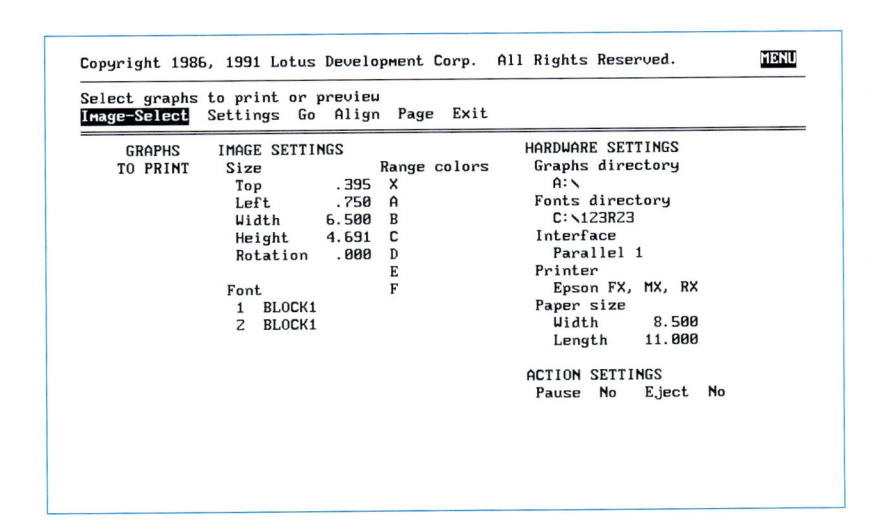

```
Copyright 1986, 1991 Lotus Development Corp.  All Rights Reserved.    MENU

Select graphs to print or preview
Image-Select  Settings  Go  Align  Page  Exit

   GRAPHS      IMAGE SETTINGS                    HARDWARE SETTINGS
   TO PRINT    Size              Range colors    Graphs directory
               Top       .395  X                   A:\
               Left      .750  A                 Fonts directory
               Width    6.500  B                   C:\123R23
               Height   4.691  C                 Interface
               Rotation  .000  D                   Parallel 1
                               E                 Printer
               Font            F                   Epson FX, MX, RX
                 1  BLOCK1                       Paper size
                 2  BLOCK1                         Width     8.500
                                                   Length   11.000

                                                 ACTION SETTINGS
                                                 Pause  No   Eject  No
```

Figure 8.10

The PrintGraph Utility's opening screen appears when you select the PrintGraph option from the Lotus Access System.

At the top of the screen, below the copyright information, is a command menu similar to the command menus you see in 1-2-3. You select commands in the same way that you do in 1-2-3. The only difference is that option explanations or option submenus are displayed above the options rather than below them.

The rest of the screen displays the settings currently in effect for printing graphs. Some of the settings were selected when Lotus 1-2-3 was installed on your system. You might want to change other settings, depending on the graph you print. For example, you might want to change the size of the graph and/or selected fonts.

In this exercise, you will step through the basic steps for printing a graph, using the default settings provided with PrintGraph. The first step is to make sure that the current PrintGraph directory setting is correctly set to locate your graph files.

8 ▶ Type **S** to select the Settings command.

9 ▶ Type **H** to select the Hardware command.

Using the Lotus PrintGraph Utility to Print Graphs

10 ▶ Type **G** to select the Graphs directory command.

PrintGraph prompts you to enter the directory (and drive) where your graph files are stored.

11 ▶ Type **a:** (or **b:** if you do not have a hard disk).

12 ▶ Press ⏎.

The Graphs directory setting is changed, and PrintGraph returns to the previous menu level.

> Note: If your graph files are stored on another drive, or in another subdirectory, enter that drive and/or subdirectory.

13 ▶ Type **QQ** to select the Quit options that back you up to the main PrintGraph menu.

> Note: You are now ready to continue with this exercise and print one or more graph files. However, see your instructor or technical support person if you encounter an error message box that stops you. Often an incorrect PrintGraph hardware setting will prevent you from performing a PrintGraph operation.

14 ▶ Type **I** to select the Image-Select command.

PrintGraph displays another screen with a list of graph file names in the current directory. These are files with the file extension .PIC.

15 ▶ Move the pointer to the graph file 3DBSALES.

16 ▶ Press SPACEBAR to select this graph file.

PrintGraph places a pound sign (#) to the left of the graph filename, indicating that it has been selected.

At this point, it is a good idea to preview your graph before you print. The preview feature displays a miniature version of the graph document on a graphic screen. The miniature version shows you approximately how the graph will look on the printed page. Graphs take longer to print than worksheets. When you preview your graph, you can verify that it is the right graph. Also, you can spot-check that the graph is set up properly before you print.

17 ▶ Press F10 (Graph command).

The selected graph file is displayed in PrintGraph's preview.

Note: If there are any problems with the graph, press ⏎ twice to exit this screen and the previous screen. Then exit PrintGraph, and load 1-2-3. Retrieve the worksheet with the named graph settings that were used to save the graph file. Make the necessary changes to the graph. Next, use the /Graph Name Create command (/GNC) to save the setting changes with the same graph name. Also, use the /Graph Save command (/GS) to save the modified graph to the same graph filename. Then make sure you save the changes to the worksheet file. Finally, exit 1-2-3 and return to PrintGraph to print the corrected graph file.

18 ▶ Press ⏎ to exit PrintGraph's print preview screen.

19 ▶ Press ⏎ again to select this graph file and return to the PrintGraph menu.

PrintGraph displays the name of the graph file that you selected under the column entitled "Graphs to Print."

20 ▶ Make sure that your printer is on and has paper. Also, make sure that the paper is properly aligned.

21 ▶ Type **A** to select the Align command.

Like the same option in 1-2-3, the Align command tells PrintGraph that your printer is ready to print.

22 ▶ Type **G** to select the Go command.

The graph prints.

Note: If an error message appears, perhaps the hardware settings within PrintGraph are not properly set. Ask your instructor or a technical support person to help you correct any problems.

23 ▶ Type **P** to select the Page command.

If you have a dot-matrix printer, the paper advances one sheet. If you have a laser printer, the printed page ejects if it has not already ejected.

Using the Lotus PrintGraph Utility to Print Graphs

After printing a graph, you can print another graph or you can exit the PrintGraph utility. If you want to print another graph, use the Image-Select command to redisplay the list of graph files. Move the pointer to the graph filename you just printed, and press the SPACEBAR to "deselect" it. Then select the other graph file you want to print. You can also select more than one graph filename to be printed. Repeat the printing process to print the selected graph file or files.

24 ▶ When you are ready to exit PrintGraph, type **E** to select the Exit command.

PrintGraph prompts you to indicate whether you want to exit the PrintGraph session.

25 ▶ Type **Y** to select the Yes option and exit PrintGraph.

Depending on how you accessed the PrintGraph utility, you will see either the Lotus Access Menu screen or the DOS prompt.

26 ▶ If you see the Lotus Access Menu screen, type **E** to select the Exit command.

You return to the system DOS prompt.

Concept Summary ▷ ▷ ▷ ▷ ▷ ▷

■ Spreadsheet software often has graphing capabilities that let you graph worksheet data. Graphs are another tool for analyzing and understanding information in a worksheet.

■ Most spreadsheet software lets you create line, bar, pie, stacked-bar, and a variety of other graphs. Many formatting options are available to improve the appearance of graphs. Different types of graphs can be created for the same data ranges, so you can choose the type that best presents your message.

■ By giving a name to a group of graph settings, you can always access a particular graph for editing and enhancement.

■ Unless the spreadsheet software package lets you print a graph directly from the program, you can save graphs in special graph files that can be printed later, usually through a utility program.

■ Graphs are dynamically linked with their associated worksheets. Thus any changes to worksheet data are reflected in the graph automatically.

8 ▶ Graphing Worksheet Data

Command Summary

/Graph Type (/GT) [Line XY Bar Stacked bar Pie HLCO Mixed]
specifies one of seven graph types for the current graph

/Graph X (/GX)
specifies the X data range for the graph's x-axis

/Graph A (/GA) [B C D E F]
specifies worksheet ranges to be graphed

/Graph View (/GV)
displays the current graph on screen

/Graph Options Titles (/GOT) [First Second X-Axis Y-Axis]
specifies text labels as graph titles or axis labels

/Graph Name Create (/GNC)
names the current graph settings

/Graph Save (/GS)
saves the current graph settings to a graph file (.PIC format)

/Graph Name Use (/GNU)
makes named graph settings the current graph

/Graph Reset Graph (/GRG)
clears all the current graph settings

/Graph Options Legends (/GOL) [A B C D E F]
specifies legends that identify graphed data ranges

F10 (Graph command)
displays the current graph when 1-2-3 is in READY mode
displays a selected graph in PrintGraph's print preview

LOTUS (at DOS prompt)
loads the Lotus Access System menu

PrintGraph (from Lotus Access System menu)
loads the PrintGraph utility program

PGRAPH (at DOS prompt)
loads the PrintGraph utility program from DOS

Settings Hardware Graphs-Directory (in PrintGraph)
specifies the drive and/or directory that contains graph files (.PIC format)

Image-Select (in PrintGraph)
selects one or more graph files for printing

Align Go (in PrintGraph)
tells PrintGraph that the printer is ready and prints a selected graph

Page (in PrintGraph)
advances the paper in the printer after printing a graph

Exit (in PrintGraph)
quits (leaves) the PrintGraph utility program and returns to the Lotus Access System menu or the DOS prompt

Exit (from Lotus Access System menu)
quits (leaves) the Lotus Access System menu and returns to the DOS prompt

Applications

Applications

Begin doing the applications by loading 1-2-3, if necessary. Place your student data disk in drive A (or drive B if you do not have a hard disk). Change the current directory to the drive that contains the student data disk. Also, change the Clock setting in the Global Settings dialog box so that the current filename is displayed on the status line.

Business

Sales Analysis

1. Along with the sales comparison data, you want to send the branch managers a graph that shows 1994 sales levels versus 1995 sales levels. Retrieve the file SALES7.WK1 and create the line graph shown in Figure 8.11. Be sure to enter the first and second titles, the y-axis title, and legends as shown in the figure.

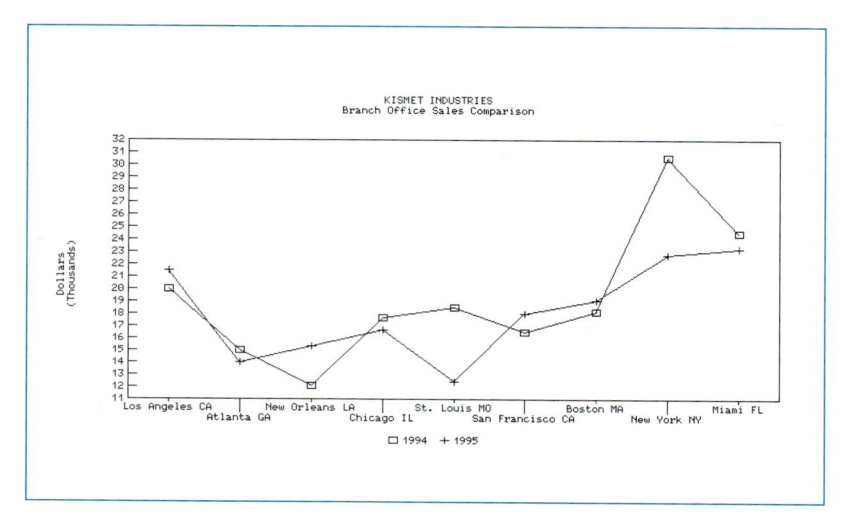

Figure 8.11

Create the line graph shown here for application 1 (Sales Analysis).

Specify the branch office locations as the X data range, 1994 sales figures as the A data range, and 1995 sales figures as the B data range. If your monitor can display graphics, look at the graph. Assign the name SALESCOMPLINE to the current graph settings. Save the graph to a graph file called SALES8.PIC, and then save the worksheet as SALES8.WK1. Then exit 1-2-3 and access the PrintGraph utility program. Print the line graph, and then exit PrintGraph and the Lotus Access System (if necessary).

If you have some extra time, load 1-2-3, retrieve the file SALES8.WK1, and create a bar graph that shows the overall change in sales for each office. Name the graph settings, save the bar graph to a graph file, and then save the changes to the worksheet file. If your printer can print graphics, use the PrintGraph utility to print the bar graph.

Business

Small Business

2. You will include a bar graph with your break-even analysis to hand in with the worksheet data. Retrieve the file PRFLOSS8.WK1, and create the three-dimensional bar graph shown in Figure 8.12. To complete this application, perform the following steps:

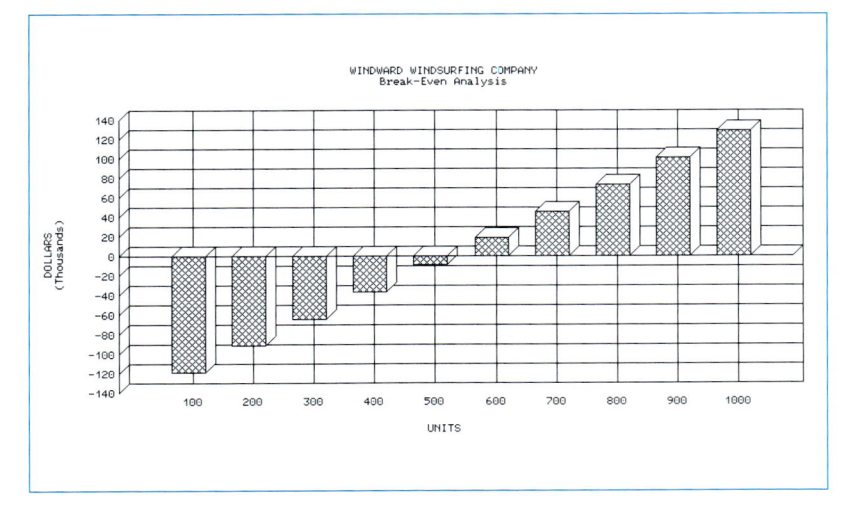

Figure 8.12

Follow the instructions in application 2 (Small Business) to create this graph.

a. Specify the Units Made values as the X data range and the Total Profit(Loss) values as the A data range.

b. Enter the first, second, y-axis, and x-axis titles as shown in the figure.

c. Enhance the graph with vertical and horizontal grid lines and 3-D bars.

d. If your monitor can display graphics, view the graph.

e. Assign the name 3DBARBREAKEVEN to the current graph settings. Save the graph as PROFIT8.PIC.

f. Save the worksheet as PROFIT8.WK1, and exit 1-2-3.

g. If your printer can print graphics, use the PrintGraph utility to print the bar graph. Exit the PrintGraph utility after printing the graph.

Business

Accounting

3. As a part of your project, you will include two pie graphs that show the ending debit and credit account balances for April. Retrieve the file WORKSHT8.WK1, and create the pie graphs shown in Figures 8.13 and 8.14. The pie graph of balance sheet debit accounts will represent the eight account names in the range A9..A16 and their debit balances in the range S9..S16. The pie graph of balance sheet credit accounts will represent the four account names in the range A19..A22 and their credit balances in the range U19..U22.

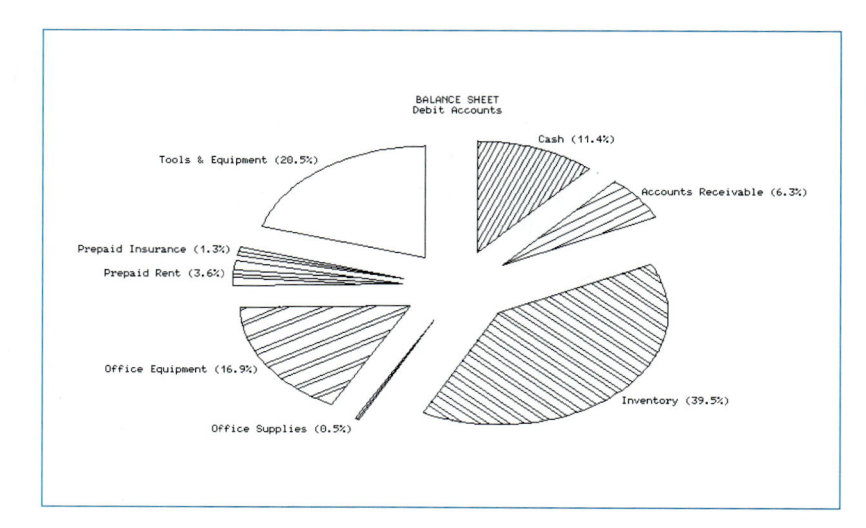

Figure 8.13

Follow the instructions in application 3 (Accounting) to create this pie graph of balance sheet debit accounts.

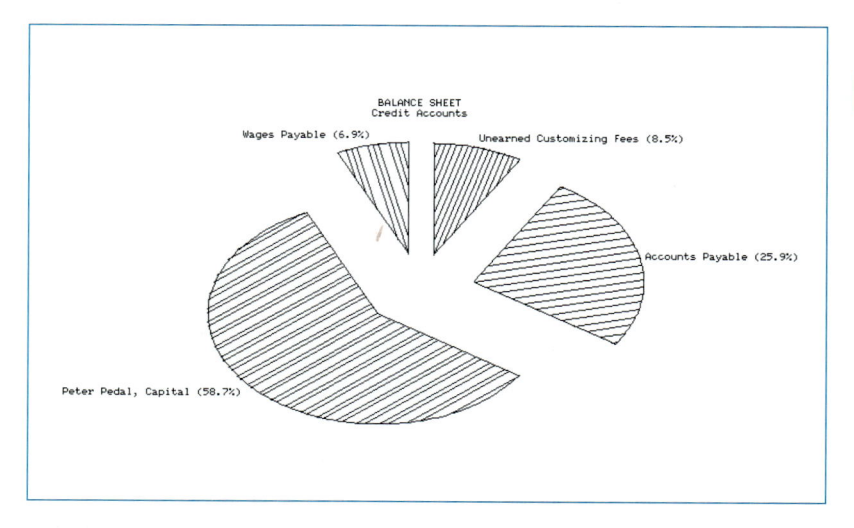

Figure 8.14

Follow the instructions in application 3 (Accounting) to create this pie graph of balance sheet credit accounts.

To enhance the graphs with hatch patterns and exploded pie slices, enter and specify B data ranges that correspond to each account in column W.

Name the debits pie graph BALSHTDEBS-PIE, and save it in a graph file named DBALNCE8.PIC. Name the credits pie graph BALSHTCRED-PIE, and save it in a graph file named CBALNCE8.PIC. Save the changes to the worksheet as BALANCE8.WK1. Exit 1-2-3, and use the PrintGraph utility to print the pie graphs.

HINT

Add 100 to each hatch pattern number to separate, or explode, the slices.

Social Studies

Student Survey

4. Studying survey results can be more enjoyable when you look at graphic representations of response data. Create a pie graph that illustrates attitude responses for football as parts of a whole and a bar graph that compares responses for football, baseball, and basketball. First you need to make some changes to the worksheet's format to simplify the graphing process. Retrieve the file SURVEY7.WK1, and do the following tasks:

   a. Edit the labels in the range A5..A7 to remove the word "Varsity" from each label.

   b. Delete the columns labeled "Rating" and "Variance," and then delete each column labeled "Percent."

   c. Create the pie graph shown in Figure 8.15. Specify the range of rating categories (column headings) as the X data range. Specify the range of responses for football (in row 5) as the A range.

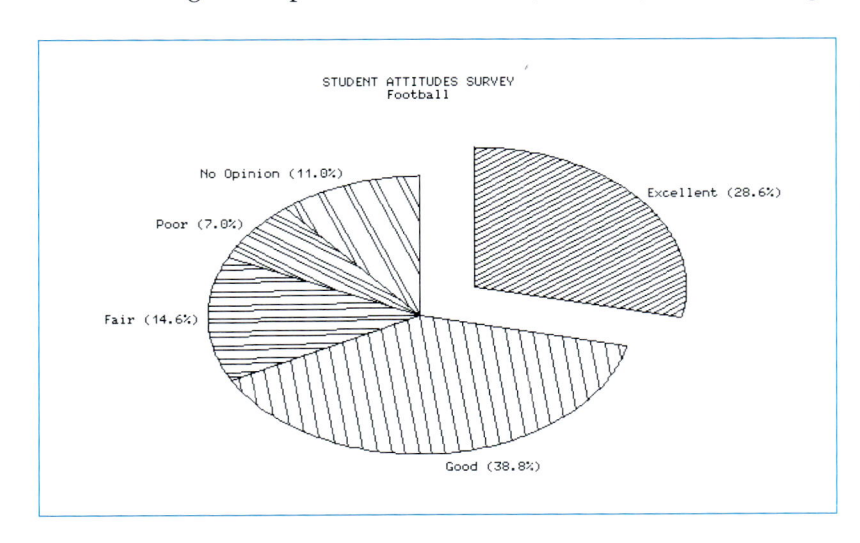

Figure 8.15

Follow the instructions in application 4 (Student Survey) to create this pie graph of student responses to football.

   d. Enter a range of hatch pattern numbers in row 2, placing one number above each column heading. Add 100 to the hatch pattern number above the label "Excellent." Specify this range as the graph's B data range.

   e. Enter the graph's first and second titles, as shown in Figure 8.15.

   f. If your monitor can display graphics, view the graph.

   g. Name the pie graph settings as PIE-FOOTBALL, and save the graph as PSURVEY8.PIC.

   h. Use the /Graph Reset Graph command (/GRG) to clear the current graph settings.

   i. Create the bar graph shown in Figure 8.16.

Applications 263

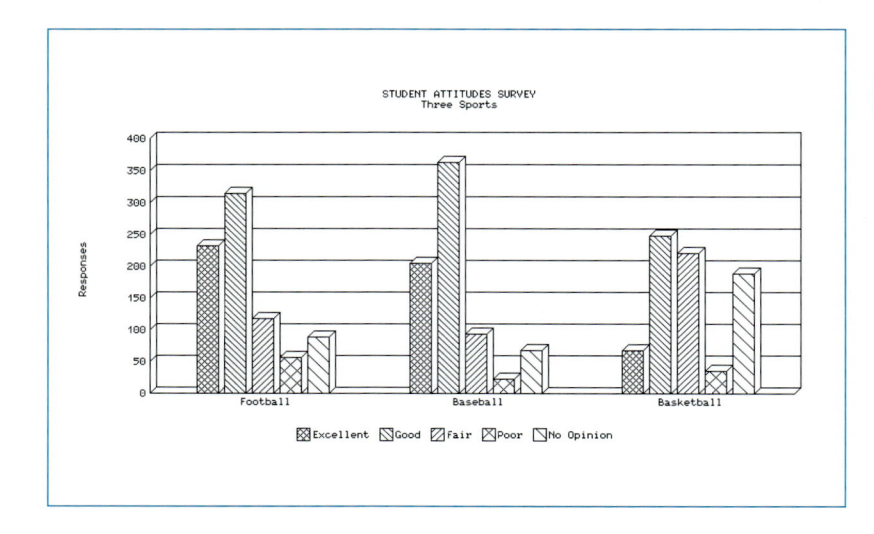

Figure 8.16

Follow the instructions in application 4 (Student Survey) to create this bar graph that compares survey responses for three sports.

j. For each sport (football, baseball, and basketball), specify the range of "excellent" responses as the graph's A data range. Specify the range of "good" responses as the B data range and the range of "fair" responses as the C data range. Specify the range of "poor" responses as the D data range and the range of "no opinion" responses as the E data range.

k. Enter the first, second, and y-axis titles as shown in Figure 8.16.

l. Enter legends for the range of response categories (column headings), and enhance the graph with the 3-D bars option.

m. If your monitor can display graphics, view the graph.

n. Name the bar graph BAR-SPORTS, save the graph as BSURVEY8.PIC, and then save the worksheet changes as SURVEY8.WK1.

o. If your printer can print graphics, use the PrintGraph utility to print the graphs.

Social Studies

Geography

5. Continue with your world population analysis. You will create a line graph that compares estimated population for each continent with growth projections, as shown in Figure 8.17. The graph's X data range will be the continents, the A data range will be the estimated population values, and the B data range will be the growth projection results. Retrieve the file WRLDPOP7.WK1 and enter the titles and legends as shown in the figure. View the graph if your monitor can display graphics. Name the graph settings WORLDPOPLINE, and save the graph as LINEPOP8.PIC. Then change the graph type to a bar graph, name the settings WORLDPOPBAR, and save the graph as BARPOP8.PIC. Save the current changes to the worksheet as WRLDPOP8.WK1. Exit 1-2-3, and print both graphs if your printer can print graphics.

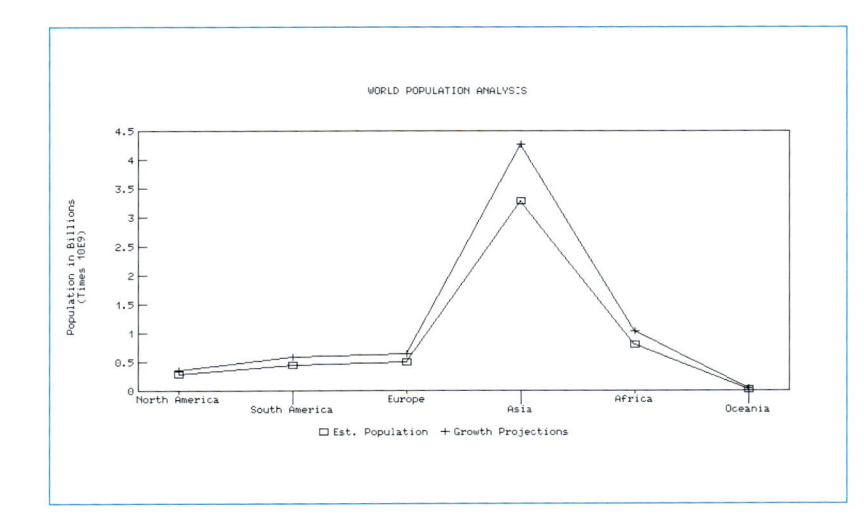

Figure 8.17

Follow the instructions in application 5 (Geography) to create this line graph. The graph shows a comparison between estimated population and growth projections for each continent.

Social Studies

American Government

6. Graphically represent a comparison of the percentages of popular and electoral votes in the 1960 election, as shown in Figure 8.18. Retrieve the file ELECTN7.WK1, and do the following tasks to create the graph:

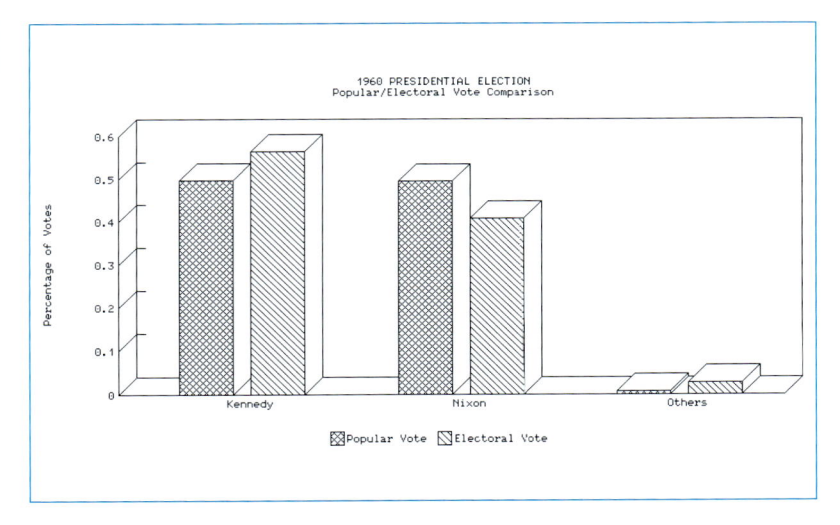

Figure 8.18

Follow the instructions in application 6 (American Government) to create this bar graph.

   a. Specify the range of candidates' names as the graph's X data range and the range of popular vote percentages as the A data range. Specify the range of electoral vote percentages as the B data range.
   b. Enter the graph's first, second, and y-axis titles as shown in the figure.
   c. Enter legends as shown in the figure, to identify which vote the bars represent.
   d. If your monitor can display graphics, view the graph.
   e. Name the graph settings 60VOTECOMPBAR, and save the graph as ELECTN8.PIC.
   f. Save the changes to the worksheet as ELECTN8.WK1.

Applications 265

g. If you have some extra time, create similar bar graphs for the other two election years in the worksheet. Assign names to the particular graph settings, and save them as graph files. Be sure to save the change to the worksheet when you have completed creating graphs.

h. Exit 1-2-3, and if your printer can print graphics, use the PrintGraph utility to print the graphs.

Science/Mathematics

Astronomy

7. Create a graph that shows a comparison of nearest and greatest orbital distances from the sun for the four planets closest to the sun. You will tackle this assignment by creating a stacked-bar graph. Stacked-bar graphs show comparisons between individual and total values. Retrieve the file PLANETS7.WK1, and do the following steps to create the stacked-bar graph shown in Figure 8.19:

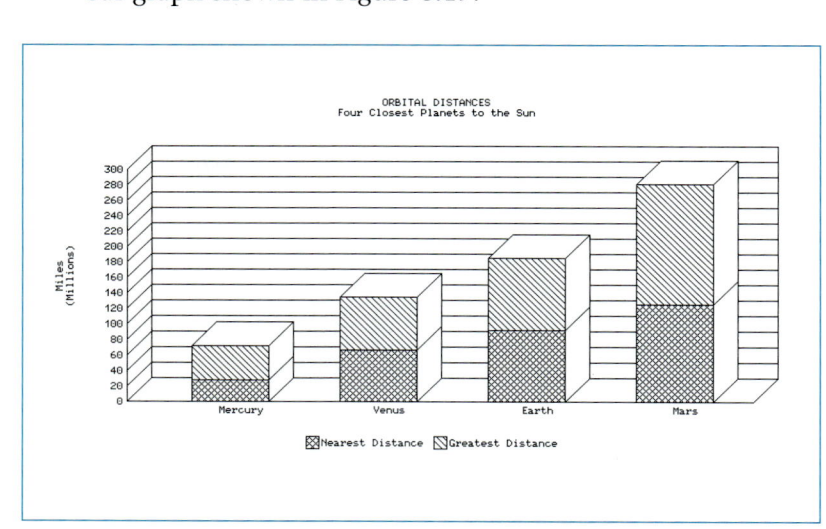

Figure 8.19

Follow the instructions in application 7 (Astronomy) to create this stacked-bar graph. This graph illustrates a comparison of nearest and greatest orbital distances for the four planets closest to the Sun.

a. Specify the X data range to include the names for the four planets closest to the sun.

b. Specify the nearest orbital distances for the four planets as the graph's A data range. Specify the greatest orbital distances for the same planets as the graph's B data range.

c. Enter the graph's first, second, and y-axis titles as shown in the figure.

d. Enhance the graph with the 3-D bars setting and horizontal grid lines. Specify legends to identify the bars, as shown in the figure.

e. If your monitor can display graphics, view the graph.

f. Assign the name SBARORBITS to the graph settings, and save the graph as SBORBIT8.PIC.

g. Modify the current graph settings to remove the grid lines and turn off the 3-D bar settings. Change the graph type to a line graph.

8 ▶ Graphing Worksheet Data

h. Assign the name LINEORBITS to the current graph settings, and save the graph as LNORBIT8.PIC.

i. Save the changes to the worksheet as PLANETS8.WK1, and exit 1-2-3.

j. If your printer can print graphics, use the PrintGraph utility to print the graphs.

Science/Mathematics

Mathematics

8. Recall the uniform motion problem you completed in Lesson 5. You will now create a line graph that graphically represents the results calculated in that worksheet. Retrieve the file MATH5.WK1, and create the graph shown in Figure 8.20 as outlined in the following steps:

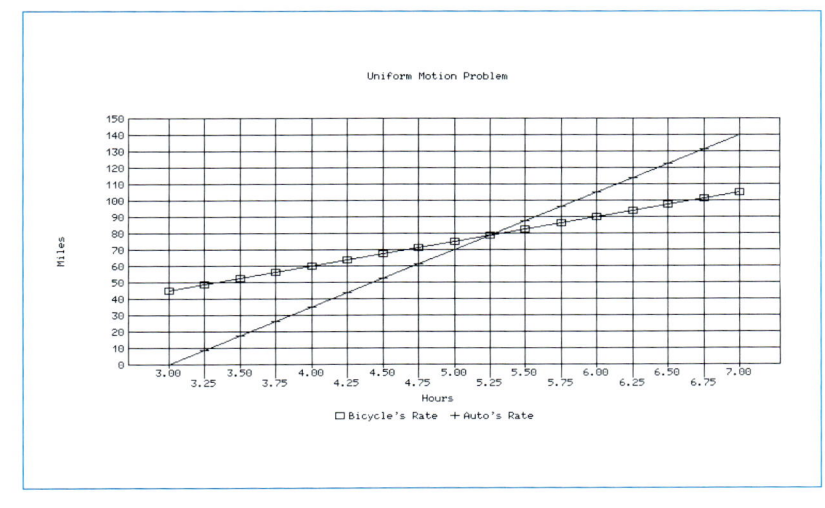

Figure 8.20

Follow the instructions in application 8 (Mathematics) to create this line graph.

a. Specify the values representing the amount of time spent on the bicycle as the X data range.

b. Specify the bicycle's distance as data range A and the auto's distance as data range B.

c. Enter the graph's first, y-axis, and x-axis titles as shown in the figure.

d. Specify legends for the symbols in the graph as shown in the figure.

e. Enhance the graph with horizontal and vertical grid lines.

f. Name the graph settings LINEUNIMOPROB, and save the graph as MATH8.PIC.

g. Save the worksheet as MATH8.WK1.

h. Exit 1-2-3; if your printer can print graphics, use the PrintGraph utility to print the line graph.

Applications

Health

Nutrition

9. You want to create a graph from selected data in the dietary nutrient information worksheet. The graph will show the percentages of nutrient intake. Retrieve the file DALYNUT8.WK1, and create the pie graph shown in Figure 8.21, as outlined in the following steps:

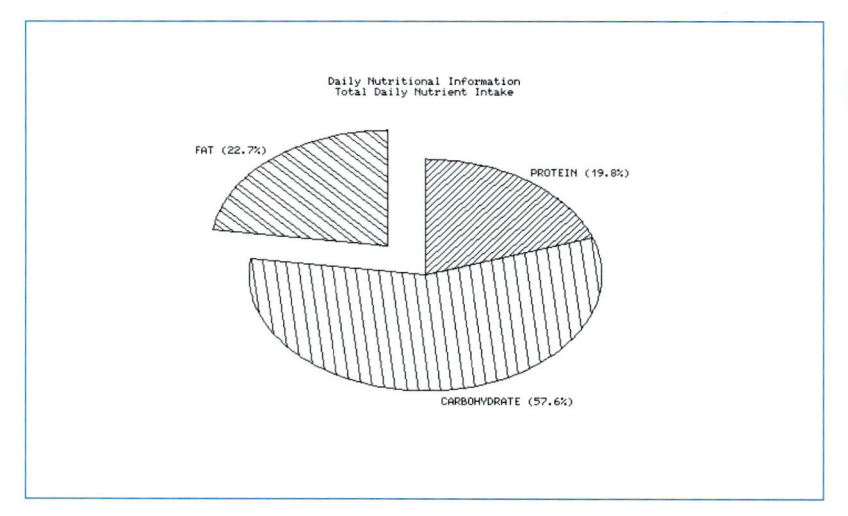

Figure 8.21

Follow the instructions in application 9 (Nutrition) to create this pie graph.

a. Specify the range of nutrient labels in row 3 as the graph's X data range.
b. Specify the range of daily nutrient gram totals in row 36 as the A data range.
c. Enter a range of hatch pattern numbers in row 2 directly above the nutrient column heading labels. Add 100 to the hatch pattern number for the "FAT" slice.
d. Specify the range of hatch pattern numbers as the B data range.
e. Enter the first and second titles as shown in the figure.
f. Name the current graph settings DAILYNUTPIE, and save the graph as NUTRINF8.PIC.
g. Press (HOME), and save the worksheet as NUTRINF8.WK1.
h. Exit 1-2-3; if your printer can print graphics, use the PrintGraph utility to print the pie graph. Exit PrintGraph.

Health

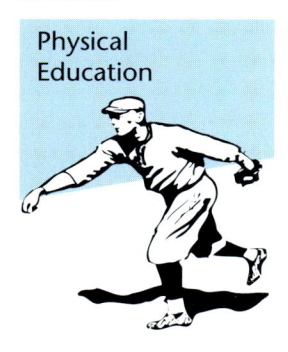

Physical Education

10. The Washington High School softball team coach would like a graph that compares players' batting averages and slugging percentages. Retrieve the file SBGAME7.WK1 and create the bar graph shown in Figure 8.22, as outlined in the following steps:

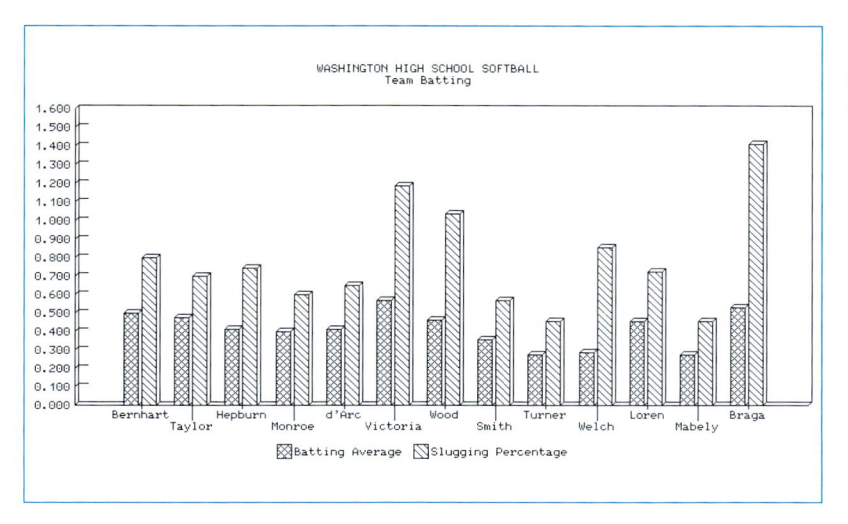

Figure 8.22

Follow the instructions in application 10 (Physical Education) to create this bar graph. This graph shows a comparison of each player's batting average and slugging percentage.

a. Specify the players' names as the graph's X data range. Specify their batting averages as the A data range and their slugging percentages as the B data range.

b. Enter the graph's first, second, and x-axis titles as shown in the figure.

c. Enter the legends that identify the bars for batting averages and slugging percentages, as shown in the figure.

d. If you would like, experiment with some more advanced graph settings. Use the /Graph Options Scale Y-Axis command (/GOSY) to format the y-axis values as fixed decimals with three decimal places. This will make the y-axis values look like batting averages, as shown in the figure.

e. If your monitor can display graphics, view the graph.

f. Name the current graph settings BARTEAM_AVGS, and save the graph as SBGAME8.PIC.

g. Save the current changes to the worksheet as SBGAME8.WK1.

h. Exit 1-2-3; and if your printer can print graphics, use the PrintGraph utility to print the bar graph.

Applications

9 Using Wysiwyg to Create Presentation-Quality Documents

Objectives

- Attach and invoke the Wysiwyg add-in program.
- Use Wysiwyg command menus.
- Detach Wysiwyg to remove it from memory.
- Change fonts for selected text.
- Format text with font attributes.
- Format a range to print reverse against a solid background.
- Format a range to print with a background shade.
- Underline a range of values.
- Use Wysiwyg's print preview.
- Add a graph to a document.
- Use Wysiwyg features to enhance a graph.
- Enter text in a Wysiwyg document.
- Reformat a range of text into a paragraph.
- Select a printer in Wysiwyg.
- Print a presentation-quality document.

Lotus 1-2-3, Release 2.3 includes a special spreadsheet publishing program called Wysiwyg. Wysiwyg can be used to turn your spreadsheets and graphs into polished documents. In this lesson you will learn how to attach and detach Wysiwyg and use the Wysiwyg menu system. You will also learn how to select fonts, add graphic elements, and combine a graph with worksheet data in a document.

Note: If you are working with 1-2-3 on a floppy disk (you do not have a hard disk), skip Lesson 9 and go on to Lesson 10. Wysiwyg is not available for systems without hard disks.

Exercise 9.1 Attaching and Using the Wysiwyg Add-In

Objectives

After completing this exercise, you will be able to
- Attach and invoke the Wysiwyg add-in program.
- Use Wysiwyg command menus.
- Detach Wysiwyg to remove it from memory.

ADD-IN PROGRAM
A separate software program that can exist in a computer's memory along with the 1-2-3 program. Add-in programs provide additional features or enhance the use of 1-2-3.

Lotus 1-2-3, Release 2.3 includes several add-in programs. *Add-in programs* are separate programs that can be present in your computer's memory while you run 1-2-3. This lesson will show you how to use Wysiwyg (pronounced "WÍ-SEE-WIG"). *Wysiwyg* is a spreadsheet publishing add-in program. You can use Wysiwyg to customize the on-screen appearance of worksheet data and to print appealing presentation-quality documents.

"Wysiwyg" stands for "What you see is what you get." This means that the data you view on screen looks very similar to the way it will look on the printed page. When you attach Wysiwyg, your computer's monitor switches to graphics mode (if your system supports graphics).

In many business situations, 1-2-3 users must often include worksheet data in a document or report. Usually the document will be reviewed by staff members, managers, board members, clients, and so on. Depending on the audience, it is often preferable to give the report a polished appearance. Wysiwyg provides a means of formatting worksheet data and graphs into sharp-looking documents.

WYSIWYG
An acronym for "What you see is what you get." This add-in program displays 1-2-3 worksheet data and graphs on screen so that they appear very close to the way they will appear on paper (hard copy). The program is also used to specify fonts and other graphic elements to print presentation-quality documents.

INVOKE
To activate an add-in program's main menu.

You attach the Wysiwyg add-in by selecting the /Add-In Attach command (/AA). From the Add-In command submenu, you select the file WYSIWYG.ADN from a list of add-in program filenames. When Wysiwyg is attached, you will see a big difference in the way your screen looks. However, the screen still has a control panel, worksheet area, and status line. Each screen component works in the same way as when 1-2-3 runs alone. In fact, all 1-2-3 commands, operations, and keystrokes can be used exactly as when Wysiwyg is not attached.

However, Wysiwyg has its own command menu system. There are two ways to access this menu system. You can press and hold the [ALT] key and then press a function key ([F7], [F8], [F9], or [F10]), or you can type a colon (:). Lotus 1-2-3 prompts you to select the function key you want to use to *invoke* Wysiwyg when you select the /Attach Add-In command. "Invoking Wysiwyg" simply means accessing its Main Menu. In the exercises in this lesson, you will use the [ALT]-[F7] key assignment to invoke Wysiwyg.

In this exercise, you will retrieve a worksheet file that is a slight variation on the SUMSALES.WK1 file. You will use this file to create a document that contains the worksheet data, a bar graph, and a short memo. The owner wants to send the document to the store's investors. To begin, you will attach the Wysiwyg add-in program. Then you will learn how to use the Wysiwyg command menu. Finally, you will learn how to detach Wysiwyg to remove it from memory.

1 ▶ If necessary, start 1-2-3. Use the /File Directory command to change the current directory to the drive that contains the student data disk.

2 ▶ Press the Slash key (/) to access the Main Menu.

3 ▶ Type **AA** to select the Add-In and Attach commands.

Lotus 1-2-3 prompts you to enter the add-in you want to attach (load into memory). A list of add-in program filenames is displayed on the third line of the control panel, if the directory that contains the add-in programs is displayed at the prompt.

> Note: If Wysiwyg is being attached for the first time, Lotus 1-2-3 looks for add-in filenames in the directory from which you loaded 1-2-3. If add-in filenames are not displayed, press [F3]. Move the menu pointer to the directory that contains the add-in programs and press [←]. If you are not able to do this, press [ESC] and type the name of the directory that contains the programs. (Generally, this is the directory that contains the 1-2-3 program files.)

4 ▶ Move the menu pointer to the filename WYSIWYG.ADN.

5 ▶ Press [←].

A submenu of key assignment options appears on the second line of the control panel. The first option, No-key, is highlighted. The number options (7–10) correspond to the function keys [F7], [F8], [F9], [F10].

9 ▶ Using Wysiwyg to Create Presentation-Quality Documents

6 ▶ Type **7**

The Wysiwyg add-in's "invoke" key is selected, and Wysiwyg is attached. The screen's appearance changes noticeably, as shown in Figure 9.1. Notice that the 1-2-3 Add-In command menu is activated on the control panel.

Add-in command submenu

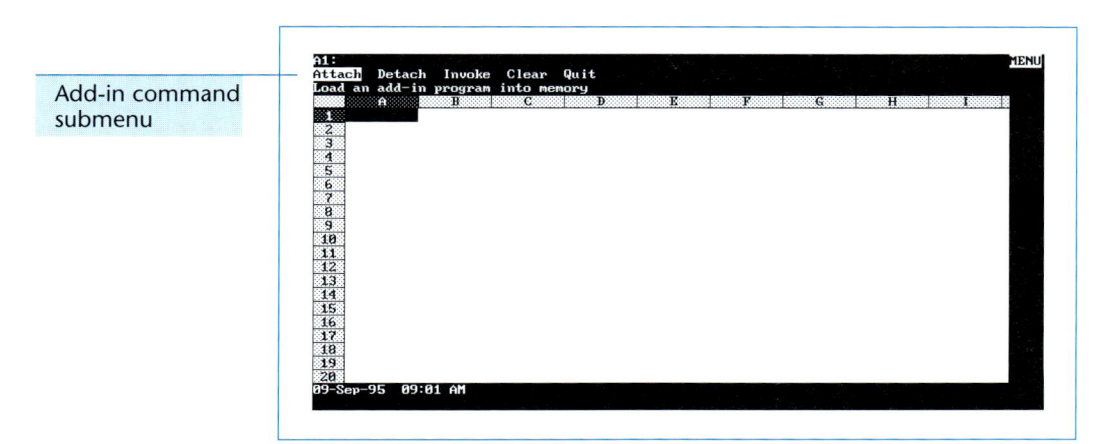

Figure 9.1

After you attach the Wysiwyg add-in program, the screen display switches to graphics mode. The Add-In command submenu reappears on the control panel.

Note: You can select the Invoke command to display the Wysiwyg Main Menu. However, you will quit this menu so you can practice using the ALT-F7 key you just assigned.

7 ▶ Type **Q** to select the Add-In command submenu's Quit option.

Lotus 1-2-3 returns to READY mode.

Now you will retrieve the file WYSSALES.WK1 so that you can enhance the worksheet with Wysiwyg commands.

8 ▶ Press the Slash key (/) to access the 1-2-3 Main Menu.

The 1-2-3 Main Menu is displayed.

Although Wysiwyg is attached, you still use 1-2-3 menus and commands the same way you do when Wysiwyg is not attached.

9 ▶ Retrieve the file WYSSALES.WK1.

Now you will get to know the Wysiwyg display and some of its command menus.

Attaching and Using the Wysiwyg Add-In **273**

10 ▶ Press ALT-F7.

The Wysiwyg Main Menu is displayed, as shown in Figure 9.2.

Wysiwyg Main Menu

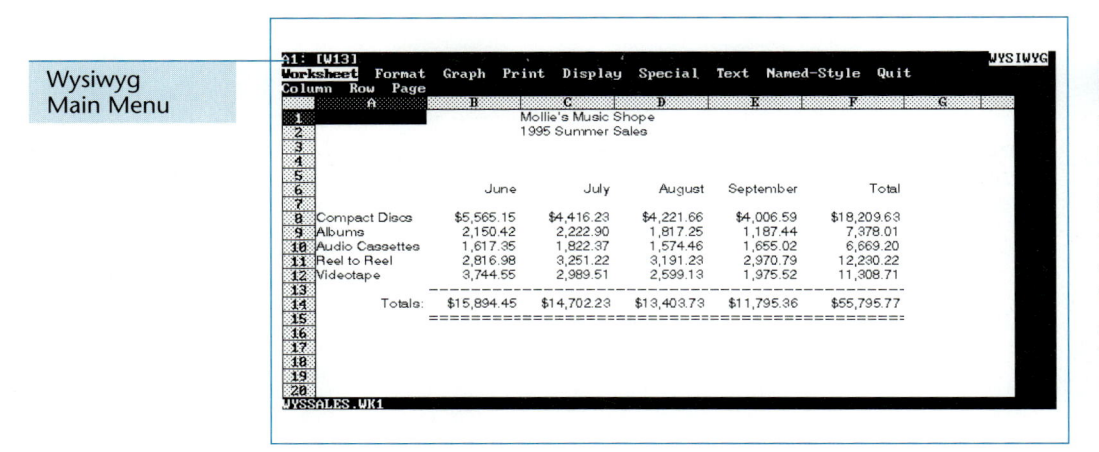

Figure 9.2

The Wysiwyg Main Menu appears when you press the Wysiwyg invoke key that you assigned when you attached Wysiwyg. You can also type a colon (:) to access the Wysiwyg Main Menu.

11 ▶ Type **W** to select the Worksheet command.

The Wysiwyg Worksheet command submenu appears.

The first option allows you to change the width of columns (just like 1-2-3's /Worksheet Column Set-Width or /Worksheet Column Column-Range Set-Width commands). The Rows option allows you to change the height of rows. The Page option is used to insert page breaks.

12 ▶ Press ESC.

The Wysiwyg Main Menu reappears. Wysiwyg menu keys operate in the same way as 1-2-3 menu keys.

13 ▶ Type **D** to select the Display command.

The Display command submenu appears. This submenu contains a variety of commands that can be used to customize the Wysiwyg display.

14 ▶ Type **Z** to select the Zoom command.

The Zoom command submenu is displayed. This submenu contains options that allow you to reduce or enlarge the worksheet in the worksheet area.

15 ▶ Type **T** to select the Tiny command.

The worksheet's display reduces to display more columns and rows, as shown in Figure 9.3.

Size reduction indicator

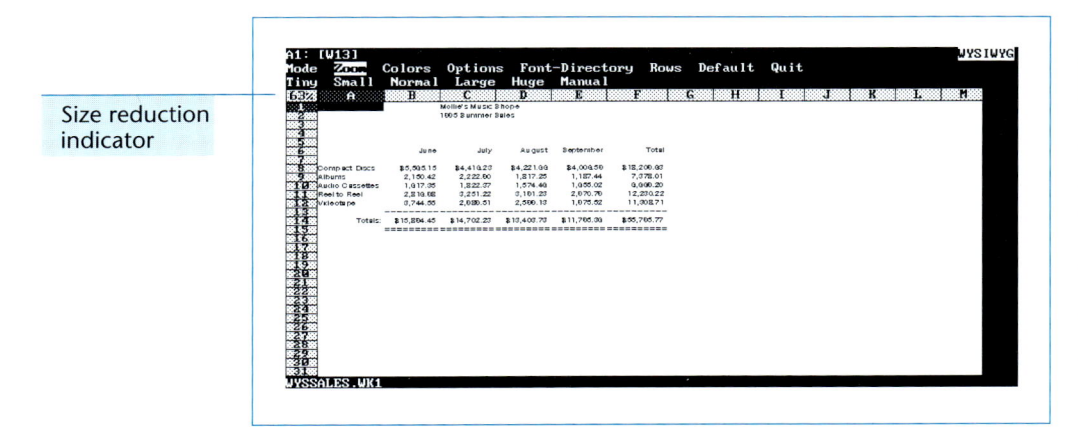

Figure 9.3

When you select the Tiny option on the Zoom command submenu, the Wysiwyg worksheet area displays more columns and rows. This reduces the size of the worksheet.

Note: The number of rows and columns shown will vary, depending on your system's monitor and graphics.

16 ▶ Type **ZH** to select the Zoom command and Huge option.

The worksheet's display enlarges to display a closeup of its upper-left corner.

17 ▶ Type **ZN** to select the Zoom command and Normal option.

The worksheet's display returns to normal view.

18 ▶ Type **Q** to select the Display command submenu's Quit option.

Lotus 1-2-3 returns to READY mode.

Now you will experiment a little with Wysiwyg's text-editing feature to fix the misspelling in the worksheet's title. When Wysiwyg is attached, you can still edit a label in EDIT mode. You also have the option of editing a range of text directly in the worksheet area in Wysiwyg's TEXT mode. You can use the same editing keystrokes in Wysiwyg's TEXT mode that you learned to use in 1-2-3's EDIT mode. There are only two differences between EDIT mode and TEXT mode. In TEXT mode, you edit text in the worksheet directly, rather than on the control panel. Also, you use an insertion bar, instead of a cursor, to insert, delete, or overtype text.

19 ▶ Move the cell pointer to cell C1.

20 ▶ Press [ALT]-[F7].

The Wysiwyg Main Menu is displayed.

21 ▶ Type **T** to select the Text command.

The Text command submenu is displayed. This submenu contains options to edit and format text in the worksheet.

Attaching and Using the Wysiwyg Add-In

22 ▶ Type **E** to select the Edit command.

Lotus 1-2-3 prompts you to select a text range to edit. The current cell is anchored.

23 ▶ Press →.

The range C1..D1 is highlighted. Because the worksheet's title extends into column D, you need to extend the text range to that column.

24 ▶ Press ←.

Lotus 1-2-3 switches to Wysiwyg TEXT mode, and the cell pointer is no longer displayed. An insertion bar is at the beginning of the text range. Notice that the control panel displays the row and column location of the insertion bar within the text range.

25 ▶ Press → 5 times.

The insertion bar moves five characters to the right and seems to be between the "i" and the "e" in the name "Mollie's."

26 ▶ Press END.

The insertion bar moves to the last character on the line. Notice that the control panel shows that the insertion bar is in text column 20.

27 ▶ Press ← once.

28 ▶ Type **p**

The letter "p" is inserted to correct the text.

29 ▶ Press ESC.

The worksheet's title text is corrected, 1-2-3 returns to READY mode, and the cell pointer returns.

After learning to use Wysiwyg, you may find yourself doing the majority of your work with Wysiwyg attached. Wysiwyg is especially useful when you are formatting or enhancing worksheets. However, because attaching Wysiwyg takes up memory space, you may sometimes need to detach it. You may need more of your computer's memory to work with a large amount of worksheet data or complex formulas. To complete your introduction to the Wysiwyg add-in, you will now detach the program. You use 1-2-3's /Add-In Detach command (/AD) to detach Wysiwyg. Detaching Wysiwyg means that you remove it from your computer's memory.

30 ▶ Press the Slash key (/) to access the 1-2-3 Main Menu.

31 ▶ Type **AD** to select the Add-In and Detach commands.

Lotus 1-2-3 prompts you to enter the add-in to detach. The third line of the control panel displays a list of currently attached add-in programs. Wysiwyg should be the only add-in program listed.

32 ▶ Press ⏎.

Wysiwyg is detached, and the Add-In command submenu is displayed.

33 ▶ Type **Q** to select the Add-In command submenu's quit option.

Lotus 1-2-3 returns to READY mode.

34 ▶ Press HOME, if necessary, and save the changes to the same file.

In the next exercise, you will learn to change fonts and font attributes for the data in your worksheet.

Exercise 9.2 Changing Fonts and Font Attributes

Objectives

After completing this exercise, you will be able to
- Change fonts for selected text.
- Format text with font attributes.

TYPEFACE
Printed or displayed (on a monitor screen) characters that belong to a particular family or group based on their design characteristics.

POINT
A unit of measurement that equals 1/72 of an inch. Points are used to measure the height of a character. For example, a 12-point typeface is a font whose characters are approximately 1/6 of an inch high.

When you work with Wysiwyg, you need a basic understanding of certain typographical terms. Typography is the art of arranging type on a printed page to achieve a certain appearance. A *typeface* is a specific design for characters. For example, the typeface for the text in this paragraph is Stone Serif. Times Roman, Helvetica, and Courier are just three of many typefaces available for printed documents.

Typefaces range in many sizes, which are expressed in points. A *point* is a unit of measurement that equals 1/72 of an inch and determines the height of a character. A *font* is a typeface that is a particular size. For example, the font used for the text in this sentence is 10-point Stone Serif. The following are examples of other fonts:

`This text is set in 12-point Courier.`

This text is set in 24-point Times Roman.

This text is set in 8-point Helvetica.

In addition, fonts can be enhanced with certain *font attributes*—such as bold, italics, and underline—that help to emphasize characters in a particular way, as shown in the following examples:

`This text is 12-point Courier with boldface.`

Changing Fonts and Font Attributes 277

FONT
A typeface that is a specific size (measured in points).

FONT ATTRIBUTE
An enhancement or formatting characteristic for printed characters, such as boldface, italics, and underlining.

This text is 14-point Times Roman with italics.

This text is 10-point Helvetica with underlining.

The data you have printed in previous lessons with the 1-2-3 /Print Printer command (/PP) printed in one font. Most likely this was 12-point Courier. With Wysiwyg attached, you have the flexibility of using a variety of fonts and font attributes. Fonts and font attributes add a lot to the appearance of a document.

Specifying fonts and font attributes for a document is a very important formatting technique. An important rule is to keep it simple. Rarely should you use more than two or three fonts in a document. Too many fonts can make a document look awkward or make it too hard to read.

You will now begin formatting the summer sales document that the owner wants to send to investors. You will attach Wysiwyg, change selected fonts, and emphasize selected text with font attributes.

1 ▶ Make sure that the WYSSALES.WK1 worksheet is displayed and 1-2-3 is in READY mode.

2 ▶ Press the Slash key (/) to access the 1-2-3 Main Menu.

3 ▶ Type **AA** to select the Add-In and Attach commands.

Lotus 1-2-3 prompts you to enter an add-in program to attach.

4 ▶ Move the menu pointer to the filename WYSIWYG.ADN.

5 ▶ Press ⏎.

Lotus 1-2-3 prompts you to select an invoke key assignment.

6 ▶ Type **7**

The Wysiwyg add-in program is attached, and the Add-In command submenu reappears.

7 ▶ Type **Q** to select the Add-In command submenu's Quit option.

Lotus 1-2-3 is in READY mode.

8 ▶ Move the cell pointer to cell C1.

The cell pointer is on the cell that contains the company's name.

9 ▶ Press [ALT]-[F7].

The Wysiwyg Main Menu is displayed.

10 ▶ Type **F** to select the Format command.

The Format command submenu is displayed. This submenu contains options that you can use to specify fonts, font attributes, lines, shading, and other formatting features.

278 9 ▶ Using Wysiwyg to Create Presentation-Quality Documents

11 ▶ Type **F** to select the Font command.

The Wysiwyg Font Selection box is displayed, as shown in Figure 9.4.

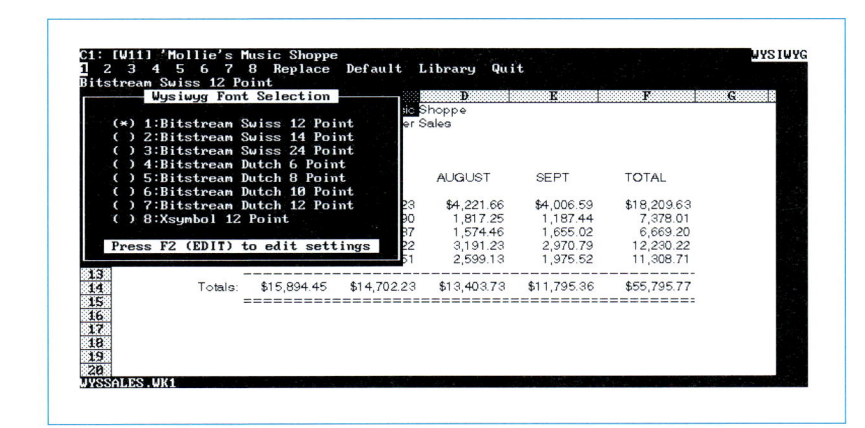

Figure 9.4

When you select the Wysiwyg Format Font command, the Wysiwyg Font Selection box is displayed. Notice that the first font on the list, Swiss 12 point, is the default selection for the entire worksheet.

12 ▶ Type **3** to select the Swiss 24 point font.

Lotus 1-2-3 prompts you to enter the range of text to format.

Note: Your Wysiwyg Font Selection box may contain font options other than those shown in Figure 9.4. If so, select a font that is as close as possible to Swiss 24 point.

13 ▶ Press ⏎.

The font is changed for the worksheet's main title, and the text enlarges in the worksheet area. Notice also that the height of row 1 changed automatically to accommodate the new point size.

14 ▶ Press ↓.

The cell pointer moves to cell C2, which contains the worksheet's subtitle.

15 ▶ Press ALT-F7.

The Wysiwyg Main Menu is displayed.

16 ▶ Type **FF2** to select the Format and Font commands and the Swiss 14 point font.

Lotus 1-2-3 prompts you to enter the range to format.

17 ▶ Press ⏎.

The label in cell C2 is formatted with another font.

18 ▶ Press ↑.

The cell pointer moves back to cell C1.

Now you will specify the boldface font attribute for the title and subtitle.

Changing Fonts and Font Attributes

19 ▶ Press ALT-F7.

The Wysiwyg Main Menu is displayed.

20 ▶ Type **FB** to select the Format and Bold commands.

The Bold command submenu is displayed. You use this submenu to set or remove the attribute from selected text.

21 ▶ Type **S** to select the Set option.

Lotus 1-2-3 prompts you to enter the range to change.

22 ▶ Press ↓ once.

The worksheet's title labels are selected.

23 ▶ Press ↵.

The boldface attribute is selected for the worksheet's title, and the text appears boldfaced in the worksheet area.

24 ▶ Move the cell pointer to cell A8.

To get a closer look at the formatting changes, you will use the Zoom command to enlarge the display of the worksheet.

25 ▶ Press ALT-F7.

The Wysiwyg Main Menu is displayed.

26 ▶ Type **DZL** to select the Display, Zoom, and Large commands.

The worksheet enlarges, as shown in Figure 9.5.

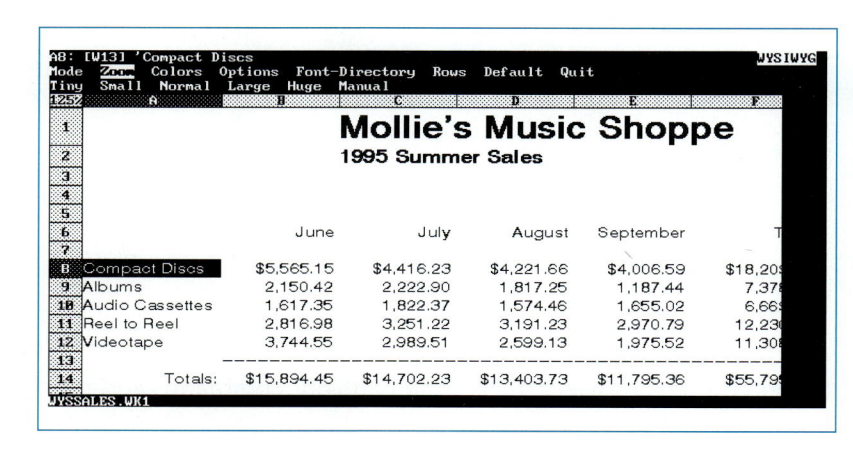

Figure 9.5

After you select the Wysiwyg Display Zoom Large command, the view of your worksheet should look like this.

27 ▶ Press ESC.

The Wysiwyg Main Menu is activated on the control panel.

28 ▶ Type **FIS** to select the Format, Italics, and Set commands.

Lotus 1-2-3 prompts you to enter the range to be formatted.

9 ▶ Using Wysiwyg to Create Presentation-Quality Documents

29 ▶ Press ⬇ 6 times.

   The range of column A labels is highlighted.

30 ▶ Press ⏎.

   The column A labels are italicized.

31 ▶ Move the cell pointer to cell A14.

   The cell pointer is on the cell that contains the right-aligned label "Totals:."

32 ▶ Press ALT-F7.

   The Wysiwyg Main Menu is displayed.

33 ▶ Type **FBS** to select the Format, Bold, and Set commands.

   Lotus 1-2-3 prompts you to enter the range to format.

34 ▶ Press ⏎.

   The italicized label in cell A14 is also boldfaced.

The label "Totals:" in cell A14 would probably look better if it were not italicized. So you will clear the italics attribute from the label.

35 ▶ Make sure the cell pointer is on cell A14.

36 ▶ Press ALT-F7.

   The Wysiwyg Main Menu is displayed.

37 ▶ Type **FIC** to select the Format, Italics, and Clear commands.

   Lotus 1-2-3 prompts you to enter the range in which you want to clear the formatting.

38 ▶ Press ⏎.

   The italics attribute is removed from the label.

39 ▶ Press HOME, and save the changes to the same file.

In the next exercise, you will learn how to enhance the worksheet document with other Wysiwyg features.

Changing Fonts and Font Attributes

Exercise 9.3

Enhancing Ranges with Lines and Shading

Objectives

After completing this exercise, you will be able to
- Format a range to print reverse against a solid background.
- Format a range to print with a background shade.
- Underline a range of values.
- Use Wysiwyg's print preview.

REVERSE TYPE
Characters that appear white against a black or solid background.

You will continue using Wysiwyg formatting features to enhance the worksheet data in the summer sales document. To enhance the document, you will display the month column headings in *reverse type* against a black or solid background. You will also add shading, to emphasize the range of totals, and underline the videotape sales figures in row 12.

When working with Wysiwyg attached, you can use Wysiwyg's print preview to check the arrangement of elements in your document. The print preview feature displays a miniature version of a document page on screen. The miniature page represents the approximate appearance of elements on the printed page. You will begin this lesson by preselecting the range of column heading labels.

1 ▶ Move the cell pointer to cell B6.

The cell pointer is on the cell that contains the label "June."

2 ▶ Press [F4].

Lotus 1-2-3 prompts you to enter a range.

3 ▶ Press [END], and then press [→].

4 ▶ Press [↵].

The range B6..F6 is highlighted.

5 ▶ Press [ALT]-[F7].

The Wysiwyg Main Menu is displayed.

6 ▶ Type **FC** to select the Format and Color commands.

The Color command submenu appears. You can use this submenu to change display colors for particular ranges or display a range in reverse type against a solid background.

7 ▶ Type **R** to select the Reverse command.

The preselected range is formatted to print reverse characters against a solid background.

> Note: If you are using a monochrome monitor, the reverse type may not be apparent because the range remains highlighted.

To make the reverse text really stand out, you will apply the boldface font attribute to the same range.

8 ▶ Press ALT-F7.

The Wysiwyg Main Menu is displayed.

9 ▶ Type **FBS** to select the Format, Bold, and Set commands.

The reverse text is formatted with the boldface font attribute.

10 ▶ Press HOME.

The cell pointer moves to cell A1.

PRINT PREVIEW
A graphic display screen in which a reduced version of a document page is displayed. The displayed document page represents the approximate appearance of elements on the printed page.

Now would be a good opportunity to view the document in Wysiwyg's print preview. Print preview gives you a good idea of how the data will appear on the overall page. *Print preview* is a special graphic screen that displays a miniature document page. This feature is very useful for quickly checking how well text is centered on the page. You can also get a rough idea of how well fonts match or exactly where pages break. To view a document in print preview, you must first specify a print range. You will continue this exercise by selecting a print range and viewing the document in print preview.

11 ▶ Press ALT-F7.

The Wysiwyg Main Menu is displayed.

12 ▶ Type **P** to select the Print command.

The Wysiwyg Print Settings dialog box is displayed, as shown in Figure 9.6.

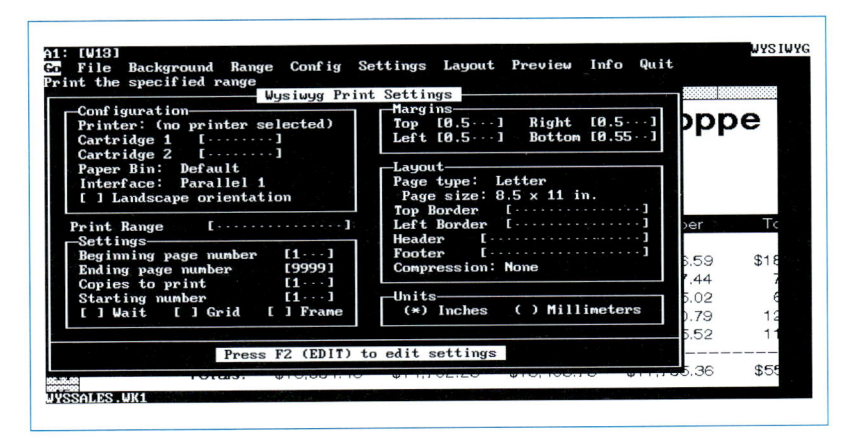

Figure 9.6

The Wysiwyg Print Settings dialog box appears when you select the Wysiwyg Print command.

Enhancing Ranges with Lines and Shading

13 ▶ Type **RS** to select the Range and Set commands.

Lotus 1-2-3 prompts you to enter the range to print. The current cell is not anchored.

14 ▶ Type **.** (a period) to anchor the current cell.

15 ▶ Press (END), and then press (HOME).

The range A1..F15 is highlighted.

16 ▶ Press (←).

The print range is specified, and the Wysiwyg Print Settings dialog box reappears. The Wysiwyg Print command submenu is activated on the control panel.

17 ▶ Type **P** to select the Preview command.

The print preview screen displays a miniature version of the way the document page will look when printed. Notice that the worksheet's title could be better centered on the page, as shown in Figure 9.7.

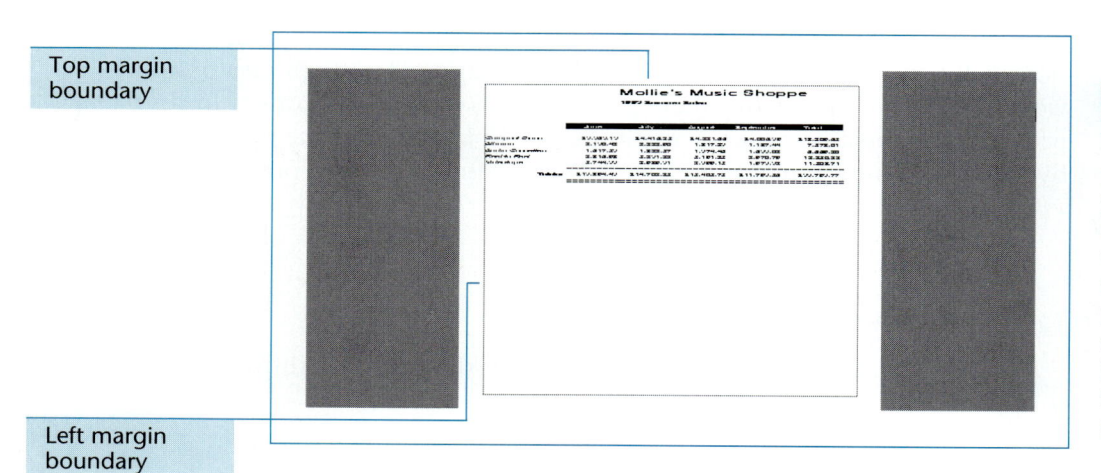

Top margin boundary

Left margin boundary

Figure 9.7

The Wysiwyg print preview screen shows you how the document will look when printed. Notice that the current margin settings are marked with dotted lines and the current formatting and fonts are shown.

18 ▶ Press SPACEBAR, or any other key.

The Wysiwyg Print Settings dialog box and Print command submenu reappear.

19 ▶ Type **Q** to select the Print command submenu's Quit option.

Lotus 1-2-3 returns to READY mode.

Now you will center the worksheet's title labels.

20 ▶ Move the cell pointer to cell C1.

The cell pointer is on the cell that contains the worksheet's title.

21 ▶ Press (ALT)-(F7).

The Wysiwyg Main Menu is displayed.

22 ▶ Type **TA** to select the Text and Align commands.

The Align command submenu displays four alignment options.

23 ▶ Type **C** to select the Center option.

Lotus 1-2-3 prompts you to select the range to align. Cell C1 is anchored.

24 ▶ Press → 3 times.

25 ▶ Press ↓.

The range C1..F2 is highlighted.

26 ▶ Press ←┘.

The title labels are centered.

Now you will delete the repeating-character labels that make the single and double underlines.

27 ▶ Move the cell pointer to cell B13.

28 ▶ Use the 1-2-3 /Range Erase command (/RE) to erase the repeating-character labels in the range B13..F13.

29 ▶ Move the cell pointer to cell B15.

30 ▶ Use the 1-2-3 /Range Erase command (/RE) to erase the repeating-character labels in row 15.

31 ▶ Move the cell pointer to cell B12.

32 ▶ Press ALT-F7.

The Wysiwyg Main Menu is displayed.

33 ▶ Type **FU** to select the Format and Underline commands.

The Underline command submenu is displayed.

34 ▶ Type **S** to select the Single command.

Lotus 1-2-3 prompts you to enter the range to change.

35 ▶ Press END, and then press →.

The range of sales figures for videotape is highlighted.

36 ▶ Press ←┘.

Each value in the selected range is underlined. Notice that only the characters are underlined, not the spaces between the figures.

Enhancing Ranges with Lines and Shading

285

BACKGROUND SHADING
A tint or screen that provides a background contrast for a range of data and is usually specified as a percentage of a solid background (black).

To complete this exercise, you will format the range of sales totals in row 14 with a light background shading. *Background shading* is a screen or tint effect. It is used to emphasize text or contrast a range of values that are of particular interest to the reader.

37 ▶ Move the cell pointer to cell B14.

38 ▶ Press ALT-F7.

The Wysiwyg Main Menu is displayed.

39 ▶ Type **FS** to select the Format and Shade commands.

The Shading command submenu appears. Use this submenu to select a desired background shade.

40 ▶ Type **L** to select the Light command.

Lotus 1-2-3 prompts you to enter the range to change.

41 ▶ Press END, and then press →.

42 ▶ Press ←.

A light background shade is selected for the range and is displayed in the worksheet area.

Now you will return the Wysiwyg display to normal view.

43 ▶ Press ALT-F7.

The Wysiwyg Main Menu is displayed.

44 ▶ Type **DZN** to select the Display, Zoom, and Normal commands.

45 ▶ Type **Q** to return to READY mode.

46 ▶ Press HOME, and save the current changes to the same file.

Your worksheet should look similar to Figure 9.8. Notice that dashed lines mark the current print range.

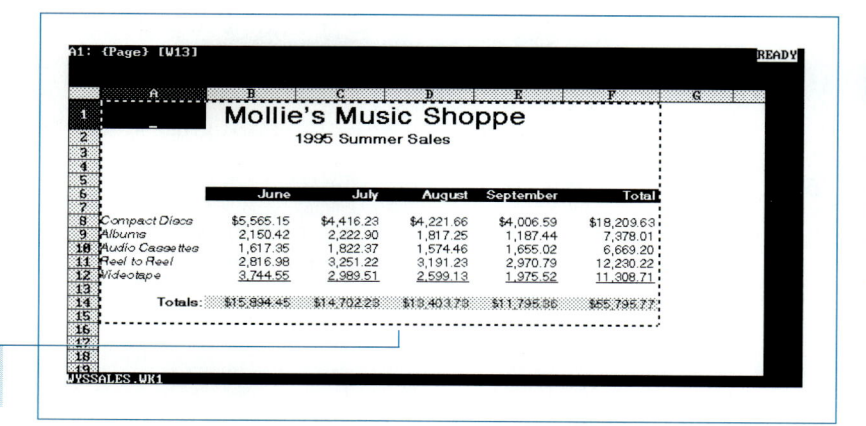

Print range boundary

Figure 9.8
The worksheet's display returns to normal view. Notice that dashed lines surround the current print range.

9 ▶ Using Wysiwyg to Create Presentation-Quality Documents

The last two exercises showed how you can use 1-2-3 and Wysiwyg operations interchangeably to format and enhance worksheet data in a document. Now you will learn how to add a graph of worksheet data to the same document.

Exercise 9.4 — Using Wysiwyg to Add a Graph to a Document

Objectives

After completing this exercise, you will be able to
- Add a graph to a document.
- Use Wysiwyg features to enhance a graph.

Wysiwyg lets you add a graph of worksheet data to a document. This is one of the most enjoyable Wysiwyg features to use. You can add the current graph, a named graph, a graph file, or other graphic formats. Often a graph is placed on the same page or in the same document with the data it represents.

Once you add the graph to the document, you can use a variety of features to enhance the graph. For instance, you can add text, lines, boxes, polygon shapes, symbols, and shading effects. You can also experiment with many other Wysiwyg features to invert, rotate, move, or copy a graphic element. In short, Wysiwyg offers a great deal of flexibility in formatting and enhancing graphs.

You will continue creating the document that the owner wants to send to the store's investors. To begin this exercise, you will insert a new column A. Then you will change the widths of columns A and H to center all the elements on the page. You will also add the current graph to the document. To add a graph you must select a specific range as the *graph range*. Finally, you will enhance both the worksheet and graph ranges with a box and drop shadow.

GRAPH RANGE
A range in a Wysiwyg document that designates the location of a 1-2-3 graph that is added to the document.

1 ▶ Make sure the file WYSSALES.WK1 is loaded, 1-2-3 is in READY mode, and the cell pointer is on cell A1.

2 ▶ Use the 1-2-3 /Worksheet Insert Column command (/WIC) to insert a new column A.

3 ▶ Press ALT-F7.

The Wysiwyg Main Menu is displayed.

Using Wysiwyg to Add a Graph to a Document

287

4 ▶ Type **WCS** to select the Wysiwyg Worksheet, Column, and Set-Width commands.

Lotus 1-2-3 prompts you to enter the column range to adjust.

5 ▶ Press ⏎.

Lotus 1-2-3 prompts you to enter the new width.

6 ▶ Type **2**

7 ▶ Press ⏎.

Column A is reduced to a width of two characters.

8 ▶ Move the cell pointer to any cell in column H.

9 ▶ Repeat steps 3–7 to set the width of column H to two characters.

10 ▶ Press F10.

The current graph is displayed. This is a three-dimensional bar graph that shows sales of each item for each month.

11 ▶ Press SPACEBAR, or any other key.

12 ▶ Press F5.

Lotus 1-2-3 prompts you to enter the cell address where you want to move the cell pointer.

13 ▶ Type **b28**

14 ▶ Press ⏎.

The cell pointer moves to cell B28, and the worksheet scrolls so that the current cell is in the upper-left corner of the worksheet area.

15 ▶ Press ALT-F7.

The Wysiwyg Main Menu is displayed.

16 ▶ Type **G** to select the Wysiwyg Graph command.

You can use this submenu to add, enhance, or remove graphs.

17 ▶ Type **A** to select the Add command.

The Add command submenu is displayed. This submenu contains options to add graphs associated with the current worksheet or other graph files.

18 ▶ Type **C** to select the Current option.

Lotus 1-2-3 prompts you to enter the display range, which is where you want the graph to be located. The current cell is not anchored.

19 ▶ Type **.** (a period) to anchor the current cell.

20 ▶ Press ↓ 18 times.

21 ▶ Press → 6 times.

The range B28..H46 is highlighted.

22 ▶ Press ↵.

The graph's display range is entered, and the graph is displayed in the worksheet area, as shown in Figure 9.9. The Graph command submenu is active on the control panel.

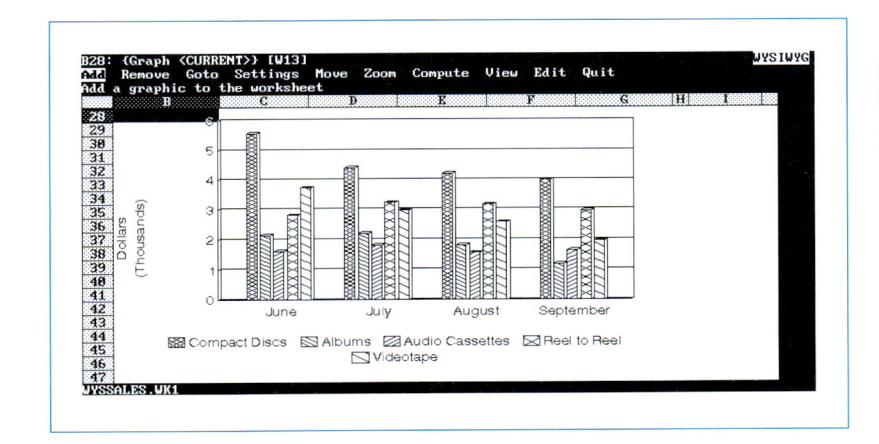

Figure 9.9

After you select the Wysiwyg Graph Add command and specify the graph range, the selected graph is displayed.

23 ▶ Type **Q** to return to READY mode.

Now you will enhance the graph range with an *outline* (box) and a drop shadow. You will begin by preselecting the range.

OUTLINE
Four connected lines of uniform width that surround an element to create a box.

24 ▶ Move the cell pointer to cell A27.

25 ▶ Press F4.

Lotus 1-2-3 prompts you to enter a range.

26 ▶ Press ↓ 20 times.

27 ▶ Press → 7 times.

The range A27..H47 is highlighted.

28 ▶ Press ↵.

29 ▶ Press ALT-F7.

The Wysiwyg Main Menu is displayed.

30 ▶ Type **FLO** to select the Format, Lines, and Outline commands.

The selected range is outlined.

31 ▶ Press ALT-F7.

The Wysiwyg Main Menu displays.

32 ▶ Type **FLS** to select the Format, Lines, and Shadow commands.

The Shadow command submenu is displayed.

Using Wysiwyg to Add a Graph to a Document

289

33 ▶ Type **S** to select the Set command.

The selected range is formatted with a drop shadow.

DROP SHADOW
A graphic effect in which a thick, solid line borders the right and bottom edges of an element to give the element a three-dimensional appearance.

Take a moment to move the cell pointer so you can see the box and *drop shadow* around the graph. Now you will apply the same enhancements to the range of worksheet data at the top of the document.

34 ▶ Move the cell pointer to cell B5.

35 ▶ Press [F4].

Lotus 1-2-3 prompts you to enter a range.

36 ▶ Press [↓] 10 times, and press [→] 6 times.

The range B5..H15 is highlighted.

37 ▶ Press [←].

38 ▶ Press [ALT]-[F7].

The Wysiwyg Main Menu is displayed.

39 ▶ Type **FLO** to select the Format, Lines, and Outline commands.

The selected range is formatted with an outline.

40 ▶ Press [ALT]-[F7].

The Wysiwyg Main Menu is displayed.

41 ▶ Type **FLSS** to select the Format, Lines, Shadow, and Set commands.

The selected range is formatted with a drop shadow.

42 ▶ Press [HOME], and save the current changes to the same file.

Now that the current graph is in the document, any changes made to the worksheet data will be reflected in the graph. Now you will temporarily change one of the worksheet values to see how this works. To begin, you will use Wysiwyg's Display command to change the view of the document. You will adjust the view to see both the graph and part of the worksheet data in the worksheet area.

43 ▶ Press [ALT]-[F7].

The Wysiwyg Main Menu is displayed.

44 ▶ Type **DZT** to select the Display, Zoom, and Tiny commands.

The document's display reduces to show more columns and rows.

45 ▶ Type **Q** to return to READY mode.

46 ▶ Press [SCROLL LOCK]. Scroll the document so that you can see the row of videotape sales figures and the bar graph, as shown in Figure 9.10.

9 ▶ Using Wysiwyg to Create Presentation-Quality Documents

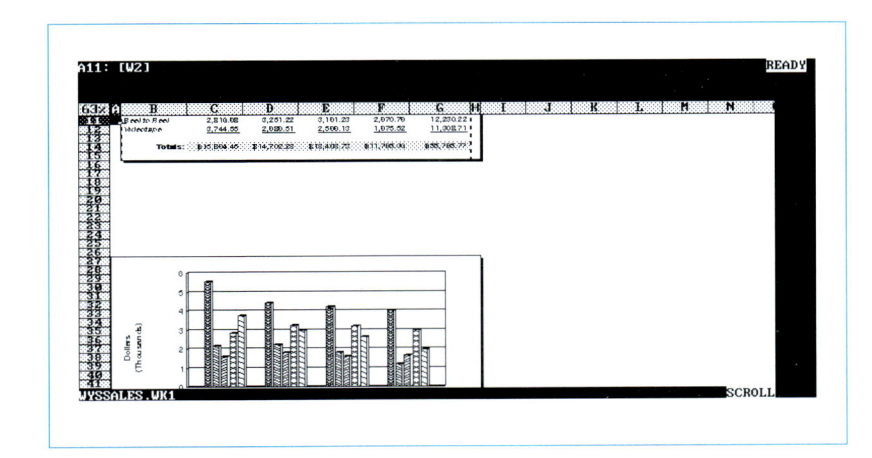

Figure 9.10

Scroll your document so that you can see the videotape sales figures and the bar graph.

47 ▶ Press SCROLL LOCK to turn it off, and move the cell pointer to cell F12.

The cell pointer is on the cell that contains the September sales figure for videotape.

48 ▶ Type **5500**

49 ▶ Press ⏎.

The value is changed, and 1-2-3 redraws the bar graph. Notice that the bar representing September videotape sales reflects the change to the worksheet data.

Now you will change the value back to the original figure and then change the view of the document back to normal.

50 ▶ Make sure the cell pointer is in cell F12.

51 ▶ Type **1975.52**

52 ▶ Press ⏎.

53 ▶ Press ALT-F7.

The Wysiwyg Main Menu is displayed.

54 ▶ Type **DZN** to select the Display, Zoom, and Normal commands.

55 ▶ Type **Q** to return to READY mode.

56 ▶ Press HOME, and save the current changes to the same file.

In the next exercise, you will complete the document by entering text to create a short memo.

Using Wysiwyg to Add a Graph to a Document

Exercise 9.5

Using Wysiwyg to Format Text

Objectives

After completing this exercise, you will be able to
- Enter text in a Wysiwyg document.
- Reformat a range of text into a paragraph.

REFORMAT
An operation in which very long labels can be entered into a single cell and then reformatted into a range as a paragraph.

Adding a memo or note into a worksheet is very easy to do. The best way is to enter the text into a few cells down a column. Because cells can hold up to 240 text characters, you can enter a lot of information into a single cell. If the memo or note is longer than 240 characters, you can move the cell pointer down one cell. Continue entering the text in the next cell in the column. After you enter the text, you can use the Wysiwyg Text Reformat command to *reformat* the text into a paragraph.

To complete the document, you will type a short memo that the owner has given you written in longhand. You will enter the memo's text in the space between the worksheet data and the graph.

TIP
This can also be done in 1-2-3 (without Wysiwyg attached) by selecting the /Range Justify command.

1 ▶ Make sure 1-2-3 is in READY mode.

2 ▶ Move the cell pointer to cell B17.

The cell pointer is on the cell where you will enter the first label in the memo header.

3 ▶ Type "**TO:**

4 ▶ Press ↓.

5 ▶ Type "**FROM:**

6 ▶ Press ↓.

7 ▶ Type "**SUBJECT:**

8 ▶ Press ↓.

9 ▶ Type "**DATE:**

10 ▶ Move the cell pointer to cell C17.

11 ▶ Type **Investors**

12 ▶ Press ↓.

292 9 ▶ Using Wysiwyg to Create Presentation-Quality Documents

13 ▶ Type **Mollie Muzak**

14 ▶ Press ⬇.

15 ▶ Type **Final Summer Sales Figures**

16 ▶ Press ⬇.

17 ▶ Type **October 1, 1995**

18 ▶ Press ⬇ twice.

    The cell pointer moves to cell C22. This is the cell where you will begin entering the memo text.

19 ▶ Type the following sentence:

    Here are the final sales figures for the summer season.

20 ▶ Press **SPACEBAR** twice.

    Two spaces are entered after the period.

21 ▶ Type the following sentences:

    The graph below shows that CD and videotape sales declined slightly during the summer. However, albums, cassettes, and reel-to-reel tapes held steady sales levels.

22 ▶ Press **SPACEBAR** twice.

    Two spaces are entered after the period.

23 ▶ Press ⬇.

    The first two sentences of the memo text are entered as a long label in cell C22. The cell pointer is on cell C23, which is where you will enter the last sentence in the memo.

24 ▶ Type the following sentence:

    We are looking forward to healthy sales in the next quarter.

25 ▶ Press ⬆.

    The memo text is entered as two long labels in the range C22..C23. The cell pointer is on cell C22.

Now you will reformat the long labels into a paragraph.

26 ▶ Press **ALT**-**F7**.

    The Wysiwyg Main Menu is displayed.

27 ▶ Type **TR** to select the Text and Reformat commands.

    Lotus 1-2-3 prompts you to enter the range to reformat. The current cell is anchored.

28 ▶ Press ⬇ 4 times.

29 ▶ Press ➡ 4 times.

Using Wysiwyg to Format Text

30 ▶ Press ⏎.

The text is reformatted into a paragraph in the range C22..G25.

Now you will preview the document, and then save the changes to the current file. To preview all the elements on the page, you will need to first adjust the current print range.

31 ▶ Press ALT-F7.

The Wysiwyg Main Menu is displayed.

32 ▶ Type **PRS** to select the Print, Range, and Set commands.

33 ▶ Press ESC.

The range is cleared, and the cell pointer is on cell B1.

34 ▶ Move the cell pointer to cell A1.

35 ▶ Type **.** (a period) to anchor the current cell.

36 ▶ Press END, and then press HOME.

The range A1..H47 is highlighted.

37 ▶ Press ⏎.

The print range is adjusted, and the Print command submenu is active on the control panel.

38 ▶ Type **P** to select the Preview command.

The preview screen displays a reduced version of the printed page, as shown in Figure 9.11.

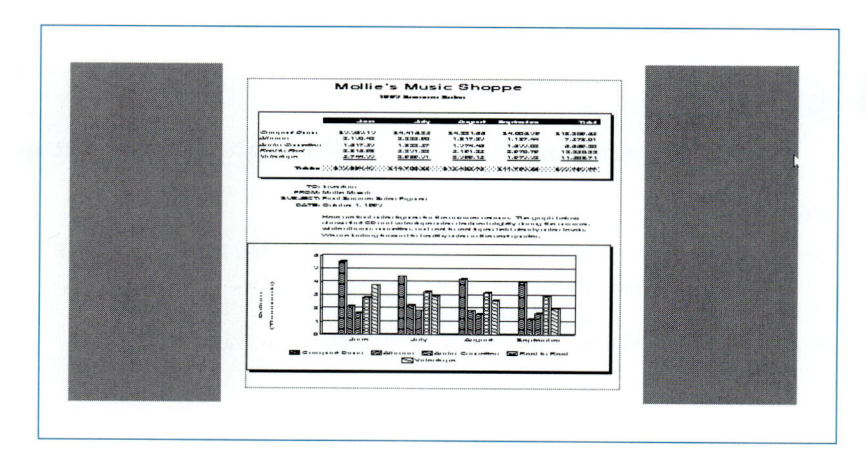

Figure 9.11

After you enter the memo text, your document should look like this on the Wysiwyg print preview screen.

39 ▶ Press SPACEBAR, or any other key.

The Wysiwyg Print Settings dialog box is displayed, and the Print command submenu is active on the control panel.

40 ▶ Type **Q** to return to READY mode.

294 9 ▶ **Using Wysiwyg to Create Presentation-Quality Documents**

41 ▶ Press [HOME], and save the current changes to the same file.

To complete this lesson, you will use Wysiwyg to print the document.

Exercise 9.6 Using Wysiwyg to Print a Document

Objectives

After completing this exercise, you will be able to
- Select a printer in Wysiwyg.
- Print a presentation-quality document.

You can use Wysiwyg to print documents that you have formatted with Wysiwyg features. Before you can print with Wysiwyg, you must check the Wysiwyg print settings. You want to make sure that the print settings are set to recognize the printer attached to your system.

You have already used the Wysiwyg Print Settings dialog box to check the print range setting. As with the 1-2-3 Print Settings dialog box, you can adjust settings directly in the Wysiwyg Print Settings dialog box, or you can use the Wysiwyg Print command submenu.

You will complete this lesson by printing the memo document. You will begin by adjusting the current Wysiwyg print settings to recognize your system's printer configuration. The printer *configuration* is the printer model, port, and interface setup that connects to your computer. The *interface* is the location on your computer system where the printer's cable is attached to the computer.

Adjusting the Wysiwyg print settings means that you select the correct printer model that is connected to your computer. You also select the proper interface. You may need to check with your instructor or technical support person for the correct printer model and interface.

CONFIGURATION
The collection of hardware devices connected to a computer system, including the computer (CPU) itself, monitor, keyboard, printer, mouse, modem, or any other devices.

INTERFACE
A port or connector on a computer through which a printer, or any other independent device, is connected. An interface allows information, in the form of electronic impulses, to be communicated between two hardware components.

1 ▶ Make sure 1-2-3 is in READY mode.

2 ▶ Press [ALT]-[F7].

The Wysiwyg Main Menu is displayed.

3 ▶ Type **P** to select the Print command.

The Wysiwyg Print Settings dialog box is displayed.

4 ▶ Press F2.

The Wysiwyg Print Settings dialog box is activated.

5 ▶ Type **CP** to select the Configuration and Printer setting options.

A Printer Selection box is displayed with a list of printer options that have been installed with the Lotus Install program.

6 ▶ If only one printer is listed, press ⏎ and go to step 8; otherwise, skip this step and go to step 7.

7 ▶ If more than one printer is listed, move the pointer to a printer that can print graphics, and press ⏎.

> Notes: If you do not know which printer can print graphics, check with your instructor or technical support person.
>
> If you are using a dot-matrix printer, check the list for a low-density option and a high-density option. If you have these options, move the pointer to the high-density option.

After you select a printer, the dialog box pointer moves to the Paper Bin setting option.

8 ▶ Press TAB.

The pointer moves to the Interface setting option.

9 ▶ Press ⏎.

A Printer Interface selection box displays a list of interface options.

10 ▶ Move the pointer to the option that is correct for your system's configuration.

> Note: Check with your instructor or technical support person if you are not sure which interface option to choose.

11 ▶ Press ⏎ 3 times.

The Wysiwyg Print command menu is activated on the control panel.

12 ▶ Check that the current print range is properly set.

The print range should be A1..H47.

13 ▶ Make sure your printer is turned on and has paper. Also, make sure that the paper is properly aligned.

9 ▶ Using Wysiwyg to Create Presentation-Quality Documents

14 ▶ Type **G** to select the Go command.

A message appears on the third line of the control panel that indicates that the print data is being processed. After the printing operation has completed, 1-2-3 returns to READY mode.

15 ▶ Press [HOME], if necessary, and save the current changes to the same file.

Now you will detach Wysiwyg to remove it from memory.

16 ▶ Press the Slash key (/) to access the 1-2-3 Main Menu.

17 ▶ Type **AD** to select the Add-In and Detach commands.

Lotus 1-2-3 prompts you to enter the add-in to detach. A list of all the currently attached add-in program files is displayed on the third line of the control panel. Wysiwyg should be the only add-in listed.

18 ▶ Press [←].

Wysiwyg is removed from memory, and the Add-In command submenu reappears.

19 ▶ Type **Q** to return to READY mode.

20 ▶ Erase the worksheet.

You can now begin the Lesson 9 applications that follow the Concept Summary, or you can go on to Lesson 10. Otherwise, quit 1-2-3 if you are through with this 1-2-3 session.

Concept Summary ▶▶▶▶▶▶

- Leading spreadsheet software is now becoming available with separate programs or utilities that use desktop publishing features to generate polished spreadsheet documents.

- These publishing programs use graphics mode to display on screen a version of your document that looks very close to the way it will look on the printed page.

- Spreadsheet publishing programs let you specify a variety of fonts; attributes, such as boldface and italics; and lines, boxes, and shading. You can also incorporate graphs into a document along with worksheet data.

- Spreadsheet publishing programs also let you edit and format text directly in the worksheet.

- The ability to preview a document on screen before it is printed is another very useful capability offered by spreadsheet publishing programs. You can use the preview feature to check formatting and the location of elements on the page before you print.

Using Wysiwyg to Print a Document

Command Summary

1-2-3 Commands

/Add-In Attach (/AA)
loads an add-in program into memory with 1-2-3

/Add-In Detach (/AD)
removes an add-in program from memory

/Range Justify (/RJ)
reformats a range of labels (text) into a paragraph within another range

Wysiwyg Commands

ALT-(F7, F8, F9, or F10) or : (a colon)
invokes the Wysiwyg Main Menu

Worksheet (W)
provides options to adjust column widths or row heights, or insert page breaks

Display Zoom (DZ)
[Tiny Small Normal Large Huge]
adjusts the display size of the worksheet in the worksheet area

Text Edit (TE)
switches 1-2-3 to TEXT mode for editing a range of text

Format Font (FF)
sets a font for a range of data

Format Bold (FB) [Set Clear]
sets or clears the boldface font attribute for a range of data

Format Italics (FI) [Set Clear]
sets or clears the italics font attribute for a range of data

Format Shade Light (FSL)
sets a light (10 percent) background shade for a range of data

Worksheet Column Set-Width (WCS)
adjusts the width of a single column or a range of columns

Format Line Outline (FLO)
sets lines around the outside edges of a cell or cell range

Format Line Shadow (FLS)
sets a drop shadow effect for a selected range

Graph Add (GA)
adds a 1-2-3 graph or any graphic format to the worksheet document

Text Reformat (TR)
reformats a range of labels (text) into a paragraph within another range

Applications

Begin doing the applications by loading 1-2-3, if necessary. Attach the Wysiwyg add-in program. Place your student data disk in drive A. Change the current directory to the drive that contains the student data disk. Also, change the Clock setting in the Global Settings dialog box so that the current filename is displayed on the status line.

> Note: Most of these Lesson 9 applications require that you add graphs created in Lesson 8. If you did not complete the Lesson 8 applications, or if you do not have access to those graphs, either complete the Lesson 8 applications or skip the instructions for adding graphs.

Business

Sales Analysis

1. You will use the Wysiwyg add-in program to create a presentation-quality document that contains the sales analysis information for branch managers. The document will include the sales data and the named line graph that compares sales for 1994 and 1995. Retrieve the file SALES8.WK1, and perform the following formatting operations:

    a. Edit the worksheet first by inserting a new column C and changing its width to three characters. Enter the state abbreviations in the new column C. In EDIT mode, delete the state abbreviations that follow the cities in column B.

    b. Specify fonts and font attributes for various text elements as follows:

    > title and subtitle—Swiss 14 point bold
    > "submit financial results"—bold, italics
    > all column headings—Dutch 12 point bold
    > columns B and C labels—Dutch 10 point
    > all values—Dutch 12 point

    c. Erase the single lines created by repeating-character labels in rows 8 and 18. Replace them with a range of dark shading.

    d. Reverse and bold the four totals in row 19.

    e. Add the named line graph associated with the current worksheet in the range A27..I44.

    f. Because you inserted a new column C, use the 1-2-3 Graph command menu to adjust the legend settings so that they reference the year labels in columns D and F. Be sure to rename the current graph settings with the same name.

HINT Use the /Graph Name Create command (/GNC).

g. Save the document as SALES9.WK1. Use Wysiwyg to set the print range and print the document. Save the changes to the same file, and erase the worksheet.

Business

Small Business

2. You have an upcoming class report on your break-even analysis for the windsurfing board business. For the report, you will create a document that combines a bar graph and the analysis worksheet data. Retrieve the file PROFIT8.WK1. Perform the following formatting tasks to create a document that appears similar to the one shown on the print preview screen in Figure 9.12.

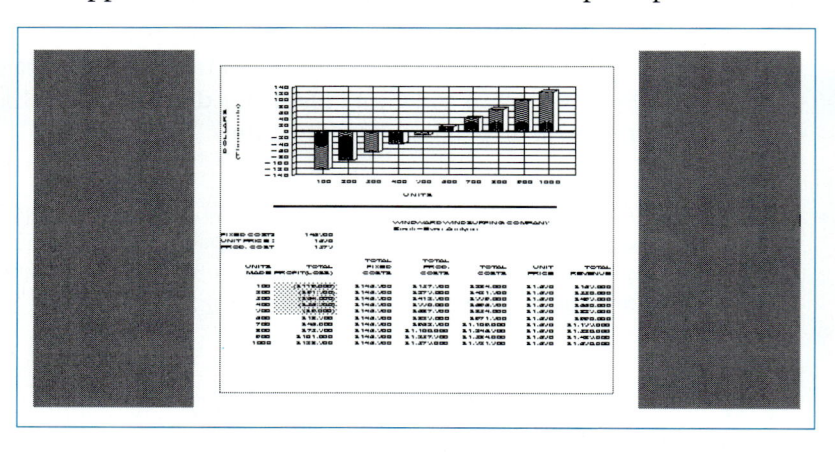

Figure 9.12

Follow the instructions in application 2 (Small Business) to create a document that looks like this when you see it in Wysiwyg's print preview.

a. Move the entire range of data (A3..G20) to the range A28..G45. Move the labels in the range A28..A30 to C28..C30, and then move the cost values in the range B28..B30 to the range D28..D30.

b. Use the 1-2-3 /Range Format Currency command (/RFC) to format the cost values in the range D28..D30 as currency with no decimal places.

c. Add the current three-dimensional bar graph to the graph range A3..G23.

d. Format the blank range B25..F25 with a double line along the top edge of the cells.

HINT
Use the Wysiwyg Format Lines Double command.

e. Specify fonts of your choice for the document's title labels, column heading labels, and the cost labels and values below the double line.

f. Edit the document's title labels so they appear centered on the page.

g. Format the loss values in the range B37..B41 with a light background shade.

h. Save the document as PROFIT9.WK1. Preview and print the document, and then save the changes to the same file. Erase the worksheet.

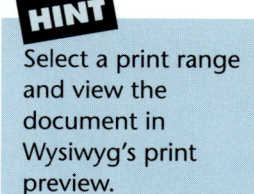

HINT
Select a print range and view the document in Wysiwyg's print preview.

300   9 ▶ Using Wysiwyg to Create Presentation-Quality Documents

Business

Accounting

3. Create a polished general worksheet that shows all the accounting for the month of April. You will create a document that you would submit to your supervisor. The document will show all your worksheet columns. Begin by retrieving the file WORKSHT9.WK1, and then perform the following tasks.

   a. Set column A's width to 21 characters. Adjust the widths of each debit and credit column to 7 characters.

   b. Format the range A4..U5 with an outline. Format row 6 with reverse print.

   HINT
   Use the Wysiwyg Format Color Reverse command.

   c. Create vertical lines that separate the columns, as shown in Figure 9.13. Create the vertical lines by formatting the first one-character-wide column (B) with a single line along the right side of the range. Then use the Wysiwyg Special Copy command to copy the range to the other one-character-wide columns. Format the range of account labels in column A with a single line along the left side of the range.

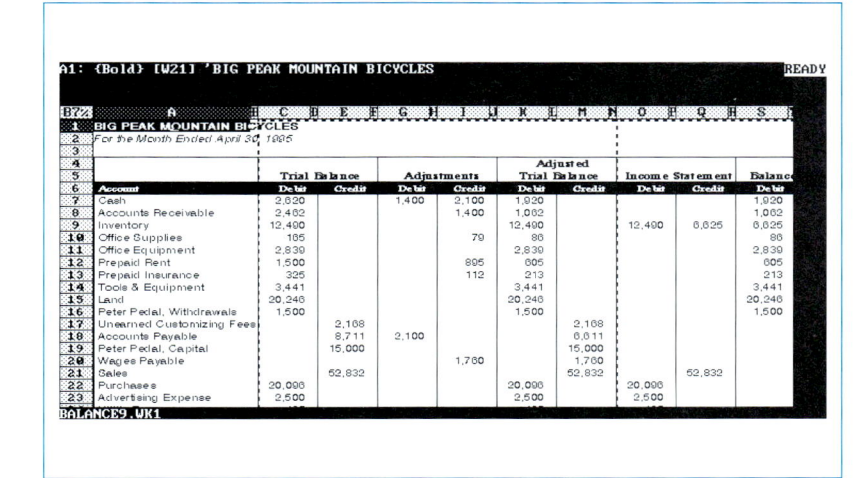

Figure 9.13

Follow the instructions to create a polished worksheet document for the company's April accounting figures. The finished document should look like this on screen.

   Specify the following fonts and font attributes:

   category labels in rows 4 and 5—Dutch 12 point bold

   row 6 labels—Dutch 10 point bold

   title—bold

   subtitle—italics

   d. Format all ranges that contain the column totals with single lines along the top edge and double lines along the bottom edge.

   e. Use the Wysiwyg Print Layout Borders Left command to specify columns A and B as a print border. Then specify the range C1..V36.

   f. Save the file as BALANCE9.WK1. Preview the document, and then print it. Save the changes to the same file, and erase the worksheet.

Applications

Social Studies

Student Survey

4. The school newspaper has asked you to submit a hard copy of the results you have gathered from the student attitudes questionnaire. You decide that you will also provide the bar and pie graphs that you saved as graph files. Retrieve the file WYSSRVY9.WK1, and do the following formatting tasks to create a polished document showing survey results:

   a. Format the following text elements with the specified fonts and/or font attributes:

   title in cell A1—Swiss 14 point bold

   label in cell B3—italics

   category labels in cells A7, A13, and A18—reverse print bold

   column heading labels—bold

   labels in cells A25 and A27—bold

   b. Insert a column between the "Variance" column and the "Excellent" column. Adjust the width of this column to one character. Insert one-character-wide columns after every column labeled "Percent."

   c. Format the range E8..F23 with a shadow. Do this for the ranges H8..I23, K8..L23, N8..O23, and Q8..R23.

   d. Format the three ranges of Ratings with a light background shade.

   e. Add the graph file PSURVEY8.PIC to the graph range A31..J50. Add the graph file BSURVEY8.PIC to the range L31..T49.

   Note: If you do not have these two graph files, go back and do application 4 (Student Survey) in Lesson 8.

   f. Specify a print range that includes all the worksheet data and the two graphs. Preview the two-page document.

   g. Save the worksheet as SURVEY9.WK1, and print the document. Save any changes to the same file, and erase the worksheet.

Social Studies

Geography

5. Use Wysiwyg formatting techniques to create a polished document that features the world population analysis data and the worksheet's current bar graph. Retrieve the file WRLDPOP8.WK1, and do the following formatting tasks:

   a. Use the /Worksheet Global Protection Disable command to remove worksheet protection.

   b. Move the worksheet's title to cell A1.

   c. Specify the following fonts and font attributes:

   title—Swiss 24 point

   column headings—Dutch 10 point bold

   continent names—italics

   d. Right-align the column headings with the Wysiwyg Text Align command.

   e. Enter a light background shade in row 8 below the column heads.

9 ▶ Using Wysiwyg to Create Presentation-Quality Documents

f. Delete row 15, and then delete row 16. Delete column G. Insert a new column A, and change its width to three characters.

g. Format the range B14..G14 with a single line on the bottom edge of the range. This range contains the values for Oceania.

h. Add the current graph to the document in the graph range B24..G44. Outline the range A23..G45. Add a drop shadow to the range A23..G45.

i. Specify a print range that includes the data and graph. Preview the document, and then save the document as WRLDPOP9.WK1.

j. Print the document, save any changes to the same file, and erase the worksheet.

Social Studies

American Government

6. Use Wysiwyg formatting techniques to create a document that graphically enhances the election comparison data. You can use the hard copy to make an overhead transparency that you can display during your report to the class. Retrieve the file ELECTN8.WK1, and perform the following formatting tasks:

    a. Insert and delete rows, as necessary, to arrange the blocks of data as shown on the print preview screen in Figure 9.14. Each election year label should be the only data in its respective row.

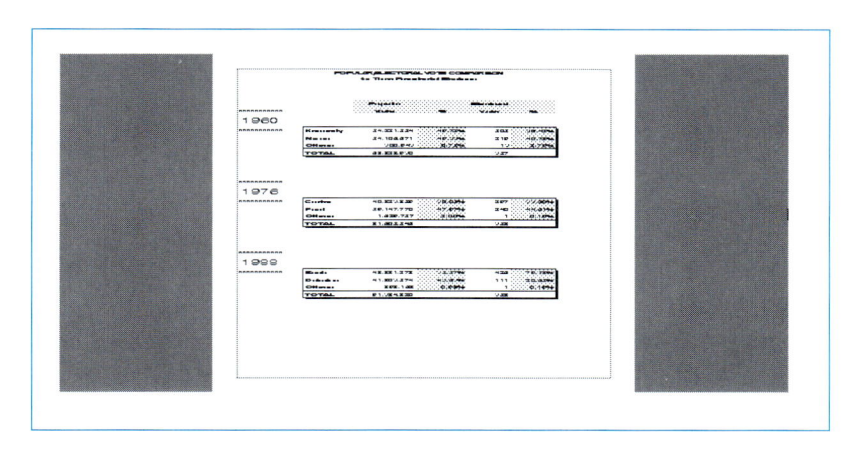

Figure 9.14

Follow the instructions in application 6 (American Government) to create a document that looks like this in print preview.

    b. Specify Swiss 24-point for the three election year labels. Specify Swiss 14-point bold for the column headings, candidate names, and "TOTAL" labels.

    c. Format each year's range of election data with an outline and drop shadow. Format the six ranges of vote percentages and the column heading range with a light background shade.

    d. Center the title and subtitle text within the range A1..H2.

    e. Specify a print range that includes all the data, and preview the document. Compare it with the screen shown in Figure 9.14 and make any necessary changes.

    f. Save the document as ELECTN9.WK1, and print the document.

    g. Save any changes to the same file, and erase the worksheet.

Science/ Mathematics

Astronomy

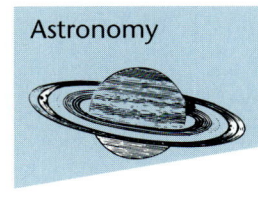

7. For your astronomy class, you want to create a document that combines part of your data with the stacked-bar graph you created in Lesson 8. Retrieve the file PLANETS8.WK1, and do the following formatting tasks:

   a. Use the 1-2-3 /Move command (/M) to move the conversion factor range (A3..C4) to B20..D21.

   b. Reorder the columns by first moving the diameter data in column E to column K and the gravity data in column G to column L. Then delete blank columns E and G.

   c. Delete two rows between the worksheet's title and the first row of column headings. Then use the 1-2-3 /Range Erase command (/RE) to erase the single line in row 6.

   d. Adjust column widths as follows: column A = 8; columns B, C, D, and F = 10; and column G = 7.

   e. Format the title text as follows: center it in the range D1..F1, and specify the Swiss 14 point bold font. Then format the range D1..F1 with a wide line on the bottom edge.

   f. Specify Dutch 10 point bold for the column headings, and format the range of planet names (A7..A15) with bold italics and reverse print.

   g. Format the range B6..H6 with a light background shade. Format the range B21..G21 with a solid background shade. Use the Wysiwyg Special Copy command to copy the solid background to the range B42..G42.

   h. Add the named graph SBARORBITS to the graph range B23..G40.

   i. Save the document as PLANETS9.WK1. Specify a print range that includes the graph and data columns A through H. Do not include columns I and J. Preview the document, and then print it.

   j. Save any changes to the same file, and erase the worksheet.

Science/ Mathematics

Mathematics

8. Your mathematics instructor would like you to explain to the class how you set up your calculations in Lotus 1-2-3 to solve the uniform motion problem. You decide to create a document that includes your data and the line graph to share with the class. Retrieve the file MATH8.WK1, and do the following formatting tasks:

   a. Move the worksheet's title to cell B1, and then delete the blank column A.

   b. Specify the Swiss 14 point font for the title. Specify the bold and italics font attributes for the title.

c. Specify the bold attribute for the labels and miles-per-hour factors in the range A3..E4.

d. Erase all the horizontal and vertical lines created by the repeating-character labels.

e. Format the range A5..D5 with a solid background shade to create a wide rule. Format the range A8..D8 with a wide line along the top edge of the range.

f. Format the range B6..B25 with a single line along the right edge of the range to create a vertical divider line.

g. Adjust column widths as follows: column A = 11 and columns C and D = 8.

h. Add the current line graph to the graph range A30..I50.

i. If you have time, enter a brief note in any column F cells. The note will briefly describe your calculations and state the final result (the approximate time the auto catches the bicycle). Reformat the text as a paragraph in the upper-right corner of the document.

j. Save the document as MATH9.WK1. Set the print range to include the data and graph range. Preview the document, and then print it.

k. Save any changes to the same file, and erase the worksheet.

Health

Nutrition

9. You decide to post your daily nutritional data on the bulletin board in your health class. You will use Wysiwyg formatting features to create the document. Retrieve the file NUTRINF8.WK1, and do the following formatting tasks:

a. Format the title with Swiss 24-point bold, and then format the range A1..D1 with a double line along the bottom edge of the range.

b. Delete the range of hatch pattern numbers in row 2. Then delete rows 9, 19, and 29 (the rows that contain repeating-character labels that create the separation lines).

c. Format the column headings with Dutch 10-point bold, and then format all the column B labels with Dutch 10-point.

d. Format the ranges of values in rows 8, 18, and 28 with a single line along the bottom edge of the range.

e. Format the three ranges that show "Energy in kilocalories" values (in rows 10, 20, and 30) with a light background shade.

f. Format the labels "BREAKFAST," "LUNCH," and "DINNER" with reverse print and the boldface attribute.

g. Erase the range of repeating-character labels that make the separation lines in rows 12, 22, and 32. Format the ranges A12..H12, A22..H22, and A32..H32 with wide lines along the bottom edges of the ranges.

h. Format the range G5..G35 with a wide line along the left edge of the range.

HINT
Format the first range, and then use the Wysiwyg Special Copy command to copy the attributes to the other range.

Applications

i. Move the label in cell C41 to cell D41, and then delete the blank column C. Adjust the column widths as follows: column B = 14, columns C, E, F, and G = 8, column D = 14, and column H = 4.

j. In EDIT mode, edit the labels in cells B38 and B39 to delete the spaces between the label formatting prefixes and the text.

k. Press [HOME], and save the document as NUTRINF9.WK1. Specify a print range that includes all data in columns A through H, and then preview the document. Print the document.

l. Save any changes to the same file, and erase the worksheet.

Health

Physical Education

10. For the school newspaper, you will create a document that contains the softball team's current batting statistics. The document will also contain the bar graph that compares each player's batting average and slugging percentage. Retrieve the file SBGAME8.WK1, and do the following formatting tasks:

a. Format the worksheet's title with Swiss 14 point bold, and then center the title within the range B1..J1.

b. Delete the label in cell C3, move the cell pointer to cell A3, and then type the label "Composite Batting." Format the label with the bold and italics attributes, and then format the range A3..B3 with reverse print.

c. Insert a new row 4.

d. Format the range A5..K5 with a double line along the top edge of the range. Format the range A6..K6 with a double line along the bottom edge of the range. Then format the range A5..K6 with a light background shade.

e. Format the totals range (A22..K22) with reverse print and the bold attribute. Erase the repeating-character labels in row 21 that make the single separation line.

f. Format the range of team averages (A24..I27) with an outline and a drop shadow.

g. Move the range of slugging percentage factors (A29..C31) to the range L2..N4.

h. Add the current bar graph to the graph range B31..J45. Use the 1-2-3 /Graph Options Titles command (/GOT) to delete the first and second titles' text.

i. Save the document as SBGAME9.WK1. Set the print range to include all data and the graph in columns A through K. Preview the document, and then print it.

j. Save any changes to the same file, and erase the worksheet.

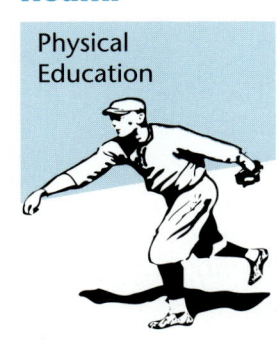

10 ▶ Creating Worksheet Databases

Objectives

- Define database terms.
- Describe the structure of a database.
- Define a database.
- Enter field names in a worksheet.
- Enter records in a database.
- Insert database records.
- Delete database records.
- Sort database records.

A telephone book, a checkbook, a Rolodex, and a file cabinet are common examples of databases. Databases are files that store and organize information for ease of use. You can store data in your 1-2-3 worksheet as a database. Then you can perform special database operations to use, manage, and maintain the information.

Exercise 10.1

Introduction to Databases

Objectives

After completing this exercise, you will be able to
- Define database terms.
- Describe the structure of a database.
- Define a database.

This first Lesson 10 exercise will introduce you to the basic concepts and structure of a database. This exercise contains introductory information only, not step-by-step operations. Before you begin working with a database, it is important to understand the definition of a database, its structure, and how it is used.

DATABASE
An organized collection of information that is stored in a file.

A *database* is an organized collection of related information. Telephone books, mailing lists, and personnel files in a filing cabinet are just a few examples of typical databases used every day. Figure 10.1 shows the structure of a database in a 1-2-3 worksheet. It is similar to the database you will set up later in this lesson.

```
A1: [W14] 'Mollie's Music Shoppe                                READY

         A              B              C         D      E      F     G
 1  Mollie's Music Shoppe
 2  Inventory
 3
 4  ARTIST         TITLE          CATEGORY  TYPE   SKU#   QUANT. COST
 5  Beagles        Tabbey Lane    Rock      CD     9366    4    6.80
 6  Doris Spyder   Web of Time    Soul      CD     8962    4    5.85
 7  Falcons        Free Flight Funk Jazz    Album  9634    6    6.30
 8  Noggins        Keep Your Head Rock      Tape   3856    2    4.00
 9  Poptartz       Breakfast Sonatas Class. CD     9224    8    5.50
10  Potholes       Long, Rough Road Country CD     8788    3    5.90
11  Shambles       Wrecking Ball  Rock      Album  8966    2    6.20
12  Silly Filly    Chompin' At The Bit Class. Tape 9754    5    5.95
13  Silly Filly    Trottin'       Class.    CD     8993    3    6.50
14  The Windows    Awning Blues   Rock      CD     8546    8    6.50
15
16
17
18
19
20
INVNTORY.WK1
```

Field names → (rows 4)
Records → (rows 5–14)

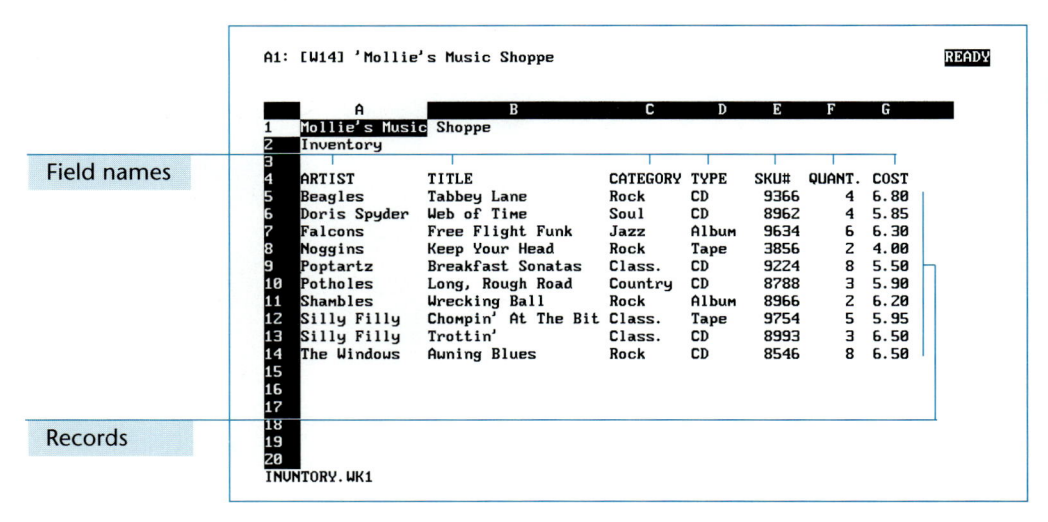

Figure 10.1

This is a typical database structure set up in a 1-2-3 worksheet. It lists an inventory of recordings. The first row contains field names that identify the items of information in each column. Each row is one database record, which is a complete set of information for each product.

10 ▶ Creating Worksheet Databases

FIELD
A column of data in a 1-2-3 database that has a specific name. A field holds an item of information for each record in a database.

FIELD NAME
A label that identifies a specific column of data in a 1-2-3 database worksheet.

RECORD
A row of data in a 1-2-3 database that holds information for each individual or part of a database. Each record's information is organized by fields.

Notice in Figure 10.1 that the first row in the database contains field names in uppercase characters. A *field* is an item of information. For example, in a telephone book, each phone number is an item of information. In a 1-2-3 database worksheet, fields are arranged in columns. *Field names* are labels that identify the type of data stored in each column. Field names do not have to be entered in all uppercase characters. However, they are easier to refer to when they are entered that way.

Each row in a 1-2-3 worksheet database contains a related set of information, called a record. A *record* is a logical unit in a database. For example, each person's name, address, and telephone number is a record, or logical unit, in a telephone book. The field columns organize the information for each record. In the inventory database shown in Figure 10.1, each record is composed of seven fields of information.

When you create a database, you want to break the information down into as many fields as necessary. This simplifies database operations, such as searching for information or rearranging records in the database. For example, if you are creating a mailing list database, consider using two fields for names instead of one. One field is for first names, and one field is for last names. This makes it much easier to rearrange, or sort, the database records alphabetically by last name. Here are some other guidelines for creating a database with 1-2-3:

▶ The database must not contain any blank rows between the row of field names and the last record. The database must not contain any blank columns.

▶ Any one record need not contain data in every field, but it must contain data in at least one field.

▶ The first row must hold the field names, or column headings.

▶ Field names cannot hold operators, such as +, —, *, /, or ^.

▶ A field name must be unique, and it cannot be used more than once.

▶ All the data in a field must be entered the same way. For example, a zip code field should not contain both numbers and text. The entries should be stored either as values or as labels.

▶ Do not use repeating-character labels to create separation lines for any row in the database range.

▶ A field can contain a formula or function that refers to other fields within a record (on the same row).

Go on to the next exercise to begin setting up a database structure.

Exercise 10.2 Creating a Database

Objectives

After completing this exercise, you will be able to
- Enter field names in a worksheet.
- Enter records in a database.

As part of your job responsibilities at Mollie's Music Shoppe, you will set up a database for the merchandise inventory. The database will contain the following fields of information:

▶ artist

▶ title

▶ category

▶ type

▶ SKU number

▶ quantity

▶ cost

▶ price

The "type" field will contain labels that describe the type of recording for each product, as follows: "Album"; "CD" (compact disc); and "Tape" (cassette tape). The SKU number field will hold the Stock Keeping Unit, which is a unique number assigned to each product. The store uses the SKU number to help maintain control over inventory. The cost field represents the store's cost for each unit it purchases from the manufacturer. The price field represents the retail price that the store charges for the item. This field will hold a formula for each record that increases the cost value by a specific markup value.

Now you will create a database for the inventory of recording products. Begin by entering a title for the database and the row of field names.

1 ▶ If necessary, start 1-2-3. Use the /File Directory command (/FD) to change the current directory to the drive that contains the student data disk.

2 ▶ Make sure that you have a blank worksheet area, the cell pointer is in cell A1, and Wysiwyg is not attached.

3 ▶ If necessary, change the clock setting so that the current filename will be displayed on the status line.

4 ▶ Type **Mollie's Music Shoppe**

5 ▶ Press ⬇.

6 ▶ Type **Inventory**

7 ▶ Press ⬇ twice.

The cell pointer is on cell A4, which will contain the first field name.

8 ▶ Press CAPS LOCK.

9 ▶ Type **ARTIST** and press →.

10 ▶ Type **TITLE** and press →.

11 ▶ Type **CATEGORY** and press →.

12 ▶ Type **TYPE** and press →.

13 ▶ Type **SKU#** and press →.

14 ▶ Type **QUANT.** and press →.

15 ▶ Type **COST** and press →.

16 ▶ Type **PRICE** and press ←.

17 ▶ Press CAPS LOCK.

Uppercase status mode is turned off.

18 ▶ Press END, and then press ←.

The cell pointer moves to the cell that contains the field name "ARTIST." Your worksheet should look like Figure 10.2.

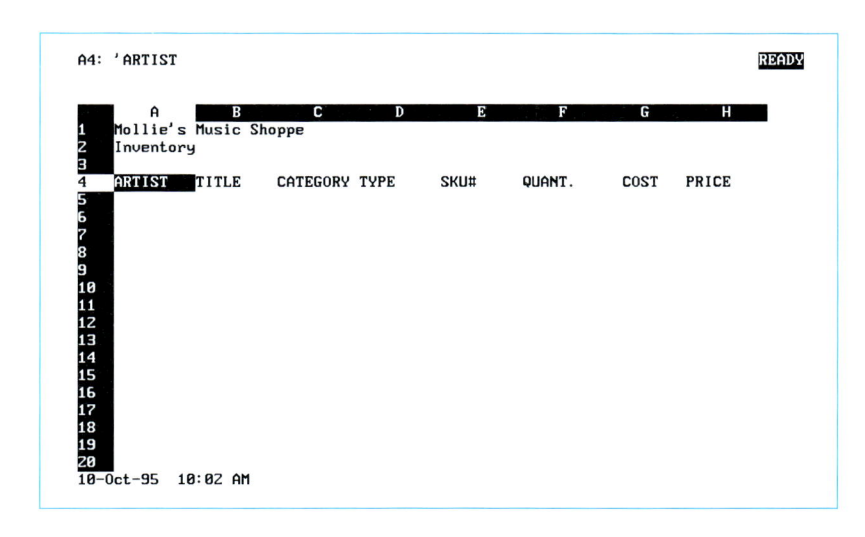

Figure 10.2

After you enter the database field names, your worksheet should look like this.

Now you are ready to enter the information for the first record.

19 ▶ Move the cell pointer to cell A5.

The cell pointer is directly beneath the first field name.

20 ▶ Type **The Windows** and press →.

Creating a Database   **311**

21 ▶ Type **Awning Blues** and press →.

22 ▶ Type **Rock** and press →.

23 ▶ Type **CD** and press →.

24 ▶ Type **8546** and press →.

25 ▶ Type **8** and press →.

26 ▶ Type **6.50** and press →.

For the first record's price field, you will enter a formula that calculates the retail price for each unit. This formula will add a markup of four dollars to the value in the "COST" field.

27 ▶ Type **+** (a plus sign).

28 ▶ Press ←.

> The cell pointer is on the cell that contains the cost for the first item, and the cell address G5 is displayed on the control panel.

29 ▶ Type **+** (a plus sign).

> The cell pointer returns to cell H5.

30 ▶ Type **4** and press ↵.

> The formula is entered, and the result, 10.5, is displayed.

Now you will change the widths of various columns to display their contents fully.

31 ▶ Press END, and then press ←.

> The cell pointer is on cell A5.

32 ▶ Use the /Worksheet Column Set-Width command (/WCS) to increase the width of column A to 14 characters.

33 ▶ Move the cell pointer to column B, and increase its width to 20 characters.

34 ▶ Move the cell pointer to cell A6.

> The cell pointer is on the next row of the database. Your database should look like Figure 10.3.

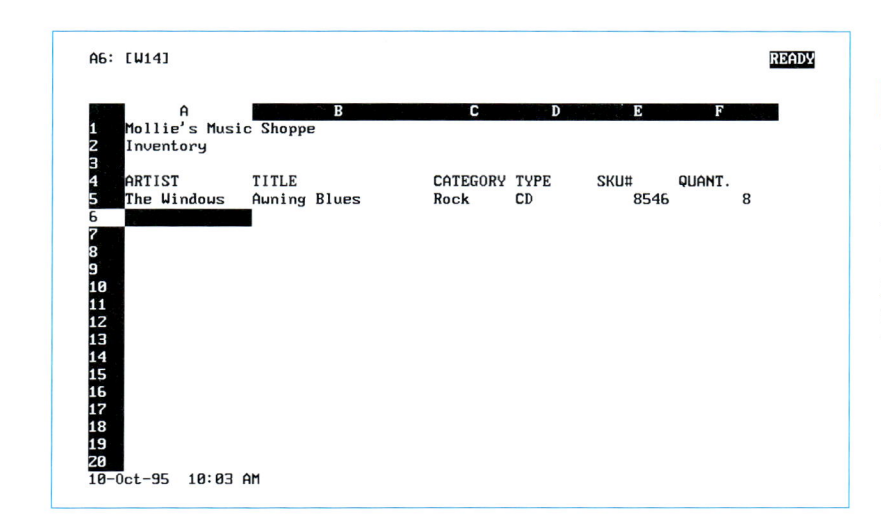

Figure 10.3

After you enter the first record's information in the field columns and adjust column widths, your database worksheet should look like this.

Now you are ready to enter more records in your inventory database.

35 ▶ Enter the following records to complete the inventory database.

> Note: Do not enter formulas in the "PRICE" field; you will use the /Copy command (/C) later to do that for you.

Artist	Title	Category	Type	SKU#	Quantity	Cost
Beagles	Tabbey Lane	Rock	CD	9366	4	6.80
Falcons	Free Flight Funk	Jazz	Album	9634	6	6.30
Shale	Boulder Youth	Rock	CD	3665	2	4.70
Silly Filly	Trottin'	Class.	CD	8993	3	6.50
Noggins	Keep Your Head	Rock	Tape	3856	2	4.00
Potholes	Long, Rough Road	Country	CD	8788	3	5.90
Doris Spyder	Web of Time	Soul	CD	8962	4	5.85
Shambles	Wrecking Ball	Rock	Album	8966	2	6.20
Silly Filly	Chompin' at the Bit	Class.	Tape	9754	5	5.95

36 ▶ Move the cell pointer to cell H5.

The current cell contains the formula that calculates the retail price for the first record.

37 ▶ Use the /Copy command (/C) to copy the formula in the current cell down the column to calculate retail price for the other records.

38 ▶ Press HOME, and save the database as INVNTORY.WK1.

You will complete this exercise by adjusting the widths of the remaining columns and formatting values in the database so that the data is easier to read and use.

Creating a Database 313

39 ▶ Use the /Worksheet Column Set-Width command (/WCS) to adjust column D to 7 characters and columns E–H to 6 characters.

40 ▶ Move the cell pointer to cell G5.

The cell pointer is on the cell that contains the cost for the first record.

41 ▶ Press the Slash key (/) to access the Main Menu.

42 ▶ Type **RF** to select the Range and Format commands.

43 ▶ Type **,** (a comma) to select the Comma format option.

Lotus 1-2-3 prompts you to enter the number of decimal places.

44 ▶ Press ⏎.

Lotus 1-2-3 prompts you to enter the range to format.

45 ▶ Press END, and then press ↓.

46 ▶ Press →.

The range G5..H14 is highlighted.

47 ▶ Press ⏎.

The range of "COST" values and "PRICE" formula results is formatted.

48 ▶ Press HOME, and save the changes to the same file.

You have created a database structure and entered labels and values to create records. Your worksheet should look like Figure 10.4. Formatting the database worksheet helps to make it easier to read and understand.

```
A1: [W14] 'Mollie's Music Shoppe                                    READY

              A              B              C       D      E     F     G
 1    Mollie's Music Shoppe
 2    Inventory
 3
 4    ARTIST         TITLE           CATEGORY TYPE  SKU#  QUANT. COST
 5    The Windows    Awning Blues    Rock     CD    8546    8    6.50
 6    Beagles        Tabbey Lane     Rock     CD    9366    4    6.80
 7    Falcons        Free Flight Funk Jazz    Album 9634    6    6.30
 8    Shale          Boulder Youth   Rock     CD    3665    2    4.70
 9    Silly Filly    Trottin'        Class.   CD    8993    3    6.50
10    Noggins        Keep Your Head  Rock     Tape  3856    2    4.00
11    Potholes       Long, Rough Road Rock    Tape  8788    3    5.90
12    Doris Spyder   Web of Time     Soul     CD    8962    4    5.85
13    Shambles       Wrecking Ball   Rock     Album 8966    2    6.20
14    Silly Filly    Chompin' At The Bit Class. Tape 9754   5    5.95
15
16
17
18
19
20
INVNTORY.WK1
```

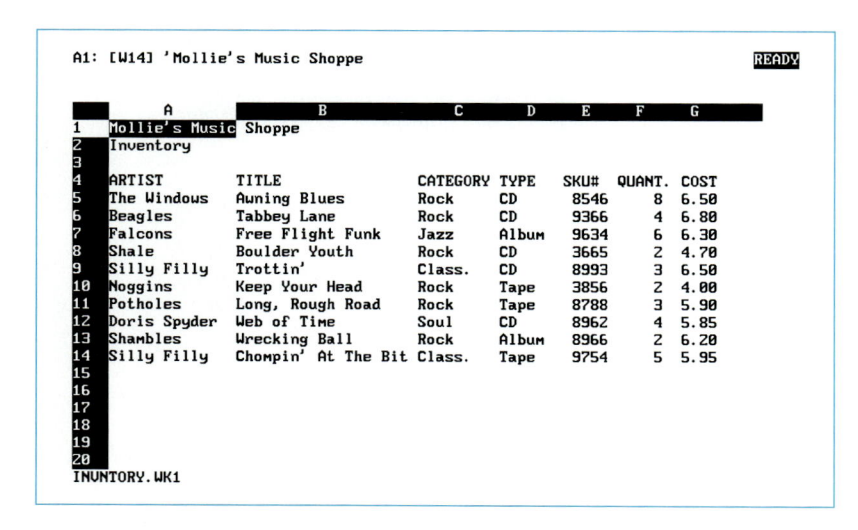

Figure 10.4

After you enter all the information for each record, your database worksheet should look like this.

Exercise 10.3

Inserting and Deleting Records to Maintain a Database

Objectives

After completing this exercise, you will be able to
- Insert database records.
- Delete database records.

In the business world, database information must be continuously maintained because information is constantly changing. Periodic database maintenance requires that you insert new records and delete obsolete records, as necessary. This helps keep the database up to date.

The recordings by the now-defunct band Shale were given away as a donation to a local organization. (The CDs never did sell all that well, anyway.) You will update the inventory by deleting this record from the database.

1 ▶ Move the cell pointer to cell A8.

2 ▶ Press the Slash key (/) to access the Main Menu.

3 ▶ Type **WDR** to select the Worksheet, Delete, and Row commands.

Lotus 1-2-3 prompts you to enter the range of rows to be deleted.

4 ▶ Press ⏎.

Row 8, containing the obsolete record, is deleted, and the rows below move up one row.

Next you will add a new shipment of product to the database. The easiest way to add records to a database is to enter the data for the new record at the end of the database. Later in this lesson, you will learn how to sort database records into a specific order arrangement.

5 ▶ Move the cell pointer to cell A14.

6 ▶ Enter the following record's data in the range A14..G14:

Poptartz   Breakfast Sonatas   Class.   CD   9224   8   5.50

Notice that when you entered the cost value in cell G14, the value did not appear with the comma format.

7 ▶ Move the cell pointer to cell G14, if necessary.

8 ▶ Press the Slash key (/) to access the Main Menu.

9 ▶ Type **RF** to select the Range, Format, and Comma commands.

Lotus 1-2-3 prompts you to enter the number of decimal places.

10 ▶ Press (↵).

Lotus 1-2-3 prompts you to enter the range to format.

11 ▶ Press (→).

12 ▶ Press (↵).

The cost value for the new record and the column H cell, which will store the record's price value, are formatted.

13 ▶ Move the cell pointer to cell H13.

The cell pointer is on the cell that contains the retail price for the Silly Filly CD.

14 ▶ Use the /Copy command (/C) to copy the formula in the current cell to cell H14.

The formula copy will calculate the retail price for the added record.

15 ▶ Press (HOME), and save the changes to the same file.

Your database should look like Figure 10.5.

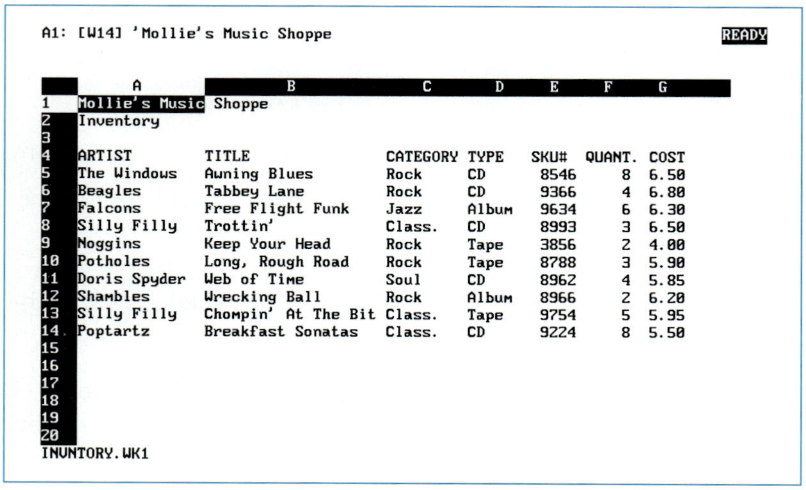
A1: [W14] 'Mollie's Music Shoppe READY

	A	B	C	D	E	F	G
1	Mollie's Music	Shoppe					
2	Inventory						
3							
4	ARTIST	TITLE	CATEGORY	TYPE	SKU#	QUANT.	COST
5	The Windows	Awning Blues	Rock	CD	8546	8	6.50
6	Beagles	Tabbey Lane	Rock	CD	9366	4	6.80
7	Falcons	Free Flight Funk	Jazz	Album	9634	6	6.30
8	Silly Filly	Trottin'	Class.	CD	8993	3	6.50
9	Noggins	Keep Your Head	Rock	Tape	3856	2	4.00
10	Potholes	Long, Rough Road	Rock	Tape	8788	3	5.90
11	Doris Spyder	Web of Time	Soul	CD	8962	4	5.85
12	Shambles	Wrecking Ball	Rock	Album	8966	2	6.20
13	Silly Filly	Chompin' At The Bit	Class.	Tape	9754	5	5.95
14	Poptartz	Breakfast Sonatas	Class.	CD	9224	8	5.50
15							
16							
17							
18							
19							
20							

INVNTORY.WK1

Figure 10.5

After you have added the new record and deleted an obsolete record, your worksheet should look like this.

Now you will learn how to sort the records in a database.

Exercise 10.4

Sorting Records

Objective

After completing this exercise, you will be able to
- Sort database records.

SORT
To arrange database records in a specific order, such as numerical order or alphabetical order.

KEY FIELD
The field, or column, used to determine the order of records that results from a database sort operation.

When you create a database, you can enter the records in any order you want. However, at some point you will want to rearrange the records in a specific order. For example, records in a telephone book are organized alphabetically by last name.

You organize database records by performing a *sort* operation. For example, you could sort your inventory database to arrange the records in alphabetical order by the name of the artist. You could also sort the database records in numerical order by the SKU number. Or you might even want to sort the database so that the records are arranged by product type. To sort database records, you select the /Data Sort command (/DS).

When sorting records, you must choose a field that will be used to determine the order of the records. This field is called a *key field*. If you want the records in alphabetical order by artist, then the "ARTIST" field (column) would be the key field.

In some cases, you might want to use two key fields to determine the arrangement of database records. If you use two key fields, the first key field, or column, is called the *primary key*. The second key field, or column, is called the *secondary key*. For example, suppose you specify the "ARTIST" field as the primary key and the "TITLE" field as the secondary key. After you sort the records, they will be in alphabetical order by artist. Then, all records with the same artist will be in alphabetical order by title.

Before 1-2-3 sorts the records, you must tell 1-2-3 whether you want the records sorted in ascending or descending order. An *ascending sort* organizes alphabetic data from A to Z and numeric data in numerical order (0, 1, 2, 3, etc.). A *descending sort* organizes alphabetic data from Z to A and numeric data in reverse numerical order (100, 99, 98, etc.).

You will first sort the database records alphabetically by artist.

1 ▶ Press the Slash key (/) to access the Main Menu.

2 ▶ Type **D** to select the Data command.

The Data command submenu is displayed. Use this submenu to sort records or specify ranges for query operations.

> Note: You will learn about database query operations in the next lesson.

3 ▶ Type **S** to select the Sort command.

Lotus 1-2-3 displays the Sort Settings dialog box. You will use the Sort command submenu to select the database range you want 1-2-3 to sort.

4 ▶ Type **D** to select the Data range command.

Lotus 1-2-3 prompts you to enter the range to be sorted.

5 ▶ Move the cell pointer to cell A5.

The cell pointer is on the cell that contains the artist information for the first record in the database.

> Caution: Do not include the row with the field names in the data range. Otherwise, that row will be sorted along with the records.

6 ▶ Type **.** (a period) to anchor the current cell.

7 ▶ Press (END), and then press (↓).

The first field column is highlighted.

8 ▶ Press (END), and then press (→).

All the records in the database are highlighted.

9 ▶ Press (↵).

The Sort Settings dialog box reappears. Notice that the range A5..H14 is displayed to the right of the Data range option, as shown in Figure 10.6.

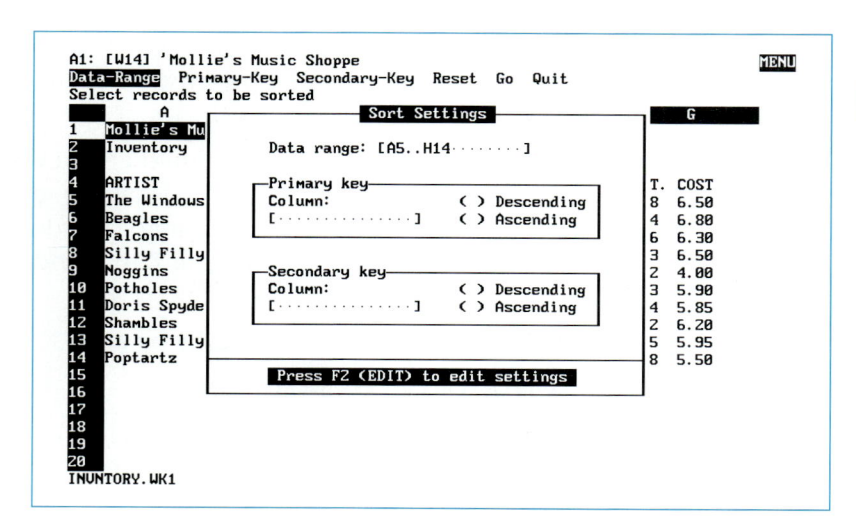

Figure 10.6

Before performing a sort operation, you must tell 1-2-3 the range of data to be sorted. The Sort Settings dialog box displays the sort option settings.

318   **10 ▶ Creating Worksheet Databases**

PRIMARY KEY
The primary or first database field (column) used to perform a sort operation.

10 ▶ Type **P** to select the Primary-Key command.

   Lotus 1-2-3 prompts you to enter the primary sort key.

11 ▶ Move the cell pointer to cell A4.

   The cell pointer is on the cell that contains the field name "ARTIST."

12 ▶ Press ⏎.

   Lotus 1-2-3 prompts you to specify an ascending or descending sort order.

ASCENDING SORT
A sort order in which labels are arranged alphabetically, from A to Z, or values are arranged in numerical order.

13 ▶ Type **A** to select Ascending sort order.

14 ▶ Press ⏎.

   The Sort Settings dialog box displays the current settings.

Now you are ready to perform the sort operation.

15 ▶ Type **G** to select the Go command.

   The records are arranged in alphabetical order by artist, as shown in Figure 10.7.

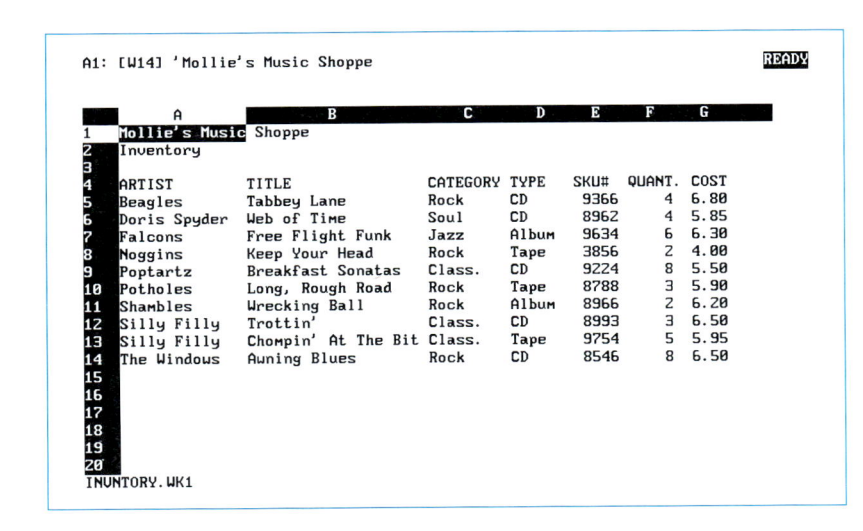

Figure 10.7

After you perform the sort operation, the records are arranged in alphabetical order by artist's name.

Notice that the titles for the recordings by the group Silly Filly are not arranged in alphabetical order. You will perform another sort operation, this time using a secondary key field.

16 ▶ Press the Slash key (/) to access the Main Menu.

17 ▶ Type **DS** to select the Data and Sort commands.

   The Sort command submenu is displayed.

SECONDARY KEY
The second database field (column) used to perform a sort operation.

18 ▶ Type **S** to select the Secondary-Key command.

   Lotus 1-2-3 prompts you to enter the secondary key field.

Sorting Records   319

19 ▶ Move the cell pointer to cell B4.

The cell pointer is on the cell that contains the "TITLE" field name.

20 ▶ Press ⏎.

Lotus 1-2-3 prompts you to specify the sort order.

21 ▶ Type **A** to select Ascending sort.

22 ▶ Press ⏎.

23 ▶ Type **G** to select the Go command.

The database range is sorted again, as shown in Figure 10.8.

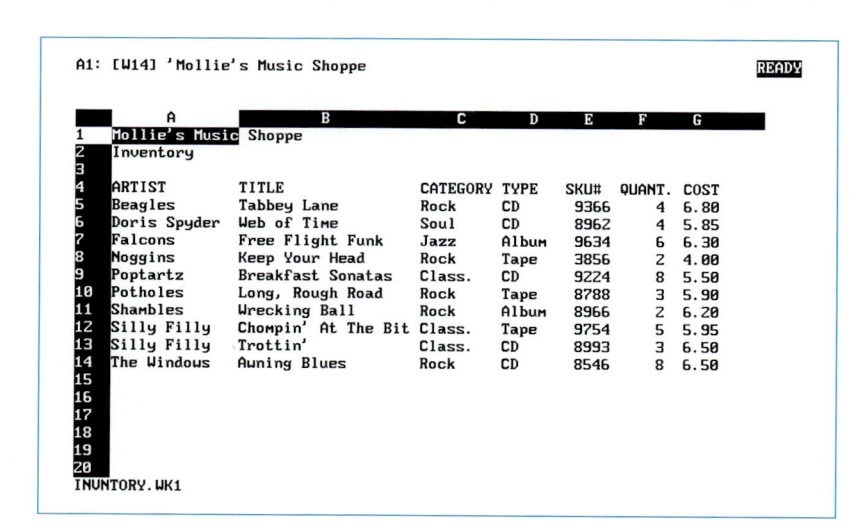

Figure 10.8

The same data range is sorted again, this time with a primary and secondary sort key. Notice that the two recordings by Silly Filly are in alphabetical order by title.

```
A1: [W14] 'Mollie's Music Shoppe                              READY

        A             B              C        D      E     F     G
 1  Mollie's Music Shoppe
 2  Inventory
 3
 4  ARTIST       TITLE              CATEGORY TYPE   SKU#  QUANT. COST
 5  Beagles      Tabbey Lane        Rock     CD     9366    4    6.80
 6  Doris Spyder Web of Time        Soul     CD     8962    4    5.85
 7  Falcons      Free Flight Funk   Jazz     Album  9634    6    6.30
 8  Noggins      Keep Your Head     Rock     Tape   3856    2    4.00
 9  Poptartz     Breakfast Sonatas  Class.   CD     9224    8    5.50
10  Potholes     Long, Rough Road   Rock     Tape   8788    3    5.90
11  Shambles    Wrecking Ball       Rock     Album  8966    2    6.20
12  Silly Filly  Chompin' At The Bit Class.  Tape   9754    5    5.95
13  Silly Filly  Trottin'           Class.   CD     8993    3    6.50
14  The Windows  Awning Blues       Rock     CD     8546    8    6.50
15
16
17
18
19
20
INVNTORY.WK1
```

The records are now in alphabetical order by artist. Also, the records for the same artist are in alphabetical order by title. Now that you have completed the sort operation, you have several choices about what to do next. You can print the results, save the results in a file, or perform another sort operation. For now, you will save the results of this sort operation to the same file. Then you will sort the database again by SKU number and save that version in a different file.

24 ▶ Press HOME, and save the changes to the same file.

25 ▶ Make sure the worksheet file INVNTORY.WKl is loaded and 1-2-3 is in READY mode.

26 ▶ Press the Slash key (/) to access the Main Menu.

27 ▶ Type **DS** to select the Data and Sort commands.

28 ▶ Type **P** to select the Primary-Key command.

Lotus 1-2-3 prompts you to enter the primary key field.

DESCENDING SORT
A sort order in which labels are arranged in reverse alphabetical order, from Z to A, or values are arranged from the highest value to the lowest value.

29 ▶ Move the cell pointer to cell E4.

The cell pointer is on the cell that contains the field name SKU#.

30 ▶ Press ⏎.

Lotus 1-2-3 prompts you to specify the sort order.

31 ▶ Type **D** to select Descending sort.

32 ▶ Press ⏎.

As you can see in the Sort Settings dialog box, 1-2-3 remembers the secondary key that you used last time. You don't need to change (or use) the secondary key here because each entry in the SKU# field is unique.

33 ▶ Type **G** to select the Go command.

The records are sorted. Notice that the first record has the highest SKU number and the last record has the lowest.

34 ▶ Press HOME, and save the current changes to a file named SKUINV.WK1.

Now you will print the SKUINV.WK1 database that is sorted by SKU number.

35 ▶ Press the Slash key (/) to access the Main Menu.

36 ▶ Type **PPR** to select the Print, Printer, and Range commands.

Lotus 1-2-3 prompts you to enter the print range.

37 ▶ Type **.** (a period) to anchor the current cell.

38 ▶ Press END, and then press HOME.

The entire database range is highlighted.

Caution: If 1-2-3 highlights additional blank columns and rows, press LEFT and UP, as necessary, to redefine the print range as Al..H14.

39 ▶ Press ⏎.

The print range is selected, and the Print Settings dialog box and Printer command submenu reappear.

Because you want to print the worksheet across one page, you will adjust your margin settings. Edit the Margins setting options in the Print Settings dialog box.

40 ▶ Press F2.

The Print Settings dialog box is activated.

Sorting Records 321

41 ▶ Type **M** to move the pointer to the Margins setting option.

42 ▶ Type **L** to select the Left option.

43 ▶ Type **2**

44 ▶ Press [TAB].

> The Left margin setting is changed, and the pointer moves to the Right option.

45 ▶ Type **80**

46 ▶ Press [←].

> The pointer moves to the Top margin setting.

47 ▶ Press [ESC].

> The pointer moves to the Margins setting option.

48 ▶ Press [↑] 4 times.

> The pointer moves to the OK command button.

49 ▶ Press [←].

> The Printer command submenu is activated on the control panel.

50 ▶ Make sure that the printer is on and has paper. Also, make sure that the paper is properly aligned.

51 ▶ Type **AG** to select the Align and Go commands.

> If you are using a dot-matrix printer, the range prints; if you are using a laser printer, the data is processed.

52 ▶ Type **P** to select the Page command.

> If you are using a dot-matrix printer, the paper advances. If you are using a laser printer, the printed page ejects.

53 ▶ Type **Q** to return to READY mode.

54 ▶ Press [HOME], if necessary, and save the print settings to the same file.

55 ▶ Erase the worksheet.

Concept Summary

- Spreadsheet software commonly provides commands that let you set up, organize, and maintain a database in a worksheet.

- Databases are composed of individual records that are logically related. For example, names, addresses, and phone numbers in a telephone directory or on a mailing list are logically related. Records generally occupy rows in a database worksheet.

- Database records group specific items of information that are called fields. Fields are identified by field names and generally occupy columns in a database worksheet.

- You can use basic worksheet editing techniques to maintain (update) a database periodically. Database maintenance requires adding new records and deleting obsolete records.

- Database features in spreadsheet software include methods for sorting database records into any arrangement. For example, database records can be sorted alphabetically by individuals' last names or numerically by part numbers.

- Different arrangements of database records can be saved in separate files to create multiple databases from a single database.

Command Summary

/Data Sort (/DS)
provides access commands for sorting database records

/Data Sort Data-Range (/DSD)
sets the range of database records to be sorted

/Data Sort Primary-Key (/DSP)
sets the primary sort key field

/Data Sort Secondary-Key (/DSS)
sets the secondary sort key field

/Data Sort Go (/DSG)
sorts database records in a selected arrangement

Sorting Records

Applications

Begin doing the applications by loading 1-2-3, if necessary. Place your student data disk in drive A (or drive B if you do not have a hard disk). Change the current directory to the drive that contains the student data disk. Also, change the Clock setting in the Global Settings dialog box to display the current filename on the status line.

Business
Sales Analysis

1. As part of your duties, you maintain a database of all the salespeople in the company. Retrieve the file SALSDB10.WK1, and do the following database maintenance tasks:

   a. Adjust column widths, as necessary, to display all the data.

   b. Format the values in column E as percentages with two decimal places.

   c. Dexter Liebrandt has left the company. Delete his record from the database.

   d. The Boston office has hired a new salesperson. Enter the following information in the row below the record for Harry Darby:

   Redding   Ruby   Boston   (617) 555-1919   .06   3

   e. Center the "PHONE" field name.

   f. Sort the database alphabetically by last name.

   g. Save this version of the database in a file called SALES10.WK1.

   h. Sort the database alphabetically by branch. In the same sort operation, sort the records for each branch by commission in descending order.

   i. Erase the worksheet without saving the file.

Business
Small Business

2. The company likes to keep track of its customers who purchase windsurfing boards. You will create a mailing list database out of a worksheet file that lists names, addresses, and phone numbers. Retrieve the file WWCMAIL.WK1, and do the following tasks to create and maintain the mailing list:

   a. Enter the following field names in row 4, directly above the first record in the list.

   LAST   FIRST   ADDRESS   CITY   ST   ZIP   AREA   PHONE

b. Starting in row 24, enter the following records for three new customers.

Sol Beach, 1969 Rays Street, Pescadero, CA 97999 (408) 555-2893

Rocky Coast, 1988 Broken Board Wy., San Luis Obispo, CA 93621 (805) 555-9176

Gracie Swell, 1975 Sea Spray Drive, Stinson Beach, CA 94822 (415) 555-5566

HINT
Enter the addresses, zip codes, area codes, and phone numbers as labels.

c. Delete the records for Ralph Tuna and Jeff Jellyfish. They have moved and left no forwarding address.

d. Sort the mailing list alphabetically by last name. Make sure the list is sorted alphabetically by first name for any records where the last name is the same.

e. Sort the database alphabetically by state ("ST" field) and numerically by zip code. This is the order you want the list to be in for a mailing.

f. Press (HOME), and save the file as PROFIT10.WK1.

g. Print the mailing list. Use a setup string to print the list in condensed print.

h. Save the print settings to the same file, and erase the worksheet.

Business
Accounting

3. Like any manufacturer, Big Peak Mountain Bicycles must maintain an inventory of parts. Retrieve the file PARTS10.WK1. This file is a database of bicycle parts that the company uses to manufacture its bicycles. Do the following database maintenance tasks to update the inventory:

a. The database includes only rear derailers. Add the following records for the front derailers:

90772703	Derailer-SPR (F)	M232	295	6
90772403	Derailer-RAC (F)	H328	220	12
50172003	Derailer-BAS (F)	H322	173	14

b. Format the "COST" field values as fixed with two decimal places. Format the "VALUE" field values with the comma format and two decimal places.

c. The eight Frame-XTs in inventory were sold off because the company no longer manufactures bicycles with that frame. Delete the record for this part from the inventory database.

d. Sort the records in ascending numerical order by "PART NUMBER."

e. Press (HOME), and save the file as DBPART10.WK1. Erase the worksheet.

Social Studies

Student Survey

4. The raw questionnaire data can be set up as a database. Retrieve the worksheet file SRVYDB10.WK1. Perform a variety of sort operations, as outlined in the following steps:

   a. Add the following record after the last record in the database:

      Spring Play   233   306   88   44   52

   b. Copy one of the formulas in the "Total" column to calculate a total for the new activity record.

   c. Sort the records in descending numeric order for "GOOD" responses. Which activity rated highest for this category? Which activity rated the lowest?

   d. Sort the records in descending numeric order for "POOR" responses. Which activity or facility rated the most "POOR" responses in this category? (Not surprisingly, the cafeteria!) Which activity or facility rated the least number of "POOR" responses?

   e. Sort the records in ascending numeric order for "EXCELLENT" responses. Which activity rated the most number of "EXCELLENT" responses? Which activity or facility rated the least number of "EXCELLENT" responses? Which rated the most?

   f. Press HOME, and save the sorted worksheet as SURVEY10.WK1. Erase the worksheet.

Social Studies

Geography

5. To further examine world populations, you will modify a database containing population data for African countries. Retrieve the file POPDB10.WK1, and do the following database maintenance tasks:

   a. Starting in row 23, enter the following data into the appropriate columns:

      | Algeria | 30500000 | 35200000 |
      | Egypt | 58900000 | 65200000 |
      | Libya | 5200000 | 6100000 |
      | Morocco | 31900000 | 36300000 |
      | Sudan | 28700000 | 32900000 |
      | Tunisia | 8900000 | 9700000 |

   b. Format the new data with the comma format and no decimal places.

   c. Sort the records in alphabetical order by country. Save the file as WLDPOP10.WK1.

   d. Sort the records in descending order by population. Which country has the highest population?

   e. Sort the records in ascending order by projected population in five years. Which country has the lowest projected population?

   f. Erase the worksheet without saving the changes.

326   10 ▶ Creating Worksheet Databases

Social Studies

American Government

6. In order to examine popular votes in the 1988 presidential election, you will work with a database that organizes population and electoral vote data for each state in the election. Use 1-2-3 database operations to find out which states have the most electoral votes. Retrieve the file ELECDB10.WKl. Each record in this database contains a state's name, its population, and its number of electoral votes. Do the following database maintenance tasks:

   a. Starting in row 51, enter the following four records into the database:

Washington	4657000	10
West Virginia	18456000	6
Wisconsin	4808000	11
Wyoming	502000	3

   b. Sort the records in alphabetical order by state.

   c. Press (HOME), and save the file as ELECTN10.WK1.

   d. Sort the records in descending numerical order by electoral votes. Which state has the most? Which state has the least?

   e. Sort the records in ascending numerical order by population. How many electoral votes does the state with the largest population have? Which state has the smallest population? How many electoral votes does that state have?

   f. Erase the worksheet without saving the file.

Science/Mathematics

Astronomy

7. The worksheet with planetary data that you have created and worked with in Lessons 1–9 is actually a database. Retrieve the file PLANDB10.WK1. This worksheet is very similar to the worksheets you have been working with. However, it has been converted into a database structure. Do the following database management tasks:

   a. Sort the records in ascending numerical order by "AVG DIST" (average orbital distance). The arrangement of the records after the sort should be the same order the planets are in from the sun to the outer reaches of the solar system.

   b. Press (HOME), and save the file as PLANET10.WK1.

   c. Sort the records so that they are in descending numerical order by "DENSITY." Which planet is at the top of the list with the greatest density?

   d. Sort the records in ascending numerical order by "FAR DIST" (farthest distance from the sum). Which planet's farthest orbital distance is closer to the sun than the rest?

   e. Erase the worksheet without saving the changes.

Applications

Science/Mathematics

Mathematics

8. For a mathematics exercise, your instructor would like you to use 1-2-3 to solve a payroll problem. Retrieve the file PYRLDB10.WK1. This file contains a database of employees, their hourly wages, and their hours worked in the current pay period. Column E is blank. In this column, you will enter a formula to calculate each employee's gross income. Before you do, take a look at the rest of the worksheet. Columns F through J contain formulas that will calculate each employee's deductions automatically based on the gross income results. Column K is blank. In this column you will enter formulas to calculate each employee's net pay.

To calculate each employee's gross pay, you must multiply her or his hourly wage and number of hours worked. However, notice that some employees have worked more than 80 hours. Any hours over 80 for this period are considered overtime hours. The company pays an overtime rate of 1 1/2 times an employee's hourly wage for any overtime hours worked. Gross income for 80 hours or less and gross income for 80 hours or more can be expressed mathematically, as follows:

$$W * H = GI, \text{ if } H = 80 \text{ or less}$$

$$W * H + (0.5 * W) * (H - 80) = GI, \text{ if } H = 81 \text{ or more}$$

where W = wage, H = hours, and GI = gross income

To solve this problem, your calculation is best handled with an @IF function. Set up the @IF function to multiply the hourly wage and number of hours worked for each employee who worked 80 hours or less. Otherwise, the @IF function must calculate the extra pay that is added to the result of multiplying the employee's wage and the total hours worked.

After building the first @IF function, copy it down the column to calculate gross pay for all employees. Look at column E in Figure 10.9 to check your results.

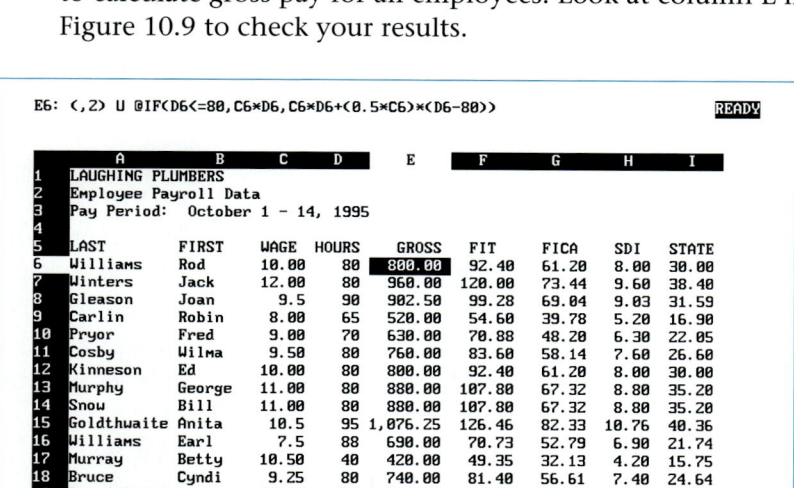

HINT

The third part of the @IF function's argument will be a formula. The formula can be structured like the mathematical expression that calculates gross income with overtime pay included. Be sure to use parentheses where necessary in the @IF function's argument.

Figure 10.9

After you enter the @IF function calculations for the employees' gross wages, you should get the results shown in column E. If you get different results, check your @IF function in cell E6 against the one shown in the figure.

```
E6:  (,2) U @IF(D6<=80,C6*D6,C6*D6+(0.5*C6)*(D6-80))                READY

         A          B         C       D        E        F       G       H       I
  1  LAUGHING PLUMBERS
  2  Employee Payroll Data
  3  Pay Period:  October 1 - 14, 1995
  4
  5  LAST        FIRST     WAGE    HOURS    GROSS     FIT     FICA    SDI    STATE
  6  Williams    Rod       10.00     80      800.00   92.40   61.20   8.00   30.00
  7  Winters     Jack      12.00     80      960.00  120.00   73.44   9.60   38.40
  8  Gleason     Joan       9.5      90      902.50   99.28   69.04   9.03   31.59
  9  Carlin      Robin      8.00     65      520.00   54.60   39.78   5.20   16.90
 10  Pryor       Fred       9.00     70      630.00   70.88   48.20   6.30   22.05
 11  Cosby       Wilma      9.50     80      760.00   83.60   58.14   7.60   26.60
 12  Kinneson    Ed        10.00     80      800.00   92.40   61.20   8.00   30.00
 13  Murphy      George    11.00     80      880.00  107.80   67.32   8.80   35.20
 14  Snow        Bill      11.00     80      880.00  107.80   67.32   8.80   35.20
 15  Goldthwaite Anita     10.5      95    1,076.25  126.46   82.33  10.76   40.36
 16  Williams    Earl       7.5      88      690.00   70.73   52.79   6.90   21.74
 17  Murray      Betty     10.50     40      420.00   49.35   32.13   4.20   15.75
 18  Bruce       Cyndi      9.25     80      740.00   81.40   56.61   7.40   24.64
 19  Dangerfield Danny     10.75     70      752.50   90.30   57.57   7.53   28.97
 20  Murphy      Linda     12.00     80      960.00  122.40   73.44   9.60   38.40
     PYRLDB10.WK1
```

Now enter the formulas in column K to calculate each employee's net pay. This formula must subtract the sum of all deductions in columns F through J from the gross income in column E.

After building the first formula in column K, copy the formula down the column to calculate net pay for all employees.

Finally, sort the records alphabetically by last name, and alphabetically by first name for records with the same last names. Save the file as MATH10.WK1, and erase the worksheet.

> **HINT**
> Include an @SUM function in the formula to total the deductions.

Health

Nutrition

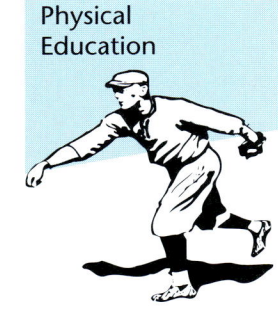

9. For your health class, you will work with a database file that lists selected daily allowances of vitamins and minerals. Retrieve the file DIETDB10.WK1. Perform the following database maintenance operations:

   a. Enter the following records into the database:

   | Females | 23-50 | 120 | 64 | 44 | .06 | .008 | .001 | .0013 | .13 | .018 | .3 | .8 |
   | Males | 23-50 | 154 | 70 | 56 | .06 | .01 | .0014 | .0016 | .018 | .01 | .35 | .8 |

   b. Sort the records in alphabetical order by category. For records with the same category labels, sort the records in ascending order by age range.

   c. Save the file as NUTINF10.WK1.

   d. Sort the records in descending numerical order by WEIGHT.

   e. Erase the worksheet without saving the changes.

Health

Physical Education

10. The softball team's coach asked you to prepare a database of the team's final batting statistics. Retrieve the file SFTBDB10.WK1, and do the following database maintenance tasks:

    a. Add the following records to the database by inserting them between the records for Loren and Mabely.

    | Smith | C | 66 | 10 | 19 | 2 | 1 | 3 | 9 |
    | Turner | P | 42 | 4 | 8 | 0 | 1 | 0 | 6 |
    | Braga | C | 68 | 19 | 26 | 7 | 2 | 8 | 18 |

    b. Copy batting average and slugging percentage formulas in columns J and K for the three new records.

    c. Sort the records in descending numerical order by "BATTING AVERAGE." Which player has the highest batting average? Which player has the lowest?

    d. Sort the records in descending numerical order by "SLUGGING PCT." Which player has the highest slugging percentage? Which has the lowest?

    e. Sort the records in alphabetical order by player.

    f. Press (HOME), and save the file as SBGAME10.WK1. Erase the worksheet.

> Note: Do not include the "TEAM" record in the last row of the database range.

Applications

11 ▶ Database Queries and @Functions

Objectives

- Assign a name to a range.
- Define the input range.
- Create and define a criteria range.
- Create and define an output range.
- Search the database to locate records in FIND mode.
- Extract records to the output range.
- Specify criteria (multiple conditions) in a criteria range.

Lotus 1-2-3's powerful database operations give you many ways to locate records and use database information. In this lesson, you will learn to use 1-2-3's database query operations to locate and extract records from a database. You will also learn how to use several database @functions that perform complex operations on database information.

Exercise 11.1

Creating, Naming, and Defining Input, Criteria, and Output Ranges

Objectives

After completing this exercise, you will be able to
- Assign a name to a range.
- Define the input range.
- Create and define a criteria range.
- Create and define an output range.

QUERY
A 1-2-3 database operation in which you request the location of particular records based on search criteria.

Using 1-2-3's database query operations, you can ask 1-2-3 to search the database and locate records. Records are located based on one or more conditions. A search condition is called a *criterion* (more than one search condition are called *criteria*).

You use the /Data Query command (/DQ) to perform search, or query, operations. The term *query* means a question, or to ask a question. When you query a 1-2-3 database, you ask 1-2-3 to locate one or more records based on pre-established criteria. To execute a data query operation, 1-2-3 needs to know the location, or range addresses, of the following three ranges:

The *input range* is the database range. It includes the row of field names and all the records you want to query or search. Usually, the input range is the entire database.

The *criteria range* is the range that contains the search conditions, or criteria. It includes two or three rows. The first row contains the database field names that you want to search. Usually you copy all the database field names to the criteria range's first row. The second row contains the criteria or conditions for the search. For some data query operations, the criteria range has a third row with additional criteria.

The *output range* is the range that collects copies of criteria-matching records during a certain data query operation. The first row of this range also contains the database field names that you want to search. Usually you copy all the database field names to the first row of the output range. This range is used when you want to create a smaller database of selected records from the input range.

To perform a query operation, you have to first create each of these ranges, and then use the /Data Query command (/DQ) to tell 1-2-3 where the ranges are located. This is called "defining the ranges."

The owner of Mollie's Music Shoppe wants you to locate specific records in the inventory database. The first group of records you will locate are all the rock recordings. Before you can locate the records, you need to create the criteria and output ranges. You will create these ranges, and then you will define all three ranges so that 1-2-3 knows their location.

1 ▶ If necessary, start 1-2-3. Use the /File Directory command (/FD) to change the current directory to the drive that contains the student data disk.

2 ▶ Retrieve the database file RECORDS.WK1.

This database contains the same information you entered in Lesson 10. It also contains additional records.

3 ▶ Move the cell pointer to cell A4.

The pointer is on the cell that contains the "ARTIST" field name.

4 ▶ Use the /Copy command (/C) to copy the range of field names to the range J4..Q4.

The criteria range consists of the row with the field names and at least one other row, directly beneath the range of field names. Now you will enter the search criterion.

CRITERION (CRITERIA)
A condition (criterion) or conditions (criteria) that 1-2-3 uses to search a database range for specific records.

5 ▶ Move the cell pointer to cell L5.

The cell pointer is on the cell directly below the "CATEGORY" field name.

6 ▶ Type **Rock**

7 ▶ Press ⏎.

The search criterion is entered, as shown in Figure 11.1.

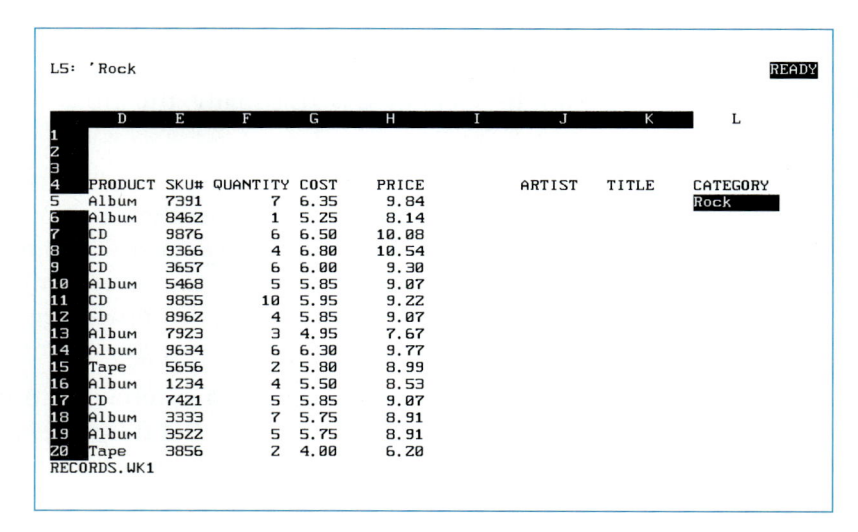

Figure 11.1

After you copy the database field names and enter the first search criterion, your criteria range should look like this.

332 11 ▶ Database Queries and @Functions

You will create a separate list of all the records that match this criterion. To do this, you will create an output range.

8 ▶ Move the cell pointer to cell J4.

9 ▶ Use the /Copy command (/C) to copy the field names in the range J4..Q4 to the range J8..Q8.

Before you define the input, criteria, and output ranges, you will assign a name to each range. Although this step may seem unnecessary, database query operations can be performed more efficiently when the ranges are named. For example, naming the database range INPUT makes it easier to remember when you specify the range for query operations.

You use the /Range Name Create command (/RNC) to assign a name to any 1-2-3 range. Range names are very useful for any 1-2-3 operation. A range name (for example, sales) is more meaningful than an address (for example, C6..F12). Range names can be 15 characters or fewer. Now you will continue this exercise by assigning names to the input, criteria, and output ranges.

10 ▶ Move the cell pointer to cell A4.

The cell pointer is on the first field name in the database.

11 ▶ Press the Slash key (/) to access the Main Menu.

12 ▶ Type **RNC** to select the Range, Name, and Create commands.

Lotus 1-2-3 prompts you to enter a range name.

INPUT RANGE
The range of records in a database that you want to query.

13 ▶ Type **input**

14 ▶ Press ⏎.

Lotus 1-2-3 prompts you to enter the range to name. The current cell is anchored.

15 ▶ Press END, and then press ↓.

16 ▶ Press END, and then press →.

17 ▶ Press ⏎.

The database range is named INPUT.

18 ▶ Move the cell pointer to cell J4.

The cell pointer is on the cell that contains the first field name in the criteria range.

CRITERIA RANGE
A range that contains some or all of the field names that are in the database (input) range and the search conditions for a data query operation.

19 ▶ Press the Slash key (/) to access the Main Menu.

20 ▶ Type **RNC** to select the Range, Name, and Create commands.

Lotus 1-2-3 prompts you to enter a range name.

21 ▶ Type **criteria**

22 ▶ Press ⏎.

Lotus 1-2-3 prompts you to enter the range to be named.

Creating, Naming, and Defining Input, Criteria, and Output Ranges

23 ▶ Press END, and then press →.

24 ▶ Press ↓.

The range J4..Q5 is highlighted.

25 ▶ Press ↵.

The criteria range is named.

26 ▶ Move the cell pointer to cell J8.

The cell pointer is on the cell that contains the first field name in the output range.

OUTPUT RANGE
A range in which 1-2-3 stores selected records from the input range that meet the conditions in the criteria range. The first row in the output range contains some or all of the field names that are in the database (input) range.

27 ▶ Repeat the procedure described in steps 19–25 to assign the name OUTPUT to the output range (J8..Q8).

Note: For the output range, you only need to name the row of field names.

You are now ready to use the /Data Query command (/DQ) to define the input, criteria, and output ranges. This command tells 1-2-3 where these ranges are located. First you will define the input range, which is the database you want to search.

28 ▶ Press the Slash key (/) to access the Main Menu.

29 ▶ Type **D** to select the Data command.

The Data command submenu is activated on the control panel.

30 ▶ Type **Q** to select the Query command.

The Query Settings dialog box appears, as shown in Figure 11.2.

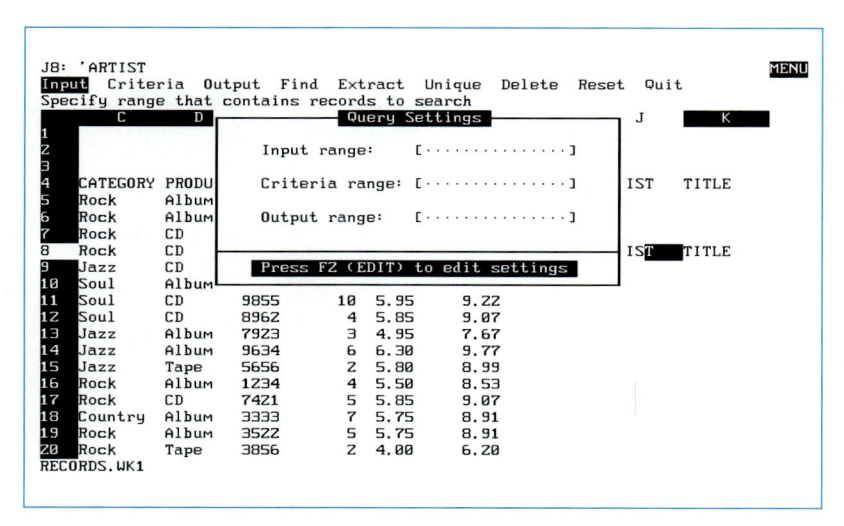

Figure 11.2

The Query Settings dialog box appears when you select the /Data Query command (/DQ). You can use the Query command submenu or edit the dialog box directly to define the input, criteria, and output ranges.

334   11 ▶ Database Queries and @Functions

31 ▶ Type **I** to select the Input command.

Lotus 1-2-3 prompts you to enter the input range.

32 ▶ Type **input**

33 ▶ Press ⏎.

The input range is defined. Notice that the Data Query dialog box displays the range name "INPUT" for the Input range setting. The Data command submenu is activated on the control panel.

Now you will define the criteria range.

34 ▶ Type **C** to select the Criteria command.

Lotus 1-2-3 prompts you to enter the criteria range.

35 ▶ Type **criteria**

36 ▶ Press ⏎.

The criteria range is defined, and the range name "CRITERIA" is displayed in the Query Settings dialog box.

37 ▶ Type **O** to select the Output command.

Lotus 1-2-3 prompts you to enter the output range.

38 ▶ Type **output**

39 ▶ Press ⏎.

The output range is defined.

You only need to define the row of field names for the output range. Lotus 1-2-3 will use as many rows as it needs to store copies of extracted records. You will learn how to extract records in the next exercise.

Exercise 11.2

Locating and Extracting Records

Objectives

After completing this exercise, you will be able to
- Search the database to locate records in FIND mode.
- Extract records to the output range.

Now that you have created and defined the input, criteria, and output ranges, you can perform data query operations. You can simply locate criteria-matching records by selecting the /Data Find (/DF) command.

Locating and Extracting Records

335

Criteria-matching records are those records that contain the criteria that are in the criteria range.

The /Data Find command (/DF) causes 1-2-3 to search the database in FIND mode. When a criteria-matching record is located, 1-2-3 highlights the record. In FIND mode, you can press the ↓ key to highlight the next criteria-matching record. After the last criteria-matching record has been located, your system will beep the next time you press ↓. You can press ↑ to go back to any previous criteria-matching record, or press ESC to exit FIND mode. You will now locate and highlight the criteria-matching records in the inventory database.

1 ▶ Make sure the Query command submenu is displayed.

2 ▶ Type **F** to select the Find command.

Lotus 1-2-3 highlights the first record in the database that matches the current criteria, as shown in Figure 11.3.

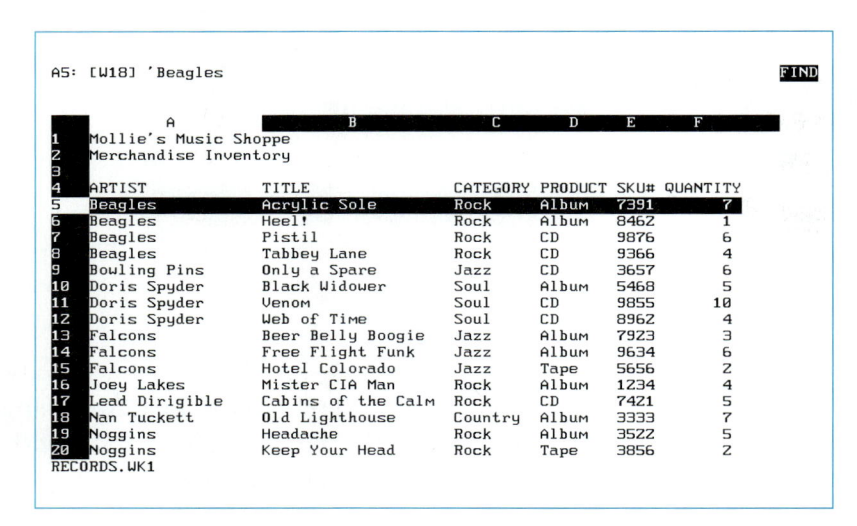

Figure 11.3

When you select the /Data Find command (/DF), 1-2-3 searches the database and highlights the first criteria-matching record. In this case, the first rock recording is highlighted.

3 ▶ Press ↓.

The second record is highlighted because it is also a rock recording.

4 ▶ Press ↓.

The next criteria-matching record is highlighted.

5 ▶ Press ↓.

The next criteria-matching record is highlighted.

6 ▶ Press ↓.

The twelfth record in the database is highlighted.

7 ▶ Press ↓ 10 times.

The last record in the database is highlighted.

8 ▶ Press ⬇.

> Your system beeps, indicating that there are no more records in the input range that meet the criterion.

9 ▶ Press ⬆.

> The previous criteria-matching record is highlighted.

10 ▶ Press ⏎.

> Lotus 1-2-3 switches from FIND mode to MENU mode. The Query command submenu is activated on the control panel.

In addition to locating records, you can perform an extract operation. You use the /Data Query Extract command (/DQE) to extract criteria-matching records. When you select this command, 1-2-3 searches the database and copies the criteria-matching records to the output range. Now you will extract the records that meet the current criterion.

11 ▶ Type **E** to select the Extract command.

> The records that meet the criterion copy to the output range.

12 ▶ Type **Q** to select the Quit command.

> Lotus 1-2-3 returns to READY mode.

13 ▶ Move the cell pointer to cell J8, if necessary.

14 ▶ Press SCROLL LOCK to lock the cell pointer.

15 ▶ Use the Arrow keys to scroll your worksheet so that the 15 extracted rock recordings are displayed, as shown in Figure 11.4.

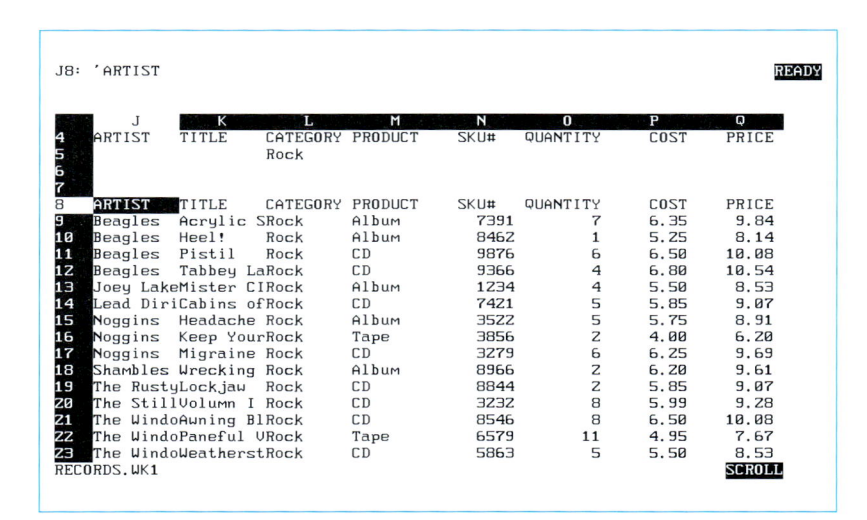

Figure 11.4

After you select the /Data Extract command (/DE), all the criteria-matching records are copied to the output range.

```
J8: 'ARTIST                                                          READY

        J          K          L        M        N         O       P       Q
4   ARTIST     TITLE      CATEGORY PRODUCT    SKU#     QUANTITY  COST   PRICE
5                         Rock
6
7
8   ARTIST     TITLE      CATEGORY PRODUCT    SKU#     QUANTITY  COST   PRICE
9   Beagles    Acrylic S  Rock     Album      7391        7      6.35    9.84
10  Beagles    Heel!      Rock     Album      8462        1      5.25    8.14
11  Beagles    Pistil     Rock     CD         9876        6      6.50   10.08
12  Beagles    Tabbey La  Rock     CD         9366        4      6.80   10.54
13  Joey LakeMister CI    Rock     Album      1234        4      5.50    8.53
14  Lead DiriCabins of    Rock     CD         7421        5      5.85    9.07
15  Noggins    Headache   Rock     Album      3522        5      5.75    8.91
16  Noggins    Keep Your  Rock     Tape       3856        2      4.00    6.20
17  Noggins    Migraine   Rock     CD         3279        6      6.25    9.69
18  Shambles Wrecking     Rock     Album      8966        2      6.20    9.61
19  The RustyLockjaw      Rock     CD         8844        2      5.85    9.07
20  The StillVolum I      Rock     CD         3232        8      5.99    9.28
21  The WindoAwning Bl    Rock     CD         8546        8      6.50   10.08
22  The WindoPaneful V    Rock     Tape       6579       11      4.95    7.67
23  The WindoWeatherst    Rock     CD         5863        5      5.50    8.53
RECORDS.WK1                                                           SCROLL
```

16 ▶ Press SCROLL LOCK to unlock the cell pointer.

Next you will locate all the classical recordings. To do this, you will change the search condition.

Locating and Extracting Records   337

17 ▶ Move the cell pointer to cell L5.

18 ▶ Type **Class**.

19 ▶ Press ⏎.

Note: Make sure you type the period (.) after "Class," or your criterion will not work.

Rather than select the /Data Query Extract command (/DQE) to perform another extract operation, you can use the Query command (F7). When you press F7, 1-2-3 uses the current data query settings and repeats the last Data Query operation. Now you will use the Query command (F7) to extract the classical recordings from the database.

20 ▶ Press F7.

The seven classical recordings in the input range are copied to the output range, as shown in Figure 11.5. Notice that the result of this extract operation replaced the previous contents in the output range.

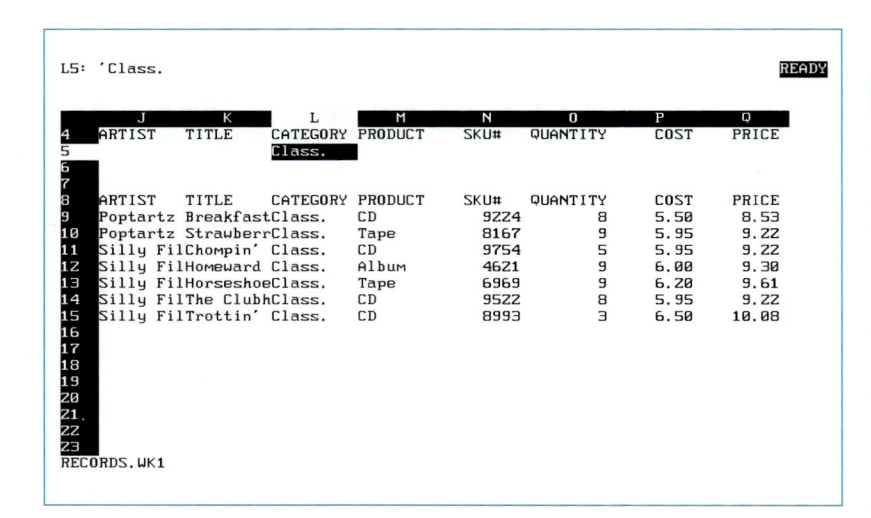

Figure 11.5

After you change the criterion in the criteria range and press F7 (Query command), 1-2-3 performs the last data query operation. In this case the last operation was the /Data Query Extract command (/DQE), so 1-2-3 extracts all the classical recordings from the database.

You can also use a formula in your criteria range to find records. For example, your next selection requires you to locate all the titles that have retail prices greater than $10. You will begin to perform the next extract operation by erasing the current criterion and entering a new one.

21 ▶ Move the cell pointer to cell L5, if necessary.

22 ▶ Press DEL.

The criterion in the current cell is erased.

23 ▶ Move the cell pointer to cell Q5.

In the current cell, you will enter a formula that compares the first calculated value in the "PRICE" field to see if it is greater than $10. The first formula for the first record is stored in cell H5.

24 ▶ Type **+H5>10**

25 ▶ Press ⏎.

The result, 0, is displayed.

Lotus 1-2-3 checks the value in cell H5 to see if it is greater than $10. If the condition is true, 1-2-3 displays a 1 in cell Q5. If the condition is false, 1-2-3 displays a 0. Here, the condition is false. The retail price for the first record is less than $10.

26 ▶ Press F7.

The four records that meet the criterion appear in the output range, as shown in Figure 11.6.

HINT

You can display this formula instead of the true or false result. To do this, use the /Range Format Text command (/RFT) to change the display format of the cell.

Formula criterion

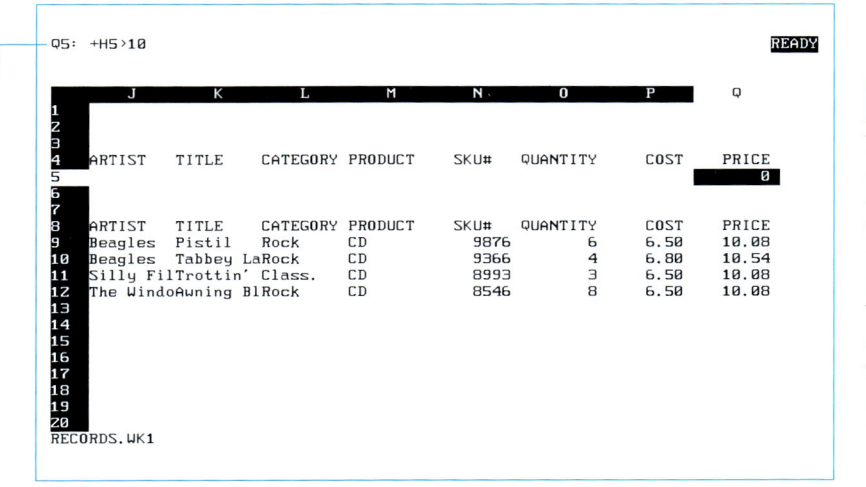

```
Q5: +H5>10                                                    READY

        J       K         L       M       N.      O       P       Q
1
2
3
4    ARTIST   TITLE    CATEGORY PRODUCT  SKU#   QUANTITY   COST   PRICE
5                                                                   0
6
7
8    ARTIST   TITLE    CATEGORY PRODUCT  SKU#   QUANTITY   COST   PRICE
9    Beagles  Pistil   Rock     CD       9876       6      6.50   10.08
10   Beagles  Tabbey LaRock     CD       9366       4      6.80   10.54
11   Silly FilTrottin' Class.   CD       8993       3      6.50   10.08
12   The WindoAwning BlRock     CD       8546       8      6.50   10.08
13
14
15
16
17
18
19
20
RECORDS.WK1
```

Figure 11.6

The formula in the criteria range compares whether the value in each record's "PRICE" field is greater than $10. The next extract operation copies all the criteria-matching records to the output range.

There are other types of operators that can be used in formulas to compare one value to another. These operators are listed in Table 11.1.

Operator	Operation
>	compares two values to see if the first value is greater than the second value
>=	compares two values to see if the first value is greater than or equal to the second value
<	compares two values to see if the first value is less than the second value
<=	compares two values to see if the first value is less than or equal to the second value
=	compares two values to see if the first value is equal to the second value
<>	compares two values to see if the first value is not equal to the second value

Table 11.1

Relational operators compare two values to determine whether the criterion specified in the formula is true or false.

Locating and Extracting Records

339

For all the data query operations you have performed thus far, you have specified a single criterion in the criteria range. You can also specify two or more criteria.

Exercise 11.3: Specifying Multiple Criteria

After completing this exercise, you will be able to
- Specify criteria (multiple conditions) in a criteria range.

Objective

The owner wants you to extract all the records for compact disc recordings by the group Silly Filly. Because there are also tapes and albums by this group in the database, you have to specify two conditions in the criteria range: "Silly Filly" for the "ARTIST" field and "CD" for the "CATEGORY" field. You want to extract only the records that meet both conditions. Therefore you must create an AND condition by entering the criteria on the same row in the criteria range. You will begin by erasing the previous criterion.

1 ▶ Move the cell pointer to cell Q5, if necessary.

The cell pointer is on the cell that contains the formula criterion.

2 ▶ Press DEL.

The formula criterion in cell Q5 is erased.

3 ▶ Press ← 7 times.

The cell pointer is on cell J5, below the "ARTIST" field name.

4 ▶ Type **Silly Filly**

5 ▶ Press → 3 times.

The cell pointer is on cell M5, in the "PRODUCT" field column.

6 ▶ Type **CD**

7 ▶ Press ←.

The criteria are entered in the criteria range to create an AND condition.

8 ▶ Press F7.

Lotus 1-2-3 searches the input range and copies all the criteria-matching records to the output range, as shown in Figure 11.7.

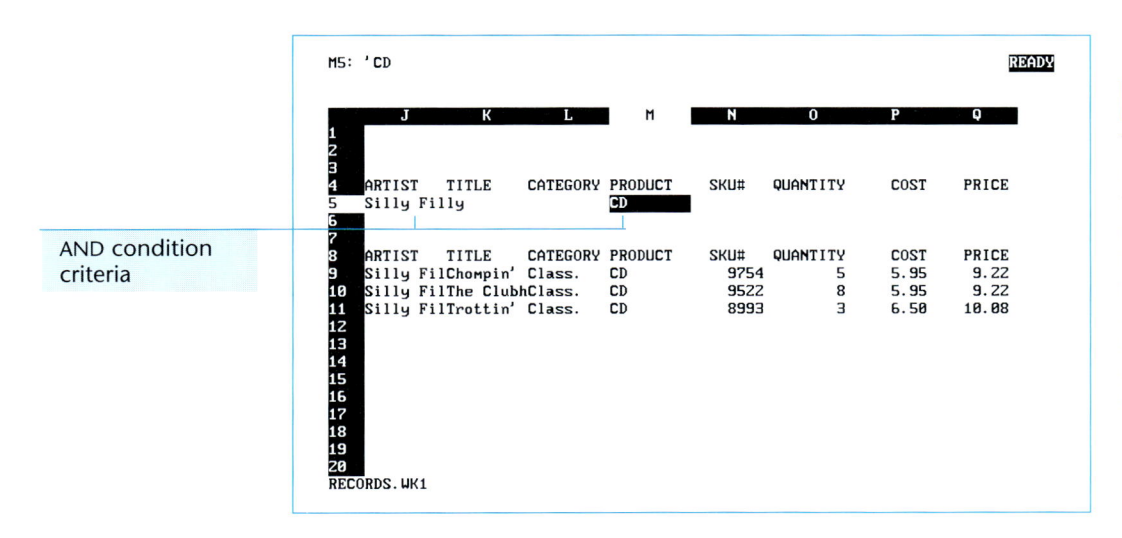

Figure 11.7

```
M5: 'CD                                                          READY

         J         K         L        M       N        O        P        Q
 1
 2
 3
 4    ARTIST    TITLE    CATEGORY PRODUCT   SKU#    QUANTITY   COST    PRICE
 5    Silly Filly                  CD
 6
 7
 8    ARTIST    TITLE    CATEGORY PRODUCT   SKU#    QUANTITY   COST    PRICE
 9    Silly FilChompin' Class.     CD       9754        5      5.95    9.22
10    Silly FilThe ClubhClass.     CD       9522        8      5.95    9.22
11    Silly FilTrottin' Class.     CD       8993        3      6.50   10.08
12
13
14
15
16
17
18
19
20
RECORDS.WK1
```

AND condition criteria

The extract operation copies all the records that match the AND condition in the criteria range to the output range. In this case, all the compact disc recordings by the group Silly Filly are extracted.

AND CONDITION
A combination of two or more criteria, all of which must be met in order to select records. Criteria are entered on the same row in the criteria range to create an AND condition.

OR CONDITION
A combination of two or more criteria in which only one criterion must be met to select records. Criteria are entered on separate rows in the criteria range to create an OR condition.

Three records meet the AND condition. When you specify multiple criteria on the same row in the criteria range, you are specifying an *AND condition*.

You can enter criteria in two criteria range rows to locate records that meet the criteria on one row or the other. This is called an *OR condition*. When you enter an OR condition, you must redefine the criteria range so that 1-2-3 knows it has an extra row.

Now you will enter an OR condition into the criteria range. You want to extract all recording titles by the Beagles or Doris Spyder. You will begin by erasing the existing criteria.

9 ▶ Make sure the cell pointer is on cell M5.

   The cell pointer is on the cell that contains the criterion in the "PRODUCT" field.

10 ▶ Press the Slash key (/) to access the Main Menu.

11 ▶ Type **RE** to select the Range and Erase commands.

12 ▶ Press (END), and then press (←).

   The range extends so that it includes both criteria.

13 ▶ Press (←).

   The criteria are erased.

14 ▶ Move the cell pointer to cell J5.

15 ▶ Type **Beagles**

16 ▶ Press (↓).

17 ▶ Type **Doris Spyder**

18 ▶ Press (←).

Specifying Multiple Criteria 341

Now you will redefine the criteria range.

19 ▶ Press the Slash key (/) to access the Main Menu.

20 ▶ Type **DQC** to select the Data, Query, and Criteria commands.

The current criteria range is highlighted.

21 ▶ Press ⬇.

The range J4..Q6 is highlighted.

22 ▶ Press ⏎.

The criteria range is redefined to include the additional row.

23 ▶ Type **Q** to select the Quit command.

Lotus 1-2-3 returns to READY mode.

24 ▶ Press F7 to perform another extract operation.

Lotus 1-2-3 searches the input range and locates all records that satisfy either condition in the criteria range. The criteria-matching records are copied to the output range, as shown in Figure 11.8.

OR condition criteria

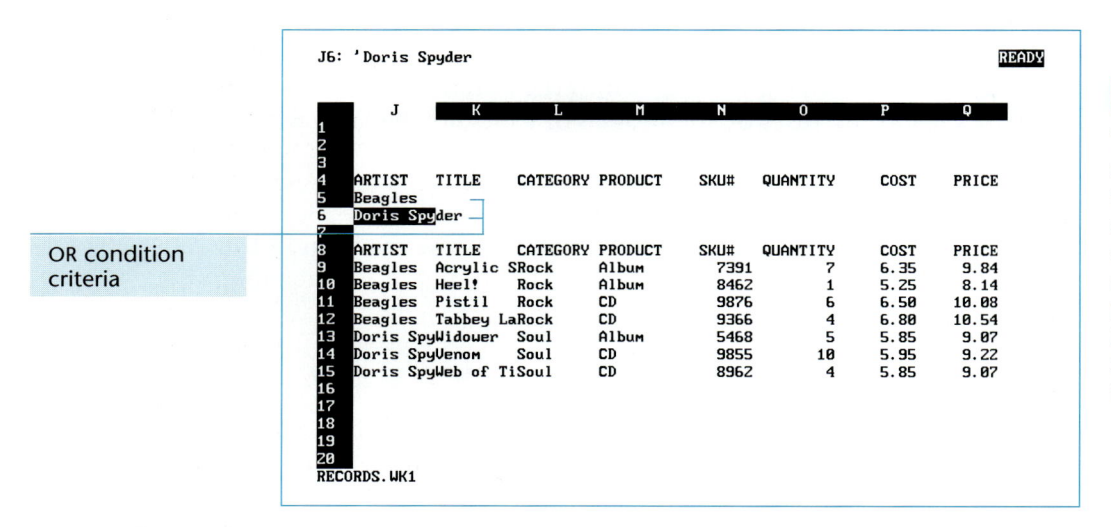

```
J6: 'Doris Spyder                                                    READY

       J        K         L        M        N        O        P        Q
1
2
3
4   ARTIST    TITLE     CATEGORY PRODUCT  SKU#     QUANTITY COST     PRICE
5   Beagles
6   Doris Spyder
7
8   ARTIST    TITLE     CATEGORY PRODUCT  SKU#     QUANTITY COST     PRICE
9   Beagles   Acrylic   SRock    Album    7391     7        6.35     9.84
10  Beagles   Heel!     Rock     Album    8462     1        5.25     8.14
11  Beagles   Pistil    Rock     CD       9876     6        6.50    10.08
12  Beagles   Tabbey LaRock      CD       9366     4        6.80    10.54
13  Doris SpyWidower    Soul     Album    5468     5        5.85     9.07
14  Doris SpyVenom      Soul     CD       9855    10        5.95     9.22
15  Doris SpyWeb of TiSoul       CD       8962     4        5.85     9.07
16
17
18
19
20
RECORDS.WK1
```

Figure 11.8

The extract operation copies all the records that match the OR condition in the criteria range. In this case, all the recordings by the Beagles and Doris Spyder are copied to the output range.

As you can see, 1-2-3 provides you with different ways in which you specify criteria. This gives you a good deal of flexibility for locating records and manipulating data in a database. In the next lesson, you will learn to use 1-2-3 database @functions. Database @functions provide even more database management capabilities.

Exercise 11.4

Using 1-2-3 Database @Functions

Objective

After completing this exercise, you will be able to
- Use 1-2-3 database @functions in criteria ranges.

The 1-2-3 database @functions let you locate records based on quantitative criteria. For example, you can use database @functions to calculate an average or a sum of values in a field. You can also enter database @functions that locate the highest (maximum) value in a field or the lowest (minimum) value.

Like other 1-2-3 @functions you have learned to use, database @functions also require an argument. To calculate a value, the argument in a database @function contains three parts: the input range, the column-offset, and the criteria range. You are already familiar with the input and criteria range concepts. The *column-offset* is the field column that contains the values the database @function will use to calculate a result. A database @function checks the input range and finds all the records that meet the criteria in the criteria range. Then the database @function calculates a result using the values in the column offset. Lotus 1-2-3 considers the first column in the database (input range) to be column-offset 0 (zero). Therefore, the second column is column-offset 1, the third is column-offset 2, and so on.

COLUMN-OFFSET
A number that represents the column of values in the input range that a database @function must use to perform a calculation. The column-offset is included in a 1-2-3 database @function's argument. Lotus 1-2-3 considers the first database column to be column-offset 0 (zero).

The first database @function that you will learn to use is the @DSUM function. It operates very much like the @SUM function, in that you use it to sum values. The @DSUM function sums values in a column in the input range. The general format, or syntax, for entering the @DSUM function is as follows:

    @DSUM(input range,column-offset,criteria range)

Although you can enter range addresses for the input and criteria ranges, it is usually easier to use range names. Ranges in a database @function argument are easier to identify when you use range names instead of range addresses. You have already named these ranges in an earlier exercise.

The owner has asked you for the average, total, highest, and lowest retail prices for rock and classical recordings. Also, she wants a count for the criteria-matching records. You will complete a summary range into which you will enter the following database @functions:

@DSUM	to calculate a sum for selected records
@DAVG	to calculate an average for selected records
@DMAX	to find the highest value for selected records
@DMIN	to find the lowest value for selected records
@DCOUNT	to count the number of selected records

Each of these database @functions will use the same argument ranges and column offsets. You will begin by erasing the current criteria in the criteria range. You will then enter a new criterion so that you can see the results as you enter the database @functions.

1 ▶ Move the cell pointer to cell J5.

The cell pointer is on the cell that contains a current criterion.

2 ▶ Press the Slash key (/) to access the Main Menu.

3 ▶ Type **RE** to select the Range and Erase commands.

4 ▶ Press ↓.

5 ▶ Press ⏎.

The previous OR condition is erased.

6 ▶ Move the cell pointer to cell L5.

The cell pointer is on the cell directly below the "CATEGORY" field in the criteria range.

7 ▶ Type **Rock** and press ⏎.

You will now display another area of the worksheet, where a summary range has already been set up for you. You will enter database @functions into this range to create a table of calculated values for the "PRICE" field.

8 ▶ Move the cell pointer to cell T4.

The cell pointer is on the cell where you will enter the first database @function. The database @function will sum all values in the input range's "PRICE" column for the criteria-matching records.

9 ▶ Type **@dsum(input,**

> Note: Do not enter a space before or after the comma.

The next element you must enter in the argument is the column-offset. If you start with the "ARTIST" field in your database and count columns to the right, the "PRICE" field is column number 8. However, because 1-2-3 considers the first column to be column 0 (zero), the column-offset representing the "PRICE" field is 7. You will enter 7 as the column-offset in the @DSUM function's argument.

10 ▶ Type **7,criteria)**

11 ▶ Press ↓.

> The @DSUM function is entered, the result $135.22 is displayed, and the cell pointer is on cell T5, as shown in Figure 11.9
>
> Note: If you obtained some other result, check the @function and its arguments. Make sure the column-offset is 7.

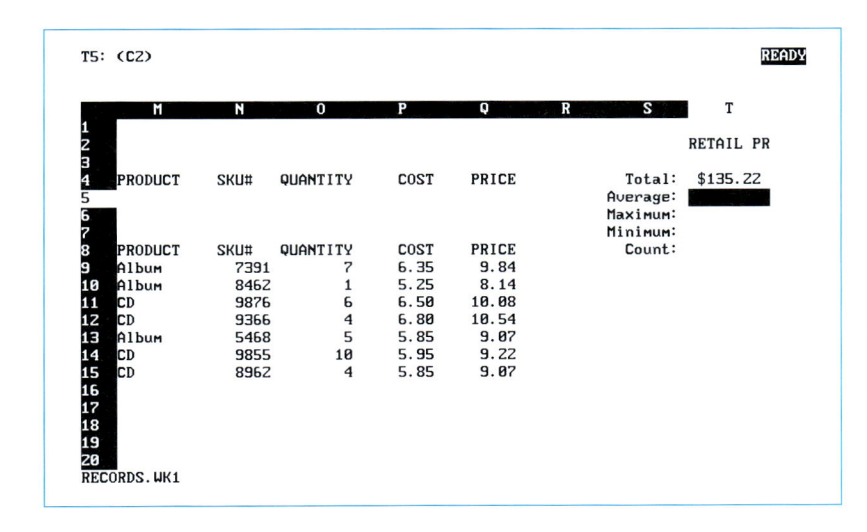

Figure 11.9

The @DSUM function returns the sum of retail prices for all rock recordings in the database. The result is displayed in the worksheet's summary table. The records shown in the output range are the result of the last extract operation you did in Exercise 11.3.

```
T5: (C2)                                                    READY

         M       N       O       P       Q       R    S       T
1
2                                                         RETAIL PR
3
4   PRODUCT    SKU#   QUANTITY   COST    PRICE     Total:   $135.22
5                                                Average:
6                                                Maximum:
7                                                Minimum:
8   PRODUCT    SKU#   QUANTITY   COST    PRICE     Count:
9   Album      7391      7       6.35    9.84
10  Album      8462      1       5.25    8.14
11  CD         9876      6       6.50    10.08
12  CD         9366      4       6.80    10.54
13  Album      5468      5       5.85    9.07
14  CD         9855     10       5.95    9.22
15  CD         8962      4       5.85    9.07
16
17
18
19
20
RECORDS.WK1
```

This result represents the sum of retail prices for all rock recordings in the input range. The @DSUM function caused 1-2-3 to search the input range and locate all the criteria-matching records. Then, the @DSUM function calculated the sum of retail price values for the criteria-matching records.

12 ▶ Make sure the cell pointer is on cell T5.

13 ▶ Type **@davg(input,7,criteria)**

14 ▶ Press ↓.

> The database @function is entered, and the result, $9.01, is displayed. This is the average retail price for the rock recordings.

15 ▶ Type **@dmax(input,7,criteria)**

16 ▶ Press ↓.

> The highest, or maximum, retail price for the rock recordings is $10.54.

17 ▶ Type **@dmin(input,7,criteria)**

18 ▶ Press ↓.

> The lowest retail price for the rock recordings is $6.20.

19 ▶ Type **@dcount(input,7,criteria)**

20 ▶ Press ⏎.

The result, 15, is displayed, telling you there are fifteen criteria-matching records in the input range.

Check your results against those shown in Figure 11.10. If they don't match, check your database @functions.

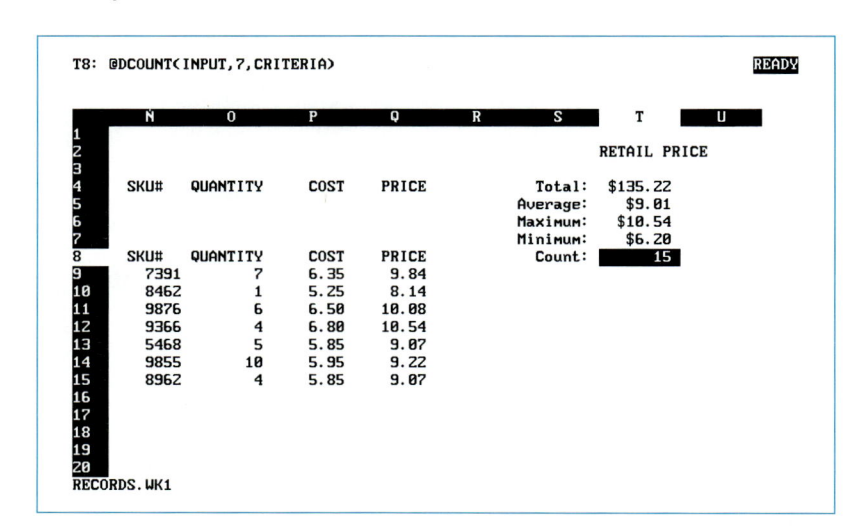

Figure 11.10

After you enter all the database @functions for the current criteria, the summary table in your worksheet should look like this.

Now you will change the criterion in the criteria range to calculate values for the classical recordings. First, you will split the worksheet area into vertical windows so that you can immediately observe the results.

21 ▶ Scroll the worksheet so that column L is the first column on the left side of the worksheet area.

22 ▶ Move the cell pointer to any cell in column O.

23 ▶ Use the /Worksheet Window Vertical command (/WWV) to split the worksheet area into vertical windows.

24 ▶ Press F6, and scroll the worksheet so that your screen looks like Figure 11.11.

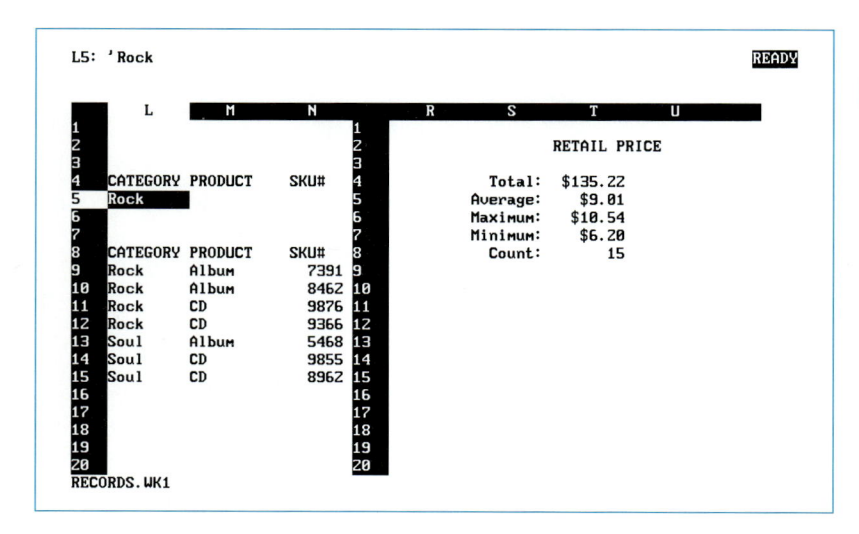

Figure 11.11

After you change the criterion in the left window, the summary table's database @function results adjust in the right window.

25 ▶ Press **Key caps**.

26 ▶ Move the cell pointer to cell L5.

The cell pointer is on the cell that contains the criterion label "Rock."

27 ▶ Type **Class.** and press ⏎.

The database @functions calculate new values for the classical recordings, as shown in Figure 11.12.

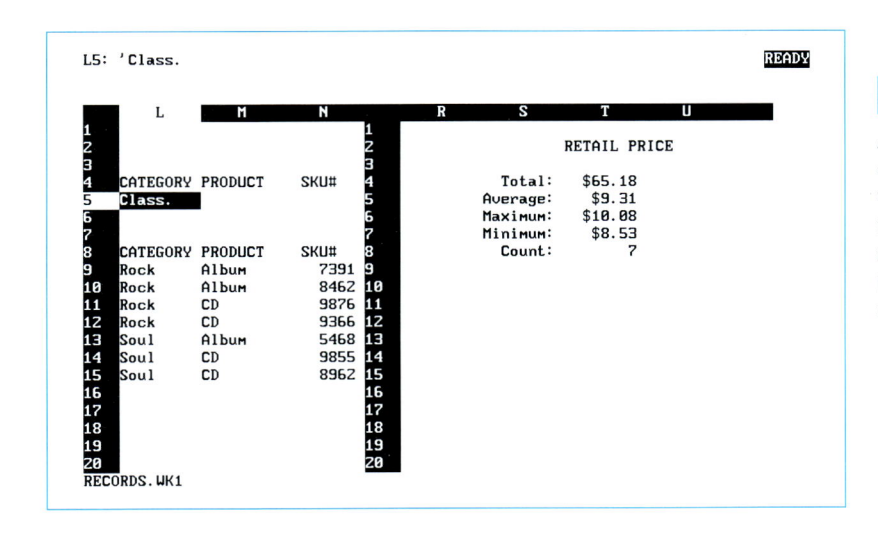

```
L5: 'Class.                                                    READY

         L         M         N           R         S       T       U
 1                                     1
 2                                     2             RETAIL PRICE
 3                                     3
 4   CATEGORY  PRODUCT    SKU#         4    Total:          $65.18
 5   Class.                            5    Average:         $9.31
 6                                     6    Maximum:        $10.08
 7                                     7    Minimum:         $8.53
 8   CATEGORY  PRODUCT    SKU#         8    Count:               7
 9   Rock      Album      7391         9
10   Rock      Album      8462        10
11   Rock      CD         9876        11
12   Rock      CD         9366        12
13   Soul      Album      5468        13
14   Soul      CD         9855        14
15   Soul      CD         8962        15
16                                    16
17                                    17
18                                    18
19                                    19
20                                    20
RECORDS.WK1
```

Figure 11.12

After you change the criterion in the left window, the summary table's database @function results adjust in the right window.

These new values are for all the classical recordings in the input range.

Once you have set up the data summary table, you can change the criteria and immediately see the results. Now you will clear the vertical window split. Then you will save your modified database so that you can use it again if the need arises.

28 ▶ Use the /Worksheet Windows Clear command (/WWC) to clear the vertical window split.

29 ▶ Press HOME, and save the changes to the same file.

30 ▶ Erase the worksheet.

Using 1-2-3 Database @Functions

Concept Summary

▶ Spreadsheet software generally includes special commands that let you query a database. Data query operations let you manipulate the data in a database.

▶ Data query operations require at least two ranges: an input range and a criteria range. The input range is the range that contains the database field names and records. The criteria range contains field names and one or two rows that contain search conditions. A search condition is an item of information that exists in a particular field for one or more records.

▶ Some data query operations require a third range, called an output range. The output range collects copies of criteria-matching records after an extract operation has been performed. This range also contains the database field names in its first row.

▶ Entering two or more criteria on the same row in a criteria range creates an AND condition. When an AND condition exists in a criteria range, 1-2-3 only locates all records that meet both conditions.

▶ Entering two criteria into separate rows creates an OR condition. When an OR condition exists in a criteria range, 1-2-3 only locates records that meet either condition.

▶ Most spreadsheet software packages provide special functions that operate on database fields to calculate quantitative data for criteria-matching records.

Command Summary

/Data Query (/DQ)
accesses a submenu of options for manipulating data in a database

/Range Name Create (/RNC)
assigns a name, 15 characters or fewer, to a range of data

/Data Query Input (/DQI)
defines the input (database) range for 1-2-3 database query operations

/Data Query Criteria (/DQC)
defines the criteria range for 1-2-3 database query operations

/Data Query Output (/DQO)
defines the output range for 1-2-3 database query operations

/Data Query Extract (/DQE)
copies all records that match criteria to the output range

/Data Find (/DF)
locates database records that match existing criteria in the criteria range

/Range Format Text (/RFT)
displays formulas in cells rather than the formulas' results

11 ▶ Database Queries and @Functions

Applications

Begin doing the applications by loading 1-2-3, if necessary. Place your student data disk in drive A (or drive B if you do not have a hard disk). Change the current directory to the drive that contains the student data disk. Also, change the Clock setting in the Global Settings dialog box to display the current filename on the status line.

Business

Sales Analysis

1. Retrieve the worksheet SALES10.WK1, and do the following database query operations:

   a. Set up a criteria range to the right of the database range, beginning in column H. Set up an output range five or six rows down from the criteria range field names.

   b. Enter the formula criterion +F5>=18 in column M below the 95 "SALES" field name. This criterion will be used to locate all records that have 18 or more sales in 1995.

   c. Name and define the input, criteria, and output ranges.

   d. Perform an extract operation to copy the criteria-matching records to the output range.

   e. Enter an OR condition in the criteria range. The criteria will locate records with 18 or more sales in 1995 or a commission of 8 percent or higher.

   f. Find each record that meets the OR condition in FIND mode. Then extract these records.

   g. Erase the OR condition criteria. Enter the criterion Los Angeles in the "BRANCH" field of the criteria range.

   h. Go to any cell that is clear of the input, criteria, and output ranges. Enter the heading "Financial Summary." Create a table below the heading in which you will enter database @functions to analyze numbers of sales. Calculate a sum, average, maximum, and minimum value for the "95 SALES" field. Also, obtain a count of the number of criteria-matching records.

   i. Change the criterion to locate records for other branches, and observe the results in the "Financial Summary" table. Split the worksheet area into windows, if necessary.

   j. Save the changes to the file SALES11.WK1. Erase the worksheet.

HINT
Leave the current formula criterion in the first row, and enter the other formula criterion in the second row. Be sure to redefine the criteria range.

Business

Small Business

2. Continue working with the mailing list database you modified in Lesson 10. Retrieve the file PROFIT10.WK1, and do the following database query operations:

   a. Set up the criteria and output ranges by copying the field names. Begin the ranges in column J, to the right of the database range.

   b. Name and define the input, criteria, and output ranges.

   c. Enter a criterion to find all records that have a 408 area code. Find the criteria-matching records in FIND mode.

   d. Replace the current criteria with a criterion that will locate all records for California customers.

   e. Perform an extract operation to copy all the records for California customers to the output range.

   f. Enter the label "CA Customers:" in cell D2. Then enter a database @function in cell G2 that returns a count of the current criteria-matching records.

   g. Change the criteria and locate the customer who lives in Santa Cruz.

   h. Press (HOME), and save the file as PROFIT11.WK1.

   i. Sort the mailing list alphabetically by last name and alphabetically by first name for records that have the same last name.

   j. Print the range A1..H24. Adjust the right margin and use the setup string that switches your printer to condensed-print mode.

   k. Save the print settings to the same file. Erase the worksheet.

Business

Accounting

3. You will continue to work with the company's parts inventory by manipulating the database. Retrieve the file DBPART10.WK1. Do the following data query tasks:

   a. Set up the criteria and output ranges by copying the field names to other ranges, beginning in column H.

   b. Name and define the input, criteria, and output ranges.

   c. Enter a criterion that can be used to locate all records with an inventory value greater than $1,000.

   d. Locate the first five criteria-matching records.

   e. Escape from FIND mode, and extract the criteria-matching records to the output range.

   f. Create an AND condition to locate all records that contain 20 or more parts in inventory that each cost $1,000 or more.

   g. Extract the criteria-matching records. How many criteria-matching records satisfy the AND condition?

HINT

f. Leave the current criterion intact, and specify the other criterion on the same line in the criteria range.

h. Enter the formula criterion +A5>50200000 in cell H5. Then, in a clear area of the worksheet, create a summary table that looks like this:

	INVENTORY SUMMARY		
	COST	AMOUNT	VALUE
Total:			
Average:			
Minimum:			
Maximum:			
Count:			

i. Enter the appropriate database @functions to complete the table. Be sure to use the correct column-offsets in the database @functions' arguments.

j. Change the formula criterion to +A5<50000000, and observe the changes in the summary table.

k. Press (HOME), and save the worksheet as DBPART11.WK1. Erase the worksheet.

Social Studies

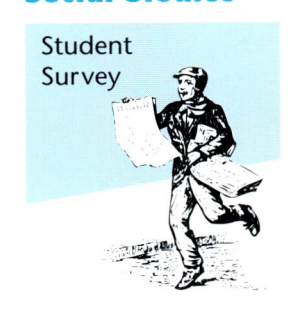

Student Survey

4. Continue analyzing the raw data from the student survey by doing a variety of data query operations. Retrieve the file SURVEY10.WK1, and do the following tasks:

   a. Copy the database's field names to the ranges I1..O1 and I5..O5 to set up a criteria range and an output range.

   b. Name and define the input, criteria, and output ranges.

   c. Enter a formula criterion that locates all records with 150 or more "POOR" responses. Locate the criteria-matching records in FIND mode. How many records are there?

   d. Enter an AND condition in the criteria range that locates all records with less than 150 "EXCELLENT" responses and more than 50 "POOR" responses. Extract the criteria-matching records to the output range. How many records satisfy the AND condition?

   e. Enter an OR condition that locates all records with more than 300 "FAIR" responses or less than 50 "FAIR" responses. Be sure you redefine the criteria range. Extract the criteria-matching records. How many records satisfy the OR condition?

   f. Enter a formula criterion that locates all records with 150 or more "EXCELLENT" responses. Extract the criteria-matching records.

g. Set up a summary table in the range I15..O21, as shown in Figure 11.13. Enter database @functions to complete the summary table for all criteria-matching records.

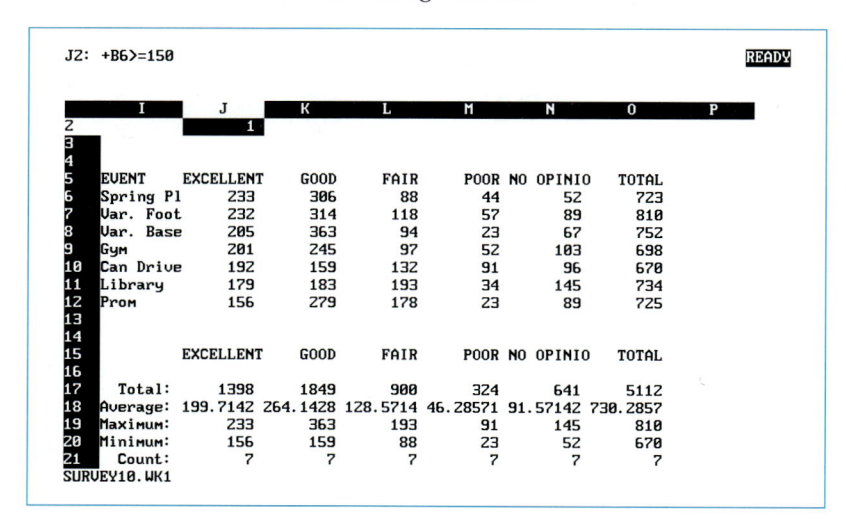

```
J2: +B6>=150                                                    READY

              I        J       K       L       M       N       O       P
 2                     1
 3
 4
 5         EVENT    EXCELLENT GOOD    FAIR    POOR  NO OPINIO TOTAL
 6         Spring Pl   233    306      88      44      52      723
 7         Var. Foot   232    314     118      57      89      810
 8         Var. Base   205    363      94      23      67      752
 9         Gym         201    245      97      52     103      698
10         Can Drive   192    159     132      91      96      670
11         Library     179    183     193      34     145      734
12         Prom        156    279     178      23      89      725
13
14
15                  EXCELLENT GOOD    FAIR    POOR  NO OPINIO TOTAL
16
17         Total:     1398    1849    900     324     641    5112
18         Average: 199.7142 264.1428 128.5714 46.28571 91.57142 730.2857
19         Maximum:    233    363     193      91     145     810
20         Minimum:    156    159      88      23      52     670
21         Count:        7      7       7       7       7       7
SURVEY10.WK1
```

Figure 11.13

Set up a summary table for the questionnaire's response options, as shown in the range I15..O21. Be sure you enter the appropriate database @functions and the correct column-offsets.

h. Change the criteria to a condition of your choice, and observe the changes.

i. Press (HOME), and save the file as SURVEY11.WK1. Erase the worksheet.

Social Studies

Geography

5. You will use data query operations to take a closer look at the population data for African countries. Retrieve the file WLDPOP10.WK1, and do the following tasks:

a. Set up the criteria and output ranges by copying the field names to the ranges E5..G5 and E9..G9, respectively. Enter a criterion to locate all records with populations greater than 10 million.

b. Name and define the input, criteria, and output ranges. Locate the criteria-matching records in FIND mode. How many records are there?

c. Enter formula criteria to create an AND condition. The AND condition locates records with populations over 20 million and five-year projections that increase by 20 percent or more over the populations.

d. Perform an extract operation to copy the criteria-matching records to the output range. How many African countries are projected to have population increases over 20 percent in five years?

e. Delete the criterion for the "FIVE-YEAR PROJECTION" field.

f. Set up a summary table that lists the labels "Total," "Average," "Maximum," "Minimum," and "Count" down column J, beginning in cell J5. Enter the label "POPULATION" in cell K4.

HINT

c. The formula in the criteria range's "FIVE-YEAR PROJECTION" field will test whether the projections in column C are greater than or equal to the result of a formula. The formula calculates a 20 percent increase over the current population figure; that is, +C6>= B6+(B6*.20).

352   11 ▶ Database Queries and @Functions

g. Enter the appropriate database @functions down column K to calculate results for the criteria-matching records. Be sure to enter the correct column-offset. How many criteria-matching records are there? What is the average population for the criteria-matching records?

h. Change the criterion to locate records with populations over 30 million. How many criteria-matching records are there? What is the maximum population figure among these records?

i. Press HOME, and save the file as WLDPOP11.WK1. Erase the worksheet.

Social Studies

American Government

6. Continue analyzing the electoral college voting system by performing a variety of data query operations. Retrieve the file ELECTN10.WK1, and do the following tasks:

a. Set up a criteria range and an output range by copying the field names to the ranges E5..G5 and E9..G9, respectively.

b. Suppose you want to locate states that have populations lower than 4 million people. Enter a formula criterion that locates the records for these states.

c. Name and define the input, criteria, and output ranges.

d. Extract the criteria-matching records. Sort the records in the output range in ascending numerical order by electoral votes. Which state with a population of under 4 million has the most electoral votes?

e. Enter an OR condition in the criteria range. You want to locate all records that have more than 4 million people or more than 8 electoral votes. Be sure you define the criteria range to include the third row. Extract the criteria-matching records that meet the OR condition. How many states are listed?

f. Move the criterion in the electoral vote column so it is on the same row as the other criterion. This creates an AND condition. Extract the criteria-matching records. Which states with fewer than 4 million people have more than 8 electoral votes?

g. Delete the current criteria, and enter a criterion to locate all records that have populations greater than 3.5 million.

h. Enter the labels "Total," "Average," "Maximum," "Minimum," and "Count" in column I, starting in cell I4. Enter the appropriate database @functions in columns J and K to create a summary table of calculations for the criteria-matching records. How many criteria-matching records are there? What is the average number of electoral votes for the criteria-matching records?

i. Edit the criterion to locate all records with populations over 10 million. How many states meet this criterion? What is the minimum number of electoral votes in this group?

j. Press HOME, and save the file as ELECTN11.WK1. Erase the worksheet.

Applications

Science/Mathematics

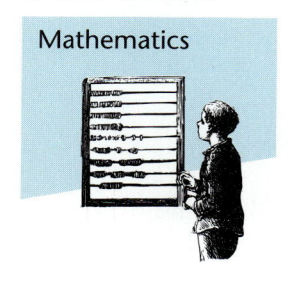

Astronomy

7. Use data query operations to continue your analysis of the planets in the solar system. Retrieve the file PLANET10.WK1, and perform the following tasks:

   a. Set up a criteria range and an output range by copying the field names to the ranges J1..Q1 and J6..Q6, respectively.

   b. Enter a criterion to locate all records with a diameter value less than 1. (Recall that each planet's diameter is expressed as a percentage of Earth's diameter.)

   c. Highlight the criteria-matching records in FIND mode. Then extract the same criteria-matching records to the output range. Sort the output range records in alphabetical order by planet.

   d. Create an AND condition in the criteria range. Locate all records that have a diameter value greater than 1 and a gravity value less than 1. (Recall that each planet's gravity value is expressed as a percentage of Earth's gravity.)

   e. Extract the criteria-matching records to the output range. Which planet meets the criteria?

   f. Erase the worksheet without saving the changes.

Science/Mathematics

Mathematics

8. Continue working with mathematical calculations and data query operations in the payroll database. Retrieve the file MATH10.WK1. Do the following tasks:

   a. Set up a criteria and output range by copying the field names to the ranges M1..W1 and M5..W5, respectively.

   b. Enter a formula criterion in row 2 of the criteria range to locate all records for employees who earn $10 or more an hour.

   c. Name and define the input, criteria, and output ranges. Locate the criteria-matching records in FIND mode.

   d. Extract the criteria-matching records to the output range. Sort the output range records in descending numerical order by gross income ("GROSS"). Which employee, earning $10 or more per hour, earned the most money for the current pay period?

   e. Sort the output records in descending numerical order by net pay ("NET"). Which employee making $10 or more per hour took home the biggest paycheck?

   f. Delete the criterion, and enter another formula criterion to locate all records for employees who worked 80 or more hours during the period.

   g. Create the summary table shown in Figure 11.14. Enter the database @functions in the appropriate columns, and format the results with the comma format and two decimal places. Do not format the result of the @DCOUNT function in column Z. What was the total Federal Income Tax ("FIT") withheld from employees who worked full time or overtime? How many criteria-matching records are there? What was the highest state tax ("STATE") deduction from among the criteria-matching records?

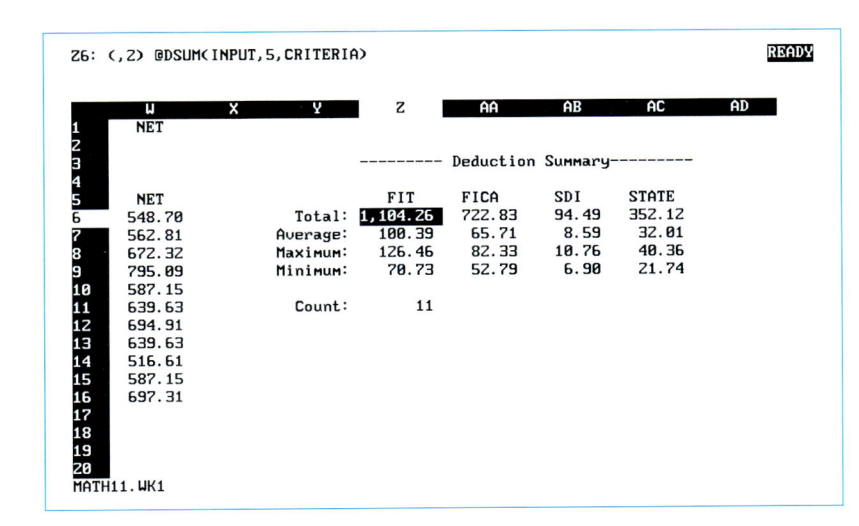

```
Z6: (,2) @DSUM(INPUT,5,CRITERIA)                                    READY

         W        X          Y        Z         AA       AB       AC       AD
    1   NET
    2
    3                                ---------- Deduction Summary ----------
    4
    5   NET                          FIT        FICA     SDI      STATE
    6   548.70          Total:    1,104.26     722.83   94.49    352.12
    7   562.81          Average:    100.39      65.71    8.59     32.01
    8   672.32          Maximum:    126.46      82.33   10.76     40.36
    9   795.09          Minimum:     70.73      52.79    6.90     21.74
   10   587.15
   11   639.63          Count:       11
   12   694.91
   13   639.63
   14   516.61
   15   587.15
   16   697.31
   17
   18
   19
   20
   MATH11.WK1
```

Figure 11.14

Set up the summary table for payroll deductions as shown here. Enter the appropriate database @functions, including the correct column-offsets.

h. Delete the criterion, and observe the recalculated results in the summary table. These are summarized calculations for all records in the database.

i. Press HOME, and save the file as MATH11.WK1. Erase the worksheet.

Health

Nutrition

9. Continue working with the database file that contains daily nutritional allowances. Retrieve the file NUTINF10.WK1, and perform the following data query operations:

   a. Set up the criteria and output ranges by copying the field names to the ranges A23..M23 and A27..M27, respectively.

   b. Enter a formula criterion in the criteria range to locate all records with greater than 0.01 grams of iron as a daily allowance.

   c. Name and define the input, criteria, and output ranges.

   d. Extract the criteria-matching records to the output range. How many records require more than 0.01 grams of daily iron? Are any children in the group?

   e. Delete the current criterion. Enter an AND condition that locates all records with daily allowances of protein less than 35 grams and vitamin C greater than or equal to 0.05 grams. Extract the criteria-matching records. Are there any adults in the criteria-matching records?

   f. Press HOME, and save the file as NUTINF11.WK1. Erase the worksheet.

Health

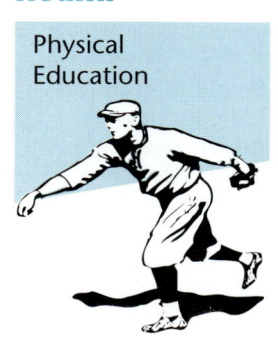

Physical Education

10. Continue working with the database of final batting statistics for the Washington High School softball team. Retrieve the file SBGAME10.WK1. Do the following data query operations to analyze the batting statistics in more detail:

   a. Set up criteria and output ranges by copying field names to the ranges A24..K24 and A28..K28, respectively.

   b. Enter a criterion to locate all outfielders' ("OF") records.

   c. Name and define the input, criteria, and output ranges. Locate the criteria-matching records in FIND mode.

   d. Enter another criterion that creates an AND condition to locate all records for outfielders with five or more home runs. Extract the criteria-matching records. How many players meet the criteria?

   e. Create an OR condition in the criteria range by moving the criterion in the home run ("HR") column down one row. Extract the criteria-matching records. How many players meet these criteria? Sort the records in the output range in descending numerical order by batting average. Who has the highest average among the group?

   f. Enter a criterion to locate records for players whose batting averages are .333 or better. Extract the criteria-matching records.

   g. Create a summary table by copying the field names "HITS," "2B," "3B," and "HR" to the range N28..Q28. Enter the right-aligned labels "Total:", "Average:", "Maximum:", "Minimum:", and "Count:" in the range M29..M33.

   h. Enter the appropriate database @functions in the table to get results for the criteria-matching records. How many total hits did the five players with batting averages over .333 get collectively? What was the maximum number of doubles? What was the minimum number of home runs?

   i. Press (HOME), and save the file as SBGAME11.WK1. Erase the worksheet.

11 ▶ Database Queries and @Functions

12 Automating Your Work with Macros

Objectives

- Write a macro.
- Name a macro.
- Run a macro.
- Write a macro that selects a 1-2-3 command.
- Step through a macro in STEP mode.
- Select a learn range.
- Record macro keystrokes in a learn range.
- Assign a descriptive name to a macro.
- Select a macro name to run a macro.
- Write an interactive macro.
- Attach the Macro Manager add-in program.
- Create and use a macro library.

Throughout this course, you have performed many 1-2-3 operations over and over again (for example, the /Copy command). This means that you used the same keystrokes repeatedly. In this lesson, you will learn how to store a series of keystrokes in a macro. Macros automate your work by entering data and selecting commands automatically.

Exercise 12.1

Writing, Naming, and Running Macros

Objectives

After completing this exercise, you will be able to
- Write a macro.
- Name a macro.
- Run a macro.

Many 1-2-3 operations require you to step through the same set of keystrokes over and over again. For example, budget worksheets often have column headings for the months of the year. Database worksheets often have records with similar items of information. Each time you enter these kinds of data in a new worksheet, you step through exactly the same set of keystrokes.

MACRO
A set of named keystrokes that are stored in a worksheet and can be played back with a single command.

Rather than type the same keystrokes each time you create similar worksheets, you can store these keystrokes in a macro. A *macro* is a named set of keystrokes that is stored with a worksheet. When you run a macro, it works very much like a tape recorder playing back recorded information. A macro carries out each keystroke automatically. Macros can enter labels and values, move the cell pointer, and select commands. And while the macro runs, you do not even have to touch the keyboard!

Lotus 1-2-3 macro keystrokes are entered as labels down a column. When a macro is run, 1-2-3 steps through each keystroke, one by one. It continues all the way down the column until it reaches an empty cell.

You can run a macro in one of two ways. You can select the macro's name from a list of names associated with the worksheet. Or you can assign a name that consists of the backslash character (\) and a single alphabetic character (for example, \A). This allows you to run the macro by pressing and holding [ALT] and pressing the alphabetic character (for example, [ALT]-A).

Now that you are a skilled 1-2-3 user, you decide to write some macros to automate your work. The macros will reduce the time and effort you spend building worksheets and doing repeated operations. The first macro you will create will enter the company's name into a worksheet automatically. When you entered the company's name in earlier lessons, you typed the name and pressed ⏎. You want your macro to do the same thing. You will begin by entering a label that you will use later to name the macro.

1 ▶ If necessary, start 1-2-3. Use the /File Directory command (/FD) to change the current directory to the drive that contains the student data disk.

2 ▶ Make sure that you have a blank worksheet area and Wysiwyg is not attached.

3 ▶ Move the cell pointer to cell B21.

4 ▶ Type '\N

> Note: The macro name must be a label. So you must enter a label-formatting prefix character before the backslash character (\). Otherwise, 1-2-3 would interpret the backslash as the label-formatting prefix used to create repeating-character labels.

5 ▶ Press →.

The label for the macro's name is entered. The cell pointer is on cell C21, which is where you will begin entering macro keystrokes.

6 ▶ Type **Mollie's Music Shoppe**

TILDE (~)
A macro command symbol, or keystroke, that represents pressing the ⏎ key during a macro's run.

The next keystroke you want in the macro must represent pressing the ⏎ key. For 1-2-3 macros, you enter a character called a *tilde* (~) to represent pressing ⏎. When 1-2-3 finds a tilde while a macro is running, it tells 1-2-3 to press the ⏎ key.

7 ▶ Type ~ (a tilde)

8 ▶ Press ⏎.

The macro's keystrokes are stored in the worksheet, as shown in Figure 12.1.

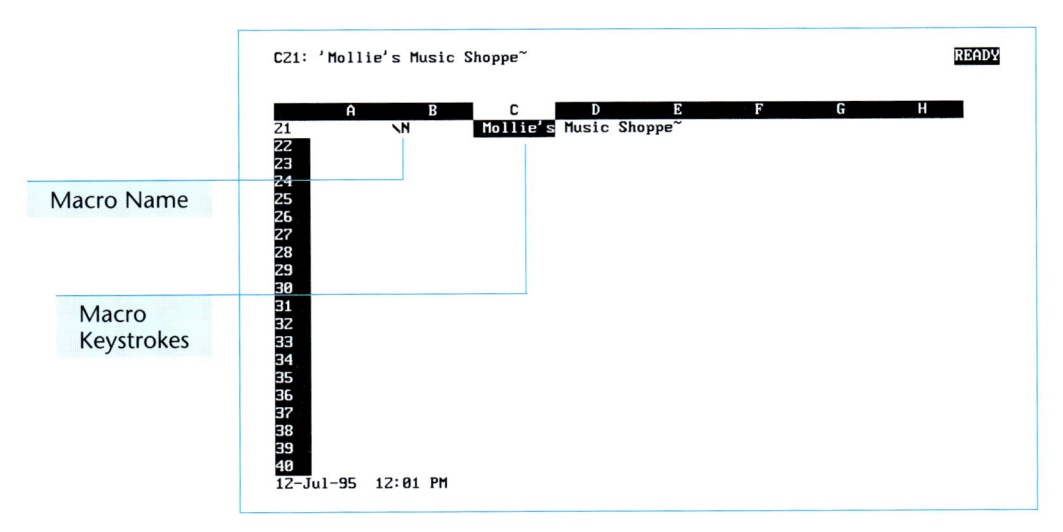

Figure 12.1

The macro keystrokes are stored as a label in the current cell. The tilde (~) represents pressing the ⏎ key. The label "\N" will be assigned as the macro's name.

(Macro Name; Macro Keystrokes)

This macro consists of the text that you enter when you type the company's name and the tilde character. The tilde (~) tells 1-2-3 to press ⏎.

Writing, Naming, and Running Macros 359

The label in cell B21 (\N) will be the macro's name. So that 1-2-3 recognizes the macro name, you can use the /Range Name Label Right command (/RNLR). This command assigns the label in the current cell as a name for the data in the cell to the right. The cell to the right is the first cell in the macro. (In this case it is also the only cell.) Then, when you run the macro (press [ALT]-N), 1-2-3 goes to the named cell and enters the keystrokes. Lotus 1-2-3 will continue entering the keystrokes in each cell down the column until it encounters a blank cell.

9 ▶ Move the cell pointer to cell B21.

10 ▶ Press the Slash key (/) to access the Main Menu.

11 ▶ Type **RN** to select the Range and Name commands.

12 ▶ Type **L** to select the Labels command.

Lotus 1-2-3 displays a submenu that allows you to select the location of the cell to be named. The cell you want to name is to the right of the current cell.

13 ▶ Type **R** to select the Right option.

Lotus 1-2-3 prompts you to enter the label range. The cell pointer is already on the cell with the label that you want to use as a name.

14 ▶ Press ⏎.

Lotus 1-2-3 assigns the name \N in cell B21 for the label that represents macro keystrokes in cell C21.

Now you are ready to test the macro. You will press [ALT]-N to run this macro. You will begin by moving the cell pointer to a blank area of the worksheet.

15 ▶ Press [HOME] to move the cell pointer to cell A1.

16 ▶ Press [ALT]-N.

Lotus 1-2-3 enters the company's name into the current cell, as shown in Figure 12.2.

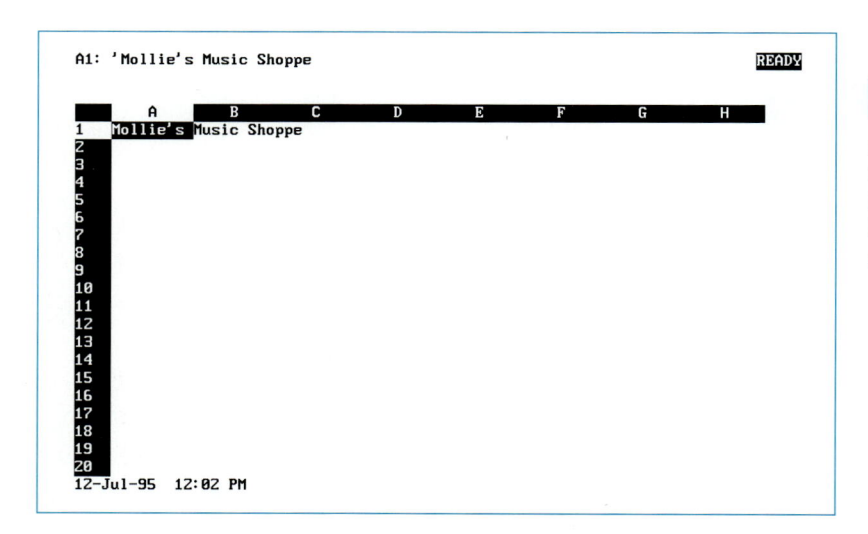

Figure 12.2

After you run the \N macro, the company's name is entered as a label in the current cell.

Note: If you hear a beep and nothing happens, you did not assign the name to your macro correctly. Repeat steps 9–14 to assign the label in cell B21 as the name for your macro.

When you pressed ALT-N, 1-2-3 looked at cell C21, the cell to the right of the macro's name (which is in cell B21). Lotus 1-2-3 then stepped through each of the keystrokes in the macro. Starting with the first keystroke, 1-2-3 worked its way to the right until it reached the last keystroke. Because the first keystroke was an alphabetic character, 1-2-3 interpreted the entry as a label and switched to LABEL mode. When 1-2-3 encountered the tilde (~), it pressed the ⏎ key and stored the label in the cell.

If you type this label yourself, you use 22 keystrokes. Now that the keystrokes are stored in a macro, you just press two keys and 1-2-3 steps through all 22 keystrokes. Thus you have automated a routine task. More importantly, you have learned that with two keystrokes you can automate operations that would otherwise require hundreds of keystrokes.

You have created a macro by typing its keystrokes into a cell. This is called "writing a macro." Later in this lesson you will learn how to record keystrokes for a macro. In the next exercise, you will learn to write another macro that selects a 1-2-3 command.

Exercise 12.2: Writing a Command Macro

Objective

After completing this exercise, you will be able to
- Write a macro that selects a 1-2-3 command.

The macro you wrote in the last exercise entered a label into the worksheet. That macro is a good example of how you can automate data entry. But you can also automate command selection with a 1-2-3 macro. The ability to automate command selection is a powerful 1-2-3 feature.

For instance, can you guess the 1-2-3 command that you have used most throughout the exercises in this book? Without giving it much thought, you would likely guess the /File Save Replace command. And you would be correct. After all, it certainly should be the most frequently used command during any 1-2-3 session.

Suppose you wanted to automate the operation to save changes to a worksheet file. As with a macro that enters data, you can do this simply by entering the command's keystrokes as a label. In this exercise, you will write a macro that selects the /File Save Replace command. You will begin by erasing the label in cell A1 that was entered when you tested the \N macro.

1 ▶ Make sure the cell pointer is on cell A1.

2 ▶ Press DEL.

The label is erased.

3 ▶ Move the cell pointer to cell B23.

4 ▶ Type '\S

5 ▶ Press →.

The label for the macro's name is entered, and the cell pointer is on cell C23. You will enter the macro's keystrokes in this cell.

6 ▶ Type '/fs~r

7 ▶ Press ←.

The macro keystrokes for saving changes to a file are entered. The cell pointer is on the cell that contains the label that will name the macro.

Now you will assign the macro's name to the macro cell.

8 ▶ Press the Slash key (/) to access the Main Menu.

9 ▶ Type **RNL** to select the Range, Name, and Labels commands.

10 ▶ Type **R** to select the Right option.

Lotus 1-2-3 prompts you to enter the label range.

11 ▶ Press ←.

The macro in cell C23 is assigned the name \S in cell B23.

Remember that a macro ends when 1-2-3 comes to a blank cell. For this reason you must be sure to leave at least one blank row between two macros. If a blank cell does not separate two macros, 1-2-3 will run all the keystrokes for both macros. This may produce undesirable results.

Now you will test your macro. But first you will use the command menu to save the current worksheet as MACROS.WK1. The current worksheet has not yet been saved. Your \S macro was written to update existing files, not save new files.

12 ▶ Press HOME, and save the worksheet as MACROS.WK1.

13 ▶ Press ALT-N.

The \N macro is run, and the company's name is entered in the current cell.

14 ▶ Press ALT-S.

The changes are saved to the MACROS.WK1 file.

In the next exercise, you will learn another way to test a macro so that you can find keystroke errors.

Exercise 12.3 — Testing a Macro in STEP Mode

Objective

After completing this exercise, you will be able to
- Step through a macro in STEP mode.

When you write a macro, it is very easy to make a mistake. You might forget to include a keystroke, you might add one too many keystrokes, or you might transpose (reverse) keystrokes. A macro that contains errors stops running or produces unexpected results, and 1-2-3 may display an error message. As you have seen, macros step through keystrokes very quickly when you run them. So if a macro contains errors, it can be impossible to see which keystrokes need correcting (or are missing).

Fortunately, 1-2-3 includes a feature that runs a macro by pausing after each keystroke. This is called "running the macro in STEP mode." You press ALT-F2 to switch 1-2-3 to STEP mode and then you run the macro. In *STEP mode,* the STEP mode indicator and the address of the first macro cell are displayed on the status line. The macro keystrokes in the first macro cell are displayed to the right of the cell address. Also, the first keystroke on the status line is highlighted.

STEP MODE
A 1-2-3 status mode in which you run a macro one step at time to find errors or observe its operation. When STEP mode is activated, you control the macro's operation by pressing any keyboard key (usually the SPACEBAR key) to execute one keystroke.

You must press any key on the keyboard to run the macro's first keystroke. The SPACEBAR is usually the easiest key to press. After you press a key, the first macro keystroke is run, the macro pauses, and the next keystroke is highlighted. Press any key again to run the next keystroke. After a keystroke is run, 1-2-3 highlights the next macro keystroke on the status line.

By running a macro in STEP mode, you control how fast the macro steps through each keystroke. This lets you see exactly where any errors in the macro occur. After you have stepped through a macro, you press ALT-F2 a second time to turn off STEP mode. If you press ALT-F2 before the macro has completed its run, the macro will run the remaining keystrokes without pausing.

Now you will run your \S macro in STEP mode.

1 ▶ Make sure the cell pointer is on cell A1.

2 ▶ Press DEL.

The label in cell A1 is erased.

3 ▶ Press ALT-F2.

The STEP indicator is displayed on the status line.

4 ▶ Press ALT-S.

In the lower-left corner of the screen, 1-2-3 displays the cell address C23, as shown in Figure 12.3. This is the cell that contains the macro keystrokes.

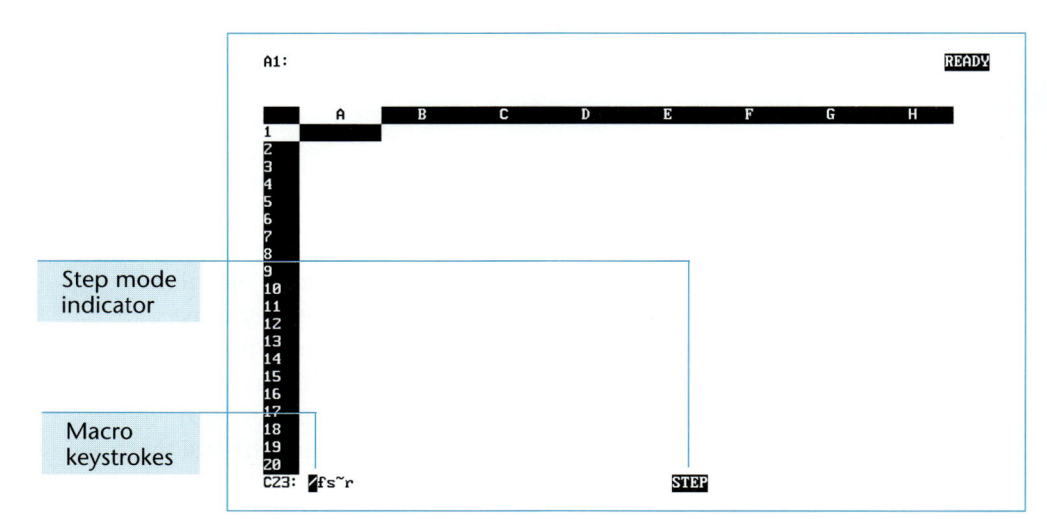

Figure 12.3

When you run a macro in STEP mode, the first macro cell's address and contents appear on the status line in the lower left corner of the screen. The first keystroke (the "/") is highlighted. As soon as you press any key, 1-2-3 will carry out the first keystroke and highlight the next.

(Step mode indicator; Macro keystrokes)

5 ▶ Press SPACEBAR once.

Lotus 1-2-3 runs the first keystroke in the macro—the slash key (/). The Main Menu is displayed on the control panel. The next keystroke ("f") in the macro is highlighted on the status line. Notice that 1-2-3 has switched to MENU mode.

6 ▶ Press SPACEBAR twice.

The File and Save commands are selected. Lotus 1-2-3 prompts you to enter a filename, and the current directory and filename are displayed with the prompt. Notice that the tilde (~) is highlighted on the status line.

7 ▶ Press SPACEBAR.

The macro's next keystroke, the tilde (~), is run, and 1-2-3 presses the ⏎ key. The submenu of save options appearson the control panel, and the "r" is highlighted on the status line.

8 ▶ Press SPACEBAR.

The Replace command is selected. The file is saved.

9 ▶ Press ALT-F2.

> The STEP indicator no longer is displayed. STEP mode is turned off.

Now you will edit the \S macro to introduce an error in the macro. Then you will run the macro again in STEP mode.

10 ▶ Move the cell pointer to cell C23.

11 ▶ Press F2.

> Lotus 1-2-3 switches to EDIT mode.

12 ▶ Press ←.

> The cursor is under the "r."

13 ▶ Press SPACEBAR.

> The tilde (~) is deleted.

14 ▶ Press ↵.

> The macro is edited.

15 ▶ Press HOME.

16 ▶ Press ALT-F2.

> The STEP indicator appears on the status line.

17 ▶ Press ALT-S.

> The macro cell's address and the macro keystrokes are displayed in the lower left corner of the screen. The slash keystroke (/) is highlighted.

18 ▶ Press SPACEBAR 3 times.

> The /File Save command is selected, and 1-2-3 prompts you to enter the name of the file to save. The current filename is displayed to the right of the prompt.

19 ▶ Press SPACEBAR.

> The existing filename is replaced by an "r."

Now you can see how to identify a macro error in STEP mode. Because the tilde (~) was deleted, the macro enters the "r" as a new filename to replace the existing filename. The "r" was meant to select the Replace command, not enter a new filename.

Now you will complete this exercise by fixing the macro's error.

20 ▶ Press CTRL-BREAK.

> The /File Save command is interrupted, and 1-2-3 returns to READY mode.

21 ▶ Press ALT-F2.

> The STEP indicator disappears, and STEP mode is turned off.

Testing a Macro in STEP Mode

22 ▶ Move the cell pointer to cell C23.

23 ▶ In EDIT mode, insert a tilde (~) between the "s" and the "r" in the macro label.

24 ▶ Press (HOME), and run the \S macro to save the changes to the same file.

This exercise stresses the importance of checking your macros in STEP mode. When you ran the \S macro in Exercise 12.2, it ran very quickly. So quickly, in fact, that you probably did not see the menus appear, or you saw them flash by briefly. You would not have noticed the missing tilde (~) error if you had run the macro without STEP mode active.

In the next exercise, you will learn how to record keystrokes to create a macro.

Exercise 12.4 Recording Macro Keystrokes in a Learn Range

Objectives

After completing this exercise, you will be able to
- Select a learn range.
- Record macro keystrokes in a learn range.
- Assign a descriptive name to a macro.
- Select a macro name to run a macro.

LEARN RANGE
A special range that collects and stores recorded keystrokes to create a macro.

An easier way to create a macro is to record your keystrokes while you do an operation. You do this with the 1-2-3 Learn feature. When you use the Learn feature, 1-2-3 records your keystrokes as labels and stores them in a learn range. You specify the *learn range* by selecting the /Worksheet Learn Range command (/WLR). As with other commands that operate on ranges, you can use the pointing method to select the range.

Once the learn range is selected, move the cell pointer to any location where you want to begin an operation. To start recording, press (ALT)-(F5). The LEARN indicator appears on the status line. Lotus 1-2-3 will record the next keystrokes that you enter. Press (ALT)-(F5) again when you want to stop recording keystrokes. The keystrokes will be displayed as labels in the learn range. Once you have finished entering keystrokes, you can assign a name to the macro in the learn range. When you use the Learn feature, there is less chance of entering an error in a macro.

To practice recording keystrokes to create a macro, you will enter labels to set up a worksheet model. You will begin by selecting the learn range.

1 ▶ Move the cell pointer to cell C25.

2 ▶ Press the Slash key (/) to access the Main Menu.

3 ▶ Type **WL** to select the Worksheet and Learn commands.

4 ▶ Type **R** to select the Range option.

Lotus 1-2-3 prompts you to enter a learn range.

5 ▶ Type **.** (a period) to anchor the current cell.

6 ▶ Press ↓ 6 times.

> Note: You want to select a range large enough to hold all your keystrokes. This range is adequate for the keystrokes you are about to record.

7 ▶ Press ⏎.

The learn range is selected.

Now you are ready to begin recording keystrokes.

8 ▶ Press ALT-F5.

The LEARN indicator appears on the status line. Your next keystrokes will be recorded.

9 ▶ Press F5 to select the Go To command.

Lotus 1-2-3 prompts you to enter the cell address where you want to move the cell pointer.

10 ▶ Type **c5** and press ⏎.

The cell pointer moves to cell C5, which is in the upper-left corner of the worksheet area.

11 ▶ Press CAPS LOCK.

12 ▶ Type **JANUARY** and press →.

13 ▶ Type **FEBRUARY** and press →.

14 ▶ Type **MARCH** and press →.

15 ▶ Type **APRIL** and press →.

16 ▶ Type **MAY** and press →.

17 ▶ Type **JUNE**

18 ▶ Press END, and then press ⏎ twice.

19 ▶ Press ↓.

20 ▶ Press CAPS LOCK.

21 ▶ Type **Compact Discs** and press ↓.

22 ▶ Type **Albums** and press ↓.

HINT

9 ▶ Use the Go To command (F5) when you want to begin entering data in a certain cell while recording macro keystrokes. That way you can be sure the cell pointer goes to the correct cell no matter where it is located when you run the macro.

Recording Macro Keystrokes in a Learn Range

23 ▶ Type **Audio Cassettes** and press ⬇.

24 ▶ Type **Reel to Reel** and press ⬇.

25 ▶ Type **Videotapes**

26 ▶ Press END, press ⬆, and then press ➡.

27 ▶ Press ALT-F5.

> The LEARN indicator disappears, and the CALC indicator is displayed on the status line.

The CALC indicator is displayed when automatic recalculation is slowed down. Certain 1-2-3 operations, such as running macros, can slow down automatic recalculation. You can press F9 (the Calculate command) to update the worksheet and turn off the CALC indicator. However, in this case all you really need to do is press any key. The CALC indicator will disappear. Your next keystroke will scroll the worksheet so you can view the macro's keystrokes in the learn range.

28 ▶ Press PGDN.

> The recorded keystrokes are displayed in the learn range, as shown in Figure 12.4. Notice that the CALC indicator is no longer displayed.

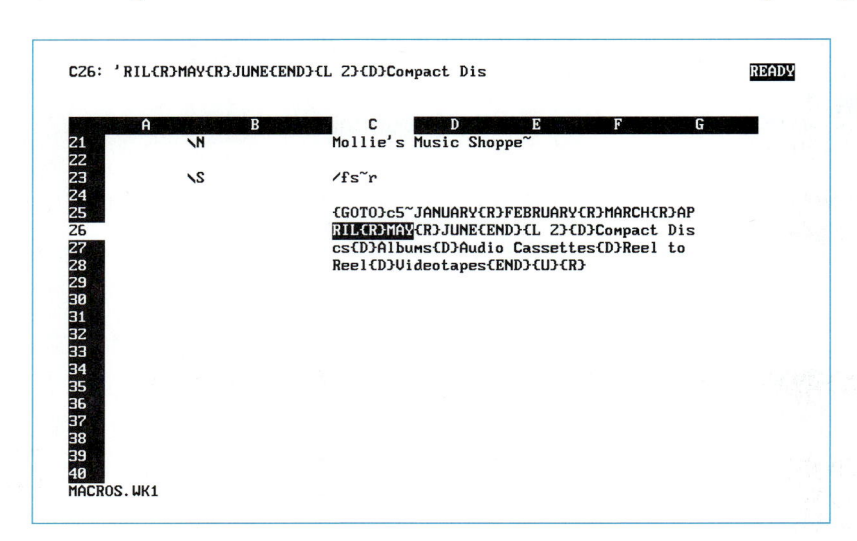

Figure 12.4

After you press ALT-F5 to turn off the recording of keystrokes, 1-2-3 stores the recorded keystrokes in the designated learn range. The macro can be named and edited after you record the keystrokes.

Lotus 1-2-3 used four cells to store all the keystrokes that you entered. Each "{R}" in the macro is the macro command for pressing the ➡ key. Each "{D}" in the macro is the macro command for pressing the ⬇ key. When you run the macro, these commands tell 1-2-3 to move the cell pointer in those directions.

If you made any mistakes as you typed keystrokes, those mistakes were included in the macro. You can edit a macro cell in EDIT mode, just as you would edit any label.

You could assign a similar name to this macro using the Backslash key (\). However, 1-2-3 allows you to assign a descriptive name to a macro. For example, you could assign the name \MODEL to this macro to tell you that it enters labels for a model worksheet. When you are ready to run the macro, you can press ALT-F3 to select the macro's name from a list. One advantage to using a descriptive name is that it is easier to identify the macro's purpose. A minor disadvantage to this type of name is that you use a few more keystrokes to run the macro. The backslash (\) must be included in front of the name to distinguish macro names from other range names.

You will continue with this exercise by assigning the name \MODEL to the keystrokes in the learn range. Then you will run the macro.

29 ▶ Move the cell pointer to cell B25.

The cell pointer is on the blank cell to the left of the first macro cell.

30 ▶ Type '**\MODEL**

31 ▶ Press ⏎.

32 ▶ Press the Slash key (/) to access the Main Menu.

33 ▶ Type **RNL** to select the Range, Name, and Labels commands.

34 ▶ Type **R** to select the Right option.

Lotus 1-2-3 prompts you to enter the label range.

35 ▶ Press ⏎.

The label in cell B25 is assigned as the name for the macro in cell C25.

Now you will test run the macro by selecting its name. You will begin by erasing the labels that you entered to record the macro's keystrokes.

36 ▶ Move the cell pointer to cell B5.

37 ▶ Use the /Range Erase command to erase the data in the range B5..H10.

38 ▶ Press HOME.

39 ▶ Press ALT-F3.

Lotus 1-2-3 prompts you to select a macro to run. A list of the macro names associated with the current worksheet are displayed on the control panel, as shown in Figure 12.5.

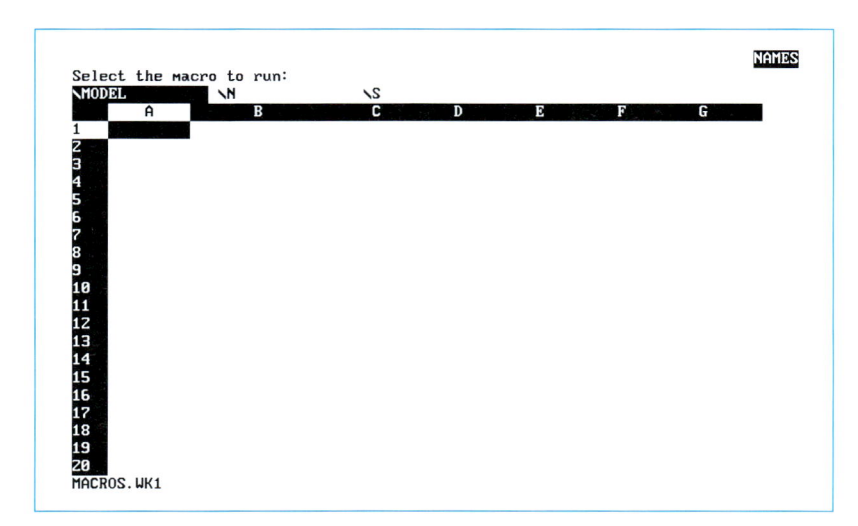

Figure 12.5

To run a named macro, you press ALT-F3. Lotus 1-2-3 prompts you to select a macro and displays on the control panel a list of all macro names that are associated with the current worksheet. Select the macro by moving the menu pointer to a macro name and pressing ⏎.

Recording Macro Keystrokes in a Learn Range

40 ▶ Move the menu pointer to the \MODEL macro name, if necessary.

41 ▶ Press ⏎.

The macro is run, and the labels are entered.

42 ▶ Press HOME, and then run the \S macro to save the changes to the same file.

So far, the macros you have created run nonstop, from the first keystroke to the last. In the next exercise, you will learn how to write a macro so that it pauses for user input.

Exercise 12.5 Writing an Interactive Macro

Objective

After completing this exercise, you will be able to
- Write an interactive macro.

As you become more comfortable with macros, you will discover there are many commands that can make macros more flexible. One such command is the {?} command (pause). This command stops a macro temporarily so that you can enter information before the macro completes its run. Use the {?} command (pause) to enter a response to a command prompt or move the cell pointer to another location. After you enter the information, press ⏎ and the macro will continue stepping through its keystrokes.

INTERACTIVE MACRO
A macro that pauses so that a user can provide additional information that 1-2-3 uses to complete the macro's operation.

The {?} command (pause) makes a macro an *interactive macro*. The word "interactive" means that there is information exchanged between the user and the macro. For example, a macro might contain keystrokes that select the /Copy command (/C) in front of a {?} command (pause). This pauses the macro and displays a prompt asking you to enter the "Copy what?" range. When you type or point to the range in response to the prompt, you are communicating information to the macro. So you and the macro are "interacting."

You will begin this exercise by editing the \MODEL macro to insert keystrokes that widen a column. The inserted keystrokes will include the {?} command (pause) so you can respond to a command prompt during the macro's run.

1 ▶ Move the cell pointer to cell C28.

> The cell pointer is on the cell that contains the last keystrokes in the \MODEL macro.

2 ▶ Press F2.

> Lotus 1-2-3 switches to EDIT mode.

3 ▶ Press ← 3 times.

> The cursor is on the "{" in front of the "R."

4 ▶ Type **/wcs{?}~**

> These keystrokes select the /Worksheet Column Set-Width command (/WCS), pause the macro for user input, and press ←.

5 ▶ Press ←. The edited macro is shown in Figure 12.6.

```
C28: 'Reel{D}Videotapes{END}{U}/wcs{?}~{R}                                READY

          A           B              C            D         E         F         G
    21                \N             Mollie's Music Shoppe~
    22
    23                \S             /fs~r
    24
    25                \MODEL         {GOTO}c5~JANUARY{R}FEBRUARY{R}MARCH{R}AP
    26                               RIL{R}MAY{R}JUNE{END}{L 2}{D}Compact Dis
    27                               cs{D}Albums{D}Audio Cassettes{D}Reel to
    28                               Reel{D}Videotapes{END}{U}/wcs{?}~{R}
    29
    30
    31
    32
    33
    34
    35
    36
    37
    38
    39
    40
    MACROS.WK1
```

Interactive {?} command (pause)

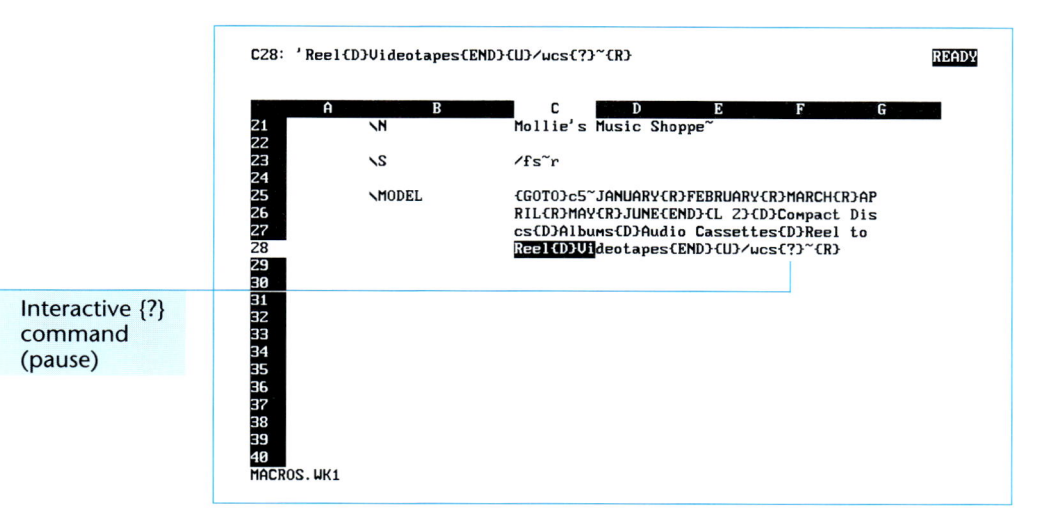

Figure 12.6

A macro becomes interactive when you include a {?} command (pause). An interactive macro stops the macro's run temporarily so that you can respond to a command prompt or move the cell pointer. You can include a {?} command when you write a macro, or you can add it to an existing macro in EDIT mode.

6 ▶ Move the cell pointer to cell B5.

Now you will erase the data entered when you last tested the \MODEL macro. Then you will test the edited version.

7 ▶ Use the /Range Erase command to erase the data in the range B5..H10.

8 ▶ Press ALT-F3.

> Lotus 1-2-3 prompts you to select a macro to run. A list of macro names associated with the current worksheet are displayed on the control panel.

9 ▶ Move the pointer to the \MODEL macro name, if necessary.

10 ▶ Press ←.

> The macro runs.

Notice that the macro entered column headings and then the cell pointer moved to column B. The macro then entered the row labels and moved the cell pointer up to cell B6. The macro then selected the /Worksheet Column

Set-Width command (/WCS) and paused after displaying the command's prompt. You will continue the exercise by responding to the prompt.

11 ▶ Press → 7 times.

The column's width increases to 16 characters.

12 ▶ Press ←.

The new width for column B is entered, and the macro completes its run by moving the cell pointer right one column.

Now you will save the current changes to the file. Then you will write another interactive macro to print a range of data.

13 ▶ Press HOME, and then use the \S macro to save the changes to the same file.

14 ▶ Move the cell pointer to cell B30.

15 ▶ Type '**\P**

16 ▶ Press →.

17 ▶ Type '**/ppr{?}~agpq**

18 ▶ Press ←.

The macro keystrokes for printing a range are entered. The {?} command pauses the macro so you can enter a print range.

Now you will name the macro and test it in STEP mode.

19 ▶ Make sure the cell pointer is on the cell that contains the label "\P."

20 ▶ Press the Slash key (/) to access the Main Menu.

21 ▶ Type **RNL** to select the Range, Name, and Labels commands.

22 ▶ Type **R** to select the Right option.

Lotus 1-2-3 prompts you to enter the label range.

23 ▶ Press ←.

The macro in cell C30 is assigned the name \P in cell B30.

24 ▶ Press ALT-F2.

The STEP mode indicator appears on the status line.

25 ▶ Press ALT-**P**.

The macro cell's address and keystrokes appears on the status line.

26 ▶ Press SPACEBAR 5 times to step through the macro's first five keystrokes.

A blinking SST indicator is displayed on the status line. This indicator reminds you that 1-2-3 is still in STEP mode while you enter information.

27 ▶ Type **b5.h10**

28 ▶ Press ←.

The tilde (~) is highlighted on the status line.

29 ▶ Press SPACEBAR 3 times.

> The next three keystrokes are run to select the tilde, the Align command, and the Go command. The selected range prints.

30 ▶ Press SPACEBAR twice.

> The Page command and Quit option are selected. The macro completes its run.

31 ▶ Press ALT-F2.

> STEP mode is turned off.

32 ▶ Press HOME, and use the \S macro to save the changes to the same file.

You have created four macros that automate common 1-2-3 operations. These operations include data entry, formatting data, saving changes to a current file, and printing a range of data. You will complete this lesson by learning how to manage macros so that you can use them in other worksheets.

Exercise 12.6 Creating and Using a Macro Library

Objectives

After completing this exercise, you will be able to
- Attach the Macro Manager add-in program.
- Create and use a macro library.

MACRO MANAGER
An add-in program that is used to create and manage macro library files.

Now that you have created several macros, where do you store them? Your macros are currently saved in a worksheet file, but you are limited to using them in that file only. However, later you might want to use them in other worksheet files.

To make your macros available to all worksheets, you can use the Macro Manager add-in program. *Macro Manager* can be used to save your macros in special macro library files. The special library files can be retrieved so that the macros are available for any worksheet file.

Recall that you learned about the Wysiwyg add-in program in Lesson 9. As with Wysiwyg, you can load the Macro Manager add-in program into memory to work along with 1-2-3. You use the same /Add-In Attach command (/AA) to load Macro Manager into the computer's memory. Once Macro Manager is loaded, you can retrieve your macro library file. All the macros in the file can then be used with the current worksheet.

You will begin the final exercise in this lesson by attaching the Macro Manager add-in program. Then you will retrieve your macro library file.

1 ▶ Press the Slash key (/) to access the Main Menu.

2 ▶ Type **AA** to select the Add-in and Attach commands.

Lotus 1-2-3 prompts you to select an Add-in program. A list of add-in program filenames is displayed.

3 ▶ Move the menu pointer to the MACROMGR.ADN filename, and press ⏎.

The invoke key menu appears.

This is the same menu you get when you attach the Wysiwyg add-in program. You can choose a function key that is pressed with the ALT key to invoke, or display, the Macro Manager main menu. The numbers displayed on the menu—7, 8, 9, and 10—refer to the F7, F8, F9, and F10 keys, respectively.

4 ▶ Type **8**

The F8 key is selected, and the 1-2-3 Add-In command menu is displayed.

5 ▶ Type **Q** to select the Quit option.

Lotus 1-2-3 returns to READY mode.

MACRO LIBRARY FILE
A file that contains macros that can be used with any worksheet.

You can now use Macro Manager to save your macros in a special *macro library file*. Macros are saved with the Macro Manager by selecting the range that contains the macros and the macro names. Now you will invoke Macro Manager so you can save your macros.

6 ▶ Press ALT-F8.

The Macro Manager main menu appears.

7 ▶ Type **S** to select the Save command.

Macro Manager prompts you to enter the name of the library file that will store your macros.

8 ▶ Type **admin** and press ⏎.

Macro Manager prompts you to enter the macro library range. Cell A1 is anchored.

9 ▶ Press ESC.

The current cell is not anchored.

10 ▶ Move the cell pointer to cell B21.

The cell pointer is on the cell that contains the name of the first macro.

11 ▶ Type **.** (a period) to anchor the current cell.

12 ▶ Press →.

13 ▶ Press ⬇ 9 times.

   The range with all the macros and their names is highlighted.

14 ▶ Press ⏎.

   Macro Manager asks you whether you want to enter a password to lock the macro library file.

15 ▶ Type **N**

Macro Manager saves the macros in the new macro library file called ADMIN.MLB. The .MLB extension indicates that the file is a macro library file. Notice that the macros have disappeared from the current worksheet.

You can now use these macros with any worksheet or to create a new worksheet. Now you will begin creating a new worksheet to test two of the macros.

16 ▶ Use the /Worksheet Erase Yes command to erase the current worksheet data.

   Your system beeps, and the control panel displays a message telling you that the current changes have not been saved. Lotus 1-2-3 prompts you to indicate whether you want to erase the worksheet anyway.

17 ▶ Type **Y**

   The worksheet area is clear.

You will begin creating a new worksheet by entering the company's name as a worksheet title with the \N macro.

18 ▶ Press ALT-N.

   The label "Mollie's Music Shoppe" is entered as the worksheet's title in cell A1.

19 ▶ Press ALT-F3.

   Lotus 1-2-3 prompts you to enter the macro to run.

20 ▶ Move the menu pointer to the \MODEL macro name, if necessary.

21 ▶ Press ⏎.

   The worksheet model's labels are entered. At the {?} command (pause), the macro pauses so you can respond to the prompt.

22 ▶ Press ➡ 7 times.

23 ▶ Press ⏎.

As you can see, Macro Manager can be very useful. After you create a macro, you can attach Macro Manager and use it to save your macro to a macro library file.

To use the macros in a macro library file, you must select the Macro Manager's Load command. This loads the macros into the computer's memory. This step was not necessary in this exercise. The macros were

Creating and Using a Macro Library

loaded automatically when you saved them to the ADMIN.MLB file. However, when you use 1-2-3 again, you must attach Macro Manager and then use the Load command. Then you can use the macros in that file for any worksheet.

To complete this course, you will do one more 1-2-3 operation: erase the current worksheet data.

24 ▶ Use the /Worksheet Erase Yes command (/WEY) to clear the worksheet area.

25 ▶ Type **Y** again to erase the worksheet without saving changes.

Congratulations! You have completed the High School Edition of Lotus 1-2-3, Release 2.3 course. You can now begin the Lesson 12 applications that follow the Concept Summary. Or you can quit 1-2-3 if you are through with this session.

Concept Summary

■ Many spreadsheet software packages allow you to create simple and complex macros. Macros are stored sets of keystrokes that can be used over and over to automate spreadsheet operations.

■ When macros are run, they operate much like a tape recorder that plays back information. Macros can enter data, move the cell pointer around a worksheet, and select commands.

■ Most programs let you either write a macro from scratch or record an operation's keystrokes into a macro. With some programs, you can assign special names to macros that allow you to run them with as few as two keystrokes.

■ Interactive macros include a special command that pauses the macro's run so that a user can enter information. The information is used to complete the macro's operation (for example, a response to a command prompt).

■ Some software packages include special add-in programs that let you store macros in special macro library files. These macro library files are stored in the computer's RAM so that their macros can be used with any worksheet.

Command Summary
▶ ▶ ▶ ▶ ▶

Range Name Labels Right command (/RNLR)
assigns a label as a range name, or macro name, for the contents in the cell to the right

ALT- (any alphabet character)
runs a macro that has been assigned a name that consists of a backslash character (\) and an alphabet character

ALT-F2
turns STEP mode on and off for testing macros

/Worksheet Learn Range command (/WLR)
sets a range that collects recorded macro keystrokes

ALT-F5
turns the 1-2-3 Learn Feature on and off for recording macro keystrokes

{?} command (pause)
an advanced 1-2-3 macro command that pauses a macro for user input

ALT-F3
displays a list of named macros

Applications

Begin doing the applications by loading 1-2-3, if necessary. Place your student data disk in drive A (or drive B if you do not have a hard disk). Change the current directory to the drive that contains the student data disk.

Business

Sales Analysis

1. You will conclude your sales analysis work by creating some macros. Retrieve the file SLSMCR12.WK1. This file contains 1995 sales figures for all the branches and their 1996 projected sales. Create three macros, as outlined in the following steps:

   a. Move the cell pointer to an empty area in the worksheet. Enter the label "\S" in the current cell. Move the cell pointer one cell to the right.

   b. Use the /Worksheet Learn command (/WL) to set up a learn range. The learn range can include two or three cells down the column.

   c. Move the cell pointer to cell C17. Press ALT-F5 to begin recording keystrokes, and enter the following keystrokes:

   @sum(↑ END ↑ **.** END ↓ **)** ⏎

   Note: Notice that the formulas in column D no longer display ERR.

   d. Press ALT-F5, and then move the cell pointer to the cell that contains the macro's name label, "\S." Use the /Range Name Labels Right command (/RNLR) to assign the macro's name.

Applications 377

e. Move the cell pointer to cell E17. Run the \S macro to enter an @SUM function, and calculate a total for projected 1996 sales.

f. Move the cell pointer two rows down from the \S macro. Write the following macro keystrokes:

'/wir~\-~/c~.{?}~

The macro inserts a row and enters a dashed line. Notice that it pauses for the user to point to the Copy command's "Where To?" range. Enter the label "\L" in the cell that is one cell to the left of the macro's first cell. Assign the name to the macro.

> **HINT**
>
> f. Use the ? command (pause) so that the cell pointer can be moved to highlight the copy command's "Where To?" range during the macro's run.

g. Move the cell pointer to cell C8. Turn on STEP mode, and test run the \L macro. Did it work correctly? If not, find the problem and fix the macro.

h. Turn off STEP mode, move the cell pointer to cell C18, and run the \L macro again.

i. Write another macro that enters a double dashed line into a range. Assign the name "\D" to the macro.

j. Move the cell pointer to cell C20. Test the macro to enter a double dashed line in the range C20..E20.

k. Attach the Macro Manager add-in program. Specify F8 as the invoke key. Save the range of macros to a macro library named FORMATS.MLB.

l. Press HOME, and save the file as SALES12.WK1. Erase the worksheet.

Business

Small Business

2. You decide to write a macro that will speed up the process of adding records for new customers to your database. The macro will insert a new record into the database and then sort the records in alphabetical order by last name. Retrieve the file WWCMAC12.WK1, and do the following:

a. Move the cell pointer to cell A5. This is where you will begin a record for a new customer. Enter the following record in the appropriate database field:

Wipeout	**Wendy**	**1979 Broken Nose Ct.**
Santa Monica	**CA**	**90033** **(213) 555-1515**

b. Move the cell pointer to cell J1, and enter the macro name label "\I."

c. Use the /Worksheet Learn command (/WL) to set up the learn range as K1..K6.

d. You will record keystrokes that will (1) move the cell pointer to cell A5; (2) select the /Move command (/M) and move the new customer's record to the end of the database range; (3) select the /Data Sort Data-Range command (/DSDR); (4) expand the data range to include the new record; (5) select the "LAST" field as the primary sort key and the "FIRST" field as the secondary sort key; (6) select the Go command to sort the records in the data range; and (7) press HOME, and move the cell pointer back down to cell A5 so that the next new customer record can be entered. Press ALT-F5 to begin recording, enter the keystrokes, and then press ALT-F5 again to turn off recording.

e. Move the cell pointer to cell J1, and assign the label in that cell as the macro's name.

f. Test-run the macro in STEP mode. Fix any problems you find, and then turn off STEP mode.

g. Enter the following record in the new customer range:

| **Wipeout** | **Wally** | **1979 Broken Nose Ct.** | |
| **Santa Monica** | **CA** | **90033** | **(213) 555-1515** |

h. Run the macro. Check the data range after the macro has completed its run. Did the macro correctly sort the two new records?

i. Attach the Macro Manager add-in program. (Select F8 as the invoke key.) Save the macro range to the macro library file DBUPDATE.MLB.

j. Enter your name, address, and phone number in the new customer range. Run the macro.

k. Press HOME, and save the changes to the file PROFIT12.WK1. Erase the worksheet.

Business

Accounting

3. You will write a macro that creates a template for other accounting periods by editing your general accounting worksheet. Retrieve the file ACCMAC12.WK1. Your macro will carry out several editing operations. First, it must replace the trial balance values (in columns C and E) with the adjusted trial balance values (in columns K and M). The macro should begin by copying data in the columns headed "Adjusted Trial Balance" to the "Trial Balance" columns. Then the macro will do a series of operations to erase the data in the columns headed "Adjustments" and "Adjusted Trial Balance" columns. In a blank area of the worksheet, enter the label "\T." Use the /Range Name Labels Right command (/RNLR) to assign it as a macro name for the next cell to the right. Beginning in the first macro cell, structure your macro so it does the following:

   a. Moves the cell pointer to cell K9

   b. Copies the data in the adjusted trial balance's debit column to the trial balance's debit column

   c. Copies the data in the adjusted trial balance's credit column to the trial balance's credit column

   > Note: For the /Copy command's "Copy what?" ranges, be sure to include the totals in row 39.

   d. Erases the data in the "Adjustments" debit and credit columns

   e. Erases the data in the "Adjusted Trial Balance" debit and credit columns

   f. Moves the cell pointer to cell O40 and deletes the value that adjusts the income statement's debit balance

   g. Moves the cell pointer to cell U40 and deletes the value that adjusts the balance sheet's credit balance

   h. Moves the cell pointer to cell A2 so that the worksheet's date can be edited

   Test the macro. If the macro does not run properly, check to see if your macro matches the macro shown in Figure 12.7. Attach the Macro Manager add-in program. Save the macro to a macro library file named WSTEMPL.MLB. Save the changes to the worksheet as BALANC12.WK1. Retrieve the file ACCMAC12.WK1 again. Run the macro to create the template again. When the macro completes its run, edit the label in cell A2 to change the date to May 31, 1995. Press (HOME), and save the changes to the file BALANC12.WK1. Erase the worksheet.

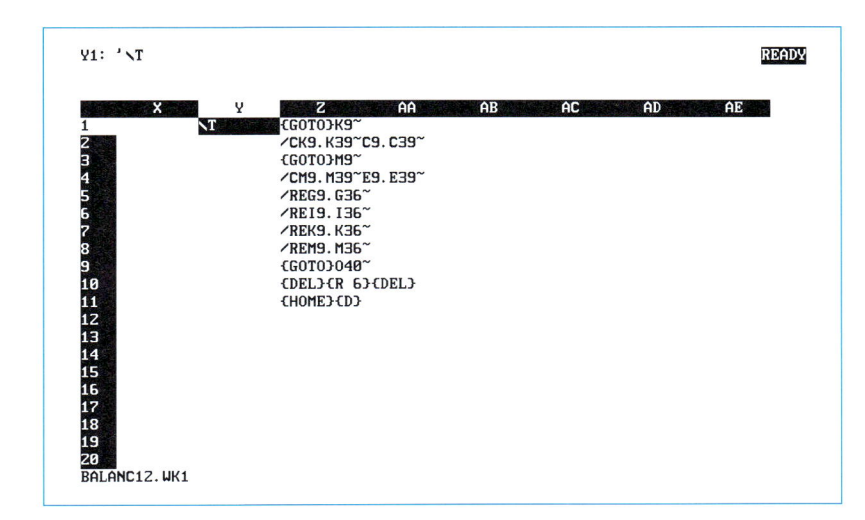

Figure 12.7

```
Y1: '\T                                           READY

              X     Y    Z       AA     AB    AC    AD    AE
         1         \T   {GOTO}K9~
         2              /CK9.K39~C9.C39~
         3              {GOTO}M9~
         4              /CM9.M39~E9.E39~
         5              /REG9.G36~
         6              /REI9.I36~
         7              /REK9.K36~
         8              /REM9.M36~
         9              {GOTO}O40~
        10              {DEL}{R 6}{DEL}
        11              {HOME}{D}
        12
        13
        14
        15
        16
        17
        18
        19
        20
BALANC12.WK1
```

This macro edits an existing worksheet to create a template for the next accounting cycle. If your macro does not run without errors, check to see if the keystrokes are the same as those shown here. If they are not, edit the macro.

Social Studies

Student Survey

4. To help you work more efficiently, you will write a macro that formats a range of values. Retrieve the file SRVMAC12.WK1. Notice that the percentages in columns C, E, G, I, K, and M are not formatted. To create the macro, do the following:

   a. Record keystrokes to a learn range to create a macro called \P that formats values as percentages with two decimal places. Begin the macro by using the [F4] key to preselect a range within a column by using the cell pointer movement keys.

   b. Test the macro in STEP mode to format the values in column C. If the macro does not work properly, edit it until it does.

   c. Use the \P macro to format the values in columns E, G, I, K, and M.

   d. Edit the \P macro so that it pauses for you to select the range you want to format.

   e. Test the macro by formatting the range of values in row 26.

   f. Press [HOME], and save the worksheet as SURVEY12.WK1. Erase the worksheet.

HINT

d. You can do this in two ways. You can delete the keystrokes that pre-select the range and enter a {?} command after selecting the /Range Format command (/RF). Or you can enter a {?} command after the keystroke that presses [F4].

Applications   **381**

Social Studies

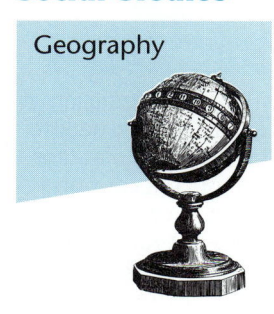

Geography

5. To help you manipulate your database of African populations, you will write macros that sort and print ranges. Retrieve the file POPMAC12.WK1, and do the following to write and test the macros:

   a. Write a macro named \N that sorts the records in alphabetical order by country. The macro will select the /Data Sort command (/DS), specify the data range, specify a primary sort key, and sort the records.

   b. Write another macro named \R that sorts the records in ascending numerical order by population. This macro will be set up in the same way as to the \N macro. Include a {?} command so you can enter a new data range or accept the current range.

   c. Write a macro named \F that sorts the records in descending numerical order by projected population. Include a {?} command so you can enter a new data range or accept the current range.

   d. Test the \N macro in STEP mode. If it does not work properly, edit it until it does. Test the other two macros in STEP mode, and edit any errors that occur.

   e. Edit each macro to include the keystrokes that will specify and print the range A1..D28.

   f. Run the three macros to print the three sorted versions of the database worksheet.

   g. Attach the Macro Manager add-in program. Save the three macros in a macro library file named SORTS.MLB.

   h. Press (HOME), and save the file as WLDPOP12.WK1. Erase the worksheet.

Social Studies

American Government

6. To help you with your work, you will write a macro that sums a range of values that are listed in a column. Retrieve the file VOTMAC12.WK1. Notice that the percentage formulas display ERR because there are no calculated vote totals. Write a macro that enters an @SUM function wherever you locate the cell pointer, as follows:

   a. Write a macro named \A that enters an @SUM function and uses the pointing method to specify the range.

   b. Test the macro in STEP mode by using it to total the 1960 popular votes in row 9. If the macro does not run properly, edit it until it does.

   c. Turn off STEP mode. Press (HOME), and save the file as ELECTN12.WK1.

   d. Use the \A macro to calculate totals on rows 9, 16, and 23 for popular and electoral votes.

HINT

a. Use the macro commands for the arrow and (END) keys to highlight the range that you want to put in the @SUM function's argument.

382   12▶ Automating Your Work with Macros

e. Write a macro named \S that moves the cell pointer to cell A1 and saves the changes to the same filename. Run the macro to save the file.

f. Attach the Macro Manager add-in program, if necessary. Save the macros in the macro library file SUM.MLB.

g. Use the \S macro again to save the changes to ELECTN12.WK1. Erase the worksheet.

Science/Mathematics

Astronomy

7. To speed up your analysis work with the solar system worksheet, you will write some macros that sort the information. Retrieve the file PLNMAC12.WK1. Create the macros by doing the following:

   a. Write a macro named \D that sorts the planets in descending numerical order by diameter percentages. Include a {?} command (pause) so you can highlight a data range in response to the data range prompt.

   b. Test the \D macro in STEP mode. If there are any problems with the macro, fix them until it runs smoothly.

   c. Write a macro named \ORBORD that sorts the planets in ascending numerical order by average orbital distance. Run the macro by pressing ALT-F2 to test it in STEP mode. Fix any errors that may occur.

   d. Press HOME, and save the file as PLANET12.WK1.

   e. Write a macro that prints the entire range of data. Test run the macro to print the current range of worksheet data.

   f. Run the \D macro again to sort the planets by diameter percentages. Then run the print macro again to print this data arrangement.

   g. Press HOME, and save the current changes to PLANET12.WK1. Erase the worksheet.

Science/Mathematics

Mathematics

8. To see how you can combine common arithmetic and 1-2-3 macros to complete a job, retrieve the file MTHMAC12.WK1. Suppose you run a business installing wall-to-wall carpeting. You would like to save time putting together written estimates for customers. You will write a macro that does some arithmetic and then prints an estimate sheet. You plan your macro to do the following:

▶ Enter the customer's name and address

▶ Increase the measured area of the job by 5 percent (the waste factor) to calculate the total area of material necessary for the job

▶ Select the price (per square foot) of the carpeting the customer wants from the list in the worksheet

▶ Print the range of estimate figures

▶ Clear the template for the next estimate

Applications

Before you record the macro keystrokes, complete the template by entering formulas that will make automatic calculations as the macro runs. Then record the macro keystrokes.

a. Enter a formula in cell B11 that calculates the job cost. The formula will multiply the total area value in cell B9 times the price of the carpet in cell B10.

b. Enter a formula in cell B13 that calculates sales tax. The formula will multiply the job cost times 7.25 percent.

c. Enter a formula in cell B15 that calculates the total cost of the job. This formula adds the job cost to the sales tax.

d. Now you are ready to record the macro keystrokes. Specify the range D20..D25 as a learn range. Enter the label "\E" as a name for the macro in cell C20. Assign the label as a macro name for cell D20.

e. When you record the keystrokes, you will enter job estimate information for a customer named Smith. The measured area for carpet installation is 388 square feet. Enter the value 388 in cell E13.

f. Begin recording keystrokes that do the following:

> Move the cell pointer to cell B5

> Enter the customer's name (Smith) and address (1415 Plush Rd.)

> Move the cell pointer to cell B9 and enter a formula that calculates total area

HINT
f. Use the Go To command (F5).

Note: The calculation can be a formula or @function that adds 5 percent of the job area to the job area value.

> Move the cell pointer to cell B10, select the /Copy command (/C), unanchor the current cell, and move the cell pointer to the price for nylon pile carpeting to copy that price to cell B10

> Select and print the range A1..C15

> Erase the ranges B5..B6, B9..B10, and the cell E13

> Return the cell pointer to cell A1

HINT
Type the range address.

g. Stop recording keystrokes once you have completed the macro. Scroll the worksheet so you can see the macro keystrokes in the learn range. Edit the macro by replacing the keystrokes "Smith" and "1214 Plush Rd." with {?} commands (pause). Enter a {?} command (pause) between the keystrokes that move the cell pointer to the price list and the two tildes (~~).

Note: This will allow you to move the cell pointer to any carpet price during the macro's next run.

h. Press HOME, and save the file as MATH12.WK1.

i. Test the macro in STEP mode for a customer named "Andrade" at "103 8th St." who wants indoor-outdoor carpeting for a 1,250-square-foot patio. Be sure to enter the measurement in cell E13 before you run the macro. If there is any problem with the macro, edit the keystrokes so they match those shown in Figure 12.8.

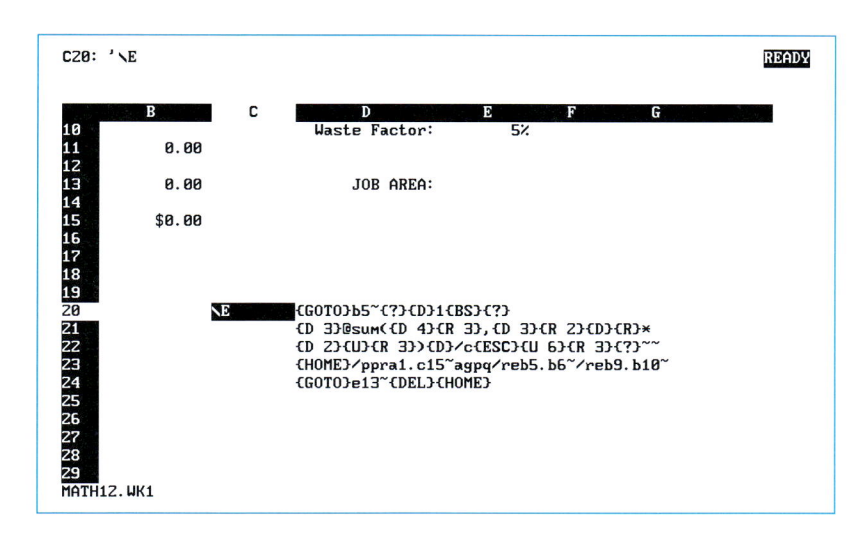

```
C20: '\E                                                    READY

       B          C          D          E        F       G
10                           Waste Factor:       5%
11               0.00
12
13               0.00                  JOB AREA:
14
15              $0.00
16
17
18
19
20                          \E     {GOTO}b5~{?}{D}1{BS}{?}
21                                 {D 3}@sum({D 4}{R 3},{D 3}{R 2}{D}{R}*
22                                 {D 2}{U}{R 3}){D}/c{ESC}{U 6}{R 3}{?}~~
23                                 {HOME}/ppra1.c15~agpq/reb5.b6~/reb9.b10~
24                                 {GOTO}e13~{DEL}{HOME}
25
26
27
28
29
MATH12.WK1
```

Figure 12.8

This macro calculates a carpet installation estimate, prints the estimate for the customer, and clears the template. If your macro does not run without errors, check to see if the keystrokes are the same as those shown here. If they are not, edit the macro.

j. Turn off STEP mode. Run your macro again for a customer named "Najim" at "1222 Goff Ave." who wants polyester shag for a 530-square-foot room.

k. Erase the worksheet without saving the changes.

Health

Nutrition

9. To continue working with your health and dietary analysis, you will write a series of macros that do unit conversions. Retrieve the file NUTMAC12.WK1, and do the following steps:

a. Write a macro that converts a column of gram units to milligram units. The macro will switch 1-2-3 to EDIT mode, and multiply the value in the current cell times 10^3. The macro will then move the cell pointer down one cell to the next value to repeat the edit.

b. Edit the last macro cell to add keystrokes that move the cell pointer up to the column heading and then one cell to the right.

c. Name the macro \M, and test it in STEP mode by converting the vitamin C gram units. Fix any errors that you may find during the macro's run.

d. Write a similar macro that converts gram units to centigram units.

e. Name this second macro \C, and test it in STEP mode to convert the column of vitamin E gram units. Fix any errors that may occur during the macro's run.

HINT

a. Use the caret symbol (^) to enter the power of 10 exponent (for example, 10^3). Enter the keystrokes to edit the first cell in the column. Then copy the keystrokes down the column to the next seven cells to speed up writing the macro.

f. Write another macro that edits converted units back to gram units. This macro will switch 1-2-3 to EDIT mode and press BACKSPACE 5 times to erase the characters "*10^3" or "*10^2." Name this macro \G, and test it in STEP mode by reconverting the vitamin C units. Fix any errors that may occur during the macro's run.

g. Turn off STEP mode, and run the \G macro to reconvert the vitamin E units.

h. Attach the Macro Manager add-in program, and save the macros to a macro library file named CONVERT.MLB.

i. Press (HOME), and save the file as NUTINF12.WK1. Erase the worksheet.

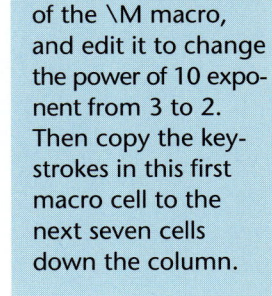

> **HINT**
>
> d. Copy the first cell of the \M macro, and edit it to change the power of 10 exponent from 3 to 2. Then copy the keystrokes in this first macro cell to the next seven cells down the column.

10. To conclude the softball season, you will write a series of macros that sort the batting statistics database in a variety of ways. Retrieve the file SFBMAC12.WK1, and do the following:

    a. Write a macro named \A that sorts the players' records in descending numerical order by batting average.

    > Note: Do not include the record for the team's statistics on row 19.

    b. Test the macro in STEP mode. Fix any errors that may occur during the macro's run.

    c. Write another macro named \S that sorts the players' records in descending numerical order by slugging percentage. Test this macro in STEP mode, and fix any errors.

    d. Write another macro named \H that sorts the players' records in ascending numerical order by home runs. Test this macro in STEP mode and fix any errors.

    e. Turn off STEP mode, and run the macros in succession a few times. Observe the effects on the list.

    f. Attach the Macro Manager add-in program, and save the macros in a macro library file named LISTS.MLB.

    g. Save the file as SBGAME12.WK1. Set up a learn range. Record keystrokes to create a macro that sets up a criteria range and an output range. The macro will also name and define the input, criteria, and output ranges. Name the macro \QUERY, and test it in STEP mode.

    h. Save the \QUERY macro to the macro library file LISTS.MLB. Erase the worksheet, and then retrieve the file SBGAME12.WK1. Run the \QUERY macro to set up and/or name and define the input, criteria, and output ranges.

    i. Erase the worksheet without saving the changes to the file.

Appendix A

Using DOS and DOS Commands

This appendix provides a brief introduction to your computer's Disk Operating System (DOS). DOS is the widely used operating system software with IBM-compatible personal computers (PCs). A basic understanding of DOS is very useful when you are learning to use a software application such as Lotus 1-2-3, Release 2.3.

An *operating system* is a special master program that controls your computer's operation. DOS makes it easier to run other software programs, such as Lotus 1-2-3, Release 2.3. There are several versions of DOS. Each new version improves or enhances the features of the previous version. There are a few basic DOS commands and operations that work the same way no matter which version of DOS you are using. Those commands and operations are discussed in the following sections.

Starting Your Computer

To begin working with a computer, you must first turn it on by flipping its ON/OFF switch to the ON position. This action provides electric current to "wake up" the computer. When you do this, the computer reads a special built-in program that is in a microcomputer chip inside the computer. The program does a two-step startup procedure. The first step checks the computer to make sure everything is in proper working order, and then it reads the first part of a disk. Special DOS instructions are on this part of the disk. The second step uses these instructions to read the rest of DOS that is necessary to get the operating system up and running.

This process is called "booting" DOS. The term "booting" comes from the expression "to pull (something) up by its bootstraps." So when you start a microcomputer, it checks itself and then "pulls DOS up by its bootstraps."

Booting DOS from a Hard Disk Drive

If your computer is equipped with a hard disk drive, the hard disk very likely has DOS already installed. So when you start the computer, its built-in program looks at the first part of the hard disk to begin booting DOS. Use the following procedure to boot DOS from a hard disk drive:

1 ▶ Turn on the computer and its monitor, if the monitor has its own power switch.

After a few moments, you may see a small, blinking cursor in the upper left corner of the screen. Then you may see one or more messages. Finally, you may see a message that looks like this:

Current date is Tue 1-01-1980

Enter new date (mm-dd-yy):

If you see a DOS prompt, DOS has successfully booted, and you can skip steps 2 and 3.

2 ▶ Type the current date as numbers for the month, day, and year (MM-DD-YY), and press ⏎.

Separate each number with a hyphen (-) or slash (/). For example, if the current date is October 3, 1992, type "10-3-92" or "10/3/92." After you press ⏎, the operating system asks you to enter the current time, by displaying the following message:

Current time is 0:00:01.23

Enter new time:

3 ▶ Type the current time as numbers for the hours and minutes (in the format HH:MM), and press ⏎.

Separate the numbers with a colon. For example, type 4:15 if it is a quarter past four. With newer versions of DOS, you can specify a.m. or p.m. by typing an "a" or a "p" after the time (for example, 4:15p). If you are using an older version of DOS, you can only specify a p.m. time by using a 24-hour clock entry. For example, if the current time is 4:15 p.m., type "16:15." After you press ⏎, you will see a DOS prompt (C:\> or C>). Your DOS prompt may look different from those shown here.

If DOS booted from your hard disk without asking you for the date and time, DOS received this information automatically. DOS does this if your computer has an internal clock battery. An internal clock battery keeps the current date and time even when the computer is switched off.

Booting DOS from a Dual Floppy Disk Drive Computer

If your computer is a dual floppy disk drive system, then you need to boot DOS from a DOS disk in the primary drive. On most dual floppy systems, this drive is called drive A. To begin this procedure, your computer must be off.

1 ▶ Place a DOS disk in drive A, and close the drive's door.

2 ▶ Turn on the computer and its monitor, if the monitor has its own power switch.

After a few moments you may see a small, blinking cursor in the upper left corner of the screen. Then you will likely see a message that looks like this:

Current date is Tue 1-01-1980

Enter new date (mm-dd-yy):

3 ▶ Type the current date as numbers for the month, day, and year (in the format MM-DD-YY), and press ⏎.

Separate each number with a hyphen (-) or slash (/). For example, if the current date is October 3, 1992, type "10-3-92" or "10/3/92." After you press ⏎, the operating system asks you to enter the current time, by displaying the following message:

Current time is 0:00:01.23

Enter new time:

4 ▶ Type the current time as numbers for the hours and minutes (HH:MM), and press ⏎.

Separate the numbers with a colon. For example, type 4:15 if it is a quarter past four. With newer versions of DOS you can specify A.M. or P.M. by typing an "a" or a "p" after the time (for example, 4:15p). If you are using an older version of DOS, you can only specify a P.M. time by using a 24-hour clock entry. For example, if the current time is 4:15 P.M., type "16:15."

Appendix A

After you press ⏎, you will see a DOS prompt (A:\> or A>). Your DOS prompt may look different from those shown here.

Using the DOS Prompt

The DOS prompt is how DOS tells you that it is ready to receive information from you. The DOS prompt contains a letter that indicates the disk drive that DOS is currently using to receive and store information. This is called the *current drive*. Your DOS prompt may have a backslash character (\) that follows the drive letter or colon (for example, A\> or C:\>). This tells you that DOS is working in the main directory, also called the *root directory*.

The root directory is always located at the very beginning of any disk. This includes hard disks and floppy disks. So even if your DOS prompt does not display a backslash character (\), DOS is working in the root directory unless your system has been specially set up to do otherwise. Directories are discussed in further detail later.

Moving Between Disk Drives

You can make another disk drive current by simply typing the drive letter and a colon (:), and pressing ⏎. For example, if disk drive C is current and you want to make disk drive A current, you type a: at the DOS prompt.

After you press ⏎, the DOS prompt changes from C:\> to A:>, or something similar. To return to disk drive C, simply type c: and press ⏎. If your computer has two floppy disk drives but no hard disk and disk drive A is current, you can type b: to make disk drive B current. When referring to any disk drive in DOS commands, you must always include the colon (:). Never include a space between the drive letter and the colon (for example, a :). Doing so will cause DOS to display the following message:

    Bad command or file name

The DOS prompt is where you type commands to give DOS instructions. Entering commands is discussed in the next section.

Entering DOS Commands

Commands are instructions that you use to communicate with DOS. A command is a name for a program that you want the computer to run. The command (program) can be the name of a program or an application program you have bought (such as Lotus 1-2-3, Release 2.3). A command can also be the name of a program that you have written or the name of a DOS program.

The next section provides a brief introduction to data disks. The remaining sections discuss files, directories, and a few DOS commands, beginning with the FORMAT command. These commands will help you to work more comfortably with an IBM-compatible personal computer.

Data Disks

You store data on disks—both hard disks and floppy disks. If you have a hard disk, it is generally more convenient to store and use data on the hard disk. But we advise you to periodically save copies of your important data on a floppy disk for safekeeping. That way, if anything should happen to your hard disk, you will be able to transport your important data to another computer. Copying data is discussed later.

A *floppy disk* is a very thin, round plastic object that has a magnetic coating. The disk itself is permanently encased in a soft or hard plastic cover or jacket. The magnetic coating allows data to be stored electronically. A hard disk is similar, except that it is a metallic disk encased in a sealed boxlike structure that is mounted inside the computer.

Several types of floppy disks are available for use with IBM-compatible PCs. The biggest difference among the floppy disk types is storage capacity. Storage capacity is measured in either kilobytes (KB) or megabytes (MB). Sometimes you will hear the terms "low density" and "high density" used to describe floppy disks. High-density disks store more data than do low-density disks. Table 1 provides the specifications for each type of floppy diskette.

Table 1

Size	Cover	Storage Capacity	Density
3.5 inch	hard	720KB	low
3.5 inch	hard	1.4MB	high
3.5 inch	hard	2.8MB	high
5.25 inch	soft	360KB	low
5.25 inch	soft	1.2MB	high

1KB = 1,000 bytes
1MB = 1,000,000 bytes

A disk's density is important to consider when determining the correct disk drive for a floppy disk. High-density disks require a high-density disk drive; they cannot be used in a low-density disk drive. However, a low-density disk can be used in a high-density disk drive. Be sure you know which type of disk drive is installed in your computer.

Managing Data in Files

When you use DOS-based software applications, such as Lotus 1-2-3, Release 2.3, you save your data in *files*. Like files in a filing cabinet, computer files hold, or store, data. Data can be documents you typed in a word processor or numbers you entered into a spreadsheet. Data can also be sets of instructions called *programs*. Often you create files when you save your work while using a specific DOS-based program such as 1-2-3.

Files are identified by unique names. The names are unique because no two names within any directory can be the same. (Directories are discussed in the next section.) A file's name is composed of two parts: the filename and the extension. A period separates the filename from the extension (for example, FILENAME.EXT). The filename is the unique name that you give to the file (for example, saving a worksheet file named BUDGET). The extension, in many cases, identifies the type of data that is stored in the file. (For example, 1-2-3 worksheet files are automatically given the .WK1 extension.) However, a file's name does not have to include an extension.

The following rules apply to files created in DOS-based applications:

▶ Filenames can be any name from one to eight characters long.

▶ Extensions can be any three characters separated from filenames by a period.

▶ Filenames and extensions can include the letters of the alphabet (A–Z); the digits 0–9; and the following punctuation symbols: tilde (~); exclamation point (!); pound sign (#); dollar sign ($); percent sign (%); caret (^); ampersand (&); opening parenthesis ((); closing parenthesis ()); hyphen (-); opening brace ({); closing brace (}); and underscore (_).

▶ Filenames and extensions cannot include a blank space.

Managing Files in Directories

A directory is an area on any disk (hard or floppy) where files can be stored and organized. In discussions of DOS operations, the terms *directory* and *subdirectory* tend to be used interchangeably. They are really one and the same. The only clear distinction you need remember is the difference between the root directory and other directories or subdirectories. The root directory is the starting point. It stores directories and files; directories also can store other directories and files. But all directories branch off the root directory. One example of a disk's directory structure is shown in Figure 1.

```
ROOT DIRECTORY
    \SUBDIRECTORY A
                            \SUBDIRECTORY A1        FILE A1a
                                                    FILE A1b
                                                    FILE A1c

                            \SUBDIRECTORY A2        FILE A2a
                                                    FILE A2b

                            FILE A1

                            FILE A2

    \SUBDIRECTORY B
                                                    FILE B1a
                            \SUBDIRECTORY B1        FILE B1b
                                                    FILE B1c
                            FILE B1                 FILE B1d
                                                    FILE B1e
                            FILE B2

                            FILE B3

    \SUBDIRECTORY C
                                                    FILE C1a
                                                    FILE C1b
                            \SUBDIRECTORY C1        FILE C1c
                                                    FILE C1d
                                                    FILE C1e

                                                    FILE C2a
                            \SUBDIRECTORY C2        FILE C2b
                                                    FILE C2c
                                                    FILE C2d

                                                    FILE C3a
                            \SUBDIRECTORY C3        FILE C3b
                                                    FILE C3c
                                                    FILE C3d
                                                    FILE C3e
                                                    FILE C3f

                            FILE C1

                            FILE C2

    FILE 1

    FILE 2

    FILE 3
```

Figure 1

The easiest way to understand directories is to think of your hard disk or floppy disk as a filing cabinet. A filing cabinet contains drawers that hold file folders. Just as filing cabinet drawers hold file folders, directories hold, or store, a group of files. Going one step further, just as file folders store documents, files on disk store data. Unlike filing cabinet drawers, however, disk directories can store other directories.

Files on a disk are usually related in some way. For example, suppose you have many files that contain worksheets you created using Lotus 1-2-3, Release 2.3. You might store those files in a directory called WRKSHTS. If your computer has a hard disk, try to organize your data files in directories. This makes finding particular files easier and will help keep your root directory uncluttered.

Creating a Directory   You create a directory on a disk by using the MKDIR command, which is short for "make directory." DOS lets you shorten the command to MD. To create a directory, you simply type the command, a backslash character (\), and the name of the directory. The directory name can be eight characters or fewer, just like filenames. For example, if you want to create a directory called WRKSHTS in the root directory on a hard disk, at the DOS prompt (C:\>) you enter the following command:

md\wrkshts

This command creates the directory in the root directory on drive C. You can create directories on floppy disks using the same command format.

You sometimes may want to create directories within directories. For example, suppose you want to organize files that contain sales data within the WRKSHTS directory. To do this, at the DOS prompt (C:\>) you enter the following command:

md\wrkshts\sales

Notice that you must enter the directory name that will contain the new directory. If you type "md\sales," DOS will create the directory on the root directory, not in the WRKSHTS directory.

Using Paths   When you enter directory levels to identify the location of a file, you are telling DOS the file's specific path. A pathname includes the drive letter, all relevant directory levels, and a file's name (for example, C:\DIRECTRY\FILENAME.EXT). Each element in a pathname is separated by a backslash character (\). Let's say that you have a 1-2-3 worksheet file named JULYDATA.WK1. The file is in a directory named SALES that is within the directory named WRKSHTS. The WRKSHTS directory is in the root directory on a hard disk. The pathname for this file is as follows:

C:\WRKSHTS\SALES\JULYDATA.WK1

Knowing how to use pathnames in DOS commands is a very important technique. Paths let you communicate to DOS the exact location of files when you give DOS commands.

Making a Directory Current   Just as you can readily make any disk drive current, you can also make any directory current. To work in, or make current, a directory, you can use the CHDIR command, which is short for "change directory." As with the MKDIR command, you can enter the shortened version, CD. To enter this command, you type the command name, a backslash character (\), and the name of the directory you want to make current, as follows:

cd\wrkshts

When you use the CHDIR command, the DOS prompt may change to show you which directory you are in (for example, C:\WRKSHTS>). Or the DOS prompt may look the same. It depends on how your system is set up. To return to the root directory from any directory, at the DOS prompt type:

cd

After you press ⏎, you will be working in the root directory on the current disk drive.

You can also make current a directory that is within a directory. Using the same example, you type the following at the DOS prompt to work in the directory SALES:

cd\wrkshts\sales

Notice that you must include all directory levels in this command, as well. In this case, if you enter "cd\sales," DOS displays the following message:

> Invalid directory.

DOS not only lets you create directories and make them current, but also lets you remove them when you no longer need them.

Removing a Directory from a Disk

You remove (delete) directories from a disk when you no longer need them. Clearing obsolete data (files and directories) from a disk is just as important as creating data. Before you remove a directory, you must first make sure it is empty. It must not contain any files or other directories. If the directory does contain files, you must first delete them (assuming you no longer need them). How to delete files is discussed later. Also, the directory you are removing cannot be the current directory.

Use the DOS command RMDIR, which is short for "remove directory," to delete a directory. As with the MKDIR and CHDIR commands, you can shorten the RMDIR command to RD, and you must include the exact path to the directory. For example, suppose you want to remove the directory SALES that is within the directory WRKSHTS. First, you make sure that the directory is empty and that you are working in a directory other than \WRKSHTS\SALES. Then, at the DOS prompt, you enter the following command:

> **rd\wrkshts\sales**

The three commands MKDIR (MD), CHDIR (CD), and RMDIR (RD) let you efficiently organize your files and directories on any disk.

Using the DIR Command

The DIR command (short for "directory") is one of the most frequently used DOS commands. You use the DIR command to list the files and directories on a disk or in a directory. Next to each file or directory name, DOS lists its size and the date and time it was created or last modified. The DIR command also shows the disk space that the current files and directories occupy and the free space that remains on the disk.

If you enter this command by itself, DOS lists files and directories on the current disk in the current directory. For example, suppose you enter the DIR command at the DOS prompt C:\>.

After you press ⏎, DOS displays a list of all the files and directories in the root directory on hard disk drive C.

You can also enter this command by including a drive letter and/or directory other than the current drive or directory. For example, suppose you want to list the files on a floppy disk in drive A while disk drive C is current. At the DOS prompt, you enter:

> **dir a:**

Or suppose you are in the root directory on drive C and you want to display a list of files and directories in the directory WRKSHTS. At the DOS prompt, you enter the following command:

> **dir \wrkshts**

The DIR command is extremely useful. Use it to check on your file's vital information before you execute commands that affect your files.

Using Wildcard Characters

DOS lets you include wildcard characters with certain commands. Wildcard characters are very useful with the DIR command. They let you display lists of selected files, instead of all the files in a directory or on a disk. The asterisk (*) and the question mark (?) are DOS wildcard characters.

The asterisk (*) is used to represent any string, or group, of characters. It is often useful for listing a related group of files. For example, suppose you want to list just the 1-2-3 worksheet files within a directory. To do this at the DOS prompt, you type the following command:

dir *.wk1

This command lists all files with the WK1 extension in the current directory. The asterisk wildcard makes using the DIR command very flexible. For instance, if you want to list all files that begin with a "T" on the current disk or directory, you enter the following:

dir t*.*

As you might guess, entering the command dir *.* would produce the same result as the command all by itself (DIR)—it lists all files in the current directory.

The question mark (?) wildcard character is used to represent any single character. This wildcard character is useful if you want to list a number of files that you know have similar names. For example, suppose you have a number of 1-2-3 worksheet files that you named by date (for example, MAY12SLS.WK1). You could enter the following command to list only those files:

dir may??sls.wk1

As you become more familiar with DOS, you will learn that these wildcard characters can be very useful with other DOS commands.

Using the FORMAT Command to Prepare Floppy Disks

To use brand-new floppy disks, you must first prepare them so that they can be used with your particular system. This preparation process is called "formatting" a disk. Without going into technical detail on floppy disk construction, formatting is a process that divides the disk surface into sections called *sectors*. Sectors serve as guidelines or areas that DOS uses in a special way to store data. So when you command DOS to format a disk, it creates sectors on the disk and sets up an empty root directory.

Formatting a Floppy Disk on a Computer with a Hard Disk

You must use the FORMAT command to format, or prepare, a floppy disk for use. The command is simple to use. Depending on how your system is set up, you may have to make the directory that contains DOS files current. Use the following procedure to format a floppy disk on a computer equipped with a hard disk:

1 ▶ Insert a blank, unformatted floppy disk into a floppy disk drive (for example, drive A). Make sure the drive door is closed properly.

2 ▶ At the DOS prompt, type **format a:**

> Note: Be sure to type the colon (:). A colon must always follow a drive letter when you refer to a disk drive in DOS commands.

3 ▶ Press ⏎.

DOS will display the following message:

> Insert new diskette for drive A:
>
> and press ENTER when ready...

> Note: If DOS displays the message "Bad command or file name," you must make the directory that contains DOS files current. Use the DIR command to check the name of your DOS directory, and then use the CD command to make that directory current.

394   Appendix A

4 ▶ Press ⏎.

DOS may display an indicator that shows what percentage of the disk has been formatted as the disk is being formatted.

When the formatting process has completed, DOS may display a message that asks you to enter a volume label. This gives you the option of naming or labeling the floppy disk. You do not have to assign a volume label to a disk. However, it is often useful to identify your disks with a volume label. Enter any name you wish for the volume label. Volume labels can be up to 11 characters.

5 ▶ Whether or not you enter a volume label, press ⏎.

The FORMAT program will display a small report that provides information on the formatted disk's capacity. Following the format report, the FORMAT program asks you a question that usually appears as follows:

> Format another (Y/N)?

6 ▶ Type **Y** (for "yes"), and press ⏎ if you want to format another disk. Then repeat the format procedure. Otherwise, type **N** (for "no") and press ⏎. The DOS prompt will appear.

Formatting a Floppy Disk on a Dual Floppy Disk Drive Computer

To format floppy disks on a computer equipped with dual floppy disk drives, you must use the DOS disk to access the FORMAT command. Use the following procedure:

1 ▶ Insert your DOS disk into drive A, and close the drive door.

2 ▶ Insert a blank, unformatted floppy disk into the other floppy disk drive (for example, drive B). Make sure the drive door is closed properly.

3 ▶ At the DOS prompt, type **format b**:

> Note: Be sure to type the colon (:). A colon must always follow a drive letter when you refer to a disk drive in DOS commands.

4 ▶ Press ⏎.

DOS will display the following message:

> Insert new diskette for drive B:
>
> and press ENTER when ready. . .

5 ▶ Press ⏎.

DOS may display an indicator that shows what percentage of the disk has been formatted as the disk is being formatted.

When the formatting process has completed, DOS may display a message that asks you to enter a volume label. This gives you the option of naming or labeling the floppy disk. You do not have to assign a volume label to a disk. However, it is often useful to identify your disks with a volume label. Enter any name you wish, up to 11 characters, for the volume label.

6 ▶ Whether or not you enter a volume label, press ⏎.

The FORMAT program will display a small report that provides information on the formatted disk's capacity. Following the format report, the FORMAT program asks you a question that usually appears as follows:

> Format another (Y/N)?

7 ▶ Type **Y** (for "yes"), and press ⏎ if you want to format another disk. Then repeat the format procedure. Otherwise, type **N** (for "no") and press ⏎. The DOS prompt will appear.

Formatting Tips

Sometimes the format report will tell you that the formatted disk includes bad sectors. Bad sectors cannot be used to store data. If the format report tells you that a disk has bad sectors, it is wise to discard the disk. The chances of losing data on such a disk are very high and replacing the disk is relatively inexpensive.

Because formatting disks takes some time, you may find it useful to format several at one time. This helps you to avoid interrupting your work if you suddenly need a floppy disk and you do not have one already formatted.

Do be careful with the FORMAT command. If you format a disk that already contains data, the data will be lost forever. If your computer has a hard disk, never enter the FORMAT command by itself. If the hard disk drive is current, include the drive letter that contains the floppy disk you are formatting. Otherwise, make sure the disk drive with the unformatted disk is current before you enter the FORMAT command by itself.

Formatting Low-Density Disks in High-Density Drives

It is worth noting that you may have to enter some additional information with the FORMAT command. This depends on the type of disk you want to format and the type of disk drive on your computer. For example, if you have a high-density 5 1/4-inch disk drive and you want to format a 5 1/4-inch 360KB (low-density) floppy disk, enter the FORMAT command as follows:

format a:/f:360

The characters "/f:" represent what is called a *switch*. In this example, the switch tells DOS to format the floppy disk in drive A as a low-density 360KB disk.

If you do not include the switch, the high-density drive will format the disk as if it had 1.2MB of storage capacity. After formatting, the format report will tell you that the disk had bad sectors in addition to the space it could format. This is important to know because you will not be able to use such a disk on a standard 360KB disk drive. And it is very likely that you will encounter problems with a disk formatted this way if you try to use it on a high-density disk drive.

The same switch can be used when you format 3 1/2-inch disks in a 3 1/2-inch drive. Disk drives for 3 1/2-inch disk drives can read and write information on 720KB or 1.4MB 3 1/2-inch disks. For example, to format a 3 1/2-inch 720KB disk in disk drive B, you enter the following command:

format b:/f:720KB

Using the COPY Command

The COPY command is another frequently used and very flexible DOS command. You use it to create duplicates of files. Although you cannot store two files with the same name in any one directory, you can copy a file to other directories or disks. For example, if you want to copy the file OCT_DATA.WK1, which is on a disk in the current drive A, to a disk in drive B, you can enter the following:

copy oct_data.wk1 b:

This command creates an exact duplicate file of OCT_DATA.WK1 on the disk in drive B and gives it the same name. Notice that you must include a space between the file's name and the destination drive letter. Another way to do this same copy operation is to copy the file from disk drive A while drive B is current. In this case, you enter the command as follows:

copy a:\oct_data.wk1

Now suppose you want to copy the same file on disk drive A to a file named OCTSALES.WK1 on a disk in drive B. You enter the command as follows:

copy oct_data.wk1 b:\octsales.wk1

This command copies the file OCT_DATA.WK1 on the disk in drive A and stores the duplicate in the root directory on the disk in drive B. The duplicate file, however, is named OCTSALES.WK1.

Using Wildcard Characters with the COPY Command to Back Up Data

Wildcard characters make the COPY command even more powerful. Let's suppose you want to back up all the files stored in a directory on your hard disk. Use the following procedure:

1 ▶ Make sure you have a blank, formatted floppy disk.

2 ▶ Insert the blank, formatted floppy disk into drive A, and close the drive door.

3 ▶ Use the CD command to make the hard disk directory you want to back up the current directory.

4 ▶ At the DOS prompt, type **copy *.* a:**

> Note: From the root directory (or any other directory), you can enter the command with the directory's name; for example,
>
> **copy \directry*.* a:**

5 ▶ Press ⏎.

DOS copies all the files in the current directory to the floppy disk in drive A. The copied files on the disk in drive A will have the same names as the original files on the hard disk.

Using the DISKCOPY Command to Back Up a Floppy Disk

The easiest way to back up a floppy disk is to use the DOS DISKCOPY command. This command copies all the files on one disk to another disk. The copied files have the same names as the original files. To use this command on a dual floppy disk system, you must have a DOS disk, a floppy disk with the original files, and a blank, formatted disk. Use drive A for the DOS disk, and drive B for the source and target disks. The source disk is the disk that contains the original files. The target disk is the blank disk. Use the following procedure to copy a disk on a dual floppy disk system:

1 ▶ Make sure you have a blank, formatted floppy diskette.

2 ▶ Insert the DOS disk into drive A, and close the drive door.

3 ▶ Insert the disk with the original files in drive B, and close the drive door.

4 ▶ Make sure drive A is the current drive.

5 ▶ Type **diskcopy b: b:**

The DISKCOPY command (program) prompts you to insert the source disk into drive B.

6 ▶ Press ⏎.

The computer reads information from the source disk and stores it temporarily in random access memory (RAM). After it reads information, the DISKCOPY program prompts you to insert the target disk into drive B.

7 ▶ Remove the disk in drive B, and insert the blank disk into drive B. Make sure the drive door is closed properly.

8 ▶ Press ⏎.

The information stored temporarily in RAM is copied (written to) the target disk in drive B.

Depending on the type of disk being copied, the program may ask you to reinsert the source disk to read remaining information. If this occurs, remove the target disk from drive B, and reinsert the source disk into drive B. Then press ⏎ to continue. Follow the instructions in any additional prompts you see on screen.

Using the DISKCOPY Command on a Computer with a Hard Disk

The DISKCOPY command is used very similarly on computers with hard disk drives. Follow this procedure:

1 ▶ Make sure you have a blank, formatted disk.

2 ▶ If necessary, use the CD command to make the directory with DOS files current.

3 ▶ If you have only one floppy disk drive for the type of disk you are backing up, type **diskcopy a: a:** (otherwise, go to step 4).

The DISKCOPY program prompts you to insert the source disk into drive A.

4 ▶ If you have two floppy disk drives for the type of disks you are using, type **diskcopy a: b:** (otherwise, skip this step and go to step 5).

The DISKCOPY program will prompt you to insert the source disk into drive A and the target disk into drive B.

5 ▶ Press ⏎.

If you have only one floppy disk drive, the program reads the information from the disk in drive A and stores it temporarily in RAM. Then it prompts you to insert the target disk into drive A. If you have two floppy disk drives, the files on the source disk are copied to the target disk, and you are done.

6 ▶ If you only have one floppy disk drive, remove the source disk from drive A and insert the target disk into drive A.

7 ▶ Press ⏎.

The original files are copied from RAM to the target disk.

Depending on the type of disk being copied, the program may ask you to reinsert the source disk to read remaining information. If this occurs, remove the target disk from drive A, and reinsert the source disk into drive A. Then press ⏎ to continue. Follow the instructions in any additional prompts you see on screen.

Using the DELETE and ERASE Commands

The DELETE and ERASE commands perform the same function: they remove files from a disk. Careless use of these commands can be very dangerous. Be absolutely certain you do not want any file that you delete because once you have deleted it, it is gone forever. DOS lets you shorten the DELETE command to DEL. DEL and ERASE are useful when you need to remove files you no longer need. This also clears some disk space; disks can become surprisingly full very fast. You can delete a single file in any directory, as shown in the following examples:

    del nov_data.wk1

or

    del c:\wrkshts\nov_data.wk1

You can also use wildcard characters with this command. For example, suppose you want to delete all the worksheet files that store data for November in the directory \WRKSHTS\SALES while working in the root directory on drive C. You enter the command as follows:

del \wrkshts\sales\nov*.wk1

This command deletes all files in the specified directory that begin with the characters "NOV" and that have the extension ".WK1."

You may find that you need to use this command to clear some disk space on your work disks as you work through the exercises and applications in this book. To do this, it is wise to first use the DIR command to list the files on the disk. Write down the file names you no longer need, and then use the DEL command (or the ERASE command) to delete the files. You also have the option of removing files from the while you are working in Lotus 1-2-3, Release 2.3. This is discussed in the next section.

Deleting Files While Working with Lotus 1-2-3 Release 2.3

As you work through the exercises and applications in this book, you will save many files. At some point you may encounter an error message box that tells you the current disk is full when you try to save a file. When working at the computer, you should always try to have an extra disk nearby that has some disk space available. That way you can simply replace the full disk with the extra disk. Then press ESC and enter the /File Save command (/FS) again to save the file to the extra disk.

However, if you find yourself in the difficult position of having no extra disk space available, don't panic. There are two courses of action you can take without losing your work. You can temporarily exit 1-2-3 to DOS and use the DEL or ERASE command to delete from the current disk. Or you can use a 1-2-3 command to delete files you no longer need without exiting to DOS. Either way, this will give you some extra disk space so you can save your current work.

If you want to exit to DOS to delete files, use the /System command (/S) to temporarily exit 1-2-3. Do not quit 1-2-3! Then you can use the DOS command DEL or ERASE to delete one or more files. Be sure you use the DIR command to first check your disk for the file names you are sure you want to delete. Once you have cleared some disk space, type "exit" at the DOS prompt to return to 1-2-3.

You might find it easier to just delete one or more files without temporarily exiting 1-2-3 to DOS. Use the following procedure to delete files from the current disk, if you get a "Disk full" error message while saving a 1-2-3 file:

1 ▶ Press ESC to return to READY mode.

2 ▶ Press the Slash key (/) to access the Main Menu.

3 ▶ Type FEO to select the File, Erase, and Other commands.

> Note: The Other command lets you delete any type of file (worksheet, graph, non-1-2-3 file, and so on) that is on the current disk.

4 ▶ Press [F3] to display a full-screen list of all the files on the current disk (and directory).

5 ▶ Move the menu pointer to the name of a file that you want to delete.

6 ▶ Press [↵].

You may have to delete more than one file, depending on how much disk space you need to save your work in a new file. If so, simply repeat the preceding steps as many times as necessary.

As you can see, you can use DOS commands to organize your files and manage disk space. Many software applications also include commands that let you do file and disk management tasks without having to exit to DOS. If you want more information about DOS, we recommend you consult your DOS reference manual. There are also many books on DOS that have been written by noteworthy experts in the computing field.

Appendix B

Using a Mouse with 1-2-3

Using a mouse makes certain tasks, like positioning a pointer or cursor, easier than using the Arrow keys on a keyboard. Selecting commands and doing certain editing operations can also be easier when you use a mouse. This appendix describes the mouse, techniques for using a mouse, and how to do some basic Lotus 1-2-3, Release 2.3 operations with a mouse.

What Is a Mouse?

A mouse is a hand-held input device that you use in combination with your keyboard. The mouse is connected to your system with a thin insulated (covered) wire that plugs into a connection port on your computer system.

You place your fingers and the upper part of your palm over the top of the mouse. Although mouse shapes vary among manufacturers, each shape is designed to fit comfortably under your extended fingers when you place your hand over the device. Your wrist rests behind the mouse on the desktop or mouse pad so that you can comfortably slide the mouse in any direction. Rather than actually holding a mouse, use your hand to guide its movement.

The bottom of a mouse has a small hole where the partial surface of a hard, round rubber ball sticks out. The ball (it looks like a miniature handball) rests inside a small compartment with rollers that touch the surface of the ball. Just enough of the ball's surface is exposed through the hole that the mouse slides easily as the ball rolls within its compartment.

Depending on the particular model, a mouse may have one, two, or three buttons on top. The buttons lie conveniently beneath your fingertips and serve different functions, depending on the software being used. If your mouse has two or three buttons, you will use the left button the most. (However, you can change this within 1-2-3 or many other applications.) Depending on the software you are using, the right button can also be used for certain operations. However, it tends to be used less often than the left button.

If you have a single button, there may be a few operations that a two- or three-button mouse can do that you cannot, depending on the software being used. You will learn more about the functions of these buttons in 1-2-3 later in this appendix.

For left-handed mouse users, the left and right buttons can be switched. Most software applications let you do this by changing specific settings. The Lotus Install program lets you switch mouse buttons for 1-2-3 operations. You will learn how to do this later in this appendix.

Identifying the Mouse Pointer and Icons

When a mouse is properly installed with your system, you will see an object on screen called a *mouse pointer*. The shape and size of the mouse pointer depends on the software application being used. In Lotus 1-2-3, Release 2.3, the mouse pointer looks like a small, solid rectangle (▌). If you have attached the Wysiwyg add-in program, the mouse pointer looks like a small arrow pointing upward and slightly to the left (↖).

As you slide the mouse pointer around a relatively small area on your desktop (or on a special foam mouse pad), the mouse pointer moves around the screen area. The mouse pointer moves in the same direction you move the mouse. For example, if you slide the mouse to the right on your desktop (or mouse pad), the mouse pointer moves to the right. You do not have to slide the mouse very far to move the mouse pointer a considerable distance across the screen.

Depending on the software in use, there may be several other objects on screen when a mouse is properly installed with your system. These objects are called *icons*. An icon is any object that can be selected with the mouse to perform specific operations. You will learn more about 1-2-3's mouse icons later. However, it is very important that you first learn about some basic mouse techniques.

Basic Mouse Techniques

If you are new to the use of a mouse, it is a good idea to familiarize yourself with basic mouse usage terms, or techniques. These techniques are described as follows:

Clicking

You click a mouse button by pressing and releasing it. You do not hold the mouse button down, but press and release it within a fraction of a second. Often you will hear or read an instruction that tells you to "click on" something. This means that you must move the mouse pointer over an object (icon) or special area on screen and click a mouse button while the mouse pointer remains on the object.

Dragging

Dragging is a technique by which you can highlight something on screen or select something by expanding the boundaries of a temporary outline around an object. You begin to drag a highlight or temporary outline by moving the mouse pointer to a starting location. Then you press and hold down a mouse button while sliding the mouse to expand the highlight or temporary outline to an ending location. For example, you highlight a range of cells in a 1-2-3 worksheet by dragging the mouse so that the range of cells is highlighted in the worksheet area.

Double-Clicking

Double-clicking a button is very similar to clicking a button. You press and release a mouse button twice in rapid succession. Often you will hear or read an instruction that tells you to "double-click on" something. As with clicking, you move the mouse pointer over an object (icon) or special area on screen and double-click the mouse button while the mouse pointer remains on the object.

Pressing

To use this technique, you press the mouse button and hold it down while the mouse pointer is positioned over an object on screen. This technique tends to be used for scrolling a list of options, spreadsheet, or document. There also can be other uses for pressing, depending on the software application in use. To press a mouse button, you hold it down until the option or area you are looking for comes into view. Then you release the button.

Now that you are familiar with mouse technique terms, read further to understand how the mouse can be used with Lotus 1-2-3, Release 2.3.

Switching Mouse Buttons

If you are left-handed, or if you would rather use the right-hand mouse button primarily, you can use the Lotus Install program to switch mouse button functions. This makes the right button the primary mouse button that you use to select objects in 1-2-3. Use the following procedure to switch mouse buttons:

1. ▶ Make sure a DOS prompt displays on your screen.
2. ▶ Type **LOTUS** to display the Lotus Access System menu screen.
3. ▶ Type **I** to select the Install command.

    The Install program registration screen appears.

4. ▶ Press ⏎.

    The Install program's main menu screen displays.

5. ▶ Move the pointer to the "Change Selected Equipment" option, and press ⏎.

    The Change Selected Equipment screen displays.

6. ▶ Move the pointer down to highlight the "Switch Mouse Buttons" option.

    The Switch Mouse Buttons screen displays. The Lotus Install program prompts you to specify the mouse button you want to use to select objects in 1-2-3.

7. ▶ Highlight the "Right" option, and press ⏎.

    The Change Selected Equipment screen reappears.

8. ▶ To save this change permanently, so that it will be in effect the next time you use 1-2-3, highlight the "Save the Current Driver Set" option, and press ⏎.

    The Lotus Install program prompts you to save the changes to the current driver set.

9. ▶ Press ⏎.

    The changes are saved.

10. ▶ Press ESC as many times as necessary to return to the "Change Selected Equipment" screen.

11. ▶ Move the pointer, if necessary, to highlight the "Return to Main Menu" option, and press ⏎.

12. ▶ Move the pointer to highlight the "End Install" option, and press ⏎.

    Lotus asks you whether you want to end the Install program.

13. ▶ Move the pointer to highlight the "Yes" option, and press ⏎.

    The Lotus Access menu reappears.

14. ▶ Type **E** to select the Exit command.

    A DOS prompt is displayed.

As mouse operations in 1-2-3 are discussed throughout the remainder of this appendix, assume that the left-hand button is to be used unless the right-hand button is stated. If you have switched mouse buttons before you read through this material, then assume the opposite.

Moving the Cell Pointer

When Lotus 1-2-3 was installed on your system, it detected automatically whether a mouse was installed. If a mouse is properly installed, the opening 1-2-3 screen will display five mouse icons on the right edge of the worksheet area. They are also directly below the 1-2-3 mode indicator. (See Figure B.1.)

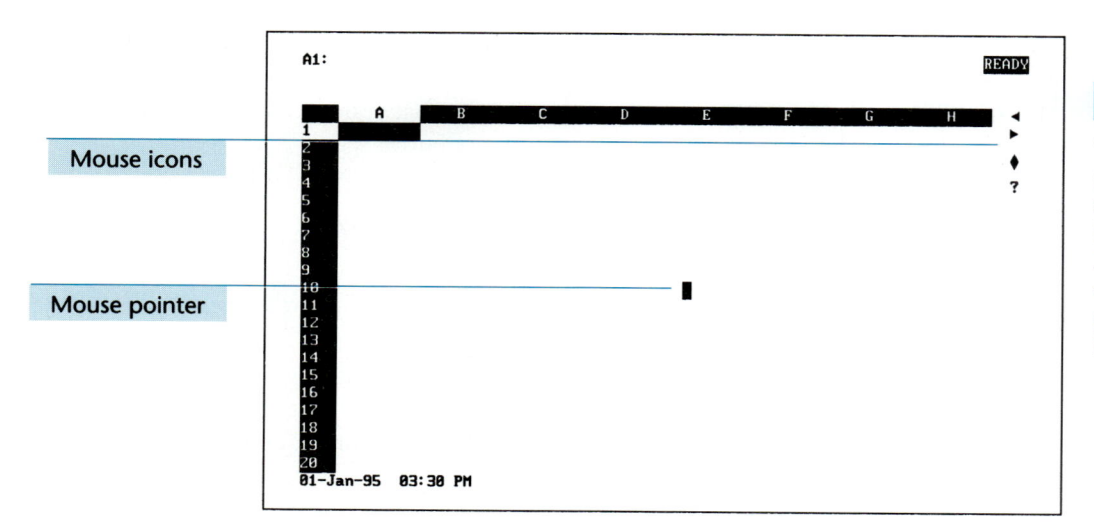

Figure B.1

When a mouse is properly installed on a computer system, the Lotus 1-2-3, Release 2.3 opening screen displays a mouse pointer and five mouse icons.

- Mouse icons
- Mouse pointer

> Note: If the Install program did not detect the mouse installation when Lotus 1-2-3 was installed, you can use the Install program to select your mouse type and driver.

The first four icons from the top look like tiny arrowheads. These "directional" icons are used to move the cell pointer. To move the cell pointer cell by cell, simply click on an icon. The cell pointer will move one cell in the direction you selected. For example, if the cell pointer is on cell A1 and you want to move it to cell B1, click on the arrowhead that points to the right (the second icon from the top).

If you want to move the cell pointer rapidly in any one direction, move the mouse pointer over a directional icon and use the press technique. Remember, the press technique means that you press and hold down the left button (right button if you have switched mouse buttons). This is also how you can use the mouse to scroll the worksheet. Just like scrolling with the keyboard, the worksheet scrolls as the cell pointer moves past the last visible row or column.

To move the cell pointer to any cell that is visible in the worksheet area, simply click on the cell. For example, suppose you want to move the cell pointer to cell G14 on the opening 1-2-3 screen display. Simply click on cell G14.

Accessing Help

The last icon from the top is a question mark (?). You can access the 1-2-3 Help facility when you click on this icon. When you click on the question mark icon (?) in READY mode, the 1-2-3 Help index screen is displayed. If you want context-sensitive help on a 1-2-3 command, select (highlight) the command, and then click on the question mark icon (?).

Selecting 1-2-3 Commands

Selecting 1-2-3 commands is a much quicker process when you use a mouse. To access (display) the 1-2-3 Main Menu, simply move the mouse pointer up into the control panel area. Lotus 1-2-3 switches to MENU mode, and the Main Menu of 1-2-3 commands is displayed automatically. This is the same as pressing the Slash key (/). If you move the mouse pointer out of the control panel before selecting a command, the Main Menu disappears and 1-2-3 returns to READY mode.

With the Main Menu displayed, you select a command by simply moving the mouse pointer over a command name and clicking on it. This selects the command, displaying its submenu of command options or executing an operation, depending on the command you select.

If you decide that you want to go back to a previous command menu level, click the right-hand mouse button. This is the same as pressing the (ESC) key. The previous menu level will reappear. To return to READY mode, keep clicking the right-hand mouse button until you exit the Main Menu.

> Note: If your mouse has only one button, use the menu keys discussed in Lesson 1 to exit from command menus.

Selecting Wysiwyg Commands

If you have attached the Wysiwyg add-in program, the right-hand mouse button (or left, if you have switched buttons) works a little differently. When you move the mouse pointer into the control panel area, the 1-2-3 Main Menu is displayed just as when Wysiwyg is not attached. However, if you press the right-hand mouse button, the Wysiwyg main menu is displayed. In fact, the right-hand button acts as a toggle between the 1-2-3 Main Menu and the Wysiwyg main menu. After you select a command in either menu, you can use the right-hand button like the (ESC) key to return to the previous menu level.

Another important point to remember when you have Wysiwyg attached: The last main menu you were working in (1-2-3 or Wysiwyg) will be displayed the next time you move the mouse pointer into the control panel area. So do not be confused if you see one menu when you want to access a command in the other. Just click the right-hand button to toggle to the other menu. For example, suppose you want to use a 1-2-3 command and the Wysiwyg main menu appears when you move the mouse pointer over the control panel area. Simply click the right-hand mouse button to display the 1-2-3 Main Menu.

Selecting Ranges

Probably the most useful mouse operation while using 1-2-3 is selecting (highlighting) a range. You use the dragging technique to highlight a range. To select a range, move the mouse pointer over the beginning cell, the cell that you want in the upper-left corner of the range. Press and hold the left mouse button, and drag the highlight to the last or lower-right cell in the range. Then release the mouse button.

You can a highlight a range before you select a command. This is the same as pressing (F4) to preselect a range. In fact, as soon as you begin dragging the highlight, 1-2-3 displays the same range select prompt on the control panel. After you release the button, the control panel briefly displays the selected range's address, and then the prompt disappears. The range remains highlighted in the worksheet area, ready for you to select a command.

You can also use the mouse to select a range in response to a 1-2-3 command prompt. To do this, use the mouse or keyboard to select the command. When 1-2-3 prompts you to enter a range, use the dragging technique to highlight the range. The prompt will display the address of the range you have highlighted. Press the left button to tell 1-2-3 that you have selected the range. In this case, pressing the left (primary) mouse button acts like pressing the (↵) key. If you highlight the wrong range, press the right mouse button. Just as when you press the (ESC) key, the range will no longer be highlighted and the current cell will be unanchored. Then simply select the range you want.

Changing Column Widths

With Wysiwyg attached, you can use the mouse to quickly adjust column widths on screen without using the command menus. To do this, move the mouse pointer over the vertical line that is to the right of the column letter. Then simply drag the vertical line right or left until the column is the width you want. As soon as you press the left button to begin dragging the vertical line, the column will be marked by two vertical dashed lines. Also, the mouse pointer changes to a small cross with right and left arrowheads. The dashed lines help you adjust the column's width in relation to the data in your worksheet.

You can adjust the height of rows (when Wysiwyg is attached) in a similar manner. Move the mouse pointer over the horizontal line that is below the row number, and drag the horizontal line up or down to adjust the row's height.

You can also use the mouse to reset a column width or row height to its default setting. To do this, you must use the keyboard and mouse together. First move the mouse pointer over the vertical line to the right of a column letter or the horizontal line below a row number. Then press and hold down the [SHIFT] key with your free hand, and click the left mouse button.

Splitting the Worksheet Area into Windows

When Wysiwyg is attached, you can use the mouse to split the worksheet area into two vertical or horizontal windows. To begin, you move the mouse pointer over the box in the upper-left corner of the worksheet frame. The box is to the left of column letter A and above row number 1, as shown in Figure B.2.

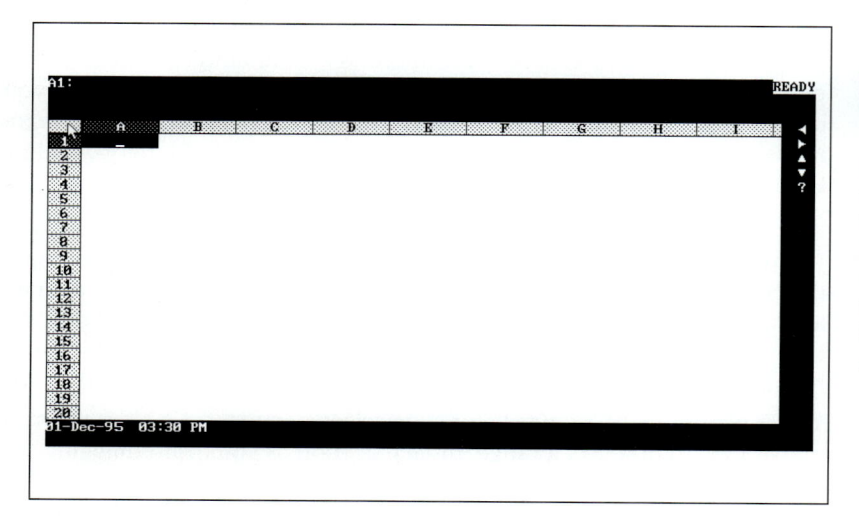

Figure B.2

The box in the upper-left corner of the worksheet frame (to the right of column letter A and above row number 1) is used to create a vertical or horizontal window split with the mouse.

You use the dragging technique to split the worksheet area into windows. Press and hold down the left button, and begin dragging the mouse pointer to the right to create a vertical split, or downward to create a horizontal split. As soon as you move the mouse in either direction, a dashed line will appear. Drag the dashed line to where you want to split the worksheet area into windows. As soon as you release the button, a second frame of row numbers will appear for a vertical window split, or a second frame of column letters will appear for a horizontal window split. Figure B.3 shows a Wysiwyg screen that is split into vertical windows.

406   **Appendix B**

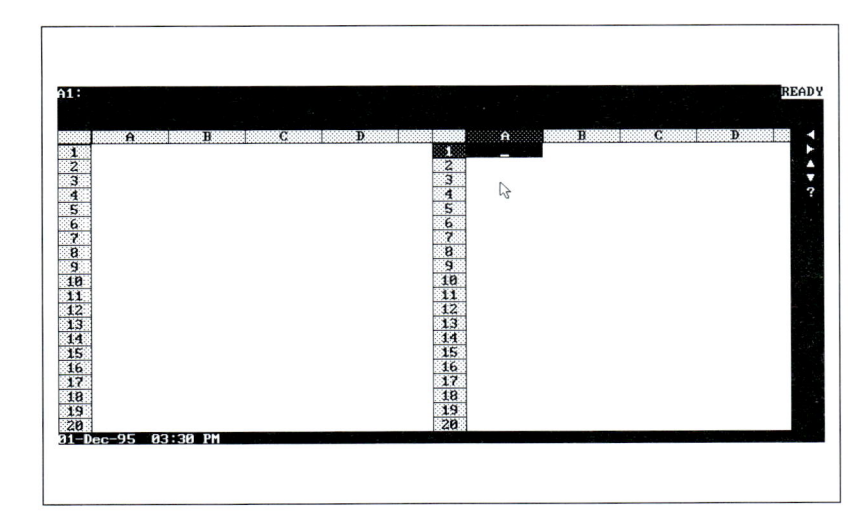

Figure B.3

This is a vertical window split created with the mouse.

Notice that above the row number 1 in the frame that divides the windows there is another blank box. You move the mouse pointer over this box and drag the split back to the left frame when you want to return the worksheet area to a single window. Similarly, you drag the second frame that divides two horizontal windows back up to the top frame when you want to close a horizontal window split.

As you become proficient with the use of a mouse, you will find that it can save you time over using the keyboard to perform certain 1-2-3 operations. And even if you are new to the mouse, do not be intimidated. With a little practice, you can quickly master mouse techniques to complement your keyboarding skills.

Index

Special Characters
  ' (apostrophe), 17
  * (asterisk)
    column width and, 70, 119
    as wildcard character, 393–394
  @ (at sign), 214
  \ (backslash)
    in DOS prompt, 389
    in graph titles, 251
    in macro names, 358, 359
    in macros, 368, 369
    pathnames and, 392
    repeating characters and, 82–83
  : (colon)
    drive names and, 389
    to invoke Wysiwyg, 272
  $ (dollar sign)
    in absolute cell references, 148
    in mixed cell references, 178
  < > (double angle brackets), 173
  ... (ellipses), 41
  = (equals sign), 176
  . (period), 50, 85
  + (plus sign)
    in formulas, 43
    linking formulas and, 174
  # (pound sign), 214
  ? (question mark), 394
  ~ (tilde), 359
  | (vertical bar), 213
ABS command (F4), 150, 178, 181
Absolute cell references, 149
  changing relative cell references to, 150
  in mixed cell references, 178
/Add-In Attach (/AA) command, 272, 373
/Add-In Detach (/AD) command, 276–277
Add-in programs, 271. *See also* Wysiwyg add-in program
  Macro Manager, 373–376
Addition, 43
Align Go command, 257
Alignment
  of labels, 17, 77–78
  of text in headers and footers, 213
Alternate (Alt) key, in macro names, 258
Anchor cell, 49, 50, 85
AND condition, 341
Apostrophe (') formatting prefix, 17
Arguments, 103–104, 115, 343
Arithmetic operators, 43

Arrow keys, 8, 11, 18–19, 44–45
Ascending sort, 317, 319, 320
Asterisk (*)
  column width and, 70, 119
  as wildcard character, 393–394
At sign (@), 214
Automatic recalculation, 49, 368
@AVG function, 115–116

Background shading, 286
Backing up, of disks, 397–398
Backslash (\)
  in DOS prompt, 389
  in graph titles, 251
  in macros, 358, 359, 368, 369
  pathnames and, 392
  repeating characters and, 82–83
Backspace key, 17, 18, 46
"Bad command or filename" message, 389
Bad sectors, 396
.BAK filename extension, 52
Bar graphs, 240–242
Blank columns, deleting, 123–124
Bookmark feature, 89
Booting, 387–389
  from dual floppy disk drives, 388–389
  from hard disk drive, 387–388
Borders, 6, 7, 10
  print, 210–212
Budget, 172
  preparation with @IF function, 182–186
Buttons, on mouse, 401, 403

CALC indicator, 368
Calculate command (F9), 368
Caps Lock key, 8, 9
CAPS status indicator, 8
Cell(s), 7
  anchor, 49, 50, 85
Cell addresses, 7, 12, 50
  formulas containing, 43
  in @function arguments, 103
Cell formulas, printing, 225–226
Cell pointer, 7
  locking in place, scrolling and, 110
  moving, 8–12, 18–19, 44–45, 403–404
Cell references
  absolute, 149, 178
  mixed, 177–182
  relative, 148–149, 178

Characters. *See also Special Characters section at beginning of index*
   deleting, 45–46
   repeating, 82–83
   in values, 20
   wildcard, 393–394
CHDIR (CD) command, 5, 392
Clicking, 402
Colon (:)
   drive names and, 389
   to invoke Wysiwyg, 272
Column(s), 7, 11
   blank, deleting, 123–124
   deleting, 123-124, 80
   determining number that can be printed, 206–207
   hiding, 217–221
   inserting, 80–81
Column-offset range, in database @functions, 343
Column width, 70
   setting, 74–76, 80, 81, 406
Comma (,) format, 69
Command(s)
   ABS (F4), 150, 178, 181
   /Add-In Attach (/AA), 272, 373
   /Add-In Detach (/AD), 276–277
   Align Go, 257
   Calculate (F9), 368
   Configuration Printer (CP), in Wysiwyg, 296
   /Copy (/C), 49–51
   /Data Find (/DF), 335–337
   /Data Query (/DQ), 331, 332, 334–335
   /Data Query Criteria (/DQC), 342
   /Data Query Extract (/DQE), 337
   /Data Query Input (/DQI), 333–334
   /Data Sort (/DS), 317, 318–322
   /Data Sort Data-range (/DSD), 318
   /Data Sort Go (/DSG), 319, 320, 321
   /Data Sort Primary-Key (/DSP), 319, 320–321
   /Data Sort Secondary-Key (/DSS), 319–320
   Display Zoom (DZ), in Wysiwyg, 274–275
   DOS. *See* DOS commands
   Edit (F2), 39–41
   Exit, 258
   /File Combine (/FC), 142–145, 173
   /File Combine Add (/FCA), 144–145
   /File Combine Copy (/FCC), 143–144
   /File Directory (/FD), 22, 23
   /File Erase Other (/FEO), 399–400
   /File Retrieve (/FR), 37–38
   /File Save (/FS), 22, 23, 52–53, 192–194
   Format Bold (FB), in Wysiwyg, 280, 281
   Format Color (FC), in Wysiwyg, 282
   Format Font (FF), in Wysiwyg, 278–279
   Format Italics (FI), in Wysiwyg, 280–281
   Format Lines Outline (FLO), in Wysiwyg, 289, 290
   Format Lines Shadow (FLS), in Wysiwyg, 289–290
   Format Lines Shadow Set (FLSS), in Wysiwyg, 290
   Format Reverse (FR), in Wysiwyg, 283
   Format Shade Light (FSL), in Wysiwyg, 286
   Format Underline (FU), in Wysiwyg, 285
   Go To (F5), 11–12, 118, 367
   /Graph (/G), 234
   /Graph A (/GA), 235
   /Graph Name Create (/GNC), 239, 246
   /Graph Name Use (/GNU), 244
   /Graph Options Titles (/GOT), 236–237
   /Graph Options Titles Y-Axis (/GOTY), 238
   /Graph Reset Graph (/GRG), 249–250
   /Graph Save (/GS), 240, 246
   /Graph Type Bar (/GTB), 241
   /Graph Type Pie (/GTP), 242
   /Graph View (/GV), 237–238
   /Graph X (/GX), 236
   Help facility and, 87–90
   Image-Select, 256–257, 258
   /Move (/M), 121–123
   Name (F3), 37, 38
   Page, 257
   Pause ({?}), 370–372
   PGRAPH, 254
   Preview (P), in Wysiwyg, 284
   Print (P), in Wysiwyg, 283, 295–296
   /Print Printer (/PP), 52, 53–54, 206
   /Print Printer Options Borders Columns (/PPOBC), 211
   /Print Printer Options Borders Rows (/PPOBR), 211–212
   /Print Printer Options Header (/PPOH), 214–215
   /Print Printer Options Margin (/PPOM), 209
   /Print Printer Options Other As-Displayed (/PPOOA), 226
   /Print Printer Options Other Cell-Formulas (/PPOOC), 225
   /Print Printer Options Setup (/PPOS), 222, 223–225
   /Print Printer Range (/PPR), 85–86
   Query (F7), 338
   {?} (pause), 370–372
   /Quit (/Q), 24
   Quit (Q), in Wysiwyg, 284
   /Range Erase (/RE), 111–112
   /Range Format (/RF), 70
   /Range Format Text (/RTF), 339
   /Range Justify (/RJ), 292
   /Range Label (/RL), 77–78
   /Range Name Create (/RNC), 333–334
   /Range Name Label Right (/RNLR), 360
   Range Set (RS), in Wysiwyg, 284
   /Range Unprotect (/RU), 189–190, 191
   selecting, 14–16, 404–405

Settings Hardware Graphs-Directory, 255–256
/System (/S), 399
Text Align (TA), in Wysiwyg, 285
Text Edit (TE), in Wysiwyg, 275–276
Text Reformat (TR), in Wysiwyg, 292, 293–294
Window (F6), 154
Worksheet (W), in Wysiwyg, 274
/Worksheet Column Column-Range Set-Width (/WCCS), 75–76
/Worksheet Column Display (/WCD), 221–222
/Worksheet Column Hide (/WCH), 218–220
Worksheet Column Set-Width (WCS), in Wysiwyg, 288–289
/Worksheet Column Set-Width (/WCS), 74–75, 80, 81
/Worksheet Delete Column (/WDC), 80
/Worksheet Delete Row (/WDR), 80
/Worksheet Erase Yes (/WEY), 55
/Worksheet Global (/WG), 70
/Worksheet Global (/WG) command, 15
/Worksheet Global Default (/WGD), 38, 40–41
/Worksheet Global Default Other Clock Filename (/WGDOCF), 38
/Worksheet Global Format (/WGF), 70, 71–74
/Worksheet Global Protection (/WGP), 189, 190
/Worksheet Insert Column (/WIC), 80–81
/Worksheet Insert Row (/WIR), 80, 81–82
/Worksheet Learn Range (/WLR), 366–370
/Worksheet Status (/WS), 16
/Worksheet Titles (/WT), 118–119
/Worksheet Titles Clear (/WTC), 117
/Worksheet Titles (/WT) command, 117
/Worksheet Titles Vertical (/WTV), 118
/Worksheet Window (/WW), 153–155
/Worksheet Window Clear (/WWC), 154
/Worksheet Window Vertical (/WWV), 154–155
Command macros, writing, 361–362
Command menus, 13–16
  accessing, 13
  leaving, 16
  selecting commands from, 14–16
  in Wysiwyg, 272
Command prompts, 8. *See also* DOS prompt
Computer, starting. *See* Booting
Condensed print, 222–225
Condition
  logical @functions and, 182, 184
  AND and OR, 341
Configuration, of printer, 295, 296
Configuration Printer (CP) command, in Wysiwyg, 296
Context-sensitive help, 87–90, 404
Control-Break key combination, 16

Control code, for printer, 222
Control panel, 7–8
COPY command, 396–397
/Copy (/C) command, 49–51
Copying
  of data and cell ranges, 49–51
  of data from other files, 143–145
  of disks, 397–398
  of files, 396–397
  of @functions, 107–108
Criteria, 331, 332
  multiple, specifying, 340–342
Criteria range, 331, 332, 333–334, 335
  in database @ functions, 343
  formulas in, 338–339
Currency format, 69
Current directory, 22, 23, 392–393
Current drive, 389
Cursor, 387, 388
{D}, in macros, 368
Data, 17
Data disks, 389–390
Data entry, 17–21
  error correction during, 17, 18
/Data Find (/DF) command, 335–337
/Data Query (/DQ) command, 331, 332, 334–335
/Data Query Criteria (/DQC) command, 342
/Data Query Extract (/DQE) command, 337
/Data Query Input (/DQI) command, 333–334
Data ranges. *See also* Range(s)
  multiple, graphs with, 249–253
/Data Sort (/DS) command, 317, 318–322
/Data Sort Data-range (/DSD) command, 318
/Data Sort Go (/DSG) command, 319, 320, 321
/Data Sort Primary-Key (/DSP) command, 319, 320–321
/Data Sort Secondary-Key (/DSS) command, 319–320
Database(s), 222, 307–323, 330–348
  creating, 310–314
  database @functions and, 343–347
  input, criteria, and output ranges and, 331–335, 338–339, 343
  inserting and deleting records in, 315–316
  locating and extracting records in, 335–339
  multiple criteria and, 340–342
  sorting records in, 317–322
Date
  entering, 4, 388
  in headers and footers, 214
@DAVG function, 344, 345
@DCOUNT function, 344, 346
Default settings, 47, 69
  for margins, 206
  for printing, 206

410 Index

DELETE command, 398–400
Delete key, 46
Deleting. *See also* Erasing
   of blank columns, 123–124
   of characters, 45–46
   of columns, 80
   of files, 398–400
   of records, 315
   of rows, 80
Descending sort, 317, 321
Dialog boxes, 15, 39–42
   activating, 39
   ellipses (...) in, 41
DIR command, 393
Directories, 391–393
   add-in programs and, 272
   changing, 5
   creating, 392
   current, 22, 23, 392–393
   within directories, 392
   files in, 391
   listing, 393
   removing, 393
   root, 5, 389, 391
   subdirectories and, 391
   using paths with, 392
Disk(s). *See also* Floppy disk(s); Hard disk
   source, 397
   target, 397
Disk drives
   changing, 389
   current, 389
   floppy, booting DOS from, 388–389
   hard, booting DOS from, 387–388
   high-density and low-density, 390, 396
Disk operating system. *See* DOS
DISKCOPY command, 397–398
Display Zoom (DZ) command, in Wysiwyg, 274–275
Displaying, of current filename, 39–42
Division, 43
@DMAX function, 344, 345
@DMIN function, 344, 345
Documents
   adding graphs to, 287–291
   printing with Wysiwyg, 295–297
Dollar sign ($)
   in absolute cell references, 148
   in mixed cell references, 178
DOS, 387–400. *See also* DOS commands
   booting, 387–389
   changing drives with, 389
   data disks and, 389–390
   managing data in files with, 390
   managing files in directories with, 391–393
   starting Lotus 1-2-3 from, 4–6
DOS commands
   CHDIR, 5
   CHDIR (CD), 392
   COPY, 396–397

   DELETE, 398–400
   DIR, 393
   DISKCOPY, 397–398
   entering, 389
   ERASE, 398–400
   FORMAT, 22, 394–396
   MKDIR (MD), 392
   RMDIR (RD), 393
   wildcard characters in, 393–394, 397
DOS prompt, 4, 387, 389
Dot-matrix printers, 54
Double angle brackets (< >), 173
Double-clicking, 402
Dragging, 402
Drives. *See* Disk drives
Drop shadow, 290
@DSUM function, 343, 344–345
Edit command (F2), 39–41
EDIT mode, 46–49
   editing macro cells in, 368
   keys in, 45–46
Editing
   of labels, 47–48
   of linking formulas, 176–177
   of macro cells, 368
   of values, 48–49
   of worksheet data, 45–49
   in Wysiwyg, 275–276
Electronic spreadsheet, 1–2. *See also* Worksheet
Ellipses (...), 41
End key, 11
END status indicator, 11
Enhanced keyboard, 8
Entering
   of data, 17–21
   of fields, 310–311
   of labels, 17–20
   of records, 312, 313
   of values, 20–21
Equals sign (=), linking files and, 176
ERASE command, 398–400
Erasing. *See also* Deleting
   of ranges, 110–114
   of worksheets, 55
Error(s), in formulas, 44
Error correction
   during data entry, 17, 18
   in macros, in STEP mode, 363–366
Error messages
   "Bad command or filename," 389
   "Invalid directory," 393
Escape (Esc) key, 16
Exit command
   in Lotus 1-2-3, 258
   in PrintGraph utility, 258
Exiting
   to DOS, temporarily, 399
   from Lotus 1-2-3, 24, 258, 399
   from PrintGraph, 258
Exponentiation, 43

Index   **411**

Fields, 309
  entering, 310–311
  key, 317, 319–320
File(s), 22, 390. *See also* Worksheet
  combining file data to worksheet and, 142–145
  deleting, 398–400
  graph, 239
  linking, 173–177
  listing, 393
  macro library, 374
  naming, 390
  relationship among, 391
  saving, 22–23
  source, 173, 174
  target, 173, 175
  WYSIWYG.ADN, 272
/File Combine Add (/FCA) command, 144–145
/File Combine (/FC) command, 142–145, 173
/File Combine Copy (/FCC) command, 143–144
/File Directory (/FD) command, 22, 23
/File Erase Other (/FEO) command, 399–400
/File Retrieve (/FR) command, 37–38
/File Save (/FS) command, 22, 23, 52–53
  passwords and, 192–194
Filename(s), 22, 390
  current, displaying, 39–42
Filename extensions, 23, 239, 253, 375, 390
FILES mode, 37, 38
FIND mode, 336
Fiscal year, 172
Fixed format, 69
Floppy disk(s), 389, 390
  backing up, 397–398
  formatting, 22, 394–396
  low- and high density, 390, 396
Floppy disk drives. *See* Disk drives
Fonts, 277–281
  font attributes and, 277–278
Footers, 213
  printing, 213–217
Format(s), 69
  value, 69–70
Format Bold (FB) command, in Wysiwyg, 280, 281
Format Color (FC) command, in Wysiwyg, 282
FORMAT command, 22, 394–396
Format Font (FF) command, in Wysiwyg, 278–279
Format Italics (FI) command, in Wysiwyg, 280–281
Format Lines Outline (FLO) command, in Wysiwyg, 289, 290
Format Lines Shadow (FLS) command, in Wysiwyg, 289–290
Format Lines Shadow Set (FLSS) command, in Wysiwyg, 290

Format Reverse (FR) command, in Wysiwyg, 283
Format Shade Light (FSL) command, in Wysiwyg, 286
Format Underline (FU) command, in Wysiwyg, 285
Formatting
  of floppy disks, 22, 394–396
  fonts and font attributes and, 278–281
  of labels, 77–79
  lines and shading and, 282–286
  of text, 278–286, 292–295
  of values, 69–74
  of worksheet, 108–109
  with Wysiwyg, 278–286, 292–295
Formula(s), 43
  containing cell addresses, 43
  copying, 49–51, 149–152
  creating, 42–45
  in criteria range, 338–339
  linking, 173–177
  pointing and, 44–45, 149–152
  printing, 225–226
@Function(s), 103–108
  arguments and, 103–104, 115
  creating and copying, 103–108
  database, 343–347
  logical, 182
Function keys, 11–12
General format, 70
Go To command (F5), 11–12, 118, 367
Graph(s), 233–259
  adding to documents, 287–291
  bar, creating, 240–242
  grid line settings and, 252
  legends in, 251
  line, creating and displaying, 234–238
  with multiple data ranges, creating, 249–253
  naming and saving, 239–240
  pie, creating, 242–243
  printing, 239, 253–258
  selecting and enhancing, 244–248
  titles in, 251
/Graph A (/GA) command, 235
/Graph (/G) command, 234
Graph files, 239
Graph name(s), 239
/Graph Name Create (/GNC) command, 239, 246
/Graph Name Use (/GNU) command, 244
/Graph Options Titles (/GOT) command, 236–237
/Graph Options Titles Y-Axis (/GOTY) command, 238
Graph range, 287
/Graph Reset Graph (/GRG) command, 249–250
/Graph Save (/GS) command, 240, 246
/Graph Type Bar (/GTB) command, 241
/Graph Type Pie (/GTP) command, 242
/Graph View (/GV) command, 237–238

/Graph X (/GX) command, 236
Grid line settings, 252
Hard copy, 52
Hard disk, 389–390
   creating directories on, 392
   DISKCOPY command with, 398
   formatting floppy disks and, 394–395
   removing directories from, 393
Hard disk drive. See Disk drives
Hatch patterns, enhancing graphs with, 246–247
Headers, 213
   printing, 213–217
Help facility, 87–90
   accessing, 404
Hidden format, 70
Hiding, of columns, 217–221
High-density disks, 390, 396
High-density drives, formatting low-density disks in, 396
Icons
   mouse, 8, 402, 404
   question mark (?), 8
@IF function, 182–186
Image-Select command, 256–257, 258
Information screen, 16
Input range, 331, 332, 333, 335
   in database @ functions, 343
Insert key, 46
Inserting
   of characters, 45–46
   of columns, 80–81
   of rows, 80, 81–82
Insertion bar, in Wysiwyg, 276
Interactive macros, writing, 370–373
Interface, 295
"Invalid directory" message, 393
Invoking, 272
Key(s)
   Alternate, in macro names, 258
   arrow, 8, 11, 18–19, 44–45
   Backspace, 17, 18, 46
   Caps Lock, 8, 9
   Delete, 46
   in EDIT mode, 45–46
   End, 11
   Escape, 16
   function, 11–12
   Insert, 46
   Num Lock, 8, 9
   Scroll Lock, 110
   slash (/), 13
   toggle, 9
Key assignment options, in Wysiwyg, 272
Key field, 317, 319–320
Keyboard, enhanced, 8
Keystrokes, macro, 358, 366–370
Kilobytes (KB), 390
Label(s), 17
   aligning, 17, 77–78
   copying, 49–51
   editing, 47–48
   entering, 17–20
   formatting, 77–79
   macro names as, 359
   print borders and, 210
   truncated, 47
Label-formatting prefixes, 17, 77, 82–83
   in macro names, 359
Laser printers, 54
Learn range, recording macro keystrokes in, 366–370
Legends, in graphs, 251
Line graph, 234
   creating and displaying, 234–238
Linking, of worksheet files, 173–177
Linking formulas, 173–177
   editing, 176–177
Loading, 4–6, 5
Locking, of worksheet titles, 117–120
Logical @functions, 182
Logical operators, 183
Lotus 1-2-3
   display of, 6–12
   exiting temporarily, 399
   quitting, 24
   starting, 4–6
Lotus Access System, 253, 254
Low-density disks, 390
   formatting in high-density drives, 396
Macro(s), 356–377
   command, 361–362
   interactive, 370–373
   keystrokes in, 358, 366–370
   naming, 358, 359–360, 368–370
   recording keystrokes in learn range and, 366–370
   running, 358, 360–361, 363–366
   testing in STEP mode, 363–366
   writing, 358–360, 361–362, 370–373
Macro libraries, 373–376
Macro library file, 374
Macro Manager, 373–376
   attaching, 375–376
Main directory. See Root directory
Main Menu, 13–16
   accessing with mouse, 404
Margins, 206
   default settings for, 206
   setting, 206–209, 215
Megabytes (MB), 390
Memory, random access (RAM), 22, 397
Memos, adding to worksheet, 292–295
Menu(s), 13–16
   Main, 13–16, 404
MENU mode, 13
Menu pointer, 13, 14
Mixed cell references, 177–182
MKDIR (MD) command, 392
.MLB filename extension, 375
Mode indicator, 8
Model. See Worksheet models

Mouse, 401–407
   accessing Help facility with, 404
   buttons on, 401, 403
   changing column widths with, 406
   moving cell pointer with, 403–404
   selecting commands with, 404–405
   selecting ranges with, 405
   splitting worksheet area into windows with, 406–407
   techniques for, 402
Mouse icons, 8, 402, 404
Mouse pad, 402
Mouse pointer, 402
/Move (/M) command, 121–123
Moving
   of cell pointer, 8–12, 18–19, 44–45, 403–404
   of ranges, 120–124
Multiplication, 43
Name command (F3), 37, 38
NAMES mode, 37
Naming
   of files. *See* Filename(s); Filename extensions
   of graphs, 239
   of macros, 358, 359–360, 368–370
Negative numbers, 43
Num Lock key, 8, 9
NUM status indicator, 8
Numeric keypad, 8
On-line help. *See* Help facility
Operands, 43
Operating system, 387. *See also* DOS; DOS commands; DOS prompt
Operators
   arithmetic, 43
   logical, 183
   relational, 339
OR condition, 341
Order of precedence, 43
   overriding, 43
Output range, 331, 332, 334, 335
Overtyping, 45–46
Page command, 257
Page numbers, in headers and footers, 214
Parentheses, in arguments, 103
Passwords, 192–194
Pathnames, 392
Pause ({?}) command, 370–372
Percent format, 70
Period (.), anchoring cells and, 50, 85
PGRAPH command, 254
.PIC filename extension, 239, 253
Pie graphs, 242
   creating, 242–243
   enhancing display of, 246–247
Pipe (|), 213
Plus sign (+)
   in formulas, 43
   linking formulas and, 174
Plus/minus (+/-) format, 70
Point, 277

POINT mode, highlighting ranges in, 49
Pointer
   cell. *See* Cell pointer
   menu, 13, 14
   mouse, 402
Pointing method
   building formulas by, 44–45
   to copy formulas, 149–152
   to enter range arguments in @functions, 104
Positive numbers, 43
Pound sign (#), 214
Pressing, 402
Preview (P) command, in Wysiwyg, 284
Primary key, 317, 319
Print (P) command, in Wysiwyg, 283, 295–296
Print preview, in Wysiwyg, 282, 283–284
/Print Printer (/PP) command, 52, 53–54, 206
/Print Printer Options Borders Columns (/PPOBC) command, 211
/Print Printer Options Borders Rows (/PPOBR) command, 211–212
/Print Printer Options Header (/PPOH) command, 214–215
/Print Printer Options Margin (/PPOM) command, 209
/Print Printer Options Other As-Displayed (/PPOOA) command, 226
/Print Printer Options Other Cell-Formulas (/PPOOC) command, 225
/Print Printer Options Setup (/PPOS) command, 222, 223–225
/Print Printer Range (/PPR) command, 85–86
Printer(s)
   configuration of, 295
   number of columns printed by, 54
Printer control code, 222
PrintGraph utility, accessing, 254
PrintGraph utility program, 239, 253–258
Printing, 206–227
   adjusting margins for, 206–209
   of cell formulas, 225–226
   with condensed print, 222–225
   of databases, 321–322
   determining number of columns that can be printed and, 206–207
   of graphs, 239
   of headers and footers, 213–217
   hiding columns and, 217–221
   setting borders for, 210–212
   of worksheet ranges, 52–55
   with Wysiwyg, 295–297
Programs, 390
Prompts
   command, 8
   DOS, 4, 387, 389
Protection, of worksheets, 189–194
Quarter, 172
Query, 331–335, 338–339, 343

414 Index

Query command (F7), 338
Question mark (?), as wildcard character, 394
{?} command (pause), 370–372
Question mark (?) icon, 8
/Quit (/Q) command, 24
Quit (Q) command, in Wysiwyg, 284
Quitting, of Lotus 1-2-3, 24, 258
{R}, in macros, 368
Random access memory (RAM), 22, 397
Range(s), 49
   adjusting, 84–86
   column-offset, 343
   criteria, 331, 332, 333–334, 335, 338–339, 343
   erasing, 110–114
   in @function arguments, 103, 104
   graph, 287
   highlighting in POINT mode, 49
   input, 331, 332, 333, 335, 343
   moving, 120–124
   multiple, graphs with, 249–253
   output, 331, 332, 334, 335
   selecting with mouse, 405
   specifying for graphs, 235–236
   x-axis, 234
Range addresses, 49
/Range Erase (/RE) command, 111–112
/Range Format (/RF) command, 70
/Range Format Text (/RFT) command, 339
/Range Justify (/RJ) command, 292
/Range Label (/RL) command, 77–78
/Range Name Create (/RNC) command, 333–334
/Range Name Label Right (/RNLR) command, 360
Range names, as input and criteria ranges, 343
Range Set (RS) command, in Wysiwyg, 284
/Range Unprotect (/RU) command, 189–190, 191
Recalculation, automatic, 49, 368
Records, 309
   entering, 312, 313
   inserting and deleting, 315–316
   locating and extracting, 335–339
   sorting, 317–322
Relational operators, 339
Relative cell references, 148–149
   changing to absolute cell references, 150
   in mixed cell references, 178
Repeating characters, 82–83
Reset format, 70
Retrieving, of worksheets, 37–38
Reverse type, 282–283
RMDIR (RD) command, 393
Root directory, 5, 389, 391
Rows, 7, 11
   adjusting height of, 406
   deleting, 80
   inserting, 80, 81–82

Saving, of worksheet files, 22–23
Sci format, 69
Screen
   information, 16
   Lotus 1-2-3, 6–12
   reverse type and, 283
   Wysiwyg and. *See* Wysiwyg add-in program
Scroll Lock key, 110
Scrolling, 9–11
   with cell pointer locked in place, 110
Secondary key, 317, 319–320
Sectors, 394
   bad, 396
Separator line, 82
Settings, 15
   default, 69. *See* Default settings
   editing, 40–41
   print, 206
Settings Hardware Graphs-Directory command, 255–256
SETTINGS mode, 40
Setup string, for printer, 222
Shading, background, 286
Shadow, drop, 290
Slash key (/), 13
Sorting, of records, 317–322
Source disk, 397
Source file, linking files and, 173, 174
Spreadsheet, 1–2. *See also* Worksheet(s)
Status indicators, 8, 9
Status line, 8
STEP mode, testing macros in, 363–366
Storage capacity, of floppy disks, 390
Subdirectory, 391. *See also* Directories
Submenus, 8, 14
Subtraction, 43
@SUM function, 103, 104–108, 111
Switch, 396
/System (/S) command, 399
Target disk, 397
Target file, linking files and, 173, 175
Templates, 187–189
Text
   editing, in Wysiwyg, 275–276
   formatting with Wysiwyg, 278–286, 292–295
Text Align (TA) command, in Wysiwyg, 285
Text Edit (TE) command, in Wysiwyg, 275–276
Text format, 70
Text Reformat (TR) command, in Wysiwyg, 292, 293–294
Text string, 183
Tilde (~), in macros, 359
Time, entering, 5, 388–389
Titles
   entering in graphs, 251
   worksheet, locking, 117–120
Toggle keys, 9

Index **415**

Truncation, 47
Typeface, 277. *See also* Fonts
Value(s), 20
   copying, 49–51
   editing, 48–49
   entering, 20–21
   formatting, 69–74
Value formats, 69–70
VALUE mode, 20, 43
Vertical bar (|), 213
Volume label, 395
What-if problems, 155–158
Wildcard characters, 393–394
   with COPY command, 397
Window(s), splitting worksheet area into, 153–155, 406–407
Window command (F6), 154
.WK1 filename extension, 23, 52, 390
Worksheet(s). *See also* Spreadsheet
   adding memos to, 292–295
   borders of, 6, 7, 10
   editing, 45–49
   erasing, 55
   graphing data from. *See* Graph(s)
   linking, 173–177
   locking titles and, 117–120
   name of. *See* Filename(s); Filename extensions
   printing. *See* Printing
   protecting, 189–194
   reformatting, 108–109
   retrieving, 37–38
   saving, 22–23
Worksheet area, 6
   splitting into windows, 153–155, 406–407
/Worksheet Column Column-Range Set-Width (/WCCS) command, 75–76
/Worksheet Column Display (/WCD) command, 221–222
/Worksheet Column Hide (/WCH) command, 218–220
Worksheet Column Set-Width (WCS) command, in Wysiwyg, 288–289
/Worksheet Column Set-Width (/WCS) command, 74–75, 80, 81
Worksheet (W) command, in Wysiwyg, 274
/Worksheet Delete Column (/WDC) command, 80
/Worksheet Delete Row (/WDR) command, 80
/Worksheet Erase Yes (/WEY) command, 55
/Worksheet Global (/WG) command, 15, 70
/Worksheet Global Default (/WGD) command, 38, 40–41
/Worksheet Global Default Other Clock Filename (/WGDOCF) command, 38
/Worksheet Global Format (/WGF) command, 70, 71–74
/Worksheet Global Protection (/WGP) command, 189, 190
/Worksheet Insert Column (/WIC) command, 80–81
/Worksheet Insert Row (/WIR) command, 80, 81–82
/Worksheet Learn Range (/WLR) command, 366–370
Worksheet models, 137–159
   combining data from other files and, 142–145
   relative and absolute cell addresses and, 146–153
   setting up, 138–141
   solving what-if problems with, 155–158
   splitting worksheet area into windows and, 153–155
/Worksheet Status (/WS) command, 16
Worksheet templates, 187–189
/Worksheet Titles Clear (/WTC) command, 117
/Worksheet Titles (/WT) command, 117, 118–119
/Worksheet Titles Vertical (/WTV) command, 118
/Worksheet Window Clear (/WWC) command, 154
/Worksheet Window (/WW) command, 153–155
/Worksheet Window Vertical (/WWV) command, 154–155
Wysiwyg add-in program, 270–298
   adding graphs to documents with, 287–291
   attaching, 272
   changing column widths with, 406
   enhancing ranges with lines and shading and, 282–286
   fonts and font attributes and, 277–281
   formatting text with, 292–295
   printing documents with, 295–297
   selecting commands in, 405
   splitting worksheet area into windows with, 406–407
   using mouse with, 405, 406–407
WYSIWYG.ADN file, 272
x-axis, 238
X-axis range, 234
y-axis, 238